TWENTIETH-CENTURY MUSIC

The Norton Introduction to Music History

TWENTIETH-CENTURY MUSIC

A History of Musical Style in Modern Europe and America

ROBERT P. MORGAN

Yale University

W · W · NORTON & COMPANY

New York · London

Printed in the United States of America.

This book is composed in Bembo.
Composition and manufacturing by The Maple-Vail Book Manufacturing
Group.

First Edition.

Library of Congress Cataloging in Publication Data
Morgan, Robert P.
    Twentieth-century music : a history of musical style in modern
    Europe and America / Robert P. Morgan.
        p.   cm. — (The Norton introduction to music history)
    Includes bibliographical references.
    ISBN 0-393-95272-X
    1. Music—20th century—History and criticism.   2. Style, Musical.
    I. Title.   II. Series.
    ML197.M675   1990
    780'.9'04—dc20   90-6986
                                                                          CIP
                                                                          MN

ISBN 0-393-95272-X

W.W. Norton & Company, Inc., 500 Fifth Avenue, New York, N.Y. 10110
W.W. Norton & Company, Ltd., 10 Coptic Street, London WC1A 1PU
1 2 3 4 5 6 7 8 9 0

Contents

List of Illustrations

Preface

To help shape what might otherwise seem a chaotic succession of passing events, historians like to divide the course of time into discrete periods, each exhibiting a significant number of common characteristics. These temporal divisions, not necessarily rigid, undergo continuous examination and revision as new scholars propose alternate possibilities. Nevertheless, however tenuous and changeable, these groupings are indispensable in organizing the complex fabric of historical evolution.

This book deals with the most recent of the large historical segments commonly distinguished by music historians, the one usually referred to as the "modern" period or simply—as in the title of the present book—"twentieth-century music." But precisely when does the history of twentieth-century music begin? From a strictly chronological point of view, the answer is obvious: 1900. But twentieth-century music is a stylistic as well as a temporal category: this music is different from that of the previous century, not just because it was composed in the subsequent one, but because it is based upon significantly different esthetic and technical assumptions and therefore manifests quite distinct stylistic qualities. That fact, quite aside from the convenience of dating, explains what makes it a meaningful historical category and, despite the unprecedented variety of twentieth-century music, an integral whole.

The passage from the "old" music to the "new" music, from nineteenth-century Romanticism to twentieth-century modernism, did not happen all at once, but was the result of historical processes that unfolded gradually over an extended period. Just when these processes reached a critical stage, beyond which music moved indisputably into a new era, is a question with no definite answer. The most convenient date, and the one adopted here (in that the first of the three main divisions of the book commences there), is the turn of the century, a reference point precise and easily remembered but in other respects relatively arbitrary.

A stronger case might be made for several alternate dates. In terms of the modern period's technical foundations, the years 1907–8, when Arnold Schoenberg first broke completely with the traditional tonal system, mark perhaps the single most significant turning point. Yet Schoenberg's early nontonal works remain manifestations of nineteenth-century German Romanticism and its esthetic of personal expression—an esthetic emphasizing the originality and individuality that were surely an essential prerequisite for Schoenberg's radical break with earlier conventions. If we wish to view modern music in terms not only of new compositional techniques, but of new esthetic orientations as well, Schoenberg's early post-tonal music could be considered the final phase of nineteenth-century music. From this perspective a better place for the dividing line would be at the end of World War I, when a widespread anti-Romantic reaction arose against (among many other things) the cult of personal expression that had persisted through the first two decades of the century—notably, though not uniquely, in the prewar expressionist movement with which Schoenberg was associated.

Yet neither the esthetic nor the technical features commonly associated with twentieth-century music surfaced at one precise moment. Tonality had been under siege for some time, not only in Schoenberg's earlier works but in those of many contemporaries and predecessors. Indeed, the history of music throughout the nineteenth century can profitably be viewed in terms of a gradual yet steady weakening of the basic principles of the traditional tonal system inherited from the eighteenth. Similarly, anti-Romantic esthetic sentiments had been expressed by such composers as Erik Satie well before 1918, even before the turn of the century.

This overlapping is characteristic of most—if not all—historical periodization, and cannot be ignored for the sake of neat compartmentalization. In the case of the present book, the nineteenth-century background to the twentieth century's revolutionary developments is treated in an introductory chapter preceding the text's three main divisions, while the first of those divisions begins with a chapter devoted to transitional figures with roots firmly planted in the nineteenth century who also contributed substantially to the earliest developments in new music. This first part continues with Schoenberg's revolutionary break with tonality and closely related technical developments in such composers as Stravinsky and Bartók, while Part II focuses on the critical changes in esthetic attitudes that emerged after World War I. World War II constitutes a third watershed, in both technical and esthetic terms, and Part III deals with the developments since then.

Beyond such problems of origins and chronological sequence, the historian of recent music must confront difficult decisions about overall focus. In its largest dimensions, music history may concern itself with—among other possibilities—music's role in society, its reception by audiences, its relationship to other arts and to political and economic factors, its performance practice, and its theory and pedagogy. Taken more narrowly, however, music history is above all the study of music itself, and the present book is primarily focused on this dimension—on compositional ideas and on the composers most responsible for their formulation. All the broader issues mentioned above arise during the course of our study, however, and the larger context has not been ignored. Each of the three principal divisions opens with a chapter discussing the prevalent social and intellectual climate, providing indispensable background to understanding the transformations that took place in music, and throughout the text the attempt is made to relate musical developments to significant aspects of contemporary life and thought.

An additional concern for the music historian, especially one dealing with the current epoch, is geographical compass. As its subtitle indicates, this study confines itself to Western music, including that of all of Europe and the Americas. Although the primary goal is to provide a general survey of the music of the entire region, particular emphasis is placed on central Europe, especially Germanic and French music, which—at least until recently—has been especially influential for the area as a whole. The treatment of the United States is also comparatively extensive, not only because of the book's origin and intended readership, but because of this country's particular role in nourishing the more experimental strains that form one of the century's enduring and characteristic features. In a broader historical sense as well, of course, the United States has acquired an ever more central role as the century has progressed, eventually achieving a position of unquestioned (if sometimes lamented) worldwide prominence.

Another decision concerns the types of music to be included. Here the scope has been limited almost entirely to Western "art" music, with popular music, folk music, and jazz, as well as non-Western music of all types, touched upon only insofar as they have directly influenced concert music. Since the increasing interaction of these "other" musics with concert music forms a distinctive feature of the modern tradition, such a decision is necessarily problematic. However, given the constraints of space, it seemed unwise to try to cover such a rich and varied field, itself encompassing many different types of music, each with its own traditions, in the highly synoptic manner necessary within a more general survey. Nevertheless, the chapters devoted to more recent musical developments, in which the interaction between art and popular musics, between Western and non-Western musics, becomes so common as to constitute almost a norm, incorporate frequent and specific references to these other kinds of music.

Even a historian working within the relatively circumscribed framework of the Western concert tradition, focusing mainly on the music itself, must deal with and reconcile several interrelated yet competing topics; the musical ideas per se, their historical evolution, and the lives and works of the composers responsible for them. Equally important, these strains are in a sense inseparable, and any effort to seek a balance carries with it certain conflicts, which the present volume addresses by incorporating three distinct, partially independent levels of organization. At the highest level stand the three previously mentioned parts, each corresponding to a major historical phase. The first, covering the period from 1900 to the end of World War I, witnesses the breakup of the traditional tonal system and its replacement by a number of new compositional approaches. The second, extending from the end of World War I to the end of World War II, reveals a general tendency toward consolidation, with efforts to forge new links with the tradition, and a strong reaction against the subjective, outwardly emotional features of musical Romanticism. The third, covering the years since World War II, differs from the first two in being less clearly defined by a single dominant line of development; rather, its most salient characteristic would appear to be an ability to accommodate, within an all-encompassing pluralism, many distinct tendencies, some of them contradictory.

These groupings, supported to a remarkable degree by a pervasive unanimity in artistic and musical orientation, provide a convincing structure for the music of the century as a whole, and reveal it to be, despite all its richness and diversity, a meaningful and comprehensible historical unit. Nevertheless, due consideration is given in Parts I and II to numerous, often quite significant currents running counter to the prevailing norm; in the third division, on the other hand, such countercurrents themselves become the norm.

At the chapter level the contents are primarily focused by the major strands of musical development within each phase. A third level is found in the extensive subsections in Parts I and II devoted to the composers principally responsible for defining these developments. This necessarily entails a selective treatment of individuals, since the more one attempts to give a broad picture of compositional activity, including as many composers as possible, the more difficult it becomes to devote adequate discussion to the musical issues themselves. Consequently, many gifted figures, some of whom might be of equal or even greater importance if viewed from a different perspective, have been omitted, touched upon only briefly, or included in several geographically organized chapters devoted to composers primarily active outside the central European area.

In this process of selection the more conservative composers tend to be neglected; although many attained positions of great prominence in their own day, they rarely exerted a significant long-range influence. This in itself reflects a point of great historical significance: musical modernism has defined itself more through emphasis on the new, on what was musically unprecedented and thus distinct from the older tradition, than through any other single attribute—an important reason for the concentration on technical issues in the study of twentieth-century music, and for the continuing use of the designation "modern" to refer to an extensive body of work now almost a century old. For all that new developments are consequently stressed, the strong and unbroken continuity of traditional attitudes, in extreme cases encompassing the tenets of common-practice tonality in unaltered form, has also been an important and telling feature of this century's music, and has not been disregarded.

In Part III the shift of focus away from individual composers mirrors a fundamental transformation in the dynamics of twentieth-century music itself. During the first half of the century, musical developments were dominated to a remarkable extent by a very small number of composers, most of them belonging to a single generation born during the latter part of the nineteenth century. From today's perspective it seems possible that they represented the last of the musical "giants" of Western music—composers responsible for shaping the essential musical directions of their time, comparable to such now quasi-mythical figures as Bach, Haydn, Mozart, Beethoven, and Wagner. The most important of them (above all Schoenberg and Stravinsky, to a lesser degree Bartók and Berg) play principal roles through most of the first half-century, and are accorded extensive consideration in both Parts I and II. Others, somewhat older or younger (Mahler and Debussy among the former, Hindemith and Shostakovich the latter), can accordingly be viewed as "predecessors" or "followers." Still others (Vaughan Williams and Janáček, for instance) attained only a more localized significance, or (like Webern, Varèse, and especially Ives) occupied relatively peripheral positions in the musical life of their times, acquiring prominence only as a result of more recent historical developments.

Within the third and most recent phase of twentieth-century music, on the other hand, it is increasingly difficult to identify a small group of composers who define the most essential features of the period. First, compositional orientations now change quickly, so that a single composer may assume several quite different points of view within a relatively short span of time. In addition, talent and musical activity now appear to be more widely dispersed. Thus the book's shift away from individuals reflects, not a deterioration in compositional talent, but a change in the nature of musical style and musical society itself, within which the now-current trend of radical eclecticism militates against the establishment of highly distinctive personal idioms. Part III thus deals with composers more in terms of their contributions to particular stylistic directions and technical innovations than as individual personalities; they are often treated briefly and, in some instances, under several separate headings.

In time, our picture of today's music may take on a more evident order. After all, we are still in the course of a continuing development, and so close to the most recent trends that it is extremely difficult to grasp the larger picture. In fact, only when we have seen the historical consequences of current musical events will we be in a position to measure their eventual significance. To the extent that the history of the newest music concerns itself with such matters (and it is difficult to imagine any serious historical writing that would not), it must necessarily be largely speculative.

Conceivably, of course, we may eventually come to recognize a principal line of musical evolution encompassing current music, an historical "mainstream" comparable to, and extending, that of Western music from the birth of polyphony through the period of functional tonality and onward. If, for example, in the not-too-distant future there should coalesce a new "common practice," with basic technical and stylistic assumptions shared by a majority of composers, today's overriding pluralism, its seemingly contradictory and disparate tendencies, might come to be understood as directed toward a new, as yet unimagined, musical era.

Equally possible, however, is that music, along with contemporary life in general, is moving into a "post-historical" phase where notions of directed chronological development no longer apply. If so, we may be at the beginning of an extended period of musical pluralism, in which styles are exchanged and combined freely, with no single one assuming a position of dominance. The history of twentieth-century music as a whole is certainly suggestive in this respect. The appearance of three major historical turning points, or musical "revolutions," in less than fifty years reflects an age of considerable historical and stylistic uncertainty. The fact that the first two of these revolutions, although pointing in somewhat contradictory directions (the dissolution of tonality and neoclassicism, respectively), were essentially the work of the same composers is striking and anticipates the current stage, where a single composer often experiments simultaneously with a number of alternative approaches.

All these changes may eventually come to be seen as inextricably interconnected, even as part of a single pluralistic musical culture characterized more by inconstancy and diversity than by stylistic homogeneity. Should this occur, the history of future music may well require a new kind of historian, equipped with entirely new ways of thinking about historical connections.

A book dealing with such a wide range of music necessarily owes much to many different scholars, specializing in many different areas. I have drawn on the work of countless others throughout this volume for factual information of all types. As far as I am aware, the interpretation of this material is essentially my own, though it overlaps frequently with the views of others. On a more personal level, the book has benefitted from conversations with numerous friends and colleagues, in some instances in specific ways, in others more indirectly. Above all, I should mention the faculty and students at the Department of Music of the University of Chicago, where I taught when I was writing this book, among them especially Joseph Auner, Philip Bohlman, Easley Blackwood, Howard Brown, Peter Burkholder, Richard Cohn, David Gable, Philip Gossett, Ellen Harris, and Shulamit Ran. Marilyn McCoy and Philip Rupprecht deserve special thanks for their excellent help with the bibliographies. Claire Brook, Music Editor at W. W. Norton surprised me by suggesting that I write the book in the first place and has remained a loyal friend and source of much-needed encouragement through the vicissitudes of a very long period of gestation. My debt to David Hamilton, who edited the entire volume, cannot be adequately expressed. Suffice it to say that there is literally no page of this book that has not benefited substantially from his sympathetic advice. I count myself very fortunate indeed to have had someone working closely with me who, in addition to being a good friend of many years' standing, has such broad understanding of twentieth-century music and enviable command of the English language. Finally, I take special pleasure in thanking my wife Carole Morgan, who, in addition to helping me in countless ways to survive difficult periods during the writing of the book, managed to remain patient and supportive throughout what must have seemed an interminable process.

New Haven, Connecticut
April 1990

An Anthology of Twentieth-Century Music is in preparation; it will include examples from the composers and trends discussed in this history, along with brief analytical essays on each of the pieces included.

Introduction: The Nineteenth-Century Musical Background

It is impossible to say precisely when twentieth-century music, as a stylistic and esthetic phenomenon, began. Even the year 1900, despite obvious advantages, is not a particularly satisfactory candidate. Among other possible choices, perhaps the most appealing is 1907, the year Arnold Schoenberg made a final break with the traditional tonal system that the new century had inherited from the previous two. The collapse of traditional tonality,[1] particularly emphatic in Schoenberg but evident in all the major younger composers of the century's first decade, was from a technical point of view the single most significant factor in shaping modern music. After a two-hundred-year period of relative agreement about basic technical matters, Western music was suddenly confronted with a radically new set of compositional possibilities, with basic new compositional decisions, and it is by no means farfetched to see subsequent music in the large as a series of conscious stratagems designed to compensate for tonality's loss.

Yet traditional tonality did not collapse at once. The entire nineteenth century—arguably even the common-practice period as a whole—had witnessed a progressive weakening of its constructive force, along with corresponding shifts in compositional esthetic. Any effort to under-

1.   In this Introduction the word "tonality" is used in a restricted sense to encompass only the so-called "common practice" period of the eighteenth and nineteenth centuries. The term "functional tonality" is sometimes used to distinguish this particular form of tonality from others, such as those encountered in other cultures or in earlier European music.

1

stand twentieth-century music must consider its relationship to these earlier developments out of which it grew, in part as their extension, in part as a set of new departures. To this extent the history of twentieth-century music and its nineteenth-century background are inseparable, and can be thought of as two links within a single, more encompassing chain of musical evolution.

Before discussing some of these nineteenth-century developments, it should be pointed out that when we speak of "common-practice tonality," we mean more than just a system in which pitches are organized so that one particular pitch predominates, forming a "center" in relationship to which all the others have their own unique position and from which they acquire their own particular meaning. We also mean the kind of rhythmic and formal structures that developed in conjunction with this system. One of the most characteristic features of tonality is its ability to invest extended spans of music with a sense of clearly defined, goal-directed motion. The property of modulation, of temporarily replacing the original center with a new one whose ultimate meaning still depends upon its eventual resolution to the original tonic, enabled composers to conceive long and autonomous musical structures that were logical in construction and thus meaningful in effect.

A number of generalized formal types, such as the sonata form, the song form, and the rondo, developed in conjunction with tonality. But common to all these forms is a hierarchical system of relationships in which shorter musical units combine to produce longer ones, such as phrases; phrases combine to form periods; periods combine to produce sections; and so on until a complete movement evolves, which itself is a single and ultimately indivisible unit held together by the dynamic system of relationships provided by functional tonality. That is, the smaller units do not simply connect up with one another in an additive sense; they balance and complete one another in a complex network of delayed and eventually fulfilled expectations. Such music has a remarkably strong "syntactic" component, a logical pattern of formal connections that makes sense to a listener not unlike the way the succession of clauses, sentences, paragraphs, and chapters does to the reader of a novel.

Of course, the tonal system, and the kinds of extended formal structures associated with it, did not develop at once, any more than it dissolved at once; it evolved gradually over a considerable span of music history. But by the end of the eighteenth century, its evolution had made it a sort of "universal musical language," commonly accepted throughout Europe despite minor—though often significant and interesting—variations attributable to personal and geographical differences. The flexibility of this language, and the power and range of its applicability, is evident in its accommodation of such diverse personalities as, for example, Gluck, Haydn, Mozart, and Beethoven, all active in the latter part of the eighteenth century. Despite their many differences, however, these composers were all, in an essential way, speaking a shared musical tongue.

Indeed, it is just because the sense of a mutual musical framework was preserved to such a degree throughout the two centuries in which tonality flourished, from c. 1700 to c. 1900, that we refer to them as the "common practice" period. Nevertheless, the main currents of musical development in the nineteenth century considerably undermined this common foundation. Perhaps the most important reason for this gradual turning away from an essentially "universal" style lay in a growing preference for a more personal kind of musical expression. As the nineteenth century progressed and the esthetics of musical Romanticism became more fully established, a new emphasis—one unthinkable in the eighteenth century, with its Classical concern for universality—was placed upon the unique as opposed to the general. Interestingly, the tonal system proved to be remarkably adaptable to this spreading desire for personalism; although originally evolved as a set of shared conventions, it could be modified to produce effects that were strikingly individual and thus intensely expressive in nature. Already in the later works of Haydn and Mozart and the earlier works of Beethoven, a tendency to treat the system in a highly personal way was evident, but in the nineteenth century it became much more pronounced. From Beethoven on, one feels a growing determination to give each composition its own unmistakable expressive stamp, distinct from that of all others.

This striving for individuality is evident in virtually all aspects of nineteenth-century music. Thematic material became more strikingly profiled in rhythmic and melodic contour (an example is Beethoven's Fifth Symphony). Compositions frequently began in distinctive registers (e.g., unusually high, as in the Prelude to Wagner's *Lohengrin*, or unusually low, as in the Prelude to his *Das Rheingold*). A characteristic instrumental color was chosen to lend an arresting quality to a particular passage (the unison horn statement of the melody that announces the opening of Schubert's Ninth Symphony). But the most striking innovations were encountered within the tonal system itself, which was similarly exploited to produce "special effects" of various kinds. By the middle of the century chromaticism and dissonance, always associated with expressivity in Western music, were stressed to a point where it became difficult to ascertain the consonant and diatonic basis from which they represented a departure. What this meant, in fact, was that both chromaticism and dissonance were no longer really thought of as "departures," but rather as norms.

Moreover, if dissonance is conceived as applying not only to individ-

Nowhere is the nineteenth-century view of the artist as individualist more evident than in this sculpture of Beethoven (1897–1902) by the German artist, Max Klinger. The variety of materials—marble, alabaster, ivory, bronze, amber, and semi-precious stones—reaches new heights of extravagance. (Museum der bildenden Künste, Leipzig)

ual notes but also to secondary keys at varying distances from the tonic, an equally radical extension of earlier practice can be observed. Whereas in the eighteenth century only those keys most closely associated with the tonic (i.e., the dominant and, in minor, the relative major) were commonly exploited for prolonged modulations, in the nineteenth century more remote tonal regions appeared with ever greater frequency and emphasis. Already in compositions dating from the earliest years of the century, Beethoven showed an interest in choosing a particular set of unusual—and therefore "characteristic"—key relationships for a specific work (as in the String Quartet in E minor, Op. 59, No. 2, especially its final movement), a practice developed and extended by virtually all later tonal composers. Key relations, no longer conventional, took on a "motivic" aspect; they contributed to what was singular in a given composition.

Another important development in nineteenth-century tonality (exemplified especially in Wagner's *Tristan und Isolde*) is that key centers came to be defined more by implication than by actual statement. Although tonal motion was still directed toward a goal, the goal itself might never actually appear, producing a sort of "suspended" tonality regulated primarily by cadences of a "deceptive" nature. This produced a more fluid type of harmonic motion, with key centers so tenuously defined that they seem to melt almost imperceptibly into one another. The balance between tonal stability and instability, a distinction fundamental to the functional definition of formal segments in the Classical style, tipped precariously toward the latter. Even in works written relatively early in the century (e.g., Chopin's Piano Sonata in B minor), one finds opening thematic material that is motivically developmental and tonally uncertain from the outset, obscuring the traditional distinction between what is expositional and what is developmental or transitional.

Such innovations undermined the foundation of Classical form, the counterpoising of key-defining passages with modulatory ones in a carefully controlled system of tensions and resolutions designed to produce ultimate tonal confirmation. As nineteenth-century composers exploited ever more exaggerated levels of chromaticism and tonal ambiguity, music approached a condition of almost unbroken flux, within which formal boundaries were largely eradicated. Composition became an "art of transition," as Wagner proclaimed of his work. In place of the Classical ideal of form as an interaction among well-defined and functionally differentiated units (thematic, transitional, developmental, closing, etc.), a new Romantic ideal emerged of form as process, of music as a continuum of uninterrupted growth and evolution. Form thereby acquired a more "open" quality, quite different from the "closed" character of Classical musical structure. This can be seen with special clarity in openings and closings: instead of beginning with a definite thematic statement, compositions often seem to emerge only gradually out of the preceding silence, as if putting themselves together bit by bit (e.g., Liszt's Piano Sonata in B minor); or, rather than ending with a definite cadence, they drift off imperceptibly into final extinction (e.g., Tchaikovsky's Sixth Symphony). Clarity is no longer necessarily a desideratum; ambiguity, even obscurity, is embraced as the countersign of a new formal sensibility.

Supporting these technical innovations was the nineteenth century's embrace of "program music"—the idea that music was not a purely abstract, "absolute" art, but one related to and reflective of various extramusical concerns. Program music contributed to the breakup of tonality in at least two important ways. First, it led to musical conceptions that were essentially dramatic, coloristic, or descriptive in nature, conceptions that would have been literally "unthinkable" within a strictly abstract musical context. Second, it provided composers with justification for writing passages that could not have been adequately explained in traditional theoretical or purely musical terms. It is no coincidence, certainly, that the most radical musical developments of the century took place, almost without exception, in the area of program music and opera (the latter being a kind of explicit program music).

Another significant factor was the rise of nationalism during the nineteenth century. The traditional tonal system, though generally adhered to throughout Europe, was above all a creation of the Germanic countries, Italy, and, to a lesser extent, France. The principal line of development within these countries was mainly an "internal" one: the musical properties inherent in the system itself were extended— through increased chromaticism, more distant modulation, etc. But a second, and largely independent, way of enriching tonal relationships was discovered by composers in countries on the edges of Europe, who drew upon the very different musical qualities found in the folk and ethnic music of their own lands. Modal relationships, essentially foreign to the tonal system, were exploited, producing new melodic and harmonic effects that, although not dependent upon increased chromaticism, also called into question the basic organizational principles of traditional tonality (especially the uniquely privileged role of the dominant chord as the basic key-defining agent). Moreover, non-European composers, such as Musorgsky in Russia, began to model their music's rhythmic structure on the speech rhythms of their native languages, creating a freer, more plastic kind of phrase structure, quite different from the largely balanced metrical types of European Classicism.

The inevitable combined result of these tendencies was to weaken the structural foundations of traditional tonality. In place of the basic major and minor scales of tonality, the nationalists offered a complex set of modal possibilities, while the chromatic composers of central Europe moved toward a single twelve-note scale that made available all possible types of triadic chord formations on all possible scale degrees. By the end of the century it was often difficult, if not impossible, to determine the key of an ostensibly tonal work. The relationships might be so ambiguous, as in Debussy, that the key center only barely emerges as a last tenuous resting point; or, as in Strauss and Mahler, two (or more) keys might compete on substantially equal terms, raising the possibility that either one could eventually assume final control. The last movement of Mahler's Symphony No. 4, completed in 1900, closes in E major after having begun in G major, and the two centers, E and G, alternate throughout the movement to form a sort of "paired" tonality seemingly capable of resolution in either direction. Similarly, in Strauss's *Also sprach Zarathustra* the keys of C and B compete throughout, their tonics juxtaposed right up to the last bar.

A final matter, equally contributory to the breakup of traditional musical form, was the increasingly autonomous position occupied by music, as well as the other arts, during the nineteenth century. Music's gradual separation from the larger social and cultural framework, produced by the dissolution of the old patronage system under which church and court had given it specific functions, enabled composers to act more

Aubrey Beardsley's grotesque pen and ink illustration for Oscar Wilde's play, *Salome* (1893), was a strange mixture of many of the aspects of art in the 1890s: the fusion of words and images, the embracing of obscure and ambiguous symbols, and the refinement of abstract decorative patterns. *Salome with the Head of John the Baptist.* (Princeton University Library)

and more as "free agents." As their ties to social, political, and religious institutions loosened, they could increasingly fashion their work solely according to the dictates of their own consciences. Beholden to no higher authority than creative imagination, the progressive composer could experiment at will, following the inclination of the age to pursue the unique and unusual at the expense of the conventional and accepted. This new artistic freedom went hand in hand with the period's overall esthetic orientation, for the more music was able to follow an independent course, without concern for the comprehension and receptivity of a broadly based public, the more it was able to serve as a vehicle for personal expression and to assume its new role as a symbol of individuality or, eventually, of open revolt.

As an outcome of these tendencies, music had at the close of the nineteenth century reached a position fundamentally different from the one it occupied at the beginning. A musical language once dominated by an international style that, despite significant geographical and personal variants, was solidly based upon common esthetic principles and shared compositional conventions was now fragmented into many divergent compositional tendencies. And whereas composers of 1800 had been closely linked to the social milieu within which they worked and were thus significantly bound by accepted stylistic norms, their 1900 counterparts were autonomous creators committed to the musically exceptional, who defined a purely personal milieu by breaking away from what had preceded them.

The repercussions were decisive for the future course of music. The twentieth century inherited a tonal system shaken to its foundations and already well on its way to total collapse. A final rupture was inevitable, and it was both the achievement and burden of the new century to complete the break and shoulder its consequences. Of course, many composers continued to write tonal music of a traditional sort (as many continue to do right up to the present). But the single most important and encompassing feature of twentieth-century music has unquestionably been its move beyond functional tonality, and to a lesser extent beyond the traditional musical forms associated with it, either to new kinds of tonal organization achieved through novel means, or to nontonal systems based upon entirely new compositional methods.

PART I

Beyond Tonality: From 1900 to World War I

In this apocalyptic illustration for Albert Robida's novel, *La Vie électrique,* published in 1892, the old world is shown being broken up, with tradition carted away like so much rubbish. Overseeing all is a robot made up of a chemical retort, an electric light, a T-square, and cog and wheels. In the distance, smoking factories—the world of the twentieth century.

CHAPTER I

The Historical Context: Europe at the Turn of the Century

Europe entered the twentieth century in a euphoria of optimism, full of bright hopes for the future. International tensions, long a consistent feature of life on the Continent, were at a relatively low point, peace having reigned since the close of the Franco-Prussian War in 1871. In 1900 the Western world found itself on the crest of a long and profitable wave of unprecedented growth. To most of its citizens, mankind appeared to be moving triumphantly forward in the quest for an improved existence and a more equitable standard of life. Recent scientific and technical discoveries brought increasing control over the environment, permitting a level of material comfort unimaginable even a few years previously.

Europe, considered by the majority of its inhabitants to comprise the entire civilized world, had extended its colonial dominion in an ever-widening arc over the outlying regions of the earth, producing an unparalleled economic boom. Expansion and improvement were everywhere apparent. Industrialization continued to rise, transportation and communications to reach further, health care to advance, and public services to attain new levels of excellence. The continental population was also increasing dramatically, and this contributed further to the general condition of prosperity and expansion.

The sense of achievement characterizing the time was nowhere more strongly evident than in the sciences. Indeed, scientific progress formed the true foundation of the age, and its advances encompassed such diverse inventions as the telephone, electric light, moving pictures, and X-rays, and such engineering feats as the Suez Canal. Developments in medicine produced improved surgical techniques and better control over infectious diseases. To many it seemed as if mankind, bolstered by the advances in scientific thought, was finally in a position to solve all its material problems, perhaps even its social ones as well.

The controlling scientific idea for these developments, providing the period with its dominant conceptual image, was the theory of evolution formulated shortly after the middle of the nineteenth century by the English naturalist Charles Darwin. This theory offered an explanation of the evolution of plant and animal species through processes of hereditary choice, governed by a principle of preservation called natural selection. In Darwin's view this principle led to "the improvement of each creature in relation to its organic and inorganic conditions of life; and consequently, in most cases, to what must be regarded as an advance in organization." Darwin's ideas were subsequently extended by his followers to incorporate a much wider range of phenomena, including the evolution of social classes, the rise and fall of nations, and ultimately almost all aspects of human life. They provided the foundation for a view of the world as a complex organism steadily moving toward its own perfection, controlled through the mechanism of a universal law. "Progress" became the watchword of the period.

The Viennese novelist Stefan Zweig, in his reminiscences of the years preceding World War I, described the general prevailing attitude:

> This faith in an uninterrupted and irresistible "progress" truly had the force of a religion for that generation. One began to believe more in this "progress" than in the Bible, and its gospel appeared ultimate because of the daily new wonders of science and technology. In fact, at the end of the peaceful century, a general advance became more marked, more rapid, more varied. . . . Comfort made its way from the houses of the fashionable to those of the middle class. It was no longer necessary to fetch water from the pump or the hallway, or to take the trouble to build a fire in the fireplace. Hygiene spread and filth disappeared. People became handsomer, stronger, healthier, more robust. . . . Small wonder then that this century sunned itself in its own accomplishments and looked upon each completed decade as the prelude to a better one. There was as little belief in the possibility of such barbaric declines as wars between the nations of Europe as there was in witches and ghosts. Our fathers were comfortably saturated with confidence in the unfailing and binding power of tolerance and conciliation. They honestly believed that the divergencies and the boundaries between nations and sects would gradually melt away into a common humanity and that peace and security, the highest of treasures, would be shared by all mankind.[1]

1.   *The World of Yesterday* (New York, 1943), pp. 3–4.

World War I put an end to such optimism. Its effects were devastating, bringing a magnitude of physical destruction and human misery unknown in previous human history. To most, such a conflict among modern civilized nations had seemed impossible. Yet, although the complex political and strategic origins of the war are still hotly debated, in retrospect it appears evident that the seeds of the conflict had been planted long before hostilities broke out in 1914. Moreover, signs of personal unrest and social disintegration were clearly visible even during the halcyon days of late nineteenth-century prosperity—indeed, formed an inseparable component of the very way of life they would ultimately help to destroy. One of the main conditions necessary for the era's prosperity, for example, was absolute political and social stability, which those in power did everything possible to maintain. Each person was accorded a fixed and prescribed place in an unchanging social order, severely limiting the possibilities for individual advancement. Creative thought was heavily circumscribed; the more radical its nature, the more actively it was suppressed. To the day's more progressive artists and thinkers, life seemed all too predictable and intolerably boring; one knew not only how the world was presently constituted, but also how it was to remain in the future. Reaction was inevitable in a society that allowed such a limited range of personal mobility. Extreme individualism and revolt against the prevailing value system became a rallying point for a small but vocal group of freethinkers determined to expose the lies hidden beneath the surface of well-being and complacency.

Paradoxically, science itself contributed to the breakdown by calling into question the old, comfortable belief in a predictable and mechanical universe. The tenets of quantum mechanics, which emerged near the turn of the century, indicated that essential features of the physical world were chaotic and unpredictable; and Einstein's theory of relativity, published in 1905, suggested that the entire notion of a stable and mechanically ordered universe was no longer viable. At the same time, Freud's newly proposed psychoanalytic theories emphasized the irrational side of human behavior and reaffirmed the primacy of the sexual impulse. The suggestion that the human psyche was divided into two separate compartments, one conscious and the other unconscious, and that the unconscious, instinctual side to a significant degree controlled the conscious one shook current assumptions of human nature to their foundations. (That Freud himself, according to his biographer Ernst Jones, considered his own discoveries to be "contrary to nature" offers a telling indication of the extraordinary inner tensions and contradictions that typified the period.)

But it is turn–of–the–century art that shows perhaps most vividly the

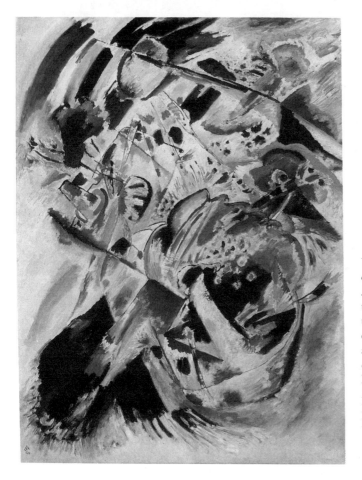

Wassily Kandinsky's 1914 oil *Winter (Painting Number 201)* suggests something of the nature of the season through the descriptive, expressive powers of abstract means. (Oil on canvas, 64¼ × 48¼". Collection, The Museum of Modern Art, New York. Nelson A. Rockefeller Fund (by exchange)

disillusionment and dissatisfaction hiding beneath the civilized veneer, the determination to break away from the outworn conventions of an old and dying way of life. The period between 1900 and 1914 is one of the most turbulent in the entire history of the arts, one that produced a series of revolutionary developments fundamentally affecting all subsequent endeavors.

These years witnessed the end of the realist tradition that had dominated Western art since the Renaissance. As nineteenth-century painters turned increasingly inward, drawing inspiration more and more from their own internal psychological experiences at the expense of a faithful mirroring of external objects and events, their work moved inexorably toward a state of pure abstraction. The final breakthrough occurred with Wassily Kandinsky, the first major artist to create completely non-representational paintings, in Munich during the years immediately preceding World War I.

But the tendency to distort objective reality in favor of a more personalized and emotionally charged vision was evident throughout the

Oskar Kokoschka. *Hans Tietze and Erica Tietze-Conrat* (1909). This well-known double portrait seems to bare the souls of the two art historians who are its uneasy subjects. (Oil on canvas, 30⅛ × 53⅝″. Collection, The Museum of Modern Art, New York. Abby Aldrich Rockefeller Fund)

art world in the early years of the century, in the Norwegian Edvard Munch, the Austrian Oskar Kokoschka, and the Italian Carlo Carrà, among others. In France it took a particularly characteristic turn, as Pablo Picasso and Georges Braque developed a stylized approach to representation, known as cubism, that ignored all assumptions of a rationally ordered three-dimensional space. Heavily influenced by primitive art, which had begun to be taken seriously as a basis for a possible alternative to European realism, the cubist painters broke up objects into their constituent parts, emphasizing their basic geometrical features such as planes, cubes, etc., and rearranged them into new, more abstract configurations. The impact of these visual innovations on contemporary consciousness can scarcely be exaggerated. The English novelist Virginia Woolf, after viewing the first exhibit of post-Impressionist painting in London, went so far as to observe: "On or about December 1910 human character changed."

Analogous tendencies were evident elsewhere in the arts. Writers such as the Austrian Robert Musil portrayed the dissolution of the old social order, while others like the Belgian Maurice Maeterlinck attempted to escape from the present altogether by projecting a world of historical fantasy and psychological symbolism. Reality began to be depicted from new and uniquely modern perspectives, as in the work of the French novelist Marcel Proust, who employed a "stream of consciousness" technique to present events according to the random sequence of memory and inner reflection, ignoring chronology, logical continuity, and distinctions between conflicting temporal and spatial levels. Similarly dramatic transformations occurred in architecture, as in the buildings of the Viennese Otto Wagner, who rejected the official eclectic, ornament-heavy style in favor of a simpler, more functionally conceived architecture that stressed utility in place of monumentality.

In music the fall of traditional tonality brought in its wake new principles of organization that corresponded closely to these revolutionary developments in the other arts. In the Introduction, we noted how older musical conventions were under considerable strain even before the turn of the century. For many these conventions represented the absolute and inviolable dictates of a "natural"—thus presumably eternal—musical order, the artistic counterpart to the innate scheme of rank, privilege, and regulation on which nineteenth-century political and social life rested. Viewed in this light, the overthrow of tonality was but one of many symptoms of a widespread determination to lay the foundation for a new way of life by destroying the basis of the old one. In all areas of artistic activity innovative works attacked the accepted, long-accustomed assumptions of a discredited past.

Thus an undeniable element of negation and provocation can be perceived in musical developments during the earlier years of the twentieth century. A radical, aggressively new type of music required the brutal destruction of habits ingrained during the long and unbroken reign of

The leading Viennese architect, Otto Wagner, avoiding the flamboyant historical references so characteristic of earlier nineteenth-century Viennese buildings, designed this modern and comfortable apartment house in 1890–91. Gustav Mahler lived in it from 1898 to 1909. (Plan- und Schriftenkammer der Stadt Wien)

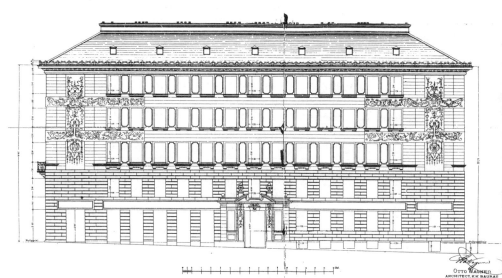

traditional tonality. Considered positively, however, the downfall of tonality allowed for a moment of extraordinary liberation and release, one that made available a seemingly limitless range of previously unimagined possibilities. No longer confined by the constraints of the old system, composers began investigating largely unexplored areas of musical thought. Much of the music of the period preceding World War I evinces a marked "experimental" aspect. It was as if suddenly, after two centuries of domination by a single prevailing musical dogma, a whole new world had miraculously materialized. Fundamental choices had to be made by every composer—indeed, for every composition. By comparison with those of the previous century, the range and variety of these choices consequently seemed—and to a large extent still seems—baffling. Certain composers, such as the Futurists, seized the opportunity to construct works that defied virtually all the basic tenets of the older esthetics. More commonly, however, some principles of tonal music, especially those relating to general formal, rhythmic, and thematic concerns, were preserved.

Since the new music also retained, with few exceptions, the dominant esthetic of personal expression inherited from the previous century, the music of the early years of the twentieth century should perhaps be understood as the final gasp of late nineteenth-century Romanticism. From a technical point of view, as opposed to a general esthetic one, however, the new and unprecedented seems most characteristic of this music, lending it a prominent place among the many manifestations of a changing temperament evident in all the arts of the period. Above all, it is the "spirit of the new" that defined the age, driving its most influential figures and producing such profound cultural transformations. As the French poet Charles Péguy commented at the time: "The world has changed less since the time of Jesus Christ than it has in the last thirty years."

CHAPTER II

Some Transitional Figures

In this chapter we will consider several composers born in the 1860s and early 1870s. Though they reached musical maturity under the dominating influence of nineteenth-century musical ideals, they all, in their own ways, contributed significantly to the radical stylistic changes of the early years of the modern period. Transitional figures, these composers provided a foundation for the future by transforming what they inherited from the past. By the end of their lives, all were creating music that could only have been conceived in the new century—unlike many of their contemporaries, who remained more closely tied to their nineteenth-century beginnings (for example, Elgar and Rachmaninov). With one major exception they all died while the new century was still relatively young, so their role in the twentieth century was limited to the period leading up to World War I. And, as we shall see, the exception, Richard Strauss, followed a course of evolution that was to place his later work somewhat outside the main historical currents of the postwar years.

AUSTRIA: MAHLER

Though born in a small town that is now part of Czechoslovakia, Gustav Mahler (1860–1911) studied at the Vienna Conservatory and eventually adopted the Austrian capital as the center of his musical activities. Enormously gifted as a performer, Mahler pursued throughout his life a career as a conductor, and became one of the most prominent of his time. He held positions with opera houses in Leipzig, Budapest, and

A 1904 photograph showing a typically preoccupied Gustav Mahler leaving the Viennese opera house, where he set new standards of artistic excellence during his ten-year reign as Director. (Bild-Archiv der Osterreichischen National-bibliothek, Wien)

Hamburg before becoming in 1897 music director of the Vienna Court Opera, among the most important artistic posts in all Europe. During his ten-year reign Mahler brought the company to new heights of achievement, producing a golden age in Viennese music that has never been equaled. He tightened the company's musical discipline, sought the collaboration of important visual artists, insisted upon integration of musical and dramatic elements, and in general raised performance standards considerably. He also provided valuable support to younger colleagues such as Schoenberg.

Despite its basically conservative core, Mahler's Vienna was a center of intense artistic and cultural activity, engendering some of the most radical currents in turn-of-the-century European thought. As the seat of the Austro-Hungarian Empire, symbolized by the aging Emperor Franz Josef (1848–1916), Vienna was both guardian and arbiter of the cultural and political order; and as the birthplace of musical Classicism, it was especially proud and protective of its distinguished artistic heritage. Yet signs of unrest were clearly apparent as the new century dawned.

Independent political and nationalist movements challenged the authority of the central government, presaging the ultimate disintegration of the empire at the end of World War I. Uncertainty about the future became a prevalent concern.

These tensions were embodied in the work of a remarkable group of radical artists and intellectuals who were concentrated in Vienna at the turn of the century, whose ideas would become profoundly influential. Among them were the scientist Sigmund Freud, the political thinker Theodor Herzl, the architects Otto Wagner and Adolph Loos, the painters Gustav Klimt, Egon Schiele, and Oskar Kokoschka, the writers Arthur Schnitzler, Hugo von Hofmannsthal, and Karl Kraus, and the composers Arnold Schoenberg and Mahler himself. All were committed to restructuring traditional beliefs, to developing new modes of thought, new manners of verbal expression, new ways of seeing and hearing. Collectively they helped lay the intellectual and artistic foundations of the modern age.

Thus one might say that Vienna encompassed both past and future in a manner unequaled by any other European city of the period; and its contradictory role as a bastion of tradition and a caldron for the new found a precise artistic counterpart in Gustav Mahler's complex musical temperament. As an opera conductor Mahler was deeply committed to preserving the masterpieces of the standard repertory, yet his productions were considered revolutionary in both musical conception and scenic design. And as a composer his output betrayed similar tensions between nostalgia for the past and a constant search for innovative means of musical expression.

From one perspective Mahler can be seen as the last major link in the great chain of Austro-German symphonic composers, extending from Haydn and Mozart through Beethoven and Schubert to Brahms and Bruckner and, finally, Mahler himself. Mahler owed much to this tradition, and he continued and brought to a culmination many of its most characteristic developments. The tendency toward greater length and ever larger orchestral forces, evident throughout the history of the symphony, reached a point in his work beyond which further evolution seemed both pointless and impractical. A quality of lyricism, introduced especially by Schubert and Bruckner into the symphonic conception, pervades his music with even greater emphasis. Three of Mahler's first four symphonies require voices (the exception is the First), an indication both of a strongly lyrical inclination and of a debt to the precedent of Beethoven's Ninth Symphony. Moreover, the first three symphonies contain instrumental movements that rework, without voices, earlier Mahler songs, including settings of texts drawn from the famous collection of German folk poetry *Des Knaben Wunderhorn* (The Youth's Magic Horn); and the last movement of the Fourth Symphony

The beginning of the third movement of *Das Lied von der Erde* in draft score. Mahler worked on this composition during the summer of 1908, three years before his death. (Gesellschaft der Musikfreunde, Archiv, Vienna)

is a vocal setting, freshly composed, of a text from the same collection.

The first four symphonies span the years 1888–1900. With the Fifth Symphony of 1902, which Mahler himself considered a stylistic turning point, comes a shift of emphasis toward purely instrumental conceptions. The Fifth, Sixth (1904), and Seventh (1905) Symphonies are all purely orchestral, as are the Ninth (1909) and Tenth (1910, left unfinished at the composer's death). Only the Eighth (1906), a monumental choral symphony in two parts (based on, respectively, the Latin hymn text *Veni, creator spiritus* and the closing scene of Goethe's *Faust,* Part II), and *Das Lied von der Erde* (The Song of the Earth, 1909), an extended symphonic setting, for contralto and tenor soloists, of Chinese poems in German translation, relate back to the earlier vocal symphonies. In addition, a number of songs to poems by Friedrich Rückert date from the early 1900s, five of them grouped into a cycle with orchestral accompaniment known as *Kindertotenlieder* (Songs on the Death of Children).

In his compositions after the turn of the century, extended multi-movement works requiring enormous performing forces, Mahler developed a strikingly new conception of the formal and expressive possibilities of symphonic music. A tendency, evident even in his earliest works, toward constant variation, toward a continuous evolution of new material out of old, was refined with ever greater technical assurance. Related to this was Mahler's essentially polyphonic conception of texture, influenced by the music of Bach, whom he greatly admired. Accompanimental "filler," so characteristic of the harmonic conception of other late nineteenth-century composers, was shunned in favor of textures whose individual strands took on true melodic significance, producing a rich web of subtle and varied motivic correspondences.

Mahler's mature works display a quality of ambivalence and uncertainty that seems uniquely modern in character, most clearly evident in the area of harmony and tonal relationships. On the one hand, the music often seems deceptively "conservative" in nature, as there is far less chromaticism than in contemporary works by such composers as Strauss and Reger, or even in the later operas of Wagner; and undisguised dominant relationships still continue to play an essential structural role. Despite moments of extraordinary daring (such as chords built in fourths in the Seventh Symphony and dissonant polychordal combinations in the Sixth), the harmonic language remains for the most part unexceptional. Yet at the same time, tonality in Mahler comes close to reaching its final stage of dissolution: complete works, and even individual movements, no longer necessarily define a single key, but explore a range of related and interconnected regions, often closing in a different key from the one in which they began.

The Seventh Symphony offers an instructive example. The first movement is in E minor (though, typically, it begins in B minor), while the final movement is in C major. Yet what matters is precisely the opposition and interconnection of these two tonal areas, E and C, an opposition that controls most of the important tonal relationships of the symphony as a whole and that is already set up within the first movement when the main contrasting theme appears in C major. Moreover, the E-minor ending of the first movement is followed immediately by the C-minor opening of the second; and the main theme of the last movement, though itself in C, pointedly juxtaposes the chords of E minor and C major at its beginning.

Even more striking, because of the distance of the keys, is the Ninth Symphony: the first movement is in D major, the fourth and last in D♭ major. The third movement mediates between the two: in A minor, it contains a long D-major section and closes with a cadence in which a D♭-major chord figures prominently. This chord prepares for the key of the immediately following final movement in D♭, just as the latter in turn refers back to its predecessor with the dramatic appearance of an A-major chord in its third measure. Such procedures alter the very meaning of tonality, which becomes a complex network of interchangeable relationships, rather than a closed system that ultimately pulls in a single, uncontested direction.

These tonal practices stem from Mahler's innovative conception of musical form as a succession of individual episodes, held together by the kinds of tonal connections indicated above and by an elaborately developed system of motivic correspondences. Although in most of his works traditional formal types, such as sonata forms, are at least superficially adhered to, the actual dynamics of the formal process are fundamentally different. In place of the traditional balance among connecting sections whose functional relationships to one another—whether expositional, transitional, or developmental—are never seriously in doubt, Mahler presents a pattern of abrupt oppositions between formal units that differ radically in both character and structure.

Musical continuity in Mahler is marked by a high degree of disjunction and juxtaposition, of rapid crosscutting back and forth among widely contrasting (and often seemingly unrelated) ideas. The concept of recapitulation, one of the cornerstones of the traditional view of form, also acquires a different significance. Musical segments do recur, but they are invariably transformed through the process of constant variation that pervades all of Mahler's mature work. As the composer himself once said, "Music is governed by the law of eternal evolution, eternal development—just as the world, even in one and the same spot, is always changing, eternally fresh and new."[1] The resulting effect of an unending musical flux—and a corresponding loss in constancy, in the sense of a firm and immutable foundation—goes far in explaining the revolutionary impact of Mahler's music upon his contemporaries.

For some of these aspects of Mahler's work, precedents can be found—for example, in Bruckner. But the degree of contrast and the range of character in the musical materials is fundamentally new. Whereas Classical form offered a closed system of musical relationships, capable of accommodating only a limited range of thematic and formal types, Mahler's more open conception enabled him to incorporate materials whose extreme contrasts would destroy the internal consistency of a more traditional context. Mahler once commented, "To me 'symphony' means constructing a world with all the technical means at one's disposal."[2] This world is remarkably inclusive in nature, for the symphonies are pervaded by music of a popular, even "vulgar" quality—a marked departure from the more restricted content of earlier concert music. Music evoking popular dances and folk songs is joined with bugle calls, marches, and grotesque parodies to create what can seem an almost collagelike jumble, a juxtaposition of discordant qualities made possible by a more episodic approach to form.

1.   Natalie Bauer-Lechner, *Recollections of Gustav Mahler,* ed. Peter Franklin, trans. Dika Newlin (London, 1980), p. 130.
2.   Ibid., p. 40.

By such means Mahler was able to shape epic structures of enormous length (several of his symphonies last in the neighborhood of ninety minutes), affording time and place for the most divergent and contrasting types of musical substance, over which hangs nevertheless the threat of impending chaos. Indeed, the music is, at times, almost frightening in its impact. As the composer himself once asked after conducting a performance of his First Symphony: "What sort of world is it that brings forth such sounds and shapes as its representation?"[3]

Mahler was one of the major conductors of his age, a fact that had both a positive and negative effect upon his compositional career. Although it forced him to relegate composing almost entirely to the summer months, Mahler's conducting career also gave him an unmatched knowledge of orchestral technique and the possibilities of instrumental combination. Indeed, his use of the orchestra represents one of Mahler's most important areas of innovation. During the nineteenth century composers had increasingly experimented with novel orchestral effects and with coloristic possibilities made available by larger ensembles. Mahler retained and even expanded the huge forces of his predecessors, but, particularly in the later works, he used the Romantic orchestra not so much as a medium for massed, large-scale effects but as a repository of instruments from which to draw many smaller, essentially chamber-like combinations, each with a distinct timbral character. The skillful alternation of these groups gives his music an arresting quality that depends upon intricate and subtle transformations of color.

Yet Mahler's orchestration is never solely a matter of color; it also defines essential musical relationships. Thus in the symphonies interlocking melodic contours are differentiated by means of timbral contrast and a careful balancing of the instrumental forces. Mahler often makes use of what might be characterized as "analytic" instrumentation: the individual motivic units of an extended melodic line are set off from one another through the alternation of different instruments or instrumental groups, creating a sort of "melody of timbres." This technique was to have a pronounced influence upon later composers, especially Schoenberg.

Something of the quality of Mahler's music can be gathered from the main theme of the second movement of the Seventh Symphony (Example II-1). At first hearing, this music may seem almost too simple, even naive in construction and character. An unprepossessing little march tune in C major appears in two phrases, the first cadencing on the dominant (m. 36) and the second on the tonic (m. 43, followed by a three-measure extension)—a tonal organization in no way exceptional. Though there are many accidentals, these result almost entirely from the juxta-

3.   *Gustav Mahler Briefe, 1879–1911,* ed. Alma Maria Mahler (Berlin, 1924), p. 419.

position of major and minor elements (a characteristic trait of Mahler's style), so that the music remains essentially diatonic and triadic throughout.

Example II-1: MAHLER, Symphony No. 7, second movement, mm. 29–46

Especially interesting, however, is the internal construction of the principal melodic line (heard first in the horn, then in the violins), pieced together from a number of recurring motivic units that are varied and rearranged so that no literal repetitions occur, either within the first phrase or between the first and the second. The latter, although clearly an altered version of the opening phrase, begins with a motivic figure derived not from its first measure but from m. 34. This figure dominates the first part of the second phrase, its relation to m. 34 becoming especially evident at m. 40. Moreover, Mahler disturbs the expected rhythmic balance between the phrases by cadencing the second a measure "too soon" (at m. 43 rather than m. 44, thus avoiding an 8 + 8 correspondence), and by prolonging the cadential chord over four measures (mm. 43–46). When the melodic material of mm. 29–30 finally does reappear in the viola in mm. 43–44, one at first expects a repeat of the theme, but after the opening two measures appear once more in a lower register, they lead into a new and contrasting section (not included in the example).

Another characteristic of the passage is the degree to which the details of the accompaniment are motivated by contrapuntal considerations. The cellos freely imitate the principal melody at a distance of one measure (mm. 30–32) and, after proceeding more independently, do so again at mm. 41–44, now at a distance of only a half measure. At m. 31 the bassoons add a motivic correspondence, anticipating the outline of the horn melody in m. 34. Notable too is the way the horns, having apparently finished their first phrase in m. 36, continue in mm. 36–38 with a descending half-step motive derived from their ascending half step in mm. 29–30. Mahler's use of a percussive march rhythm—which in a lesser composer might sound like a cliché, a stock item found in countless marches—is particularly revealing: it appears only as an isolated fragment (in mm. 32 and 36 in the violins, then not again until mm. 45–46 in the oboe), a momentary yet evocative reference to the march genre that completely transcends its banal origins.

The passage also illustrates certain more general characteristics of Mahler's style. Its curious blend of simplicity and complexity, of the ordinary mixed with the extraordinary, is very much at the heart of his music. Something that on one level seems familiar and conventional has been transformed on another into something strangely compelling and intensely beautiful. This quality is found in countless passages throughout his work: e.g., in the minor-mode version of the tune *Frère Jacques,* used as the basis for a canon in the third movement of the First Symphony; in the series of dislocated march tunes that dominate the first movement of the Third; in the bugle calls that open the Fifth; and in the "serenade" (complete with mandolin and guitar) that forms the third movement of the Seventh. Again and again, one is struck by

Mahler's ability to take from diverse sources an immense range of materials, often unassuming and of apparently little interest in themselves, and to integrate them into a complex and cohesive structure that lends them new and unexpected significance. Consistency in Mahler is no longer a matter of the individual materials themselves, but of an encompassing compositional attitude that transforms them all into integrated and expressively forceful musical statements.

It is perhaps this aspect of Mahler's music, more than any other, that has led certain commentators to label him the first truly modern composer. (As we shall see, a similar claim has been made, though on different grounds, for Debussy, as well as for other composers treated in this section.) Others feel that Mahler was limited in that he wrote no chamber music or operas. Yet if we measure Mahler's achievement by what he did, rather than did not, accomplish, then there can be little doubt that he fundamentally altered the face of music, at least in the Germanic world. His influence on Schoenberg and his followers was emphatic. And in more recent years, as Mahler's works have finally acquired their due recognition from the general public, it has become apparent that he anticipated many facets of the music of the period after World War II.

As a figure poised between two musical epochs, Mahler presents a curiously mixed and even contradictory impression. On the one hand, his message is one of nostalgia, of great sadness at the dissolution of the world of nineteenth-century Romanticism, a condition his music reflects more poignantly than that of perhaps any other twentieth-century composer. The prevalent diatonicism and unabashed melodic expressivity recall a simpler and more gracious time, but they are now tinged with a pronounced element of discordance, ambiguity, and uncertainty. For Mahler also stands at the threshold of a new age, the musical possibilities of which he had already begun to explore with great imagination and inventiveness in the early years of the century.

GERMANY: RICHARD STRAUSS

Richard Strauss (1864–1951) composed in most of the major musical genres (the exception being chamber music): opera, symphonic music, songs, and choral works. He shared marked similarities with his contemporary Mahler. Both were conductors of international fame, with a profound knowledge of the resources of the modern orchestra. (Strauss's 1905 edition of Berlioz's famous *Treatise on Instrumentation,* incorporating the latest innovations of the Wagnerian and post-Wagnerian orchestra, remains to this day a standard text on nineteenth-century orchestral technique.) Both composed extended symphonic works of programmatic origins, requiring very large orchestral forces. And despite distinct differences in character and expressive intent, their music shares important technical traits. But whereas Mahler suffered from the widespread incomprehension of contemporary listeners, Strauss, though certainly controversial, was widely recognized by the turn of the century as the leading figure of the post-Wagnerian generation of German composers.

Strauss, the son of a well-known Munich horn player, was unusually precocious. His first published work, an orchestral march, appeared when he was only twelve, and by the middle of the 1880s, while still a student, he had amassed an impressive body of works in a conservative style largely derived from Mendelssohn. (Strauss's father apparently insisted that the young musician study only the classics.) These youthful compositions were taken up by major soloists and ensembles, and by his twentieth year Strauss enjoyed a degree of prominence that many older composers would have envied.

The symphonic fantasy *Aus Italien* (From Italy, 1886) marked an important turning point in Strauss's development toward a more progressive style influenced by the "new German" school of Wagner and Liszt. A series of eight "tone poems" (a term coined by Strauss in preference to the older "symphonic poem") followed, extending from *Don Juan* (1888) to the *Symphonia domestica* (Domestic Symphony, 1903), works that brought the composer unrivaled popular success and established him at the forefront of the most advanced compositional tendencies of the age. At the same time, Strauss achieved equal renown as a conductor, succeeding the famous Hans von Bülow in Meiningen in 1885 and then assuming major posts in Munich (1886–89), Weimar (1889–94), Berlin (1894–1918), and Vienna (1919–24). He also traveled widely as a guest conductor, and his compositions were performed frequently throughout the Western world. Even Debussy, a composer in most respects diametrically opposed to Strauss's compositional esthetic, referred to him as "the dominating genius of our time."

Strauss's musical prominence as the new century began is easy to understand. His tone poems are brilliant compositions of supreme technical polish, and they exude an aura of irresistible confidence and power that offered an appropriate musical symbol for the expansionist mood of Germany at the time. After victory in the Austro-Prussian War of 1866 (which led to the formation of the first truly unified German confederation, under Prussian domination) and triumph in the Franco-Prussian War of 1870–71, Germany emerged as the principal political and industrial power of Europe. German science and technology were unmatched on the Continent. National pride was at an unprecedented peak, and Strauss, having successfully streamlined the esthetic and musical principles he inherited from Wagner to fit the requirements of a more modern age, was ideally suited to give expression to his country's newly found optimism.

The image of confidence projected by Strauss's tone poems contrasts strikingly to the profound questioning so deeply embedded in Mahler's music. Mahler, the Bohemian Jew beset by uncertainty, feeling himself an outsider even while occupying the most important artistic position in Vienna, harbored a much more pessimistic view of the world, a view that left unmistakable traces in his music. The typical Mahler conclusion offers a gradual extinction, an ultimate dissolution into silence (as at the ends of the Sixth and Ninth Symphonies). Strauss, on the other hand, favors endings that bring about a final consummation and glorification of the principal musical materials (as in the last section of the symphonic poem *Tod und Verklärung* (*Death and Transfiguration,* 1889). Strauss was supremely certain of himself and of his position in the world, a characteristic that distinguishes him not only from Mahler but from most other major twentieth-century composers. This self-confidence and assurance found their most blatant (if somewhat tongue-in-cheek) expression in the tone poem *Ein Heldenleben* (*A Hero's Life,* 1898), wherein the hero—explicitly identified with Strauss himself—is depicted as a kind of "superman" who, through unique powers and indomitable strength of will, overcomes all obstacles and adversaries.

The question of program music is critical for Strauss. Unlike Mahler, who later withdrew the programs for his earlier symphonies and for whom programs had in any event only a very generalized relation to the overall characteristics of his music, Strauss favored programs that were quite detailed in content, with definite correlations to specific musical events in his compositions. This is not to say that the music can be followed only with knowledge of its extramusical basis; the works do have an inherent musical logic. As Strauss himself remarked: "In my opinion . . . a poetic programme is nothing but a pretext for the purely musical expression and development of my emotions, and not a simple *musical description* of concrete everyday facts."[4] Yet the musical possibilities suggested by his programs were essential in enabling Strauss to develop large-scale forms quite different from those he inherited from the Classical tradition.

In most of the tone poems the shell of a traditional formal type is still recognizable: sonata form in *Don Juan* and *Tod und Verklärung,* rondo in *Till Eulenspiegels lustige Streiche* (*Till Eulenspiegel's Merry Pranks,* 1895), theme and variations in *Don Quixote* (1897). But, as in Mahler, the actual sense of the form is fundamentally innovative. Indeed, in its overall formal characteristics, the music of Strauss has much in common with

---

4.   From a letter of July 1905, in *Richard Strauss and Romain Rolland: Correspondence,* ed. Rollo Myers (London, 1968), p. 29.

that of his Austrian contemporary—notably a similar tendency toward episodic structures featuring distinct and highly differentiated sections, each with its own individual character. But in Strauss this tendency is intimately tied to a portrayal of the various events and psychological moods associated with the programs. And despite its sectional variety, Strauss's music, with its more obvious consistency, projects little of the quality of stylistic opposition and confrontation, of the unresolved and ambivalent emotional complexity, so marked in Mahler.

The technical innovations introduced by Strauss in the symphonic works of the 1890s proved of considerable importance in the development of twentieth-century music. Extending Wagner's practice, he carried the leitmotif over into a purely instrumental context. Using an array of very brief, though readily identifiable, melodic figures presented in rapid alternation and shifting combinations, Strauss fashioned complex polyphonic textures only barely contained within a highly inflected and intensely chromatic harmonic framework. The pacing of this music reveals something quite new: an unprecedented amount of musical material is often compressed into a very short span of time, although the exceptional activity is primarily a matter of rapid transformations of surface details. (The larger structure is in fact less complex than might be expected from the explosive nature of the moment-by-moment succession.)

The virtuosity with which Strauss manipulated the orchestra in this new, intensified musical context made a profound impression upon his contemporaries. He demanded a level of instrumental playing far beyond that required by other composers of his generation (with the notable exception of Mahler). Experimenting with novel effects of instrumental color and atmosphere, usually suggested by programmatic considerations, he revolutionized the whole concept of orchestral sound—as, for example, in the effect, bordering on sheer noise, of the battle scene from *Ein Heldenleben,* with its percussive ostinato, sharp pizzicatos, and swirling woodwind figures (intended to suggest clashing swords); and the depiction of bleating sheep in *Don Quixote,* produced by muted brass playing flutter-tongue in dissonant combinations. Music could never again be the same after the admission of such previously unheard elements, which by any traditional standard were considered "foreign" and "unmusical" in nature.

During the period of his symphonic poems Strauss wrote only two operas: *Guntram* (1893) and *Feuersnot* (1901), neither of which was to gain a permanent place in the repertory. After 1904, however, he began directing his compositional efforts almost exclusively to the stage, producing two operas that are pivotal in the history of twentieth-century music. *Salome* (1905) and *Elektra* (1908) might be described as staged tone poems, for they logically extend the line followed by Strauss in his earlier symphonic works. Here the program has simply been made theatrically manifest, presented on the stage as a visual and vocal "accompaniment" to the orchestral music, which responds to its emotional and expressive content. Like the tone poems, each opera is conceived as a single "movement" that presents its action in an unbroken succession. But in *Salome* and *Elektra* the technical developments encountered in the earlier works are carried to a new and critical stage: the tonal underpinnings are now strained to the breaking point, and the unfolding of the musical argument achieves an almost unbearable level of intensity and complexity.

Much of the extraordinary effect of these operas derives from their plots, which deal in graphic and lurid detail with the compulsive obsessions and murderous desires of their respective protagonists. Always sensitive to unusual extramusical suggestions, Strauss treats these plots as provocations to drive his compositional inclinations ever nearer their ultimate consequences. The musical results vividly communicate the eroticism, physical horror, and psychological depravity of the stories and characters. Tonality, though still present as an underlying control, is stretched to its outermost limits. The chordal succession increasingly takes on the character of a series of momentary coloristic effects, rather than a logical, key-defining progression. Dissonances are handled with unprecedented freedom, and the extreme chromaticism often blurs the triadic harmonic basis to the point of unrecognizability. Melodic ideas interact with one another with great freedom, breaking up the larger line into a sequence of isolated motivic fragments.

There are moments of relative repose (although even these are characterized by considerable activity), and the larger shape of the operas is to a degree still controlled by an alternation of passages of greater and lesser stability. But what impresses the listener most is the sense of an unending succession of violent interruptions, generated by the abrupt— and, at least from a purely musical point of view, seemingly unmotivated—contrasts that mirror the furious pace and brutal intensity of the stage action.

An example of the new harmonic constructions explored by Strauss

Example II-2: STRAUSS, *Elektra,* mm. 1–2 after No. 27.

Alfred Roller, the leading stage designer for the Vienna Opera during the earlier years of the twentieth century, created this set for Act III of the original 1911 production of Strauss's *Der Rosenkavalier.* The legend below reads: "Private room in a small inn." (By permission of Boosey & Hawkes, Inc.)

is found in a passage from *Elektra* (Example II-2), where a C♭-major triad is superimposed over an open fifth D-A, producing a dissonant clash of a minor ninth between D and E♭. This chord is then moved down chromatically in parallel motion until it returns to its original pitch level an octave lower. The resolution of dissonance is delayed so long that the dissonant chordal complex temporarily becomes the norm, rather than merely a departure from a triadic foundation, and thus itself forms the basis for the descending progression.

The degree of chromatic saturation and tonal instability reached in *Salome* and, especially, *Elektra* brought musical developments in the first decade of the century to a critical point: it became impossible to continue in the same direction without completely, and irrevocably, undermining the foundation of the old tonal system. In fact, the fatal step that carried music beyond tonality into a new stage of technical evolution was taken not by Strauss but by Schoenberg, at approximately the same time that *Elektra* was being completed. Thereafter, however, Strauss took a different path. Recognizing the impossibility of continuing along the lines of the technical innovations in his two great operas, he chose to turn in the opposite direction from Schoenberg—a step that, from a historical point of view, must be viewed as "backward." His next opera, *Der Rosenkavalier* (*The Cavalier of the Rose,* 1910), is much more traditional in conception than either *Salome* or *Elektra.* The tonal basis again becomes clearer and firmer; and the libretto, although like that of *Elektra* written by the brilliant Austrian poet Hugo von Hofmannsthal (with whom Strauss would also collaborate on several later operas), recounts an amusing and bittersweet love story set in eighteenth-century Vienna, far removed from the pathological excesses of the preceding operas.

Der Rosenkavalier, with its gay and sparkling (if anachronistic) waltzes and its soaring Romantic lyricism so evocative of a less troubled past, is brilliantly accomplished and contains some of Strauss's most beautiful music. (It remains to this day his most popular opera.) But to the radical young composers of the time, it must have seemed a betrayal of all that was most progressive in his earlier scores. It marked a decisive turning point in Strauss's development: he never again went back to the extremes of *Salome* and *Elektra,* but followed instead a more traditional course during the remainder of his long and fruitful career.

Strauss wrote four more operas with Hofmannsthal: *Ariadne auf Naxos* (*Ariadne on Naxos,* 1912, revised in 1916), *Die Frau ohne Schatten* (*The Woman without a Shadow,* 1918), *Die ägyptische Helena* (*The Egyptian Helen,* 1927), and *Arabella* (1932). Historically, *Ariadne* is the most interesting for its early indication of neo-classical tendencies. The original version was particularly daring in conception, consisting of a spoken performance of Molière's play *Le Bourgeois Gentilhomme* with incidental music by Strauss, followed by a one-act opera in which the Molière characters interacted with *opera seria* and *commedia dell'arte* players. (It was not a success, however, and in the revised version a sung prologue was substituted for the play.) In *Ariadne* Strauss used relatively small forces (an orchestra of only thirty-seven, for instance), and pared down his textures considerably to create a score that, by his standards, was notably economical. But the next opera, *Die Frau ohne Schatten,* again wears *Der Rosenkavalier*'s rich garb of late Romanticism, as also do *Die ägyptische Helena* and, to a lesser extent, *Arabella.*

In 1923 Strauss completed *Intermezzo,* a semiautobiographical opera to his own libretto, in a more conversational style, and after Hofmannsthal's death (in 1929) he remained active as an opera composer, creating four additional stage works between 1933 and 1941. These operas, all conceived and premiered under the Hitler regime, do not measure up to the earlier scores—partly from the absence of a librettist comparable in stature to Hofmannsthal, but surely also because of the repressive cultural atmosphere in Germany and Austria during this period. In 1933 Strauss allowed himself to be appointed president of the State Music Office by Joseph Goebbels, Hitler's minister of propaganda, but soon after became disillusioned with Nazi cultural and racial policies. He was publicly denounced for working with the Jewish writer Stefan Zweig, librettist for the first post-Hofmannsthal opera, *Die schweigsame Frau* (The Silent Woman, 1934). Strauss refused to remove Zweig's name from the program book and posters for the opera; performances of the opera were banned in Germany, and Strauss was forced to resign his party position in 1935. Though thereafter politically inactive, he continued to live in Germany and Austria and to be celebrated as the nation's most renowned composer.

Capriccio, Strauss's final opera, appeared in 1941. Following the war the composer enjoyed a resurgence of creative energy and, despite his advanced years, produced several of his most beautiful compositions, including the *Metamorphosen* for twenty-three strings (1945) and the *Four Last Songs* for voice and orchestra (1948). Yet with respect to the evolution of twentieth-century musical language, all of Strauss's music after *Elektra* seems curiously "unhistorical," giving the impression of having been composed in a time warp. Although this fact need not reflect on its quality (and Strauss's technical mastery has never been questioned), it does explain why the later work has played a relatively minor role in the development of subsequent music.

BUSONI

Although Ferruccio Busoni (1866–1924) was born in Italy of an Italian father, his mother was of German descent, his musical education was acquired mainly in Graz and Leipzig, and his professional career was centered largely in Berlin. Busoni was one of the most celebrated pianists of his age, greatly admired for the freely Romantic style of his playing and for his virtuosic transcriptions of Bach keyboard compositions. He was also a noted conductor, and introduced works by most of the important composers of the younger generation, including Schoenberg and Bartók.

Though active as a composer from his earliest years, Busoni's interest in composition seems to have increased markedly after the turn of the century. Whereas his earlier works, culminating in the gigantic Piano Concerto of 1904 (which introduced a male chorus in the finale), were written in an expansive, full-blown style typical of the late Romantic period, his subsequent music began to take on a leaner, more economical quality and a more forward-looking technical basis. The *Elegies* for piano, composed in 1907, were considered by Busoni to be the first works in which he completely found his own voice. During the following years he wrote a series of compositions, mostly of modest length, that are notable for their exploration of new compositional tendencies.

Busoni formally announced this change in attitude in a small volume entitled *Sketch of a New Esthetic of Music,* published in 1907, which represents the earliest attempt to formulate a comprehensive philosophical statement of the technical and esthetic foundations of a new twentieth-century music. A critical document in the history of the early modern movement, the *New Esthetic* had considerable influence on the younger composers of the time. It argues for the liberation of music from what Busoni considered to be the confining shackles of outmoded compositional practices. New music should be infinite and absolute, unencumbered on the one hand by the representative and descriptive limitations of program music, and on the other by the rigid and stereotyped formal schemata of "absolute music" as defined and prescribed by the academic theoreticians. Traditional musical "laws" were not to be accepted in blind faith, for the music of the future must be free to develop according to the requirements of its own inherent potentialities.

In place of what he refers to as the "tyranny of the major and minor system," with its rigid distinction between consonance and dissonance, Busoni proposes an undoctrinaire use of new scalar possibilities (which, as he remarks, had only just begun to be investigated in the music of such composers as Strauss and Debussy). He even sketches out a system of microtonal divisions of the octave, and discusses the potential of electronic instruments and new notational strategies in opening up as yet unimagined possibilities of entirely new musical systems. Busoni later gave the name "Young Classicism" to this visionary conception of a hoped-for new music, which would take into account "all the gains of previous experiments and their inclusion in strong and beautiful forms." This turn away from Romanticism toward a new kind of classicism was to prove remarkably prophetic, as we shall see, especially when we consider musical developments following World War I.

In his works after the publication of the *New Esthetic,* Busoni himself attempted at least a first step toward the kind of music he envisioned in his theoretical writings. Notable in this regard are the six sonatinas for piano, composed between 1910 and 1920. In these relatively short works, largely contrapuntal in conception and strongly influenced by the music of Bach, Busoni explored a number of novel compositional techniques: bitonal chordal complexes, "artificial" scalar patterns (such as wholetone), and unmetered rhythm, for example, can all be found in the Second Sonatina of 1912. Example II-3a, notated without indication of meter, represents the opening of the first main thematic idea, heard over a dissonant, arpeggiated chordal complex that forms the harmonic basis for the entire first section of the piece. In Example II-3b multiple levels of triadic harmonies move in parallel motion and combine with one another to form richly sonorous "polytonal" aggregates.

Equally suggestive is Busoni's wish to combine and reconcile stylistic traits drawn from diverse historical periods, in keeping with his view of the interconnection and ultimate oneness of all musical expression (an attitude he forcefully argued in a famous essay entitled "The Unity of Music"). This view is particularly evident in his later works. Both the Fifth (1919) and Sixth (1920) Sonatinas, for example, make explicit use of earlier music (Bach's D-minor Fantasy and Fugue and Bizet's *Carmen,* respectively), mixing actual quotations with freely composed distortions of the borrowed material, producing a distinctly modern effect that has parallels with Stravinsky's music of the same time.

Even in his most chromatic and experimental works, such as the Second Sonatina, Busoni never completely gave up the notion of tonality.

Example II-3: BUSONI, Second Sonatina

a. mm. 4–5

b. mm. 74–76

But tonality is here something quite different from what it formerly was—more inclusive and encompassing, capable of combining pure diatonicism with extreme chromaticism, major and minor scales with unusual new modalities, and traditional harmonic successions with complex vertical aggregates that, despite their dissonant structure, function as referential sonorities for entire sections.

Busoni's later works include three operas. *Arlecchino* (1916) and *Turandot* (1917) both contain spoken dialogue and rely upon eighteenth-century *commedia dell'arte* precedents, another reflection of Busoni's interest in revitalizing older traditions in modern guises. *Doktor Faust,* left unfinished at the composer's death in 1924, was completed by his friend the Spanish-German composer Philipp Jarnach; with its clearly defined numbers and traditional forms, it also exemplifies Busoni's very personal idea of Young Classicism. Based on old German puppet versions of the legend rather than on Goethe's *Faust,* the opera is, somewhat like the composer himself, a curious mixture of seemingly incompatible elements. At once remote yet visionary, it combines dramatic austerity with musical opulence.

Busoni is a puzzling figure, difficult to place within the larger picture of twentieth-century music. Especially in its moments of uninterrupted diatonicism and its frequent adherence to an unambiguously triadic harmonic structure, his music looks backward, yet it also contains innovations that point to the future. In his eclectic vision of a new music that would draw upon the widest possible range of technical and stylistic sources, Busoni helped stake out one of the principal paths that subsequent music would follow.

PFITZNER

Another German composer of this period deserving mention is Hans Pfitzner (1869–1949). Pfitzner's music is rarely performed outside his native Germany (a condition shared, though to a lesser extent, by Busoni), and he is of interest to us mainly as a counterweight, for, unlike the contemporaries we have discussed, Pfitzner remained entirely a faithful child of the nineteenth century. His compositions, though they give ample evidence of distinct and individual musical intelligence, never pass beyond the limits of late Romantic tonal and harmonic practice. The opera *Palestrina* (1915), based on an apocryphal episode in the life of the famed sixteenth-century Italian composer, is his best-known and most representative work.

In his numerous writings Pfitzner assumed an active role in defending the principles of a bygone musical era against those of a new age. His militant and polemical pamphlet *Futuristengefahr* (Danger of the Futurists), written in 1917 as a rebuttal to Busoni's *New Esthetic of Music,* was widely read and heatedly debated, and was followed two years later by a companion piece entitled *The New Esthetic of Musical Impotence.* In these essays Pfitzner defended the nineteenth-century esthetic of feeling and inspiration against what he felt to be the intellectual calculations and expressive paralysis of musical modernism, thus initiating an argument that has continued to rage in one form or another down to the present day.

REGER

In the brief forty-three-year span of his life, Max Reger (1873–1916) produced a staggering amount of music, ranging over every compositional genre except opera. Like his good friend Busoni, Reger reached musical maturity under the pervasive influence of post-Wagnerian chromaticism, but learned to temper its more extreme tendencies through an intimate knowledge of the music of Bach. Reger, a student of the arch-conservative theorist Hugo Riemann, maintained throughout his career a much closer and more specific tie with his musical heritage.

One finds little in his music of the pronounced experimental quality so noticeable in the later works of Busoni. Reger's intense chromaticism is invariably held in check by a clear triadic background that, although highly inflected and capable of moving with extraordinary speed to seemingly remote key regions, ultimately preserves its tonal mooring.

Reger's unrivaled contrapuntal virtuosity, learned mainly from the keyboard works of Bach, is everywhere in evidence in his work, especially in the numerous compositions for organ. A passage from the Symphonic Fantasy and Fugue for Organ, Op. 57 (1910), representing the most extreme stage in the composer's development toward increased chromaticism, indicates the density and complexity of Reger's contrapuntal fabric and chromatic voice-leading—and also the degree to which the motion is rooted within a firmly grounded triadic framework that provides a constant check on the freedom of the individual voices (Example II-4). The harmonic basis of the first part of the passage is a straightforward alternation of major or minor triads with diminished-seventh chords, the latter in each case reinterpreted in relation to the key of the following chord. Moreover, despite a liberal use of all degrees of the chromatic scale, the controlling D-minor tonality is never really in question, as tonic triads reappear as points of reference several times throughout the passage.

Example II-4: REGER, Symphonic Fantasy and Fugue for Organ, Op. 57, m. 57

Reger's highly developed chromaticism and mastery of strict contrapuntal procedures within complex multivoiced textures gave him a prominent position in the early years of the century. Though admired by Schoenberg, who counted him among the major innovators of the period, Reger never ventured beyond the edge of tonality, and even his most daring polyphonic constructions are ordered within essentially traditional formal contexts (notably the traditional contrapuntal genres used in his many organ works), which lend his music an almost archaic, even "classicistic," quality. The Variations and Fugue on a Theme of Mozart, Op. 132 (1914), probably his best-known orchestral composition, is a fascinating example of this peculiar blend of progressive and conservative elements (again in certain respects reminiscent of Busoni).

Reger's music would provide a point of departure for one of the major composers of the postwar generation of German musicians, Paul Hindemith. Indeed, Reger's belief in the beneficial effects of the music of Bach could stand as a watchword for many of the leading figures of that generation: "Sebastian Bach is for me the beginning and end of all music, the solid foundation of *any* true progress! . . . a sure cure, not only for all those composers and musicians who are sick of 'indigestible Wagner,' but for all those 'contemporaries' who suffer from any sort of spinal atrophy."[5]

FRANCE: DEBUSSY

In the late nineteenth century Paris was indisputably the cultural center of Europe. The arts flourished in the French capital, where a well-established avant-garde tradition had existed since at least the middle of the century and would have considerable impact on the evolution of modern art. The symbolist poets Stéphane Mallarmé, Paul Verlaine, and Arthur Rimbaud, and the post-Impressionist painters Paul Gauguin, Georges Seurat, and Paul Cézanne, placing unprecedented emphasis on purely formal elements at the expense of conventional representational ones, had completely overthrown the main assumptions of nineteenth-century realism, so that by the turn of the century France was already poised at the edge of a new artistic epoch.

Despite that progressive tradition in literature and the visual arts, French music remained curiously underdeveloped, and was still significantly under the influence of Germanic formal types and esthetic aims. Yet signs of a more independent direction began to appear before the century was out. The developments traced in the previous chapter, emphasizing increased chromaticism and heightened expressivity, represented an intensification of purely Germanic aspects of musical Romanticism that were essentially alien to the French temperament. In France, where the principles of functional tonality had never been so strongly anchored as in Germany, musical evolution was destined to follow a different path.

As early as 1871, in an attempt to counter the pervasive influence of Wagner and the trend toward late Romantic chromaticism, a national society of music (the Société Nationale de Musique) was founded by a group of young composers that included Camille Saint-Saëns (1835–

---

5. "Rundfrage: Was ist mir Johann Sebastian Bach und was bedeutet er für unsere Zeit," *Die Musik,* 5 / 1 (1905–6): 74.

Georges Seurat was one of the French painters at the turn of the century who emphasized purely formal elements at the expense of conventional representational ones. *Le Chahut* (1889–90) (Riijksmuseum Kröller-Müller, Otterlo)

1921), Emmanuel Chabrier (1841–94), and Gabriel Fauré (1845–1924), with the purpose of inspiring a musical renaissance of a specifically French character. Particular emphasis was placed on the resurrection of absolute music and a return to the principles of order, clarity, and restraint traditionally regarded as most characteristic of the great masterpieces of France's artistic past. Although the impact of Wagnerism, as well as other outside influences, proved too strong to be completely overcome—and indeed led in the 1880s to a split among the members of the Société—the goals set out by its founders had a decisive bearing on the future of French music.

Claude Debussy (1862–1918), the man who would be largely responsible for setting French music on a new course, matured in the atmosphere of this "renaissance" and, more than anyone else, was responsible for bringing it to full fruition. Born near Paris, he attended the Conservatory there and, although considered something of a "difficult" student, succeeded in winning the coveted Prix de Rome in 1884 for his cantata *L'Enfant prodigue*. Throughout his adult life Debussy lived in Paris, assuming a major position in the city's cultural life and establishing contacts with many prominent artistic figures of the time.

Debussy's youthful works reveal the influence of Chabrier and Fauré—especially the latter, who offered the young composer a precedent in his search for a new approach to tonality that, although essentially diatonic, would be free of the constraints of the traditional functional system. An interest in Russian music, particularly that of Musorgsky, reflected a similar concern. In Debussy's Baudelaire songs (1889) and String Quartet (1893) innovative modal combinations are used in conjunction with more standard harmonic progressions. The opening phrase of the Quartet (Example II-5) is typical. Here the diatonic modal degrees of the unraised seventh (F♮) and lowered second (A♭) appear with particular emphasis, especially in the cello's bass line, where F♮ replaces the traditional raised leading tone on the last beat of m. 1 before a return to the tonic G-minor chord. The A♭ also functions as a kind of substitute leading tone, in this case an "upper" one, on the last beat of m. 2, again before a return to the tonic.

Although the String Quartet still clings to the outlines of traditional formal types and employs the by-then-standard principle of cyclic construction, it also reflects, albeit at a relatively early stage, Debussy's growing concern for textural and timbral development. The elaborate exploitation of the purely sonic possibilities of the four instruments is characteristic, and in certain passages (most notably in the second movement) no doubt reflects the profound effect made upon Debussy by the Javanese gamelan music he heard at the Paris Universal Exposition of 1889. One of the most interesting aspects of his musical devel-

Example II-5: DEBUSSY, String Quartet, mm. 1–3

opment, which increasingly distinguished him not only from German contemporaries but also from the composers of the Société Nationale, was his interest in expanding traditional compositional resources from "without" (as opposed to the "internal" expansion of chromaticism), by importing ideas and techniques from traditions that were distant temporally (as in the case of medieval modes) and geographically (as in gamelan music).

The music of Wagner, toward whom Debussy harbored distinctly ambivalent feelings, also occupied an important place in the formation of his compositional personality. Well aware of the strength and uniqueness of Wagner's artistic achievement, Debussy came to distrust him as a force capable of undermining his own musical inclinations. Even when following a course in many respects opposed to the tenets of Wagnerianism, however, Debussy owed much to the German, especially the notion of a more naturalistic kind of music, intimately tied to the continuity of linguistic expression—both in a literal sense, as in the case of opera, and in a figurative one—and to the flow of dramatic events and psychological feelings. This became increasingly evident in the 1890s, when Debussy abandoned his earlier preference for abstract music in favor of a more programmatic conception. Yet the relation of Debussy's music to extramusical considerations is quite different from that of Wagner. In place of Wagner's complex and highly developed system of explicit musical references, Debussy favored a more generalized poetic evocation of moods, impressions, and atmospheric landscapes—"an emotional interpretation of what is invisible in Nature," as he once said in reference to Beethoven's *Pastoral Symphony*.

This attitude is reflected in the first great orchestral masterpieces of Debussy's maturity: the *Prélude à "L'Après-midi d'un faune"* (*Prelude to "The Afternoon of a Faun,"* 1894), the three Nocturnes (1900; the third, *Sirènes,* introduces a wordless female chorus), and the opera *Pelléas et Mélisande* (1893–1902), in which, despite the presence of a "story," the music seems to respond primarily to an interior action taking place in the minds of its characters and to the gloomy atmosphere evoked by its forest setting. The opening of the *Faune,* with its gently undulating flute solo (which will serve as a model for most of the important melodic transformation to come), illustrates the type of free ornamental melody of "natural curves" that the composer came to characterize as the "arabesque." Debussy recognized the source of the arabesque in what he described as the "delicate tracery" of Gregorian chant, which he felt could provide an archetype for the modern composer seeking new expressive life and freedom in his music.

Indeed, the concept of theme or melody in the traditional sense seems often inappropriate in relation to Debussy's music, which consists of collections of brief motivic particles that are mutually interconnected variations of one another, rather than derivations of a single primary melodic source stated as a point of departure at the outset. Thus a Debussy composition often seems not so much to "begin" as to gradually form itself out of an indistinct and atmospheric background.

The opening of the piano prelude *La Cathédrale engloutie* (*The Sunken Cathedral,* 1910) is exemplary (Example II-6). To the extent that there is a real melody, it does not commence until m. 7, where it emerges almost imperceptibly out of the remains of the opening harmonic complexes, after they have been reduced to a single E doubled in octaves (m. 6). This doubled E then becomes the first note of a more continuous linear statement, and also serves as an accompanying pedal point throughout mm. 7–13.

This passage also illustrates important characteristics of the new tonal and harmonic language developed by Debussy. No accidentals are used in the six introductory measures; all seven "white" notes combine to make up a static harmonic field, within which they sound in free combination. The open fifth on the first beat of m. 1 is combined with a series of parallel chords (also consisting of open fifths and fourths) that move upward through a pentatonic scale; the pitches, accumulated by the sustaining pedal (indicated by the ties), form a massed harmonic complex that, although dissonant by traditional standards, is treated as a "fused" consonance. Similarly, when the original fifth is retained in the right hand in mm. 3 and 5, the left hand moves downward in stepwise motion to form rich new sonorities, again combining with the parallel chords, which continue as before.

In such contexts harmony takes on a new role: rather than a dynamic agent of musical motion, it becomes a largely static means for producing atmospheric and coloristic effects of sonority. Typically, when a change of pitch focus occurs, as at mm. 6–7, where E emerges unambiguously as the center for the next segment, the change represents not a "modulation" in the traditional sense—that is, a transition from one functional key area to another—but simply a shift of mode from E Phrygian (no accidentals) to E Lydian (five sharps), the note E serving as a common reference within both scales.

The presence of pentatonic, Phrygian, and Lydian scales in this passage points to a basic element of Debussy's style. Since harmonies are chosen as much for their color, resonant quality, and general sonorous effect as for their functional position within a larger harmonic sequence, he feels free to employ various "exotic" scalar types as a basis for new kinds of vertical combinations. One such type particularly associated with the composer's name is the whole-tone scale, in which the octave is divided into six equal whole steps—unlike the diatonic scale, purely symmetrical in structure and thus tonally ambiguous. Although the whole-tone scale had appeared previously in the music of such com-

Example II-6: DEBUSSY, *La Cathédrale engloutie,* mm. 1–13

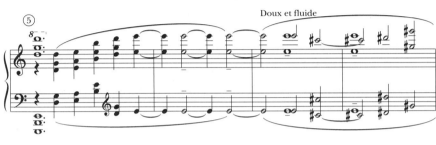

posers as Liszt (and was especially popular in Russia, back at least as far as Glinka), Debussy was the first to use it with any real consistency. Even in his work, however, it is normally employed only as one of a variety of scalar types (including pentatonic, diatonic, and symmetrical) that are combined and integrated into a larger complex of related scalar divisions with impressive freedom and skill. (The prelude *Voiles,* which uses the whole-tone scale exclusively save in one brief contrasting section, is an exceptional case.)

Debussy's new approach to scale, harmony, and tonality represents one of his most significant contributions to early twentieth-century music, as far-reaching in its historical implications as the continued development of chromaticism in Germany and Austria. Indeed, Debussy's compositional procedures altered the very way in which music could be experienced. Traditional Western music is heard largely as a motion directed toward a tonal goal, and so one tends to listen to any given musical moment mainly in terms of where it is coming from and, especially, where it is headed. In Debussy, on the other hand, tonality is treated in a more stable way, defined by a series of related yet essentially stationary blocks of largely static harmony. Thus the listener tends to experience each musical moment more in terms of its own inherent properties, less in relationship to what precedes and follows it.

This difference had a decisive influence on all aspects of Debussy's style. The "surface" of the music—its texture, color, dynamic nuances, etc.—assumes an unprecedented prominence and importance. A concern with sound for its own sake is especially apparent in Debussy's orchestration, where a new level of finesse is achieved in the production of novel timbral effects. The opening of the second of the three orchestral sketches *La Mer* (*The Sea,* 1905), entitled "Jeux de vagues" (Play of the Waves), provides a relatively simple, yet representative, instance (Example II-7). The entire passage is based on a single stationary sonority consisting mainly of the pitches C♯, G♯, and A (the low strings add an F♯ on the second beat of m. 1 and m. 3). Only the underlying structure of the chord is stable, however; its surface is constantly varied by delicate dynamic gradations and by a continuous pattern of rising and falling fifths in the upper strings, coupled with intermittent arpeggiations in the glockenspiel and harps. Other touches are the use of cymbal, pianissimo, to punctuate the return of the upper strings to their original position (third beat of mm. 2 and 4) and the addition of two flutes in m. 4. The latter will provide the first truly "melodic" element in the following measure (not included in the example); but up to this point the entire effect is one of shifting orchestral colors and rhythmic patterns that arise from the interaction of the various textural components.

The orchestration of the opening of "Jeux de vagues" breaks up the underlying sonority into a number of individual elements, producing a musical effect that has been compared to the dissolving of the surface in Impressionist painting through the use of numerous individual brush strokes. Because of such techniques of fragmentation, as well as his general interest in effects of atmosphere and color, Debussy is commonly referred to as a musical "Impressionist." This is a useful term in distinguishing him from the musical "expressionists" of the German school of the day, but one cannot take the parallels between music and painting too literally (for one thing, the Impressionist painters were active long before Debussy). Moreover, there is perhaps an even stronger parallel with another art, that of literature, as represented by the symbolist writers active in France in the later years of the nineteenth century. In the poems of Mallarmé (1842–98), for example, there is a closely analogous tendency to dissolve traditional syntax so as to allow individual words to be appreciated more fully for their purely sonic values,

Example II-7: DEBUSSY, *La Mer,* "Jeux de vagues," mm. 1–4

and to evoke instantaneous impressions through isolated and motionless images. (Significantly, Mallarmé's poem *L'Après-midi d'un faune* provided the programmatic basis for Debussy's orchestral composition.)

Whereas in traditional tonal music harmonic progression is basically a matter of combining chords that are essentially different from one another in effect (since they occupy different positions within the key system), in Debussy it becomes more a matter of combining chords that are similar in both quality and structure. This is illustrated in its purest form in one of the composer's most common techniques: the use of chords in parallel motion, so that a single sonority is simply moved about in melodic sequence (as in m. 1 of Example II-6). Similarly, a particular harmonic sound may dominate an entire section or even a complete piece. One among many examples is the piano prelude *Le Vent dans la plaine (The Wind in the Plain),* most of which is pervaded by a tonally ambiguous, texturally elaborated sonority that is stated at the opening and then reiterated almost incessantly, varied through subtle inflections to produce a remarkably unified overall effect.

By the turn of the century Debussy often avoided the traditional means of establishing a tonal center through dominant-tonic harmonic relationships. To replace them, he had to devise new methods, essentially of a melodic and rhythmic rather than harmonic nature, for creating key centers. Repetition became perhaps the most important means of providing a tonal focus. In *La Cathédrale engloutie* (Example II-6) a continuous pedal point provides the focus for the passage at mm. 7–13, and even the opening of "Jeux de vagues" (Example II-7) produces a sense of tonal orientation through the extension of the first chord by various means of repetition, although here the primary focus is not a single pitch but a dissonant chordal complex.

These new technical procedures combine to produce equally innovative formal characteristics in Debussy's music. A comparison with more traditional practice is again instructive. The dynamic and progressive nature of large-scale Classical and Romantic designs gives way in Debussy to "additive" structures, in which musical segments of varying degrees of similarity follow one another in an essentially "flat" and nondevelopmental linear order. (This device again recalls an attribute of much of the painting of the time, which favors two-dimensional perspectives conforming to—and thus emphasizing—the flat surface of a canvas.) The basic formal technique involves subtle variations of repeated musical units, often by means of apparently insubstantial transformations, and the mediation of contrasting units through the retention of common elements. The structure of Debussy's music often resembles a mosaic: seemingly separate and self-enclosed units combine into larger configurations, the individual discontinuities thereby being dissolved into a continuous, unbroken flow. The dynamic thrust toward points of climactic emphasis, typical of German music of the time, is replaced by a sort of floating balance among subtly interconnected musical entities, giving rise to wavelike motions characterized by extremely fine gradations of color, pacing, and intensity.

In his ground-breaking painting *Les Demoiselles d'Avignon* (1907), Pablo Picasso transformed the human figure into a series of geometric planes to conform with the two-dimensional surface of the canvas. Inspired by African sculpture, he rendered the faces of two of the women as masks. (Oil on canvas, $8' \times 7'8''$. Collection, The Museum of Modern Art, New York. Acquired through the Lillie P. Bliss Bequest)

It was Debussy's achievement to provide these forms with a strong sense of structural integrity. The music never degenerates into a series of pleasant yet unrelated effects, a succession of isolated musical moments; everything is held together by a tight network of melodic, rhythmic, and harmonic associations. Nevertheless, the type of musical form he developed is more loosely connected and more "permeable" (in the sense that any given section seems capable of flowing into or out of any other) than that of traditional tonal music. His conception of form as essentially "open" in character was to have an important influence on much later twentieth-century music.

Debussy increasingly refined his ideas in a series of revolutionary works that appeared in the early years of the century, most notably in the *Estampes* (*Prints,* 1903), *Images* (*Pictures,* Books I and II, 1905), and Preludes (Book I, 1910; Book II, 1913) for piano, and *La Mer* and the third set of *Images* (1905–12) for orchestra. They reached their most advanced form in the music for the ballet *Jeux* (*Games,* 1913), which most of Debussy's contemporaries considered an incomprehensible puzzle but which has greatly interested composers in recent years.

The last few years of his life manifest a distinct shift in compositional attitudes. The poetic titles disappear, replaced by those of abstract music (thus completing a circle taking the composer back to his earliest works, which also favored abstract formal designations); and his music loses much of the surface voluptuousness so typical of the works of the previous years. Already in the Études for piano (1913) one notes a renewed tendency toward textural and formal economy, a development that reaches its zenith in the three Sonatas of 1915–17 (for cello and piano, violin and piano, and flute, viola, and harp, respectively), all of which are characterized by a restraint bordering on austerity. In this respect they have something in common with the widespread development toward neo-classicism that was to come a few years later.

SATIE

As we have noted, one of the most essential elements in the evolution of musical modernism in France was the rejection of German Romanticism, with its emphasis on intense personal feeling and exalted expression. The composer who, even more than Debussy, set the tone for this rejection was Erik Satie (1866–1925). There is no more puzzling, nor controversial, figure in twentieth-century music than Satie. Although widely considered a composer of modest technical accomplishments, he was nevertheless one of the key figures of the modern age, an eccentric visionary whose conception of music as a simple, less pretentious, more popular and "democratic" art form represented a critical ingredient in the Parisian artistic scene of the early decades of the new century.

Although Satie attended the Paris Conservatory, he achieved little success as a student and was dismissed without a diploma in 1882. He had, in any event, little sympathy for the academic approach favored at the Conservatory, and his first mature works, dating from the later 1880s, demonstrated an original, if somewhat quirky, musical mind. In the second *Gymnopédie,* one of three short piano pieces with this name composed in 1888, a flowing, nondevelopmental melodic line of disarming simplicity is placed above an accompaniment of mildly disso-

Example II-8: SATIE, *Gymnopédie* No. 2, mm. 5–8

nant harmonies and "circular," nondirected model progressions (Example II-8). The static effect is further emphasized by the regularity of the rhythm, especially in the accompaniment, which remains absolutely constant throughout. No doubt some of the harmonic flavor of the *Gymnopédie* is derived from Chabrier and Fauré, and its rhythmic and textural austerity reflects something of the ideals of the composers of the Société Nationale. Yet, typically, Satie goes much further than his contemporaries in reacting against the dominant musical forces of late Romanticism: passionate intensity, chromaticism, and Wagnerian giganticism. Here music seems to be reduced to its purest core, shorn of all emotional and expressive ambitions.

Even more than Debussy, Satie during his earlier years found inspiration in things removed from his own everyday surroundings. He avidly studied Gothic art and medieval music, and like Debussy believed that Gregorian chant could form the basis for a new kind of post-Romantic melody. He too was strongly affected by the Oriental music heard at the 1889 Paris Exhibition. In 1891 Satie joined the "Rose + Croix," the French branch of the Rosicrucian Brotherhood, a mystical religious sect modeled on the secret societies of the Middle Ages, for which he wrote a number of compositions. Among these are the three preludes for a play entitled *Le Fils des étoiles* (*The Son of the Stars,* 1891), which contain, among other innovations, passages featuring parallel chords built in fourths, usually moving in steady rhythmic successions and written without bar lines (Example II-9). Although modern in har-

Example II-9: SATIE, *Le Fils des étoiles,* opening

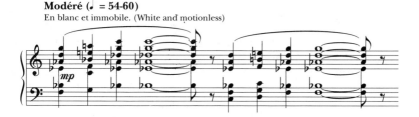

monic conception, the basic idea is derived from medieval parallel organum, which Satie especially admired at this time.

Many of the early works also display remarkably modern formal characteristics. Especially favored are mosaiclike structures, in which various more or less "fixed" musical units are combined into apparently random successions with no strictly logical connections among them, so that any unit may precede or follow any other one. (This characteristic led a later composer, Edgard Varèse, to refer to these pieces as "pre-electronic music.") Here again one recognizes a certain similarity to the music of Debussy, with whom Satie shared a long, if often strained, friendship—and the obvious parallels between the composers have occasioned heated discussion about priority and mutual influence. Clearly each owes something to the other, yet their differences seem more fundamental and important. Debussy's music normally exhibits a degree of complexity and ambition far exceeding anything found in Satie, who was increasingly content to write what he referred to as "music of every day." And Debussy could have had little sympathy for Satie's contention that "all great artists are amateurs." Moreover, in 1898 Satie began earning his living as a cabaret pianist and composer of music-hall songs; and although he considered this occupation "a great lowering," the musical style he practiced there had an unmistakable influence on his more "serious" compositions. He often incorporated his popular songs into his concert works; and in fact, the distinction between what is serious or otherwise hardly seems applicable in the case of this music.

As early as the *Gnossiennes* of 1890, Satie inaugurated a practice of writing humorous verbal indications in his scores. Some of these can be taken as ironic and playful performance instructions (e.g., "Slow down politely" or "Very seriously silent"), but the meanings of others (such as "Open the head") are more enigmatic. Satie continued this practice throughout most of his career and clearly considered these verbal asides an important part of his work, yet explanations of their purpose have always proved troubling. Certainly one of their functions is to deflate pretension. More specifically, they provide a modern, and essentially parodistic, substitute for traditional performance indications, which Satie felt had been contaminated by the emotional excess of Romanticism.

Humorous titles—so unlike the highly poetic ones favored by Debussy—serve a similar purpose: e.g., *Flabby Preludes, Dried-Up Embryos,* and the most famous of all, *Three Pieces in the Shape of a Pear* (actually a set of *seven* pieces for piano four-hands, traditionally believed, although apparently without foundation, to have been presented to Debussy in response to his complaint that Satie's music lacked form). Nor is Satie's wit confined to verbal indications and titles; it can take on a structural aspect, as in the much-publicized piano piece *Vexations* (c. 1893), which contains the instruction that it be repeated 840 times. A psychological explanation sometimes given for this aspect of Satie is that by making fun of himself and his music, he attempts to hide his own technical inadequacies. But more to the point, surely, is that he is making fun of the nineteenth-century's carefully nurtured conception of the artist as prophet and seer, as someone with a special insight into the mysteries of life and creation. For Satie, music is—or at least should be—an everyday occurrence, an activity much like any other. At the time, this belief was unheard of, although in later years it would gain many adherents.

In the early years of the century Satie's output declined markedly. In 1905, at the age of forty, to everyone's amazement, he entered the Schola Cantorum, a music school known for its conservatism and rigid curriculum, where he undertook basic studies in music theory with two prominent French composers of the day, Vincent d'Indy and Albert Roussel. Satie applied himself conscientiously (Roussel spoke of him as "a very docile and assiduous student"), and although still far from a distinguished pupil, he received his diploma three years later. Typically, Satie did not let the experience turn his head or detract him from the compositional direction he had followed in his earlier works. Although his first compositions after attending the Schola were a chorale and fugue, indicating a new interest in more traditional compositional procedures, he published them under the title *Disagreeable Observations*. Yet, technically considered, the Schola did have its effect on Satie. His later music completely rejects the rich parallel harmonies and more full-bodied accompaniments found in the youthful pieces, in favor of leaner (usually two-part) textures of essentially linear conception.

This more economical style is exemplified in the piano pieces *Heures séculaires et instantanées (Century-Old and Instantaneous Hours)* and *Sports et divertissements,* both of which appeared in 1914. Here Satie's old penchant for occasional verbal asides is extended to commentaries that run throughout the music, offering a kind of humorous description of its "content." Although placed parallel to the music, the words are not intended to be read aloud, only silently by the performer as the piece proceeds. (These literary commentaries, along with the music they accompany, can perhaps be understood as a lighthearted parody, or demystification, of nineteenth-century notions of program music.)

Typical is the text accompanying *La Balançoire (The Swing),* the first of the twenty "sketches" that, along with a brief introductory chorale, comprise the *Sports et divertissements.* (In the preface to the score Satie comments on the chorale: "I have written a chorale, sober and suitable. This makes a sort of bitter prelude, a kind of introduction quite austere

The opening measures of *La Balançoire,* complete with amusing vignette in Satie's own hand.

and unfrivolous. Into it I have put all I know about boredom. I dedicate this chorale to those who do not like me.") The entire text for *La Balançoire* reads, in English: "It is my heart that is swinging so. It is not feeling dizzy. What small feet it has. Will it want to come back inside my breast again?"

The music of the *Sports et divertissements* is an ideal introduction to Satie's later style. Each of these musical miniatures beautifully and simply matches the flavor of its text. Word paintings abound, as in the rocking accompanimental ostinato, consisting solely of two alternating E♮s two octaves apart, that evokes the "swing" of the opening piece. Parodistic quotations of well-known tunes pop up in unlikely contexts, mood and texture undergo sudden alterations, and, especially, the whole is pervaded with a sense of calculated naïveté that is unique to Satie. Everything is done with the light touch of a master of understatement.

Although regarded with great skepticism by most composers of his own generation, by 1915 Satie was beginning to attract considerable interest among younger French musicians. In the following years he produced a series of relatively extended compositions involving orchestra (up to this point his output had been limited primarily to brief piano pieces) that gained him additional fame and thrust him into the center of developments in French music during the postwar years. We will return to this phase of his career later.

RUSSIA: SKRYABIN

The course of musical developments in Russia during the nineteenth century can be viewed in terms of two main stylistic currents. On the one hand, a conservative tradition, supported by long-established cultural ties between Russia and the West, was represented by composers, such as Anton Rubinstein, who based their compositions firmly upon Western models. Others, however, cultivated indigenous musical characteristics in order to create a uniquely Russian music largely independent of Western influences, a tendency consistent with the generally nationalist climate found in Europe in the latter part of the century. The composers in this second group, notably the so-called "Mighty Handful" or "Russian Five" (Balakirev, Cui, Borodin, Musorgsky, and Rimsky-Korsakov), gained increasing prominence as the century progressed, and the novel approaches to musical structure they explored would provide an important precedent for later developments in twentieth-century music.

A tradition of musical experimentation, based in part on indigenous folk sources and to some degree independent of Western tonality, was thus well established during the nineteenth century in Russia, extending in a line from Glinka through Dargomïzhsky and Musorgsky to Rimsky-Korsakov. A prominent feature of this line was the use of modal and "exotic" non-Western scales, especially those with symmetrical qualities such as the whole-tone and the eight-tone, or octatonic, scale (regularly alternating half steps and whole steps). These were typically combined with cyclic, essentially nonfunctional harmonic progressions that moved through chains of major or minor thirds or by tritone. In the later works of Nikolay Rimsky-Korsakov (1849–1908) one finds a remarkably extensive and systematic exploitation of such symmetrical pitch relationships. The Russian composer who carried out this tendency most consequentially, however, was Alexander Skryabin (1872–1915), who in the early years of the twentieth century developed a completely new approach to harmony and tonality, based on artificial scales, that was as revolutionary in its way as the innovations introduced by Mahler, Strauss, and Debussy in Western Europe at the same time.

Curiously, Skryabin was not himself nationalist in orientation. He studied at the traditionally oriented Moscow Conservatory of Music, which had been founded by Anton Rubinstein's brother and close associate Nikolay Rubinstein, and he spent much of his adult life away from his native land, living in Switzerland. Moreover, Skryabin's esthetic views were colored by a highly romantic vision of the artist as a Nietzschean superman, a view that placed matters of personal expression well above those of national identity. Skryabin's early works, consisting mainly of piano pieces (although there are also three symphonies, the last of which appeared in 1904), were written under the dominant influence of Chopin and give only a faint indication of his later development. Clearly tonal in outline, with strong and easily recognizable harmonic root movements, they appear to be basically conservative and unadventurous. Yet almost from the beginning is evident a tendency to color the underlying triadic structure with pronounced chromatic inflections and to suspend the resolution of unstable harmonies, especially those representing dominant functions, for ever longer stretches of time.

In the works written shortly after the turn of the century, tonal resolution appears to become more a matter of convention than of necessity, and key centers are defined more by implication than by explicit
statement. These developments reach a critical stage in the Fifth Piano
Sonata (1907), one of the last Skryabin pieces to carry a key signature.
The Bb-major tonality of the principal contrasting theme of the exposition, for example, depends almost entirely upon suggestion rather than
overt statement, and is principally delineated by an unresolved, richly
decorated, chromatically altered dominant chord on F (Example II-10).

Example II-10: SKRYABIN, Piano Sonata No. 5, first movement, mm. 120–
22

Moreover, the larger tonal relationships of the piece (which, like all
Skryabin's later sonatas, is in a single movement) are extremely ambiguous. Although the key signature at the opening suggests F♯ major,
only the first statement of the main theme appears in this key, and even
here the tonality is weakly defined, as the leading tone is completely
avoided. Only near the end of the sonata, when Eb major is established
with considerable emphasis, does a single key begin to take on sufficient weight to provide a stable anchor for the movement as a whole.
But even this center proves abortive, as the sonata is framed by a brief
introductory and concluding passage (the latter identical to the last part
of the former) that focuses on the tritone A–D♯, with the result that the
work both begins and ends in tonal obscurity.

Immediately following the composition of the Fifth Sonata, Skryabin
made a final break with traditional tonality. *Prometheus,* an extended
orchestral work composed between 1908 and 1910 (subtitled *The Poem
of Fire,* a designation relating it to the somewhat earlier orchestral *Poem
of Ecstasy*), is written entirely according to a new system of tonal relationships (with one exception: it ends, incongruously, with a C-major
triad). Skryabin was to explore this system exclusively in his final years.
Along with *Prometheus,* the last five of the ten piano sonatas and a number of shorter piano compositions written between 1908 and 1913 are
all based on a single underlying dissonant harmony, the so-called "mystic
chord"; this, or slight variations thereof, serves as a harmonic reference
point and pitch source for everything in the music. The most common

Example II-11: SKRYABIN, the "mystic chord"

form of the chord is given above, presented as a series of rising fourths, the way in which the composer apparently originally conceived it (a), and as a six-note scale (b), as well as in two additional chordal versions (c and d).

The "mystic chord"—also sometimes referred to as the *"Prometheus chord,"* since it first appeared prominently in that work—is not unlike an altered dominant (with the addition of the note G, it can be ordered as a series of thirds, as in Example II-11c, to form a "dominant thirteenth" with a raised eleventh), and it can at least partially be understood as an extension of the dominant-type constructions found in the earlier works (as in Example II-10). But in Skryabin's later music this chord loses its traditional inclination to resolve to a stable tonic triad. It becomes, in fact, a sort of tonic itself, but a new kind of "artificial" and unstable tonic, unlike anything found in previous music.

When put in scalar form (as in Example II-11b) the chord closely resembles a whole-tone scale, except that an A♮ replaces A♭. This lends Skryabin's music a certain similarity to passages in Debussy. But unlike Debussy, Skryabin thinks primarily in harmonic terms and orders the larger motion mainly through root-movement progressions from one chord to the next. Since the underlying chordal type remains basically the same, however, these progressions normally end by merely transposing the same harmonic entity from one scale degree to another. The music's slow-moving harmonic rhythm gives rise to extended blocks of static harmony, again reminiscent of Debussy, enlivened through virtuosic instrumental elaborations that also recall the textural techniques of Impressionism. Furthermore, in actual practice the chordal foundation not only functions vertically as a harmonic unit, but also serves as a general repository of pitches that determines the melodic details of the music as well. In other words, harmonic and melodic aspects are derived from a single source, a characteristic that relates Skryabin's music to that of a number of his contemporaries, including both Debussy and Schoenberg. The question of whether the basic underlying structure should be thought of primarily as a chord (as Skryabin did) or as a scale is in a sense beside the point. As the composer himself once remarked: "The melody is dissolved harmony; the harmony is a vertically compressed melody."[6]

6.   Quoted in Lev Danilevich, *Alexander Nikolajewitsch Skrjabin* (Leipzig, 1954), p. 98.

After 1908 Skryabin devoted himself with almost demonic single-mindedness to the exploration of the compositional possibilities contained within this "mystic chord," developing a remarkably self-enclosed system based solely on its own particular properties. This system is not so inflexible as might at first seem to be the case. For one thing, the chord can be stated in a number of different forms: as a series of fourths, as a series of thirds, or in various other configurations (of which Example II–11d offers one possibility). And all notes of the basic chord, except its root, can be altered. Indeed, it is as often as not an altered form that serves as the norm for a particular section or even an entire composition. (A common technique, especially in the larger works such as the sonatas, is to distinguish contrasting sections by the use of different forms. See Example II–12 below.) Moreover, not all notes of the chord need be present at any given moment, and additional notes may be added at will. The latter are either handled as "nonharmonic" departures, in which case they are treated in an almost traditional way, as neighbor notes, passing notes, etc.—or they become attached to the chord to form a part of the basic harmonic sound. Given the highly chromatic context in which all of the notes appear, it is often impossible to distinguish definitely between what is "chordal" and what is "accessory."

Passages from the two principal themes of the exposition of the Seventh Sonata illustrate many of these characteristics. The opening measures of the sonata (Example II–12a) are based on a slightly altered version of the "mystic chord," built on the root C, in the form given in Example II–11d. (The alteration consists of a D♭ instead of D♮, producing a minor ninth with the root C, in place of the major ninth of the original.) All pitches up to the final chord in m. 2 are exclusively derived from this six-note chord, which provides not only the harmonic foundation but

Example II–12: SKRYABIN, Piano Sonata No. 7, first movement

a. mm. 1–6

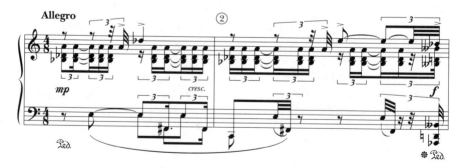

b. mm. 29–33

also the three pitches of the fanfarelike melodic idea (A and D♭ in m. 1, A and E in m. 2).

Starting with the last chord in m. 2 and extending through m. 4, the music is based on a transposition of this chord down a major third, so that the new root is A♭. (Although the pitches are exactly transposed, their registral layout is no longer the same as in mm. 1–2. In scalar form the pitches now read: A♭–B♭–C–D–F–G♭.) Here, however, the new chordal tones are not all introduced immediately. And nonchordal tones appear as well: the D♭ in the top voice at the end of m. 2 is held over from the first complex as a suspension (note that it repeats one of the three melodic pitches of mm. 1–2), resolving upward to the chordal D♮ in m. 3; and in m. 4 the chordal D moves to C♯ with the D still retained, forming a chromatic passing tone that resolves in m. 5 to C, the only chordal tone still missing from this transposition. C then serves as a "pivot" (illustrating one of Skryabin's most common transpositional techniques): the note also represents a member of the next transposition, up a tritone from A♭, and initiates a sequential repetition of mm. 1–2, built on D instead of the original C.

The main contrasting theme (Example II-12b), on the other hand, is partially based on the *unaltered* "mystic chord," here constructed on G♯ (in scalar form, G♯–A♯–B♯–C♯–E♯–F♯). When the main melodic line enters on the fourth eighth of m. 29, however, it sounds A♮, the minor–ninth version of the chord, thus recalling the form used at the opening of the sonata. But the A resolves to A♯ in m. 30, forming the unaltered major ninth, and it is this note that is then treated chordally. A♮ returns in m. 31, first as a lower neighbor to A♯ in m. 33; and C♯ is replaced by D♯ in m. 33. This passage also illustrates Skryabin's practice of enlivening the static harmonic foundation of his music through complex textural and rhythmic manipulations: in mm. 29–32 the left hand subdivides the measure in units of three, while the right hand subdivides in two (the reason for the different meter signatures in the two staves).

Despite the originality of his harmonic techniques, Skryabin's conception of form remained firmly rooted in the nineteenth century. He continued to make use of traditional types, especially sonata forms and, in shorter pieces, straightforward binary and ternary designs, which in his hands became little more than empty containers for the musical content. (Skryabin's compositional sketches, in fact, often consist only of numbered measures, empty except for occasional indications for the harmonic root movement, to which the actual music was only later added.) Perhaps the greatest limitation of his compositional approach is that sequential transposition becomes virtually the sole means for producing large-scale musical motion; and the persistence of the same basic harmony throughout an entire composition, however varied in details, causes undeniable problems of both a formal and expressive nature. Nevertheless, Skryabin's effort to create what was in effect an entirely new system of tonal organization as a replacement for the traditional one marked an important stage in musical developments during the early years of the century.

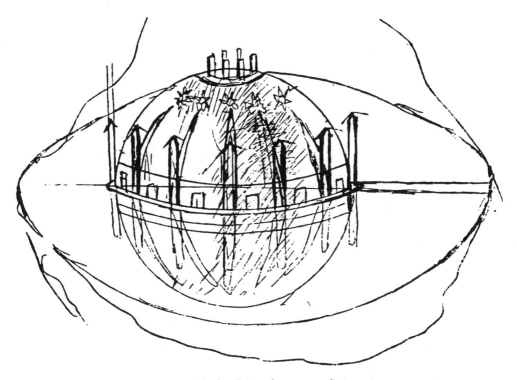

Skryabin's sketch of a temple for the performance of *Mysterium*

Along with an almost limitless ego, a strong mystical strain was deeply embedded in Skryabin's personality and became increasingly pronounced toward the end of his life. His final years were consumed with the notion of writing an immense visionary work entitled *Mysterium,* which was to incorporate theater, painting, and dance as well as music. Skryabin conceived of this work as a means to transform humanity, to achieve a new level of consciousness, and to foster "the celebration of a collective joy." Although only sketches for the music of *Mysterium* remain, all of Skryabin's later work was written in its spirit, and much of it was apparently intended to be included in the larger work. The surviving sketches give at least one further indication of the extraordinary inventiveness of Skryabin's musical mind: the use of massive chords containing all twelve notes of the chromatic scale sounding simultaneously. It is difficult to imagine a more apt symbol of the composer's belief in the self-enclosed yet all-encompassing nature of musical expression and the transfiguring power of its message.

CHAPTER III

The Atonal Revolution

SCHOENBERG

With Arnold Schoenberg (1871–1951) we reach the first of several major composers who, though nurtured in the world of late Romanticism, attained their musical maturity in the early years of the new century and then proceeded to define the principal lines of stylistic evolution for its first fifty years. None had a greater impact on compositional practice than Schoenberg, who carried the implications of late nineteenth-century chromaticism to their ultimate—and in his view necessary and logical—consequences. This course led him eventually to abandon the tonal and harmonic conventions of common-practice music entirely, thereby opening up an important new dimension for compositional exploration.

Schoenberg was born in Vienna and spent much of his life there, with brief periods in Berlin in 1901–3, 1911–15, and—as Busoni's successor at the Prussian Academy of Arts—1925–33; in 1933 he emigrated to the United States, where he taught at the University of California, Los Angeles until 1944. While still quite young, he learned to play the violin and cello, and although largely self-taught in composition, he did study briefly with Alexander von Zemlinsky, a prominent Austrian composer of the time. The young Schoenberg immersed himself completely in the musical life of his native city, studying scores avidly and learning intimately the literature of both the Classical and post-Wagnerian schools. He became part of a group of progressive musicians and artists closely associated with Mahler, who was unique among the members of the musical establishment in supporting Schoenberg. A

An odd quintet in Austrian garb, ca. 1895: (from left to right) Louis Savant, horn; Fritz Kreisler, violin; Arnold Schoenberg, cello; Eduard Gartner, violin; and Karl Redlich, flageolet. (Used by permission of Belmont Music Publishers)

close follower of developments in Viennese intellectual circles, Schoenberg was caught up in the prevailing atmosphere of ferment and change that enveloped the city as the century began, to which he was to make his own significant contribution.

Among Schoenberg's earliest surviving works is a string quartet composed in 1897, a solidly crafted tonal piece written under the influence of Brahms and revealing a Classical orientation that would persist in varying degrees throughout his life. In the string sextet that followed, *Verklärte Nacht* (*Transfigured Night,* 1899), and the orchestral tone poem *Pelleas und Melisande* (1903), where Schoenberg's own personality emerges more clearly, the influence of Wagner predominates: both works are programmatic in conception, make use of leitmotifs, and are intensely chromatic. Even more Wagnerian is the *Gurrelieder* (Songs of Gurre), a massive oratorio composed mainly in 1901–3 (though the scoring was only completed some ten years later), which rivals Mahler in the size of its vocal and instrumental forces and represents a kind of final summation of the main currents of German Romanticism.

In *Pelleas und Melisande,* and in a number of songs written in the early

years of the century, Schoenberg approaches the edges of traditional
tonality, pursuing a degree of chromaticism comparable to that used by
Strauss at the same time. The extent to which chromatic voice-leading
inflects and obscures the triadic basis and controls the sequence of harmonies can be seen in two brief passages from the song *Verlassen,* Op.
6, No. 4 (1903). The opening measure (Example III-1a) tentatively defines
the key of E♭ minor through a highly inflected presentation of the tonic
triad (note the chromatic lines in both hands). This measure is repeated
five times as an accompanimental ostinato (something of a rarity in
Schoenberg), but in mm. 7–8 (Example III-1b) its chromatic implications are more fully realized. The top voice develops upward through
sequential repetition and extension, moving from F♭ in m. 7 to E♭ (an
octave higher) in m. 8; the previous chromatic ascent in the left hand
now continues upward to D; and the root E♭ (also in the left hand),
after being sustained for seven beats, descends chromatically, also to D
(thus joining with the rising chromatic line). The chord on the last beat
of m. 8 looks like an inflected dominant seventh, but, typically, it too
moves chromatically, the bass descending to C♯.

This stage of Schoenberg's evolution culminates in two nonpro-
grammatic instrumental compositions that appeared, respectively, at

Example III-1: SCHOENBERG, *Verlassen,* Op. 6, No. 4

a. m. 1

b. mm. 7–9

the same times as Strauss's *Salome* and *Elektra:* the First String Quartet of 1905 (the earlier quartet was not published until after Schoenberg's death) and the Chamber Symphony of 1907. Here the style of the younger Schoenberg reaches its definitive formulation in a strikingly personal fusion of the previously distinct Wagnerian and Brahmsian sides of his development. The Quartet is remarkable for its extraordinary complexity and elaborate organization. Although some fifty minutes in duration, it derives its thematic content almost entirely through motivic transformation of the materials set out in the first few measures. This thematic integration is also reflected formally: the four separate movements of a traditional sonata-type construction are interwoven with one another into a single gigantic design, played without pause; for example, the recapitulation of the first movement appears only after two further movements have been heard. Although the Quartet is still tonal (it begins and ends in D, and the major structural divisions are defined by important harmonic arrivals), the degree of chromaticism is extreme; and in certain sections, especially transitional ones, the music appears to be in a state of almost complete tonal flux, held together almost entirely by motivic connections.

The complexity of Schoenberg's compositional thinking is evident in all aspects of his music. Two technical points, somewhat later formulated theoretically by the composer but already apparent in practice in the First Quartet, deserve particular mention. One is the concept of "developing variation," the continuous evolution and transformation of the thematic substance, strictly avoiding literal repetition. A closely related concept is that of "musical prose," the constant unfolding of an unbroken musical argument without recourse to the symmetrical balances produced by phrases or sections of equal length and corresponding thematic content (exemplified most clearly in the Classical formal unit known as a "period"). The result is a richly structured and densely polyphonic musical continuum in which all parts, including ostensibly "secondary" ones, are equally developmental and motivically derived. Harmonic "padding" and surface effects of textural figuration, both characteristic of much late nineteenth-century music, are shunned.

The Chamber Symphony resembles the Quartet in many respects, particularly in its interlacing of a multimovement conception into a single uninterrupted design. However, the level of tonal ambiguity and chromaticism is even more pronounced, and the musical argument has been radically compressed (despite their formal similarities, the Chamber Symphony lasts only half as long as the earlier work). An especially interesting feature of the composition is the prominence of whole-tone scales and chords built in fourths. Although this might suggest a relationship with the contemporaneous music of Debussy and Skryabin, Schoenberg conceives of these new structures from a more traditional

German point of view: as harmonic and linear departures from a more stable underlying framework, rather than as quasi-independent pitch collections forming static harmonic fields without any particular inclination toward resolution.

This view is illustrated by Example III-2, which presents a harmonic reduction of the first two phrases of the Chamber Symphony. The chord in perfect fourths that builds up gradually in mm. 1–2 is altered in m. 3 to become an augmented-sixth chord on G♭ (the standard "French sixth" with an added A♭, producing five of the six notes of a whole-tone scale), which then resolves in "normal" fashion to an F-major chord in m. 4 (Example III-2a). Similarly, the famous sequence of fourths announced by the horns in m. 5 also gives way to a whole-tone complex, here presented as a series of augmented triads in descending parallel motion; and these are transformed in m. 8 into a functional tonal chord, a diminished seventh (with an added D♮ in the bass) built on the seventh degree of E major, the main key of the work. The diminished seventh then resolves in an essentially traditional manner to E, on the second beat of m. 8 (Example III-2b).

However, at certain striking points in the Chamber Symphony Schoenberg delays the resolutions of such whole-tone and fourth complexes for an unusually long time (most notably near the climax of the development section); yet even here his conception of these complexes as the consequence of chromatic voice-leading, rather than as the abso-

Example III-2: SCHOENBERG, Chamber Symphony, harmonic reduction

a. mm. 1–4

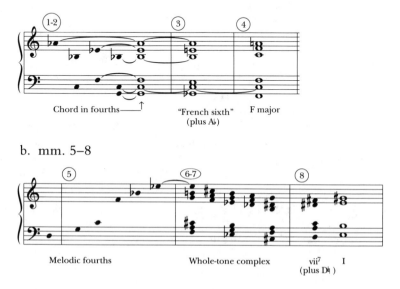

b. mm. 5–8

lute sonic entities found in Debussy and Skryabin, is ultimately confirmed. This distinction is fundamental, and helps explain the radically different direction Schoenberg's music would take during the coming years.

With the Chamber Symphony we have reached the absolute limits of traditional chromatic tonality. The period immediately following its appearance was critical in Schoenberg's development—and indeed, largely because of the direction he took, one of the most important in the entire evolution of Western music. In a two-year period of astonishing creative activity, from 1907 to 1909, Schoenberg made his final break with tonality and triadic harmony and moved into the previously uncharted area of free chromaticism, producing a series of works that fundamentally altered the course of music: the Second String Quartet, Op. 10; Three Piano Pieces, Op. 11; Two Songs, Op. 14; the song cycle *Das Buch der hängenden Gärten (The Book of the Hanging Gardens)*, Op. 15; Five Orchestral Pieces, Op. 16; and the monodrama *Erwartung (Expectation)*, Op. 17. In one sense Schoenberg's break with tonality can be understood simply as the next step in a continuous development, for in his music the role of triads and key centers had already been weakened to a point of virtual extinction. But this step was decisive, producing a difference in kind rather than merely of degree. As Schoenberg himself proclaimed in the program for the first performance of his Op. 15 songs: "For the first time I have succeeded in coming near an ideal of expression and form which I had in mind for years. . . . Now that I have finally embarked on the path I am conscious that I have broken all barriers of a past esthetic."[1]

Schoenberg's revolutionary new conception of pitch organization entails two essential aspects. First, the degree of emphasis on nonharmonic tones finally reaches a point where these tones lose their inclination to resolve at all, thus making it impossible for the listener to infer even a latent triadic background. Schoenberg referred to this as the "emancipation of dissonance": the dissonant harmonic complexes are no longer regulated by underlying triadic successions but are "set free" as absolute harmonic entities, capable of standing on their own and related solely to one another rather than to a single harmonic type representing a universal norm. For the first time in Western music since the Renaissance, the triad was no longer accepted as the sole harmonic reference from which all other vertical sonorities were derived and to which they owed their meaning. What is new in Schoenberg's music of this period is thus not so much the dissonant chords themselves (for such chords had always been used) but the fact that these chords are no longer related to a simpler, more consonant triadic basis.

1.   Quoted in Egon Wellesz, *Arnold Schönberg* (Leipzig, 1921), p. 34.

The second aspect, closely connected to the first, is the more or less complete abandonment of conventional tonal functions in Schoenberg's music during the 1907–9 period. No longer does a single pitch, or the major or minor triad based upon this pitch, act as a constant functional reference for the other tones (and the triads built upon them). It is as if Schoenberg's music has learned to move in a free chromatic space where there are fundamentally new principles of organization. Such music was labeled by the composer's critics as "atonal" (that is, having no tonality), a term that Schoenberg objected to but that has remained in common use down to the present day.

Despite these revolutionary tendencies, however, it should be emphasized that there is no absolute demarcation between Schoenberg's last tonal works and his first atonal ones; indeed, the first "purely" atonal composition cannot be identified with any real precision. Formally, the new works extend the principles of "developing variation" and "musical prose" already established in earlier compositions in a consistent—if admittedly extreme—manner. Moreover, all the new works retain at least faint traces of tonal thinking. Finally, the chronology of these years is unusually complicated. Schoenberg always wrote quickly, in bursts of inspiration, and in this period of especially intense creative activity he worked on several pieces simultaneously. For these reasons the transition from tonal to atonal is so gradual that an attempt to locate a precise moment of fundamental change is meaningless.

The Second String Quartet, completed in 1908, is particularly instructive, as it constitutes a sort of bridge from the old methods to the new ones. The first two movements are still basically tonal (in F♯ and D, respectively), and the second even opens and closes with a repeated tonic pedal in the cello. Yet the individual voices of the basically polyphonic textures now move with such freedom as to only rarely produce triadically derived harmonies. In the last two movements (both of which are settings for soprano and quartet of poems by Stefan George) the sense of key is weakened to almost total dissolution, although even here a specific triad is used as an occasional point of reference (E♭ minor in the third, F♯ major in the fourth). In the second of these movements, however, this reference only gradually emerges as the end of the quartet approaches; the entire earlier part seems suspended in midair, as it were, floating in a new kind of musical space, freed from the gravitational pull of key relationships. In a "programmatic" proclamation of new musical context, the opening line of George's poem announces: "I feel the air of other planets."

Schoenberg, himself acutely conscious (as perhaps only a composer of the twentieth century could be) of the critical point he had reached, commented on the Quartet (in words that also suggest the ambiguity of the tonal-atonal dichotomy):

In the first and second movements there are many sections in which the individual parts proceed regardless of whether or not their meeting results in codified harmonies. Still, here, and also in the third and fourth movements, the key is presented distinctly at all the main dividing-points of the formal organization. Yet the overwhelming multitude of dissonances cannot be counterbalanced any longer by occasional returns to such tonal triads as represent a key. It seemed inadequate to force a movement into the Procrustean bed of a tonality without supporting it by harmonic progressions that pertain to it. This dilemma was my concern, and it should have occupied the minds of all my contemporaries also. That I was the first to venture the decisive step will not be considered universally a merit—a fact I regret, but have to ignore.[2]

Even the works that follow the Quartet retain, as mentioned, faint and occasional echoes of tonal orientation. To cite just two examples, the piano piece Op. 11, No. 2, features a recurring ostinato that suggests D minor; and the song Op. 14, No. 1, despite the absence of clear triadic harmony elsewhere, closes on an unadorned B-minor chord. Nevertheless, most of the pieces avoid triadic structures entirely; and even when traditional references appear, they do so more as isolated occurrences than as the result of any consistently applied principles. The methods and procedures for shaping the music have become basically different. It would be difficult, however, to list them in a comprehensive way, since what is most revolutionary about this music is precisely that each work establishes its own methods, its own special set of references. There is no "given" language, no grammar of relationships that can be assumed in advance and then relied upon in the process of composition and of listening. Musical structure has become "contextual," defined by the network of referential associations set out within each separate composition.

Generalization about the organizational properties of such music is obviously difficult, but one particularly prevalent feature is the uncompromisingly linear and contrapuntal character. In the absence of any given referential harmonic norm such as the triad, even harmony is conceived largely as a kind of vertical melody. Indeed, the distinction between harmony and melody becomes, as in Skryabin, indistinct; they are simply two different ways of presenting the same underlying pitch content. This content consists mainly of small groups of related pitches, today usually referred to as pitch "cells" or "sets," that are manipulated in various ways to produce new material. At least theoretically, any cell may be chosen for use in a particular piece; and a single piece normally uses many such cells, although these will usually share certain similarities (such as related intervallic content).

2. *Style and Idea: Selected Writings,* ed. Leonard Stein, trans. Leo Black (Berkeley, 1975), p. 86.

The song cycle *Das Buch der hängenden Gärten,* sometimes described (as we have seen, by Schoenberg himself among others) as the first work written completely in the new style, offers a rich repository of examples. Each of the fifteen songs is uniquely organized, articulating—and in turn articulated by—its own structural context (although there are also shared correspondences that link a number of the songs).

Example III-3: SCHOENBERG, *Das Buch der hängenden Gärten,* No. 7

a. mm. 1–3

b. mm. 13–19

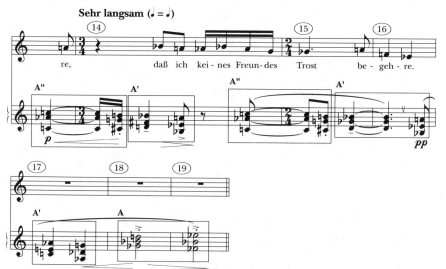

c. mm. 9–11

The seventh song, for instance, sets out its basic structural idea in the opening measure (Example III-3a)—not so much an abstract set of unordered pitches, used in various forms, as a particular compositional configuration: a two-chord sequence **(A)** that, though stated as a harmonic succession, is basically linear in origin. The outer voices of an augmented triad move in stepwise contrary motion, while the middle voice repeats, to form a chord built of two fourths, one perfect and one augmented (a chord especially favored by Schoenberg during this period, no doubt for its "nontonal" quality).

After a measure of parallel minor thirds in the piano, the succession returns in an altered form **(A')** in m. 3 to articulate the close of the first phrase. It also appears prominently in the middle of the song and, especially, at the end (Example III-3b), first in the altered form **(A'),** then in various transpositions as well as yet a third form **(A"),** and finally, in the last two measures, in its original version (with augmented rhythm) at the original pitch level (providing another example of a vague, yet audible, quasi-tonal effect). A clear demonstration of the derivation of linear material from this basic unit is found in the vocal part of Example III-3a, where, through the first half of m. 2, the voice unfolds pitches heard simultaneously in the piano. (The first three measures of Example III-3b are similar in this regard.) A further example is provided by the piano part of mm. 9–11 (Example III-3c), which almost entirely comprises linear and vertical statements of transpositions of the basic cell's second chord.

The use of a cell predominantly as an abstract, unordered group of pitches—or "set," to use the term favored by music theorists—is illustrated by the eleventh song. In m. 1 (Example III-4a; see p. 72) the first four notes in the right hand of the piano present the basic set **(A):** B♭-D♭-D♮-F (in unordered, or scalar, form). (The left-hand figure, consisting of three sequential statements of a four-note cell, although not strictly derived from the basic set, is nevertheless closely related, as it is made up entirely of minor seconds and major thirds, both important intervals within the **A** cell.) In mm. 8–10 (Example III-4b) the first seven notes of the vocal line—except for a B♭ that here might be considered as a sort of "passing tone"—form a transposition of the original four-note set down a whole step: A♭-C♭-C♮-E♭. Each of the subsequent vocal minor thirds, A-C and D-F, combines with a sustained note in the piano accompaniment to form a transposition of a three-note "subset," consisting of a minor third plus a minor second, drawn from the complete **A** cell: A-C with C♯, D-F with F♯. (Note that these two units are linked by yet another transposition of this subset: C♯ from the first with D-F of the second.) Finally, the last segment of the vocal line, from the high C (penultimate note of m. 9), presents two additional forms of the complete four-note **A** set (with D♯ common to both): G♯-B-C-D♯ and C-D♯-E-G. (This same tightly constructed passage returns, in a somewhat modified form, to close the song.)

Example III-4: SCHOENBERG, *Das Buch der hängenden Gärten,* No. 11

a. m. 1

These brief examples should not give the impression that Schoenberg used such procedures consciously (at least completely so) or systematically during the atonal period. On the contrary, he seems to have worked intuitively, adjusting his method to suit the requirements of particular pieces. The first three of the Five Orchestral Pieces, Op. 16, illustrate the variety of techniques employed: the first relies heavily upon canonic devices; the second features a recurring dissonant chord (a sort of dissonant "tonic") that appears at important formal divisions, as well as a number of ostinatos that supply a more stable background for the less stable surface; and the third (the well-known and highly influential *Farben,* or "Colors") is based on a recurring, slow-moving harmonic progression (again canonically derived), with particular emphasis placed on subtle timbral transformations in the orchestra. In all of these pieces pitch cells are used as a controlling device, but with widely varying degrees of consistency and within ever-changing compositional contexts.

Moreover, as Schoenberg reached the end of this two-year period of intense creative experimentation, he began to rely less and less upon explicit motivic correspondences and conscious structural strategies, such as canon, to integrate his music. Thus the last three pieces composed in 1909—the third of the Op. 11 piano pieces, the last of the Op. 16 orchestral pieces, and *Erwartung*—are not only atonal but essentially "athematic" as well. *Erwartung,* an extended (c. twenty minutes) monodrama for soprano and orchestra with text by Marie Pappenheim and one of Schoenberg's most remarkable achievements, offers perhaps the most extreme instance: an outpouring of freely unfolding, continuously changing, and violently eruptive music that seems to have surfaced directly—without intervention of conscious control—from the composer's innermost subliminal thought processes. (The entire work was composed in piano score in seventeen days, suggesting that the music must have formed itself almost by free association.)

The text of *Erwartung* presents the interior monologue of a woman waiting to meet her lover in a forest. When he fails to appear, she becomes increasingly frantic; eventually, while running desperately through the woods, she stumbles over his dead body. (There is at least a hint that she herself may have killed him.) The quality of hysteria evoked by the text, much of it fragmentary, stream-of-consciousness recollections of previous events, is faithfully mirrored in the turbulent character of Schoenberg's score, which responds graphically and instantaneously to the mercurial changes in the woman's emotional state. Although brief melodic patterns are occasionally repeated immediately, the overall effect is of constant transformation, the musical equivalent to the instability of the protagonist's psyche. *Erwartung* almost completely defies rational musical analysis, at least along traditional lines, yet it is unquestionably a work of extraordinary psychological depth and evocative power. With its vivid suggestion of impending disaster and emotional disintegration, it is a true child of the new age.

That Schoenberg should have reached maturity in Vienna, the home

Schoenberg's own sketch for the setting of *Erwartung*. (Used by permission of Belmont Music Publishers)

of Sigmund Freud and a major center of the "expressionist" movement that, especially in Germany and Austria, dominated the plastic arts during the early years of the twentieth century, is more than mere historical coincidence. Believing that art should reflect internal rather than external aspects of reality, the expressionist painters eventually came to abandon traditional pictorial conventions in favor of nonrepresentational or "abstract" art, which enables the artist to project his emotions and feelings directly without interference from the "outside" world. Schoenberg, himself an amateur painter of considerable ability, exchanged ideas with Wassily Kandinsky, a leading figure in the expressionist movement during this critical period, and he abandoned the conventions of traditional tonality at approximately the same time Kandinsky's first purely abstract paintings appeared. Atonality and athematicism, the last evolutionary stage of Schoenberg's concepts of developing variation and musical prose, seemingly freed him from all previous restraints. Music, without recourse to "outside" rule or system, became—or at least so Schoenberg believed at the time—more immediately communicative, more directly a summoning of the composer's inner life. Because of these parallels, the years from 1907 to World War I are often referred to as Schoenberg's expressionist period (much as Debussy is called an Impressionist, but with perhaps more justification).

The impact of Schoenberg's music of this period on the course of twentieth-century music in general was profound, far exceeding that of his own personal compositional style. The influence of the latter was primarily limited to musicians closely associated with Schoenberg, principally his students, and only a relatively small number of composers actually adopted atonality in any form during Schoenberg's lifetime. Yet his conception of music as comprising a free twelve-note chromatic field, within which any configuration of pitches could act as a "norm," completely redefined the limits of what was considered possible, or permissible, in the realm of musical composition. To a degree, every modern composer was forced to consider his own work in reference to these expanded possibilities. In effect, Schoenberg's atonal music established a new set of boundaries, within which each composer, Schoenberg included, staked out a personal terrain. Indeed, the notion of contextual music, which applies in varying degrees to all twentieth-century music no longer adhering to functional triadic tonality, can be adequately understood only in relation to these new limits: within the enormous new range of available possibilities, each work had to define its own particular vocabulary and compositional methods.

Following the great burst of creative energy during the 1907–9 period, Schoenberg continued to compose steadily, though less prolifically. The Six Little Piano Pieces, Op. 19, and the song *Herzgewächse (Heartbloom)*, Op. 20, appeared in 1911; *Pierrot lunaire (Moonstruck Pierrot)*, Op. 21, in 1912; the one-act "drama with music" *Die glückliche Hand (The Lucky Hand)*, Op. 18, in 1913; and the Four Orchestral Songs, Op. 22, in 1916. Of these, the most influential was *Pierrot lunaire,* a setting of twenty-one poems by the French poet Albert Giraud, in German translations, for *Sprechstimme* and five instrumentalists (two of whom double, so that seven different instruments are called for). *Sprechstimme* (literally, "speaking voice") is a type of vocal delivery somewhere between speech and song, and its eerie, almost inhuman, quality vividly reflects the world of madness and decadence depicted in Giraud's poetry. Each of the twenty-one songs has its own special instrumental setting (only the last one uses all seven instruments) and creates a unique and unforgettable atmosphere that is intimately joined to its text.

Historically, *Pierrot* is of particular interest as it gives the first indication of a change in Schoenberg's thinking that was to become more evident in later years. Several of the songs feature elaborate contrapuntal structures of a relatively strict kind, marking a turn from the freer approach of the preceding works. *Die Nacht (The Night)* is based almost entirely upon manipulations of a single three-note cell (Schoenberg subtitles the song "Passacaglia"), while *Der Mondfleck (The Moonfleck)* contains an elaborate double canon that proceeds to the song's midpoint and then moves backward, in retrograde motion, until its opening is reached again. In *Pierrot* these techniques remain isolated occurrences, used contextually to shape individual songs; but we shall see that in the postwar years Schoenberg would eventually incorporate them into a new general compositional system.

That Schoenberg would eventually chart a new course seems, in retrospect, unsurprising, for the limitations of his compositional approach during the atonal period were in truth severe. Without the aid of tonal moorings or explicit motivic and thematic correspondences, it was difficult to sustain coherent musical structures of extended duration. It is noteworthy that all the larger atonal works are vocal and thus rely upon a text as an "outside" agent of control and comprehensibility, while the purely instrumental pieces are all relatively brief. (The longest of the Op. 16 orchestral pieces lasts no more than a few minutes, while the Op. 19 piano pieces are little more than fragments.) Whatever the expressive strength of this music (which is considerable: many still find these Schoenberg's most original and important works), the possibility and advisability of continued development along the same lines seemed increasingly questionable.

Chromaticism had always provided the most potent expressive force in Western music, but this force had been tied to its role as a departure from an implied diatonic substructure. Once that structure was removed, total chromaticism acquired a new freedom, as well as a pronounced shock value, that Schoenberg exploited with consummate mastery. Yet the sense of shock—of both intoxication and provocation—could not be indefinitely sustained. Ironically, free chromaticism, in rendering everything more or less equally chromatic and thus equally intense, tended ultimately to neutralize its own expressive basis.

No one was more aware of these problems than Schoenberg himself, and it is significant that he published no new piece for a period of seven years after 1916. These were not years of inactivity, but rather of intense searching, and the new works that began to appear after 1923 were the fruits of a distinct shift in technical and stylistic orientation.

SCHOENBERG AS THEORIST AND TEACHER

A notable feature of nineteenth-century musical life was the emergence of the composer as commentator on music and esthetics; such prominent figures as Weber, Schumann, Berlioz, and Wagner not only wrote music but also wrote extensively *about* it, in books, pamphlets, journals, and newspapers. Schoenberg carried on this tradition, actively publishing articles about his own work and that of others throughout his professional life. Unlike his predecessors, he did not confine himself to general analytical, critical, and philosophical matters; he wrote extensively on the technical aspects of music, establishing himself as a music theorist of major importance (the first prominent composer to do so in modern times). Schoenberg's *Harmonielehre* (Theory of Harmony), published in 1911, is one of the twentieth century's central documents of musical thought, and his later books include studies of counterpoint, composition, and the relationship of harmony to musical form.

Given his interest in the theoretical side of music, it is not surprising that Schoenberg was an important teacher of composition, perhaps the most influential of his day. In Austria and Germany, and later in the United States, he guided a large number of prominent younger composers, among them such diverse figures as the German Hanns Eisler, the Spaniard Roberto Gerhard, and the Americans John Cage and Leon Kirchner.

However, the two composers most closely associated with Schoenberg were the Austrians Anton Webern and Alban Berg, both of whom rank with the most important figures in twentieth century music. Webern and Berg were among Schoenberg's earliest students in Vienna and both remained in close contact with him throughout most of their lives, relying upon him as a musical adviser and general counselor long after they ceased formal study. So closely did the three composers come to be associated that they were referred to as the "Second Viennese School," distinguishing them from the earlier "school" of Haydn, Mozart, Beethoven, and Schubert. The role of turn-of-the-century Vienna as a breeding ground for influential and formative new ideas is nowhere more impressively revealed than in the appearance of these three musicians, born within fifteen years of one another and intimately linked through musical and personal associations.

Despite many common musical attitudes inherited from Schoenberg, Webern and Berg were fully independent composers with entirely distinct artistic personalities. Each put his own unique stamp on the development of prewar tonality, integrating esthetic conceptions and technical procedures acquired from Schoenberg within an unmistakably personal stylistic framework.

WEBERN

Although some ten years Schoenberg's junior, Anton Webern (1883–1945) was, almost as much as his master, a product of late Germanic Romanticism. His earliest compositions, written in the opening years of the century though published only recently, have their roots in Wagner and Mahler yet also already suggest the understatement and economy so characteristic of Webern's later works. Textures are relatively transparent, the thematic development is unusually compact, and a curious blend of intensity and restraint pervades most of the music. Despite chromaticism and frequent tonal ambiguity, these pieces seem detached and reserved when compared with the full-blown expressivity of most Germanic music of this period, including that of Webern's future teacher Schoenberg. It was to be Webern's mission, and achievement, to adapt Schoenberg's ideas to his own more introverted and circumscribed musical temperament—and in the process to focus on their most basic features with a consistency far exceeding that of the older composer.

Although born in Vienna, Webern spent much of his early life in two smaller Austrian cities, Graz and Klagenfurt. In 1902 he returned to pursue studies in music history at the University of Vienna under Guido Adler, one of the principal founders of modern musicology, and was awarded a doctorate in 1906 for a dissertation on the fifteenth-century Flemish composer Heinrich Isaac. Webern was greatly impressed by Isaac's ability to shape tightly controlled musical forms through strict canonic procedures and by the pronounced independence of his part writing—characteristics that were to have considerable relevance for his own work. In Isaac, Webern noted, "every voice has its own development and is a complete, wonderfully spirited structure, closed and understandable within itself."[3]

Webern composed a sizable body of music before and during his early university years, and Adler, aware of his interest in composition, recommended him to Schoenberg for instruction. Under the latter's guidance from 1904, Webern quickly developed an extremely personal compositional manner. His first published works, the Passacaglia, Op. 1, for orchestra and *Entflieht auf leichten Kähnen,* Op. 2, for a cappella chorus, both completed in 1908 (when Schoenberg was writing his first atonal works), were the last composed under his teacher's guidance, and they clearly suggest the direction Webern's future work would take. The Passacaglia remains tonal (more so, even, than five settings of poems by Richard Dehmel, written about the same time though published only posthumously), and its extended developmental form adheres to late nineteenth-century models, although the main influence has now become Brahms rather than Wagner. Yet there are also clear hints of the Webern to come in the rigorous contrapuntal writing and the use of a strict variational form. The Op. 2 chorus, while still carrying a key signature and closing with an unadorned tonic G-major triad, is tonally and harmonically freer. The entire work is conceived canonically, again showing Webern's predilection for strict contrapuntal procedures.

Following Schoenberg's lead, Webern abandoned traditional tonality in his next composition, Five Songs on texts by Stefan George, Op. 3 (1909). Here the characteristic features of his mature style become more readily apparent: nontriadic vertical combinations favoring minor seconds, sevenths, and ninths; wide intervallic leaps; and continuous development through diverse variational techniques. Especially notable is the determination to derive the entire musical substance from the smallest possible source. The compositional starting point is often no

---

3.   *Denkmäler der Tonkunst in Österreich,* 16, part 1: *Heinrich Isaac: Choralis Constantinus II* (Vienna, 1909), p. viii.

Alban Berg and Anton
Webern

longer a melodic idea with clearly defined rhythmic characteristics, but
a more abstract set of pitches that can be molded into any number of
different compositional formations. All of these characteristics clearly
betray the influence of Schoenberg, but Webern employs them with a
constancy and intensity that is his own. It is as if he views his materials
through a microscope, examining them for their essential properties,
which he presents in their most distilled form. The result is music of
striking compactness and brevity; the longest of the songs contains only
sixteen measures, the shortest only ten.

A typical example (although we should remember that, as with
Schoenberg's atonal music, each piece tends to unfold according to its
own procedures) is provided by the two measures that constitute the
entire middle section of the first song in Op. 3 (Example III-5). The
first seven notes in the voice part present the basic material in its simplest form (m. 6). The right hand of the piano doubles the voice an
octave higher (and doubles itself a third below) for four notes, then
plays a varied version of the last three of these four notes (retaining the
pitches E♭ and D) before continuing in m. 7 with the remainder of the
seven–note set (G♯–B, now doubled with sixths, and the last note elab-

Example III-5: WEBERN, Five Songs, Op. 3, No. 1, mm. 5–8

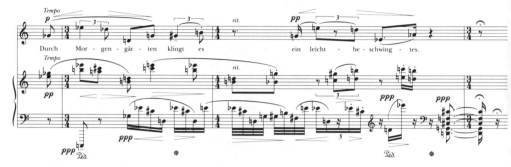

orated by an upper-neighbor C). The left hand is derived from the same seven-note set, but with a completely different rhythm. The first four notes appear in order; the last three of the four are then repeated twice, the second time with an added E♮ (echoing the right hand's E♮ in the previous beat). The final three notes of the seven-note set (G–G♯–B) then continue in order, after which the series resumes from the beginning (spelled F♯ instead of G♭), using first the varied form (with E♮) of notes 2–4. Meanwhile, in m. 7 the voice has begun a new statement of the first five notes, transposed up a half step and thus also rising to a high E♮. The left hand of the accompaniment continues by repeating the E♭–C♯–D♮ group with registral displacements, the final C♯ and D forming the outer notes of the chord that closes the section. The entire conception is therefore quasi-canonic.

The concentration of elements in this passage is noteworthy: a great deal of musical activity takes place in a very short time—as if the expressive intensity of Mahler or Schoenberg had been compressed into a different time scale, transformed from an extended cry into a brief and compacted utterance. As Schoenberg wrote in his preface to Webern's Bagatelles for string quartet, Op. 9, "Consider what moderation is required to express oneself so briefly. You can stretch every glance out into a poem, every sigh into a novel. But to express a novel in a single gesture, joy in a breath—such concentration can only be present in proportion to the absence of self-pity." Although the tendency to shorter compositions is evident in the atonal music of all three composers of the Second Viennese School, in Schoenberg and Berg it occupies only a limited and essentially exceptional period in their development; with Webern it becomes a lifelong obsession. His entire published output, consisting of thirty-one opus numbers, lasts no longer than a single composition of many other composers.

Following Op. 4 (another group of George settings dating from the same time) Webern devoted himself during the years 1909–14 principally to instrumental composition. In the seven works of this period (Opp. 5–11, among which only Op. 8 is vocal) he cultivated his inclination toward succinct statement in a series of miniature masterpieces that have achieved a unique position in music history. The individual movements of these pieces, each a tiny jewel unlike anything heard before, are intimate expressions of pure lyricism, fleeting musical visions that communicate as much by suggestion as by statement, by silence as by sound. Thematic and motivic correspondences, already weakened in Opp. 3–5, become even more tenuous; and the canonic procedures so prominent in the earlier works are dropped completely. As in Schoenberg's works of these years, musical content is reduced to basic intervallic successions dissociated from explicit, recurring rhythmic or motivic patterns. Moreover, in Webern these intervals are increasingly presented as isolated units, cut off from one another by registral, instrumental, and dynamic oppositions. Only rarely do more than a few notes occur in a continuous group; the overall texture is broken up into a series of separate gestures, giving rise to a quality that has been described (once again by analogy with a technique in painting) as "pointillistic"— that is, made up of a number of individual "points."

Webern's progressive development toward "athematicism" can be illustrated by comparing the opening of the first of the Five Pieces for String Quartet, Op. 5 (1909), with the third of the Four Pieces for Violin and Piano, Op. 7 (1910). In the former (Example III-6) the initial rising sixteenth-note motion in m. 1 (C-C♯, followed by F-E) still provides a semblance of motivic content in the traditional sense. Both intervallically and rhythmically, it gives rise to the quasi-sequential development in the first violin (m. 2), which is imitated canonically by the second violin (m. 3) and, briefly, by all the other instruments (m.

Example III-6: WEBERN, Five Pieces for String Quartet, Op. 5, No. 1, mm. 1–4

4). Similar melodic–rhythmic gestures appear in readily recognizable form throughout the movement, and they are played off against contrasting material, presented at a slower tempo, in a way that lends the movement something of the quality of a miniature sonata form.

In the violin piece one can no longer speak of themes or motives. Only 14 measures in length, the piece is put together from a number of highly individualized elements, all more or less equal in weight and importance. Considering the extreme brevity, the number and variety of these elements is surprisingly high, since, except for the ostinato-like violin passage in mm. 6–9 (which sets these measures off as a contrasting middle section), repetitions of larger units are strictly avoided.

Unity is achieved not by readily evident recurrences, but by highly elliptical—one might say "hidden"—associations. For example, a faint suggestion of reprise is achieved when the extended opening pitch A in mm. 1–3 in the violin (Example III-7a) returns in mm. 10–11, immediately following the middle section (Example III-7b), heard again in conjunction with half-step relationships (with B♭ and A♭ in mm. 1–3, with G in mm. 10–11); and the repeated-note idea of mm. 1–2 (the piano's B♭s) also recurs, transformed into the tremolos in the violin (mm. 10–11). Despite its contrasting character, the middle section is also prepared by the opening measures. The predominant interval of a perfect fourth in the violin's ostinato figure (which consists of the notes A–D–E♭–A♭, played in ascending direction) is anticipated in m. 4 in the piano (B♭–E♭); while three of the ostinato's four pitches, as well as its four-note rhythmic grouping and linking of fourths by half steps, derives from the violin figure in m. 4 (Example III-7a).

Also characteristic is the use of half-step connections and a related tendency to fill out chromatic scale segments. Thus the opening sustained A immediately branches out chromatically (ignoring octave transpositions), to B♭ in m. 1, to A♭ in m. 3; and the violin's G♯-A in m. 10 is expanded chromatically upward by the piano's sustained A♯-B-C. This tendency to produce chromatic blocks, found in all of Webern's music of this period, is evident throughout the piece; every note appears in close conjunction with a note a half step away (or an octave transposition thereof).

As in all of Webern's music from this period, much of the effect of the violin piece stems from the instrumental writing. Webern's penchant for taking an idea of Schoenberg's to its ultimate consequences is again illustrated—in this case the concept of *Klangfarbenmelodie* (tone-color melody), of music structured by transformations of color rather than pitch and rhythmic development. Striking and unusual timbral effects are characteristic of all of his works of the prewar years. The most extreme examples are found in the Five Pieces for small orchestra, Op. 10, completed in 1913. But even in the violin piece, where the

Example III-7: WEBERN, Four Pieces for Violin and Piano, Op. 7, No. 3

a. mm. 1–4

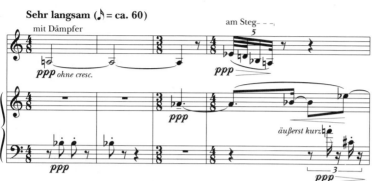

b. mm. 10–11

instrumental resources are severely limited, one recognizes a special concern for timbral matters. Every note sounded by the violin, except the first, is played either on the bridge (*am Steg*) or with the wood of the bow (*col legno*), and the alternation of the two is essential in differentiating the three brief formal segments (the outer sections are both *am Steg,* the middle one is *col legno*). The "normal" note becomes the exception.

The aphoristic, fragmentary quality of Webern's atonal compositions is underscored by a preference for soft dynamic levels. The entire violin part of Op. 7, No. 3, for example, is played with mute (*mit Dämpfer*), and the prevailing dynamic level is *ppp*. In addition, the closing segment is marked "scarcely audible" (*kaum hörbar*)! Not only has the extreme brevity pared down the statement to an almost unbearably concentrated form; it is matched by a dynamic range that reduces the actual sound to an absolute minimum. Music here seems to verge on its own extinction; it threatens to consume itself with silence. In no other music of the period are the overwhelming effects of the loss of tonality more dramatically, or more poignantly, reflected.

BERG

Alban Berg (1885–1935), the third and youngest member of the Second Viennese School, acquired his musical training almost exclusively from Schoenberg. Born into a well-to-do Viennese family, Berg enjoyed the advantages of a cultivated household in which music and the arts had a prominent role. Although his early musical training seems to have been limited, he did learn to play the piano reasonably well, and he began composing songs while still in his early teens. The young Berg enjoyed the company of some of the leading intellectual and artistic personalities of the day, those then in the process of undermining the conservative conventions upon which Vienna's traditional cultural life rested. Among his friends and acquaintances were the painters Gustav Klimt and Oskar Kokoschka and the writers Stefan Zweig, Karl Kraus, and Peter Altenberg.

Despite the stimulating environment in which he matured, Berg was an undistinguished student, more given to imaginative pursuits of an artistic and intellectual nature than to the restricted format and rote learning of traditional Austrian education. He passed his final school examination only with difficulty, and the second time around, in 1904. Shortly thereafter Berg began musical studies with Schoenberg, working formally with him for six years but continuing to show him his compositions well beyond this point.

The Seven Early Songs, written during the earlier years of instruction (1905–8) but not published until 1928 (in both piano and orchestral versions, the latter having been prepared only at this later time), display something of the warm lyricism characteristic of Berg's mature music. Although the songs vary widely in quality and style, there are definite indications of future directions: e.g., the rich chromaticism of *Traumgekrönt* and the whole-tone features of *Nacht*.

The Piano Sonata, Op. 1, completed in 1908, was the first extended composition Berg considered worthy of publication. Like Schoenberg's First Quartet and Chamber Symphony, it is in one unbroken movement (though it does not combine characteristics of different movements within this single span); and like them, it pushes traditional tonality to its outermost fringes. Although a B-minor center is established at both the beginning and end, elsewhere the tonal motion is in constant flux, with at best veiled suggestions of specific key centers at important formal divisions (often defined by means of dominants whose tonics never actually appear). The combination of a rather straightforward, if highly compressed, traditional sonata-type structure with rich contrapuntal textures derived from densely woven motivic developments lends the sonata a curious tension and undeniable fascination. At the same time, the disparity between outer structure and inner detail means that the piece seems to stand poised uneasily between past and future. In his next large instrumental work, the String Quartet, Op. 3, Berg was to find a more successful resolution of the conflict between traditional form and tonal dissolution.

Before this quartet appeared, however, Berg wrote the Four Songs, Op. 2, brief settings of poems by Hebbel and Mombert, which mark an important milestone in his ultimate rejection of the conventions of functional tonality. Only two of the songs, the first and third, end with unadorned triads (and in one of these, the third, it is a dominant rather than a tonic chord); and all four are full of richly chromatic harmonic structures that, though closely resembling the dissonant triad-based chords found in late nineteenth-century music, tend to be used here as "absolute" harmonies that avoid resolution.

An example is the opening harmonic succession of the second song (Example III-8a), which is based entirely on transpositions of a single dissonant chord. This chord, consisting in its first statement of the pitches Bb–D–Fb–Ab, is identical in structure, though not in function, to a traditional "French" augmented-sixth chord (it also contains four of the

Example III-8: BERG, Four Songs, Op. 2, No. 2

a. Opening measures

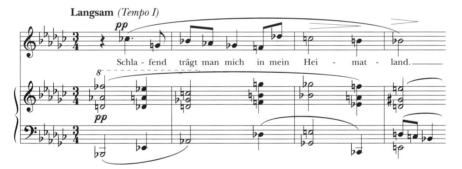

b. Closing measures

By permission of the original publisher, Robert Lienau, Berlin.

six notes of a whole-tone scale), and forms the basic sonority for the entire song, completely dominating the opening and closing measures. (It also returns prominently in the final measures of the last song, tying together the set as a whole.) As is typical throughout Berg's later work, traditional tonal associations are constantly suggested, but are weakened and made ambiguous through contextual means. The opening harmonic progression moves through a circle of falling fifths (or rising fourths)—yet there is little sense of tonal definition or resolution, as all of the chords retain the same underlying dissonant structure.

The altered tonal context becomes even more evident in the song's closing measures (Example III-8b). These begin with a compressed version of the opening phrase, with the voice starting on the sixth note (F) of its first line and holding the eighth note (C) while the piano repeats its first seven chords (with slight modifications, mainly confined to octave displacements) at a faster rhythm. Rather than resolving to a final consonance, however, the progression is left suspended over yet another transposition of the basic sonority, E♭-G-A-D♭ (the A is sustained by the voice only to the downbeat of the last measure). Thus the dissonant sonority retains its role as the tonal "norm," in direct contradiction to its traditional inclination toward triadic resolution.

The Quartet, Op. 3, completed in 1910, is one of the most remarkable products of the Viennese atonal period. Although traces of tonality remain, the harmonic structure is now essentially nontriadic, determined primarily by linear considerations and internal intervallic consistency. Among the purely instrumental works of the Viennese School at this time, Berg's Quartet is unique for its extended length and for the passionate, unrestrained expressivity of its musical language. Here Berg reveals for the first time the full extent of his ability to conceive large-scale musical forms of extraordinary dramatic power. Technically, the work still owes much to Schoenberg, especially its individual adaptation of the notion of developing variation and its use of basic pitch cells. But Berg remains closer to the spirit of the nineteenth century than either his mentor Schoenberg or his close friend Webern. The expansive thematic gestures, which impel the music forward through cumulative points of climactic emphasis, closely recall models drawn from the Romantic tradition and match them in emotional intensity.

Although the Quartet is divided into two movements, which can be analyzed, respectively, according to traditional sonata and rondo patterns, its sense and logic are really that of a single uninterrupted argument (thus following Berg's own Op. 1 and its Schoenbergian precedents). The second movement takes up from the point reached at the end of the first (its first three melodic pitches are directly derived from the last three notes in the top voice of the first movement's accompaniment), and there are numerous connections between the principal melodic materials of the two. Moreover, as the second move-ment progresses, elements from the first movement begin to reappear in an increasingly literal form and ultimately become dominant. A marked holdover from tonal thinking is discernible in the fact that when the main themes of both movements are repeated at important formal junc-tures, they usually begin with the same pitches. In addition, the closing section of the last movement seems clearly to be directed toward a final cadence on D, and a D-minor triad actually appears in the last mea-sure—only to be followed by a dissonant chordal cluster that leaves the question of tonal focus ultimately unresolved.

Berg's next two works follow the tendency toward concentration previously noted in both Schoenberg and Webern. Although requiring quite a large orchestral apparatus, the Five Orchestral Songs, Op. 4 (1912), are intimate settings that mirror something of the "snapshot" quality of the texts by Peter Altenberg, which were written on—and comment upon—picture postcards. Berg's first work with orchestra, these songs give impressive evidence of his remarkable skill in instru-mentation. Deriving from Schoenberg and Mahler a conception of the orchestra as a collection of varied chamberlike groupings, Berg pro-duces a colorful, constantly changing timbral surface, enlivened by spe-cial instrumental techniques such as flutter-tonguing and glissandos. Especially notable is the scoring of a chord containing all twelve pitches that opens and closes the third song: while the pitches remain unchanged during the first seven measures, the music develops entirely through orchestral transformations, as different instruments take over different notes in a manner somewhat reminiscent of Schoenberg's orchestral piece *Farben*, Op. 16, No. 3. Also of interest is the use, in the last song, of a passacaglia-like structure, which echoes Schoenberg's return at this time to stricter contrapuntal procedures in portions of *Pierrot lunaire*. Berg's passacaglia actually involves several recurring themes, one of which consists of a series of twelve different pitches, derived from a similar theme in the first movement.

Berg's only contributions to the type of brief instrumental composi-tions especially favored by Webern during this period are the Four Pieces for Clarinet and Piano, Op. 5. Yet despite their brevity, these clarinet pieces display little of Webern's textural sparseness and aphoristic con-cision. Berg's typically full-blown dramatic melodic gestures are still in evidence, only here compressed into as compact a space as possible. To subvert his natural inclination toward expansion, Berg introduces repetitive patterns that freeze the motion each time it seems to get fully under way, producing a strangely beautiful disparity between the strong forward thrust of the thematic ideas and the ostinato-like barriers set up to thwart them.

Berg's last prewar composition, the Three Pieces for Orchestra, Op.

6 (1914), reveals perhaps more effectively than any other work of this period his special ability to relate the new musical language of atonality to the fading tradition of late Romanticism. Mahler's always strong influence on Berg is especially noticeable: in the great sweep of the melodic lines, in the brilliant and meticulous orchestration, and in the clear evocation of popular forms of music (explicitly acknowledged in the titles of two of the three pieces: *Reigen,* or "round dance," and March). The opening piece, entitled Prelude, begins with percussion alone, to which oscillating pitches are slowly added, creating the impression of "music" only gradually forming itself out of the opening "noise." This process is then reversed at the end of the piece, yielding an arch form, a type much favored by Berg, who liked to open and close movements with the same pitches (Op. 4, Nos. 2 and 4), the same chord or interval (Op. 4, No. 3; Op. 5, No. 2), or the same thematic statement (Op. 3, No. 1). Later, after his adoption of the twelve-tone system developed by Schoenberg in the early postwar years, this tendency found more systematic expression in the composer's use of strict retrograde forms.

CHAPTER IV

New Tonalities

STRAVINSKY

At the beginning of his autobiography, published in Paris during the 1930s, Igor Stravinsky (1882–1972) recalls two of his earliest musical memories:

> An enormous peasant . . . would begin to sing. This song was composed of two syllables, the only ones he could pronounce. They were devoid of any meaning, but he made them alternate with incredible dexterity in a very rapid tempo. . . . Another memory which often comes back is the singing of the women of the neighboring village. There were a great many of them, and regularly every evening they sang in unison on their way home after the day's work. To this day I clearly remember the tune, and the way they sang it . . .[1]

It is notable that both these memories are concerned with music performed by simple people of the Russian countryside, for Stravinsky's national origins and the character of his native folk music were of special importance to his work. Although one of the ironies of his life was that he spent most of it as an expatriate, cut off from his homeland, Stravinsky's Russian heritage would always remain a critical factor in his stylistic development.

We have noted the tension that characterized the growth of nineteenth-century Russian music, pulled between allegiance to traditional Western models and the drive to establish an indigenous musical tradition. This tension was intensified in Stravinsky, acquiring a specifically

1. *An Autobiography* (New York, 1936), pp. 3–5.

twentieth-century coloration as a result of the composer's isolation from his native country. The intellectual or artistic refugee, removed from his own soil and forced to adapt to an alien culture, has been a characteristic figure in contemporary life; and the image of the artistic outsider or "extraterritorial" has found one of its most complex and richly developed realizations in Stravinsky's work.

Stravinsky's father was a prominent operatic bass at the imperial opera in St. Petersburg, and the composer's early years were divided between winters in the city and summers on various country estates owned by his mother's well-to-do family. The young Stravinsky matured in an environment in which the importance of music was taken for granted. He received piano lessons from the age of nine and later also instruction in harmony and counterpoint. Yet his family was opposed to a career in music, so he enrolled at the University of St. Petersburg in 1901 as a student in law and legal philosophy. Only in 1903, in his twenty-first year, shortly following his father's death, did Stravinsky commence composition studies with Rimsky-Korsakov, whom he had met the previous year through family connections. Thus was initiated a warm and musically rewarding association that lasted until Rimsky's death in 1908, and the master's decisive influence is evident in various aspects of the younger composer's music, notably its emphasis on non-Western scales and its brilliant and colorful orchestration.

Under Rimsky's supervision Stravinsky composed a number of works following strict classical models, including a Symphony in E♭ major (1905–7). But the marks of a distinct and highly personal compositional style first become recognizable in two brief orchestral works written in the year of Rimsky's death, the *Scherzo fantastique* and *Fireworks*. The former is a study in octatonic pitch relationships—an interest Stravinsky had acquired from his teacher and would retain as an important aspect of his compositional approach; the latter illustrates his enduring preference for static, nondevelopmental harmonic areas. *Fireworks* is almost completely anchored in the home key of E major, remaining largely bound to the tonic triad. To compensate for the absence of tonal progression, Stravinsky concentrates on manipulating small motivic units, mostly confined to the same pitch repertory, and enlivens the essentially motionless harmonic background through virtuosic instrumentation, anticipating two of the most characteristic features of his later style.

The premieres of these two orchestral works on a single concert in 1909 gained Stravinsky sudden recognition, most significantly through the interest of the famed Russian artistic impresario Sergey Diaghilev, who was in attendance. Diaghilev was then in the process of forming the Ballets Russes, a company of dancers, choreographers, artists, and

Igor Stravinsky in his study at Ustilug, 1912, the year before the premiere of *The Rite of Spring*. (Courtesy Paul Sacher Stiftung)

musicians working in close collaboration that was to become one of the major forces in the performing arts in the first quarter of the twentieth century. Greatly impressed by the young composer's brilliant orchestral works, Diaghilev invited Stravinsky to join the undertaking, thus initiating one of the modern period's most fruitful artistic associations.

Among the members of Diaghilev's company were some of the most important Russian artists of the day, including the dancers and choreographers Mikhail Fokine and Vaslav Nijinsky and the artists and designers Leon Bakst and Alexandre Benois. Stravinsky was enormously stimulated by his association with this group, and he composed for the company three major ballet scores that are numbered among his most important compositions: *The Firebird* (1910, choreography by Fokine), *Petrushka* (1911, also with Fokine), and *The Rite of Spring* (1913, choreography by Nijinsky). The music for each was conceived as an integral part of a complete artistic conception that also encompassed drama, dance, staging, and set design; and Stravinsky worked in close collaboration with the other artists on all aspects of the production (the scenario of *The Rite of Spring,* for example, originated from one of his own ideas). The fact that the music was designed to complement a total staged presentation had a pronounced effect on the formal characteristics and compositional planning, giving rise to a new conception of musical structure that in its own way would prove as influential for later musical developments as the atonal works of Schoenberg, Webern, and Berg.

In certain respects the first of the ballets, *The Firebird,* is a holdover from the past. One still perceives the direct influence of Rimsky, notably in the association of chromaticism with the supernatural elements of the traditional Russian fairy tale upon which it is based. Much of the music—that for the mortal characters—remains diatonic and traditionally tonal, and adheres to nineteenth-century conceptions of melodic development. (Not surprisingly, this has remained by far Stravinsky's most popular score, a circumstance much resented in later years by the composer, who felt that his more innovative works deserved comparable public recognition.) Yet certain sections hint at new formal possibilities. The introduction works with two opposing groups of material, alternated in abrupt juxtaposition. Especially telling is the way the individual segments are not necessarily rounded off at their endings, but interrupted in mid-course by the presentation of the next new or recurring contrasting segment. This creates a formal rhythm characterized by sudden opposition that seems more closely related to film techniques than traditional musical ones. (The essays of the Russian film director Sergey Eisenstein, written some years later, often read like descriptions of Stravinskian compositional procedures.) Undoubtedly Stravinsky's concern for an intimate coordination between his music and the shifting spatial designs of the dance movements onstage played a critical part in the development of this new approach.

In *Petrushka* the direction of this approach becomes more clearly focused. The story of the ballet, a love triangle involving three circus puppets, is—unlike that of *Firebird*—unmistakably modern and anti-Romantic in flavor; and Stravinsky's score effectively mirrors its essentially sardonic quality with a lean, hard-edged complexion in sharp contrast to the richly sensuous textures still predominating in the earlier work. The very opening measures (Example IV-1), with their chamberlike scoring and minimal motivic content, illustrate a new economy. All the notes in the flute melody up to m. 9 are drawn from the four pitches (D-E-G-A) stated at the outset by the clarinets and horns in the tremolo accompaniment. Moreover, this melody is pieced together from a limited number of fixed melodic and rhythmic modules that remain largely unchanged in themselves, acquiring variety mainly through their shifting combinations (a technique that will remain, as we shall see, a basic aspect of Stravinsky's melodic style).

Example IV-1: STRAVINSKY, *Petrushka,* mm. 1–11

Thus the opening rising fourth A-D occurs no fewer than seven times in the first five measures, alternating with the rising and falling triplet figure (m. 3, m. 4) that fills out the upper fifth D-A. The cello line beginning in m. 6 is closely related: its boundaries are also defined by a perfect fourth (B-E), and its content is similarly limited to four pitches (B-C♯-D-E). Two of these, D and E, are taken from the original collection of the accompaniment, while B and C♯ are new, producing a total combined collection consisting of six of the seven notes of a D-major scale (only F♯ is missing). The cello line, like that of the flute, is made up of brief melodic reiterations that emphasize the outer notes of its fourth B-E. When the flute melody continues after its long A in m. 6, it now reflects the influence of the cellos: the motive of the fourth is now also grouped in falling patterns, and the pitch B, first introduced by the cellos, is added in mm. 9–10.

This passage is unambiguously centered on D, yet the key is presented as a static tonal field rather than a result of dynamic harmonic relationships. The motionless quality is especially apparent in the accompanimental ostinato that continues unchanged throughout, its outer pitches presenting the key-defining fifth D-A; but the flute line also incessantly emphasizes the pitches D and A. When the cellos produce a shift to B-E, the effect is unlike a modulation—it happens instantaneously, without any preparation such as a pivot chord, and the accompaniment continues, completely unaffected by the cellos. In addition, the flute picks up its melody again before the cellos have stopped, so that the two different pitch modules temporarily overlap with each other.

Even this brief segment gives an idea of the new formal processes used by Stravinsky in *Petrushka*. The crosscutting from flute module to cello module and back again (in this case with overlapping) forms a basic structural model for the entire piece. Indeed, the musical shape of the whole first tableau of the ballet, which depicts in musical form the intense activity of a pre-Lenten fair, can be understood as an extension of this idea; it too cuts abruptly back and forth between clearly differentiated musical segments, mirroring the shifting focus of the stage action from generalized crowd scenes to various smaller groups of characters (a small group of merrymakers, an organ grinder with a dancer, etc.). Stravinsky does not hesitate to imitate the "popular" character of fair music, deriving melodic material from folk songs and popular tunes; he even imitates the sound of a barrel organ and a music box. Typically, after being introduced separately, the music for the latter two is combined in a multileveled texture that features striking rhythmic conflicts between the two distinct layers.

The first tableau of *Petrushka* is almost entirely diatonic; yet only when the composer mimics the quality of the music of street dancers does he resort to traditional dominant and tonic relationships (and even then these are distorted in a typically Stravinskian manner). Otherwise, key centers are established as in the opening measures: by melodic and rhythmic emphasis, allowing the tonal focus to shift suddenly as one segment gives way to the next. The effect of the whole is not unlike a colorful, constantly changing musical kaleidoscope.

The second tableau, which is considerably more chromatic than the first, contains a famous dissonant chord consisting of two superim-

Example IV-2: STRAVINSKY, the "Petrushka chord"

posed major triads with roots a tritone apart (F♯ major and C major), a chord of such striking effect that it has become known as the "Petrushka chord."

Because of this two-part structure, the chord, and the music based upon it, are often described as "bitonal." The term is somewhat misleading, for it suggests that traditional tonal procedures are still employed, but here with reference to two simultaneous keys; and it emphasizes the separateness of the two triadic components. But Stravinsky conceives of the chord as a total chromatic complex, much as he conceives of the opening accompanimental ostinato of the first tableau as a diatonic complex from which he can draw pitches. Example IV-3 on p. 96 shows a typical passage based on the chord.

As in the ballet's opening segment, there is an ostinato accompaniment consisting of tremolos, in this case alternating the two major triads (played by flutes, oboes, English horn, piano, and strings). With the F♯ triad in first inversion, stepwise motion is emphasized in the tremolos (another correspondence with the opening). The lower woodwinds, however, play arpeggiated figures that mix together notes from both triads. The overall effect is that of a single fused harmonic complex (in this case using notes of the octatonic scale C-D♭-E♭-E-F♯-G-A-B♭-C, rather than the diatonic scale of the opening), from which the trumpets and trombones derive the principal melodic material.

If the Paris productions of *The Firebird* and *Petrushka* established Stravinsky as a major composer of international reputation, the score for his third Diaghilev ballet, *The Rite of Spring,* made him the most widely recognized composer of his age. The premiere of *The Rite* in Paris on May 29, 1913, is probably the most famous (or notorious) premiere in the history of music. The ballet's scenic evocation of pagan Russian rituals elicited from Stravinsky a score of unprecedented primitive force, in which music seemed to be distilled to its rhythmic essence, hammered out by the orchestra with unrestrained percussive intensity. Shaken by the radical nature of both score and ballet, the opening-night audience was in an uproar from the beginning, with those both for and against shouting at one another in heated debate. The noise level was

Example IV-3: STRAVINSKY, *Petrushka,* second tableau, mm. 5–8 after
No. 51

so high that most of the music remained inaudible; yet, if nothing else, the sensational aspect of the event placed Stravinsky at the forefront of the musical revolutions of the time. For contemporary listeners of *The Rite,* as for those of the first atonal works of Schoenberg, music could never be the same again.

In many respects *The Rite* extended, and intensified, techniques already nurtured in the earlier ballets, especially *Petrushka*. What was new was the tone: an aggressive, propulsive quality sets the music apart from the exoticism of *The Firebird* or the detached humor and athletic brilliance of *Petrushka*. *The Rite* makes its points with brutal force, even its quieter moments projecting an expressive intensity that was new to Stravinsky (and that was to remain something of an exception in his work).

Contributing to the harshness of *The Rite* is the high level of dissonance and chromaticism, illustrated by the reiterated chord (Example IV-4a) that opens the "Augurs of Spring," the first section of the ballet following the introduction. The chord is hammered out in the strings in a stream of eighth notes, some accented by the addition of horns to produce complex rhythmic patterns superimposed over the steady underlying pattern. Like the "Petrushka chord," this one can also be viewed as a combination of two triadic structures, a dominant seventh chord built on E♭ and a major triad on F♭; but it too functions basically as an integrated sonority with octatonic qualities (it is largely, though not exclusively, drawn from the scale E♭–E–F♯–G–A–B♭–C–D♭–E♭). As in the earlier work, the chord provides a basic pitch reference, or tonal focus, for the entire section: twice interrupted by contrasting segments, it returns in unaltered form.

Even the interruptions reveal the influence of this chord, as is illustrated by the beginning of the first contrasting segment (Example IV-4b; see p. 98), which contains all seven notes of the original chord, plus the new pitch C♮ (thereby bringing the total content still closer to the octatonic scale mentioned above). In the opening of the second departure (Example IV-4c) the lower fifth C♭–F♭ of the original chord has dropped to B♭–E♭ (pitches already in the original sonority), which become the lowest two notes of a series of rising and falling perfect fifths, while the violas restate in a different form the C-major chord played by bassoons and cellos in the previous example. Throughout both contrasting segments, the English horn plays an ostinato figure comprising three of the four notes of the "E♭ portion" of the reference chord (E♭–D♭–B♭).

Examples IV-4b and 4c also illustrate a pervasive rhythmic technique of *The Rite:* the superimposition of multiple ostinatos with different rhythmic values and unequal total durations. Example IV-4c features three such recurring units: six eighth notes (basses and cellos), four eighth notes (English horn), and six eighth-note triplets (violas). The resulting three-level rhythmic structure requires three full measures before the beginnings of all of the units again coincide with one another.

The Rite also shares with *Petrushka* an emphasis on brief melodic fragments of folklike simplicity that combine to produce more complex larger units. In the later work these fragments, still normally diatonic in themselves, usually appear in chromatic contexts. Thus the dissonant

Example IV-4: STRAVINSKY, *The Rite of Spring,* "Augurs of Spring"

a. mm. 1–4 after No. 13

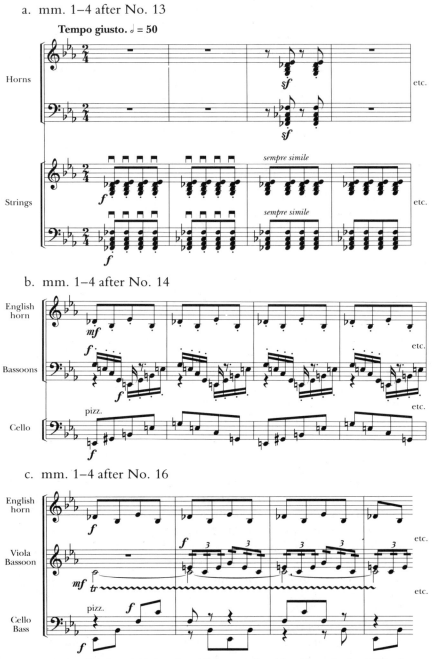

b. mm. 1–4 after No. 14

c. mm. 1–4 after No. 16

chord of Example IV-4a later (at rehearsal No. 19) forms an accompaniment for a series of brief melodic statements made up entirely of reorderings of the pitches of the scale segment F-G-A♭-B♭. (Afterward, at rehearsal No. 21, these statements are combined contrapuntally in a sort of primitive canon.) The most striking instance of Stravinsky's "modular" approach to melody is seen in Example IV-5, a flute melody that consists entirely of an uninterrupted presentation of five different motivic units **(a-e)** in changing successions:

Example IV-5: STRAVINSKY, *The Rite of Spring,* "Augurs of Spring," mm. 1–11 after No. 28, flute part

A significant rhythmic feature of *The Rite* is evident in passages whose meter changes almost continuously. The most extreme example occurs in the final section, the "Sacrificial Dance," the opening measures of which are given in Example IV-6 (see p. 100). Here we see yet another outgrowth of Stravinsky's familiar technique of linking individual musical units into longer chains through irregular combination. In this brief excerpt there are only two such units, first introduced in m. 1 and m. 5, respectively. The changes of meter reflect differences in the total durations of the two basic units: the first unit may last either three sixteenths (as in mm. 1, 3, 4, 7, 8, and 10) or two (as in mm. 2 and 6), while the second (mm. 5 and 9) always needs four sixteenths (expressed as 2 / 8).

The kind of rhythmic structure evident in this passage represents a basic alteration of traditional Western rhythmic conceptions, as radical in its implications as the abandonment of functional tonality; durations are organized, not—as in most tonal music—by the regular subdivision of a constant larger unit (such as the measure), but by the addition of unequal shorter units into larger, irregular patterns. This is reflected in the pronounced difficulties Stravinsky experienced in notating the section. Even after having completely composed it mentally and played it frequently on the piano, the composer was still uncertain about how it could be written down. The traditional Western notational system,

Example IV-6: STRAVINSKY, *The Rite of Spring,* "Sacrificial Dance," mm. 1–10

designed to indicate relationships based principally upon subdivisions of a common denominator, was not easily adaptable to his new rhythmic conception. Indeed, after devising the notation seen in Example IV-6, Stravinsky apparently remained dissatisfied, as he twice renotated it in subsequent revisions of the work.

The entire "Sacrificial Dance" section offers an excellent opportunity for study of Stravinsky's "combinational" technique, which, though simple enough in principle, produces unprecedented rhythmic complexity. The concentration on purely rhythmic effects reaches a high point in the first contrasting section of the final dance (rehearsal No. 149), where the first twenty-nine measures consist primarily of a single chord reiterated without change no less than forty-one times, the only variation·resulting from differences in the durations between attacks. It has been remarked that the radically new sound of *The Rite* derives in part from the fact that frequently, as here, the orchestra seems to be treated like a gigantic percussion instrument. As in all good music, however, the orchestral approach is dictated by the overall compositional approach; and in Stravinsky the latter might itself be character-

The artist Valentine Hugo's sketches for the "Sacrificial Dance" from *The Rite of Spring,* made during rehearsals for the original 1913 production. The choreography, costumes, and sets were considered to be as shocking as Stravinsky's music. (Collection André Meyer)

ized as "percussive" in nature, as it emphasizes the manipulation of basically "fixed" musical elements.

An essential aspect of this technique is a new conception of tonality that, although largely independent of the traditional one, is capable of integrating extended musical structures. While emphatically asserting that "tonality is my discipline," Stravinsky himself remarked in his *Poetics of Music* (published in 1942): "My chief concern is not so much with what is known as tonality as what one might term the polar attraction of sound, of an interval, or even a complex of tones."[2] This new and more broadly defined sense of tonal centricity transformed what had been basically a dynamic, and essentially diatonic, concept into a largely static one (at least in the larger dimensions) that was equally applicable to diatonic or chromatic contexts. For example, both diatonic and chromatic passages occur in *Petrushka* and *The Rite of Spring,* diatonic ones being particularly characteristic of the former work, chromatic ones of the latter. But, as we have seen, the basic principle of "polar attraction" (to borrow Stravinsky's term)—that is, of a referential pitch complex that serves as a center of focus for the events that form it and surround (or elaborate) it—is equally applicable to both compositions.

Moreover, it is this new type of tonality that makes possible the formal techniques developed by Stravinsky in his three great ballets. The abrupt crosscutting between harmonically static planes, with one strand of music cut off suddenly by another only to be picked up again later as if nothing had intervened, would be impossible to sustain within a traditional tonal context, as would continuous permutations of a set of fixed melodic modules. Of course, the compositional methods Stravinsky evolved during this period were not unprecedented. We have observed similar techniques in Debussy (and precedents for Debussy can be found in still earlier composers, notably Musorgsky and Liszt). But Stravinsky carried these techniques to new levels of potential, particularly in the area of rhythm.

Stravinsky completed no other large-scale compositions during the period of the three early ballets, although he found time to compose a few songs and the brief cantata *Zvezdoliki* (*The Star-Faced One,* 1912). Before beginning work on *The Firebird,* however, he had finished the first act of an opera, *The Nightingale;* and, after *The Rite of Spring,* he took it up again four years later, composing the second and third acts in 1913–14. This brief (c. forty-five minutes) work, based on a fairy tale by Hans Christian Andersen, is a fascinating document of the great stylistic change the composer had undergone during the critical four-year period of its interruption. (In his autobiography Stravinsky later acknowledged a stylistic disparity in the score, although he found it

2.   *Poetics of Music* (Cambridge, Mass., 1947), p. 36.

justified by the fact that the first act is a kind of prologue with no action, which stands somewhat apart from the rest of the work.)

By 1914 Stravinsky was living and working primarily in Switzerland, returning to Russia only for the summer months. The advent of war, however, cut him off completely from his native country, and the Russian Revolution of 1917 left him a permanent exile in Western Europe and, later, in the United States. (He did not return to his homeland until a visit in 1962.) We shall see that this change in residence accompanied an important shift in stylistic orientation, and was thus to have a profound effect on the future course of Stravinsky's music.

BARTÓK

When Béla Bartók (1881–1945) decided in 1899 to pursue advanced musical studies at the Budapest Academy of Music, remaining in his native land rather than going to Vienna like most other promising Hungarian musicians of the time, he revealed a deep concern for national identity that would be central to his life as a composer. Although art music in Hungary had previously developed as a peripheral variant of Western European traditions, Bartók's profoundly nationalist outlook led him to instill his work with an unmistakable Hungarian flavor. Taking Liszt as his first model, he explored the musical traditions of his homeland and ultimately achieved a remarkable personal synthesis of elements drawn in approximately equal measure from Hungarian folk and Western art sources, thereby charting one of the most characteristic lines of twentieth-century musical development.

Bartók was born into a highly musical family and was himself something of a musical prodigy (curiously, the only such among major composers of the twentieth century). He began piano lessons at the age of five and was composing actively by the time he was ten. It seems to have been assumed all along that he would undertake a career as a professional musician. He studied both piano and composition at the Budapest Academy, at first distinguishing himself primarily as a pianist. A performance of Strauss's *Also sprach Zarathustra* in 1902, however, reignited the spark of composition ("At last I saw the way that lay before me," he later commented), the result being the symphonic poem *Kossuth* (1903), a work of considerable scope and technical achievement. Significantly, the program for *Kossuth* concerns the life of a Hungarian national hero, a leader in the 1848–49 war of independence; and the music, despite affinities to Strauss, also reflects the influence of Liszt, the only Hungarian composer before Bartók to earn international recognition.

The Lisztian strain becomes yet more pronounced in the Rhapsody,

A young Béla Bartók recording folk songs in a Transylvanian mountain village, ca. 1904. (Picture taken by Zoltan Kodály)

Op. 1, originally for piano solo, later arranged for piano and orchestra (1904). Its form is based on the traditional structure of Hungarian Gypsy music—a slow introductory section ("Lassu") followed by a fast, dancelike one ("Friss")—which Liszt had employed in his Hungarian Rhapsodies. From this point on, the influence of Strauss declined. And although that of Liszt always remained evident to some extent in Bartók's virtuosic piano writing, it too was sharply modified after 1904. In that year Bartók made a discovery that was to be of special significance for his future work: the folk music of his native Hungary.

Interested in the popular music of Hungary himself, Liszt had even written a small book on the subject, *The Gypsies and Their Music in Hungary* (1859). But, as the title indicates, Liszt was exclusively concerned with the music of the Gypsies, whom he considered the founders of an indigenous Hungarian national style. The music of the Hungarian peasants, on the other hand, he considered to be not only inferior in quality but entirely derived from—and thus a perversion of—Gypsy music. This view, still generally accepted in the early years of the twentieth century, was embraced by Bartók as well, at least by implication, in such works as the 1904 Rhapsody and the Suite No. 1 for Orchestra, completed the following year.

In 1904, however, when Bartók began to go out in the countryside to hear and write down folk melodies, he found that the opposite was the case: the music of the farmers and peasants was the true folk music of Hungary, of which Gypsy music was an urban and largely commercial adaptation, incorporating numerous Western influences. Encouraged by his fellow composer and compatriot Zoltán Kodály (1882–1967), he set out to make a thorough study of this authentic folk music. As he later pointed out in an important article, "On the Significance of Folk Music," those in countries with little or no musical tradition could find their own musical heritage: "For an artist it is not only right to have his roots in the art of some former times, it is a necessity. Well, in our case it is peasant music which holds our roots." Bartók concluded by quoting Kodály: "Folk music must for us replace the remains of our old music. . . . A German musician will be able to find in Bach and Beethoven what we had to search for in our villages: the continuity of a national musical tradition."[3]

Using a wax cylinder phonograph, Bartók recorded the singing of the local people in their own environment, later transcribing the results for study and categorization. Working together, Bartók and Kodály helped lay the foundation for the discipline we now know as ethnomusicology—the study of indigenous music within its cultural context, as a basic form of human and social expression. Throughout his life Bartók maintained an active interest in these studies, and wrote a number of ground-breaking books and articles in the field.

Most significant for Bartók the composer, however, were the new possibilities for the enrichment of his own musical language that this contact with folk music suggested. In his own words: "The outcome of these studies was of decisive influence upon my work, because it freed me from the tyrannical rule of the major and minor keys."[4] Once again we find a wish to move beyond traditional tonality, now viewed as an outmoded system in need of new life and energy.

In Bartók's case the source of this new energy was native folk music. Instead of major and minor scales, folk music favors older modes no longer found in Western music. Some of these are similar to the traditional church modes, but pentatonic and chromatic modes occur as well. The melodies also exhibit great flexibility and variety. "Measures" (which must be in quotes, since there are no bar lines in the music itself, only in the scholar's transcription thereof) are often made up of unequal groupings of twos and threes, phrases are highly·varied in length, and tempos often fluctuate freely. Equally important for Bartók were the music's harmonic implications. Even though the original folk music is entirely monophonic (one of the "corruptions" of Gypsy music was its introduction of triadic harmony), Bartók thought it possible to develop a harmonic language consistent with the intervallic characteristics of the

3.   "On the Significance of Folk Music [1931]," in *Essays,* ed. Benjamin Suchoff (New York, 1976), pp. 345ff.
4.   "Autobiography [1921]," ibid., p. 410.

melodies. The frequent use of seconds, fourths, and sevenths, for instance, suggested the possibility of employing these same intervals as basic concords.

All these musical characteristics are reminiscent of stylistic traits we have observed in other composers of the early twentieth century. The melodic and rhythmic features bear resemblances to those of Stravinsky (who owed much to the folk music of his own country, though certainly less consciously and systematically than Bartók); the derivation of melody and harmony from a common interval source recalls Debussy, Skryabin, and Schoenberg, as well as Stravinsky. Furthermore, Bartók shared with all of these composers—except Schoenberg—a desire to move beyond traditional tonality by redefining its meaning, not by rejecting it altogether. Here again the influence of folk music is evident: as Bartók himself pointed out, it is "always tonal."

Equally important for Bartók, as well as for other composers of the time (again one thinks of Stravinsky), was that folk music offered the prospect of a new musical esthetic, free from the expressive pretensions and the cult of personality inherited from musical Romanticism. Folk music was a collective creation, the unaffected expression of simple people still breathing clean country air, untouched by the numbing effects of urban industrialization. It was, in a word, "healthy" music, a firm basis for a new kind of art music rooted in soil that, though rich in cultural tradition, was uncontaminated by the decadence of the recent musical past.

Bartók began to draw upon folk music for his own compositions almost immediately upon his first contact with it, but only after several years did he succeed in integrating the new elements completely within a personal style. This process of integration is traced most readily in a series of compositions, mostly for piano, that he based on actual folk tunes. In the first, Twenty Hungarian Folk Songs (1906), brought out jointly by Bartók and Kodály, the melodies are provided with very simple harmonizations (the first ten by Bartók, the remainder by Kodály), completely triadic and, though mildly modal in flavor, based on essentially conventional chord progressions. During the following years, however, Bartók relied increasingly upon harmonic characteristics derived from the melodies themselves.

Example IV-7 illustrates two stages in this progression. In the first (7a), from the collection For Children, a set of eighty-five folk-tune settings (1909), the prominent major seconds of the melody are reflected both chordally and melodically in the right hand's accompaniment, yet the chordal structure still retains a strong feeling of triadic underpinning. In the second (7b), the opening measures of the Improvisations on Hungarian Peasant Songs, Op. 20 (1920), triadic suggestions are completely avoided, the major seconds in the right hand (again derived from the melody) being treated as fully independent harmonic entities. This

Example IV-7: BARTÓK

a. *For Children,* II, No. 34, "Farewell," mm. 1–12

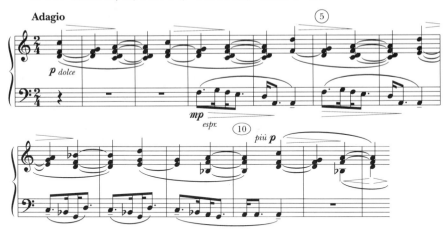

b. *Improvisations on Hungarian Peasant Songs,* No. 1, mm. 1–4

distinction is also reflected in the closings of the two settings from which these excerpts are taken: the first ultimately resolves on a pure, unaltered triad, while the second preserves its dissonant character right to the end.

Related to this development is Bartók's tendency to devise more and more elaborate accompaniments for the melodies, shifting the emphasis from the original tune to the total effect of its presentation. In *For Children* the accompaniments are still relatively simple in texture, but in the *Fifteen Hungarian Peasant Songs* (1917) one finds a wealth of pianistic variety, including doubling and elaborate registral layouts. Finally, in the Sonatina for Piano (1915) the accompaniment represents a completely integrated component of a complex compositional conception, each movement of which—as the work's title suggests—far transcends the formal scope and expressive intent of the folk material on which it is based.

Even before the Sonatina appeared Bartók had composed a work that, though unmistakably preserving the quality of folk music, was in fact entirely original. This was the *Allegro barbaro* of 1911 (Example IV-8), a keyboard piece of elemental rhythmic force whose character and title suggest a strong kinship with *The Rite of Spring,* which Stravinsky began composing in the same year. The raucous, *martellato* rhythm of the accompaniment matches the driving insistence of the melody, folklike in its repetition of brief motivic units circling around a single pitch (A). Despite the dominant suggestions in mm. 7 and 11, the accompaniment stands rooted on F♯ minor, creating a dronelike effect from which the percussive melody seems determined to escape. Yet the scalar content is not F♯ minor but "exotic" in character: in both hands G♮ replaces G♯ as the second scale degree, and in the right hand B♯ replaces B♮.

With its extended length (over two hundred measures) and sectional contrasts, the *Allegro barbaro* reveals that by 1911 Bartók had learned to accommodate his folk influences within a musical language completely of his own making. Like the Suite for piano, Op. 14, written some five years later, it can be said to represent a sort of "free imitation" of folk music, in which the folk quality has been modified to accommodate the formal and developmental ambitions of concert music. Bartók later wrote that it should be the aim of the composer "to assimilate the idiom of folk music so completely that he is able to forget all about it," so that it becomes his "mother tongue." One cannot yet say that the composer of the *Allegro barbaro* has "forgotten" folk music, since clearly one of the piece's aims is to evoke the primitive force found in certain types of native music—but he has clearly taken an important step in this direction. In Bartók's later work, moreover, it is often impossible to make

Example IV-8: BARTÓK, *Allegro barbaro,* mm. 1–13

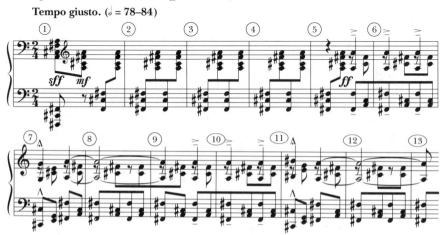

any precise distinction between what is folk-oriented and what is not; all the elements are absorbed into a single, unified vision.

Bartók's researches, which eventually encompassed the folk music not only of Hungary but of the Slavic countries, Turkey, and North Africa, convinced him that the most vital folk traditions were those having frequent contact with other cultures, allowing a mutually enriching exchange of ideas. This attitude is also evident in the eclecticism of Bartók's own mature compositional style, which draws upon many different, even seemingly opposed, sources yet synthesizes them within a completely consistent and personal idiom.

By 1908, well before the folk influence had become dominant, Bartók was already moving away from the late Romanticism of such works as *Kossuth,* the Rhapsody, Op. 1, and the two orchestral Suites, Opp. 3 and 4. In the Fourteen Bagatelles, Op. 6, for piano, published in that year, he began using a number of new techniques associated with such progressive contemporaries as Debussy (whose music Bartók had discovered, again thanks to Kodály, only in the previous year) and Schoenberg. Bartók later remarked that several of these pieces were written specifically as "experiments."

The first Bagatelle combines two different modes simultaneously, one in each hand; the two staves even bear different key signatures, although the net effect is really that of a single chromatically colored mode centered on C. Bagatelle No. 8 features series of dissonant harmonies moving in parallel motion, in a tonal context so ambiguous as to border on atonality (although it does ultimately settle on G, supported by a five-measure tonic pedal at the end). By contrast, two pieces (Nos. 4 and 5) are relatively simple modal arrangements of folk songs. Though a curious and eclectic collection, the Bagatelles mark an important milestone in Bartók's break with nineteenth-century precedents. Alongside the definite departure from conventional tonality, the austere pianistic style reveals a significant reduction of the more decorative and flamboyant manner of the earlier works.

An additional influence on Bartók was the tradition of classical instrumental music stretching back from Brahms to Haydn, Mozart, and Bach, which Bartók's earliest student compositions, written before *Kossuth,* had already explored. Characteristically, when he later set about fashioning a more personal voice that, like his native Hungary, was to some degree independent of this tradition, he did not turn away from his classical predecessors. An active and accomplished professional pianist (appointed professor of piano at the Budapest Music Academy in 1907, he made his living thereafter principally as a teacher and performer), he knew intimately and admired greatly the standard literature of Western music. Moreover, he was interested in incorporating its large-scale formal dimensions and developmental procedures into his own evolving compositional style.

In this respect the First String Quartet, completed in the same year as the Bagatelles (1908), is of special significance. Although less experimental than the Bagatelles, and with relatively little of the folk quality that was to become so pervasive in later works, the Quartet represents Bartók's first mature and fully successful realization of an extended developmental form. It inaugurates a series of six quartets that, taken as a group, form one of the major musical achievements of the first half of the century.

However, the first completely convincing synthesis of the full range of Bartók's compositional influences was achieved in the one-act opera *Bluebeard's Castle* (1911), with a libretto by the Hungarian nationalist poet Béla Balázs. Although it contains no actual folk material, the score is pervaded with the character of the native music Bartók had been intensively studying. This is partly attributable to the intimate correlation between music and text; the phonetic characteristics of the Hungarian language help shape many of the work's most characteristic rhythmic and melodic features. The opera is constructed as a series of brief scenes, each introduced by the opening of one of the doors in Duke Bluebeard's castle, each with its own distinct musical character and formal structure.

The range of Bartók's sources, and the skill and freedom with which he employs them, are evident throughout. Certain scenes are dominated by dissonant harmonic centers, built up largely in fourths, others are mainly triadic in nature; passages with pentatonic and modal scales are set off against those that are largely chromatic. Yet the score is convincingly integrated, thanks in part to the use of a characteristic "leitmotif," chromatic in structure and closely associated with the word "blood" (the libretto's dominant symbol), which recurs repeatedly until, in an extended instrumental segment near the close, it is finally developed to a shattering climax.

Following the completion of *Bluebeard's Castle,* Bartók's output declined, owing in significant measure to his disappointment at the opera's failure to achieve immediate recognition. During this fallow period he devoted much time to his folklore researches. When the war came his delicate health exempted him from military service, and he resumed composition, initiating a new phase in his development that will be taken up in Part II.

CHAPTER V

Other European Currents

RUSSIA: RACHMANINOV AND OTHERS

At the turn of the century Russia enjoyed a position of special prominence in Western musical composition. Tchaikovsky's works were widely
played throughout Europe, and those of Borodin and Rimsky-Korsakov were growing in popularity. But Russian musical life was to undergo
radical changes in the new century, during which political and social
circumstances would increasingly compromise its former centrality. To
begin with, the two principal figures of the generation that reached
maturity in the years around 1900, Skryabin and Stravinsky, failed to
have an impact on Russia's musical life comparable to that of Debussy
in France or Schoenberg in Germany and Austria. Increasingly isolated
by his highly personal mystic vision, Skryabin died prematurely in 1915,
leaving no major musical followers, while Stravinsky's first important
compositions, the early scores for Diaghilev, were written for performance in Paris, where they achieved their greatest fame and influence.
Moreover, after the first decade of the century Stravinsky spent most
of his time in Western Europe, and remained there permanently following the Russian Revolution of 1917.

Only one other Russian of this generation, Sergey Rachmaninov (1837–
1943), attained a position of international prominence, and he was a
composer almost completely tied to the older tradition, who attempted
to extend the Romanticism of such predecessors as Tchaikovsky into
the new era. Rachmaninov never abandoned the tonal and formal conventions of nineteenth-century music and thus remained throughout
his life outside the main currents of twentieth-century musical devel-

opments—yet the antimodernist sentiments of composers like him have been a persistent and important factor in modern musical life. Among the composers who continued to write as if nothing had happened, convinced that the older musical values could be retained without any significant loss, Rachmaninov was perhaps the most consistent in refusing any concessions to the increasingly dominant new currents of musical thought. He was also among the most successful in writing works that, despite their "old-fashioned" quality (or perhaps largely just because of it), had an undeniably fresh expressive appeal.

The Second and Third Piano Concertos, completed in 1901 and 1909, are Rachmaninov's best-known compositions and for many years ranked near the top of any list of the most popular concert works. Similar in general layout and effect, both illustrate the essential features of the composer's style. Textures are consistently homophonic, and the melodic lines are usually periodic in structure, the rhythmic regularity relieved by their great climactic sweep and warm expressivity. Harmonically, the richly sonorous yet only mildly chromatic music is firmly based upon traditional root progressions. The formal layout is crystal clear: highly charged thematic sections alternate with transitional and developmental segments that are often sequential in construction. Rachmaninov was one of the greatest pianists of his age, and much of the life of his music resides in the virtuoso keyboard writing. But despite the technical fireworks, an aura of sadness and melancholy pervades the concertos, perhaps reflecting the composer's regret for the loss of an older and more stable way of life.

Like Stravinsky, Rachmaninov chose exile after the 1917 revolution in Russia. Virtually all his major compositions, including the first three concertos, the three symphonies, the choral symphony *The Bells,* the symphonic poem *The Isle of the Dead,* and numerous piano pieces, were written in Russia. After settling in the United States in 1918, he composed relatively little, while continuing to enjoy an active performing career (he was also a notable conductor). Only one piece written during the American years won public favor, the *Rhapsody on a Theme of Paganini,* Op. 43, for piano and orchestra, a brilliant set of free variations that is among the composer's finest achievements.

Certainly one reason for Rachmaninov's relative compositional inactivity during the final quarter century of his life was the sense of cultural isolation induced by his exile. But the complete lack of correspondence between the composer's own musical inclinations and the prevailing musical tendencies of the age were no doubt equally important. Responding in 1934 to a question concerning his limited output, Rachmaninov remarked: "Perhaps I feel that the kind of music I care to write is not acceptable today."[1] With this straightforward and unaffected

1.   "The Composer as Interpreter: An interview with Norman Cameron," *The Monthly Musical Record,* 44 (November 1934): 201.

comment, Rachmaninov drew attention to a problem that has plagued a number of major talents of the twentieth century: a discrepancy between their own compositional tendencies and the tenor of the age. Here it is instructive to compare Rachmaninov with Charles Ives, whom we will discuss in the next chapter. Both composers felt cut off from their contemporaries, but for opposite reasons: Ives because his music was so innovative, Rachmaninov because his was traditional.

The years preceding World War I also saw the emergence of a small group of Russian composers writing highly innovative music, historically interesting although without any influence on subsequent developments. The compositions of Nikolay Roslavets (1881–1944), Efim Golishev (1897–1970), Arthur Lourié (1892–1966), and Nikolay Obukhov (1892–1954) represent, on the one hand, an outgrowth of the ideas of Skryabin and, on the other, a parallel to the atonal music of the Second Viennese School, even a partial anticipation of the twelve-tone system formulated by Schoenberg after the war. Independently of one another, yet drawing upon the already noted Russian tradition of using "artificial" scales (such as whole-tone) as compositional resources, these four composers began working with harmonic complexes containing a number of different pitches used without repetition. Roslavets, the most prominent of the group, called such complexes "synthechords," but they are not so much chords as repositories of pitches, all of which are to be "used up" before a new complex is introduced.

In his *Quasi Prélude* (1915), for example, Roslavets employs a "pitch set" (to use the modern terminology for the "synthechord") of seven notes as the basis for all the pitch material used in the work. Each time the seven notes are used up (the sequence of their appearance is not determined but can be varied at will), a new set is begun. Since the set can be transposed to any degree of the chromatic scale, new pitches can be generated—always dependent, however, upon the disposition of the original set. In many respects this procedure corresponds to Skryabin's use of pitch complexes, although here the complexes are considerably more chromatic, and the transposition levels are more varied and handled much more freely. Roslavets apparently prefers to avoid repeating transpositions if possible; the first four measures of the *Quasi Prélude*, for example, contain ten different transpositions of the set. In another Roslavets composition using a similar system, *Synthèses* (1914), complete twelve-tone sets appear, along with others containing fewer pitches.

Lourié, Golishev, and Obukhov left Russia before or after the revolution, living out the rest of their lives in relative obscurity. Roslavets remained in his native country, composing actively into the 1920s along the lines of his earlier work. The highly advanced technical aspects of his music, however, eventually aroused the displeasure of those in political power, and during the Stalin period he was heavily censured and forced to stop composing.

ITALY: THE FUTURISTS

Although Verdi died in 1901, his ghost continued to dominate Italian music in the early years of the new century. The new type of opera known as *verismo,* which developed near the end of the nineteenth century as an operatic equivalent to the literary realism of Verga, Zola, and Sardou, and which leaned heavily on Verdi's later style (especially *Otello*), continued to flourish. Opera's dominant position in Italy, which helped maintain a national musical identity independent of the pervasive German instrumental style, also tended to relegate all other musical forms to relatively minor roles. The leading composers at the turn of the century—Pietro Mascagni (1863–1945), Ruggiero Leoncavallo (1857–1919), Umberto Giordano (1867–1948), and Giacomo Puccini (1858–1924)—were all musicians of the theater who remained faithful to the traditions they inherited from the past and took little part in the development of new musical procedures prevalent elsewhere in Europe.

Among this group, Puccini was the only—and only partial—exception. A series of extraordinarily popular operas—*Manon Lescaut, La Bohème,* and *Tosca*—that appeared between 1893 and 1900 established him as the major Italian composer of the period. His melodic gifts and his sense of theatrical effect were unrivaled. In later operas he began using modal scales, unresolved dissonances, and various "exoticisms" with increasing prominence, especially in two operas with Oriental settings: *Madama Butterfly* (1904) and *Turandot* (left incomplete at his death). But these appear in a relatively mild form, tempered by the underlying presence of traditional tonal functions.

Significantly, the Italian artistic development of these years that best reflected the general European revolutionary climate was not musical in origin. This was the movement known as Futurism, founded in 1909 by the artist and writer Filippo Tommaso Marinetti. In a series of polemical manifestos, Marinetti asserted the necessity of throwing out all previous conceptions of art (he considered museums to be "cemeteries") in order to develop a new kind, suitable for an age based upon technology: "We say that the world's magnificence has been enriched by a new beauty; the beauty of speed. A racing car whose hood is adorned with great pipes, like serpents of explosive breath . . . is more beautiful than the *Victory of Samothrace* [a famous Greek statue]."

Although his movement mainly attracted painters, sculptors, and writers (some of whom achieved positions of considerable prominence in the world of art), Marinetti was also interested in promoting a Futurist music. He encouraged the composer Francesco Balilla Pratella (1880–1955) to work in this direction; and in 1910 Pratella issued a "Manifesto of Futurist Musicians" that advocated the use of microtonal scales and polyrhythmic combinations, as well as the infusion into music of the

In *Unique Forms of Continuity in Space* (1913), the futurist artist Umberto Boccioni used the structural devices of Cubism to express the movement's vision of motion and speed. (Bronze [cast 1931], 43⅞ × 34⅞ × 15¾". Collection, The Museum of Modern Art, New York. Acquired through the Lillie P. Bliss Bequest)

spirit of "the crowd, of great factories, of trains, of transatlantic lines, of battleships, of motor-cars and aeroplanes."[2]

However, the ultimate musical implications of the Futurist movement were developed not by Pratella or any other professionally trained composer but by the Italian painter Luigi Russolo (1885–1947). Stimulated by Pratella's suggestions, Russolo issued his own manifesto, "The Art of Noises," in 1913. Whereas Pratella had been primarily concerned with the extension of traditional tonal, rhythmic, and instrumental resources, Russolo demanded a radical break with all music of the past and a corresponding acceptance of any and all new available sonic possibilities. His manifesto makes the case in the strongest terms:

> The art of music at first sought and achieved purity and sweetness of sound; later, it blended diverse sounds, but always with intent to caress the ear with suave harmonies. Today, growing more complicated, it seeks those combinations of sounds that fall most dissonantly, strangely, and harshly upon the ear. We thus approach nearer and nearer to the music of noise.

2.   Marinetti, *Selected Writings,* ed. R. W. Flint, trans. R. W. Flint and Arthur A. Coppotelli (New York, 1972), p. 41.

The laboratory with noise instruments *(intonarumori)* in Milan, 1913, with Futurist composer Luigi Russolo (left) and his assistant Ugo Piatti. (Courtesy Pendragon Press)

. . . We Futurists have also loved the music of the great composers. Beethoven and Wagner for many years wrung our hearts. But now we are satiated with them and derive much greater pleasure from ideally combining the noises of street-cars, internal combustion engines, automobiles, and busy crowds than from hearing, for example, the "Eroica" or the "Pastorale." . . . Futurist musicians must substitute for the limited variety of timbres of the orchestral instruments of the day the infinite variety of the timbres of noises, reproduced by suitable mechanisms.[3]

In response to his own summons, Russolo invented a series of new instruments called *intonarumori* ("noise intoners"), divisible into six timbral types: "booms, whistles, whispers, screams, percussive sounds and vocal sounds (human and animal)." The noises were produced by setting into vibration a single stretched diaphragm, the speed of vibration being continuously variable so as to produce an uninterrupted pitch continuum. Several of Russolo's compositions for ensembles of *intonarumori,* bearing such titles as *The Wakening of a Great City* and *A Meeting of Motorcars and Aeroplanes,* were performed in Italy and London in 1914,

3.   Quoted in Nicholas Slonimsky, *Music Since 1900,* 4th ed. (New York, 1971), pp. 1299, 1301.

creating a considerable critical stir. After the interruption of the war years, he resumed activity during the 1920s (several of his "noise concerts" were given in Paris in the postwar years), but by this time the entire Futurist movement had lost most of its former energy.

Curiously, neither Russolo's musical scores, written in a special "graphic" notion devised by the composer, nor his *intonarumori* have survived. Judging from newspaper accounts and from Russolo's lack of musical training, it is perhaps safe to assume that the compositions were in themselves of limited interest. Yet Futurism stands in the history of twentieth-century music as the first clear manifestation of a major and enduring concern: the relationship between new music and modern technology. Although the Futurists apparently had no direct influence on subsequent compositional developments, their wish "to conquer the infinite variety of noise-sound" has remained a recurring interest throughout the century.

CZECHOSLOVAKIA: JANÁČEK

The leading figure in extending into the twentieth century the tradition of Czech national music initiated by Smetana and Dvořák was Leoš Janáček (1854–1928). Despite his early birth date, Janáček should be considered principally as a twentieth-century composer, for he developed his mature style at a relatively late stage in his life. Indeed, all his major works—most of them operas—were completed after 1900, and only after 1915, when his opera *Jenůfa* (1903) had a success in Prague, was he widely recognized as a major figure.

The early compositions, including the operas *Šárka* (1888) and *The Beginning of a Romance* (1891), are dominated by the influence of Smetana and Dvořák and give little indication of Janáček's very personal later style. Already in the late 1880s, however, he had begun studying the folk music of his native Moravia, an undertaking that not only produced publications of this music and studies of its stylistic characteristics, but also influenced his own work. Like Kodály and Bartók after him, Janáček was struck by the melodic and rhythmic freshness of folk music and its value as a model free of the "foreign" conventions of nineteenth-century European music.

In his opera *Jenůfa*, which he worked on from 1894 to 1903, Janáček began to develop a personal harmonic and melodic language derived from these Moravian sources, thus laying the technical foundation for his mature style. Not interested in exploiting the "exotic" quality of folk music (as had, to a degree, Smetana and Dvořák), Janáček wanted, rather, to acquire through its example a more flexible approach to tonality and to rhythmic and melodic development. Toward this end he for-

Some examples of speech melodies that Janáček jotted down during a lecture on Dante, June 6, 1921.

mulated a theory of "speech–melody" aimed at producing a more "realistic" type of vocal line, based on the natural rhythms and inflections of spoken language. (In this regard Janáček's music bears certain resemblances to Musorgsky's.) By emulating the rhythmic freedom and supple contours of the "melodic curves of speech," Janáček believed he could mirror more faithfully in music the shifting complexities of dramatic and psychological action and thus "reveal immediately a human being in one definite phase of his existence."[4] Indeed, Janáček went so far as to maintain that the melodic and rhythmic aspects of music were to be explained solely "on the basis of the melodic curves of speech."

Jenůfa was the first work in which the fruits of the composer's studies of folk music became evident. The tradition of the "number" opera is completely renounced, and the music is marked by a freely unfolding linear development that closely follows the inflections and the starkly realistic character of the prose libretto. The melodic lines consist primarily of brief repeated figures, handled with sufficient rhythmic flexibility to avoid an overly fragmented effect. Although solidly tonal and triadically based, the harmonic structure is built largely upon modal combinations, thus avoiding the strong gravitational pull of functional tonality.

In a sense Janáček's real career began with the completion of *Jenůfa*—that is, in 1903, in the composer's fiftieth year. In the works that followed, including the operas *Fate* (1905) and *The Excursions of Mr. Brouček* (1917), he intensified the stylistic elements found in *Jenůfa,* fashioning

4.   Quoted in Ian Horsburgh, *Leoš Janáček: The Field That Prospered* (London, 1981), p. 51.

a musico-dramatic style of unusual power and originality. This development culminated in a series of four operas written during the final years of his life (the last two while he was in his seventies): *Kát'a Kabanová* (1921), *The Cunning Little Vixen* (1923), *The Makropulos Affair* (1925), and *From the House of the Dead* (1928) rank among the major twentieth-century conceptions for the operatic stage. They are works of striking originality and expressive impact, in which the main sources of Janáček's mature art—the folk elements and speech-derived melodic lines—are completely integrated into the musical whole. Here the orchestra increasingly carries the principal burden of the musical argument, allowing the vocal lines to develop with ever greater freedom the irregular and shifting patterns of an essentially parlando style.

Janáček also wrote a sizable body of instrumental works, and those from his later years, such as the two String Quartets (1923, 1928), *Mládí* (Youth) for wind sextet (1924), and the Concertino for piano, strings, and winds (1925), can be counted among his major achievements. Of equal importance is the *Glagolitic Mass* (1926), a brilliant setting of the Slavonic version of the mass, for soloists, chorus, organ, and orchestra. Nevertheless, Janáček's reputation today rests principally upon his operatic production.

Despite his considerable accomplishments, Janáček had surprisingly little influence upon subsequent musical developments. One reason for this, no doubt, is that opera, his main creative area, has lost in the twentieth century the central position it enjoyed in musical developments of the preceding. Another reason may be that Janáček has been overshadowed by the importance of Bartók. Although he actually anticipated Bartók's evolution in certain striking respects (notably in his use of folk music as a compositional resource), Janáček was considerably less influenced by the "progressive" elements in twentieth-century music than was his Hungarian colleague. In any event it was Bartók who came to be viewed as the dominant compositional voice of Eastern Europe during the first half of the century.

HUNGARY: KODÁLY

As we have seen, Zoltán Kodály (1882–1967) developed an interest in Hungarian folk music well before his compatriot Bartók, and was instrumental in introducing his friend to this still largely unknown music. Like Bartók, Kodály maintained a lifelong interest in this field, publishing many collections of music and scholarly studies, and these activities had an equally important influence on his own compositional style.

Kodály's first major work, the String Quartet No. 1, Op. 2 (1909), is already rich with the flavor of Hungarian folk music. By comparison with Bartók's large-scale instrumental works, the folk material retains considerably more of its original form, and is less influenced by combination with the progressive features of contemporary musical language. Although the score is unambiguously tonal and triadic and preserves an essentially traditional formal structure, an unmistakably personal voice can be discerned.

The Quartet was followed by a series of chamber works conceived in a similar spirit, establishing Kodály as a leading figure: the Cello Sonata, Op. 4 (1910), the Duo for Violin and Cello, Op. 7 (1914), the Sonata for Solo Cello, Op. 8 (1915), and the String Quartet No. 2, Op. 10 (1918). Here Kodály refined the basic elements of his style, concentrating more and more on the creation of a strongly profiled melodic quality, which would be increasingly characteristic of his work.

Indeed, Kodály believed that song formed the basis for all music, an attitude that found its fullest creative expression in two later sacred compositions for chorus and orchestra: the *Psalmus hungaricus,* Op. 13 (1923), and the *Te Deum* (1936). In keeping with the general tendency of the interwar years, these works are structurally simpler and more easily accessible than the earlier chamber compositions. The *Psalmus hungaricus,* based on a sixteenth-century Hungarian translation of Psalm 150, makes an immediate yet powerful effect. The "popularizing" tendency noticeable here is even more evident in the opera *Háry János* (1926), in which folk elements are particularly emphasized; the orchestral suite drawn from it is perhaps Kodály's best-known composition.

In addition to his activities as a composer and folk-music specialist, Kodály played an important role in the development of music education in his native Hungary, gaining thereby—perhaps even more than through his work as a composer—the status of a national hero. His highly successful approach to the musical development of children, based primarily on group singing and universally known as the "Kodály Method," has been widely adopted in Europe and the Americas. Moreover, many of Kodály's own compositions reflect his interest in education and are intended for performance by children and nonprofessional adults.

SCANDINAVIA: SIBELIUS AND NIELSEN

At the turn of the century Finland, since 1814 a province of tsarist Russia (and before that governed by Sweden), was in the throes of asserting its identity. Around 1890, in this new atmosphere of developing national pride, the composer Jean Sibelius (1865–1957) achieved his first musical maturity and became deeply involved with the legends and folklore of his native country. His earliest major compositions—the symphony with

A portrait of the young
Sibelius (1894) by Akseli
Gallen-Kallela. © Pub-
lished through the courtesy
of Aivi Gallen-Kallela-
Sirén, Snellmaninkatu
15A4, Helsinki 17, Finland.

voices *Kullervo* (1892) and several tone poems: *En Saga* (1892), the four
Lemminkäinen Legends (1893–95), and the well-known *Finlandia* (1899)—
are all programmatic conceptions inspired by Finnish national literature.

Sibelius's development took a new turn in 1899, the year his First
Symphony appeared. Conceived in a more abstract and economical style
than the earlier programmatic pieces, it was received with great enthusiasm and became the first in a series of seven symphonies that dominated the remainder of his creative life and became the mainstay of his
reputation. Despite their essentially conservative—even antimodernist—stance, they are works of great originality, and they extended and
revitalized the nineteenth-century symphonic tradition, especially that
of Liszt and Tchaikovsky, perhaps more convincingly than any others
of the time. Sibelius was quickly acclaimed, particularly by conservative critics and listeners, and his popularity during the 1930s and 1940s,
especially in England and the United States, was unrivaled by any other
contemporary composer.

Sibelius's view of the symphony is neatly summed up in his account
of a discussion he once had with Mahler: "When our conversation touched
upon the essence of the symphony, I said that I admired its severity of

style and the profound logic that created an inner connection between all the motifs. . . . Mahler's opinion was just the reverse. 'No, a symphony must be a world. It must embrace everything.' "[5] The characteristics of economy and thematic consistency, stressed by Sibelius in contrast to Mahler's all-inclusiveness, are evident throughout his symphonic work. The seven symphonies differ widely in general layout, each following the particular course suggested by its own opening gestures (often with little concern for traditional formal types); but all are based upon the idea of constant thematic evolution, through which the original materials are gradually transformed in a process of seemingly unbroken development. Subsequent materials are derived through progressive transformations of the original motivic cells, so that secondary themes are rarely of a strongly contrasting nature, but appear as subtle mutations of what has gone before.

Although Sibelius used no actual folk material in his symphonies, their distinctly "national" flavor has always impressed listeners. This quality stems partly from the dark coloring; the unusually somber and muted orchestral writing suggests associations with the severity of the Finnish landscape and climate. In addition, the melodic material shares certain general structural similarities with much folk music: a preponderance of stepwise motion, adherence to diatonic and usually modal scales, highly restricted melodic ranges, and a tendency to circle continuously around a single note that serves as a tonal focus. These features are supported by the harmony, which is essentially triadic and modal in conception and often tonally ambiguous. Especially characteristic is the frequent emphasis on the interval of a tritone, which, counterbalancing the clear melodic focal points and long-held accompanimental pedals, tends to deprive the music of a strong gravitational pull.

The tritone is especially prominent in the Fourth Symphony (1911), whose entire structure can be viewed as a delicate balancing of the tensions and ambiguities set up by that interval. Interestingly, Sibelius conceived of this symphony, arguably his finest, as a conscious response to and reaction against what he felt to be the vices of musical modernism. ("Nothing, absolutely nothing of the circus about it," he once remarked.) Certainly the avoidance of strong contrasts, the emphasis on internal consistency, and the extension of traditional concepts of tonal and motivic development greatly distance it from Europe's more disruptive and revolutionary musical tendencies; the works of Stravinsky and Schoenberg written around 1910 make the Fourth Symphony seem very tame indeed. Yet it is, on its own terms, a remarkably complex and adventurous work, offering a highly original solution to the

5.   Karl Ekman, *Jean Sibelius: His Life and Personality*, trans. Edward Birse (New York, 1938), p. 191.

problem of extended symphonic structure within a twentieth-century musical context.

In addition to symphonic music, Sibelius wrote a Violin Concerto (1903), incidental music for several plays, many solo songs, choral and piano pieces, and a few chamber works (most notably the String Quartet of 1909, subtitled "Voces intimae"). The last two major compositions to appear from his hand were the Seventh Symphony, the final of the series, completed in 1924, and the tone poem *Tapiola,* which followed two years later and ranks among the composer's most individual creations. Although Sibelius's long life extended some thirty years after *Tapiola,* no substantial compositions followed. In 1929 he wrote a colleague that he had finished an eighth symphony, but it has never come to light, and if completed was presumably destroyed. Perhaps, like Rachmaninov, Sibelius's essential conservatism ultimately caused him to feel irrevocably out of step with his time. Yet his achievement was a large one; despite his separation from the main currents of musical developments, he stands as an imposing, if isolated, figure in early twentieth-century music.

Sibelius's most important Scandinavian contemporary was the Danish composer Carl Nielsen (1865–1931). Born in the same year, the two men share a number of common traits. Like Sibelius, Nielsen gained his reputation primarily through a series of extended symphonic works (though for Nielsen fame came much more slowly; only in recent years have his compositions been programmed with any frequency outside his native country). Nielsen also built his work firmly upon the foundation provided by the nineteenth-century symphonic tradition, renouncing the innovations introduced by other composers. Finally, Nielsen too succeeded in developing a compositional style of considerable personal character despite the strongly conservative element in his work.

Nielsen's six symphonies appeared at irregular intervals between 1892 and 1925. Although the composer refined his style considerably over this period, the symphonies are all essentially classical in conception and, unlike those of Sibelius, remain true to established formal categories. Triadic harmony supports a tonal structure firmly tied to traditional models, although there is increasing development of a type of "extended tonality" (already embryonic in the finale of the First Symphony), whereby the principal key emerges only gradually as an outcome of oppositions between competing tonal regions.

Although this approach to tonality can be seen as a direct outgrowth of tendencies in late Romantic symphonic music (in Mahler and Strauss, for example), the general character of Nielsen's music is in most respects strongly anti-Romantic. Excessive chromaticism is avoided, and the music's lightness and textural transparency produce an almost "Classical" character that sets it off not only from the earlier German and Russian symphonists but also from Sibelius. The austerity and emotional complexity of the latter's music is largely missing in Nielsen, and instead one finds a pronounced note of humor (largely lacking in Sibelius), as in the good-natured satire of modernist musical tendencies found in the second movement (entitled "Humoreske") of the Sixth Symphony.

Although the symphonies form the cornerstone of his output, Nielsen wrote many other works, including the operas *Saul and David* (1901) and *Maskarade* (1906), concertos for violin (1911), flute (1926), and clarinet (1928), plus a number of chamber works. Among the latter, the frequently performed Woodwind Quintet of 1922 is especially notable. Its expressive restraint, textural transparency, and classically oriented forms provide an excellent introduction to the most characteristic features of the composer's style.

FRANCE: RAVEL

Debussy's dominance of French musical composition during the early years of the century can hardly be exaggerated. He was deplored by the conservatives for his innovations and hailed by the progressives for opening up new areas of musical exploration—but in either case, the force of his musical personality colored the entire period.

Among the more prominent younger composers active in France at the time were Paul Dukas (1865–1935), Florent Schmitt (1870–1958), and Charles Koechlin (1867–1950), as well as that iconoclastic outsider Erik Satie. But with the exception of Satie (whose fame was to come somewhat later and within a more proscribed context), only one member of this generation attained an international reputation to rival Debussy's in any way: Maurice Ravel (1875–1937).

Ravel once stated that his sole aim as a composer was to achieve "technical perfection," and the extraordinary care and meticulousness of his workmanship reflect that attitude. So does the fact that listeners to his music are apt to be less conscious of a strongly individualized personal style than of an impressive ability to draw upon different sources and to mold diverse materials into a consistent whole, locked in forms of gemlike precision. (Stravinsky, noting this characteristic of Ravel's music, once likened him to a "Swiss watchmaker.")

Many of Ravel's works contain distinct echoes of musical elements borrowed from foreign sources: e.g., the music of exotic lands in the orchestral song cycle *Shéhérazade* (1903) and the *Rapsodie espagnole* (1908); popular dance music in the *Valses nobles et sentimentales* for piano (1911) and the ballet *La Valse* (1920); eighteenth-century dance forms in the

Maurice Ravel at work

Sonatina (1905) and *Le Tombeau de Couperin* (1917), both for piano; and American jazz in the Violin Sonata (1927) and the Piano Concerto in G major (1931). Certain scores, such as the ballet *Daphnis et Chloé* (1912), are notable for their extremely subtle gradations of timbre and shading, recalling Debussy. Others reveal a considerable dramatic flair: the brilliant orchestration of Musorgsky's piano suite *Pictures at an Exhibition* (1922) and the original ballet *Boléro* (1928). In the latter an incessantly repeated melody is clothed in ever more expansive orchestral garb, making a remarkably concentrated orchestral tour de force. Originally conceived as a kind of "experiment" in orchestral effect, it quickly became, much to Ravel's dismay, his best-known (or most notorious) composition.

Given Ravel's tendency to draw upon elements from "external" sources, it is not surprising that one finds a marked degree of detachment and objectivity in his music. Especially apparent in compositions that adhere closely to traditional formal types, such as the String Quartet (1903) and the Sonatina, these qualities are noticeable even in works of an openly "impressionist" flavor. *Jeux d'eau* (1901) and the suite *Miroirs* (1905), both for piano, and the orchestral *Rapsodie espagnole,* all strongly "atmospheric" works with richly woven textures, nevertheless maintain a clarity and expressive understatement that distinguish them from most of the music composed during the first decade of the century.

Ravel's stylistic relationship to Debussy is especially interesting. Marked similarities in their music are apparent, and Ravel himself willingly expressed his debt to his older countryman. Ravel's early interest in elaborate yet finely detailed textures clearly owes much to Debussy (although his application of Debussian textural ideas to the keyboard, notably in *Jeux d'eau,* at a time when Debussy's major piano works had not yet appeared, may in turn have influenced the older composer), and Ravel's harmonic vocabulary, with its richly structured triadic extensions and freely employed nonharmonic tones, was no doubt also in part derived from his predecessor. Further reminiscent of Debussy is a preference for brief melodic ideas, developed mainly by repetition and subtle modification.

Yet Ravel's music projects little of the ambiguity or mystery so characteristic of Debussy. To Debussy's seemingly unbroken transitional flow, it opposes lucid formal articulations, and Ravel's harmonic innovations are more firmly tied to traditional root movements, providing a stronger tonal pull. Indeed, in general Ravel's music seems more solid, more firmly anchored, than Debussy's. Its rhythmic patterns are more regular, and its cool lyricism is bound within a much more clearly delineated framework of phrase divisions.

These attributes set Ravel somewhat apart from the main currents of early twentieth-century musical development, which were still significantly colored (even in the case of Debussy) by the esthetics of late Romanticism. On the other hand, his music offers clear anticipations of the neo-classical development that was to dominate the postwar years. We have noted the presence of neo-classical tendencies even in Debussy's later works, which in some respects seem to have been conceived almost in direct opposition to his previous approach. In Ravel's case the corresponding transformations during the war years simply reflect a more marked emphasis on qualities always prominent in his work: simplicity, clarity, and technical refinement.

As early as the *Three Poems of Mallarmé* (1913) and the Piano Trio (1914), one finds a reduction of surface detail and textural complexity. The songs reflect Ravel's belated contact with the music of his non-French contemporaries, most notably Stravinsky (and, less directly, Schoenberg). The process of simplification continues in the piano suite *Le Tombeau de Couperin,* which despite its virtuosic aspects shows a renewed concern for formal directness, here influenced explicitly by eighteenth-century models. The culmination of this development toward economy and restraint comes in the postwar years, most strikingly in the almost grim austerity of the Sonata for Violin and Cello (1922),

Cover art for the score of Ravel's one-act opera, *L'Enfant et les sortilèges,* published in 1925. (© 1925 Durand S. A. Editions Musicales. Editions A.R.I.M.A. & Durand S.A. Editions Musicales. Joint Publication. Used By Permission of the Publisher. Sole Representative U.S.A., Theodore Presser Company)

which Ravel thought marked a turning point in his career, and of which he commented: "The music is stripped down to the bone."

Right through his final major works, the piano concertos of 1930 and 1931 (the first for left hand alone), Ravel continued to polish this more economical style. Occasionally he would experiment with modern harmonic techniques such as "bitonality" (notably in the one-act opera *L'Enfant et les sortilèges,* completed in 1925, which contains a number of passages written with two different key signatures), but such novelties remain basically surface elaborations applied to a still solidly tonal and triadic foundation.

Not a major innovator, Ravel was rather a master at "updating" traditional compositional techniques through the judicious use of modern procedures. Nor was his strong point large-scale symphonic writing; works such as *Daphnis et Chloé* (written for Diaghilev's Ballets Russes) and the piano concertos contain movements of some length, but Ravel was more at home in relatively restricted formal contexts. His talent was essentially lyrical in nature, and his finest achievements, though modest in scale, have a polished beauty and technical elegance that set them quite apart.

CHAPTER VI

Beyond the Continent

MUSIC IN ENGLAND

By the year 1900 England had endured a period of compositional decline—a sort of musical Dark Ages—lasting some two centuries. Although during the Tudor and Elizabethan periods English music had been remarkably distinguished, not a single composer of international reputation emerged between the death of Henry Purcell in 1695 and the beginning of the twentieth century. Among the factors contributing to this stunted growth, the most portentous was George Frideric Handel's domination of English musical life during the first half of the eighteenth century. Unable to overcome the force of this great foreign influence, native composers lost a healthy contact with their own tradition and looked instead to the Continent for musical inspiration and education. This fostered a view of composition that was essentially tame and conservative. In the nineteenth century Handel's influence was transferred to yet another foreign composer, Felix Mendelssohn—especially the more conservative Mendelssohn of the oratorios. The growth of musical life was further impeded by the character and quality of English music schools, without exception rigidly academic in viewpoint and outmoded in approach.

An end to this period of stagnation—all the more remarkable when one considers England's unusual productivity in other arts during these same years—was signaled by the advent of a new generation of composers, headed by Hubert Parry (1848–1918) and Charles Villiers Stanford (1852–1924), who shared a more cosmopolitan outlook and an interest in current musical developments in Europe. They were followed by two somewhat younger composers, Edward Elgar (1857–1934) and Frederick Delius (1862–1934), both fully aware of the most up-to-date continental tendencies (Elgar was closer to those of Germany, Delius to those of France) and producing work at a level of technical assurance and expressive individuality that set a new standard for English music. Though the originality and complexity of Elgar's music was initially better understood and appreciated on the Continent than in his native land, he was clearly a composer of major importance. The appearance in 1899 of his *"Enigma" Variations,* an extended orchestral work of unquestioned technical and expressive accomplishment, seemed to announce to the world that England was ripe for a musical rebirth—a prophecy fulfilled by the so-called "English Renaissance," which forms one of the notable chapters in the history of twentieth-century music.

Following the *"Enigma" Variations,* which established him as the leading English composer of his day, Elgar produced a series of works exploring the principal genres of the European tradition: the oratorios *The Dream of Gerontius* (1900), *The Apostles* (1903), and *The Kingdom* (1906); the concert overture *Cockaigne* (1901); the tone poem *Falstaff* (1913); concertos for violin (1910) and cello (1919); and three late chamber works, the Violin Sonata (1918), String Quartet (1918), and Piano Quartet (1919). Of special importance are Elgar's two symphonies. The First Symphony did not appear until 1908 (his fifty-first year)—a parallel with Brahms, whose music influenced Elgar considerably—and, again as with Brahms, a second soon followed (1911), as if to prove that the composer had truly passed over the symphonic hurdle. With their great sweep and richness of detail, Elgar's symphonies form worthy companions to the monumental creations of such continental figures as Brahms, Bruckner, and Franck, and they put the English symphony on a firm footing, establishing an important base for such later English composers as Vaughan Williams and Walton.

Though Elgar's music is heavily indebted to the more conservative currents of late German Romanticism, its dignified expansiveness and nobility (especially evident in the well-known *Pomp and Circumstance* marches) sound peculiarly English, strongly evoking the optimistic character of English life during the Edwardian years immediately preceding World War I. Following the war, however, Elgar felt alienated from the new tendencies dominating English music and largely withdrew from composition, producing nothing more of real significance. Though he lived through the first third of the new century, Elgar's musical convictions were largely tied to the old one. He had little stylistic influence on his younger countrymen, yet as the first internationally recognized English composer in some two hundred years, his importance for his successors should not be underestimated.

Frederick Delius occupies a more shadowy place in English music history. Though born and raised in England, Delius lived exclusively abroad from his twenty-second year, first briefly in the United States, then in Germany (where he attended the Leipzig Conservatory), and finally in France, his permanent home from 1888. There is little of a nationalistic character in his work, except perhaps a penchant for the musical depiction of pastoral scenes. Delius's vision of the English countryside is one not of down-to-earth folk songs, however, but of languorous, gently undulating chromatic harmonies and delicately shifting instrumental colors. His countrymen found him a bit precious, overly refined for their taste, and acceptance at home came more slowly than to Elgar. Even today, Delius remains something of a fringe figure, best known for his orchestral tone poems, especially *Brigg Fair* (1907), *In a Summer Garden* (1908), and *On Hearing the First Cuckoo in Spring* (1912), and for his choral-orchestral works *Sea Drift* (1904) and *A Mass of Life* (1908). Of his operas, *A Village Romeo and Juliet* (1901) has been most often revived.

VAUGHAN WILLIAMS

While Elgar and Delius forged again a strong link between English music and contemporary European developments, Ralph Vaughan Williams (1872–1958) was the first to reestablish fruitful contact with England's indigenous musical resources. Vaughan Williams studied with both Parry and Stanford at the Royal College of Music in London (where he himself taught after 1919), and also had extensive continental training, under Max Bruch in Berlin and then, relatively late in his development (from 1908 to 1910, when he was in his late thirties), with Ravel in Paris. Like Bartók and Janáček, who also developed at some distance from the main centers of the European musical tradition, he sought a fresh, vigorous, and independent foundation for his art in the folk music of his country, and, also like them, undertook a serious study of this music that continued throughout much of his life. This interest in native folk music profoundly influenced Vaughan Williams's compositional outlook, as did his study of traditional English church music (his 1906 edition of the *English Hymnal* represented the better part of two years of work). The strong simplicity and straightforward character of both of these types of music are apparent in most of his work.

The other important native influence on Vaughan Williams was the great English compositional tradition from Dunstable to Purcell (whose *Welcome Songs* he also edited). This relationship is not so much a matter of specific compositional details as of a general preference for modal-triadic harmony, and for freely unfolding rhythmic patterns quite unlike the metrically more emphatic ones of nineteenth-century Germanic

Ralph Vaughan Williams (right) and Gustav Holst on a walking tour of the Malvern Halls, September 1921. (Courtesy of The Gustav Holst Birthplace Museum, Cheltenham)

music. What Vaughan Williams wrote about the discovery of folk music—that it did not so much give English composers something new as uncover "something which had been hidden by foreign matter"— applies equally to this other side of his musical makeup. "My advice to young composers," he wrote, "is—learn your own language first, find out your own traditions, discover what you want to do."[1]

Vaughan Williams was unusually slow in reaching musical maturity; compositions displaying a fully formed personal voice did not appear until he was well into his thirties. His period of apprenticeship culminated in *A Sea Symphony,* a large-scale conception for soloists, chorus, and orchestra on a text by Walt Whitman that occupied the composer for some six years and was completed in 1909. In this same year appeared *On Wenlock Edge,* a setting of six poems by A. E. Housman for tenor, piano, and string quartet that established Vaughan Williams as a significant new figure, capable of producing serious English music of an unmistakably national character. Although the somewhat "atmospheric" quality of the string writing betrays the composer's association

1. "Nationalism and Internationalism," *Beethoven's Choral Symphony and Other Writings* (London, 1953), p. 106.

Example VI-1: VAUGHAN WILLIAMS, *On Wenlock Edge*, No. 2, mm. 1–11

with Ravel (with whom he was working at the time), the dominant vocal line demonstrates the simplicity and directness of melodic gesture typical of his own mature style.

The opening of the second song, "From Far, from Eve and Morning," nevertheless reveals what subtleties appear beneath the often placid surface of Vaughan Williams's music (Example VI-3). The contour—

but not the rhythm—of the opening phrase of the folklike vocal line (mm. 3–4) derives from the top voice of the richly triadic piano introduction (mm. 1–2), a relation intensified when voice and piano sound together in the second phrase (mm. 5–6, the voice's previous low G♯ now altered to G♮ to accommodate the accompaniment). Mm. 3–6 form an "antecedent" balanced by mm. 7–11, a considerably varied "consequent": the vocal line of mm. 3–4 is freely inverted and lengthened (by a 2/4 measure) in mm. 7–9, while the piano's top-voice figure is simplified and extended, spanning the entire phrase with a single diatonic descent to C♯ (instead of C♮ as before) in m. 10. This C♯, the first conclusive move away from E major, supplies the cadential goal for the whole segment and pulls the vocal line upward from its repeated, pedal-like B♮s, thereby also resolving the sensitive D♮ seventh—the highest voice note yet heard—from m. 8. The piano's nonfunctional parallel triads, linked by melodic association rather than dominant-directed progressions, are especially prevalent in Vaughan Williams, as are the cross-relations that occur between them (G♮ against G♯ in mm. 1, 2–3, 5, 6–7; and E♯ against E♮—here mediated by an intervening B major chord—in mm. 8–11).

The next year brought the *Fantasia on a Theme by Thomas Tallis* for strings, reflecting Vaughan Williams's growing interest in earlier English art music. Not only is the theme taken from the sixteenth-century English composer whose name it bears; the form of the one-movement piece bears close resemblances to the typical sectional structure of the Elizabethan fantasy (or "fancy"). On the other hand, the main textural idea, whereby the full string orchestra is pitted antiphonally against two smaller ensembles of four and nine players drawn from it, is derived from Baroque models. The overall formal conception, a freely evolving variational treatment of the basic melodic material, would consistently characterize Vaughan Williams's music from this point on.

The *Tallis Fantasia* was Vaughan Williams's first fully achieved instrumental composition, and, along with the *Sea Symphony,* it presaged his development as a major symphonic composer. His nine symphonies, which appeared at more or less regular intervals between 1909 and 1957, were instrumental in establishing a school of twentieth-century English symphonists bearing comparison with those of Scandinavia (Sibelius and Nielsen) and Russia (Prokofiev and Shostakovich). Despite his nationalistic concerns, Vaughan Williams by no means completely cut himself off from the European symphonic tradition, and his symphonies reveal strong connections with their Romantic forerunners: the general formal layout; a reliance on cyclic techniques of thematic recurrence between movements; in four symphonies, the use of descriptive or programmatic titles; in three, the inclusion of voice(s).

Yet something new also sets these works apart from the main line of this tradition. Most immediately noticeable is the music's essentially melodic and nondevelopmental character, consistent with the folk influence. But most original is a new way of unfolding the musical materials so as to produce large-scale formal structures, not dependent upon marked levels of contrast and thus basically nondramatic in character. Yet this melodic, nondevelopmental quality, which in a lesser composer might lead only to a series of disconnected tunes, is achieved by Vaughan Williams through variational procedures that allow each movement to evolve logically from its origins. This highly personal conception of symphonic continuity was perhaps his most important contribution to the new English school of symphonic writing.

Over the span of almost fifty years the musical language and technique of Vaughan Williams's symphonies remained remarkably stable, committed to the basic approach so slowly and carefully developed during his first four decades. Yet the expressive character varies considerably, gradually evolving from the essentially pastoral and openly national quality of the first three symphonies (all of which contain programmatic features), culminating with the *Pastoral Symphony* of 1921, to the more somber and intense atmosphere of the later works. Compared with the advanced musical developments of the age, these symphonies are decidedly conservative in outlook. The symphonic genre, so clearly a holdover from the eighteenth and nineteenth centuries, has been especially resistant to radical developments and thus largely avoided by the more revolutionary figures of the twentieth century. Yet Vaughan Williams ranks among the most prominent composers who managed to preserve and extend the symphonic heritage within the modern era.

Consistent with the primarily melodic character of his symphonies, the remainder of Vaughan Williams's output is dominated by vocal music. Along with a sizable body of songs and choral music, much of it with orchestral accompaniment, he composed three operas: *Hugh the Drover* (1914), *Sir John in Love* (1928), and *Riders to the Sea* (1932), as well as the "masque" *Job* (1930), the "morality" opera *The Pilgrim's Progress* (1949), and incidental music for stage plays, films, and radio. The composer's long life, and his continued productivity into his final years, resulted in an impressively large output.

HOLST

Next to Vaughan Williams, the most important and original English composer to attain maturity before World War I was Gustav Holst (1874–1934). Separated by only two years in age, the two men studied together at the Royal College of Music and became close friends and musical confidants, each submitting to the other his current work for comment and criticism. Though Holst, like Vaughan Williams, became deeply interested in English folk music and Elizabethan music, these had much less influence on his work. Yet the two friends were also profoundly different in other respects. Coming from a musical family with European antecedents, Holst's interests and attitudes were broader and more cosmopolitan than those of his friend. An early interest in Hindu literature and thought had a substantial impact upon his music. (He even learned to read Sanskrit so that he could become acquainted with the literary sources at first hand.) And he also studied astrology, an interest that was to lead to one of his most important compositions, *The Planets*.

Like Vaughan Williams, Holst developed relatively slowly. His youthful works were written under the spell of Wagner, and only when his growing acquaintance with English folk music tempered his early chromaticism did Holst's own musical personality begin to form itself. Exotic influences soon became apparent. The chamber opera *Sāvitri* (1908), which displays a new economy and directness in musical style, already reflects his interest in Hinduism, and the orchestral suite *Beni Mora* (1910) contains echoes of Oriental music that Holst heard while vacationing in Algeria.

The work that established Holst as one of the leading English composers of his generation was *The Planets* (1916), an orchestral suite in seven movements, each a musical portrait of the astrological "character" of one of the planets. Its generally triadic and modal quality is enlivened by a number of adventurous touches, especially by frequent "irregular" meters. Stravinsky's influence is apparent in this as in other aspects of the music, and in general the openness to advanced contemporary influences sets Holst's work apart from that of Vaughan Williams. Despite a certain lack of polish (Holst himself did not count it among his best works), *The Planets* was received with warm enthusiasm and brought the composer great fame, remaining to this day his best-known and most frequently performed composition.

Following an aggressive and turbulent first movement ("Mars, the Bringer of War"), the opening of the second ("Venus, the Bringer of Peace") offers a moment of relative calm (Example VI-2; see p. 136). An unaccompanied solo horn diatonically rises through a fourth (F-B♭), then repeats its figure as the bass for a woodwind statement of parallel triads and seventh chords in contrary motion. E♭ major, the tonic of the movement, is at first only obliquely suggested, and then seriously undermined when the first phrase cadences unexpectedly on a D♭ minor triad formed by the convergence of the flute and oboe planes (m. 5). The solo horn seizes this D♭ to initiate a sequential repetition, a major third lower, of the first five measures, which proceeds strictly (though with varied instrumentation) up to the cadential chord. The latter's B♭ minor, replacing the B♭♭ minor of a strict continuation, serves to pull

Example VI-2: HOLST, *The Planets,* "Venus, the Bringer of Peace," mm. 1–10

the music back toward the tonic region. The soft dynamics (with a diminuendo in each phrase), retarding rhythms of the woodwind phrases, falling pitch (both the linear contour of the top voice and the lowered sequential restatement), and repetitiveness give the passage a languid, peaceful character. Yet a definite element of tension, produced by tonal ambiguity and mildly dissonant polychordal harmony, creates an impression quite different from the underlying serenity of the Vaughan Williams example discussed above.

Among Holst's other major works are the oratorio *The Hymn of Jesus* (1917), the *Fugal Overture* (1922), the opera *At the Boar's Head* (1925), and the orchestral piece *Egdon Heath* (1927), which the composer viewed as his finest composition. The works of the 1920s show a renewed interest in counterpoint, and in general a more restrained compositional attitude (much of the music in *At the Boar's Head,* for example, is based upon seventeenth-century dance forms)—stylistic features in keeping with the neo-classical trend in European music of the time and which tended to minimize the nationalistic qualities in Holst. No doubt partly for this reason, Holst, rather than Vaughan Williams, had the greater influence on English composers of the next generation, who were themselves more international in orientation.

Holst's role in English music education was a significant one. He not only held appointments at the Royal College of Music and at University College, Reading, but was also active in teaching young schoolchildren and amateurs. A number of his choral works were written for amateur choir. Holst, who during his earlier years earned his living playing trombone in orchestras, also wrote several important compositions for concert band, including three suites (one of them written as the competition piece for a band contest)—an early precedent for the twentieth century's serious attention to this previously neglected ensemble.

The "Renaissance" in English music was only partly a matter of big figures such as Elgar, Delius, Vaughan Williams, and Holst. Equally significant was the presence, in the early years of the century, of a whole group of young composers, less prominent but all talented and completely professional musicians. Collectively they reenergized the English musical scene, transforming it from an unexciting provincial backwater into a center of remarkable activity. Prominent among them were Granville Bantock (1868–1946), John Ireland (1879–1962), Frank Bridge (1879–1941), and Arnold Bax (1883–1953). As if to compensate for the long "gap" in the history of English musical composition, they focused their output on the standard genres of the eighteenth and nineteenth centuries: Bantock wrote several tone poems and programmatic symphonies and Bax produced seven symphonies, while both Bridge and Ireland concentrated on chamber music. As teachers and models, this generation laid down a solid foundation for the future development of English music, and their promise has been fulfilled by the appearance throughout the century of unusually gifted composers.

CHARLES IVES AND AMERICAN MUSIC

Concert music in the United States at the turn of the century was largely dominated by European models and standards. The accepted practice was to send young musicians who displayed unusual talent to Europe for their musical education, and almost all of the major American composers of the period, including George W. Chadwick (1854–1931), Edward MacDowell (1860–1908), and Daniel Gregory Mason (1873–1953), were trained in German conservatories, where they absorbed the ideals, forms, and techniques of central European art music. Their music was thus for the most part devoid of elements drawn from America's own vernacular traditions. Even when such elements do appear, as in MacDowell's *Indian Suite* (1895) or Mason's *String Quartet on Negro Themes* (1919), they are treated as "exoticisms" within an essentially European idiom.

Characteristically, a European composer had shown these American "nationalists" the way. Invited to teach in the United States, the Czech Antonín Dvořák spent the years 1892–95 in the new land and was greatly impressed by the native music, incorporating some of it in his famous symphony *From the New World* (1893)—much as he, as a committed nationalist, had used materials from his native Bohemia in previous compositions. In an influential article written some two years after his arrival, Dvořák urged American composers to follow his lead in assimilating national musical sources in an idiom that still retained the spirit of European concert music.

By the turn of the century, however, at least one American composer was trying to break out of this European mold. Charles Ives (1874–1954) occupies a curious position in music history. Though he played a seminal role in the development of a serious American concert music of distinctly national flavor, Ives lived in almost total isolation from the public and from other musicians during the period in which he worked intensively on composition (from about 1895 to 1917). His music was virtually unperformed at this time and thus had no immediate influence on other composers. Yet it seems probable that this isolation was itself essential for Ives to develop a musical style largely unencumbered by the weight of the European past.

Ives nevertheless did receive a more or less traditional musical education. In childhood he was trained as both an organist and pianist, and thus became familiar with much of the standard keyboard literature, a knowledge often reflected in the music of his maturity. But the vernacular music of the small Connecticut town in which he grew up—its hymns, popular and patriotic songs, marches, and dance tunes—was equally important in the formation of his compositional personality. Much of Ives's musical training came from his father, George Ives, who was both village bandmaster and a church musician—and a man of boundless curiosity, who conducted musical experiments on such matters as quarter-tone tuning and the performance of pieces in several keys simultaneously. His influence on the younger Ives, as Charles often stressed, was of special importance, particularly in instilling in the young composer an open-minded attitude about what constitutes "proper" music.

Ives's intention to follow his own course is further evident in his pursuit of musical studies at Yale University rather than in Europe. At Yale Ives received a strong traditional training under the respected American composer Horatio Parker (himself trained in Germany).

Charles Ives at his home in West Redding, Connecticut, ca. 1935, some years after his creative life had ended.

Although often balking at what he considered to be the overly academic and conservative quality of his musical education, Ives learned much from Parker, for whom, despite differences, he had considerable respect and under whose supervision he composed his first extended works, including the First String Quartet (1896) and First Symphony (1898). He was awarded his degree in 1898.

Soon after leaving Yale, Ives came to a decision not to follow music as a profession. Instead, he entered the life insurance business, which he pursued with considerable success until his retirement in 1930. Various explanations have been offered for Ives's decision to compose only as an avocation. Musically, the most important consequence was that by becoming financially independent he was able to compose exactly as he wished, without regard for what the public or other musicians might think—or even for whether or not the music might ever be performed. Perhaps more than any other major composer in the history of Western music, Ives wrote his compositions strictly for himself, frequently not even bothering to put them into completely finished form. (The process of editing Ives's work, which in some cases actually involves "assembling" the music from scattered sketches, is still under way.) This is significant, for Ives's whole conception of music as an "open" art form, capable of encompassing all types of music and fusing them into a higher synthesis, completely transcended the comprehension of his contemporaries. It was something he had to pursue almost entirely in isolation.

A clear chronology is impossible to trace in Ives's output, as he worked on his compositions over long periods of time, often abandoning a work only to pick it up again years later. Indeed, Ives seems to have taken both pride and pleasure in thinking of his compositions as never being entirely "finished" but always subject to further addition and modification. Moreover, the borderline between separate works is often very vague, as material from an earlier piece would commonly be incorporated into a later one. Although the most important compositions were all worked on within the first decades of the century, many—and especially the more ambitious ones—had gestation periods spanning five or ten years, sometimes even longer.

Several pieces from Ives's earlier years already reveal extraordinary technical innovations. The *Song for Harvest Season* (1893), for example, contains a four-part fugue in which each part is in a different key; *Psalm 54* (c. 1894) includes passages written entirely in the whole-tone scale. By comparison, the works of the Yale years seem less experimental, though they give increasing evidence of Ives's mastery of extended form. Only in the works written after his graduation, however, do the full power and originality of Ives's musical vision become apparent.

The most characteristic feature of the mature style is its variety and range. Especially among the songs, many works retain traditional tonality. *The Children's Hour* (1901), *At the River* (1916), and *Two Little Flowers* (1921), for example, all preserve a simpler musical language that had long since been abandoned by Ives's progressive contemporaries. But it is characteristic of Ives's thinking that older techniques were not necessarily discarded after the invention of newer ones; they remained as part of a more inclusive music, existing side by side with the most radical and revolutionary new developments. He once remarked: "Why tonality as such should be thrown out for good, I can't see. Why it should be always present, I can't see. It depends, it seems to me, a good deal—as clothes depend on the thermometer—on what one is trying to do, and on the state of mind, the time of day or other accidents of life."[2]

---

2. *Essays Before a Sonata, The Majority, and Other Writings,* ed. Howard Boatwright (New York, 1962), p. 117.

This conception of tonality, viewed not as a "natural" system for ordering all music but as one of many possibilities available for different expressive purposes, was in its way as revolutionary as Schoenberg's conception of atonality.

Even in his simplest songs, however, Ives tends to place things slightly askew. The tonality, for example, sounds somehow "distanced," no longer heard entirely within the traditional context. Thus *Charlie Rutlage* (1920) clearly intends to evoke the character of a simple cowboy song of the American West, yet it also parodies that genre. Unexpected rhythmic complexities in the vocal line, along with occasional "wrong notes" in the harmony, work against the almost banal regularity of the opening piano accompaniment; and at the climax, when both Charlie and his horse fall, the music seems to lose all control, breaking out in a dissonant explosion of dense tone clusters covering the entire range of the piano. Similarly, *At the River* is for the most part a straightforward setting of a hymn tune consisting of two eight-measure phrases, both ending with tonic cadences; but after each cadence "normal" continuity is interrupted by a distorted reminiscence of an earlier segment of the song, pulling the music away from the key center and leaving it suspended in a state of uncertainty.

The melody of *At the River,* taken intact from a well-known hymn tune by Robert Lowry, provides an instance of one of Ives's most characteristic techniques: musical quotation. Although here Ives borrows the entire melody, more commonly he quotes only fragments from well-known tunes, and frequently mixes these together in complex, multileveled textures. His sources for quotations are typically catholic: hymn tunes are especially favored, but popular songs of the day, marches, and ragtime music also appear, and, much less commonly, fragments from standard concert works. But whatever the material, Ives never quotes simply for the sake of quotation. Invariably he transforms the borrowed material, both by placing it in new, more complex contexts and by distorting it through internal modifications.

Ives's ability to combine and reshape musical fragments from diverse sources can be observed in the opening measures of *The Things Our Fathers Loved* (1917) (Example VI-3; see p. 142). The harmonic language of the song, with its essentially triadic construction, reveals this simpler side of the composer, although the specific tonal focus of the music is actually quite ambiguous. (The song seems to begin in C major, but shifts toward F major by the end of the passage quoted and ends, after finally appearing to have settled in G major, with an unresolved dissonance in a remote key region.) The voice begins by quoting the opening of *Dixie*. After the third quarter of m. 2, however, it alludes to part of the first phrase of *My Old Kentucky Home* with a stepwise ascent from C to F. This fragmentary reference is at first obscure, cut

Example VI-3: IVES, *The Things Our Fathers Loved,* mm. 1–9

short by a syncopated repeat of the opening of *Dixie* on the second eighth of m. 3. (The accompaniment imitates both *Dixie* quotes, although in the "wrong" key.) But the fragment of *My Old Kentucky Home* is picked up again, now starting on F (m. 3, third quarter), and repeated once more (m. 4, last quarter), here finally with the correct rhythm of the original tune. A completely literal quotation, however, would produce the pitches D♮ and C♮, rather than D♯ and C♯, in mm. 4 and 5; the melodic distortion that results from raising these pitches is typical of Ives and explains their unusual spelling (D♯ and C♯ rather than E♭ and

D♭). A more or less straightforward quotation of *On the Banks of the Wabash* follows in mm. 6–7 (in G major, although the accompaniment suggests F major here); and finally, beginning with the upbeat to m. 8, there is a clear reference to the hymn *Nettleton*.

Thus the entire vocal line is patched together out of isolated fragments from borrowed tunes, reflecting the sort of special logic associated with things distantly and indistinctly remembered. This perfectly complements the song's text, by Ives himself, which includes a series of separate and (by normal standards) disconnected "snapshot" recollections. Yet how convincingly Ives manages to integrate everything into a series of continuously unfolding phrases that, despite their diverse origins, form a larger unity. He does this in part by techniques of rhythmic and pitch cohesion (overlapping phrases, linear connections, etc.), and in part by a web of interrelated motivic associations encompassing all the different materials. To cite just one instance of the latter: the falling fourth G-D, which forms the end of both the *Wabash* quote (m. 7, beats 1–2) and the *Nettleton* quote (last quarter of m. 8 to m. 9), is both anticipated (m. 6) and echoed (m. 9) in the top line of the accompaniment. Significantly, Ives must alter the last notes of both the *Wabash* and *Nettleton* quotes to produce this connection. Here, as elsewhere, the distortions of borrowed material are not arbitrary, but form part of an encompassing idea.

Ives's use of quotation led him to an entirely new approach to composition, conceived as a joining of heterogeneous elements into a larger synthesis—an approach that might be described as "combinational." The individual components that make up the music—drawn from a wide range of sources, some borrowed and some purely original—are juxtaposed both sequentially and simultaneously. Musical form becomes a matter of balancing and reconciling these divergent elements, and an important aspect of the expressive content derives from the unexpected associations called up by their conjunction. Thus, although the materials Ives uses are usually quite "ordinary," the way he uses them gives them a new and unexpected life; they are transformed by their surroundings.

Unity in Ives, then, is not just a matter of relationships among the materials (although this is important—the various borrowed elements in a single piece, for example, almost always share important musical characteristics, which Ives is at pains to exploit). A unity is also imposed upon the materials from without, by the consistency of Ives's attitude toward them and their appearance within a larger, encompassing framework. (In such respects, as well as in others, Ives resembles Mahler.)

Ives's progressive, innovative side is found in its most concentrated form in his works for small chamber combinations of varied instrumentation. As early as his college years Ives began writing for "theater orchestras," the small bands retained by theaters to supply music for their stage performances, and later he especially favored such pickup groups, ranging in size from a few instruments to chamber orchestra proportions, for short works of an openly "experimental" character. Here he tried out various new compositional techniques, often anticipating his European contemporaries (whose work he scarcely knew) by a number of years. Although there is normally no literal quotation in these pieces, something of the flavor of popular types of music, such as band music and ragtime, is nevertheless frequently detectable. We have mentioned Ives's early use of whole-tone and bitonal elements, dating back as far as the early 1890s; and this fondness for trying out new things to challenge the mind and ear, a taste inherited from his father, remained with him throughout his compositional career.

An example is the scherzo *Over the Pavements* (1906–13), a study in the combination and coordination of multiple layers of conflicting rhythmic activity. As often with Ives, the idea for the piece, which he called "a kind of take-off of street dancing," arose from an interest in evoking musically a nonmusical event: "In the early morning, the sounds

Example VI-4: IVES, *Over the Pavements,* mm. 46–48

of people going to and fro, all different steps, and sometimes all the same—the horses, fast trot, canter, sometimes slowing up into a walk . . . an occasional trolley throwing all the rhythm out (footsteps, horse and man)—then back again. I was struck with how many different and changing kinds of beats, time, rhythms, etc. went on together—but quite naturally, or at least not unnaturally when you get used to it."[3]

Example VI-4 contains the complex cross-rhythms and metric subdivisions found in *Over the Pavements*. Each downbeat of the notated 5/8 meter is announced by the drum, but the clarinet and trumpet, in imitation, divide the measure equally into two groups of 5/16, thus contradicting the notated eighth-note pulse. Meanwhile, the trombones and piano, supplemented by a bassoon, play drumlike clusters in the low register, each lasting a dotted eighth and thus dividing the three measures as a whole into ten equal subunits.

In several pieces, Ives experimented with pitch series, notably *Tone Roads No. 1* (1911) and *No. 3* (1915) and *Chromâtimelôdtune* (c. 1919). Although he thereby anticipated Schoenberg's earliest serial and twelve-tone pieces (which were not published until after 1923), unlike his Austrian contemporary Ives was not concerned with developing a unified serial system. In *Tone Roads No. 1,* for example, there are actually two series, neither of which is twelve-tone or strictly adhered to, and the serial aspect is only one element among many that affect the overall pitch organization. Even in *Chromâtimelôdtune,* where Ives uses a single series (and in this instance a twelve-tone one) with uncharacteristic consistency, the music betrays a strong tonal orientation. *From the Steeples and Mountains* (c. 1901) is based on a retrograde structure that even involves the serialization of rhythmic values: a steady reduction of the durations from half notes (eight sixteenths) to dotted eighths (three sixteenths) until the midpoint of the piece, after which the process is reversed until the original half notes are reattained. (A similar passage, though without the retrograde, occurs in the coda of *Over the Pavements.*)

Ives was also interested in the possibility of dividing larger ensembles into smaller units that could be separated from one another spatially as well as musically. *The Unanswered Question* (1906) is constructed of three distinct instrumental layers, each with its own specific musical character: offstage strings, playing simple sustained triadic music in C major continuously—though very softly—in the background; solo trumpet, presenting a chromatic two-measure figure that recurs intermittently seven times during the course of the work (representing the "question" of the title); and a quartet of four flutes, which answers the first six trumpet statements (the last remaining "unanswered" at the end of the piece), each answer becoming longer, louder, more dissonant and chromatic, and rhythmically more frenzied than the previous one.

3.   *Memos,* ed. John Kirkpatrick (New York, 1972), p. 62.

Extraordinarily advanced for its time, this multileveled structure, which clearly projects an extramusical conception, is typically Ivesian. Its seemingly unrelated stylistic elements are marked by different structural characteristics: the trumpet music remains essentially "fixed," unaltered on successive repetitions, while the flute music expands and develops, with the strings producing a neutral background against which the two other elements can be highlighted. Yet they are combined in a total design that builds convincingly toward a climax—the flutes' last answer—before dying out in uncertainty.

In reference to the flute music, Ives notes in the foreword to the score that "this part need not be played in the exact time position indicated." This is but one of many instances in his work of musical "indeterminacy"—that is, leaving to the players a certain degree of choice in performance. In Ives this can include such matters as how many times a particular passage should be repeated, or even whether it should be played at all. A humorous example of the latter is found in *Over the Pavements,* where the composer writes concerning the cadenza section: "To play or not to play? If played, to be played as not a nice one—but *EVENLY,* precise and unmusical as possible!" Ives's amusing indications, which include such gems as "Andante con scratchy" and "Allegro con fistiswatto" (in the Second String Quartet), along with his somewhat parodistic nature, are reminiscent of Satie, although rather different in both esthetic intent and musical result.

Ives is at his most characteristic in a relatively few extended, multimovement compositions that he worked on in the decade from about 1905 to 1915, for here he achieves a higher synthesis of the various techniques he used more individually in the songs and chamber orchestra works. Here too he reveals more explicitly the underlying continuity between his own music and that of the nineteenth-century tradition. The Third and Fourth Symphonies, the two orchestral sets (the first better known as *Three Places in New England*), the Second String Quartet, and the two Piano Sonatas (the second subtitled "Concord, Mass., 1840–1860") share the quality of complex inclusiveness discussed previously. These are lengthy musical statements that encompass, and somehow reconcile, a wealth of material drawn from apparently divergent musical worlds. Hymn tunes, popular songs, and marches are joined with dissonant harmonic combinations and rhythmic and multitextural techniques, all brought together in a wonderful amalgam that is not so much a unified "style" (a word suggesting a level of consistency that simply does not apply here) as a unified and highly personal vision.

The Fourth Symphony, along with the "Concord" Sonata Ives's most ambitious composition, can serve as an example. Though completed in 1916, the symphony's compositional history extends back over some twenty years, and it may be aptly characterized as a culmination and synthesis of all his previous work, so much of which is incorporated therein in one form or another. Ives's reuse of his own earlier music is most obvious in the third movement, an orchestration, with only minor changes, of a relatively traditional tonal fugue written during the Yale years, which originally served as the opening movement of the First String Quartet (1898). But some fifteen other earlier works—most existing only in fragmentary form—contributed in some way to the formation of the symphony. Moreover, the work abounds in quotations from a wide range of other composers, making it a sort of repository of fragments from Ives's musical past, a common meeting place where they are recycled and reassimilated and thus given new life.

In the symphony's opening movement an essentially triadic setting for chorus and orchestra of the hymn *Watchman, Tell Us of the Night* is combined with a number of fragmentary quotations that contribute to a texturally complex and varied orchestral accompaniment. Especially characteristic is the addition of a simultaneous, yet separate, layer of music for harp and two solo violins, designated in the score as a "distant choir" and marked "scarcely to be heard, a faint sound in the distance." This music, based on a second hymn, *Nearer, My God, to Thee,* and featuring chords built in fourths with pitches partially in conflict with those of the rest of the orchestra, creates an indistinct halo of conflicting sound that gently colors the hymn tune, rendering it ambiguous and vaguely mysterious. The music of this added layer occasionally seems to influence the main hymn setting, which introduces unexpected chromatic notes at strategic points and which, in keeping with the peculiar ambivalence of the whole, ends on a subdominant chord rather than the tonic, pointing up the text's final unanswered question: "Dost thou see its beauteous ray?"

Even more characteristically Ivesian, and unprecedented in richness and complexity, is the second movement, which the composer himself called a "comedy." The textural density far exceeds anything written previously, or anything that would appear until after the middle of the century. Here Ives pushes his "collage" approach to its ultimate consequences, combining multiple layers of music that are distinguished not only by thematic and harmonic content but by meter and tempo as well (three different conductors are required to coordinate the separate strands). Quotations abound, but in this case the emphasis is less upon savoring the individual references than in projecting an organized and carefully controlled "confusion" through their combination and superimposition. In many pages of the score it is in fact virtually impossible to pick out any individual details. Rather, the listener is conscious of variations and transformations within a densely packed textural aggregate from which specific events occasionally and briefly assert themselves. As Ives remarks of this music in a long "Conductor's Note," which deals largely with the effect of simultaneous musical occurrences on auditory perception,

> In music based to some extent on more than one or two rhythmic, melodic, harmonic schemes, the hearer has a rather active part to play. . . . As the eye, in looking at a view, may focus on the sky, clouds or distant outlines, yet sense the color and form of the foreground, and then by bringing the eye to the foreground, sense the distant outline and color, so in some similar way can the listener choose to arrange in his mind the relation of the rhythmic and harmonic and other material. In other words, in music the ear may play a role similar to the eye in the above instance.[4]

After the relatively simple fugal third movement, the fourth and last movement is almost as complex in texture as the second, although here the various layers are more traditionally related in both rhythmic and harmonic coordination. The added "distant choir" from the first movement reappears, again with references to *Nearer, My God, to Thee* (this cyclic return is one among numerous indications of Ives's strong ties to European musical Romanticism), and there is an additional percussive layer consisting of drums, cymbal, and gong that opens the movement alone and, after continuing almost imperceptibly in the background throughout, is heard alone again at the end. The chorus, not used since the first movement, returns to sing wordlessly at the end in a passage of luminous serenity.

Ives suffered a heart attack in 1918, and, partly because of failing health and partly because of the almost total lack of interest in his work on the part of other musicians (to say nothing of the general public), he composed very little during the final thirty-five years of his life. A few songs and shorter piano pieces (including *Three Quarter-Tone Pieces* for two pianos) appeared in the early 1920s, but after that there was almost complete silence. Very gradually during the 1920s and 1930s, his work began to attract attention among some younger American composers and performers, although performances remained a rarity until well into the 1950s. During the 1960s, however, Ives suddenly emerged as a sort of cult figure, recognized throughout the world as the first and foremost American composer. In 1965 the first complete performance of the Fourth Symphony attracted particular interest, and the work was hailed as a major monument of modern music. One principal reason for this belated success was that many of the new compositional techniques Ives had introduced, such as multiple tempos, polydimensional textures, and microtonal tunings, had since taken their place as part of the basic vocabulary of the music of the post–World War II period. Ives had become a prophet, and the musical world had finally caught up with him.

4.   Footnote to second movement, Symphony No. 4 (New York, 1965).

PART II

Reconstruction and New Systems: Between the Wars

Reprinted with permission from Felix Gilbert, *The End of the European Era,*
1890 to the Present (New York, Norton, 1984)

CHAPTER VII

The Historical Context: Europe after World War I

The close of World War I in late 1918 left Europe badly bruised and shaken. The treaties negotiated after the end of hostilities significantly altered the Continent's political and geographical shape. The old Austro-Hungarian Empire was completely dissolved; Poland, Czechoslovakia, Hungary, and Yugoslavia were established as independent states. Germany, humbled by defeat, was forced to relinquish the territory of Alsace-Lorraine to France and to make heavy reparation payments. Russia, which had fought on the side of the Allies against Germany and Austria, emerged from the war with a new, revolutionary government that was engaged in establishing the world's first communist state. The old Europe was largely destroyed, while a new one slowly put itself together out of the ashes of the confrontation.

Conditions were ripe for a major cultural reorientation. The war profoundly changed the attitudes of European intellectuals and artists. For the first time, the full destructive force of modern industrial society was exposed on a broad scale. Directing all of their power and resources to the military effort, the European states had been able to build war machines far exceeding the size and efficiency of any known in the past. The impersonal, all-consuming might of the new mechanized armies brought the horror and misery of war to the world's consciousness in a new and heightened way. The final death toll of the conflict was unprecedented, as was the degree of material and emotional devastation it brought in its wake.

The optimistic assumptions of the scientific-technical worldview, the general belief in continuing economic and social progress, were fundamentally shaken by these cataclysmic events. So too was the view of many prewar artists that the impact of personal artistic statements could significantly alter materialistic attitudes, that by transcending the practical realities of everyday experience they could foster a new level of consciousness founded upon individualism, imagination, and personal freedom. Both the remarkable degree of technical experimentation and the feeling of spiritual excitement and renewal in the prewar years owed much to this euphoric belief in the power of the arts to promote new modes of thought and experience. Following the destruction and suffering brought on by what came to be universally known as the Great War, however, this faith could no longer be reasonably sustained.

The change in viewpoint did not come about immediately. In the early stages of the war, some even hoped that the conflict might have a positive effect, clearing the way for the foundation of a new social order. Many leading artists and musicians of the day actually entered the war with feelings of optimism and commitment paralleling those of their esthetic positions (all three principal figures of the Second Viennese School—Schoenberg, Webern, and Berg—did so, for example). By the time of the armistice, however, most had been deeply shaken by first-hand experience with the brutality and banality of military conflict.

The first—and most extreme—artistic reaction to the war occurred in the movement known as Dada, founded by a group of independent artists living in neutral Switzerland during the war years, including the writers Hugo Ball and Tristan Tzara and the sculptor and painter Hans Arp. The Dadaists, who first came to prominence in 1916, were initially influenced by the Italian Futurists, especially in the iconoclastic nihilism and antitraditionalism most forcefully embodied in the Dada slogan "Burn the museum." But the new group did not share the Futurists' fascination with technology or their enthusiastic acceptance of the paraphernalia of the machine age.

Characteristically, the Futurists welcomed the war as an opportunity to put into use the full potential of new technological advances, all in the service of patriotism; they even entered the Italian armed forces as a unit, joining a motorcycle battalion. The Dadaists, by contrast, were repulsed by the stupidity of the war, which they considered an inevitable result of modern historical evolution, and as a consequence turned against civilization itself; if mankind was capable of such wholesale destruction and self-annihilation, they reasoned, then none of its accomplishments, either artistic or technological, could possibly be taken seriously. Human aspirations toward betterment through rational and scientific means were viewed as farcical; the sole proper response to a world gone mad was satirization and ridicule. For the Dadaists, the only viable art for the modern age was "anti-art"—a nihilistic attempt to promote disorder, irrationality, and anti-estheticism.

George Grosz's montage, conceived for an unpublished anthology that was to be called *Dadaco,* suggests something of the frenetic energy and dynamism of Germany after World War I.

Dada did not propose a new artistic style but rather a new mode of negative thinking with respect to the arts. Among the several manifestos written by Tzara, numerous comments indicated the thrust of the movement: "[Dada is] a harsh necessity without discipline or morality and we spit on humanity. . . . What we need are works that are strong, straight and precise and forever beyond understanding. Logic is a complication. . . . Let each man proclaim: there is a great negative work of destruction to be accomplished. We must sweep and clean. . . . Art is a PRETENSION . . . MUSICIANS SMASH YOUR INSTRUMENTS." Art was transformed into a sort of irreverent game designed to make fun of the artistic pretensions and ambitions of the past. In place of meaning, Dada promoted the nonsensical and accidental.

The extremity of the Dadaist position no doubt reflected the extremity of the human condition during the war years. And although its unrelieved negativism could not be sustained for an extended period, the Dada point of view has appeared off and on throughout the century, occasionally resurfacing with special force. (Its most important immediate influence was on surrealism, one of the leading movements in the visual and literary arts between the two world wars.) Yet in the light of the overall development of the arts in the postwar years, Dada's historical significance is best understood as a symbolic rejection of the inflated pretensions of post-Romantic individualism. Sobered and subdued by the war experience, European culture seemed to require a more economical and less subjective type of art, more down to earth and less swollen in its ambitions.

Thus a new attitude began to emerge in the late war years, and eventually came to dominate most important artistic movements of the next two decades. Among its chief features was a renewed respect for clarity, objectivity, and order—as if, after the chaotic artistic ferment of the century's early years, a new consolidation was desired. Although by no means universal, and evident in very different ways in the work of different artists and musicians, this new outlook brought a marked unity of underlying purpose to the arts during the years separating the two world wars. At no other time in the twentieth century—and perhaps not since the late eighteenth century—has there been such strong evidence of a community of shared artistic intentions as one finds in this brief twenty-year span.

The new attitude first appeared clearly in several prominent artistic movements originating in the final war years and the early postwar period, whose esthetic proclamations, consciously conceived and publicly announced, set the tone for the entire period. The earliest was *De Stijl,* a group of artists centered in the Netherlands, which took its name from its monthly publication, begun in 1917. Including among its members the well-known abstract painter Piet Mondrian, *De Stijl* promoted an art of almost mathematical purity, based on the simplest geometrical shapes. "The work of art," Mondrian remarked, "must be 'produced,' 'constructed.' One must create as objective as possible a representation of forms and relations." Another member, the architect J. J. P. Oud, stressed that this new objectivity was to go hand in hand with an effort "to give esthetic form to the products of technology."

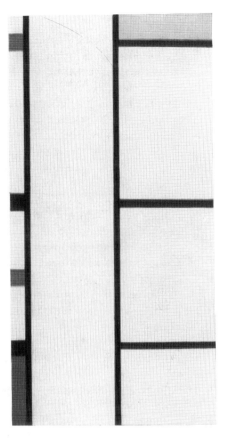

Piet Mondrian's *Composition, 1935–42* embodies the purity of means, economy of movement, and architectonic unity that characterized the *De Stijl* movement.(Collection, Mr. and Mrs. Burton Tremaine, Meriden, Conn.)

In the German city of Weimar the architect Walter Gropius formed the Bauhaus in 1919, a school of art whose faculty included such prominent artists and craftsmen as Paul Klee, Lyonel Feininger, and Wassily Kandinsky. Strongly reacting against the individualism of German expressionism in particular and of late nineteenth- and early twentieth-century art in general, the Bauhaus proposed a collective approach to art, centered in architecture but incorporating interior design, furnishings, etc., and emphasized fidelity to modern industrial materials and responsiveness to the needs of contemporary citizens. Gropius's concerns were especially focused on the relationship of design to utility, on the linking of artistic decisions to functional needs. He consequently rejected traditional distinctions between applied and fine arts: "Let us create together the new building of the future, which will be everything in one—architecture and painting."

A third group, known as the Purists, was centered in France and led by the architect Le Corbusier. Its monthly magazine *L'Esprit nouveau* (The New Spirit) proclaimed in its opening issue (1920): "There is a new spirit; it is a spirit of construction and synthesis, guided by a clear idea." Le Corbusier also emphasized simplicity, the utilization of industrial materials, and the importance of these materials in influencing design decisions. His famous characterization of a house as "a machine to live in" forcefully captured the new temper of the age.

Characteristically, these movements consisted not so much of individuals as of groups of artists collaborating closely within a framework of shared goals. Moreover, all emphasized art's practical and social role, especially its responsibility to assist in achieving adequate living conditions for all people. New technology was welcomed, but on condition that it be made to serve man's needs and, ideally, become an instrument for his liberation. The French painter Fernand Léger, in a 1924 article on "The Esthetic of the Machine" (a title that perfectly encapsulated the new orientation), drew a sharp distinction between new and old art on precisely these terms: "If the objectives of preceding architectural monuments were the predominance of the beautiful over the useful, it is undeniable that, in the mechanical order, the dominant aim is *utility*, strictly utility."

The three artistic movements discussed above centered around the plastic arts (all were concerned especially with practical construction), yet their common beliefs—e.g., emphasis on efficiency, clarity of composition, and economy of means—were also echoed in much of the music written in the postwar years. Here too a reaffirmation of tradi-

The Villa Savoye, designed by Le Corbusier (Charles-Edouard Jeanneret), built in Poissy, France in the early 30s, clearly demonstrates the architect's penchant for treating buildings as weightless volumes lifted off the ground through innovative use of strong, light building materials. (Model for Ville Savoy, Poissy, France. 1929–31. Construction, 11¼ × 25½ × 22½". Collection, The Museum of Modern Art, New York)

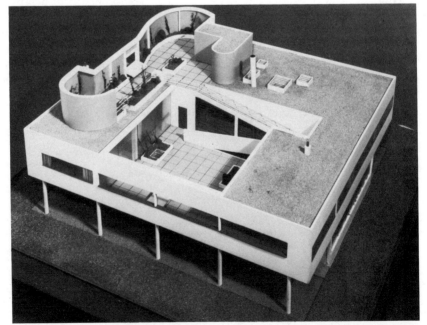

tional principles of order and clarity followed the radical innovations of the prewar years. A new interest in reestablishing ties with the more distant past appeared alongside a desire to avoid the excesses of the more immediate past—namely, late Romanticism and early twentieth-century "post-Romanticism." After a period of pronounced experimentation, which had created an aura of artistic uncertainty and, in extreme cases, even anarchy, an understandable wish for clarification and stability set in.

Like the other arts, music began to be viewed in more down-to-earth terms, as an ordering of elements and relationships rather than as a vehicle for the divine revelation of ultimate truths accessible only to the initiated. Thus Stravinsky, writing of his Wind Octet (1923), one of the most critical compositions in defining the postwar esthetic, emphasized that it was "not an 'emotive' work but a musical composition based on objective elements which are sufficient in themselves." The Romantic conception of "art for art's sake" gave way to the idea of music as an "applied" art —that is, a practical endeavor with definite social functions and responsibilities. Music became more "democratic," its simpler construction in part intended to promote greater accessibility to a larger public. An important component of the musical beliefs of the day was summarized in the term Gebrauchsmusik, or "music for use," introduced by the composer Paul Hindemith to point up "the danger of an esoteric isolationism in music."

It would be a mistake, however, to say that after the war music simply turned its back upon the technical innovations introduced during the earlier years of the century. Although many composers placed a new emphasis on tonal centricity and clarity, virtually no one (at least among the major figures) felt it desirable, or even possible, simply to resurrect the traditional tonal system of the common-practice period. Instead, new approaches to tonality were developed that retained in large measure the freely dissonant character of prewar music. As for the atonal composers, they did not abandon atonality but found new ways of controlling it. Thus the general trend was not so much to reject the innovations of the preceding years as to accommodate them within a new esthetic framework.

The sense of cooperative optimism that characterized Europe during the postwar period (so different from the more individualistic optimism of the prewar years) found its political embodiment in the League of Nations, created in 1919 in the belief that the nations of the world, if they would work together in confederation, could learn to coexist in harmony and peace. But the new optimism was not to last. By the early 1930s the political situation had greatly deteriorated: economic depression beset all the industrialized nations; national socialism seized power in Germany (fascism having already made its first appearance in Italy during the previous decade); the totalitarian regime in Russia hardened significantly; and there was growing fear that international events were pushing toward yet another worldwide confrontation, especially when civil war broke out in Spain in 1936, with Russia supporting one side, Germany and Italy the other. In the same year, Germany, having unilaterally denounced the Treaty of Versailles in 1933, remilitarized the Rhineland, setting the stage for the annexation of Austria in 1938. By this time the League of Nations had been effectively dissolved, and Europe, after less than a quarter century, found itself once again on the brink of a major war.

These developments conspired to draw a darkening shadow over the Continent's cultural life. Germany and Russia (and eventually even Italy) were cut off from the European mainstream, their totalitarian regimes brutally suppressing all progressive modern art and music as "decadent." Elsewhere, however, the more ominous atmosphere was not reflected by such dramatic changes in the arts. Although the economic hardships and political tensions of the 1930s promoted a higher degree of social consciousness on the part of many composers, especially younger ones, this did not lead to a fundamental stylistic readjustment. Rather, the trend toward simplicity and clarity continued, now underscored by an even more pronounced emphasis on music of a "popular" character capable of appealing to a larger public. Thus no significant break from the general esthetic orientation of the preceding years was required. Once again, it would take the catastrophic effects of a world war to produce a major turn in direction.

CHAPTER VIII

Neo-Classicism

THE "NEW SPIRIT" IN FRANCE

In 1918 the French poet Jean Cocteau brought forth an influential essay
entitled "Cock and Harlequin" (to be collected a few years later with
other Cocteau essays under the suggestive heading *A Call to Order*), in
which he observed that "Satie teaches what, in our age, is the greatest
audacity, simplicity."[1] One of Cocteau's points, the need for a new
French art free from German domination, was already a familiar cry.
But besides warning against the dangers of what he called "Wagnerian
fog," he equally advised the French against Debussian "mist" and the
"theatrical mysticisms" of Stravinsky's *Rite of Spring;* not only German
Romanticism, but also French Impressionism and Russian paganism
were to be avoided. Cocteau distrusted the complexity and pretension
of all such music, "its convolutions, dodges and tricks." It was too long
and had too many notes, its textures were too rich for healthy diges-
tion. "Enough of clouds, waves, aquariums, waterspirits, and nocturnal scents; what we need is a music of the earth, every-day music."[2]
This "every-day music" was to be simple in structure and modest in
scope; it should aspire to the "clairvoyance of children." Moreover, its
model should not be the music of the concert hall, but rather that of the
circus, the music hall, the *café-concert,* and jazz.

1. *A Call to Order,* trans. Rollo H. Myers (London, 1926), p. 18.
2. Ibid., p. 19.

SATIE

That Cocteau offered Satie as his prime example in this appeal to a "return to simplicity" is in one sense not surprising, for Satie's music had long reflected the musical qualities for which he argues. Unexpected, however, was the sudden thrusting to center stage of Satie, so long viewed as a figure unworthy of serious consideration and now proposed as a model for a new era in French artistic life. Not only was Satie to be taken seriously, proclaimed Cocteau, he was even to be valued above Debussy. There could be no clearer indication of the revolutionary transformations in French esthetic attitudes during the war years.

Although Cocteau's essay played a tangible role in Satie's sudden rise to prominence, there had been earlier signs that the composer was no longer to be easily dismissed. Indeed, the essay was largely the outcome of a celebrated collaborative venture of the previous year (1917) that brought Satie together with several leading artistic figures of the time under the aegis of Diaghilev's Ballets Russes: the ballet *Parade,* with story by Cocteau, sets by Picasso, and choreography by Leonid Massine.

Satie's lively score perfectly matches the light informality of the stage proceedings, which revolve around street entertainers and acrobats. Especially characteristic is the unabashed evocation of popular types of music, including jazz. Familiar formal features from Satie's earlier works are retained: brief, often seemingly unrelated musical units, mostly dominated by repetitive melodic figures, are woven together in a seemingly casual mosaic. But here these units have been molded into more extensive and continuous strands, resulting in Satie's most substantial composition to date. (*Parade* was in fact his first sizable orchestral work.) Yet there is no hint of pretension or bombast. Satie's unpredictable sense of humor is still close to the surface, perhaps most strikingly when the score calls for the sounds of a lottery wheel, a typewriter, and a revolver. Probably more than any other work, *Parade* defined the "new spirit" (a famous phrase, first used by the poet Guillaume Apollinaire in the program for the ballet's first performance) that was to characterize the arts in postwar France.

In the same year as *Parade,* Satie composed the brief *Sonatine bureaucratique* for piano, a satiric paraphrase of music by the eighteenth-century composer Muzio Clementi that is significant for anticipating the neo-classic fascination with earlier styles. His next big work, the "symphonic drama" *Socrate* (1918), is considered by many to be Satie's finest composition. This extended setting for soloists and chamber orchestra of selections from Plato's dialogues represents in some respects a departure for Satie; its seriousness and austerity, coupled with a complete

The curtain painted by Picasso for the epoch-making Diaghilev production of *Parade,* with music by Satie, scenario by Jean Cocteau, and choreography by Leonid Massine. Paris, 1917.

absence of popular elements, contrast markedly to *Parade.* Yet its understatement, linear directness, and textural simplicity equally reflect characteristic features of the new postwar esthetic. The subdued vocal line, closely tied to the inflections of the text, is laid out in unadorned diatonic phrases, joined by equally simple though rhythmically independent ostinato-like accompaniments. Everything seems to occur on an even plane, there being remarkably little contrast of any kind (dynamic, orchestral, or formal). Rarely has a work captured so faithfully those qualities of detachment and classical restraint especially admired by the French.

Before his death in 1925, Satie composed two additional ballets: *Mercure* (1924) and *Relâche* (*No Performance Today,* 1924). The most extreme embodiment of his unprepossessing attitude toward composition, however, was the *Musique d'ameublement* (*Furniture Music*), composed with Darius Milhaud in 1920. Intended for performance during the intermission of a play, it represented a radical attempt to deny all expressive intentions or artistic ambitions. The composers urged the audience "to take no notice of it and to behave during the intervals as if it did not exist. The music . . . wishes to make a contribution to life in the same way as a private conversation, a painting . . . or a chair on which you may or may not be seated."

LES SIX

During the war years Satie became a sort of musical hero to a number of younger French composers. Six of these admirers, most of whom had met while students at the Paris Conservatory, became close friends on the basis of common interests: Francis Poulenc (1899–1963), Darius Milhaud (1892–1974), Arthur Honegger (1892–1955), Georges Auric (1899–1983), Germaine Tailleferre (1892–1983), and Louis Durey (1888–1979). In 1917 they began giving joint concerts under the name "Les Nouveaux Jeunes" (The New Young People), but when a 1920 article referred to the group as "Les Six" (The Six—by analogy with "The Five" of the Russian nationalist movement), the name stuck. Eventually, the composers' differences of outlook led to the termination of their (always very informal) association, but in the early postwar days, with Cocteau as their spokesman and Satie as a sort of spiritual godfather, Les Six came to symbolize the light and bubbly flavor of postwar France. Their common espousal of music that was direct in approach, light in touch, and free of the pretensions of the concert hall defined the very essence of the "new spirit."

POULENC

Francis Poulenc probably embodied the ideals of Les Six, at least as formulated by Cocteau, more faithfully than any other composer in the group, and he also remained throughout his life more sympathetic to its original spirit than the others. Poulenc was largely self-taught in composition, but his early works, including the popular piano piece *Mouvements perpétuels* (Perpetual Motions, 1918) and the ballet *Les Biches* (The Fawns, 1923), already display the special fusion of charm, spontaneity, and fastidiousness that are characteristic of his style. The musical language is essentially conservative, incorporating a return to tonality in its simpler, more traditional forms. The harmonic structure is basically triadic, the underlying framework diatonic. Poulenc even preserves the priority of the dominant relationship as a key-defining agent, although this priority is colored by frequent modal inflections and undoctrinaire harmonic progressions. Emphasis is upon clear melodic profiles and unencumbered lyricism, and the flavor of popular music is never far away, suggesting that Poulenc (at least in his earlier work) is determined not to be taken too seriously.

Poulenc's straightforward and uncomplicated lyricism found its most natural expression in the large number of songs that he composed throughout his life. In this genre he found the ideal outlet for his talents as a miniaturist of consummate craftsmanship, and created a body of literature that ranks in size and achievement with that of any twentieth-

Francis Poulenc with the French soprano, Denise Duval, who created the leading roles in all three of his operas. (Photograph by Piccagliani)

century composer. There is never a hint of carelessness; it is music that,
despite its lightness of tone and simple, unaffected message, is written
with unforced technical finesse.

Although Poulenc remained essentially true to these general stylistic
characteristics in his later work, an increasing earnestness and intensity
can be found in the music written after his return, in the middle 1930s,
to the Roman Catholicism of his upbringing. In his later years he produced several substantial religious compositions, notably the *Stabat mater*
(1950) and *Gloria* (1959), both for soprano soloist, chorus, and orchestra, as well as an opera, *Dialogues des Carmélites* (*Dialogues of the Carme-
lites,* 1956), based on a religious subject. Another opera, the one-act *La
Voix humaine* (*The Human Voice,* 1958), sung entirely by a single character (a young woman speaking to her lover on the phone as she hears
of his intention to abandon her), made an equally powerful impression.
(These works marked a significant departure from Poulenc's only previous operatic endeavor, the highly eclectic *Les Mamelles de Tirésias* [*The
Breasts of Tiresias,* 1944], based on a surrealist play by Apollinaire and
with music ranging from the flippant to the noble.) Poulenc's reputation, little more than that of a clever but not especially significant *enfant
terrible* in his earlier years, rose dramatically with the appearance of these
substantial works, all composed within the final fifteen years of his life.

MILHAUD

Of all the members of Les Six, the closest to Satie personally was Darius Milhaud, who met the older composer in 1918 and collaborated with him on the notorious *Musique d'ameublement*. Milhaud brought to the group an already well-developed musical point of view that was consistent with the esthetic program outlined by Cocteau. Several of his early compositions created considerable scandal with their impertinence and offhand humor. Largely responsible for establishing him as a leading figure among the younger generation were two scores for ballets conceived by Cocteau: *Le Boeuf sur le toit* (*The Bull on the Roof*, 1919) and *Le Train bleu* (*The Blue Express*, 1924). The music of the former is a loose collection of popular dances from Brazil (where Milhaud had spent two years in the foreign service), while the latter is, in the composer's words, "an operetta without words . . . gay, frivolous, and frothy, in the manner of Offenbach." Another ballet score, *La Création du monde* (*The Creation of the World*, 1923), was notable as one of the first concert works significantly influenced by American jazz.

Milhaud's unprepossessing, somewhat irreverent attitude toward composition also found expression in three so-called "minute operas" (1927–28), lighthearted dramatic works freely based on themes drawn from Greek mythology and lasting only some ten minutes each. Even more pointedly satirical of conventional notions of artistic propriety and expressive suitability are the two song cycles *Machines agricoles* (1919) and *Catalogue de fleurs* (1920), based on texts taken from catalogues of, respectively, farm machinery and flowers.

A compositional technique closely associated with Milhaud during the 1920s—and especially indicative of the esthetic orientation of many French composers of the time—is "polytonality," a simultaneous combination of two or more keys. A clear example occurs in "Corcovado," from Milhaud's piano suite *Saudades do Brasil* (*Souvenirs of Brazil*, 1921).

The left hand is firmly based in G major, alternating tonic and dominant harmonies with each measure, while the right hand is in D major and similarly alternates melodic figures based on dominant and tonic functions. One does not actually hear two keys, however, for the left-

Example VIII-1: MILHAUD, *Saudades do Brasil*, "Corcovado," mm. 1–4

Fernand Léger's set design study for the original production of the ballet *La Creation du monde* (1922) echoes the strong African influences in Milhaud's score. (Pencil, 8¼ × 10⅞″. Collection, The Museum of Modern Art, New York. Gift of John Pratt)

hand bass progression encompasses, and thus controls, the entire harmony; thus the right hand is heard not as an independent key but rather as a dissonant "coloring" of the principal tonality defined by the left hand. (Significantly, Milhaud ends the piece unambiguously with an arpeggiated "pure" G-major triad.) Such "polytonality" offered a characteristic method of spicing up an essentially traditional harmonic conception, an element of "modernity" without unwanted complexity or cluttered chromaticism. The simple rhythmic regularity, punctuated only by the mild syncopations of the Brazilian dance on which the music is based, is never seriously disturbed, thus preserving a distinctly popular flavor.

Milhaud, whose compositional career spanned more than a half century, was extraordinarily prolific and blessed with unusual technical facility. Music seemed to pour from his pen with disarming ease, yielding a catalogue that includes fifteen operas, seventeen ballets, thirteen symphonies, and eighteen string quartets, as well as numerous orchestral scores (including over twenty concertos) and a large body of chamber works, songs, and choral music. Milhaud composed much incidental music for film, stage, and radio, and also numerous pieces for performance by children. Inevitably, this extraordinary productivity had an effect on the quality of the music, especially the later work; much of it is "occasional" in nature, produced quickly for a particular purpose or to satisfy a commission. Milhaud's most substantial music is probably found in his dramatic works, especially those written in collaboration with his close friend the poet Paul Claudel. The most important and ambitious of these is the opera *Christophe Colomb* (1928), which treats the discovery of America using unusually large forces and a complex dramatic apparatus (including film) to produce a powerful statement of the poet's Catholic mysticism.

HONEGGER

Among Les Six, Arthur Honegger was the one who eventually turned away most consequentially from the original ideals. Although remaining a citizen of his native Switzerland, Honegger studied at the Paris Conservatory and eventually settled in Paris permanently. In 1921 he achieved almost instantaneous fame with the appearance of the dramatic oratorio *Le Roi David (King David),* a work of powerful directness and almost aphoristic economy that compresses no less than twenty-seven episodes into a span of some forty-five minutes. Widely imitated, the piece did much to revive interest in the oratorio as a twentieth-century medium, and Honegger himself wrote a number of further compositions in the genre, including his well-known *Jeanne d'Arc au bûcher* (*Joan of Arc at the Stake,* 1935).

Much of Honegger's music of the 1920s closely parallels the esthetic ideals of Les Six—for example, both the *Pastorale d'été* (*Summer Pastorale,* 1920), a chamber work of relaxed lyricism, and the jazz-influenced Piano Concerto (1925). The postwar fascination with technology, mirroring the desire for a more streamlined approach to art, is also evident in *Pacific 231* (1923), a once-notorious orchestral "tone poem," musically evoking the sounds of a locomotive. Yet a degree of complication in Honegger's compositional outlook places him somewhat apart from

The young Arthur Honegger in Paris (Photograph by Lipinski courtesy Haags Gemeentemuseum, the Hague)

both Poulenc and Milhaud. An admirer since childhood of the music of Bach, his own work gives frequent evidence of an inclination toward complex contrapuntal thinking.

Following the 1920s Honegger's interest in larger forms and extended symphonic composition increased markedly. His five symphonies (written between 1930 and 1951) and the last two of his three string quartets (both completed in 1936) manifest greater formal complexity and a more varied, flexible approach to tonality. An interesting example of the latter is found in the opening of the Fifth Symphony (1951), where massive combinations of simultaneous conflicting triads (scored for full orchestra) offer a more differentiated example of "polytonality" than was seen in Milhaud's *Saudades*.

Here the two levels (clearly separated by register and notated on separate staves in the example) both take D minor as a point of departure, but their inversionally related motions produce independent series of parallel triads, whose combination creates richly sonorous, polytriadic harmonies.

Example VIII-2: HONEGGER, Symphony No. 5, first movement, mm. 1–4

Honegger did not achieve a position of importance and influence comparable to that of Stravinsky, Schoenberg, or Bartók, nor did any of the other members of Les Six. Curiously, despite the position of Paris as indisputably the most important cultural center in Europe during the years immediately preceding and following World War I, no French composer of the highest rank was active during this time except for Debussy, who died in 1918. The subsequent absence of a dominant figure probably explains why the members of Les Six are commonly considered as a group, even though their formal connection lasted only a few years. In addition, the idea of a composers' collective appealed greatly to an age attempting to throw off the vestiges of Romantic individualism. In any event, taken together the composers of Les Six played an essential role in shaping the atmosphere of musical life in postwar Paris and in establishing the main features of its predominant compositional style. Their combined historical significance thus clearly exceeds that of their individual attainments.

STRAVINSKY AND NEO-CLASSICISM

When protesting against the dominance of German music in his essay "Cock and Harlequin," Cocteau expressed the hope and belief that the new, simpler, "anti-Romantic" style of French music would soon "influence the world." Certainly it had some effect on Stravinsky, who moved to Paris in 1920 and remained there for almost twenty years. As he later remarked, "My feeling for clarity, my fanaticism for precision was waked through France, and my distaste for hollow twaddle and bombast, false pathos, lack of discretion in creative effusions—that was all at least strongly encouraged through my stay in Paris."[3] He also praised Satie for his "firm and clear musical language devoid of all extraneous sound painting."

Even before the new French developments, Stravinsky had begun moving toward a leaner and more economical compositional language that eschewed the large proportions and extended instrumental forces of his three great prewar ballets. Perhaps to compensate for his exile in Switzerland during the war years, he immersed himself in folk materials, both musical and textual, from his native Russia. These inspired a series of compositions, including the three *Pribaoutki* songs (1914), the chamber opera *Reynard* (1916), the choreographic scenes *The Wedding* (composed by 1917, though the final instrumental scoring—for four pianos and percussion ensemble—was not completed until 1923), and the "traveling entertainment" *Histoire du soldat* (The Soldier's Tale, 1918). All use small ensembles and feature a musical style reduced to essentials, following a tendency already suggested in the austere *Zvezdoliki*, composed in 1912 while Stravinsky was still working on *The Rite of Spring*. Purely instrumental works of the period reveal similar traits: the Three Pieces for String Quartet (1914), the two sets of *Easy Pieces* for piano four-hands (1915 and 1917), and the Three Pieces for Clarinet (1919).

Musically, these works retain many characteristics found in the earlier ballets. Even though actual quotation of Russian folk music is avoided, the melodic material is still pervaded with folk flavor, and Stravinsky continues to use fragmentary melodic ideas, incessantly repeated with slight yet telling rhythmic modifications. Ostinatos still figure prominently, and formal development is achieved through the familiar Stravinskian techniques of stratification and crosscutting. Yet differences from the earlier works are equally noticeable. The overall conception has been scaled down radically; textures are simplified, developmental processes compressed. A tone of lightness and humor is often evident, producing an effect very different from the primitive intensity of *The*

---

3.   Quoted in Charles Oulmont, "Besuch bei Stravinsky," *Melos,* 14 (1946): 107–8.

Rite or the sardonic sophistication and surface elegance of *Petrushka*. *Reynard,* designated as a "burlesque," treats the activities of barnyard animals with a childlike charm and naïveté; much of its music has a pronounced "circus-band" quality. More down-to-earth than before, this music has a new—though still peculiarly Stravinskian (and Russian)—brashness and directness.

Stravinsky's work up to about 1920 is commonly referred to as his "Russian" period, the first of three major stylistic divisions generally recognized in his work. But the tone of economy and restraint evident in these post-*Rite* works already points toward the second, so-called "neo-classical" period. Especially revealing in this regard is *Histoire du soldat,* written in collaboration with the Swiss author C. F. Ramuz and based on a Russian story (although the text is in French). This fable of a fiddle-playing soldier who matches wits with the devil is "to be read, played, and danced" by a narrator, actors, dancers, and a small mixed chamber group (clarinet, bassoon, trumpet, trombone, violin, bass, and percussion) that evokes the character of a pickup band.

Although many technical features of *Histoire,* such as the rhythmically irregular phrases juxtaposed against accompanimental ostinatos that often have independent rhythms, recall Stravinsky's earlier works, the tone and character seem quite new. Organized as a series of brief tableaux, the action is presented mainly through mime and dancing, with continuity supplied by the narrator. However, the music is solely instrumental and, though it mirrors the general mood of the action, thus forms an essentially independent strand (it is often played as a separate concert suite). The atmosphere of the entire production suggests a cabaret or an informal street entertainment, an impression enhanced by the score's tendency to mimic—and parody—well-known types of popular music: the musical characteristics of standard dances (tango, waltz, and ragtime) are evoked, and there are also a march and two chorales. The degree of distortion in the reworking of these familiar musical types is much greater, however, than in the later dancelike pieces favored by Les Six. As always in Stravinsky, the level of rhythmic complexity is quite high, and, although essentially tonal, the music is often sharply dissonant and ambiguous in tonal focus.

Typical is the duo for violin and bass that opens and persists throughout much of the first scene of *Histoire,* a sort of constant yet shifting background against which other, more melodic, elements occasionally appear (Example VIII-3; see p. 170). Although entirely diatonic, this passage is curiously ambivalent measured by traditional standards of tonality. Against a continuous four-note ostinato pattern in the base suggesting G as tonic (G is both its lowest and highest, as well as its first and last, notes), the violin plays a figure that, although occasionally supporting G, is more consistently directed toward A. The

Example VIII-3: STRAVINSKY, *Histoire du soldat,* opening scene, mm. 1–7

result, highly characteristic for Stravinsky, is a pull in two directions, neither emphatic enough to settle the matter (the absence of a leading tone to either key, G or A, is important in maintaining the uncertainty). Equally typical is the rhythmic structure. The varied though also ostinato-like opening violin figure recurs at irregular intervals and is thus set off against the absolute immobility of the bass, the encounters of the two parts producing ever-changing rhythmic combinations. (Note that the bar lines follow the violin's changing metrical structure, so that the bass figure, though matching the measure at the beginning, soon shifts out of phase.)

Stravinsky's interest in working with given musical types, treated much like existing "objects" to be subjected to external manipulation, can be traced back to the reworking of "borrowed" folk materials in the ballets. Clearly evident in the brief *Easy Pieces* for piano four-hands (including a polka, galop, etc.) written shortly before *Histoire du soldat,* his interest subsequently grew dramatically. In the same year *Histoire* was completed, for example, Stravinsky wrote *Rag-time,* for a chamber ensemble of eleven players, and in the following year (1919) the *Piano-Rag-Music* further explored the jazz rhythms and textures found in the earlier work.

This practice of working in a highly stylized way with borrowed materials reached a more advanced form in the ballet *Pulcinella* (1920). Asked by Diaghilev to orchestrate some pieces attributed to the eighteenth-century composer Pergolesi, Stravinsky decided, after beginning the project, not merely to orchestrate the music but to completely rework it in his own terms. Here, then, the borrowing process involves

Picasso's version of 18th-century Neapolitan costumes for the original production of the ballet, *Pulcinella,* in 1920.

not just general musical types but specific compositions. Moreover, Stravinsky's entire score, not just portions of it, is pieced together from the older music. The result is one of the most interesting and historically significant works of the century, especially in terms of Stravinsky's own later development. Although *Pulcinella* has the unmistakable flavor of eighteenth-century music, the original has been subtly transformed so that it takes on a new, and unexpectedly Stravinskian, character: accompanimental patterns from the original are rethought in more ostinato-like terms; added inner voices create a more dissonant harmonic structure; phrases are shortened or extended to produce rhythmic irregularities. The result is a miraculous renewal of the past through the impact of Stravinsky's irrepressibly modern musical sensibility.

From one point of view, *Pulcinella* might be seen as little more than a pastiche, a clever modern caricature of an earlier musical style. But its importance for Stravinsky's compositional outlook was profound, as he later pointed out: "*Pulcinella* was my discovery of the past, the epiphany through which the whole of my late work became possible."[4] This "discovery" led the composer to a highly personal reconsideration of the underlying structural principles of eighteenth-century Classicism, reformulated to provide a basis for his own work. The point for

4.   Stravinsky and Robert Craft, *Expositions and Developments* (New York, 1962), pp. 128–29.

Stravinsky was not to *return* to the past, however, but to revitalize certain basic traditional compositional assumptions in ways consistent with contemporary harmonic and rhythmic practice. The movement associated with this idea came to be known as neo-classicism. And although Stravinsky was himself its principal initiator and most effective and visible advocate, the neo-classical urge, taken in its broadest terms, can be seen to have influenced most of the prominent figures of the 1920s and 1930s. We have already noted its presence in the emphasis on simplicity and clarity of Les Six, and will even detect its traces in the postwar music of the Second Viennese School.

His residence in Switzerland during the war brought Stravinsky into much closer contact with the mainstream of the Western musical tradition, and it is tempting to see his move to Paris in 1920—as we have seen Stravinsky himself later did—as a symbolic expression of his turn to "classicism." However, the full extent of his stylistic transformation did not become apparent until 1923, when the premiere of the Octet for Winds created a sensation throughout the musical world. The composer many considered the most important of his time had apparently changed direction in midstream. The Russian "primitivism" of *The Rite* (and to a lesser extent even of *Histoire*) had vanished, superseded by a new set of esthetic hallmarks drawn largely from the musical heritage of the eighteenth century: formal clarity, expressive moderation, and personal detachment. In speaking of the Octet (which, characteristically, he referred to as a "musical object"), Stravinsky stressed that it was not an "emotive" piece but "a musical composition based on objective elements which are sufficient in themselves," and explained his choice of wind ensemble by referring to its ability "to render a certain rigidity of the form I had in mind."

New in the Octet, above all, are an acceptance of relatively traditional notions of contrapuntal writing and an adherence to clear-cut, standard classical forms. Throughout, the music betrays a strong linear impulse. (This characteristic especially struck contemporary listeners, and the phrase "back to Bach" became a sort of rallying cry for like-minded composers of the time.) Of the work's three movements, the first is symmetrical in structure with close similarities to sonata form, the second is a theme and variations, and the third is rondolike. Moreover, the tonal basis, especially in the outer movements, is more diatonic (and with more emphasis on major, as opposed to modal, scales) than one had come to expect of Stravinsky.

The Octet was the first of a series of compositions, covering Stravinsky's entire output up to the early 1950s, that are based on—though they often also work against—traditional compositional models and procedures. The influence of these works was enormous and formed the basis for the widespread neo-classical movement. The term "neo-classical" is somewhat misleading, however, for Stravinsky drew perhaps even more heavily on musical characteristics of the Baroque period than on those of Haydn, Mozart, and the late eighteenth century; and some commentators even prefer the designation "neo-baroque." But in fact, Stravinsky's "return to the past" was not actually tied to *any* given stylistic period, and eventually encompassed virtually every period of Western music.

Among the neo-classical works, it is important to distinguish between those (like *Pulcinella*) that use actual compositions as models and those (such as the Octet) in which only general stylistic features are taken as points of departure for completely original compositions. The majority are of the latter type, and give evidence of a remarkable range of stylistic sources. Immediately preceding the Octet, for example, Stravinsky completed the one-act opera *Mavra* (1922), which draws upon precedents from nineteenth-century Russian nationalist opera. After the Octet the sources are mainly Western in origin: Baroque keyboard concerto (Concerto for Piano and Winds [1924], Violin Concerto [1931]); concerto grosso ("Dumbarton Oaks" Concerto [1938]); Classical symphony and sonata (Piano Sonata [1924], Symphony in C [1940]); Classical serenade (Serenade in A [1925]); Baroque oratorio (*Oedipus Rex* [1927]); Classical opera (*The Rake's Progress* [1951]); and medieval liturgical music (Mass [1948]). Only once again during his middle period did Stravinsky again use specific works by another composer as the basis of his own: in the ballet *The Fairy's Kiss* (1928), where compositions by Tchaikovsky were reworked even more extensively than was the case in *Pulcinella*.

Not every work of the period, however, betrays an unmistakable stylistic prototype. Two of the most important, the *Symphony of Psalms* (1930) and the Symphony in Three Movements (1945), defy easy categorization. Baroque references abound (notably in the fugal second movement of the former work and in the *concertante* instrumental writing of the latter), but these are combined with other elements that resist unequivocal attribution. Yet in all of Stravinsky's compositions of these years one feels an emphasis on limits rather than excesses, on matters of formal construction and balance rather than personal expression.

In certain respects Stravinsky's neo-classicism parallels the esthetic program put forward by Cocteau and Les Six, but his music far exceeds that of his French contemporaries in conceptual richness and technical complexity. Stravinsky himself insisted during this period that he did not intend his music to "say" anything beyond the musical relationships themselves: "I consider that music is, by its very nature, essentially powerless to *express* anything at all," he wrote; "music is given to us with the sole purpose of establishing an order in things." Yet the very esthetic stringency of his approach—so different from the casual, even frivolous attitude cultivated by Poulenc and Milhaud in the 1920s— gave birth to musical statements of remarkable expressive power.

In his 1936 *Autobiography* Stravinsky remarked on the "need for restriction, for deliberately submitting to a style," and went on to say that "in borrowing a form already established and consecrated, the creative artist is not in the least restricting manifestation of his own personality. On the contrary, it is more detached and stands out better when it moves within the definite limits of a convention."[5] What matters to him, then, is not the specific style but the act of submission and restriction itself. The fact that Stravinsky came to the Western tradition as an "outsider" no doubt accounts for his ability to change stylistic sources so easily, and it may also help explain his capacity to fashion musical conceptions of such startling originality despite the overt use of traditional references. With his own musical roots firmly planted in Russia, he could approach Western stylistic models with a certain neutral detachment, treating them like "foreign objects" to be transformed and manipulated according to his own inclinations, in ways consistent with the basic compositional conceptions developed during his earlier years. Thus Stravinsky's neo-classical works betray the same structural techniques as those of his Russian period: tonal polarity, static harmonic progressions, rhythmic juxtaposition, formal stratification, etc. Even the pieces most closely tied to earlier stylistic models, however different they may appear on the surface, are unmistakably his own.

Brief excerpts from two piano pieces, the Sonata (1924) and Serenade in A (1925), illustrate some of the technical features characteristic of Stravinsky's neo-classicism. The opening movement of the Serenade (Example VIII-4a) is completely diatonic, confined to notes from the F-major scale, and the harmonic basis is essentially triadic. Yet there is no tonal motion at all in the traditional sense: virtually the entire passage is focused on an F-major chord in first inversion. The strongest melodic emphasis, however, is not on F but on A, which figures prominently both as the focal note around which the top line circles in mm. 1–5 and as a more or less constant pedal in the bass. The ambiguity as to whether the passage is really in A (as the melodic structure suggests) or F (as does the harmonic construction) is typical of Stravinsky. So too is the "weak" cadence on A minor at the end of the phrase (m. 6) that finally resolves the ambiguity. (It is "weak" in that there is no strong motion *toward* the tonic A, since the A has received special emphasis throughout; the only pitch change that articulates the cadence is the displacement of F by E, with both A and C remaining more or less constant throughout the passage.)

The phrase's F-major / A-minor polarity and the static harmonic conception are familiar from Stravinsky's prewar music, although their appearance within the transparent textures of the Serenade, colored by

5.   *An Autobiography* (New York, 1936), p. 132.

Example VIII-4: STRAVINSKY

a. Serenade in A, first movement, mm. 1–6

b. Piano Sonata, first movement, mm. 13–22

the bright major harmonic sound, is characteristic of his neo-classical style. Similarly, the motivic structure of the passage—especially the incessant circling of the top line around the same few notes—is based on techniques of repetition and rhythmic modification developed in the earlier work. Stravinsky's neo-classicism, then, is not so much a completely new compositional approach as a rethinking in fresh terms of an underlying method that had been firmly established long before.

Similarly, the opening of the principal theme of the first movement of the Piano Sonata (Ex. VIII-4b; see p. 175) is also based mainly upon a diatonic scale (C major) and projects an essentially triadic harmonic structure. Here, however, there is little tonal ambiguity, as both hands present material accommodated by a C-major framework. Rather, tonal tension results from the unusual coordination of the two hands, which—although equally oriented toward C—move against each other with complete harmonic independence. The accompanimental left hand alternates arpeggiations of chords that in a more traditional tonal context would indicate normal tonic and dominant functions. Yet these functions seem to have no influence on the melodic line presented in the right hand, which suggests a harmonic structure directly opposed to the one in the lower hand: that is, it tends to imply tonic support where the other offers a dominant harmony, and vice versa.

In such passages Stravinsky works with the "vocabulary" of traditional functional tonality in a manner that recalls the techniques of cubist painting, also developed in France in the early twentieth century. In both cases objects of "conventional reality"—in the case of the Sonata, the standard harmonic entities of the old tonal system—are broken up into their constituent parts and then put back together, rearranged into new, more "abstract" configurations. The "modulation" to D major in the tenth measure of the Sonata offers a striking example of such a restructuring of conventional relationships, here primarily in the area of rhythm and phrase structure. The diminished-seventh chord on the last beat of m. 9 provides a clear dominant function to the new key, establishing the new tonal area through a traditional key-defining harmonic relationship. Yet the context of the progression is completely distorted with respect to traditional practice: the modulating diminished seventh appears suddenly, without warning, following nine measures of a basically static C-major area, and then moves immediately—after only a single beat—to the new key of D major. There is no preparation, either rhythmic or harmonic. The result is a fascinating rethinking of Stravinsky's long-standing practice of abruptly juxtaposing two static tonal fields (here C and D major) into neo-classical terms.

Such purely diatonic passages, often with strong suggestions of major and minor keys, occur frequently in Stravinsky's music of this period, usually in the form of relatively static harmonic blocks. (This predilection soon gave rise to the designation "white-note music.") Tension is then maintained through polarities established by competing tonal areas, such as the pull between F major and A minor in the first movement of the *Serenade* or between C major and E minor in the first movement of the *Symphony in C*. All three movements of the *Symphony of Psalms* participate in a set of multiple tonal relationships involving C minor, E♭ major, E minor, and G major. But chromatic passages also occur in neo-classical Stravinsky, often based on elements drawn from the octatonic scale (another connection with the earlier works). Such passages are usually set off against diatonic ones, however, the two types interacting with each other in complex and often equivocal relationships.

In the first movement of the *Symphony of Psalms* octatonic and diatonic elements compete in a typically Stravinskian manner. The orchestral introduction opens with a single E-minor chord, immediately followed by two arpeggiated dominant-seventh-type chords, the first with B♭ root and the second with G root (Example VIII-5b). All three chords are related by minor thirds and are drawn from a single octatonic scale (Ex. VIII-5a). The first segment of the introduction is entirely derived from these materials. The single, heavily accented E-minor triad appears four times, alternating with music derived from the two seventh chords (another instance of crosscutting) and providing a tonal focus against which that less stable music is projected.

Example VIII-5: STRAVINSKY, *Symphony of Psalms,* first movement

a. Tonal material

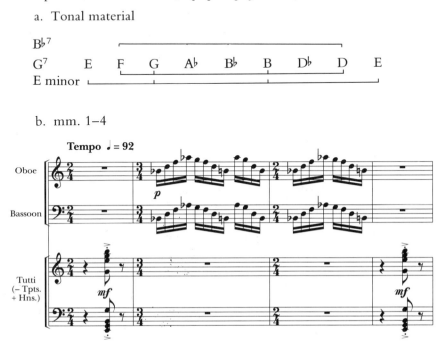

b. mm. 1–4

c. mm. 1–5 after No. 2

Fourteen measures later a new segment begins (Example VIII-5c), in which the diatonic implications of the E-minor chord are made explicit. The new segment opens with music drawn entirely from the E Phrygian scale: E-F-G-A-B-C-D-E. Since the characteristic lowered second and seventh degrees of the tonic E (F♮ and D♮), as well as the E minor triad itself, are common to both the octatonic and Phrygian collections used by Stravinsky, the two passages are closely related, even complementary. Moreover, later (not shown in the examples) both segments undergo chromatic alterations that associate them still more strongly.

Throughout his neo-classical phase Stravinsky continued to write ballet scores, including *Apollon musagète* (Apollon, Leader of the Muses, 1928), *Jeu de cartes* (Card Game, 1936), and *Orpheus* (1947). An especially significant part of his output, dating back to the years in Switzerland, was a series of innovative stage works involving acting, pantomime, singing, dancing, and narration. These works, conforming to no previous genre, established a new form of contemporary music theater that attempted to demystify and depersonalize dramatic action, to make it less realistic by making it more stylized and ritualistic.

In *The Wedding* and *Histoire du soldat* the instruments are placed on the stage in full view of the audience, while in *Histoire, Oedipus Rex,* and *Perséphone* a narrator serves to "distance" the audience from the action. In *Reynard* and *The Wedding* the singers are positioned in the orchestra and are not even associated with particular mime or dance figures onstage, rather switching from role to role (with female voices often assuming male roles and vice versa) at the composer's will. A more fundamental rejection of the realistic tenets of nineteenth-century opera and drama would be difficult to imagine. Yet this new dramatic direction did not prevent Stravinsky from also writing a fully neo-classical opera, *The Rake's Progress* (1951), for which he drew heavily upon the conventions of late eighteenth-century—especially Mozartian—opera, complete with set numbers and secco recitative.

Since, unlike the other great composers of his generation, Stravinsky lived well into the post–World War II period, participating in some of its major musical developments, we will return to him again. In many respects he reflected more acutely than any other figure of the first half of the twentieth century the altered compositional situation. Deprived of a common musical language, the modern composer had to construct artificial ones out of whatever materials were available. Stravinsky, the perennial "outsider" cut off from his native land, searched through the entire repertory of Western music history in pursuit of a basis for his own work. The preference for what he called the "impersonal formulas of a remote past"—whether literally remote, as in the models for his neo-classical "reconstructions," or figuratively so, as in those for his serial works, to be discussed in Part III—offered him a powerful symbol for the modern artist's creative isolation. His music speaks with uncommon force of a common plight.

BARTÓK

After the temporary retreat from public life brought on by the rejection of *Bluebeard's Castle,* Bartók achieved a resounding success in 1917 with the premiere of his ballet *The Wooden Prince,* based (like the opera) on a scenario by Béla Balázs. This in turn stimulated the production of the opera the following year. Signs of renewed activity on Bartók's part had already been evident: several shorter pieces, including the Suite for piano, Op. 14, and two song cycles, appeared in 1916; and in 1915 work had begun on the Second String Quartet, which would be completed in 1917, the year of the ballet.

During his years of compositional inactivity Bartók had studied the scores of his advanced European contemporaries, and this left a definite mark on his own music. *The Wooden Prince* suggests the influence of Stravinsky, while the Second Quartet reveals parallels with Schoenberg. By comparison with Bartók's First Quartet, nine years earlier, the latter work is motivically more economical, formally tighter, and more consistently contrapuntal in conception.

The new Quartet also departed completely from the triadic basis underlying almost all of Bartók's prior music. Much of the harmonic and melodic content is derived from a common intervallic source, a

Example VIII-6: BARTÓK, String Quartet No. 2, first movement

a. Beginning

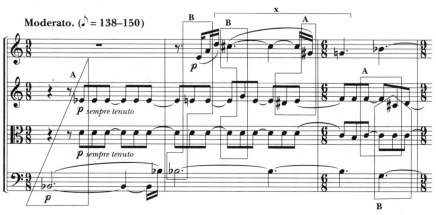

b. Beginning of recapitulation

three-note basic cell consisting of a perfect fourth and a minor second. In the opening measures (Example VIII-6a) the perfect fourth is especially emphasized, almost always associated with a minor second, which may appear either inside the fourth or outside it. (In the example, cells with internal seconds are marked **A,** those with external seconds are marked **B.**) The first violin plays a related four-note cell in which the tritone figures prominently (marked **x**); this is formed by two overlapping statements of cell **B:** D-C♯-G♯ and C♯-G♯-G♮. Although relatively unobtrusive here, it takes on considerable prominence during the course of the quartet, especially at the recapitulation (Example VIII-6b). This cell came to be especially favored by Bartók, playing an increasingly important role in his works of the 1920s and 1930s.

The recognition Bartók gained from *The Wooden Prince* soon spread westward; as a result, he acquired a Viennese publisher, assuring wider circulation for his music. (His few published works to date had circulated only in Hungary.) His music was now heard in such European centers as Vienna (thanks especially to Schoenberg's support) and London. During the 1920s he made frequent appearances throughout Europe as a concert pianist, often performing his own works.

Despite his emergence as a figure of international prominence, Bartók's artistic situation remained precarious during the interwar years. Hungary was in a state of political and economic turmoil, and the unstable political situation created serious difficulties for composers, especially those who, like Bartók, were actively involved in the effort to reestablish a national musical culture. To add to his problems, Bartók's next work, another ballet, *The Miraculous Mandarin* (1919), was banned because of the eroticism of its scenario. The ballet's heated aggressiveness and morbid tone may well reflect the emotional stress attendant upon life in Hungary at the time.

Here and in the works of the next few years, Bartók's music takes on something of the intensity of prewar European expressionism. This is most evident in the two Sonatas for violin and piano (1921 and 1922, respectively), striking in their extraordinary textual density (especially the first) and rhapsodic, freely evolving formal structures; although not yet "atonal" in the Schoenbergian sense, their tonal focus is so ambiguous as to produce a sense of unrelieved instability. (In 1920 Bartók had expressed what was, for him, an uncharacteristic opinion: "The music of our time strains decidedly toward atonality.") The harmonic structure is uncompromisingly dissonant and nontriadic, and even the motivic development—usually so transparent in Bartók's music—is obscured by constant, freely evolving transformations. Moreover, the violin and piano parts share so little common musical material that they seem to have been conceived independently of each other.

Even in the most extreme works of this period, however, Bartók never entirely abandoned the modal-tonal approach he had derived from his folk-music studies. Although largely hidden by the chromatic surface, some tonal basis is detectable even in the violin sonatas. Bartók's concern for accommodating the new elements of his postwar music to his established folk orientation is evident in the *Improvisations on Hungarian Peasant Songs,* Op. 20, the folk-song settings for piano composed in 1920 (thus just prior to the violin sonatas) that we briefly discussed earlier (see Example IV-7). As noted, the *Improvisations* differ from the earlier settings in that triads are entirely avoided, and the underlying modal basis is distorted to produce sharply dissonant and chromatic harmonies in the accompaniment. Yet since the borrowed melodic material is preserved more or less intact, a definite modal-tonal focus is retained. Here again one observes Bartók's capacity for reconciling seemingly incompatible elements.

Nevertheless, Bartók must have instinctively felt that the direction his music took in the early postwar years would eventually undermine his deeply anchored roots in Eastern European modality. It also placed him at odds with the prevailing European tendency toward neo-classicism, with which Bartók had become well acquainted during his travels as a pianist. In any event, his next composition, the Dance Suite for orchestra (1923)—a work that, although not based on actual folk sources, intentionally imitates such music—reveals a definite stylistic reversal, a move toward greater textual clarity, simpler motivic structure, and tighter tonal orientation. But then, from 1923 to 1926, Bartók produced no substantial new works at all, while still busily engaged with his folk researches, piano teaching, and performing tours—a circumstance suggesting that at this point he felt a need to take stock of his work and consider its future course.

In 1926 three major piano compositions appeared, announcing his return to creative activity: the Piano Sonata, the *Out of Doors Suite,* and the First Piano Concerto. These reveal another decided shift in purpose and direction; while retaining something of the more dissonant character of the early postwar pieces (as well as the elemental force and rhythmic vitality typical of all Bartók's music), they are more sharply defined tonally and more closely tied to traditional formal models. Indeed, in many respects this music has taken on a distinct neo-classical cast. Especially in the Piano Concerto, passages of Bach-inspired counterpoint remind one of Stravinsky's music of this period, notably the Octet and the Concerto for Piano and Winds. Yet this music is also very different from Stravinskian neo-classicism, lacking the detachment, coolness, and restraint normally associated with that style, let alone any hint of popular urban music—the music hall, circus, or jazz.

Nevertheless, in the works following 1926 Bartók did forge his own brand of "new-classical" synthesis, in which the diverse elements of his style were welded into a more tightly knit language. The compositions of the late 1920s and the 1930s incorporate a wealth of different scalar resources—including diatonic, whole-tone, octatonic, and chromatic types—into a remarkably flexible new stylistic amalgam. But even when, as often, the music is fully chromatic and thus, as in the Viennese atonalists, apparently implies the equality of all twelve pitches, the chromaticism is almost always generated by a combination of simpler, nonchromatic elements that retain a certain degree of individuality. By arriving at complex pitch configurations through the addition of simpler and more basic building blocks, Bartók was able to integrate a remarkably varied fund of pitch material, ranging from the simplest diatonicism to full twelve-tone chromaticism.

Passages from *Mikrokosmos,* a graded six-volume series of short pieces for piano students, illustrate different solutions to the integration of such opposed scalar types, in this case octatonic and diatonic. In the opening phrase of the piece "Diminished Fifth" (Example VIII-7a) the entirely octatonic scale is generated by a combination of two diatonic tetrachords a diminished fifth apart, each assigned to one of the pianist's hands in a quasi-imitative texture. At the beginning of "From the Island

Example VIII-7: BARTÓK, *Mikrokosmos*

a. No. 101, "Diminished Fifth," mm. 1–5

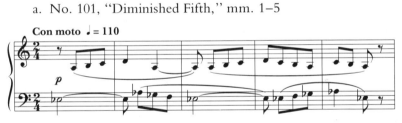

b. No. 109, "From the Island of Bali," mm. 1–4

c. No. 109, "From the Island of Bali," mm. 23–26

of Bali" (Example VIII-7b) the octatonic material is again generated by combining two four-note units in an imitative texture, but here the individual units are essentially chromatic rather than diatonic. Later in the piece (Example VIII-7c), however, Bartók alters the lower four-note group by raising its two lowest pitches (G♯ and A) a half step (to A and B♭), while omitting the upper unit entirely in favor of octave doubling. This "diatonization" of the original material momentarily lends the music a more definite tonal focus, directing it more clearly toward E♭ (the A♮, sounding like a leading tone to the dominant B♭, parallels D, the leading tone to the tonic).

Between 1927 and 1939 Bartók combined this orderly yet flexible approach to pitch organization with an increasingly rigorous conception of formal structure, in a series of substantial instrumental compositions: the Third and Fourth String Quartets (1927, 1928), the Second Piano Concerto (1931), the Fifth String Quartet (1934), the *Music for Strings, Percussion, and Celesta* (1936), the Sonata for Two Pianos and Percussion (1937), the Second Violin Concerto (1938), and the Sixth String Quartet (1939). Especially characteristic is a new emphasis on tightly organized arch forms (Bartók called them "bridge forms"), in which larger symmetrical patterns are built using movements paired by means of motivic and formal correspondences. The Third String Quartet provides a rudimentary example: in its single tripartite movement the third part is a highly compressed and varied restatement of the first. But the idea is first fully realized a year later, in the Fourth Quartet. In this five-movement plan the first and last movements are allegros based on similar thematic ideas; the second and fourth movements are scherzos, the latter a free variation of the former; and the central slow movement has a symmetrical A B A structure of its own, serving as the core for the entire A B C B A structure.

The Fifth String Quartet follows a similar plan, although here the middle movement is a scherzo, the second and fourth are complementary slow movements. The Second Piano Concerto and Violin Concerto offer three-movement versions of the arch idea. Indeed, all of Bartók's compositions of this period are characterized by unusual formal strictness, yet the expressive range of the music remains broad. The influence of folk sources, never far from the surface, is at times still very much in the foreground, as in the consciously folk-inspired *Cantata profana* of 1930. The figures of Liszt and Debussy, so important in Bartók's early stylistic evolution, also remain discernible, especially in the slow movements written in the "night music" style, setting impressionistic color effects and fragmentary melodic materials within an essentially static harmonic framework. (This style derives its name from its earliest instance, the third movement of the *Out of Doors Suite*, entitled "Night Music.") Other works exploit the coloristic effects produced by special instrumental combinations (e.g., the *Music for Strings,*

Percussion, and Celesta, which also features antiphonal division of the strings) or use novel instrumental techniques in standard ensembles; for example, Bartók's distinctly personal approach to the string quartet medium entails an elaborate use of such special effects as glissando, *sul ponticello, col legno,* and pizzicato.

In the latter part of the 1930s, especially in the Violin Concerto and Sixth String Quartet, Bartók began to return to a more traditional and functional conception of tonality that not only reincorporated triadic harmony but even included tonic-dominant relationships. This seems to have occurred, not as a reaction against the progressive aspects of his mature style, but rather as Bartók's attempt to encompass as much of his musical heritage as possible within his late work. In the Violin Concerto not only are triads frequently encountered, but also, at the other extreme, a twelve-tone row, complete with the normal serial transformations. Typically, Bartók is here again concerned with synthesis: the row is conceived in a purely thematic way (it provides the basis for the contrasting themes of both the first and last movements) and is given a strong tonal orientation.

With the approach of World War II, Bartók's intense dislike of the Nazis made it impossible for him to remain in Hungary, and he emigrated to the United States, where he settled in the fall of 1940. His early years in the new country were particularly difficult, despite a modest grant enabling him to continue folk-music studies at Columbia University for a while. The effort of making ends meet, as well as the difficulty of adjusting to his new surroundings, impeded creative work. Between 1939 and 1943, for the third time in his career, Bartók went through a period of several years without producing any large works.

During the early part of 1943 his health suffered a serious setback, and during convalescence (only temporary, unfortunately) he again took up composition. Four sizable works ensued: the Concerto for Orchestra (1943), the Sonata for Solo Violin (1944), and two others that remained unfinished at his death in 1945, the Third Piano Concerto and a Viola Concerto. (Both were completed by his friend the Hungarian-born composer Tibor Serly. The Piano Concerto only required scoring of the last seventeen bars, but the entire Viola Concerto had to be reconstructed and orchestrated from sketches.) In these works Bartók further pursued the course of simplification and codification undertaken in the late 1930s. The opening of the Third Piano Concerto, with its unabashedly tonal accompaniment and a diatonic melody of unmistakable Hungarian character, is typical (Example VIII-8; see p. 186).

Directness and simplicity also mark the formal structure of these final works, of which especially the two completed ones, despite Bartók's failing health, show little sign of artistic decline—indeed, the Concerto for Orchestra ranks among Bartók's finest compositions.

Bartók's achievement was in certain respects unique. He rethought

Example VIII-8: BARTÓK, Piano Concerto No. 3, first movement, mm. 1–5

the esthetic orientation and constructive aspects of eighteenth- and nineteenth-century music in distinctly twentieth-century terms with perhaps less sense of disruption than any of his major contemporaries. (Only Berg comes to mind as a possible rival in this regard.) Bartók's logical extension of the thematic, formal, and tonal techniques of his predecessors, and his fundamentally nationalistic orientation, reinterpreted within the more scientific orientation of a new age, combined to produce a remarkably traditional "tone" in his work. Unlike that of many of his progressive contemporaries, his music does not seem to play itself off so much "against" traditional elements (as one feels so strongly in Stravinsky, for example) as to work directly "with" them. In this light it is significant that among that small group of figures born in the 1870s and 1880s who were largely responsible for the twentieth-century musical revolution, Bartók was the only one who had from his earliest years a "normal" professional musical training. This may also explain why, of the music created by this critical group, only his has been accepted essentially whole into the standard concert repertory.

CHAPTER IX

The Twelve-Tone System

SCHOENBERG

For Schoenberg the early postwar years marked a period of reconsideration and consolidation. The outbreak of hostilities in 1914 had found the composer already in a state of artistic uncertainty. After *Pierrot lunaire* (1912) and *Die glückliche Hand* (1913) his output diminished significantly; by 1916 only the Four Orchestral Songs, Op. 22, had appeared, and thereafter no new compositions until 1923. The reduced productivity was partly accounted for by the war: Schoenberg was called into active service in December 1915, released within a year for health reasons, and then called again in September 1917.

Yet the principal cause of his creative crisis lay deeper and was essentially artistic in nature. Schoenberg had reached a point of no longer trusting the largely "intuitive" character of his prewar music. Despite the temporary sense of creative release offered by the freer and less systematic compositional methods of his atonal music, he came to believe them inadequate as a basis for extended, developmental compositions. Thus, not unlike Stravinsky, he emerged from the war years determined to reestablish stronger and more conscious links to the older Western tradition. But for a composer so deeply committed to the historical irreversibility of music's evolution toward total chromaticism, this could not take the form of a return to diatonicism or a new kind of tonality. What was needed was a system for chromatic music in some way analogous to the tonal one, a system capable of incorporating the new dissonant melodic and chordal structures characteristic of twentieth-century music within a more consciously conceived and systematically ordered framework.

Schoenberg believed it to be his own historical mission to develop such a system, and the seven-year silence (1916–23) indicates how difficult he found his self-imposed task. Yet these were not years of inactivity; he worked on a number of projects, most notably the unfinished oratorio *Die Jakobsleiter (Jacob's Ladder)*, which occupied him off and on between 1917 and 1922, and in which he first began to explore his new structural ideas. Moreover, the first three compositions he published in 1923–24 contained individual movements dating back as far as 1920.

In 1921 Schoenberg confided to one of his pupils that he had made a discovery that would "insure the supremacy of German music for the next hundred years." This was the twelve-tone system, which he believed would permit the continuation of traditional musical values in a manner consistent with the path already traversed by twentieth-century musical evolution. Writing later, Schoenberg explained that he developed the system out of a desire for more conscious control over the new chromatic materials he had heretofore employed only intuitively—in his own words, "as in a dream. . . . Strongly convincing as this dream may have been, the conviction that these new sounds obey the laws of nature and of our manner of thinking—the conviction that order, logic, comprehensibility and form cannot be present without obedience to such laws—forces the composer along the road to exploration. He must find, if not laws or rules, at least ways to justify the dissonant character of these harmonies and their successions."[1] For Schoenberg, then, the twelve-tone system was able to provide—and thus replace—the structural differentiations formerly furnished by tonality.

The system's basic principles are simply described. Each composition draws its basic pitch material from a uniquely chosen sequence of the twelve pitches of the chromatic scale, known as the twelve-tone "row" or "series." In addition to the original, or "prime" form (conventionally designated *P*) of the row, three other related forms are used (see Example IX-1). The retrograde *(R)* form reverses the sequence of pitches and intervals. In the inversion *(I)* each of the original intervals is inverted so that, for example, a perfect fifth upward becomes a perfect fifth downward (or a perfect fourth upward). Thus, the first interval in Example IX-1, the major third upward Eb-G♮, becomes a major third downward, Eb-Cb (the latter pitch is spelled B♮ in the example; enharmonic spellings are not differentiated in this totally chromatic system), which is equivalent to a minor sixth upward; the minor second downward between the fifth and sixth pitches, C♯-C♮, becomes a minor second upward, F♮-F♯, equivalent to a major seventh downward, etc. Finally,

---

1.   "Composition with Twelve Tones (1)," *Style and Idea: Selected Writings of Arnold Schoenberg*, ed. Leonard Stein (New York, 1975), p. 226.

Example IX-1: The four forms of a tone row

the retrograde may also be inverted (the "retrograde inversion" or *RI* form).

In addition, any of these four basic forms of the row may be transposed to begin on any other pitch. (The transposition level is conventionally indicated by an Arabic numeral following the designation of the row form, indicating the number of half steps upward from the untransposed form: thus the designation *P*-0 indicates the untransposed prime, *P*-5 indicates the prime transposed up a perfect fourth [i.e., five half steps], *R*-1 indicates the retrograde transposed up a minor second.) The four basic forms of the row, multiplied by their twelve possible transpositions, yield forty-eight possible versions of the original row. Normally, however, only a selection of these will be used in a given piece, the choice being determined by compositional considerations.

For example, in his first completely twelve-tone work, the Suite for Piano, Op. 25 (1924), Schoenberg uses only eight different row forms (Example IX-2; see p. 190). He limits himself to these particular forms, all related by transpositions of the tritone (i.e., six half steps), in order to exploit a significant characteristic of the chosen row: the fact that its first and last notes are a tritone apart. Thus the two "forward" forms of the untransposed row, the prime (*P*-0) and inversion (*I*-0), both begin on E and end on B♭ (since the inversion of a tritone is itself a tritone); similarly, the untransposed "backward" forms, the retrograde (*R*-0) and retrograde inversion (*RI*-0), both begin on B♭ and end on E. In addition to these four untransposed forms, Schoenberg uses only the four transpositions that are tritone-related (that is, *P*-6, *I*-6, *R*-6, and *RI*-6). He is thus able to establish a "closed" system: all eight row forms have the same two notes for their outer pitches, E and B♭ (or B♭ and E).

Although the row determines the succession of pitches used in a piece, it does not determine their registers or their durations. Nor does it prescribe (though it may influence) the music's textural layout or its form.

Example IX-2: SCHOENBERG, Piano Suite, Op. 25, eight forms of the tone
row

It is, in other words, an "abstract" structure, a set of potential relation-ships, that must be embodied in the musical details of a particular com-position. Several brief excerpts from the Piano Suite (Example IX-3) suggest the freedom and variety with which Schoenberg employs his row, even in his earliest complete twelve-tone compositions. At the beginning of the sixth movement (Gigue; Example IX-3a) one row appears at a time, in strict order: first P-0, then I-6. (Note also: [1] Schoenberg articulates the end of each row with a sforzando followed by a rest; [2] the immediate repetition of B♭—the last note of the first row and the initial note of the second—is emphasized by its retention in the same register; and [3] the tritone G-D♭, common to both rows [the third and fourth notes of each], is played as a simultaneity in both statements and returns in the same register.)

At the opening of the third movement (Musette; Example IX-3b) the row is treated as if it were three separable four-note groups (notes 1-4, 5-8, and 9-12), which can be freely combined with one another to produce the total twelve-tone aggregate. Within each group, ordering is usually (though not always) preserved, but the sequence of the four-note groups relative to one another is not; thus, in the first row, notes 9-12 precede notes 5-8. Furthermore, G, which belongs to the first four-note group of both forms used in this excerpt (again P-0 and I-6), is employed as a pedal throughout (an idea suggested by the title Musette, a dancelike piece containing a drone suggestive of a bagpipe).

Finally, at the beginning of the fourth movement (Intermezzo; Example IX-3c) the row is again divided into three four-note groups, but here the first group is used as a constantly repeating "accompaniment" (in the upper staff) for a two-part melodic idea (in the lower staff) resulting from the simultaneous presentation of notes 5-8 (upper line) and 9-12

Example IX-3: SCHOENBERG, Piano Suite, Op. 25

a. Gigue, mm. 1–2

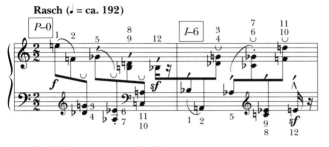

b. Musette, mm. 1–3

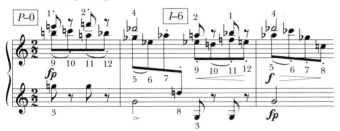

c. Intermezzo, mm. 1–3

(lower line).

Although in his later twelve-tone music Schoenberg normally tends to adhere to the order of the row much more strictly than in the Piano Suite, we shall find that the idea of treating the series as a partially unordered twelve-tone aggregate continued to interest him and led him at times to handle row orderings with considerable freedom.

Now that the basic properties of the twelve-tone system have been introduced, its position within Schoenberg's compositional development can be better understood as a gradual outgrowth of two already well-established features of the prewar works: (1) the tendency to derive melodic material from a limited number of basic intervallic cells through variation procedures and (2) the tendency toward chromatic saturation through the use of all twelve pitches in more or less constant rotation. An important step toward systemization of the latter is already found in the opening segment of the unfinished *Jakobsleiter,* in which an ostinato figure of six different pitches is combined with a sustained chordal background comprising the six remaining pitches. Thus the possibility of combining complementary six-note groups, or hexachords, to create a twelve-tone field, one of the most important principles of Schoenbergian twelve-tone music, interested the composer well before he consciously formulated the new system. A more systematic approach to intervallic aspects of atonality is also evident in passages from *Die Jakobsleiter,* but this aspect of the evolution of Schoenberg's thought can be more profitably traced in the two completed compositions that appeared one year prior to the Suite: the Five Piano Pieces, Op. 23, and the Serenade, Op. 24, both published in 1923.

While each of these works includes one movement using a complete twelve-tone series, each also contains movements with other types of ordered series consisting of either more or less than twelve notes, indicating that Schoenberg experimented with various forms of serial organization before ultimately deciding upon the twelve-tone approach. For example, the third of the Five Piano Pieces, Op. 23, is constructed largely from a five-note series, the second contains a nine-note series, and the first has a number of different series, ranging in length from three to twenty-one notes and often appearing simultaneously. But all these series share two significant attributes: they are ordered, which distinguishes them from the earlier atonal works based on unordered cells or sets, and they are treated as "abstract" intervallic successions that can be presented in different rhythmic and registral guises. Two passages from the first piece (Example IX-4a and 4b) illustrate a relatively simple transformation of an untransposed seven-note series (located in the upper staff of both excerpts). Although the order of the pitches remains the same, both rhythm and octave placement are treated independently.

It is not difficult to see why Schoenberg soon ceased experimenting with other types of series and concentrated exclusively on rows containing all twelve pitches. The latter provided him with a "closed" system encompassing all of the material available in the twelve-tone chromatic scale, as well as an orderly means for handling this material. As the first really systematic attempt to provide a rational, coherent, and inclusive framework for post-tonal chromatic music, Schoenberg's method became a topic of intense debate, which unfortunately tended to divide composers of the time into two rigidly opposed groups: those

Example IX-4: SCHOENBERG, Five Piano Pieces, Op. 23, No. 1

a. mm. 1–3

b. mm. 17–18

who, following Stravinsky, favored the preservation of some type of tonality and those who, like Schoenberg, adopted the twelve-tone system. Although this second group was confined for the most part to Schoenberg's own circle of students, the new method, because of its systematic and comprehensive nature, had an impact on the musical thought of the period far out of proportion to the limited extent of its adoption.

Moreover, in several important aspects, Schoenberg's postwar development actually mirrored that of the more tonally oriented composers. He too sought clarification and order after the uncertainty of the prewar years. Since Schoenberg worked within a rigorously atonal and chromatic context, while composers like Stravinsky used a more diatonic and tonal idiom, the differences in pitch structure are naturally fundamental, and, thanks to the still intense chromaticism and the jagged, angular melodic quality, Schoenberg's postwar music retains something of the "expressionistic" flavor of his prewar works. Yet if one considers the nonpitch components of Schoenberg's twelve-tone music, with due regard for the influence of twelve-tone thinking on his overall style, important points of contact with his contemporaries can be found. Characteristic of the Suite for Piano, for example, is a new emphasis on more lucid textures and leaner contrapuntal writing. The massive harmonic complexes so prevalent in the atonal works are now largely gone, while the motivic and formal structure has been greatly clarified.

Reconsidering from a more general stylistic point of view the three excerpts from the Suite in Example IX-3, we see that not only are the textures relatively transparent; the thematic and motivic conception are almost "classical" in layout. Thus Example IX-3a contains two symmetrically balanced formal units (each comprising a statement of the row), the second an almost exact inversion of the first, their identity of rhythmic structure and phrase length emphasized by the previously mentioned sforzandos on the final notes. In Example IX-3b the rhythmic structure of the first four quarter notes is repeated exactly in the second four, a symmetrical correspondence emphasized by the repeated rhythm and the inverted octave leap in the pedal G. Finally, the right-hand accompaniment of Example IX-3c reveals a clear pattern of repetition, against which the left hand states two rhythmically similar motivic groups. Notable in all three examples is the fact that the music's textural layout and thematic organization are closely tied to the particular disposition of the row structure.

Schoenberg's concern for establishing his own variety of "new-classicism" is also reflected in a renewed preoccupation with large-scale instrumental composition and a reliance on traditional formal types. The Piano Suite, the first completely twelve-tone composition, seems to announce this almost "programmatically" by its use of standardized Baroque dance forms. Two movements, the Musette and the Menuet and Trio, even contain exact repeats of extended sections, a practice Schoenberg had avoided completely in his "free" atonal music. (However, even in the twelve-tone music such repetitions—which also appear in certain movements of the Serenade—remain uncommon, no doubt because they are inconsistent with Schoenberg's basic principle of "developing variation.")

The Woodwind Quintet, Op. 26 (1924), which followed the Piano Suite, was the first twelve-tone piece to contain extended instrumental forms. Each of its four movements is based on a standardized Classical type: sonata form, scherzo with trio, song form (A B A), and rondo. The row of the Quintet, unlike that of the more harmonically conceived Suite, is handled in an essentially linear manner, with all the melodic and accompanimental material derived from the series and its transformations. The polyphonic construction reveals close correlations with the highly motivic structure of such earlier compositions as the First String Quartet and the first of the Five Orchestral Pieces, in which all thematic material is derived from a small number of motives stated at or near the beginning.

Indeed, the twelve-tone works might be understood simply as a more systematic version of the same intensely motivic and variational conception of thematic development, except that here the basic material—the row—is an abstract series of intervals without any motivic content of its own. Whereas a motive is a compositionally realized musical event, the row "predates" the actual piece—it is, one says, "pre-compositional." Schoenberg himself seems to have conceived of his row as a sort of pre-compositional fund for motivic possibilities, and he emphasized that he thought of it in essentially thematic terms. In a work such as the Quintet, then, *everything* becomes "motivic" in the sense that all of its material is drawn from the same basic source, the row. (Significantly, it was with the Quintet that Schoenberg, aware of the difficulty of recognizing the principal voice in such a rigorously thematic context, began using special notational signs to distinguish between main and secondary parts.)

Schoenberg's discovery of a more conscious and orderly way of controlling his compositions had a liberating effect on his output. After the long period of silence and experimentation, a flood of new works suddenly appeared, all written in the new system and all exploring the traditional genres abandoned during the atonal period. The Quintet was followed by three additional large-scale instrumental works: the Suite for seven instruments (1926), the Third String Quartet (1927), and the Variations for Orchestra (1928). Then came a period devoted to operatic composition: the one-act comic opera *Von heute auf morgen* (From Today until Tomorrow) was completed in 1929, and the first two acts of the three-act biblical opera *Moses und Aron* were written between 1930 and 1932. The latter work, which remained unfinished at Schoenberg's death (though the two completed acts have since been widely performed), is a moving statement of the composer's own spiritual philosophy, an idealistic view of religious faith and belief free from all material considerations.

In these early twelve-tone compositions Schoenberg continued to refine his use of the new system. An especially important technique, which, following a gradual evolution, was first introduced on an extended scale in the Variations for Orchestra and systematically exploited thereafter, is "combinatoriality," the simultaneous presentation of two different forms of a single row so constructed that new twelve-tone aggregates are created by the combination of their hexachords. This is illustrated by two forms of the row used in the Piano Piece, Op. 33a (1929), P-0 and I-5 (Example IX-5a). Note that the total pitch content (though not the ordering) of the first half of P-0 is identical to the second half of I-5. Since there are no pitch duplications between the first halves of the rows, they (as well as, of course, the respective second halves) can be combined to form a twelve-tone aggregate. In a passage from the same piece (Example IX-5b) the upper voices state P-0, the lowest voice I-5; and the rows are so disposed that the first hexachords are combined in

Example IX–5: SCHOENBERG, Piano Piece, Op. 33a

a. Row forms

b. mm. 14–18

the first two and a half measures, the second hexachords in the remainder. Thus combinatorial twelve-tone aggregates are formed in each of the passage's two subphrases.

Another interesting feature of this passage is the frequency of pitch repetitions, both of individual notes and groups of notes. Indeed, P–0, which supplies the pitch basis for a sort of accompaniment for the more linear disposition of I-5, is handled almost in a "chordal" manner; although the notes are all introduced in the correct order, they are then repeated almost as though they formed parts of a single six-note harmonic complex. Although I-5 is treated more "normally," each of the

left-hand subphrases begins with repeated groups of notes before proceeding through the hexachord without interruption: notes 1–2 are
repeated in mm. 14–15, while in mm. 16–18 first note 8, then 7–8, and
finally 7–10 are repeated.

This tendency toward a more "harmonic" conception of the row,
evident in much of Schoenberg's music, often appears in more extreme
forms. In the opening (Example IX-6) of the first of the Three Songs,
Op. 48 (1933), for instance, the vocal phrase presents notes 1–8 of the
prime form of the row, while the piano accompaniment has the remaining four, 9–12. First stated in correct sequence, the latter are then repeated
"freely" without concern for order, as a harmonic unit. Note too that
the phrase as a whole produces a twelve-tone aggregate—not through
hexachordal combinatoriality, however, but by the simpler technique
of presenting a segment of the row in the principal part (here the voice)
simultaneously with its remainder in the accompaniment (a technique
often used by Schoenberg and already observed in Examples IX-3b and
IX-3c from the Suite, Op. 25).

Example IX-6: SCHOENBERG, Three Songs, Op. 48, "Sommermüd," mm.
1–3

In the early postwar years Schoenberg continued to eke out a difficult
existence in Vienna through teaching and other professional activities.
Of particular interest was the Society for Private Musical Performances, founded by Schoenberg in 1919 to perform a wide range of
new music, encompassing such varied composers as Debussy, Bartók,
Reger, and Schoenberg himself, as well as his pupils. Schoenberg's idea
was to present contemporary music in circumstances conducive to its
proper appreciation: compositions were carefully rehearsed, difficult
works were repeated, publicity was avoided, and critics were barred.

Although the society was disbanded after only three years, a victim of the high rate of inflation in Austria, it furnished an early reflection of the isolation of new music from "official" concert institutions, and thus of the need to find a more specialized forum for its presentation.

Schoenberg's circumstances altered dramatically in 1925, when he was named to succeed Busoni as head of the master class in composition at the Prussian Academy of Arts in Berlin, one of the most prestigious positions in Europe. However, his employment was terminated upon Hitler's rise to power in 1933, and Schoenberg, sensing that the situation in Germany was impossible for him, emigrated, eventually making his way to the United States and in 1934 settling in Los Angeles (as Stravinsky was to do a few years later).

Schoenberg took an active role in the musical life of his adopted city. Despite diminished financial circumstances and the requirement of teaching untalented students, he was able to guide a number of prominent young American composers in their musical studies. In his creative work he carried on the "classical" tendencies evident in the earlier twelve-tone pieces, moving toward yet greater thematic clarity and formal cohesiveness. Among his major American compositions were several large-scale instrumental works based on traditional formal prototypes,

Arnold Schoenberg teaching a group of students at home in Los Angeles, 1949. (© 1953, 1981 Richard Fish, photographer)

notably the Violin Concerto, Op. 36 (1936), and the Piano Concerto, Op. 42 (1942).

An interesting, and unexpected, development in Schoenberg's American years was his renewed interest in tonality, which earlier he had viewed as a historically outmoded system, relegated to the past as a result of its "replacement" by post-tonal music. Now he began to see it again as a viable compositional method, and wrote several tonal pieces: the Suite for String Orchestra (1934), the Second Chamber Symphony, Op. 38 (a work left unfinished in 1906 and finally completed in 1939), Variations on a Recitative for Organ, Op. 40 (1941), and Theme and Variations for Wind Orchestra, Op. 43a (1943). Although this return to tonality was perhaps consistent with the composer's general inclination throughout the 1920s and 1930s to reestablish closer ties to the music of the past, Schoenberg's own attitude toward it was strongly conditioned by his continuing belief in the "progressive" nature of musical evolution. He considered his use of tonality not so much a return as an effort to add the finishing touches to an already realized musical development. In reference to the Organ Variations, for example, he remarked: "The harmony . . . fills in the gap between my Chamber Symphony and the 'dissonant' music (i.e., the atonal works). Many unused possibilities can be found therein."[2]

Nevertheless, Schoenberg's renewed interest in tonal composition does seem to have influenced at least one of his twelve-tone works. In the Ode to Napoleon, Op. 41 (1942), for reciter, string quartet, and piano (based on a poem by Byron), he uses a row that gives rise to triadic harmonic combinations, and consistently exploits these possibilities throughout the piece, even ending on an unadorned E♭-major triad. In his earlier twelve-tone works Schoenberg had carefully avoided such triadic suggestions because he felt their strong tonal associations would induce inappropriate musical expectations in the listener.

Schoenberg continued to compose actively up to the time of his death in 1951. Two of the works from his final years, the String Trio (1946) and the Phantasy for violin with piano accompaniment (1949), rank among his most original accomplishments. Both mark a departure from the relatively strict formal procedures of the preceding instrumental pieces. Both are in a single movement, and the music takes on a disruptive quality reminiscent of the expressionist works. Brief sections of widely varying character and tempo are pitted against one another, producing an effect rather like that of free recitation. Perhaps here Schoenberg was attempting a final reconciliation between the atonal and twelve-tone phases of his output, and thus a synthesis of the two apparently

---

2. *Letters,* ed. Erwin Stein, trans. Eithne Wilkins and Ernst Kaiser (New York, 1965), p. 248.

conflicting aspects—the Romantic-expressive and Classical (or Wagnerian and Brahmsian)—that made up his musical personality.

With respect to this conflict, a "contradiction" has often been noted in Schoenberg's twelve-tone music between a progressive system of chromatic, atonal pitch organization and a conservative approach to thematic, rhythmic, and formal matters. Yet Schoenberg's overall musical conception is consistent with his view of nineteenth-century musical evolution as one of increasing chromaticism and heightened thematic complexity with regard to specific details, but framed within an essentially unchanging context of general formal and esthetic assumptions. It was precisely Schoenberg's belief in cultural continuity, and thus in the necessity of extending the older tradition, that led him to establish a new compositional system; for in his view it was required by the tradition itself, which had brought the old system to a point of ultimate dissolution. Schoenberg once characterized himself as a "conservative revolutionary," but he could equally have called himself a "revolutionary conservative."

Schoenberg's importance in the development of twentieth-century music is rivaled only by Stravinsky's. Except for the early tonal works, his music has failed to achieve widespread public recognition, yet its impact on other composers has been profound. Even among those of a radically different artistic persuasion, few have been able to ignore the challenge of his work. Without Schoenberg, the course of contemporary music would undoubtedly have taken a very different turn.

WEBERN

Except for a temporary period of service in the Austrian army, Webern was able to continue composing throughout most of the war years. That he, like his mentor Schoenberg, was to undergo a stylistic reorientation in the postwar period was immediately evident in a turn away from the aphoristic instrumental miniatures that had dominated his prewar output. All of Webern's opus numbers between 12 and 19 (1915–26) are groups of two or more songs. All are for solo voice accompanied by chamber ensembles ranging in size from clarinet and guitar (Op. 18) to small chamber orchestra (Op. 13), except for Op. 19, which is for chorus, and Op. 12, which is accompanied by piano.

While retaining the "free" atonal approach to pitch organization found in Webern's prewar instrumental compositions, the earlier among these song sets, dating from the war period and immediately after, are less fragmentary in texture (partly a result of continuity provided by the text) and more consistently linear in conception. Indications of a renewed concern for stricter compositional procedures, providing a more systematic underpinning to this linear emphasis, appear in the last of the *Five Sacred Songs,* Op. 15 (composed in 1917, though not published until 1923). Conceived as a double canon in contrary motion, this song represents Webern's first use of such a strict compositional construction since his first two opus numbers.

Such strict procedures surface still more consequentially in the *Five Canons on Latin Texts,* Op. 16 (1923–24), written at the time Schoenberg's first twelve-tone compositions were appearing and all rigorously canonic in structure. In his next composition, the *Three Traditional Rhymes,* Op. 17 (1925), Webern took up the twelve-tone method himself, and used it exclusively from that point on. In these earliest twelve-tone compositions, however, Webern made no attempt to integrate the possibilities of the new system with his recently rediscovered interest in canonic procedures—although, as we shall see, this would be a main focus of his later development. His initial concern was simply for a more precise control of the formation of twelve-tone aggregates, a tendency already evident in his atonal music.

Thus the second of the Op. 17 songs uses only the original row form, and only at its original pitch level, the notes freely distributed among the voice and the accompanying instruments. As soon as the twelve pitches are used up, the same row form is presented again in a similar way, with each statement of the row thus producing a twelve-tone aggregate between voice and instruments. (The row is repeated twenty-three times in the course of the work, generating twenty-three such twelve-tone fields.) The influence of Schoenberg's aggregate conception of row use, evident in his Piano Suite, Op. 25, published the previous year, is apparent. Webern first uses all forms of the row (though still without transposition) in the second of the Three Songs, Op. 18 (also 1925), and in the third song of that set he uses for the first time more than one row form simultaneously in a linear manner, an approach that would become standard for him.

However, the first big breakthrough in the evolution of Webern's twelve-tone music came with the String Trio, Op. 20 (1927), his first instrumental composition in thirteen years. Once again the influence of Schoenberg, who had just completed his "classically" oriented Wind Quintet, is evident: the Trio's two movements follow traditional formal types—respectively, a rondo and a sonata form. But uniquely characteristic of Webern is the intimate correlation between each movement's formal structure and its underlying row structure. In the opening rondo, for example, the sections appear in the following sequence (with X representing an introductory section): X A B A C X A B A. However, the formal connections between sections with corresponding letters are not defined by recurring thematic material (as in a traditional rondo, or in the rondo finale of the Schoenberg Wind Quintet), but by the use of the same sequence of row forms. Thus, although the row structure of all the A sections is identical, the actual musical realization of these rows is quite different each time. The Trio thus reveals two critical—and closely related—characteristics of Webern's mature twelve-tone compositions: (1) the formal structure is conceived primarily in terms of the underlying serial structure rather than of "concrete" musical materials (recurring themes, for example), and (2) the row tends to retain a highly abstract character, independent of a specific motivic or thematic presentation. In both these respects Webern took a course significantly different from Schoenberg's.

This direction of Webern's later style became fully established in the work immediately following the Trio, the Symphony, Op. 21 (1928). Here for the first time are synthesized the composer's long-established interest in strict polyphonic methods and his recent encounter with the twelve-tone system. The entire first movement is constructed as a series of double canons, each canonic voice derived from the row (its basic form is shown in Example IX-7, along with *I-8*, *I-0*, and *P-4*, the first three transformations used in the work). Typically, Webern exploits certain basic features of the row compositionally. First, the second half of the row is a retrograde of the first half transposed at the tritone, suggesting the possibility of various symmetrical retrograde structures (especially prominent in the second of the Symphony's two movements). Second, the row is constructed so that notes that were adjacent in the original form remain so in certain transformations. Thus, in the four forms given in Example IX-7, the notes E and F, next to each other in *P-0*, are also adjacent in *P-4* and *I-0*. (Other adjacent pairs are also, in varying degrees, preserved.) Webern exploits this property by emphasizing the repetitions of these identical pairs, producing a tightly

Example IX-7: WEBERN, Symphony, Op. 21, basic row and first three
                transformations

woven net of quasi-motivic correspondences on the musical surface.

The compositional realization of this can be followed in the first of the three sections that make up the Symphony's opening movement. In Example IX-8 the score has been arranged so that each of the four voices of the double canon that defines this section is presented on a separate staff. The canon is strictly twelve-tone (that is, all canonic voices

Example IX-8: WEBERN, Symphony, Op. 21, first movement, opening

follow the sequence of notes determined by the row and its transformations); however, the instrumentation of each voice varies constantly,
at times changing with each new note—a practice consistent with the
"pointillistic" approach to texture noted in Webern's earlier works. The
fact that there is no timbral consistency within any given voice (as there
would be in a more traditional canon) renders it virtually impossible to
hear the voice as a "real" melodic line.

The layout of the canon is as follows: (1) *P-0* in the top voice is canonically imitated by its inversion (*I-0*) in the bottom voice; (2) *I-8* in the second voice is canonically imitated by its inversion (*P-4*) in the third voice. Since these two canons run concurrently, since they completely overlap with each other in register as well as in time, and since the instrumental presentation changes constantly within any given voice, the listener cannot actually follow the canonic structure at all. Here again we encounter Webern's conception of the row as an abstract background, a sort of underlying structural grid that "secretly" determines the piece's course without being directly tied to the audible features of its surface.

What one can—and does—hear in the Symphony's opening section results in large part from Webern's very special and entirely original use of register. With one exception, every pitch in the section is assigned to a single octave, in which it always appears. (The exception is E♭ / D♯, which appears in two different positions an octave apart.) As a result, the recurrent fixed pitch pairings described above always appear in the same register and are thus readily perceptible, especially when they occur in close proximity. Two examples: in mm. 3–4 G-A♭ in the top voice (*P-0*) is answered in the second voice (*I-8*) by an overlapping A♭-G; in mm. 5–6 B-B♭ in the fourth voice (*I-0*) is answered by an overlapping B♭-B in the third voice (*P-4*), and then, in mm. 7–8, by B-B♭ in the first voice (*P-0*)—and so on. As if by chance, these staggered repetitions pop out of the carefully ordered though largely inaudible canonic substructure to form quasi-motivic fragments that lend the work a readily perceptible surface coherence. This complex interplay between an audible "foreground" and its inaudible structural "background" constitutes one of the most fascinating aspects of Webern's music.

A further feature of the Symphony's row is exploited by Webern: since the row's first and last intervals (major sixth and minor third) are complementary, the last two notes of any given row form are identical to the first two notes of a particular transposition of the inversion. Thus *P-0* (in the first voice) ends with the notes C-E♭, which are also the first two notes of *I-3*; *I-8* (the second voice) ends with D-B, the first two notes of *P-5*—and so on. Webern allows this property to determine the sequence of row forms in all four voices, the last two notes of each of the four initial forms overlapping with the first two of the following ones (the reason these two notes are always numbered twice in Example IX-8). Moreover, this property is symmetrical: the row is constructed so that the second of each row pair leads back to the first one again. For example, not only does *P-0* overlap with *I-3* in the top voice; the last two notes of *I-3* (A-F♯) are also identical to the first two of *P-0*. This offers Webern a compelling reason for repeating the entire segment (note the double bar at the end), since the row structure literally turns back on itself and thus forms a closed system.

More than any other twelve-tone composer of the time, including Schoenberg, Webern undertook to rethink and transform traditional formal assumptions. As we have seen, Schoenberg conceived of his rows in essentially thematic terms, using them as an aid in building up large-scale forms through processes of thematic exposition and motivic development still closely analogous to those of tonal music. Webern, on the other hand, thought of the row in a more uncompromisingly abstract sense, and developed his formal structures as far as possible out of the particular characteristics of the row he was using. To him, the form and the row structure of a particular work seemed virtually identical, whereas in Schoenberg the two remained to some degree separable. As Webern remarked of his use of the series: "The twelve-note row is, as a rule, not a 'theme.' But I can also work without thematicism—that's to say much more freely, because of the unity that's now been achieved in another way; the row ensures unity."[3]

Along with this exact repetition, the Symphony's formal clarity—the first movement is clearly divided in three parts (each a double canon, with the third set up in the same manner as the first to produce a sort of "recapitulation"), and the second is in strict variation form—recalls similar practices found in Schoenberg's music of this period. Indeed, the general emphasis on strict formal control and relative textural clarity resembles not only Schoenberg's practice but also the more widespread neo-classical tendencies of the time. Particularly noticeable is the much greater simplicity and consistency of rhythm in the Symphony, compared with the extreme rhythmic differentiation of Webern's earlier music. Even the return, here as in the preceding String Trio, to traditional generic titles suggests a concern for reestablishing close ties with the music of the past.

Two additional excerpts from works by Webern provide brief illustrations of the way he draws musical implications from row structures. The row of the Concerto for Nine Instruments, Op. 24 (1934), is derived from serial transformations of its first three notes (Example IX-9a): the second trichord is an *RI* form of the first, the third an *R* form, and the fourth an *I* form. (Rows with highly structured internal relationships—a characteristic already noted in connection with the Symphony—become

Example IX-9: WEBERN, Concerto for Nine Instruments, Op. 24

a. Row

3.   *The Path to the New Music,* ed. Willi Reich, trans. Leo Black (Bryn Mawr, 1963), p. 55.

b. mm. 1–3

an almost constant feature of Webern's later music.) This structural feature is articulated at the opening of the piece (Example IX-9b) by assigning different instruments, durations, and articulations to each of the three-note units.

The main structural idea of the Piano Variations, Op. 27 (Example IX-10), is derived not so much from the row itself as from the idea of combining the original form of the row with its untransposed retrograde. Webern exploits this combination to shape the opening phrase as an exact palindrome, with its axis in the middle of m. 4; that is, the music from the last sixteenth of m. 4 through m. 7 is an exact retrograde of the music up to the beginning of m. 4. This is accomplished serially by interchanging the row material between the two hands: the

Example IX-10: WEBERN, Piano Variations, Op. 27, mm. 1–7

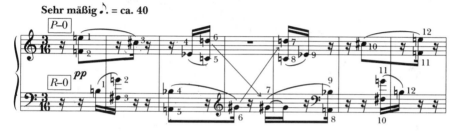

right hand begins with notes 1–6 of *P*-0 (mm. 1–3), then continues with notes 7–12 of *R*-0 (which are, of course, notes 1–6 of *P*-0 in retrograde), while the left hand begins with notes 1–6 of *R*-0 and then switches to 7–12 of *P*-0 (which are, similarly, notes 1–6 in retrograde). The passage's symmetrical disposition is also reflected in the textural layout (the number of notes sounding in each hand alternates 2–1 and 1–2 in the right hand, 1–2 and 2–1 in the left) and in the rhythmic organization (whereby the three–note units in one hand always enclose those of the other, again in an alternating fashion).

The opening of the Piano Variations (completed in 1936) alone provides ample testimony to the great stylistic distance Webern covered in his postwar evolution and to the profound effect of twelve-tone technique upon his compositional approach. With its carefully controlled symmetries, regular rhythmic successions, and emotional reserve, this music is far removed from the disjunct textures, exaggerated contrasts, and expressive intensity of the prewar output. Here again we see a reflection of the postwar turn toward clarity and objectivity.

Yet Webern's own brand of neo–classicism is very special and entirely his own. Moreover, his twelve-tone music does retain certain basic stylistic features established in the atonal works. The inclination to break up the row into smaller particles and to distinguish these from one another through instrumentation, registration, dynamics, and articulation produces a pointillistic quality reminiscent of the expressionistic works. The importance of paper-thin textures—of long stretches of silence as a backdrop for these separate units, which often consist of no more than two or three notes each—takes on, if anything, even more significance here than in the early instrumental miniatures. And Webern's preference for forming the row out of manipulations of smaller pitch groups can be seen as a more systematic development of his essentially intuitive prewar techniques of cellular construction.

But the most striking earlier characteristic retained in Webern's later work is the music's extreme brevity. His long-standing tendency to strip away all padding and unnecessary elaboration is still evident in the twelve-tone compositions and accounts for one of the more idiosyncratic aspects of his move to a more classical orientation. Despite the traditional titles of his instrumental works during the 1920s and 1930s (in addition to those already mentioned, he wrote a String Quartet, Op. 28, and Variations for Orchestra, Op. 30), these works have little of the temporal scope (no movement lasts more than a few minutes) or the dynamic developmental quality normally associated with these genres; Webern's conception of form as a function of row structure tends to produce music of an essentially lyrical character. Another significant distinction lies in the size of the forces: even in the larger works, such as the Symphony and Variations for Orchestra, the orchestra called for is in fact a relatively small chamber ensemble.

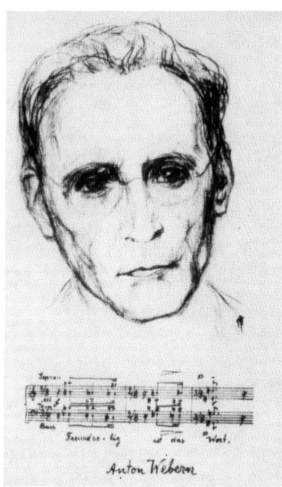

Anton Webern in 1944, as depicted in a lithograph by the poet Hildegarde Jone. The musical quotation is from the fifth movement of Webern's Second Cantata, Opus 31, the text of which is by Jone.

Webern died in 1945 as the result of a tragic accident during the final days of World War II, when he was mistakenly shot by an American soldier. The last years of his life were primarily occupied with the composition of two vocal works, the Cantatas No. 1, Op. 29 (1939), and No. 2, Op. 31 (1943), both for soloists, chorus, and small orchestra. (They were preceded by an earlier cantata, *Das Augenlicht* [Eyesight], Op. 26, composed in 1935, and sketches for an additional choral work were found after the composer's death.) Although his work was condemned by the Nazi powers, Webern had remained in Austria throughout the war years, living in almost complete isolation and in precarious financial circumstances.

But in fact his music had always been spurned by the public and, indeed, by all but a very few professional colleagues—a circumstance not difficult to understand. Although he regarded himself as a dedicated traditionalist, committed to an extension of the line of great European art music, Webern came to believe, like Schoenberg, that this continuation could be realized only through the new possibilities provided by the twelve-tone system. In this respect he was much more "faithful" to the method than its inventor. For whereas Schoenberg thought of his system mainly as an aid for organizing chromatic pitch relationships within a formal context that retained strong traditional ties, Webern accepted it as the basis for an essentially new way of thinking about musical structure. Not surprisingly, then, the unfamiliar nature of his music made it largely incomprehensible to contemporary listeners; and even today his works are widely held to be the overly specialized products of an overly intellectual composer, situated well outside the mainstream of musical developments. Yet Webern's music—no doubt to the surprise of most observers—proved to be of great historical importance. As we shall see, in the years following World War II it was to have a profound influence on some of the most important younger composers, helping to foment a second musical revolution as fundamental in its way as the one Webern himself had participated in shortly after the turn of the century.

BERG

Like Schoenberg and Webern, Alban Berg moved during the early postwar years toward a more consciously controlled compositional method, although in his case the changes were considerably less dramatic. Not only had his prewar atonal compositions remained closer to the rhythmic and harmonic character of late nineteenth-century tonal music, at least some of these pieces (most notably the final passacaglia movement of the Altenberg songs) already reflected a fondness for strict compositional procedures. Nevertheless, Berg's first postwar work, the opera *Wozzeck,* evidenced a still more detailed and comprehensive structural conception.

As early as 1914 Berg had begun thinking about an opera based on a recently discovered play, *Woyzeck,* by the nineteenth-century Austrian writer and political activist Georg Büchner, who had died in 1837 at the age of twenty-four. Through a series of brief, disconnected, and episodic scenes, Büchner's play portrays the plight of a poor soldier, exploited and victimized by his superiors. In conception, content, and structure the play is remarkably modern, and its powerful story of inhumanity and oppression provided Berg with an ideal vehicle.

Shortly after undertaking the project, however, Berg entered military service, and little work was completed until his release in 1918, whereupon he began intensive work on *Wozzeck,* completing the full score in 1922. Selecting only portions of Büchner's play, Berg arranged the material in a symmetrical plan of three acts divided into five scenes each, the scenes within each act connected by orchestral interludes. Thus

Program for the pre-
miere of *Wozzeck* at the
Berlin State Opera,
December 14, 1925.

each act forms a continuous musical structure, organized by Berg as a carefully shaped formal totality. Within the first act (conceived as a "suite" in five movements) and the second (a "symphony"), the music of each scene is based upon a traditional formal type. (The five scenes, or "movements," of the second act, for example, are respectively a sonata form, a fantasia and fugue, a slow movement in ternary—A B A—form, a scherzo, and a rondo.) The final act is cast as a set of five "inventions," or variations, each on a particular structural feature of the music (a theme, a chord, a rhythm, etc.).

In addition, close musical and dramatic correspondences between the first and third acts create a larger three-part structure (A B A) for the work as a whole; and each of the three acts ends with a varied presentation of the same "cadential" chord. The degree of formal integration is thus unusually high, and although Berg stressed that he did not expect, or even wish, listeners to be conscious of *Wozzeck*'s complex organization, its tightly conceived structural plan was clearly significant to him. In a lecture on the opera delivered in 1929, he remarked that this plan provided him with a way "to achieve the same degree of cohesion and of structural unification without the use of the hitherto accepted medium of tonality."[4]

The general character of the music of *Wozzeck,* expressively lyrical and intensely dramatic, is not essentially different from Berg's earlier works, and the pitch organization, still based on referential cells or chords, is thus basically the same as before (although—as we shall see—these cells are now at times more systematically applied). But *Wozzeck* also includes occasional passages of more or less diatonic tonality, which blend seamlessly within the prevailing atonal language. (Berg's special gift for achieving this blend without stylistic discontinuity stems largely from the pronounced tonal implications of his atonal idiom.) The composer's later adoption of the twelve-tone system is also anticipated, most notably in the last act, where in each scene a particular compositional idea functions as a constant reference from which the musical materials are derived through various types of transformation, a procedure not unlike that of twelve-tone composition. This is particularly evident in Act III, Scene 3, where the pitches are derived almost exclusively from a group of six notes. Berg himself referred to the scene as an "invention on a chord," but the six notes are in fact used like an unordered set, appearing throughout the scene in different configurations—some chordal, others essentially linear. Although an extension of the cell techniques found in Berg's earlier works, this conscious and systematic derivation of all the material from a single basic source, used in both transposed and untransposed forms, is new. In the adjacent brief passage from the scene (Example IX-11), all the notes are drawn from the untransposed original six-note unit (given in scalar form above the example). The *Sprechstimme* voice part, since it does not produce precise pitches, is not limited to the six-note unit.

The dramatic power of *Wozzeck,* and the sympathy and compassion for the title character its music communicates, has made it among the most successful of all twentieth-century operas. Its immediate success when first produced in 1925 brought Berg sudden fame and made him by far the most widely performed of the three members of the Second Viennese School.

In his next composition, the Chamber Concerto for Piano, Violin, and Thirteen Wind Instruments (1925), dedicated to Schoenberg for his fiftieth birthday, Berg pursued with even greater intensity the formal rigors found in *Wozzeck.* In a letter to his teacher, Berg described in detail the architectonic construction of the piece, which he had consciously worked out in minute detail. Especially remarkable is the mathematical exactitude with which the numbers of measures in different sections have been made to correspond to one another. In the first

4.   H. F. Redlich, *Alban Berg* (New York, 1957), p. 262 (the entire lecture is reprinted).

Example IX-11: BERG, *Wozzeck,* Act III, Scene 3

a. Six–note cell

b. Excerpt

movement, a theme with variations, the theme lasts 30 measures, the variations respectively 30, 60, 30, 30, and 60 measures. This produces a total of 240 measures, which is balanced by the 240–measure length of the second movement (a slow movement whose second half recapitulates the material of the first half in reverse order). Finally, these two movements, which together equal 480 measures, are balanced by the 480 measures of the third and final movement, a rondo that combines the music of both of the previous movements within a final synthesis.

This complex plan, with its incorporation of traditional formal schemata, shows Berg's increasingly "constructivist" leaning at this time. Moreover, although no portions of the Concerto are written strictly in the twelve-tone system, a number of twelve-tone rows do appear. Berg had already employed such rows in the Altenberg songs and in *Wozzeck* (thereby anticipating Schoenberg), but here for the first time they are subjected to the serial transformations used in Schoenberg's first twelve-tone compositions (which appeared just before the Chamber Concerto was written). The theme of the first movement, for example, is based on a twelve-tone series, and the variations of the theme present the same series not only in its original form but in inverted, retrograde, and retrograde-inverted forms as well. On the other hand, the accompanying voices for the theme and its variations are not yet twelve-tone.

The Chamber Concerto, a "transitional" work on the borderline between free atonality and twelve-tone composition, was followed by Berg's first consistently twelve-tone piece, the song *Schliesse mir die Augen beide* (1925), a setting of a poem by Theodor Storm that Berg had previously set, in 1907, in a late tonal style. Then came the first extended twelve-tone work: the *Lyric Suite* (1926) for string quartet, in six movements. Even here, however, only the first and sixth movements use the new method throughout. The third movement is twelve-tone except for its central trio, the fifth movement only in its two trios. The remaining movements—the second and fourth—contain no consistently twelve-tone episodes, although rows from the twelve-tone movements are "quoted" in each (the reappearance of material from previous movements is a characteristic feature of the piece).

Berg's ability successfully to combine twelve-tone and non-twelve-tone music in a single work suggests the smoothness with which he incorporated the new technique into his already firmly established technical and stylistic approach. Unlike Webern, whose style underwent significant transformations under the impact of the twelve-tone system, Berg retained the essential characteristics of his earlier work. As we have noted, the tendency toward more schematic formal conceptions was already well established before he began using the system. Moreover, as is already apparent in the twelve-tone sections of the *Lyric Suite,* Berg's conception of the method was considerably freer and more flexible than Schoenberg's or Webern's. For example, whereas the latter normally limited themselves to a single row within a given composition, Berg altered the row of the *Lyric Suite* from movement to movement by exchanging certain of its pitches. He once remarked that although these changes did not dramatically alter the overall "line" of the row, they did transform its "character." The row thus "submitted to fate," as he put it, undergoing modifications as it progressed through, and was influenced by, the particular course of the composition. Berg had a much less abstract conception of the row than Schoenberg or—especially—Webern. For him it represented actual "musical material," not simply an unchanging source for such material; it could be worked on and varied, just as the themes and motives of a composition are varied.

Even within the *Lyric Suite*'s first movement, one finds ample evidence of Berg's individual approach to the twelve-tone method. The basic row of this movement can be divided into two six-note groups, the second a retrograde inversion of the first (Example IX-12a). Each half contains six of the seven notes of a diatonic scale segment, and Berg

Example IX-12: BERG, *Lyric Suite*, first movement, basic row and two derivations

also reorders the six-note groups to produce two derived rows: (1) with the groups in scalar form (Example IX-12b) and (2) as a sequence of perfect fifths (Example IX-12c).

A few brief passages from the movement illustrate Berg's use of these row forms. The opening measure (Example IX-13a), introductory in function, first presents the prime form of the perfect-fifth version of the row (Example IX-12c above) in four-note groups and then repeats notes 2–7 of the same row as a six-note chord. The principal thematic idea of the movement (Example IX-13b; see p. 216), presented by the first violin immediately following the introductory measure, consists of a straightforward linear statement of the basic row (Example IX-12a above), by far the most frequently used of the three versions. Finally, in a passage that marks the end of the first half of the movement (Example IX-13c; see p. 216), the rising scalelike passages in all the strings are based on the scalar version (Example IX-12b above), while halfway

Example IX-13: BERG, *Lyric Suite*, first movement

a. m. 1

b. Main thematic idea (mm. 2–4)

c. mm. 33–36

through the second measure the cello begins a statement, played pizzicato, of the perfect-fifth version as well.

The diatonic aspect of the *Lyric Suite* row (the fact that both its hexachords contain six notes of a diatonic scale) is especially characteristic of Berg, enabling him to continue his long-established practice of evoking tonal associations in his nontonal music. Diatonicism is even more pronounced in the Violin Concerto (1935), a two-movement work whose formal symmetry and relative textural transparency reflect the general trend toward simplification and consolidation apparent in so many composers of the 1930s. The first nine notes of the Concerto's row can be considered as a series of alternating and interlocking minor and major triads a perfect fifth apart (i.e., G-minor, D-major, A-minor, E-major)— a property Berg frequently exploits to lend the work a pronounced "triadic" quality (as in Example IX-14b, from the first movement; the minor changes in note order are typical of the composer).

These strong tonal suggestions also enable Berg to introduce "borrowed" tonal material during the course of the Concerto without risking stylistic inconsistency. A Carinthian folk song appears in the closing section of the first movement, while the final Adagio section of the second movement incorporates Bach's harmonization of the Lutheran chorale *Es ist genug*. In fact, the striking opening of the latter, a whole-tone ascent spanning a tritone, is identical to the last four notes of the row (see Example IX-14). The elusive yet distinct tonal references of Berg's score become especially evident when the chorale is presented in phrases that alternate between Berg's reharmonization and Bach's version (Example IX-15; see p. 218).

Before his premature death in 1935, Berg wrote only four major twelve-tone compositions: the *Lyric Suite,* the cantata *Der Wein* (The Wine, 1929) for soprano and orchestra, the Violin Concerto, and the unfinished opera *Lulu.* Berg based the libretto of *Lulu* on two plays by the German dramatist Frank Wedekind depicting the rise and fall of an amoral woman (the title figure) and her impact upon all the other char-

Example IX-14: BERG, Violin Concerto

a. Row

b. First movement, mm. 11–15

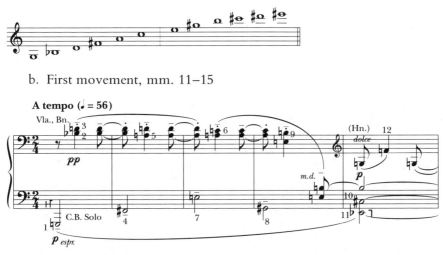

Example IX-15: BERG, Violin Concerto, second movement, Adagio section, mm. 147–52

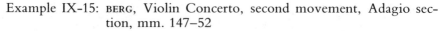

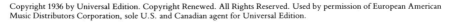

acters in the play. Although Berg had substantially completed the music before his death, he had only begun the orchestration of the third act; for many years his widow withheld the last act from performance, and most productions concluded with a brief pantomime set to the part of the finale orchestrated by Berg for a symphonic suite. In 1979, after Mrs. Berg's death, a full version was finally presented, completed from Berg's drafts by the Austrian composer Friedrich Cerha.

Because of its scandalous nature, especially as perceived at the time of its earliest performances, and its unfinished state, *Lulu* has remained less popular than *Wozzeck*. Yet, as the completed version makes particularly clear, it is a work of equal dramatic and musical richness. Although shaped as a traditional "number" opera, with arias, duets, cavatinas, etc. (all duly indicated by headings in the score), the opera's larger organization is conceived as "symphonically" as *Wozzeck*'s; and its musical and dramatic aspects are, if anything, even more tightly bound together.

Completely twelve-tone in conception, *Lulu* impressively demon-strates the dramatic possibilities of using multiple twelve-tone rows: each of the principal characters is assigned a particular series, and these series are interrelated with one another in ways that reflect the relation-ships among the characters. *Lulu*'s remarkable technical and expressive variety eloquently testifies to the adaptability of twelve-tone music for a wide range of musical and dramatic purposes.

Despite the small size of Berg's output, his works stand among the century's most important musical achievements. Thanks to his ability to reconcile contemporary techniques with stylistic characteristics retained from late nineteenth-century Romanticism, he was able to follow a continuous yet stylistically unbroken evolution, unique among the major figures of his generation. The intense and highly personal expressive-ness that characterizes all of his work remains undiminished by even the most rigorous and involved formal constructions of the postwar period.

In the previously mentioned letter to Schoenberg, after explaining the constructive intricacies of the Chamber Concerto, Berg closes by apologizing for concentrating on these technical and numerological matters: "I can tell you, dearest friend, that if it became known how much friendship, love, and a world of human and spiritual references I have smuggled into these three movements, the adherents of programme music—should there be any left—would go mad with joy. . . ."[5] One does feel, in fact, that a deep biographical basis lies behind all Berg's music (in the case of at least one composition, the *Lyric Suite*, the explicitly personal nature of its references has recently been concretely documented). This programmatic aspect, so alien to the prevalent esthetic of the neo-classical period, is essential to Berg's work, and accounts for an important feature of his extremely individual compositional voice.

5.   Willi Reich, *The Life and Work of Alban Berg,* trans. Cornelius Cardew (London, 1965), pp. 147–48.

CHAPTER X

The Influence of Politics

GERMANY

Germany's defeat in World War I brought about the collapse of the old monarchy and the foundation of the Weimar Republic. Throughout the country a strong sense of liberation from older modes of existence, both social and artistic, was experienced, and in the first decade or so following the war Germany enjoyed a period of remarkable artistic and intellectual rejuvenation. Among the younger generation the dominant impulse was to reject the past in favor of everything new and up-to-date. In the arts this took the form of a strongly anti-Romantic sentiment; a simpler, more streamlined and objective type of art was needed, responsive to the flavor of contemporary life.

The leading cultural center of postwar Germany was Berlin, which during the 1920s became a haven for all that was new and experimental in the arts, eventually rivaling Paris as a focus of avant-garde activity. Several of the most prominent composers of the age taught in Berlin during these years, including Busoni, Schoenberg, Franz Schreker, and somewhat later, Paul Hindemith. Yet activity was not limited to this one city. In Frankfurt, Baden-Baden, and elsewhere, signs of a new musical vigor reflected the extraordinarily intense and varied character of German life during the postwar years.

All this came to a sudden end with the victory of the Nationalist Socialist party in the 1933 elections and the subsequent appointment of Adolf Hitler as chancellor. Even during the 1920s, when Germany experienced an acute economic crisis marked by unemployment and rampant inflation, voices from the extreme right were heard denouncing the "cultural Bolshevism" of radical artists and composers. But with the advent of Hitler everything new in German art was abruptly stifled—indeed, banned by the regime as "degenerate." The anti-intellectual and anti-artistic attitudes of the National Socialists, along with their brutal suppression of the Jews, had a fatal impact upon the country's cultural life. Many of the leading artistic figures, Jewish and non-Jewish alike, fled during the 1930s. Artistic activity was confined exclusively to what those in power considered politically acceptable. Germany, for centuries at the forefront of important developments in European music, suddenly became, at a single stroke, a cultural backwater, cut off from the main creative currents of the time.

HINDEMITH

The exuberance and optimism of the early years of the Weimar Republic were strongly reflected in the decidedly brash and experimental eclecticism of Paul Hindemith (1895–1963), the first important new composer to emerge in Germany in the postwar years. Endowed with extraordinary musical gifts and an accomplished violinist while still a youth, Hindemith attended the Hoch Conservatory in Frankfurt in his thirteenth year, concentrating first on instrumental studies. In 1912 he began composition lessons with Arnold Mendelssohn, and later studied with Bernard Sekles. However, his first recognition came as a violinist: in 1915 he became concertmaster of the Frankfurt Opera. The Amar-Hindemith String Quartet (in which he played viola) was formed in 1921 to play Hindemith's Second String Quartet; it soon became one of the most prominent ensembles of the day, especially noted for its performances of new music.

After his appointment in 1927 as professor of composition at the Music Academy in Berlin, Hindemith reduced his active performing career; though he continued to appear as violist (and later as conductor), the quartet disbanded in 1929. His extensive early performing experience and legendary proficiency (on clarinet and piano as well as violin and viola) had a profound effect on his basic attitudes about music and musical composition. Throughout his career Hindemith maintained a strong belief in the importance of practical music making and in the necessity of a solid technical foundation for all aspects of music study.

Hindemith's earlier compositions, such as the String Quartet No. 1, in F minor, Op. 10, and the piano piece *In einer Nacht (One Night)*, Op. 15 (both 1919), are written in a late Romantic style indebted to Brahms, Strauss, and Reger, characterized by lush chromaticism and essentially triadic harmony. But during the early 1920s the young composer broke away from these traditional roots and established himself as one of the

Hindesmith's drawing for the cover of his *Piano Suite "1922"* evokes the hurly-burly of modern city life in a way reminiscent of the score it accompanies. (© B. Schott's Soehne, Mainz, 1922. © Renewed, Schott and Co. Ltd, London, 1950. All rights reserved. Used by permission of European American Music Distributors Corp., sole U.S. and Canadian agent for Schott)

more radical members of the postwar generation, quickly becoming known as the *enfant terrible* of the German contemporary musical scene. Of three one-act operas written during 1920 and 1921, two—*Mörder, Hoffnung der Frauen (Murder, the Hope of Women)* and *Sancta Susanna*—deal with highly charged sexual topics, and the third, the puppet opera *Das Nusch-Nuschi*, mockingly parodies Wagner's *Tristan und Isolde*. Hindemith's new anti-Romantic and parodistic stance is also reflected in two piano works of 1922, the *Tanzstücke (Dance Piece),* Op. 19, and the Suite "1922," Op. 26, both consisting of dancelike movements conceived in a severely linear manner, with sharp dissonances and a highly flexible, nontraditional approach to tonality. But most notable is the influence of jazz and popular music. As the composer remarked in a typically pithy autobiographical sketch, written in the same year for the *Neue Musik-Zeitung:* "I have 'tilled' the following fields of music: all sorts of chamber music, movies, cafés, dance halls, operetta, jazz band, military band."[1] The sentiment echoes Cocteau and Les Six, yet the

---

1. *Neue Musik-Zeitung, Sonderheft zum 11. Donaueschinger Kammermusikfest zur Förderung zeitgenössischer Tonkunst* (Stuttgart-Leipzig), 63 (1922): 33.

actual music, German to the core, is fundamentally different—on the one hand less graceful, on the other more complex and developed.

Another indication of the young Hindemith's "nose-thumbing" attitude, so typical of the early postwar years, is found in the *Kammermusik* No. 1, another 1922 work, which quotes a popular fox trot of the day and even employs a siren. This first *Kammermusik* (literally, "Chamber Music," a neutral title with a symbolic significance of its own, directed against the programmatic titles of the recent past) also reveals the composer's preference at this time for small and heterogeneous instrumental ensembles, ideally suited to display the music's essentially linear and nonfigurative style. It initiated a series of seven works so named that were composed between 1922 and 1927. Except for the first, all feature a solo instrument playing with a chamber group of ten or more instruments. Modeled on Baroque concerto forms and featuring Bach-like polyphonic textures and continuously unfolding motivic work, these compositions mirror the general neo-classical trend of the period and suggest a knowledge of Stravinsky's most recent compositions. But the more heavily accented metrical rhythm (a basic characteristic of most German music) and the more rigorous contrapuntal writing set them off from the music of Stravinsky and his French contemporaries.

During the middle and later 1920s Hindemith adopted a more serious and disciplined stance. Although he remained extraordinarily prolific throughout his career, the period from 1922 to 1927, during which he solidified his mature style, was particularly rich and produced many of his most original and ambitious compositions. In addition to the *Kammermusik* series, several large chamber works appeared during these years: the Third and Fourth String Quartets (1922, 1923), the First String Trio (1924), the *Kleine Kammermusik* for wind quintet (1922), and the Clarinet Quintet (1923), as well as a number of sonatas for solo string instruments, some with piano and some unaccompanied, and the song cycle *Das Marienleben* (The Life of Mary, 1923), perhaps the finest work of the period. In addition, the Concerto for Orchestra appeared in 1925 and the *Konzertmusik* for wind ensemble in 1926.

Characteristic features of Hindemith's style during this period are illustrated by the opening of the *Kammermusik* No. 2 (1924) for piano and twelve-piece chamber orchestra (Example X-1; see p. 224). Throughout the passage, accompanying instruments hold a pedal G, supplying a firm tonal focus around which the piano, after confirming the G in the opening measure, moves more freely. Thus, in m. 4 the opening material is repeated in the piano on A♭, a half step away from the accompanying pedal. (Hindemith's innovative approach to tonality is reflected in the fact that the movement concludes in E♭, a key only attained near the end, following a series of major tonal shifts usually associated with a return of the opening motivic material.) Several fea-

Example X-1: HINDEMITH, *Kammermusik* No. 2, mm. 1–4

tures illustrate the "back to Bach" attitude so prominent among composers at the time: the Baroque-like motoric rhythm, the use of brief melodic figures spun out in a continuous development, and the contrapuntal conception of the whole (e.g., from the second beat on, the left hand of the piano canonically imitates the right hand at the lower octave). Also, despite meter changes, the main beats are emphasized by the recurring motivic units in the upper hand.

The most extensive project of these years was the full-length opera *Cardillac* (1926), based on a story by E. T. A. Hoffmann. In keeping with Hindemith's then-current anti-Romanticism, it departs markedly from the Wagner-Strauss operatic tradition. Consisting of a series of clearly defined separate "numbers," the music eschews its traditional role as a conveyor of emotional content. Indeed, as in Stravinsky's theater works of the late 1910s and early 1920s, music and drama seem to run separate courses, the rhythmically driving, *concertante* quality of the music remaining aloof from the onstage happenings, responding at best in terms of general pacing and by providing contrasts to punctuate the principal formal divisions of the stage action.

Widely performed, *Cardillac* established Hindemith, only recently turned thirty, as the leading German composer of his generation. There followed the twelve-minute chamber opera *Hin und zurück* (*There and Back,* 1927), in which the stage action moves in reverse order after the midpoint until the opening situation is reattained (a reversal also reflected in the musical layout, though only in a general sense), and then by the full-length comic opera *Neues vom Tage* (*News of the Day,* 1929). The latter, dealing with modern people in contemporary situations, reflects the 1920s' fashion for operatic works on topical matters (known in Germany as *Zeitoper*—that is, opera of the time). Thanks to an office scene in which twelve typists contribute percussive parts to the music and another in which the leading lady sings an aria while bathing in a tub, *Neues vom Tage* achieved considerable notoriety.

Hindemith's extraordinary productivity is directly attributable to his view of composition as a craft to be practiced faithfully, with the mastery and dedication one brings to any respectable occupation but unburdened by grandiose thoughts of self-expression. From this followed implicitly Hindemith's emphasis upon music as a social activity rather than as a vehicle for personal communication, an attitude reflected in the unusually high percentage of chamber works in his output. During these years this concern for the utilitarian aspects of music—as something to be played rather than just listened to, and to be played by amateurs and students as well as professionals—became ever more consciously defined. From this viewpoint, shared by a number of composers of the time, came the term *Gebrauchsmusik* (literally, "music for use"). Although Hindemith himself preferred the term *Sing-und-Spielmusik* ("music for singing and playing"), *Gebrauchsmusik* has stuck and is still commonly applied to such "functional" music.

In this cause Hindemith devoted a significant portion of his output during the later 1920s and early 1930s to compositions that could be played by nonprofessionals, including choral pieces, works for string orchestra and wind ensemble, and the children's play with music *Wir bauen eine Stadt* (*Let's Build a City,* 1930). Perhaps the most important of these works is *Lehrstück* (*Teaching Piece,* 1929), a politically motivated stage work for amateur performers incorporating music, acting, dance (or film), and audience participation, based on a text by the playwright Bertolt Brecht, the most important innovator in German theater of the time. Hindemith also collaborated with Brecht on *Der Lindbergflug* (*Lindbergh's Flight,* 1929), writing the music in conjunction with Brecht's frequent collaborator Kurt Weill.

Although relatively little of Hindemith's output after the early 1930s was intended strictly for amateurs, his desire to narrow the gap between the composer and the public, between the musician as specialist and the musician as amateur, had a lasting effect upon his general compositional views. As he later acknowledged: "Once a writer's technique and style is organized in this direction, so that music which satisfies the amateur's wishes can be created, his approach to his entire work will inevitably undergo a radical change: the emphasis on moral aspects will now become recognizable also in his works written for the concertizing professional, and now he will talk with a different spirit to the general audience."[2]

This "radical change" is apparent in Hindemith's own concert works of the 1930s, which reveal a decided stylistic simplification. Tonal areas become more clearly enunciated, textures are more transparent, a new lyricism is evident in the music—while, on the other hand, the sardonic and parodistic humor of the 1920s has disappeared almost entirely. The first major work to reflect these changes was the opera *Mathis der Maler* (*Mathis the Painter,* 1935), based on the life of the sixteenth-century German painter Matthias Grünewald. The solid craftsmanship of the earlier music remains, now in the service of a new expressive weight and solemnity. Yet something of the composer's youthful fire is also missing, and although a symphony drawn from *Mathis* remains one of Hindemith's most compelling and frequently performed compositions, the stage work is rarely heard.

In 1937, two years after *Mathis,* Hindemith published the book *Unterweisung im Tonsatz (The Craft of Musical Composition),* in which he attempted to codify the principles of his new approach and establish a firm theoretical foundation for the harmonic and melodic aspects of his music. Taking the tonal principle as his starting point, he reaffirmed its priority as "a natural force, like gravity" and constructed a comprehensive pitch system in which all the possible intervallic relationships are graded according to their "absolute" degree of consonance and dissonance. Hindemith believed that this new system was capable of accommodating not only the principles of traditional tonal music but those of *any* meaningful music, including that of the twentieth century. Music that failed to conform was considered suspect. Not only did Hindemith attack the music of others, notably Schoenberg and Stravinsky, he also questioned his own earlier work in the light of his new theoretical formulations and eventually revised several earlier compositions, including such works as *Das Marienleben, Cardillac,* and *Neues vom Tage* (as well as *Frau Musica,* a choral-orchestral work for amateurs), to bring them in conformity with his new theories. (Although most feel that the revised versions lack the freshness and individuality of the originals, the

2. *A Composer's World* (Cambridge, Mass., 1953), p. 219.

works provide an unusually instructive basis for comparison between the two distinct phases of Hindemith's stylistic evolution.)

Whatever one thinks of its somewhat dogmatic approach, *The Craft of Musical Composition* is a central document of twentieth-century musical literature, one of the most conspicuous reflections of the interwar tendency toward greater compositional rigor and systemization. Although seeking, like Schoenberg, a new equivalent for traditional tonality, Hindemith differed in continuing to accept the basic principles of the older system, wishing only to extend them rather than to replace them completely. He stated his belief in tonality in the strongest possible terms: "Music, as long as it exists, will always take its departure from the major triad and return to it. The musician cannot escape it any more than the painter his primary colors, or the architect his three dimensions. In composition, the triad and its direct extensions can never be avoided for more than a short time without completely confusing the listener."[3]

The opening of the Piano Sonata No. 3 (Example X-2), composed in 1936 while Hindemith was working on his theoretical treatise, indicates the new orientation. Not entirely inconsistent with the earlier style, it entails a simplification and codification of principles already at least implicit in Hindemith's music, which had always remained basically tonal and triadically oriented, however much this may have been obscured by surface complexities. Thus, like the earlier example from the *Kammermusik* No. 2, the passage from the sonata is essentially contrapuntal

Example X-2: HINDEMITH, Piano Sonata No. 3, first movement, mm. 1–10

3.   *The Craft of Musical Composition,* trans. Arthur Mendel (New York, 1942), 1:22.

in conception; indeed, in mm. 5–7 the left hand even imitates the right in a manner reminiscent of Example X-1 (although here the imitation is free). But the texture is now considerably less complex, the basic harmonic vocabulary more consistently triadic, the tonality more firmly established. The opening phrase moves unambiguously from the tonic B♭ to the minor dominant in m. 4; after a more developmental passage progressing sequentially upward by minor thirds, B♭ returns in m. 10, along with the opening melodic idea, now doubled in a higher register. The move away from and back to the tonic is carefully planned, the final top-voice B♭ completing an ascent by minor thirds that spans the entire passage: from B♭ (m. 1) to D♭ (m. 4), then sequentially through E (m. 6) and G (m. 8) back to B♭ again (m. 10).

Hindemith began to have problems with the Nazi regime almost immediately after it came into power. The first performance of *Mathis der Maler,* which had been scheduled at the Berlin Opera, was forbidden by the authorities. Not only was the subject matter politically sensitive (in one scene Lutheran books are burned by Catholics), but Hindemith's reputation as a cultural radical, even if based primarily on his earlier work, made him suspect. Initial efforts to work within the new regime proved to be increasingly difficult for such an independent figure, and Hindemith was forced from his teaching position in Berlin in 1937. In the following year he left his homeland permanently, settling first in Switzerland and then in the United States. From 1940 until his retirement in 1953, Hindemith was teacher of composition and director of the Collegium Musicum at Yale University, after which he returned to Switzerland for the final decade of his life.

From the middle 1930s until his death in 1963, Hindemith's music remained remarkably consistent in style; once his new theoretical position had been formulated, he adhered to it faithfully. The entire body of his later work can be seen as a conscious effort to reconcile twentieth-century compositional techniques with the music of the past, a reconciliation reflected not only in reliance upon traditional forms and genres and the frequent appearance of such conventional procedures as fugue, fugato, and passacaglia, but also in the incorporation of actual earlier music in some of the scores. Examples of the latter include medieval chants in *Mathis der Maler,* folk tunes in *Der Schwanendreher (The Swan Turner,* 1935), and music of the nineteenth century in the *Symphonic Metamorphosis on Themes of Carl Maria von Weber* (1943). The differences between Hindemith and Stravinsky in this regard are especially telling. In Hindemith we find little of the "distancing" effect produced by his Russian colleague's elaborate manipulations; the borrowed matter is completely integrated into the total fabric as an essentially unexceptional component. Thus the "mannered" quality of Stravinsky's music is largely absent—but also its special brand of esthetic tension.

In his later years Hindemith turned more and more toward large-scale compositions conceived as extensions of the eighteenth- and nineteenth-century orchestral operatic traditions. The opera *Die Harmonie der Welt* (*The Harmony of the World*, 1957) is perhaps his most personal statement, in which the protagonist, the Renaissance astronomer and speculative music theorist Johannes Kepler, embodies Hindemith's beliefs in the mystical and cosmic implication of harmonic relationships. But the bulk of Hindemith's later output is purely instrumental. Between 1939 and 1942 he wrote eight concertos, six for solo instruments and two for small groups of soloists in the Baroque concerto grosso manner, and five symphonies appeared between 1940 and 1958, including one for concert band and one derived from the Kepler opera. Especially representative is the piano composition *Ludus tonalis* (*Tonal Game*, 1942), a series of preludes and fugues modeled on Bach's *Well-Tempered Clavier* and intended as a didactic demonstration of the continuing validity of traditional practices within a contemporary idiom.

Although Hindemith wrote no *Gebrauchsmusik* as such during this period, his continued commitment to the composer's practical responsibility yielded a series of twenty-five sonatas with piano accompaniment for most of the standard orchestral instruments (1935–55), among them pieces for instruments with relatively limited solo repertories, such as bassoon or tuba, that fulfill a decided need. Although varying considerably in difficulty, their level is usually not beyond the abilities of an advanced student or amateur.

Hindemith's music and theoretical ideas had their greatest impact upon younger composers during the years immediately preceding and following World War II; since then his influence has diminished. Nevertheless, he remains one of the more interesting figures of twentieth-century music, a composer of prodigious talent whose career during the interwar years mirrored with particular clarity some of the most important historical currents of that time.

WEILL

In certain outward aspects the careers of Hindemith and Kurt Weill (1900–50) followed similar courses. Both matured in the heady atmosphere of the early Weimar Republic, and both left Europe in the 1930s to settle in the United States. Yet their artistic temperaments and compositional interests were markedly different.

The son of the chief cantor at the Dessau synagogue, Weill displayed an early talent for composition and began studies with Albert Bing, himself a student of Pfitzner, when he was only fifteen. Three years later he enrolled at the Music Academy in Berlin, where he studied composition with Engelbert Humperdinck. After one year he left to take up work at the Dessau court opera, but returned to Berlin in 1920 to study with Busoni, recently named professor of composition at the Prussian Academy of the arts.

Virtually all the music Weill composed before 1921 was long lost and has only recently been rediscovered; this music and the immediately subsequent works give little indication of the direction of his later output. The Symphony No. 1, for example, written in 1921 as Weill was beginning compositional studies with Busoni, falls within the tradition of Mahler and Strauss. Its one-movement structure, richly polyphonic textures, and chromatic tonality also suggest a debt to Schoenberg's First String Quartet and Chamber Symphony. But in the years immediately following, Weill turned away from the highly charged expressivity of the Symphony toward a more restrained and economical style, reflecting the current neo-classical fashion. The Concerto for Violin and Winds, Op. 12 (1924), is more transparent in texture, its smaller instrumental forces complementing a considerably cooler musical language.

Weill's neo-classical phase reached its summit in the one-act opera *Der Protagonist,* Op. 14 (1926). Based on a libretto by the prominent playwright Georg Kaiser, it established Weill as a figure rivaled among his German contemporaries only by Hindemith. It also provided clear evidence of his natural gift for the theater. The music of two pantomimes placed within the opera's action strikingly presages the grotesque and sharply parodistic quality that was to become a hallmark of the mature Weill.

As well as his simplification of stylistic and expressive means during the earlier 1920s, Weill later in the decade gradually adopted a radical new ideology, and the two tendencies combined to produce a significant change in his work. Troubled by the pervasive moral cynicism of Germany in later years of the Weimar Republic and by the severe economic deprivation endured by many of its citizens, Weill began exploring the possibilities of using music as an agent for social change. To a degree, his new position was consistent with the contemporaneous *Gebrauchsmusik* movement, which also viewed music in terms of its utilitarian functions and its appeal to a broader public. But whereas a composer such as Hindemith aspired to renew amateur music making, Weill envisioned the resurrection of what he called the "socially creative power of art"—that is, its ability to awaken political consciousness. The most powerful medium for achieving this end, in his view, was opera. Having already proved his musico-dramatic talents, he set out to revitalize the genre, to transform it from what he saw as a "socially exclusive art" into a "community-forming or community-advancing" one.

Weill's close collaborator—and to some extent mentor—in this proj-

(left to right) Bertold Brecht, the singer-actress Lotte Lenya (Weill's wife), and Kurt Weill, ca. 1931. (Courtesy of the Weill-Lenya Research Center, Kurt Weill Foundation for Music, New York)

ect was Bertolt Brecht (1898–1956), the brilliant Marxist poet and playwright. Perhaps the most important new development in German drama of the time, Brecht's conception of a depersonalized and nonillusionist "epic theater" combined music, action, oratory, and staging within a stylized dramatic framework in order to produce a "shock of recognition" in the audience. Between 1927 and 1933 Brecht and Weill collaborated on a remarkable series of stage works that presumed nothing less than a redefinition of the concept of musical theater. Opera was to be purged of all romantic sentiment, all personalized expression, and all those "culinary" effects (such as vocal virtuosity, orchestral tone painting, and illusionistic scenery) intended solely for the distraction and entertainment of the audience. Above all, Brecht and Weill sought to simplify both musical and dramatic means so as to allow the work to speak as directly as possible to a large and varied audience. The basic musical unit was the "Song"—an English word they adopted to indicate a distinction from the traditional German *Lied* with its "exclusive," high-art connotations. Weill compared it to "the better type of American popular song," except that it was to be freer, less conventionalized in form and rhythm.

Weill's first collaboration with Brecht was the *Mahagonny-Songspiel* (1927), a series of six extended songs with instrumental interludes, set in the form of a "scenic cantata." Portraying the mythical city of Mahagonny, a false Utopia intended to symbolize Germany's contemporary moral and spiritual corruption, this work had a profound effect upon contemporary audiences, who found its explicit yet "distanced" employment of elements of popular music, jazz, dance bands, and cabaret to be remarkably affecting. Most remarkable about the *Mahagonny-Songspiel,* however, is the way it reworks these elements to avoid any hint of commercialism or cliché. From the scoring for small orchestra to the specific choice of harmony, everything sounds slightly askew— familiar yet always unexpected. Weill rethinks the ordinary to achieve extraordinary effects. Though occasionally suggesting Mahler or Stravinsky, Weill remains much more closely tied to his popular sources. This is music that really speaks in the vernacular, not in some dressed-up version thereof, and it does so with undisguised directness. Rather than good-natured and playful, the popular allusions sound bitingly sarcastic, even contemptuous. Weill's music, as a contemporary critic remarked, "calls everything secure . . . into question."

In the instrumental interludes of the *Mahagonny-Songspiel* Weill retained the complex, freely dissonant tonal language of his earlier work, and even in the songs the level of tonal and textural complication was relatively high. In his next collaboration with Brecht the composer stripped down his material yet more severely, producing an unabashed number

A scene from the original production of *Aufstieg und Fall der Stadt Mahagonny* at the Neues Theater in Leipzig, 1930. (Courtesy of the Weill-Lenya Research Center, Kurt Weill Foundation for Music, New York)

opera with spoken dialogue. This was their first full-scale work, *Die Dreigroschenoper* (*The Threepenny Opera,* 1928), based on the eighteenth-century *Beggar's Opera* of John Gay. Here Weill's populist song style simultaneously achieved new heights of simplicity and sophistication—a strikingly fresh alternative to the standardized output of the commercial music industry. Much to the composer's surprise, the work proved to be an enormous popular success.

The only other full-length dramatic product of the Brecht-Weill collaboration was *Aufstieg und Fall der Stadt Mahagonny* (*Rise and Fall of the City of Mahagonny,* 1929), an operatic adaption of material from the earlier *Mahagonny-Songspiel.* In accordance with his growing preference for a more austere and direct style, Weill dropped the complex instrumental interludes of the original, and gave the song accompaniments a more explicitly triadic and consonant harmonic basis. Yet the music retains its own special subtlety. The opening of the refrain of the "Alabama Song," one of the score's principal hits (Example X-3; see p. 234), illustrates both the popular basis of Weill's art and his extraordinary ability to circumvent the threat of banality. In an article on dramatic music, Weill himself used this passage (in its earlier *Songspiel* version) as an example of what he called the "gestic" character of music: its ability to represent objectively the basic truth of a dramatic situation or character. Weill pointed especially to the way the music defines the speech-rhythm of the text (written by Brecht in a kind of pidgin English), thereby setting its essential character.

Other significant features include an incessant ostinato-like rhythm in the accompaniment, inner voices moving to create tension with the underlying triadic foundation, and discreet yet telling chromatic inflections in the voice (mm. 6, 9, 10, 12, and 14). The latter set up a recurring if irregular pattern of half-step correspondences: D♯-E (mm. 6–7), D-C♯ (mm. 8–9), C♯-C (mm. 12–13), and E♭-D (mm. 14–15). Although in this instance the phrases are essentially regular (the excerpt includes four, each of four measures), Weill inflects the rhythm so as to achieve considerable variety. Thus, although the first (mm. 3–6) and third (mm. 11–14) phrases both begin with half-note upbeats, the second (mm. 7–10) has only a quarter note and the fourth (mm. 15–18) no upbeat at all. Also characteristic is the way the second and third phrases end on chromatic notes (C♯ and E♭), preparing for the voice's unexpected close of the final phrase on E rather than on the tonic G. This final E also forms a half step with the E♭ that closed the preceding phrase, thereby reflecting the earlier half-step relationships over a somewhat more extended scale.

After *Mahagonny* the Weill-Brecht partnership began to show signs of strain from the collaborators' diverging interests, and although the two worked together again on the school opera *Der Jasager* (*The Yes*

Example X–3: WEILL, *Aufstieg und Fall der Stadt Mahagonny*, "Alabama Song," mm. 1–17

Sayer, 1930) and later in Paris on the ballet *Die sieben Todsünden* (*The Seven Deadly Sins,* 1933), they never again undertook a major dramatic project. During the early 1930s Weill wrote two more operas, *Die*

Bürgschaft (*The Forfeit,* 1931) and *Der Silbersee* (*The Silver Lake,* 1933), the latter with his first librettist, Kaiser, but neither achieved the success or impact of the Brecht collaborations, at least in part because of worsening economic and political conditions—indeed, *Der Silbersee,* first presented just weeks before the Nazis seized power, was quickly banned from the German stage.

In March 1933 Weill fled Germany and settled briefly in France, where he completed his Second Symphony, his first large instrumental work in nine years and the last that he would compose. He then emigrated permanently to the United States, where the remaining fifteen years or so of his relatively brief life were passed primarily in New York and devoted almost exclusively to the Broadway musical theater—a period often regarded as an entirely separate and independent phase of his career. Although he remained closely tied to the conventions of the American popular song, Weill's remarkable ability to assimilate the accents and inflections of this foreign idiom enabled him to produce a number of successful musicals, including *Lady in the Dark* (1940), *One Touch of Venus* (1943), *Street Scene* (1946), and *Lost in the Stars* (1949).

Although these final works represent a softening of edges and a loosening of critical perspective by comparison with their German predecessors, they had an important influence on such later composers for the popular American stage as Leonard Bernstein and Stephen Sondheim. The narrative and musical continuity of *Street Scene,* for example, was essentially new for the Broadway musical, as was its tenement setting, while the controversial subject of *Lost in the Stars* (apartheid in South Africa) also represented a significant extension of what had previously been considered suitable for musical comedy. Moreover, despite the technical and esthetic differences between the more overtly political and experimental European works and the more smoothed-out American ones, the same general concerns underlie both: topical matters, presented in a direct, unpretentious musical and dramatic manner, and directed toward a broad audience.

RUSSIA

Even more than in the case of Germany, an understanding of the development of music in Russia requires some knowledge of its social and political background. The October Revolution of 1917, which brought to an end the old autocratic Russian Empire and led to the formation of the Union of Soviet Socialist Republics, had an immediate impact upon all facets of cultural life, including music. Although most Russian artists had disapproved of the brutally oppressive Tsarist regime, many of them feared an uncertain future under the new government and left the country immediately following the revolution. Among the musicians who cast their lot with the West were Stravinsky and Rachmaninov. We have noted the important stylistic adjustments that accompanied Stravinsky's self-exile and that were at least partly attributable to it. Yet the repercussions of the revolution would even more profoundly affect those who remained behind.

Vladimir Ilyich Lenin, the principal architect of the revolution, defined the new government's official view of art: "Art belongs to the people. It must have its deepest roots in the broad masses of workers. It must be understood and loved by them. It must be rooted in, and grow with, their feelings, thought and desires."[4] But Lenin did not simply advocate a crass popularization of art to make it accessible to all; he stressed the importance of improving the general education of the Russian people and thus their cultural receptivity. Well into the 1920s the regime fostered an open and even experimental climate for the development of music and other arts in Russia, while strong mutual contacts and shared influences with contemporary European artists were not only tolerated but encouraged.

The progressive character of these years was bolstered by the new regime's conviction that the new social order required an entirely new kind of art. To many, this meant rejection of the past and embrace of the new technical means and esthetic attitudes of the modern age. Avant-garde artists—among them the abstract painter Kasimir Malevich, the writers Vladimir Mayakovsky and Mikhail Bulgakov, and the innovative theater director Vsevolod Meyerhold—flourished in this new environment, stimulated by the prospect of creating a new kind of "involved" art that would play an honored role in shaping the new Soviet society.

Among musicians, two of the most prominent innovators were Nikolay Roslavets, who continued to develop the independent conceptions of atonal serialism discussed earlier, and Alexandr Mosolov (1900–73), who created an international stir with *The Iron Foundry,* a short symphonic episode from his ballet *Steel* (1928). Evoking with striking realism the sounds of a modern factory, Mosolov used a combination of grating ostinato figures to produce a primitive, latter-day tone poem for an era of mechanization and industrialization. Though superficially related to Honegger's somewhat earlier *Pacific 231, The Iron Foundry* explores the idea of a machine-age esthetic with much more fervor and intensity, if also less skill. Widely performed in Europe and America as well as at home, it briefly established Mosolov as an artistic celebrity of the new Russia.

But the progressive character of Soviet art during these years was not to last. Almost from the beginning, there was widespread disagreement concerning what type of art was suitable for the new society. Two directly opposed schools of composition developed, and each had its

---

4.   Quoted in Boris Schwarz, *Music and Musical Life in Soviet Russia* (Bloomington, Ind., 1983), p. 3.

Suprematism by Kasimir Malevich, a work reproduced in the *UNOVIS Almanac* No. 1, 1920. The tensions produced by the varying proportions and interactions of the flat geometrical shapes embodied the ideals of the suprematist movement as well as those of Unovis, a new kind of art school espousing "comprehensive teaching methods for modern times."

own organization. Although both agreed that music should somehow reflect the ideology of communism, the Association for Contemporary Music felt that this could only be achieved by following the most advanced tendencies of musical modernism, while the Russian Association of Proletarian Music believed that music should therefore be simple, even primitive, and free of all artistic pretension. Indeed, the more extreme members of the latter group rejected as alien to the communist ideology not only all modernist innovations, but also the great musical masterpieces of the past.

After Lenin's death in 1924, Joseph Stalin began to strengthen his position within the party hierarchy, eventually assuming complete control in the early 1930s. Stalin had little use for music, or any other art, except as a political weapon; and consequently his views accorded with those of the Russian Association of Proletarian Music: art should be direct and, above all, conventional, in idioms rooted in folk and popular traditions. During Stalin's ascent increasing pressure was applied to curtail freedom in the arts. Such composers as Roslavets and Mosolov were effectively silenced by 1930. In 1932, when Stalin had attained full power, a proclamation entitled "On the Reconstruction of Literary and Artistic Organizations" brought to a definitive halt the openness and variety that had characterized Russian art throughout much of the 1920s and inaugurated a period of repression and absolute conformity. In the same year, the government-affiliated Union of Soviet Composers was founded, replacing the two independent composers' organizations of earlier years.

From this point on, the Union of Soviet Composers became the sole arbiter of what was musically acceptable. It adhered strictly to the official Soviet view that art must "depict reality in its revolutionary development." Music, as well as the other arts, had to be "about something," namely the positive and wholesome virtues of the new society; it had to have "social content." This esthetic position, known as socialist realism, determined the direction of all art in the USSR from 1932 on. Any work that did not adhere to its principles, as determined by those in power, was condemned as "formalist"—i.e., without "content"—and likened to the "degenerate" and "decadent" art of such Western modernists as Stravinsky, Schoenberg, and Hindemith. The parallels with the views of the contemporaneous Nazi regime in Germany are striking.

Two particular instances of official intervention by the Communist Party's Central Committee attracted worldwide attention: the condemnation in 1936 of Shostakovich's opera *Lady Macbeth of the Mtsensk District,* dooming it to limbo for some twenty-five years; and the more general attack, in 1948, on every internationally prominent Soviet composer, including Prokofiev, Shostakovich, and Khachaturian, promulgated by the party's notorious "cultural tsar" Andrei Zhdanov, whose name came to epitomize the repression of art in Russia. But these were only the most extreme and explicit manifestations of the repressive atmosphere that inescapably colored all musical activities in Russia during this period. Whatever a composer wished to write, the question of its political acceptability was ever present, and artistic freedom as it existed in the West was completely unknown. Given this basic fact, the extent to which both Prokofiev and Shostakovich, the leading Soviet composers of the first half of the century, were able to continue to produce compelling works is all the more remarkable.

PROKOFIEV

Born with exceptional musical talents to parents who provided him with every cultural advantage, Sergey Prokofiev (1891–1953) developed unusually early as a composer. From his eleventh year he had a full-time summer music tutor (the young Reinhold Glière, who would himself become a prominent figure in twentieth-century Russian music), and two years later, in 1904, he entered the St. Petersburg Conservatory, where he concentrated first on composition, graduating in 1909, and then on piano, for which he won the highest student award in 1914.

By the time he entered the conservatory Prokofiev had already written a sizable quantity of music, including a short three-act opera (*The Giant*) and a symphony. Although dissatisfied with his conservatory instruction under Lyadov and Rimsky-Korsakov, both of whom he considered hopelessly outdated, he continued to develop rapidly. By 1909 Prokofiev's music was widely performed, attracting considerable public attention and even enjoying the distinction of denunciation by conservative critics as "ultra-modernist."

Prokofiev described his First Piano Concerto (1912) as his "first more or less mature composition, both as regards the conception and its realization." A remarkable achievement for a twenty-year-old, the Concerto is not only technically accomplished, but also speaks in an unmistakably personal voice. Romantic bombast and sentiment are eschewed in favor of traits that were to be consistently characteristic of the composer: formal and textural economy, incisive rhythm, and a lean, hard-edged quality (especially evident in the frequently percussive piano writing). The musical content is compressed into a single move-

An affectionate caricature of Prokofiev by the scenic designer and painter, Michel Larionov, in 1921.

ment, in which thematic sections alternate with brilliant toccata-like episodes featuring acrobatic pianistic figurations. The striking individuality of the score—its often biting and sardonic character, textural lightness, and rhythmic energy—established Prokofiev as an outstanding compositional personality. Viewed within a broader perspective, it also anticipates many stylistic characteristics that would typify the postwar neo-classical movement.

Though softened by moments of cool lyricism, Prokofiev's anti-Romanticism and anti-emotionalism were deeply ingrained in his temperament and evident from his earliest years. Indeed, "classicism" seems to have been second nature to him. In an interview he spoke of it as the trend of the time: "Therefore, I think the desire which I and many of my fellow composers feel, to attain a more simple and melodic expression, is the inevitable direction for the music of the future. . . . There is a return to classic forms which I feel very much myself. . . . In the field of instrumental or symphonic music . . . I want nothing better, nothing more flexible or more complete than the sonata form, which contains everything necessary to my structural purpose."[5]

This attitude is most clearly embodied in the well-known "Classical" Symphony (1917), which makes explicit references to eighteenth-century style, most evidently that of Haydn. (Significantly, it predates the appearance of Stravinsky's Octet by several years.) But the essential features of Prokofiev's style had already been firmly established in a series of earlier compositions: the Second Piano Concerto (1913); the Second and Third Piano Sonatas (1912, 1917); the operas *Maddalena* (1913) and *The Gambler* (1917); the First Violin Concerto (1917); and the ballets *Chout* (The Tale of the Buffoon) and *Ala and Lolli* (better known in its concert version as the *Scythian Suite*), both composed for Diaghilev and completed in 1915. Written within a five-year span (even this partial list suggests Prokofiev's extraordinary productivity), all these works display a clear preference for pre-Romantic stylistic models.

The idea of writing a work consciously evoking the style of Haydn—but a Haydn who had, in Prokofiev's words, "lived to our own day [and] retained his own style while accepting something of the new at the same time"—must thus have seemed natural to the young composer, entirely in keeping with his own musical inclinations. The "Classical" Symphony is scored for a small orchestra characteristic of the late eighteenth century, and each of its four movements follows a Classical formal prototype. Its parodistic aspect, which pokes affectionate fun at the conventions of a highly conventionalized style, distorting them through sudden and unexpected shifts of harmony and rhythm, was inherent in Prokofiev's own nature. "Whimsicality, laughter, and

5.   From an interview with Olin Downes, *New York Times,* February 2, 1930, section 8, p. 8X.

mocking" are words he himself used to describe a characteristic of his personality, also reflected in the titles of several of the early piano pieces— e.g., *Diabolical Suggestion* and *Sarcasms.*

Typical features of Prokofiev's style can be observed in the opening (Example X-4) of one of the twenty brief piano pieces written between 1915 and 1917 and collected under the title *Visions fugitives.* Although from one of the earliest of the pieces (dated 1915), the passage already exhibits the good-natured caricaturing found in the "Classical" Symphony. The two phrases, each four measures in length, can each be subdivided into two subphrases of two measures each. This balanced structure is complemented by the classical simplicity of the texture: a single-lined melody with an unprepossessing triad accompaniment— which nonetheless behaves in a distinctly nontraditional manner.

In the first two measures three root-position triads move downward by whole steps (thus producing blatant parallel fifths) to G♭, the goal of the first subphrase. This progression is answered in the second subphrase (mm. 3–4) by two additional major triads, also moving downward by whole step, but with the first one in first inversion rather than root position. The goal of the second subphrase is G major—an unexpected resolution for the final G♭ of the previous subphrase, which in retrospect sounds like a kind of harmonic leading tone (i.e., an F♯-major chord). Such unexpected and untraditional harmonic progressions are typical of Prokofiev. He uses the normal triadic vocabulary of tonal music but avoids the functional expectations traditionally associated with it. The listener seems to be wrenched away from a "normal" continuation.

Example X-4: PROKOFIEV, *Visions fugitives,* No. 5, mm. 1–8

The second phrase (mm. 5–8) is essentially a varied repetition of the first. The opening upbeat figure now appears in the left hand, inverted and extended by one sixteenth note. And now (m. 6) the G♭ chord that closes the first subphrase is preceded by its dominant, apparently signaling a return to more conventional harmonic connections. (It is now also respelled as an F♯ chord!) But this too turns out to be a kind of joke on the listener, for the phrase then continues as before, without a balancing V–I cadence on G to close it off.

By 1918, the year after the Russian Revolution, the works culminating in the "Classical" Symphony had established Prokofiev as a composer of international importance, and in May he left his native land, apparently intending at first to stay away only until the political situation had become more settled. But in fact he did not return permanently for eighteen years, living primarily in the United States until 1922 and then in Paris. Prokofiev's contact with the West eventually had a noticeable effect on his style, though its extent was not immediately evident. The two principal works of the American years (both premiered in Chicago), *The Love for Three Oranges* (1919), a satiric opera based on a fairy tale by Gozzi, and the Third Piano Concerto (1921), retain the essential features of the earlier Russian works.

After he settled in Paris, however, Prokofiev's music took on a more dissonant and complicated character. The Piano Sonata No. 5, Op. 38 (1923, later revised and simplified as Op. 135), the Quintet for Winds and Strings (1924), and the Second Symphony (1925) trace a clear line toward greater textural and formal intricacy. The first movement of the Symphony, for example, features dense blocks of sound, built up from ostinato-like layers, and a tonal environment considerably more ambiguous than before. Although ostinato figures were a familiar element in such earlier works as the *Scythian Suite* and *Chout,* here they tangle with one another instead of cooperating as before, forming complex textural patterns that recall Stravinsky's *Rite of Spring.*

Prokofiev himself was uncertain about the Second Symphony and came to believe that it had been written against his own nature—that he had been, in his words, seduced by the "effect of the Parisian atmosphere." After its first performance he wrote, "It occurred to me that I might be destined to become a second-rate composer," and in the compositions that followed he returned to a somewhat more constrained style. Two ballets for Diaghilev, *The Steel Step* (1926) and *The Prodigal Son* (1929), and the Third and Fourth Symphonies (1928, 1930) all show a tendency toward greater clarity and simplicity. So did the only opera of the Paris years, *The Fiery Angel* (1923, revised in 1927). Although it did not receive a full performance until after the composer's death, material from the opera was incorporated into the Third Symphony.

Prokofiev never felt completely at home in Western Europe. After several extended visits to Russia during the late 1920s and early 1930s, he finally resettled there permanently in 1936. His reentry into Soviet life coincided with the increasingly intense crackdown on progressive art in Russia and the emergence of socialist realism as the official style of the Communist Party. Although apparently little interested in politics, Prokofiev was inevitably drawn into the esthetic controversies raging at that time. Those in power considered his Parisian works, even the more recent ones, to be "formalist" and "decadent," conceived under the spell of undesirable foreign influences.

Prokofiev proved susceptible to the pressures exerted by the regime; as early as 1934 he had begun expressing views more to the liking of the Party. He wrote publicly that a new kind of "light-serious" or "serious-light" music was required for the "new mass audience that the modern Soviet composer must strive to reach," and that this music should be "primarily melodious, and the melody should be clear and simple." His orchestral suite *Lieutenant Kijé* (1934), based on music originally written for a film, reflected an effort to move in this direction. Indeed, all of the composer's music from this time on reveals a more conservative and "populist" tone.

Yet Prokofiev was not completely willing to compromise his musical conscience, and his attitude toward the political function of music remained ambivalent. He warned against "the danger of becoming provincial" and for the remainder of his life walked a dangerously thin line between official acceptability and the dictates of his own artistic inclinations. In Zhdanov's notorious 1948 decree attacking all the more progressive elements in Russian art, Prokofiev's entire output was officially characterized as "alien to the Soviet people," a censure not lifted until 1958, five years after the composer's death.

In his later Russian period Prokofiev continued to be remarkably prolific, despite the strained political and artistic atmosphere. During these years he completed three symphonies (Nos. 5–7); four piano sonatas (Nos. 6–9); two concertos, one for violin and one for cello; three well-received full-length ballets (*Romeo and Juliet, Cinderella,* and *The Stone Flower*); and a number of film scores, most notably two for the famous director Sergey Eisenstein, *Alexander Nevsky* (1938, source of the cantata of the same name) and *Ivan the Terrible* (1945). In addition, he produced a series of operas, most of which unfortunately encountered ideological objections and were little heard until the 1960s: *Semyon Kotko* (1939), *Betrothal in a Monastery* (1941; after Sheridan's play *The Duenna*), *War and Peace* (completed in 1943, though much revised thereafter), and *The Story of a Real Man* (1948). Of these, *War and Peace* is the most ambitious and musically arresting; cast in an essentially traditional operatic mold, it has earned a respected position among twentieth-century works for the musical stage.

Although lacking the energy of Prokofiev's youthful scores, his later music contains, as if for compensation, a more open, relaxed lyricism, a new expressive warmth. Such works as the Fifth Symphony and the Seventh Piano Sonata have undeniable power. But at heart he had always been a composer with a strong traditional orientation, so the more conservative approach of his later scores represented not so much a negation of his earlier style as a readjustment made within its own terms.

SHOSTAKOVICH

The fifteen years between Prokofiev's birth and that of Dmitry Shostakovich (1906–75) placed the younger composer in a very different relationship to the development of Soviet Russia. Prokofiev had received all his training and attained full musical maturity by the time of the revolution, and the main influences on his work throughout the two decades when he lived abroad were primarily Western. Although after his return to Russia he frequently professed his support of "the new society," Prokofiev was a "Soviet composer" in only a limited sense, and always remained something of an outsider, not actively involved in official musical deliberations. Shostakovich, on the other hand, began his professional musical training after the revolution, entering the Petrograd Conservatory in 1919. Moreover, since he remained in Russia throughout his life, his musical attitudes, as indeed his entire compositional career, were intimately tied to the growth of musical life under the new regime.

Shostakovich seems to have never doubted that every composer owes certain political and social responsibilities to the state. From the earliest years of his professional life, he unequivocally believed that music should have an ideological function and accepted the ideal of reaching as large an audience as possible. In addition, he participated actively in the musical affairs of his country and was recognized throughout Russia as a major public figure in the arts. Yet creative life was far from easy for Shostakovich, who frequently disagreed with the authorities over the type of music best suited to realize the Soviet mission. As a consequence, he suffered under the constant threat of political censorship.

In his extraordinary musical gifts and early development, Shostakovich resembled Prokofiev. His First Symphony (1925), a conservatory graduation piece written with impressive assurance in an essentially conservative tonal style, established him as an international figure at the age of nineteen. Upon leaving the academic atmosphere of the conservatory, Shostakovich began to explore the more progressive trends at that time still relatively prominent in Russian music. In two piano works, the First Sonata (1926) and *Aphorisms* (1927), we encounter a

The young Shostakovich

seemingly new composer, eager to experiment; the tightly linear textures and aggressive rhythmic drive set this music off sharply from the symphony. (Shostakovich's former composition teacher, Maximilian Steinberg, admitted that he "understood nothing" when the young composer showed him the score of the *Aphorisms*.) This development toward "abstract experimentation," as Shostakovich himself later characterized it, culminated in the Second Symphony (1927), a one-movement composition with a final choral section setting a Marxist text. The tonal freedom and general stylistic complexity of this work are remarkable; indeed, the contrapuntal writing reaches levels of such density that the listener often hears only a generalized timbral effect rather than specific melodic or harmonic content. The Third Symphony (1929), also a single movement with a choral (and Marxist) conclusion, is somewhat more relaxed despite retaining much of the Second's textural complexity.

In 1930, after completing the Third Symphony, Shostakovich began work on the fateful opera *Lady Macbeth of the Mtsensk District,* finishing it in 1932. Initially the opera met with unusual success, performed repeatedly in Leningrad and Moscow (as well as in a number of foreign cities), enthusiastically received by both public and critics, and even acclaimed as an ideal embodiment of Soviet art. But suddenly and unexpectedly, in January of 1936, after ninety-seven performances in Moscow, the official Party newspaper *Pravda* published an article entitled "Chaos Instead of Music," which attacked *Lady Macbeth* for its "negative" libretto, "petty-bourgeois innovations," and "deliberately dissonant, confused stream of sound." This article marked an important turning point in Soviet attitudes toward contemporary music, which from this moment on were to be consistently repressive. Exactly why this particular work was singled out as an example has never been clear, for it is considerably more consonant, more "melodic," and more openly tonal than the Second Symphony, Shostakovich's earlier satiric opera *The Nose* (1928), or the ballet *The Golden Age* (1930). Probably it was simply due to *Lady Macbeth*'s great success and the prominence of its composer, while the unusual international attention it attracted also may have raised suspicions that it was catering to the decadent tastes of the West. In any event, it provided the Party with a pretext to state publicly, in the strongest terms, that the liberal attitudes of the past, which had welcomed experimentation, innovation, and international contacts, would no longer be tolerated.

The Fifth Symphony (1937) was, to quote a famous remark supposedly made by Shostakovich himself, the composer's "creative answer to justified criticism." Certainly the new work, texturally much simpler than the preceding three symphonies and more straightforward thematically and tonally as well as formally, represents a stylistic retrenchment. For example, the opening of the first movement (Example X-5) sets out a canon at the octave, rhythmically arranged to expose the imitative relationship between the two parts as clearly as possible. The motivic connections between the two lines are supported by those within each line, and the new rhythmic figure in m. 3, which appears when the two voices become independent, is unmistakably derived from the opening dotted figure, as is the accompanimental rising fourth in the lower part (mm. 4ff.). Also unambiguous are the tonal focus and direction of the passage: the two canonic voices both begin on upbeat tonic Ds and at the end of the first phrase (m. 4) converge from opposite directions on A, whose dominant function is immediately confirmed by the V–I ostinato pattern in the lower strings. Finally, the melody that begins in mm. 6–7 in the first violins clearly outlines the D-minor tonic triad, gently inflected by a chromatic E♭.

To view the Fifth Symphony purely as a political concession tailored to fit the party's requirements would be an oversimplification. The music Shostakovich wrote between the Second Symphony and the 1936 attack on *Lady Macbeth* had already traced a partial withdrawal from the extremes of the former work. Both the Third and Fourth Symphonies, for example, fall more easily within the older symphonic tradition, owing in part to the influence of Mahler, which was first becoming discernible

Example X-5: SHOSTAKOVICH, Symphony No. 5, first movement, mm. 1–7

in Shostakovich's music at this time, evident in the choral finale of the Third and in the huge orchestral forces and broadly etched musical characterizations—including "populist" elements—of the Fourth. Still incomplete at the time of the *Lady Macbeth* affair, the Fourth Symphony was finished by Shostakovich in the following months, then withdrawn just before its first performance and not heard for another quarter century. And, ironically, the opera itself showed signs of further stylistic clarification.

Evidently, Shostakovich was already moving at least in the general direction of the Fifth Symphony before the *Pravda* denunciation; and although his future would no doubt have been different had there been no official rebuke, it is difficult to believe that the course he took—or was forced to take—was in any basic way antithetical to his own temperament. (Here the parallel with Prokofiev is striking.) Even in his most complex compositions, such as the Second and Third Symphonies, the chromatic and tonally obscure segments are juxtaposed against others more tonal and diatonic. Moreover, both of these symphonies have explicitly political programs, and incorporate settings of Marxist texts in a style simpler and more triadic and tonal than any other music they contain. Indeed, these symphonies suggest that Shostakovich made a definite programmatic association of, on the one hand, dissonant, structurally complex music with the Party's struggle for power, and, on the other, more straightforward tonal music with the Party's ultimate victory.

The changes in Shostakovich's style in the middle and later 1930s, even though imposed upon him, were changes he could accommodate within the framework of his own compositional beliefs. Despite its relative uncomplexity, the Fifth Symphony is a work of obvious artistic conviction, expressive power, and technical accomplishment. During the remainder of his life, Shostakovich was able to produce much more music of real interest and worth, despite the constant pressures of a dictatorial regime.

This does not mean that he was unaffected by political oppression. During the years following Zhdanov's 1948 decree, Shostakovich's productivity declined markedly. For a five-year period he concentrated mainly on film music, resuming a full range of compositional activity only after the death of Stalin in 1953 and the subsequent lifting of the decree. More broadly, his output over the four decades following the 1936 *Pravda* article is decidedly uneven in quality—a fact no doubt partly attributable to the shifting degrees of control exercised by the Party but also probably affected by fluctuations in the composer's own attitude toward the explicit inclusion of political and social "content" in his work. Several of the symphonies seem crudely populist in conception. The ponderous Seventh and Eighth, both written during World War II and with programs related to the war, are monumental in scope, overblown in expression, and extremely repetitive. (The Seventh has nevertheless achieved considerable popularity.) And the Eleventh and Twelfth (1957, 1961), also politically oriented, betray similar weaknesses.

Yet other Shostakovich symphonies from the post-Stalin period are works of great interest. The Tenth Symphony (1953), with an impressive first movement that gradually develops its basically simple melodic materials into a lengthy, climax-punctuated statement, is a considerable achievement. So is the Thirteenth (1962), a remarkably somber and sparsely textured setting for bass, male chorus, and orchestra of five poems by Yevgeny Yevtushenko (one of which, "Babi Yar," dealing with the execution of Russian Jews during World War II, had to be modified after the premiere to satisfy the censors). Equally stark and technically impressive is the Fourteenth (1969), which resembles the Thirteenth in being more an orchestral song cycle than a symphony; its eleven movements are settings of poems by eleven different poets (many of them from Western Europe) for soprano, bass, and a small chamber orchestra limited to strings and percussion. Shostakovich's last symphony, the Fifteenth (1971), is a much plainer and brighter affair, even incorporating, for ironic or enigmatic ends, quotations from Rossini and Wagner.

The eclecticism, stylistic inconsistency, and technical unevenness of the symphonies, intended for a large and diverse public, are less apparent in Shostakovich's chamber music. Most notable are the fifteen string quartets, the first dating from 1935 and the last, among the composer's final compositions, from 1974. In these more intimate statements the composer seems to have been less burdened by outside pressures and thus able to develop a more concentrated and adventurous musical language. In such works as the Eighth and Twelfth Quartets (1960, 1968) Shostakovich superimposes a highly original brand of intense chromaticism upon an essentially triadic and tonal foundation; the harmonic motion is determined mainly by linear considerations, without recourse to conventional progressions. The extension of the technical and expressive features of the Romantic instrumental tradition within a highly personal twentieth-century idiom is here reminiscent of Alban Berg.

Our picture of Shostakovich, and in particular of his relationship to the regime, has been complicated by the appearance in 1979 of his alleged "memoirs," entitled *Testimony* and edited by the exiled Russian music critic Solomon Volkov. According to Volkov, the material, first taken down in conversations with Shostakovich over a lengthy period, was then restructured by the editor into a first-person narrative. Its accuracy in many details is impossible to determine, and the book's authenticity has been much debated, especially in Russia, where a systematic attempt was at first made to discredit its reliability and to question the closeness of Volkov's association with the composer. Nevertheless, it seems likely that much of the material reflects Shostakovich's views. The bitter descriptions of the difficulties confronting the Soviet composer, particularly during the extremes of the Stalinist period, are compelling; and many of the musical opinions expressed appear to be consistent with Shostakovich's general outlook.

A final word is in order concerning the continued prominence of the symphony in twentieth-century Russia. The fact that two of the century's most important symphonists, Prokofiev and Shostakovich, were Russian in origin and (excepting Prokofiev's two decades abroad) remained mainly active in their native country is not coincidental. In central and Western Europe, the home of the symphonic tradition, the major composers, apparently convinced that it could no longer accommodate a fully modern compositional sensibility, shied away from the genre. In Russia, however, the symphony had been cultivated only since the latter part of the nineteenth century and thus represented a less weighty heritage. (Significantly, other countries where the symphony especially flourished during the first half of the present century also lie outside its original breeding ground: e.g., Finland, England, the United States.) And the generally conservative Russian political and artistic atmosphere, at least after the 1920s, was also hospitable to its growth.

In a comparison of Prokofiev's and Shostakovich's symphonic output, however, the differences between the two composers seem as prominent as the similarities. Prokofiev remained close to the eighteenth-century symphonic conception: clear textures, strongly articulated individual sections, the overall shape arising from balanced combinations of discrete, strongly contrasting formal units. Shostakovich's symphonies, on the other hand, tend toward the more freely and continuously evolving "narrative" conception found in many nineteenth-century symphonists, especially Mahler. Sectional contrasts are less marked, yielding a more ongoing and connected form, shaped by gradual alternations of graded levels of expressive and technical emphasis within an essentially unbroken temporal span.

The influence of politics on musical events has been unusually potent in the twentieth century—as attested by the overall organization of this book, divided into segments by the two world wars. Ideological conflicts have assumed an explicit role in the arts comparable to that occupied in past epochs by religion or social class. While the extent of that influence has varied considerably (waxing again in recent decades, as we shall see), at no time did such ideas and events play so large a role as during the interwar years, and in no places more than in the two countries just considered, Germany and Russia, where the establishment of totalitarian regimes fundamentally transformed the entire complexion of musical life. Yet everywhere during these decades the press of political events impinged significantly on musical activities. In Spain and Italy, where fascist regimes also (if less brutally than in Germany) kept rein on musical developments, the influence was overt; in Poland and Hungary, where nationalist sentiments increasingly affected stylistic leanings, it was more indirect; and even in the United States a strongly populist turn during the Great Depression widely altered compositional attitudes. And, as the world moved inexorably closer to all-out war, the role of the arts—including music—inevitably dwindled within the larger course of events.

CHAPTER XI

Other Europeans

ITALY: CASELLA, MALIPIERO, AND DALLAPICCOLA

In the early years of the twentieth century the continuing hold of nineteenth-century operatic conventions, especially those of the *verismo* style, represented a definite hindrance to the evolution of Italian music. Along with a marked tendency to minimize the importance of all instrumental music, including that of Italy's own highly developed Baroque and Classical tradition, the pervasive atmosphere of musical provincialism prevented acceptance of the more progressive compositional developments evident in Germany and France. Italy's only direct experience comparable to what was taking place elsewhere on the Continent in the years preceding World War I was with the Futurists, but their views were too extreme to bring about a significant change in the musical life of the country at large.

The two composers most responsible for initiating the eventual renewal of Italian music were Alfredo Casella (1883–1947) and Gian Francesco Malipiero (1882–1973). The precocious child of a family with unusually broad musical interests, Casella was sent at the age of twelve to study at the Paris Conservatory. In the French capital, which remained his principal residence for some twenty years, Casella was exposed to musical influences from all over Europe and acquired a broadly cosmopolitan musical outlook. Returning to Italy in 1916, he dedicated himself to the development of a new Italian style that, in his words, "would be based on our great instrumental past but which would also be contemporary in its musical language."[1] This essentially neo-classical stance led Casella

1. *Music in My Time,* trans. and ed. Spencer Norton (Norman, Okla., 1955), p. 90.

to ground his work on traditional formal models and to produce music that was tonal and diatonic, deriving its dissonant harmonies from the free combination of contrapuntally conceived melodic lines. Despite his lack of a marked individual personality, or of a large following even in his own country, Casella was an effective organizer, and as a composer aware of contemporary musical currents and versed in the techniques of instrumental music as well as those of opera, he provided a significant model for younger Italians.

Malipiero, although no more influential than Casella in the development of Italian music, achieved considerably more success as a composer. He too studied abroad, attending lectures by Max Bruch in Berlin in 1908, and he met Casella during a visit to Paris in 1913, where he heard—and was greatly influenced by—the premiere of *The Rite of Spring*. But the most important event in Malipiero's compositional evolution was the discovery, at the Bibliotèca Marciana in Venice in 1902, of a group of manuscripts by early Italian composers. This music, ranging from Monteverdi to Stradella and Tartini, made a lasting impression on his own work: "From the very start," he later wrote, "I reacted instinctively against musical conditions in an Italy that was suffocated by the tyranny of nineteenth-century opera."[2]

In his compositional style Malipiero attempted to integrate within a contemporary idiom not only features of this earlier Italian music but also those of more "archaic" sources, especially Gregorian chant. Although the harmony is often triadic in foundation, traditional functions are avoided in favor of a sort of neo-modality, and the music's freely developing formal character results from successions of clearly differentiated, essentially lyrical musical segments—an approach clearly at odds with the more continuous, dramatically conceived, climax-oriented music of late nineteenth-century Italian opera. Although Malipiero's long life spanned the major stylistic transformations that took place following both world wars, his own work remained essentially consistent and without noticeable evolution. Like Casella, he composed prolifically in all genres, and his output includes eleven symphonies, six piano concertos, and a large number of stage works (including over thirty operas), as well as chamber and piano music.

Malipiero's interest in earlier Italian music led him to edit and publish the work of Monteverdi and Vivaldi in modern editions. And both he and Casella wrote compositions using musical materials from Italian composers of the past: e.g., Malipiero's *Scarlattiana* (1926) and *Paganiniana* (1942), and Casella's *La Cimarosiana* (1921) and *Vivaldiana* (1952). In this practice, a manifestation of the period's neo-classical climate,

2.   Quoted in Everett Helm, "Malipiero," John Vinton, ed., *Dictionary of Contemporary Music* (New York, 1974), p. 446, col. 2.

they were joined by their contemporary Ottorino Respighi (1879–1936), who reworked material from earlier composers in his *Rossiniana* (1925) and *Antiche Arie e danze per liuto* (1917, 1924, and 1932). Respighi, however, is better known for his two popular neo-impressionist tone poems, *Fontane di Roma* (*Fountains of Rome,* 1916) and *Pini di Roma* (*Pines of Rome,* 1924).

To the next generation of Italian composers belongs Luigi Dallapiccola (1901–75), widely regarded as the country's outstanding twentieth-century composer. Dallapiccola matured in the atmosphere of classical renewal initiated by Casella and Malipiero, and his earliest fully representative work, the Partita for Orchestra (with a soprano solo in the finale; 1932), reflects the then-current concern for stylistic directness, transparent textures, and traditional formal types (the first movement, for example, is a passacaglia). Yet the diversified pitch language, incorporating significant chromatic elements within an underlying diatonicism, already hints at the gradual development toward dodecaphony that was to characterize the next phase of Dallapiccola's career.

Born of Italian parents in what was then a disputed part of Austria, Dallapiccola was interned in Graz during part of World War I, and it was there that he first became intensely interested in composition. Upon returning to Italy after the war, he undertook serious musical studies, eventually attending the Cherubini Conservatory in Florence, where he studied with Ernesto Consolo and Vito Frazzi, and where, after receiving his diploma, he himself began teaching in 1934. Dallapiccola's reputation was acquired slowly and in the face of considerable resistance within his native country. Mussolini's fascist regime, though far less repressive than the one in Germany, reacted strongly against new developments in the arts, insuring that Italy as a whole remained unreceptive to musical modernism. On the contrary, the government fostered a very narrowly conceived nationalism. Even Casella and Malipiero were attacked for their "progressivism" and "internationalism," and the still more progressive Dallapiccola was viewed by many as a traitor to his country's musical heritage. Only in the 1950s and 1960s, when a more open and tolerant atmosphere again prevailed, did Dallapiccola finally begin to be widely recognized as the most gifted and original Italian composer of his time.

As the first prominent Italian composer to adopt the twelve-tone system, Dallapiccola played a significant role in redefining the boundaries of his country's music. He also showed that the system did not irrevocably entail a Germanic stylistic orientation. Reinterpreting the system according to his own esthetic needs, Dallapiccola was able to produce a new range of expressive intentions. His path to full use of the twelve-tone system was entirely different from those taken by his Viennese predecessors. Whereas they gradually neutralized traditional tonal functions through increasing chromatic saturation, he treated more system-atically the chromatic elements he already used to enhance his music's essentially modal-diatonic basis. Thus, in the earliest instances of Dal-lapiccola's twelve-tone writing, such as *Il Coro degli zitti* (from the third series of *Cori di Michelangelo,* 1936), tone rows are used only occasion-ally, and simply as a means for controlling the chromatic content of certain melodic sequences; the accompaniment is not affected by the row at all, nor are any of the standard row operations (inversion, ret-rograde, etc.) used. Even when these operations do appear, in the *Tre Laudi* (1937), the row is still limited to a melodic role, combined with a triadic accompaniment that is not row-derived.

Dallapiccola's move toward a more systematic treatment of the total chromatic was thus extremely gradual, and accomplished without any fundamental change in the overall character of his music. The two most important works of the late 1930s and early 1940s, the one-act opera *Volo di notte* (*Night Flight,* 1939) and the choral *Canti di prigionia* (Songs of Imprisonment, 1941), continue to juxtapose modal and chromatic elements, although the balance has shifted more heavily toward the lat-ter. The first completely twelve-tone piece, *Cinque Frammenti di Saffo* (Five Fragments from Sappho), for voice and fifteen instruments, did not appear until 1942, and even here Dallapiccola's use of the method is quite free and entirely personal, as is illustrated by a passage from the fourth song (Example XI-1).

The music is not based on a single row but on two (both shown in Example XI-1a). Row I can be segmented into four three-note groups, the first, second, and fourth of which produce, respectively, major, minor, and diminished triads. In the excerpt (Example XI-1b) as throughout the song, Dallapiccola uses this row harmonically, and the resulting triadic groupings give the music a strongly traditional flavor, despite the very different meaning the triads take on in this dodeca-phonic context. Moreover, the vocal part is also entirely derived from this row, creating an essentially traditional correspondence between the principal melodic line and its accompaniment. The second row is pre-sented linearly, starting in m. 2 of the excerpt (upper piano system), appearing first in original form and then, in m. 4, in retrograde inver-

Example XI-1: DALLAPICCOLA, *Cinque Frammenti di Saffo,* No. 4

a. Tone rows

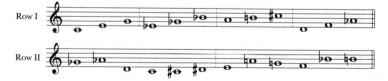

b. Excerpt (piano reduction)

sion. At the same time, another voice begins with a repetition of the original form (m. 4, lower piano system).

Dallapiccola's conception of the system as one that is open to tonal and triadic allusions (the song quoted above even closes on an unadorned C-major triad) suggests the influence of Berg, but another feature of his twelve-tone writing, a tendency to employ strict canonic structures, draws more upon the precedent of Webern. Even the relatively early "Congedo di Girolamo Savonarola" (third of the *Canti di prigionia*) contains a section with a complex canonic structure, including a strict ret-rograde, and a number of the eleven movements of the *Quaderno musicale di Annalibera*, a piano work of 1952, are strictly canonic. Indeed, Dallapiccola's preference for strict contrapuntal procedures is evident throughout much of his work, including three tonal compositions using melodic material from earlier Italian composers: the *Sonatina canonica* for piano (1943), based on Paganini, and the *Tartiniana* for violin and orchestra (1951) and *Tartiniana seconda* for violin and piano (1956).

However, such tonal compositions are the exception in Dallapiccola's mature output. During the 1950s and 1960s he continued to refine his twelve-tone writing, even moving toward a stricter and more "orthodox" conception of the method, so that triads and octave doublings, so characteristic of his earlier twelve-tone pieces, were eventually avoided. Moreover, Dallapiccola began to adopt certain techniques characteristic of post–World War II serialism, among them derivation of secondary rows through serial permutations of a single segment of a principal row and variation of small rhythmic cells through strict proportional transformations. Yet the expressive character of his music remained remarkably untouched by these technical innovations. The basic impulse continued to be fundamentally lyrical, with long melodic lines spun out in free, continuously unfolding sections, clothed in delicate instrumentation and resonant (though now nontriadic) harmonies. Especially characteristic of the later music is its "floating rhythm" (a term used by the composer), achieved by the avoidance of heavy metrical accents, steady pulses, and balanced phrase structures.

Dallapiccola was a scrupulous and severely self-critical composer with a correspondingly small compositional output. Aside from *Volo di notte* he produced two additional operas—the one-act *Il Prigioniero* (*The Prisoner,* 1948) and the full-length *Ulisse* (*Ulysses,* 1968), which proved to be his last major composition—as well as a small body of choral and instrumental music. However, the heart of Dallapiccola's oeuvre, reflecting the essentially lyrical focus of his style and spanning his entire creative life, is a series of pieces for solo voice with different groups of accompanying instruments. Here, in such works as *Tre Poemi* (1949), *Goethe Lieder* (1953), and *Parole di San Paolo* (1964), one recognizes most clearly the profoundly Italianate character of his musical personality.

Opening scene of Dallapiccola's *Il prigionero;* in the 1962 La Scala production with sets and costumes by Ita Maksimovna, direction by Günter Rennert. (Courtesy Ente Autonomo Teatro Scala, Milan)

The only other Italian of Dallapiccola's generation to achieve significant recognition outside his own country was Goffredo Petrassi (b. 1904). In compositions such as the Partita for Orchestra (1932) and the First Concerto for Orchestra (1934), Petrassi adopted a diatonic, neoclassical style derived from Stravinsky and Casella. Later, however, he began to put more emphasis on chromaticism, and eventually—a considerable time after Dallapiccola—adopted the twelve-tone system, which he employed sporadically in the cantata *Noche oscura* (1951) and then predominantly (though still not exclusively) in the Second Concerto for Orchestra (1952). In the most recent phase of his career Petrassi has favored an uncompromisingly chromatic and atonal language that, while not strictly serial, owes much to the stylistic innovations of the post–World War II generation. The String Trio (1959), for example, is athematic in conception and places special emphasis on textural and timbral features. Although a *concertante* conception of instrumental writing has remained constant throughout much of Petrassi's work, the extent to which his compositional approach has altered over the years is striking—an interesting contrast to Dallapiccola, whose music, despite its slowly evolving technical basis, remained fundamentally unchanged in overall character and intent.

GERMANY: ORFF

German composers who were not forced—as were Hindemith, Weill, and many others—to leave their country during Hitler's Third Reich faced essentially two possibilities: either to go on writing as they wished, "privately," with no immediate hope of making the music known to others, or to adopt a suitably conservative musical style that would not offend those in power. The first choice, for example, was taken by Karl Amadeus Hartmann (1905–63), who continued to compose actively, though essentially secretly, during the Nazi period, emerging after the war as one of the leading figures of the older generation, especially admired for his symphonic writing. Of those taking the second course, Carl Orff (1895–1982) was perhaps the most successful in fashioning a style that, though sufficiently simple to please the authorities, was nevertheless clearly individual and in significant respects original. That he was able to do so stemmed largely from the fact that his music stood so totally apart from the main currents of twentieth-century musical developments.

Orff's characteristic style first emerged in the scenic cantata *Carmina burana* (1937), a setting of somewhat ribald medieval Latin and German songs. Here was established his conception of music as part of a composite art form in which textual declamation assumes the dominant role. Simple syllabic settings are projected through elemental chantlike melodic figures, repeated incessantly to the percussive accompaniment of static triadic harmonies, which themselves appear in recurrent, blocklike patterns featuring highly rhythmic, though uncomplicated, ostinato figures. The closest musical precedent is Stravinsky, especially the Stravinsky of *The Wedding;* but the extremely differentiated compositional techniques of that work are here reduced to their most basic common denominator. Everything is contrived to produce a direct and instantaneous effect. The music gives something of the impression of a ritualistic incantation, but one that seems to have been purposely shorn of all mystery.

Orff was so convinced by the new manner he had fashioned for this work that he instructed his publisher to destroy all of his previous music; and he has remained essentially constant in method ever since. His inclination to view music as part of a larger spectacle incorporating words and movement led him naturally to the theater, and the bulk of his output since *Carmina burana* (which itself calls for "magic images") has been for the stage. The later works become even more stylized in conception, their dramatic content presented in uncompromisingly detached and objective, rather than personal and psychological, terms. This is already evident in two operas based on fairy tales written immediately following the cantata: *Der Mond* (*The Moon*, 1939) and *Die Kluge* (*The Clever Woman*, 1943). But the fullest realization of Orff's vision of modern ritualistic theater, with dance, action, and music occupying equal roles, is found in a trilogy of theater works (the word "opera" is no longer applicable) based on Greek subjects: *Antigonae* (1949) and *Oedipus der Tyrann* (1959) are settings of Hölderlin's free German translations of Sophocles, and *Prometheus* (1966) uses Aeschylus's original Greek. Here Orff reduces his musical content even more stringently, limiting melodic lines to the simplest possible shapes. Everything is geared to a highly stylized rhythmic projection of the text, punctuated by incisive accents from an accompanying orchestra dominated by percussion instruments.

Orff's disposition to limit pitch content to an absolute minimum reached its extreme in the theater piece *Die Bernauerin* (1947), where spoken sections alternate with purely rhythmic settings of the text, accompanied by an ensemble of unpitched percussion instruments. Only twice, once briefly during the course of the action and then again in a more extended final section, are pitches used at all, and even these are limited to a few notes, repeated over and over in the simplest possible manner.

An especially important aspect of Orff's career has been his educational work with children. In 1924 he helped found a school for gymnastics, dance, and music, for which he developed a pedagogical approach enabling young people with no formal musical training to participate immediately in ensemble performances and to improvise cooperatively within simple, yet prescribed, melodic and harmonic frameworks. (The close relation between Orff's conception of school music and his own

An important aspect of the Orff *Schulwerk* is its effectiveness with handicapped children, some of whom are shown here playing together on special xylophones of all sizes. (From Gertrud Orff, *The Orff Music Therapy,* Schott Music Corporation, New York, 1974)

musical style is noteworthy.) For these purposes he helped design special, easily playable instruments, and developed a set of graded materials, encompassing preliminary exercises, folk tunes, and dances; collectively published under the title *Orff-Schulwerk,* these are now known throughout the world for their creative approach to elementary musical education.

Despite the limited character of his compositional output and the absence of any followers, Orff occupies an important position in twentieth-century German music—the only German composer of his generation who remained at home and won widespread recognition abroad. His most significant contemporary was Werner Egk (1901–83), who also concentrated mainly on works for the theater, though in his case these took the form of more traditionally conceived operas and ballets. Both composers also shared the influence of Stravinsky, but Egk is clearly distinguished from Orff by his fondness for impressionistic coloring and more differentiated use of melodic and harmonic materials. Nevertheless, Orff is the more original and personal figure; whatever his limitations, he fashioned an entirely distinctive approach to music, quite different from any other of his time.

AUSTRIA: HAUER

One of the more interesting "outsiders" of the first half of the century, the Austrian composer Josef Matthias Hauer (1883–1959) was trained as an elementary school teacher and did not concentrate seriously on musical composition until he was twenty-eight. In a series of compositions between 1912 and 1919, he experimented with chromaticism and atonality, and after 1919 developed a systematic conception of twelve-tone composition that predated the one later proposed by Schoenberg.

Although his twelve-tone approach differed from Schoenberg's in several significant aspects, Hauer's starting point was similar: the twelve pitches of the chromatic scale were first given a specific structure, which then formed the basic source for the pitch material of a composition. Whereas for Schoenberg this structure was a serial ordering of all twelve pitches, for Hauer it consisted of a combination of two unordered hexachords that together contained all twelve pitches. Hauer referred to this twelve-tone structure as a "trope," and by 1921 he had formulated a theory according to which all possible twelve-tone collections could be reduced to forty-four such tropes, each consisting of two unordered hexachords, plus their transpositions and inversions. (Since the contents of each hexachord are unordered, the operation of retrograde is irrelevant.)

From the early 1920s on, all of Hauer's compositions were based on

Example XI-2: HAUER, Piano Piece, Op. 25, No. 8

a. Trope

b. mm. 1–8

(Accidentals apply only to notes immediately following)

By permission of the original publisher, Robert Lienau, Berlin.

his trope theory. Typical is the opening of the Piano Piece, Op. 25, No. 8 (1923; Example XI-2b). The trope on which the piece is based is shown in Example XI-2a, with the two unordered hexachords labeled **A** and **B**. Each of the first four measures—and thereafter each pair of measures—presents one of the two hexachords, which alternate so as to produce twelve-tone complexes. At first untransposed (mm. 1–2), the trope is then transposed up a minor third (mm. 3–4) and then up an additional minor third (mm. 5–8).

The stark simplicity of this music—the undifferentiated rhythmic and melodic structure, the reliance on triads for cadential emphasis—and its "neutral" expressive quality are characteristic of Hauer, whose music often gives the impression of having been conceived primarily for the purpose of illustrating his theory of twelve-tone tropes. Consequently, despite his very sizable catalogue of music, Hauer is known today primarily for the several small theoretical books in which he detailed the technical and esthetic basis of his compositional approach, notably *Von Melos zur Pauke* (From Melody to Kettledrum, 1925) and *Zwölftontechnik: Die Lehre von den Tropen* (Twelve-Tone Technique: The Theory of the Tropes, 1926).

Even as a theorist, however, Hauer's significance today is measured primarily by his relationship to Schoenberg. The two composers worked along similar lines in the years around 1920, when they were in frequent contact and actively shared ideas. Since Hauer first arrived at the notion of a systematic deployment of all twelve tones, it seems likely that he influenced Schoenberg and not vice versa. As we have seen, Schoenberg occasionally used unordered rows in his earliest twelve-tone pieces (in movements of the Suite, Op. 25), and in later works sometimes used unordered tetrachords and hexachords in "accompanimental"

contexts. The crucial, overriding difference between the two composers is that for Schoenberg twelve-tone theory seems to have been a
means for realizing what was first and foremost a compositional idea,
whereas for Hauer the theoretical idea came first.

Hauer professed a mystical conception of the place of music in the
universe. For him "the atonal Melos" was something present from the
beginning of all time, not "created" by the composer but only "heard"
by him. The atonal composer, then, was not so much a "maker of
music" as a "hearer of music," one able to perceive and preserve the
"unchangeable, untouchable eternity in the essence of things." This notion
of twelve-tone melody as something that is simply "there," to be "taken
down"—rather than "created"—by the composer, eventually led him
to view composition as an "automatic" process within which personal
decisions have no role. After 1939 he stopped calling his works "compositions," preferring the designation *Zwölftonspiele (Twelve-Tone
Games)*. He wrote these "games" according to specific sets of rules that
varied from composition to composition, designed to suppress the
"ego"—and thus the individuality—of the composer in favor of a "play
with notes for the notes' sake," achieved through constant rotations of
cyclically conceived twelve-tone fields. Hauer composed over a thousand *Zwölftonspiele,* entitled only by number and date, for instrumental
ensembles ranging from solo piano to full orchestra, but most have
apparently been lost; however, those that survive are not fundamentally
different in character from the earlier works.

KRENEK

The most prominent member of the second generation of twentieth-
century Austrian composers, Ernst Krenek (b. 1900), has had a remarkably varied career. He first made his name with the extremely popular
"jazz opera" *Jonny spielt auf* (1926), one of the most successful products
of the 1920s' *Zeitoper* trend, in which—in Krenek's words—he "returned
to the tonal idiom, to the cantilena of Puccini, seasoning the whole with
the condiments of jazz." In 1930, however, Krenek adopted the twelve-
tone system, and he has since continued to write twelve-tone or serial
music. In 1938 he emigrated to the United States, eventually settling in
southern California.

Throughout his career Krenek has proved unusually responsive to
current trends, and his style and approach have varied accordingly. Following World War II he became interested in integral serialism and
wrote several works—notably the *Sestina* of 1957—that pushed the idea
of total compositional control to its outermost limits. Somewhat later
he experimented with limited degrees of indeterminacy: e.g., *From Three*

Make Seven (1961) and *Fibonacci mobile* (1964). Krenek is endowed with a prodigious compositional technique, and all of his considerable output—which includes a number of operas, as well as a large body of orchestral, chamber, and vocal music—has an authoritative mark. Active as a teacher and writer, in many books and articles he has dealt with both twentieth-century music (especially twelve-tone composition) and earlier Western music (that of the Renaissance).

POLAND: SZYMANOWSKI

Firmly under Russian political and cultural domination until the end of World War I, and with a single composer—Chopin—monopolizing its musical heritage, Poland offered little encouragement to progressive composers in the earlier years of the twentieth century. Nevertheless, one figure of international prominence did emerge during those years: Karol Szymanowski (1882–1937). Although recognized abroad more quickly than at home, Szymanowski ultimately exerted an important influence on Polish musical life, which experienced a sudden flourishing of compositional activity following World War II.

In such early works as the Piano Preludes, Op. 1 (1900), and the Études, Op. 4 (1902), Szymanowski was heavily indebted to Skryabin, while in the orchestral works of a few years later the mark of Wagner and Strauss was evident. By then, in travels to the West (and to North Africa), he had become acquainted with the music of Debussy and Ravel and the early ballets of Stravinsky, and these diverse sources contributed to an idiom that encompassed features of both French Impressionism and Germanic expressionism.

Szymanowski's works of the war years, which he passed primarily in the Ukraine, are remarkable for their originality and intensity. Two of the most notable, the Violin Concerto No. 1 (1916) and Piano Sonata No. 3 (1917), are both one-movement pieces in a rhapsodic, seemingly improvisatory manner featuring rich chromaticism and soaring climaxes. Although both are ultimately tonal (the Concerto ends on a carefully prepared A, the Sonata on an equally conclusive E), their freely dissonant harmonic material at times brings them to the edges of atonality. Virtuosic in conception, they make severe demands upon the performers. Dense, stratified layers of musical activity bring forth ecstatic waves of sound, betraying not only the earlier pull of Skryabin but also Szymanowski's more recently acquired interest in exotic musical cultures, especially those of Arabia and Persia. (Another work of this period, the Symphony No. 3 of 1916 for soloists, chorus, and orchestra, incorporates a setting of "The Song of Night" by the thirteenth-century Iranian poet Jalāl ad-Dīn ar-Rŭmi.) But perhaps the most significant offspring of Szymanowski's "Mediterranean" style was the opera *King Roger* (1926), whose subject was Roger II of Sicily.

Although at the height of his creative powers by the end of World War I, Szymanowski was still received coolly in Poland, distrusted for his international outlook and European stylistic orientation. Newly independent Poland was enveloped in a fresh atmosphere of national consciousness. Szymanowski, caught up in these nationalist feelings, began to question the distance separating his work from the larger Polish public, and, after a period of self-examination, set out to find a more explicitly national focus for his work. Stimulated by the examples of Bartók and the Stravinsky of the "Russian" period, he undertook a serious study of his native folk music and modified his style significantly in order to achieve a more openly Polish character. Beginning with the song cycle *Slopiewnie* (1921), his music takes on a much leaner, more compressed quality; the harmony is less chromatic, the melodic writing—now dominated by folk models—simpler and more direct, shorn of the expressive intensity evident in the earlier scores.

Szymanowski retained this national focus through the rest of his life. The principal work of this final period is the *Stabat mater* (1926), a finely conceived setting of the Latin text for soloists, chorus, and orchestra, notable for its rhythmic incisiveness and stark contrapuntal textures. Here the composer combines influences from contemporary neo-classicism with those of folk music and ancient chant to produce a powerful yet succinct statement. Other works of this period include the Second String Quartet (1927) and the Second Violin Concerto (1933).

Afflicted periodically by tuberculosis, Szymanowski died at the age of fifty-four. His output was relatively small, but it encompassed all mediums, including opera. Because of his eclecticism and his significant stylistic change after World War I, he is not easily placed within the larger framework of twentieth-century music. Yet his importance for the history of Polish music in the present century can be compared only with that of Chopin in the preceding one.

CZECHOSLOVAKIA: HÁBA

A strikingly independent figure in his day was the Czech composer Alois Hába (1893–1973), who became the chief advocate of microtonal music in the interwar years. A student of Viteslav Novák in Prague, Hába became acquainted with microtones (and also attended the concerts of Schoenberg's Society for Private Musical Performances) while studying in Vienna with Schreker. In such works as the String Quartet No. 1, Op. 4 (1919), he evolved a highly chromatic style based on a principle he referred to as "tonal centrality," whereby any fundamental tone could be combined freely with any other pitches of the chromatic scale. This led him to view tonality as a broadly defined pitch field characterized by steadily changing scalar content, and he considered his interest in microtonalism to be simply a further development of this general tonal conception. In the preface to his String Quartet No. 2, Op. 7 (1920), his first work to use microtones, Hába wrote: "For me it is a matter of enriching the previous semitone system with finer tonal differentiations, not of destroying it. For me the quarter-tone system appeared not as a new language, but as an extension of the old one." The use of additional subdivisions of the whole tone made available to him a wider range of scalar resources and allowed for more subtly inflected pitch relationships; the quarter tones in the Second String Quartet are employed essentially as nuances, as added inflections to the traditional Western system of twelve chromatic pitches.

At the time of his first microtonal compositions, Hába was also developing what he called "nonthematic" music: music with no repetition or development of melodic or motivic ideas, music in which contrapuntal lines are entirely independent, unrelated melodically or rhythmically. The String Quartet No. 3 (1922), also a quarter-tone piece, was the first composition written in this nonthematic manner, which has, however, little in common with the nonthematicism of, say, Webern. Indeed, in general textural layout and overall rhythmic shape, Hába's score seems remarkably traditional. It opens with a long melody in the first violin, which unfolds freely over several extended phrases without repetition or motivic variation; although the other voices are indeed independent in a narrowly thematic sense, they are clearly shaped to achieve a balance of motion and direction when heard in conjunction with the principal line. In the composer's description: "Thematic development is avoided, the total stream of thought is ruled entirely by the idea of forward motion."

Such music, excluding all traditional ideas of thematic relationships, obviously runs the risk of seeming "neutral" in quality, and an undeniable aspect of routine in Hába's nonthematic scores (especially noticeable in his reliance upon conventional figuration) would seem to be the inevitable consequence of an essentially negative conception of musical structure. In this respect Hába's music is reminiscent of Hauer's: one feels that it has been written to realize an abstract idea of primarily theoretical origin.

Hába's microtonal works were not exclusively quarter-tone. Among those based on fifth-tone division is the String Quartet No. 16 (1967), and the sixth-tone works include the Duo for Two Violins (1937), the String Quartet No. 11 (1957), and the opera *Thy Kingdom Come* (1942). Hába wrote several books on microtonal music, the most important being the *Neue Harmonielehre* (New Theory of Harmony, 1927), in which he attempted to codify the musical principles governing four different microtonal systems: quarter-tone, third-tone, sixth-tone, and twelve-tone (the latter incorporating all of the possibilities of the previous three).

Hába's output encompasses over one hundred opus numbers, and throughout his life he continued to write in the normal semitone system as well as in microtones, although the quarter-tone opera *The Mother* (1929) is considered by many to be his masterpiece. He also stimulated the construction of a number of microtonal instruments, including a quarter-tone piano, a sixth-tone harmonium, and a quarter-tone clarinet. And from 1934 until 1951 (except during the war years, when he was ostracized by the Nazis as a "decadent") Hába directed a department of microtonal music at the Prague Conservatory.

It seems likely that Hába was influenced by the ideas of Ferruccio Busoni, who in his 1907 *Sketch of a New Esthetic of Music* had proposed an enrichment of the available musical resources through microtonal extensions. (Other passages in that book may have suggested the notion of "nonthematic" music.) Two other composers during the first half of the century, the Mexican Julián Carrillo (1875–1965) and the Russian-French Ivan Vïshnegradsky (1893–1979), devoted the main portion of their work to microtonal music, and Charles Ives made occasional use of such possibilities. Although outside the central currents of early twentieth-century music, these developments have acquired renewed significance from the increased interest in microtonal divisions during recent years.

SPAIN: FALLA

Throughout the nineteenth century Spanish musical life had been dominated by the zarzuela, a popular form of folk opera alternating singing, dancing, and spoken dialogue. Escape from the limitations of that tradition was the moving force behind the country's musical development in the new century. The first steps were taken by Isaac Albéniz (1860–1909) and Enrique Granados (1867–1916). Both wrote zarzuelas in their earlier years, but both also studied abroad (in Leipzig and Paris, respectively) and began to explore a more cosmopolitan style of musical nationalism, combining indigenous elements of popular Spanish music with more advanced contemporary techniques, especially those of French Impressionism.

Albéniz specialized in relatively brief character pieces for the piano. The principal achievement of his brief life was the *Suite Iberia,* a series of twelve piano pieces published in four books between 1906 and 1909, whose brilliant pianistic conception and stylized use of local musical color set a new standard for Spanish musical nationalism. Influenced by

Albéniz, the somewhat younger Granados also favored the piano: his best-known work is *Goyescas* (1911), a suite of six pieces, impressions of paintings by Goya in a distinctive yet characteristically national style, which later served as the basis for an opera of the same name (1916).

Manuel de Falla (1876–1946), the outstanding Spanish composer of the first half of the twentieth century, reached musical maturity within the framework of this new nationalist movement. Characteristic of Falla's early work is the opera *La Vida breve* (*The Short Life*, 1905); although hampered by a dramatically thin libretto, it contains some strikingly effective music in the then current nationalist vein. Shortly after its completion Falla went to Paris, where he remained for seven years before returning to Madrid in 1914. In the French capital he befriended such prominent French musicians as Debussy, Ravel, and Dukas, and the city's cosmopolitan musical life stimulated in his work a more varied, less local character. Yet these new influences became evident only gradually. For all its technical virtuosity, the popular *Noches en los jardines de España* (Nights in the Gardens of Spain, 1915), three pieces for piano and orchestra evoking the musical atmosphere of the *cante jondo* or *flamenco* (the folk idiom of Falla's native Andalusia), still conforms to the general stylistic prescription of Albéniz and Granados: Spanish flavor coupled with impressionistic harmony and brilliant instrumental writing.

Nevertheless, the more rounded and developed compositional technique evident in this work and in the *Seven Spanish Popular Songs* for voice and piano (1915) already sets Falla somewhat apart from his Spanish predecessors. Moreover, in his next composition, the ballet *El Amor brujo* (*Love the Magician,* 1915), and especially in the later ballet *El Sombrero de tres picos* (*The Three-Cornered Hat,* 1919), Falla began to join less specific evocations of Spanish musical character with a more classically oriented approach to structure and instrumentation. This development, no doubt influenced to a degree by Stravinsky's somewhat analogous path following *The Rite of Spring,* culminated in the two masterpieces of Falla's maturity: the highly imaginative puppet opera *El Retablo de maese Pedro* (*Master Peter's Puppet Show,* 1922, based on Cervantes) and the Harpsichord Concerto (1926). Works of great economy and concision, these display a stark, hard-edged style reflecting not only current neo-classical tendencies but, more specifically, Falla's growing interest in earlier Spanish art music. This foundation drawn from the Middle Ages, the Renaissance, and the eighteenth century (especially Domenico Scarlatti, who lived in Spain for many years) gave Falla's nationalism greater universality, and placed these two works far beyond their forerunners in technical and expressive range.

Both are scored for small instrumental ensembles: the opera for three winds, four strings, percussion, and harpsichord, the Concerto for three

Nicola Benois' stage design for the second scene of Manuel de Falla's puppet opera *El retablo de Maese Pedro.*(Museo Teatrale della Scala, Milan)

winds, two strings, and harpsichord. (The harpsichord's prominent role in both works reflected Falla's recent study of earlier keyboard music, and contributed significantly to the twentieth-century revival of this instrument.) Both are essentially episodic in structure, with little emphasis on tonal motion or large-scale thematic development. The harmonic language, though still uncompromisingly tonal, is less consistently triadic than before, and largely liberated from the traditional functions of the common practice period: major-minor tonality has given way to a flexible modality. The music's Spanish character is no longer achieved through specific allusions to local musical types, but rather has become a fully integrated component within a complex and differentiated musical whole. With these works Falla virtually single-handedly brought Spanish music into the twentieth-century mainstream.

Unfortunately, declining health then took an increasing toll on his work. After 1926 Falla worked mainly on what he envisioned as his magnum opus, the "scenic cantata" *Atlántida,* but was unable to bring it to conclusion before his death in 1946. (A version prepared from Falla's working material, with additions, by his student Ernesto Halffter, was staged in 1962.) As a result, Falla's output, taken as a whole, is extremely limited. He worked slowly and was severely self-critical (though a chamber work lasting only twelve minutes, the Harpsichord Concerto required almost three years for its completion). Yet Falla's significance to the music of his country was decisive, comparable to that of Bartók in Hungary, Sibelius in Finland, and Vaughan Williams in England.

Falla's virtual silence after 1926 left Spanish music without an active leading figure. His best-known contemporary, Joaquin Turina (1882–1949), did not achieve a compositional level even roughly comparable. Perhaps the most talented member of the next Spanish generation, a generation whose development was significantly affected by the Spanish Civil War of 1936–39, was Roberto Gerhard (1896–1970). A composer of unusual ability, Gerhard studied first in Spain with Felipe Pedrell (who had earlier been mentor to Albéniz, Granados, and Falla) and then in Vienna with Schoenberg. After the defeat of the Spanish Republicans in 1939, Gerhard took up residence—and eventually citizenship—in England. The later work for which he is now best known was written in the "international" style characteristic of much post–World War II music, and offers few clues to its composer's Spanish origins.

CHAPTER XII

England after World War I

WALTON

In the years immediately following World War I English music continued to be largely dominated by the composers who had laid the foundation for the country's prewar "musical Renaissance"—Vaughan Williams, Holst, Bax, and their colleagues. The most important new voice of the 1920s was William Walton (1902–82). Largely self-taught in composition, Walton studied music at Oxford University but left there in 1920 without receiving a degree. Subsequently, he lived for some time as the "adopted, or elected, brother" of his Oxford friends, the poets and writers Osbert and Sacheverell Sitwell. With their sister Edith, one of the more radical English poets of her generation, Walton collaborated on his first major composition, *Façade* (1922), a "drawing-room entertainment" comprising recitations of brief poems with musical accompaniments played by a small, mixed chamber ensemble. Its immediate success, tinged with a touch of the scandalous, thrust Walton, at age twenty, into the national spotlight.

Although the medium of *Façade* recalled Schoenberg's *Pierrot lunaire* (and in its final version Walton's work contained the same number of poems), the result was very different. Sitwell's down-to-earth but often abstractly treated language inspired a score very much in the contemporary French manner of Les Six, sharply differentiating Walton from English composers of the previous generation. The musical background for the recitations consists of brief, highly stylized musical vignettes that wittily parody various types of popular music: tango, lullaby, fox-trot, polka, etc. The rhythms of the recitations (but not the

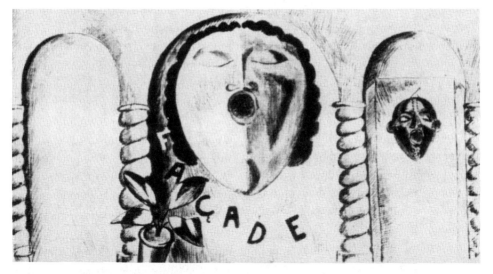

Screen design by Frank Dobson for the first public performance of Walton's
Façade, London, June 12, 1923.

pitches) are precisely notated, so that each word is carefully cued to the
musical setting. (At the first performance the detached, parodistic character was emphasized by having the verses recited through a megaphone, which protruded through a screen behind which the speaker
was hidden.) *Façade*'s light, no-nonsense anti-Romanticism quickly
captured the imagination of the younger generation in England.

Despite *Façade*'s success, Walton's development eventually led him
along a very different compositional path. Although the orchestral
overture *Portsmouth Point* (1925) retained much of the syncopated, jazz-
influenced character of the earlier work, the large-scale symphonic
aspirations of his next sizable composition, the Viola Concerto (1929),
placed him in a line of descent from Elgar. Eschewing the prevalent
nationalistic, folk-oriented style, Walton adopted a manner that aligned
him with such internationally oriented twentieth-century symphonists
as Sibelius and Prokofiev. The Concerto's warm lyricism and expres-
siveness stand in stark contrast to the concentrated brevity and emotional distance of *Façade*. While both works are unabashedly tonal, the
Concerto's form is expansive and structured after traditional symphonic models. The type of long, slowly evolving melody that initiates
the opening Andante comodo, though in some ways indebted to Elgar,
was to become one of Walton's stylistic hallmarks.

The seriousness, scope, and traditionalism of the Viola Concerto erased
Walton's earlier reputation as an *enfant terrible* and established him as the
leading English symphonic composer of his generation. His fame was
further enhanced by his next composition, the oratorio *Belshazzar's Feast*

(1931) for baritone, chorus, and orchestra, with a biblical text arranged by Osbert Sitwell. Its broad design (a sequence of connected musical numbers unbroken except for occasional fermatas), incisive musical imagery, and rhythmic intensity, plus Walton's skillful and varied handling of the chorus, make *Belshazzar* one of the most effective and powerfully expressive examples of conservative twentieth-century choral music.

After settling upon his mature style in the later 1920s, Walton remained essentially consistent in compositional approach. A slow and careful worker, he produced a relatively small catalogue during his long career, including concertos for violin (1939) and cello (1956), two symphonies (1935, 1960), a set of orchestral variations (1963, on a theme by Hindemith), the three-act opera *Troilus and Cressida* (1954, after Chaucer), the one-act comic chamber opera *The Bear* (1967, after Chekhov), and some chamber music, including two string quartets. Beginning in the middle 1930s Walton also composed for films, most notably for three Shakespeare films by the renowned actor and director Laurence Olivier: *Henry V* (1944), *Hamlet* (1947), and *Richard III* (1955).

Walton's reputation faded somewhat following World War II, partly because his music began to sound less distinctive, and his refusal to alter his style to suit current fashion made the later work sound increasingly dated. Yet it is not only for their technical polish that Walton's best scores remain in the repertory; they speak the international symphonic language with a distinctively British accent and emotional flavor.

BRITTEN

The two most gifted English composers to emerge during the 1930s were Benjamin Britten (1913–76) and Michael Tippett (b. 1905). Because together they dominated the English compositional scene in the decades after World War II, their names have been consistently associated, despite significant differences in both temperament and musical style. Britten developed early, achieving an enviable facility in composition by the time he was in his twenties. The effortless impression his music gives is reinforced by his extensive output. Tippett, on the other hand, attained musical maturity only after a long and difficult apprenticeship. Some eight years Britten's senior and thus closer in age to Walton's generation, his individuality did not become fully evident until the late 1930s, after Britten had already gained wide attention.

Although he later worked with John Ireland at the Royal College of Music in London, Britten began his compositional studies under Frank Bridge, one of the least provincial English composers of the time, who encouraged his young student's interest in advanced European music.

Written in 1932 when he was only eighteen, Britten's Op. 1, a Sinfonietta for ten instruments, contains structural complexities that set it
apart from most English music of the period, and, despite the subsequent relative simplification of his style, he always retained something
of his early interest in rigorous formal procedures. The works that followed the Sinfonietta in quick succession experimented with various
approaches and indicated, at an early date, what would be one of Britten's most enduring characteristics: an untroubled eclecticism that is
both technically assured and expressively convincing. The style of each
work seems to be shaped according to its own particular demands. What
remains constant is an essentially diatonic tonal orientation (even if, at
times, heavily colored with chromatic elements), set within a clearly
defined formal framework and transparent, contrapuntally conceived
textures.

Several compositions of the later 1930s placed Britten at the forefront
of the English younger generation. A significant factor in his development was his friendship and collaboration with the English poet W. H.
Auden, whom he met in 1935. Their joint works included the symphonic song cycle *Our Hunting Fathers* (1936, a work Britten felt to be
his first entirely personal achievement); *On This Island* (1937), a cycle
for voice and piano; and the later "operetta" *Paul Bunyan*. Before the
last of these, the composer had completed his first full-fledged masterpieces: the *Variations on a Theme of Frank Bridge* (1937) for string orchestra, in which the use of traditional forms and manners (Italian aria,
Viennese waltz, etc.) reflects a growing inclination toward neo-classicism; *Les Illuminations,* after Rimbaud, for voice and string orchestra
(1939); and the *Sinfonia da requiem* (1940). Although the influence of
Stravinsky, and to a lesser extent Mahler, is detectable in all these scores,
it is overshadowed by a directness of expression and unforced lyricism
that is both peculiarly English and Britten's own.

The slightly later *Serenade,* Op. 31, for tenor, horn, and strings (1943),
a cycle of six songs on a collection of varied English texts, confirms
these qualities. The fourth song, a setting of an anonymous fifteenth-
century Scottish dirge, is based on a six-measure vocal ostinato, which
appears unaccompanied at the opening of the song (Example XII-1) and
then recurs eight times (with minor variations to accommodate the
changing text) while the instruments unfold a fully developed fugue,
complete with expositions, episodes, and climactic stretto. The combination of a statically recurring vocal layer with an expansive and
developmental instrumental one underscores the text's grim underlying
message: the inevitable passage of all humankind toward a day of final
reckoning.

As usual in Britten, the music has a strongly tonal orientation, yet
considerable tension ensues from the vocal-instrumental polarity, which—

in a manner reminiscent of Stravinsky (who incidentally set the same text in his 1952 Cantata)—encompasses key as well as character. The vocal ostinato is firmly rooted on G (outlining a G-minor triad as it descends through the octave from G to G), yet the sense of key is complicated by several modal elements, especially the upper-neighbor Ab associated with both opening and closing tonics, which lend the music a distinctly Phrygian color. These Abs also suggest the possibility of a turn to Eb major—a possibility seized by the instruments when they ground their fugue on this pitch.

But the instruments' Eb is similarly clouded by ambiguities. The first three entrances of the subject (mm. 6, 10, and 14) are on Eb, Db, and G, respectively, outlining an incomplete dominant-seventh chord rather than establishing the traditional tonic-dominant polarity that would

Example XII-1: BRITTEN, *Serenade,* "Dirge," mm. 1–15

support a stable E♭ tonic. Moreover, the entrances on D♭ and G reinforce pitches prominent in the voice part: the latter its tonic, the former the highly characteristic inflection to D♭ in the ostinato's fourth measure.

Such complex interactions between voice and "accompaniment" (the term is not really appropriate here) typify the entire movement and, despite the prevailingly triadic harmonic basis, give it a marked quality of tonal tension and uncertainty. A particularly striking moment occurs when the horn, after remaining silent for half the movement, enters with a dramatic E-minor statement of the fugue subject (the final one preceding the climactic stretto), a pitch that confers a fresh and noticeably different harmonic coloring upon the voice's omnipresent G. Although the voice ends alone, confirming its own centrality on G, its final tonic follows close upon a low pizzicato E♭ in the basses, the terminal note in a dissolving motion that brings the fugue to an end. The music's true tonal focus is thus ultimately left unresolved.

Britten's leftist and pacifist views made him increasingly discontented with the course of events in prewar Britain, and in 1939 he emigrated to the United States, where Auden had preceded him. Although withdrawn after its first performance in 1941 (and not revived until 1976), *Paul Bunyan* marked an important turning point in Britten's career, which from this point on was to be principally devoted to music for the stage. Returning to wartime England in 1942, he began work on a commission from the Koussevitzky Foundation of Boston for his first full-scale opera. The result was *Peter Grimes,* completed in 1945. While the opera's modal–diatonic melodic style and solidly triadic harmonic foundation bespeak Britten's essential conservatism, its structure is remarkably complex. A prologue is followed by three acts, each comprising two scenes connected by an instrumental interlude—a plan owing something to Berg (with whom Britten at one time had contemplated studying). And the somber, pessimistic subject matter, presenting a sadistic title character combining characteristics of a romantic "outsider" and a psychotic social misfit, is decidedly modern in flavor.

Britten succeeded not only in bringing this material to musical life, but in humanizing the character of Grimes so as to elicit sympathy as well as revulsion. Only a composer of uncommon dramatic and compositional instincts could have so effectively brought off the range of musical moods demanded by the opera's plot, which juxtaposes such diverse elements as the impassioned ravings of Grimes, a popular round sung in a pub, the depiction of an intense storm, and the singing of a church congregation. The opera's premiere, on the occasion of the reopening of the Sadler's Wells Theater in London, just one month after the German surrender, was an event of considerable national significance. English opera, so long moribund, had so far played a distinctly

Peter Grimes (Jon Vickers) with his new apprentice. From Act II of the Metropolitan Opera production, November 1977. (© Beth Bergman 1983)

subordinate role in the "English musical Renaissance"; now it was revitalized in a single stroke. *Peter Grimes* was greeted as a masterpiece and its creator lauded as the most important English opera composer since Purcell. Not only did the work initiate a long series of operas by Britten himself, it laid the foundation for an extraordinary flowering of a new English operatic tradition, which engaged not only Britten and Tippett, but almost every major figure of the postwar generation, including Peter Maxwell Davies, Harrison Birtwistle, Alexander Goehr, and Nicholas Maw.

The success of *Peter Grimes* did not immediately lead to further opportunities for large-scale works, so Britten concentrated for a time on composing for smaller forces, especially for the English Opera Group, which he founded in 1947. Notable among these were *The Rape of Lucretia* (1946), *Albert Herring* (1947), and *The Turn of the Screw* (1954). His other principal operas included *Billy Budd* (1951), *Gloriana* (1953), *A Midsummer Night's Dream* (1960), and *Death in Venice* (1973). Britten's operas cover a wide range of musical and dramatic possibilities and are notable for their variety and technical polish. Collectively they represent an impressive attempt to reaffirm the importance of a genre—opera conceived along essentially traditional lines—that has by and large been confined to a secondary position during the twentieth century.

The operas reflect Britten's essentially eclectic approach, drawing inspiration from various sources to suit the requirements of each particular work; perhaps his most striking talent is the ability to adapt "foreign" manners so that they become his own and fulfill his own purposes. In *The Turn of the Screw,* where the music must project the complex and subtle psychological ambiguities of the Henry James novella it adapts, the constant recurrences of a twelve-tone row mirror the obsessive nature of the subject matter. Since the row consists entirely of a sequence of perfect fifths, it lends itself readily to tonal suggestion, and Britten uses it to form a score that is unmistakably his own. *The Turn of the Screw* is perhaps his most complicated musico-dramatic conception (its overall structure unified by sixteen orchestral interludes that are fashioned as a series of fifteen variations on an opening theme), organized—as are all Britten's operas—according to a carefully regulated sequence of key changes. In *A Midsummer Night's Dream* (1960), considered by many to be Britten's finest opera, three clearly differentiated types of music interact with one another without any hint of stylistic discrepancy: the hard, brightly metallic music associated with the supernatural elements of Shakespeare's play, dominated by ostinatos and high voices (Oberon is cast as a countertenor, Titania as a coloratura soprano); the more lyrical, linearly flowing music of the lovers; and the comical, harmonically dissonant and rhythmically awkward music of Bottom and the rustics. Britten plays off these highly stylized types with unfailing musical instinct, integrating them within a score of remarkable richness.

In addition to operas, Britten produced a substantial catalogue of orchestral works and concertos, choral music (notably the 1961 *War Requiem*), chamber music, and a long series of vocal works, most of them conceived for his friend the tenor Peter Pears, who also figured prominently in all his operas. From 1948 the festival he founded at Aldeburgh became the focus of his activity as composer and performer (he was himself a notable pianist and conductor).

TIPPETT

Slower to mature stylistically, Michael Tippett produced his first representative works only when he was in his early thirties. The String Quartet No. 1 (1935, later revised) and Piano Sonata No. 1 (1937) show the beginnings of an assured and personal idiom, but the first fully achieved composition, and the first with which the composer was himself completely satisfied, was the Concerto for Double String Orchestra (1939). Its modal diatonicism suggests certain parallels with Britten, although the music's intensity and richly syncopated rhythmic character are Tippett's own. Freely shifting accentual patterns, derived from English Renaissance music (especially the madrigal) and typical of much twentieth-century English music since Vaughan Williams, are carried to an unprecedented level of complexity, and combined with a new degree of textural differentiation partly attributable to the dual-orchestral conception recalling Vaughan Williams's *Tallis Fantasia*. Although the "additive" nature of the constantly changing rhythmic groupings may also owe something to Stravinsky, it is coupled with a distinctly non-Stravinskian melodic lyricism and a strongly linear impulse that gives rise to extended spans of unbroken musical continuity.

Despite the quality of the Concerto, it was the oratorio *A Child of Our Time,* completed two years later, that first attracted widespread interest in Tippett's work (not until 1944, however, did it receive a performance, largely through the help of Britten). Based on a text by the composer, the oratorio is in form an imaginative rethinking of the conventions of Bach's Passions, in content an impassioned statement of man's inhumanity to man, set within the context of the Nazi persecution of the Jews. Like its Baroque prototype, the score is clearly divided into recitatives, arias, and choruses; substituted for the traditional Lutheran chorale settings are five American Negro spirituals, simply yet effectively reharmonized by the composer for a cappella chorus. Both music and text reverberate with historical references, yet the overall tone, of ultimately unresolved questioning, is very much of its own time.

Tippett's scores, unlike Britten's, appear to have been fashioned out of both struggle and pain. This is reflected in the relatively small volume of his output, and also in the expressive depth of his music, its uneasy tension and gestural complexity. Moreover, Tippett seems to have grown with each work, producing ever more differentiated and technically ambitious musical statements, encompassing ever more of the variety of contemporary experience.

This development is apparent in the first three of Tippett's four symphonies, which are evenly distributed over the later part of his career (1945, 1957, 1972). The First Symphony, his most ambitious and extended instrumental composition to that point, resembles the earlier Concerto in general style, but the contrapuntal conception is yet more concentrated, and the previously triadic harmony is now distinguished by a more liberal use of other types of sonorities (especially chords in fourths). In the Second Symphony the harmonic language, while remaining basically diatonic, becomes still more differentiated; especially in the slow movement, there is also greater textural contrast and formal complexity, and the orchestration draws upon a wider and more varied timbral palette. Finally, the Third Symphony alternates sections of ongoing, forward-directed music, typical of Tippett's earlier compositions, with static sections based on the type of blocklike textures characteristic of much post–World War II music. In the second of the Symphony's two parts, which includes several sections featuring a soprano soloist, direct allusions to Beethoven's Ninth Symphony and to jazz (an influence at least implicit since Tippett's early period) are juxtaposed within a rich, almost collagelike fabric.

Tippett's Third Piano Sonata, written in 1973 immediately following the Third Symphony, marked a return to the more abstract conception of instrumental music evident in his earlier music. Yet the musical language reflects the composer's later maturity. The opening measures (Example XII-2) of the first of its three movements are shaped by an encompassing idea involving both a particular kind of textural opposition and the special physical possibilities of keyboard performance. Pitting the performer's two hands against each another, these measures explore the extremes of the keyboard in a consistent two-part contrapuntal layout involving registral opposition and the alternation of freely imitated melodic patterns. During the opening phrase the two lines develop freely yet vigorously, accelerating in surface rhythm and in rate of alternation between hands, and culminating in m. 5 in a moment of melodic liquidation, where the two hands first approach each other and then expand outward to lead back to a varied return of the opening idea.

The shifting, metrically unstable rhythmic groupings are a Tippett hallmark. So too is the highly ambiguous and flexible tonal language, which here inclines, if rather obliquely, toward B major: the rhythmically emphasized high notes of the right hand in mm. 1–3 (F♯-B-D♯, followed by A♯-E-D♯-C♯) outline a tonic triad and an elaborated VII chord, while the left hand reiterates prominent low F♯s in mm. 2–3 and again in m. 5. Even more than with Britten, the key emerges by veiled suggestion rather than overt statement. The constant chromatic inflections in the melodic lines, coupled with largely nontriadic harmony and extreme contrapuntal independence, produce an overriding sense of tonal flux rather than clear-cut definition.

The opening melodic idea recurs several times within the underlying sonata-form framework of this movement, both in short-term phrase repetitions (in addition to the restatement in m. 6, Example XII-2 contains the beginning of a second return in mm. 11–12) and in connection with large-scale formal returns (including a complete recapitulation that follows a more developmental middle section). Though varied in detail, these returns correspond closely in pitch structure (in this regard, compare the opening gesture in mm. 1–2 with its returns in mm. 6–7 and mm. 11–12) and thus serve not only to assure thematic unity but to provide intermittent tonal anchors for the larger structure. This very personal reformulation of traditional procedures is characteristic of Tippett's work.

Since the 1950s Tippett's output has been dominated by the composition of four full-scale operas, to his own librettos, that have earned him a place beside Britten as the leading English opera composer of the

Example XII-2: TIPPETT, Piano Sonata No. 3, first movement, mm. 1–12

century. The range of dramatic material mirrors the diversity of the composer's musical sources. *The Midsummer Marriage* (1952) is a heavily symbolic comedy that draws upon both Shakespeare and classical mythology. *King Priam* (1961) treats material related to the Trojan War on an epic scale. *The Knot Garden* (1969) explores, in an extremely concentrated and stylized way, the interrelationships among seven characters, five of whom on occasion assume roles from Shakespeare's *Tempest.* Finally, *The Ice Break* (1976) deals with contemporary situations within an essentially realistic dramatic framework (the opening scene, for example, takes place in an airport lounge).

The musical differences among the operas are equally striking. *The Midsummer Marriage* has an essentially continuous structure, based on nineteenth-century operatic models, whereas in *King Priam* relatively brief and sharply individualized musical segments punctuate the larger continuity. Moreover, the stark, thin textures of the latter work contrast markedly with the more luxurious ones of the former. The subsequent two operas are less traditional in both musical language and form. Fragmentary individual sections interact almost kaleidoscopically with one another, providing an appropriate formal vehicle for the extremely varied musical substance, which ranges from evocations of popular music (especially the blues, which Tippett particularly favors) through quotations of standard repertory (a Schubert lied is quoted at length in Act II of *The Knot Garden*) to a full range of contemporary procedures (including occasional, though unsystematic, use of twelve-tone rows).

Remarkably, Tippett's prolonged stylistic evolution, during which he has incorporated an ever-expanding range of techniques and materials, offers little suggestion of imitation or concession to current fashion. His continuous development has been achieved entirely within the framework of his own musical inclinations and has remained consistent with his own distinctive compositional voice. The growth of his reputation has matched his long and complex artistic development, to the point where some might rank him even above Britten. But the two are so different in artistic temperament that such judgments are perhaps pointless. Certainly Tippett lacks Britten's easy fluency and technical polish; his work, in fact, often seems rather labored and even awkward. Yet Tippett's music speaks with a warmth and depth of vision that is rivaled by few other composers of his generation.

CHAPTER XIII

The United States

THE NEW AMERICAN TRADITIONALISTS

In the United States the years following World War I witnessed the emergence of the first generation of home-grown composers who were totally professional in training and technique yet also unmistakably American in outlook and musical expression. Born near the turn of the century and reaching musical maturity during the 1920s, these composers gave American concert music a seriousness of purpose and a distinctive native voice that attracted international attention.

Following the pattern set by their American predecessors, all these composers received traditional musical training, and almost all studied in Europe. Despite this, they did not view European music as a model to be slavishly followed, but rather immersed themselves in the European tradition in order to broaden their own musical outlook and extend their technical capabilities. Moreover, most of the important figures in this generation studied under a single European teacher, the Frenchwoman Nadia Boulanger, who believed that to be American—or, more generally, to be non-European—was at that moment in music history an advantage: much as with nineteenth-century Russian composers, notably Musorgsky, a non-European perspective could facilitate the development of innovative compositional ideas and a fresh expressive focus.

Boulanger's importance for music in the United States between the wars can hardly be exaggerated. Under her rigorous training such Americans as Aaron Copland, Roy Harris, Virgil Thomson, and Marc Blitzstein all turned into remarkably polished composers. Indeed, of the major American composers of the period who fashioned an indigenous

Four of Nadia Boulanger's American pupils in her Paris apartment, 1924: (from left to right) Virgil Thomson, Walter Piston, Herbert Elwell, and Aaron Copland.

native style grounded in the European tradition, only one, Roger Sessions, did not study formally with Boulanger (though for a time he showed her his music)—and he worked with another European, the Swiss-born Ernest Bloch, and lived in Europe for a number of years.

Thus, despite strong American roots, these composers were "internationalists," as their years in Europe obviously suggest. More significantly, their music, despite its American spirit, indicated a mastery of the latest continental developments—especially those of Stravinsky (whom Boulanger admired above all other contemporary composers), but also of Schoenberg and his followers, Bartók, and others—and could thus assume a comfortable position within the tradition of European concert music. The stylistic focus was mainly neo-classical, especially of the Stravinskian variety, and the American elements in their work, though detectable, were not forcefully emphasized. As Copland later wrote of the Americans of the 1920s: "Our concern was not with the quotable hymn or spiritual: we wanted to find a music that would speak of universal things in a vernacular of American speech rhythms. We wanted to write music on a level that left popular music far behind—music with a largeness of utterance wholly representative of the country that Whitman had envisaged."[1]

The "vernacular" quality Copland mentions is particularly evident in the driving, sharply accented, irregular rhythms of these composers' music, and more specifically in its jazz-influenced character. Much of the most characteristic concert music written in the United States during the "jazz age" of the 1920s echoes the idiom, inflections, and spirit of this still relatively recent form of music. The most obvious instances are found in works such as Copland's Piano Concerto (1926) and the *Rhapsody in Blue* (1924) of George Gershwin (1898–1937), both conscious attempts to fuse "serious" and "popular" musical elements. (However, Copland and Gershwin moved toward this common ground from opposite directions; before the *Rhapsody* Gershwin had been exclusively a composer of popular songs.) Nevertheless, if most American music of the 1920s inevitably mirrored something of the nation's vernacular musical heritage, little conscious effort was made to exploit openly popular and folk resources other than jazz. As Copland says, the focus was upon more "universal things."

The Great Depression of the 1930s changed this. Besides fundamentally transforming the country's social and political life, it prompted a heightened concern for the role of music in society. This affected virtually every American composer, and the musical atmosphere thus changed radically from that of the 1920s: internationalism gave way to a conscious nationalism with strong political overtones. It was widely felt that composers should actively assume political responsibility and that music should be simplified, made more readily accessible to a large, democratic audience. Populist works based on American subjects, often incorporating folk and popular elements, appeared with increasing frequency.

A leading figure in the use of American vernacular materials during this period was Virgil Thomson (1896–1989), who had anticipated the development in several works of the late 1920s: the *Variations and Fugue on Sunday School Tunes* for organ (1926), the *Symphony on a Hymn Tune* (1928), and the opera *Four Saints in Three Acts* (composed in 1927–28, though not orchestrated until 1933). The latter, to a libretto by the well-known American experimental writer Gertrude Stein, is written in a deliberately simple yet highly sophisticated style, variously modeled on Protestant hymns, popular dances, and patriotic tunes. Thom-

---

1. *Music and Imagination* (Cambridge, Mass.: 1952), p. 104.

son's later opera *The Mother of Us All* (1947), also to a Stein libretto and based on the life of Susan B. Anthony, a leading figure in the women's suffrage movement in the United States, is even more a piece of pure, if ironic, Americana. (A still earlier user of vernacular materials, Charles Ives, had quite different stylistic and expressive intentions, and was working within an entirely different social and historical context.)

Despite this change of emphasis toward more popular sources, the basic technical approach of most American composers during the 1930s remained essentially neo-classical; traditional genres and forms were retained as carriers for a new, more locally focused content. Indeed, the 1930s witnessed an unexpected flowering of the American symphony, especially notable in the work of Roy Harris (1898–1979), who between 1933 and 1944 composed the first six of his fourteen symphonies. Harris's, long spun-out modal melodies, often rooted in Protestant hymnody, his widely spaced sonorities, cumulative forms, and direct, unmannered expression came to be viewed as quintessentially American. Other important American symphonists of the time included Howard Hanson (1896–1981), Walter Piston (1894–1976), Samuel Barber (1910–81), and William Schuman (b. 1910). Despite significant differences, these composers all wrote ambitious symphonic works in an essentially traditional style, addressed in a broad voice toward a large and varied public.

In this period of heightened social consciousness, the most openly political among prominent American figures was Marc Blitzstein (1905–64). Although his principal composition teachers, in Europe during the late 1920s, were Boulanger and Schoenberg, he began during the 1930s, under the influence of Kurt Weill and Bertolt Brecht, to view music as a vessel for social commentary, and like Weill developed a compositional idiom closely attuned to the popular music of the day. Blitzstein's theater piece *The Cradle Will Rock* (1937), a critical view of capitalist America set in the mythical company town Steeltown, USA, complete with crooked industrialist, quack doctor, unprincipled newspaperman, and heroic laborers, became a *cause célèbre* during a period of violent labor agitation. When the work was deemed too provocative by the administrators of the Federal Theater Project, its scheduled premiere was canceled and agents impounded the theater. Thereupon the cast marched to a second theater and staged a makeshift version, without scenery or costumes and with the composer filling in at the piano for the missing orchestra—an event that attracted widespread attention, strengthening the production's already significant political impact.

This populist trend continued unabated throughout World War II; indeed, if anything, patriotic fervor seemed to intensify the commitment to straightforward, accessible music, vividly typified by such works as Copland's *Lincoln Portrait* and *Fanfare for the Common Man* (both 1942). Of the composers mentioned in this section, only Sessions remained aloof from the general tendency toward a simpler, more conservative style of writing. Not until the war was over would widespread changes in compositional attitudes once again radically transform the character of American music. Neo–classicism, dominant in the prewar years, would then seem outdated to many younger composers, who had found renewed interest in Schoenberg and twelve-tone music.

COPLAND

A native of Brooklyn, Aaron Copland (b. 1900) has been widely recognized as the most prominent American composer of his generation. His career has mirrored with unusual clarity the changing features of American concert music since World War I. Although Copland began his compositional training in 1917, the most important milestone in his early development was the decision in 1921 to continue his studies in France, where he became the first of many Americans to work under Nadia Boulanger. She gave him the first definite indication of the direction his future development would take, and she thought highly enough of him that when he returned to the United States in 1924, she commissioned a work that she could play during a 1925 American concert tour. The result was Copland's first major composition, the Symphony No. 1 for organ and orchestra, whose broad, declamatory thematic content and jazzlike features (the latter especially apparent in the Scherzo) were to remain enduring traits of his style.

The jazz influences were even more emphatic in Copland's next pieces—the orchestral suite *Music for the Theater* (1925) and the Piano Concerto (1926). In the Concerto, however, an increasing complication of both rhythmic and harmonic language was the first suggestion of a gradual move toward a more aggressively modern style that, though retaining the basic tonal orientation and rhythmic vitality of the earlier music, was obviously directed toward a more sophisticated and "specialized" listener. After the still transitional *Vitebsk* (1928), for piano trio, and *Symphonic Ode* (1929) came the two masterpieces of this phase of Copland's development: the Piano Variations (1930) and the *Short Symphony* (1933).

The theme of the Piano Variations (given in its entirety in Example XIII-1a) is striking for its expressive stringency, textural leanness, and crisp, percussive piano setting. Not only unusually brief, the theme is confined to a relatively small number of pitches. The first phrase (mm. 1–3), punctuated by an accented eighth-note chord followed by a fermata, contains only four melodic pitches (E, C, D♯, C♯). These are retained to form the melodic content of the slightly varied second phrase (mm. 4–6), with the addition of only a D♮. After the third phrase (mm. 7–10) expands the pitch content somewhat (adding F♯, G♯, and B to the

Example XIII-1: COPLAND, Piano Variations

a. Theme

*) ◇ = press down silently.

b. Opening of second variation

continuing E, C♯, D, and C [now spelled B♯]), three of the original four pitches return again (E, D♯, and C♯) to form the final phrase (m. 11).

In the Variations Copland concentrates with remarkable persistence on these notes and the intervallic possibilities they define. For instance, the opening measures of the second variation (Example XIII-1b) use the first four pitches of the theme exclusively, rearranging them into new combinations through rhythmic, registral, and textural transformations.

Such manipulation of a small pitch cell recalls Schoenberg's pre-twelve-tone procedures, but Copland avoids the Schoenbergian tendency toward total chromaticism. Rather, he tends to circulate the same pitches in a manner resembling Stravinsky, whose neo-classical style is echoed in many other features of the Variations as well: the clear formal structure, textural transparency, rhythmic irregularities, and cool yet intense expressive quality. Moreover, despite the chromatic and dissonant character of much of the writing, the music remains resolutely tonal. C♯ is the final melodic and "cadential" pitch for the theme's first and last phrases, while the middle phrases, ending on D and B♯ respectively, surround the central C♯ by half steps. Moreover, C♯ serves as a tonal focus throughout much of the rest of the composition as well.

Following completion of the *Short Symphony* in 1933, Copland's compositional views took another significant turn. Caught up in the general climate of social consciousness, he began to consider his music in relationship to a larger and more diversified audience. As he later remarked, he wanted "to see if I couldn't say what I had to say in the simplest possible terms." His *Statements* for orchestra (1935) gives some indication of the new direction, which is first fully developed in *El salón México* (1936), a brilliant orchestral composition evoking the spirit of Mexican popular music. It was followed by the equally symptomatic "play-opera for high school students," *The Second Hurricane* (1936)—a sort of American version of *Gebrauchsmusik,* written in a simple style suitable for amateur production.

Later in his career Copland twice returned to Latin-American themes—in the *Danzón cubano* for two pianos (1942, orchestrated in 1944) and the orchestral *Three Latin American Sketches* (1972). But during the later 1930s and the 1940s his compositional interests were mainly rooted in the vernacular traditions of his own country. A more conscious and literal American orientation was especially apparent in three popular ballets: *Billy the Kid* (1938), *Rodeo* (1942), and *Appalachian Spring* (1944), where Copland occasionally employed actual American folk material to create a "homespun" musical atmosphere, much as he had done with a Mexican tune in *El salón México.* (*Billy the Kid,* for example, contains the cowboy song *Goodbye, Old Paint,* and the last section of *Appalachian Spring* is an elaborate set of variations on the Shaker tune *The Gift to Be Simple.*)

Copland's ability to transform basically simple material in musically

A scene from the 1965 production of *Appalachian Spring* by the Martha Graham Company. (Photograph by Martha Swope)

interesting and unpredictable ways, marking it with the stamp of his own personality, is illustrated by a brief passage from *Billy the Kid* (Example XIII-2). At heart nothing more than an ordinary little cowboy tune in D♭ major, the trumpet melody is subjected to irregular (though regularly alternating) groupings—4 + 3 + 4 + 3 + 4—that contradict the notated meter. The accompaniment is also irregularly grouped, yet differently: 3 + 3 + 4 + 3 + 3 + 4. (Dotted lines in Copland's score indicate these "syncopated" groupings in both melody and accompaniment.) The result is a wonderfully "off-gait" transformation of the simple tune, which seems to stumble over itself, regaining its balance only on the second beat of the last measure. Copland's ability to create such personal effects, providing the folklike material with an unexpected expressive dimension, was unrivaled among his American contemporaries, setting him quite apart from most other populist composers of the time.

In his ballets Copland collaborated with some of the most distinguished figures in American dance, including the choreographer–dancers Agnes de Mille and Martha Graham. Along with such pieces as the wartime *Lincoln Portrait* (1942), these works established him as the most prominent American composer of his time. He was commissioned to write scores for several well-known films, beginning with *Of Mice and Men* (1939) and eventually including *Our Town* (1940), *The Red Pony* (1948), and *The Heiress* (1948). But during the 1940s Copland also returned to purely abstract music, in the Piano Sonata (1941), Sonata for Violin and Piano (1943), and Third Symphony (1946), in which he attempted to reconcile the greater directness of his recent pieces with

Example XIII-2: COPLAND, *Billy the Kid,* mm. 1–5 after No. 11

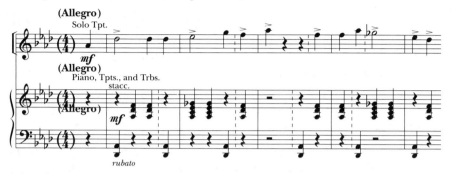

the large-scale symphonic ambitions of the earlier ones. Though the Stravinsky influence is still apparent, the music is simpler and less austere than in the instrumental pieces of the late 1920s and early 1930s; if the newer works have gained in immediacy, they have also lost something in intensity and expressive impact.

As noted earlier, the musical scene in the United States shifted radically following World War II, and this change in atmosphere eventually affected Copland himself. The complex style of the *Twelve Poems of Emily Dickinson,* a song cycle completed in 1950, recalled the works of the early 1930s, and the Quartet for Piano and Strings, composed in the same year, made use of twelve-tone procedures. In a statement remarkable for one with his former leanings, Copland declared at the time that he "found twelve-tone writing . . . especially liberating in two respects: it forces the tonal composer to unconventionalize his thinking with respect to chordal structure, and it tends to freshen his melodic and figurational imagination."[2]

Yet Copland never seemed completely comfortable with the twelve-tone approach, or—for that matter—with the course of his subsequent evolution. His output in the next two decades (no new works have appeared since the early 1970s) was greatly reduced in volume and unfocused in style. Two large orchestral scores, *Connotations* (1962) and *Inscape* (1967), continued to explore twelve-tone technique. Other pieces, such as the Nonet for Strings (1960), were more tonal yet retained a considerable level of developmental complexity. The Duo for Flute and Piano (1971), on the other hand, referred back to the more populist style of the *Appalachian Spring* period.

The decline—and stylistic uncertainty—of Copland's later output reflect a common problem in twentieth-century music: the difficulty of maintaining artistic consistency under the pressure of rapidly changing fash-

2.   *The New Music, 1900–1960* (New York, 1968), p. 168.

ions and attitudes. During the postwar period Copland found himself in an environment largely alien to his basic musical instincts, leaving him unsure of his own musical voice. Yet the compositions he wrote during the second quarter of the century are established as permanent fixtures in the repertory, and earned for Copland a secure position in the arts of the United States.

SESSIONS

Although Roger Sessions (1896–1985), like Copland, was born in Brooklyn, his musical background was very different. Both musically and intellectually precocious, Sessions graduated from Harvard at the age of nineteen and continued his studies at Yale with Horatio Parker (who had been Ives's composition teacher). However, the main influence on Sessions's early development was Ernest Bloch, the prominent Swiss composer who settled in the United States in 1916. After leaving Yale Sessions worked privately with Bloch, and from 1921 to 1925 was his assistant at the Cleveland Institute of Music. Contact with Bloch reinforced Sessions's already well-established knowledge of the European tradition, as well as his conviction that American music's most fruitful course lay in extending that tradition—a conviction further strengthened by an eight-year residence in Germany and Italy from 1925 to 1933.

Upon his return to the United States Sessions became active as a teacher of composition, eventually serving on the faculties of such centers as the University of California at Berkeley, Princeton University, and the Juilliard School of Music. In this role he had a significant impact on the development of American music for more than four decades, numbering among his pupils such prominent (and diverse) figures as Milton Babbitt, Andrew Imbrie, Donald Martino, and David Del Tredici.

Although almost all of his works are substantial in both length and content, Sessions's output was relatively small, especially in his earlier years. His first major compositions were the incidental music for Leonid Andreyev's play *The Black Maskers* (1923), the First Symphony (1927), and the First Piano Sonata (1930). Essentially neo-classical in focus, these placed Sessions squarely in the compositional mainstream, not far removed in general outlook from Copland. (Sessions and Copland were in fact closely associated at this time, and between 1928 and 1931 jointly organized an important series of contemporary concerts in New York.) Stravinsky's influence is evident in these works, notably in their essentially diatonic language and clarity of formal outline.

Yet indications that Sessions was beginning to move away from the Stravinsky orbit and toward that of Schoenberg are also detectable. By

The Swiss-American composer Ernst Bloch (right) with his eminent pupil Roger Sessions in 1923.

comparison with Stravinsky or Copland, the music has a much stronger sense of forward harmonic progression, and the underlying diatonic basis is more heavily marked by chromatic inflections. Instead of their stratified textural and formal quality, Sessions develops a more continuously evolving structure, shaped by long, goal-directed linear spans (especially evident in the Piano Sonata, whose four movements, played without pause, are thematically and formally integrated into a single, unbroken unit). Finally, his music rarely suggests the characteristic coolness and detachment of neo-classicism, or its ironic references to older musical conventions—on the contrary, the expressive quality is direct and intensely personal.

These differences led Sessions on a course away from most of his American contemporaries. To him, the more popular and accessible style they favored represented a retreat into false simplicity, and their nationalist leanings, especially as manifested in the use of folk materials, struck him as technically and expressively limited. In his words: "What is lacking . . . in the entire nationalist movement in our music is awareness of the fact that genuine national character comes from within and must develop and grow of itself, that it cannot be imposed from without, and that, in the last analysis, it is a byproduct, not an aim, of artistic expression."[3]

Sessions's music continued to develop in a consistent line toward greater complexity and differentiation. The chromatic inflections and textural complications of the earlier works were further intensified in the Violin Concerto (1935) and First String Quartet (1936), and with the Second Symphony (1946) the composer solidified a compositional approach that would remain essentially constant in subsequent years. Although the Second Symphony, with its strongly directed motion, is still in a very general sense tonal, the music has become completely chromatic, and its textures are richer and more consistently contrapuntal than before. Thematic development now assumes the form of a dense network of interconnected associations, laid out in ever-widening melodic arcs that shape the larger flow of the music. The form thus evolves from a continuous expansion of material, within which the various motivic figures appear and disappear in constant alternation and mutual interplay.

In contrast to Copland, Sessions, isolated during the prewar years by his music's complexity, found himself more at home in the altered atmosphere of the period following World War II, and his compositional output increased significantly. The Second Symphony was followed by six more between 1957 and 1968, and a ninth in 1978. Other large-scale instrumental pieces included a Piano Concerto (1956), a Double Concerto for Violin, Cello, and Orchestra (1971), and a Concerto for Orchestra (1981), as well as a number of chamber works. Vocal works from these years included two operas—*The Trial of Lucullus* (1947) and *Montezuma* (1963)—and two extended concert works with orchestra—*The Idyll of Theocritus* (1954), for soprano, and *When Lilacs Last in the Door-yard Bloom'd* (1970), for soloists and chorus.

In all these works Sessions continued to develop the established features of his style with unswerving consistency. Even the adoption of twelve-tone technique, used first in the Sonata for Unaccompanied Violin (1953) and regularly thereafter, had no profound effect on either the formal or expressive character of his work. Unlike Copland, who somewhat earlier had adopted the method in search of new sonorities and melodic material, Sessions found it useful simply as a means of more consciously controlling two features that had long marked his style: full chromaticism and motivic-intervallic cohesiveness. Like Copland, however, he employed the method with great freedom, often using pairs of unordered complementary hexachords to provide "har-

3.   *Reflections on the Music Life in the United States* (New York, [1956]), p. 151.

monic" definition without determining the note-by-note succession, or using the series primarily for the principal thematic material while allowing the subsidiary parts to be more freely constructed.

In any case, Sessions's twelve-tone music sounds essentially consistent with his earlier work—indeed, it still sounds "tonal" in the broadest sense of the term. As the composer has remarked, serialism "is a technical principle that a wide number and variety of composers have found useful for their own purposes, both because of the organizing principles they have derived from it and because of the musical resources it has opened up for them. Like any other technical principle, it yields nothing in itself; it is always for the imagination of the composer to discover what it can give him, and to mold it to his own uses."[4]

The richness and complexity of Sessions's music have slowed its public acceptance; performances have been relatively rare and often technically unsatisfactory, owing to the music's uncommon difficulty. Yet both performers and audiences are gradually accustoming themselves to the density of his musical thought. Sessions is arguably the finest symphonist yet produced in the United States, whose large-scale orchestral works deserve a place beside those of the twentieth-century composers, such as Sibelius and Shostakovich, who have contributed most to the preservation and continued evolution of this traditional genre. Moreover, his symphonies have defined a unique course of evolution, tracing—perhaps more than those of any other composer of his generation—a direct descent from the German symphonic heritage, from Strauss's tone poems through the orchestral works of Schoenberg. Yet to this tradition Sessions adds his own distinctly American voice, evident above all in the buoyancy and vigor of his rhythmic ideas.

THE EXPERIMENTAL TRADITION IN AMERICAN MUSIC

To this point the present chapter has stressed the strong ties binding music in the United States between the wars to the European tradition, focusing upon composers who, though often consciously striving for a distinctly "American" quality in their work, did so within the well-established forms and genres of the Western tradition. This close bond with Europe was entirely natural—the early colonization of the States had been exclusively European; and throughout its history the country has maintained its closest political, social, and cultural ties with the countries of Western Europe and the British Isles.

4. "Problems and Issues Facing the Composer Today" (1960), in *Roger Sessions on Music,* ed. Edward T. Cone (Princeton, 1979), p. 82.

Nevertheless, the geographical peculiarities of the United States—its enormous spaces and varied terrain—and the pioneering spirit that these fostered have tended to shape the country and its people in a quite different mold from that of the Old World. Early settlers were forced to rely largely upon their own ingenuity, making do with resources at hand in responding to the harsh demands of an unfamiliar environment, and something of the pragmatic invention and improvisation encouraged by this experience has been preserved in the national character. In addition, social forms have tended to develop in a less conventionalized and structured way than in Europe. The resulting tradition of tolerance toward a broad range of individual differences has been supported by the belief that one should make of one's life whatever one wishes, even to the extent of defying generally accepted norms. Though mythologized—and trivialized—in the popular media to the point of meaninglessness, the ideal of the "rugged American individualist" has a concrete historical basis in the special circumstances of the nation's development.

Thus a figure like Charles Ives would simply have been unthinkable in a European country during the early years of the twentieth century. Despite his very strong ties to Old World music, Ives's work betrays a distinctly non-European esthetic eclecticism and openness to vernacular influences. His is the voice of an authentic American maverick, who forged an entirely personal musical vision, in virtual isolation from the rest of the world and answerable only to his own conscience.

Copland and Sessions have both written in praise of Ives's music, yet—significantly—not without a certain reserve. For them he is a fascinatingly original composer, yet one with something of the amateur about him; despite a fertile musical imagination, he is undisciplined and unpolished. Indeed, among those within the musical mainstream who thought about Ives at all, this was the generally accepted view.

But another, smaller group of composers and musical commentators have seen in Ives a model for what a truly *American* composer might be. They have viewed him as the initiator of an "alternative" stream in twentieth-century American music, dedicated to the pursuit of highly personal compositional approaches largely unencumbered by European precedents. The composers in this group are for the most part uncompromisingly individual and, like Ives, have worked in relative isolation. Yet they tend to share at least one of two important characteristics: a willingness to experiment with sound for its own sake, without consideration of accepted formal or technical practice (in which regard they have something in common with certain radical European composers, such as the Futurists), and a tendency to draw inspiration not only from local folk sources but from "exotic" cultures far removed from the European orbit, especially those of the Orient.

Despite its historical connections with the Old World, the United States is geographically as close to the Orient as it is to Europe, and, not surprisingly, many Americans, especially those in the western part of the country, have felt a strong affinity for Eastern cultures. Among them have been a series of composers who have studied various forms of Eastern music and incorporated some of its technical procedures and esthetic assumptions into their own work. These include Henry Cowell (1897–1965), Harry Partch (1901–74), the Franco-American Dane Rudhyar (1895–1985), Alan Hovhaness (b. 1911), Lou Harrison (b. 1917), and the Canadian Colin McPhee (1901–64). At the same time, others have concentrated upon the invention of new rhythmic and textural effects in a more "abstract" context, without reference to exotic materials: e.g., Carl Ruggles (1876–1971), Ruth Crawford Seeger (1901–53), Henry Brant (b. 1913), and Conlon Nancarrow (b. 1912). Also belonging to this latter group is the Franco-American Edgard Varèse (1883–1965).

All of these composers, if in varying degrees, manifest a marked experimental strain. They share an interest in exploring new musical terrain and an urge to break free from what they perceive as the outworn artistic heritage of Western culture, to rejuvenate an old and exhausted tradition with something fresh and youthful.

COWELL

Henry Cowell was born in San Francisco, and, despite frequent periods of absence, California remained his principal residence for the first forty years of his life. Raised in simple circumstances, the youthful Cowell was exposed to a considerably more varied range of music than any American composer we have previously considered. He knew Oriental music from the Chinese quarter of San Francisco, and folk music from many parts of the world through contact with the city's other ethnic groups. Like Ives, he was creatively stimulated by these vernacular sources (though unlike Ives, he had access to an international range). Accepting them all as a normal part of his environment, Cowell once remarked: "I want to live in the *whole world* of music."

Cowell's musical independence was evident at an early age. *The Tides of Manaunaum,* a piano piece composed in 1912 when he was fifteen, already makes use of "tone clusters"—chordal blocks consisting of all the notes (or, alternatively, all the white or black notes) between two indicated pitches, played with the fist, flat of the hand, or forearm, depending on the width of the cluster. In a series of innovative piano pieces over the next decade, Cowell experimented with various types of clusters, and after 1923 further expanded his repertory of new sonic

The autograph mansucript of the opening measures of Henry Cowell's innovative piano piece, *The Aeolian Harp* (ca. 1923). Courtesy of the Library of Congress.

possibilities for the instrument through such then-unprecedented techniques as plucking, strumming, or banging on the strings (*The Banshee,* 1925), applying "mutes" to the strings to alter the timbre (*Sinister Resonance,* 1930), and depressing keys silently while simultaneously strumming the strings (*Aeolian Harp,* 1923).

For these effects, Cowell had to develop a special notation. For example, in *The Banshee* (whose opening measures are given in Example XIII-3) circled letters designate the way the string is to be set in vibration (twelve different possibilities are used in the complete piece): Ⓐ indicates the player is to "sweep with the flesh of the finger from the lowest string up to the note given"; Ⓑ, "sweep lengthwise along the string of the note given with flesh of finger"; Ⓒ, "sweep up and back from lowest A to highest B♭ given in this composition." The piece requires two performers, one to play on the strings and another to hold down the damper pedal throughout so that the strings can vibrate freely.

Although best known for their explorations of new timbral and textural techniques, the piano pieces of these years are also remarkable for their combination of these experimental features with unexceptional triadic harmony or simple folklike melodies. Here one sees a characteristic trait Cowell shares with Ives: an all-embracing eclecticism. Though the unfamiliar timbral effect at the opening of *The Banshee* seems closer to recent electronic music than to the sound of a normal piano, the melodic material consists of a descending sequence of rising pairs of whole tones, their durations limited to half and whole notes, answered

Example XIII-3: COWELL, *The Banshee,* mm. 1–8

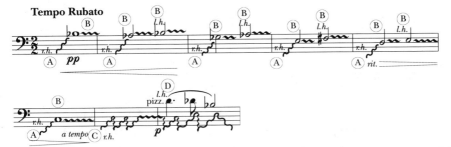

by a dotted three-note figure played "pizzicato" that ends on B♭, the same pitch with which the previous idea began. Most of the piano pieces reveal such stylistic dichotomies, although several have a more consistently dissonant harmonic and melodic character, among them *Advertisement* (1914) and *Tiger* (1928). But, as those dates indicate, there is no direct stylistic evolution toward more complex pitch materials. Rather, Cowell evidently regards dissonant textures as one among many possibilities, to be used when desired but not exclusively.

Cowell did not study music formally until he was seventeen, when he began work at the University of California at Berkeley with Charles Seeger, who encouraged him to develop a more systematic approach to composition. This stimulus led to the ground-breaking theoretical treatise *New Musical Resources,* completed in 1919 but not published until 1930, in a slightly revised version. The book treats such new possibilities of pitch structure as "poly-harmony," dissonant counterpoint, quarter tones, quartal harmony (i.e., chords built in fourths), and tone clusters, but its most remarkable section concerns rhythm. Starting from the premise that there is a "physical identity between rhythm and harmony," Cowell shows that since both intervallic and rhythmic relationships can be reduced to common mathematical ratios, the latter can be derived from the former. As an instance, the C-major triad given in Example XIII-4 (see p. 300) incorporates the ratios 2:4 (from the low C to middle C), 4:5 (from middle C to E), and 5:6 (from E to G); these can then be translated into rhythmic values incorporating the same ratios, as in the second example.

While working on his treatise Cowell wrote two compositions illustrating this rhythmic concept: the *Quartet Romantic* (1917) and the *Quartet Euphometric* (1919). To produce the former, he composed a simple choralelike piece in four parts, converted its intervallic ratios into rhythmic ones (as described above), and then used the latter as rhythmic structure for a new set of independent pitches. (Thus the chorale serves as the

Example XIII-4: COWELL, from *New Musical Resources*

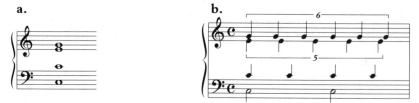

source of the piece's rhythms, but not its pitches.) Each of the first three measures of the *Quartet Romantic* (Example XIII-5) is rhythmically derived from the C-major chord given in Example XIII-4 (it is the first chord used in the chorale).

The procedures Cowell developed for this work offered him a way of generating and controlling complex new rhythmic relationships; unlike anything attempted before his time, they bear resemblances to methods used by certain serial composers during the 1950s. To grasp the extent of this complexity, one must remember that the ratios shown in Example XIII-4 are only those of the first chord of the "generating" chorale; and since the chords change constantly as the chorale progresses, so do the rhythmic relationships among the four instruments of the Quartet. Although it has been both performed and recorded since his death, Cowell assumed that the piece was unplayable, and some years later asked the French inventor Lev Termen to build a machine that could play such complex polyrhythms. This led to the "rhythmicon," a mechanical percussive instrument for which Cowell wrote several compositions, including a Concerto for Rhythmicon and Orchestra (1931).

Another Cowell innovation is the use of indeterminacy. Even within the earliest piano pieces, the decision about how many times to repeat a particular passage may be left to the performer. And in a 1924 piece

Example XIII-5: COWELL, *Quartet Romantic*, mm. 1–3

entitled *Ensemble,* for string quintet and three thundersticks (a type of string drum used by Southwestern American Indians), the three percussion parts are indicated only "graphically," by squiggly lines. The most extreme instance of indeterminacy is found in the *Mosaic Quartet* (1935), conceived in what the composer called "elastic form": its five brief movements may be played in any order and with any number of repetitions of individual movements.

The unparalleled audacity of Cowell's earlier compositions attracted widespread attention both at home and abroad, and during the decade between 1923 and 1933, a time of free international exchange and interest in the new and experimental, he made five successful concert tours throughout Europe, performing his own piano music and establishing contact with a number of the leading European musicians of the day (including Schoenberg, who invited Cowell to play for his composition class in Berlin).

In the middle 1930s, like most of his American colleagues, Cowell altered somewhat the course of his work, turning toward a simpler music, more suitable for a large audience. Abandoning his earlier rhythmic complexities and textural innovations, he concentrated more upon the folk-music roots that had always been evident to some degree in his work. Even his most dissonant and experimental pieces retained a clear basis in song, and he avoided the wide melodic leaps typical of advanced European music (especially Schoenberg and his school) in favor of a simpler and more continuous melodic flow, usually with clear motivic recurrences. Thus, although the String Quartet No. 2 (1934) ranks among the composer's more tonally and harmonically complex pieces, it nevertheless retains a strong sense of linear continuity.

So the change in Cowell's music was less extreme than it might at first appear. Moreover, whereas the developments of the later 1930s led a composer like Copland to the adoption of a more explicitly "American" voice, they encouraged Cowell—true to his eclectic preferences—to draw upon folk music from all over the world. Already in 1931 Cowell had undertaken a study of non-Western music at the University of Berlin, and subsequently began incorporating exotic influences in his own music. The *United Quartet* (1936), one of the earliest manifestations of this new turn, was described by Cowell as an attempt to create "a more universal style," with elements "suggested from many places and peoples." Although direct quotation is avoided, the work emphasizes constructive principles especially characteristic of non-Western music: static harmonic backgrounds, often with drones of some kind; highly repetitive melodic materials confined to a few pitches appearing in changing combinations; scales suggestive of Oriental modes. As its title suggests, the *United Quartet* seeks to combine a rich variety of compositional styles and techniques (including twentieth-century dissonant counterpoint) into an integrated whole.

In his later years Cowell continued to embody the character and structure of non-Western music via Western musical genres and ensembles; e.g., the *Persian Set* for chamber orchestra (1957), and *Homage to Iran* for violin, piano, and Persian drum (1959). Nor did he neglect American musical sources. Between 1943 and 1963 an extended series of compositions entitled *Hymn and Fuguing Tune,* scored for various ensembles, was based on a traditional two-part form favored by eighteenth-century New England composers such as William Billings.

At the same time there emerged a new interest in more abstract forms of music. All but the first of Cowell's twenty symphonies were written between 1939 and 1965. Even here folk elements are found: the Andante of the Seventh Symphony (1952) has a pronounced Oriental flavor, while the opening of the third movement has the character of an Irish jig. (Some of the symphonies bear titles explicitly acknowledging their exotic influences, such as *Thesis* and *Icelandic*.) Yet the balance has tipped toward more abstract musical concerns, with even an occasional return to the earlier innovative procedures: e.g., tone clusters in the fifth movement of the Symphony No. 11 (1954). Indeed, this work, subtitled "Seven Rituals of Music," seems to attempt a sort of personal synthesis, its seven connected movements forming a catalogue of the many different faces of Cowell's musical style (although generally lacking the exuberance and experimental daring of the earlier music).

In addition to his work as a composer, Cowell was a prominent editor, writer, and teacher. In 1927 he founded the New Music Edition, primarily dedicated to publishing scores by contemporary North and South American composers. He was also instrumental in drawing public attention to the music of Ives, on whom he, with his wife, wrote the first book-length study. An earlier book, *American Composers on American Music,* which Cowell compiled in 1933 and for which he wrote a number of essays, especially reflects the breadth of his perspective. Not only does it include articles on a remarkably varied group of younger American composers (including some of radically different persuasion); it contains essays on such topics as Mexican music, Cuban music, jazz in American music (by George Gershwin), Oriental influences on American music, and "An Afro-American Composer's Point of View" (by the black composer William Grant Still). The book is an eloquent testimonial to Cowell's all-embracing musical personality.

PARTCH

Harry Partch (1901–74) was born in California, which remained his principal home throughout most of his adult life, although he grew up in Arizona and lived off and on in other parts of the American West and Midwest. Largely self-taught in composition, Partch wrote a large body of conventional music in his earlier years, including a symphonic poem, a piano concerto, a string quartet, and many songs, all of which he destroyed in the middle 1920s following a period of intense self-examination, when he radically altered his musical attitudes. In 1928 Partch set down his new philosophy in a book, *Genesis of a Music* (eventually published, in a later version, in 1949). Here he developed a musical esthetic derived from an eclectic range of influences, including (as he later noted) "Yaqui Indians, Chinese lullabies, Hebrew chants for the dead, Christian hymns, Congo puberty rites, Chinese music hall (San Francisco), lumber yards and junk shops, . . . Boris Godunov."[5]

Unlike Cowell, who wished to integrate a comparable diversity of sources into the language of art music, Partch came to a radical rejection of Western music—its harmonic system, its equal-tempered tuning, indeed its very notion of autonomous concert music—in order to create an entirely new kind of music, modeled on the ancient musical cultures of Greece and Asia and employing the "pure" intervals of just intonation. To this end he developed a forty-three-note scale that could produce pure, untempered consonances. In addition, his new music was to be "corporeal," with the tactile aspects of the performance—the physical motions of singing and playing—as important as the actual sounds; and it was to be "monophonic," conceived in terms of the human voice, its spoken words and speech inflections. The instruments had to be specially constructed, not only to permit Partch's special tunings but to project this character of "voice" basic to the entire conception.

The first work Partch composed in his new manner was the *Li Po Songs* (1930–33), a setting of seventeen Chinese lyrics for "intoning" voice and "adapted" viola. The voice inflects the words in a manner resembling speech more than music (more so, even, than Gregorian chant); though occasionally blossoming into song, it more often sounds like a highly stylized and exaggerated reading of the text. It is accompanied by unobtrusive yet strangely evocative melodic and rhythmic patterns in the adapted viola, the first of a long series of instruments specially created for Partch's music (although in this case—as in other early pieces—simply an altered form of a familiar Western instrument). The music, characterized above all by its naive, unforced simplicity, has virtually nothing in common with traditional Western art music.

The isolation Partch experienced in producing music so utterly out of step, not only with the musical mainstream but also with the avant-garde of the time, is difficult to appreciate fully in today's more experimental climate. Under the impact of the Great Depression he temporarily stopped composing entirely, living for six years as a hobo wandering back and forth across the United States. Only in 1941 did he again

---

5. From a letter to Ben Johnston, June 1, 1968, quoted in Johnston, "Partch," in John Vinton, ed., *Dictionary of Contemporary Music* (New York, 1974), p. 555, col. 2.

Harry Partch with two of his remarkable musical instruments: gourd tree and cone gongs. Courtesy of BMI Archives.

begin producing "intoning voice" pieces, now using words drawn from his recent experiences: hitchhiker inscriptions collected from highway railings (*Barstow,* 1941), excerpts from a letter written by a hobo friend (*The Letter,* 1943), texts collected during a cross-country trip (*U.S. Highball,* 1943), and the cries of newsboys (*San Francisco,* 1943). This phase of Partch's career, lasting through most of World War II, mirrored the social concern of most American composers of the time. During the middle 1940s, however, his interests began to expand: two pieces written in 1944 used texts from James Joyce's *Finnegan's Wake,* and in 1951 he finished a full-scale dramatic setting entitled *Oedipus,* based on the play of Sophocles.

By this time Partch had built a number of new and completely original instruments for the performance of his music. They bore such colorful names as "cloud chamber bowls," "spoils of war," "diamond marimba," and "harmonic canon," and were as notable for their physical beauty as for their unusual timbral and intonational characteristics. (While claiming to be a "philosophic music-man seduced into carpentry" and refusing to be described as an instrument builder, Partch obviously had an extraordinary gift for such work.)

During the postwar years Partch began to view music as an element of a universal drama encompassing all of the arts, in which his instruments occupied a central position, not only as sources of sound but also as features of the total physical environment constructed for the performance. His work became a sort of ritualistic presentation incorporating dancing, mime, and the movements of the musicians on the stage, as well as vocal and instrumental music. (Partch once offered this view of the performer's role: "I believe in musicians who are total constituents of the moment, irreplaceable, who may sing, shout, whistle, stamp their feet; in costume always, or perhaps half naked, and I do not care which half."[6]

Moving toward his conception of a total musical theater, Partch's music took on a more differentiated quality. Its rhythmic and melodic structure became more highly profiled, and, thanks to the strikingly sensual resonances of the new instruments, its textural features acquired greater complexity and individuality. With their brief, repetitive melodic figures, Partch's later compositions are in one sense still "primitive," but their highly flexible, nonmetrical rhythm and microtonal pitch relationships, in conjunction with a fascinating interplay of textures and timbres, produce remarkably colorful musical surfaces.

The occasional purely instrumental works of Partch's later years, most notably *And on the Seventh Day Petals Fell on Petaluma* (1964), were products more of necessity (as a result of the difficulties involved in assembling sufficient performing forces for the dramatic works) than of preference. For he now believed that music could achieve its full nature and power only as a contributing component within a larger and more comprehensive unity. "My trinity," he once observed, is "sound-magic, visual beauty, experience-ritual."

The major creation of Partch's final years was *Delusion of the Fury* (1966), a large-scale dramatic work based on a Japanese Noh play. In this ritualized drama, featuring colorful costumes (including fantastic headpieces), the main currents of the composer's artistic development achieved an apt culmination. There is no actual libretto; all the action is either danced or mimed, and the voices sing only meaningless syllables. The positioning of the instruments (some of them quite large) and the motions entailed in playing them form part of the overall dramatic plan. As in all of Partch's work, the musicians are expected to play from memory, for they are as much actors as musicians.

In his later years Partch occasionally received assistance from foundations or universities, and held brief "research" appointments at several Midwestern colleges. Yet throughout his life he remained an essentially isolated figure, both professionally and personally. Despite severe financial hardships, he pursued his vision of a new kind of dramatically integrated, performance-oriented music with unswerving dedication, always in the face of professional rejection and public apathy. Partch's determination to construct his own unique musical universe in the face of such widespread neglect sets him off as a notable figure in twentieth-century music. (Webern and Varèse, who might come to mind as possible comparisons, were both much more fully

---

6.   "Remark made for a BMI brochure, 1968, but not used there," quoted in Johnston, "Partch," ibid., p. 556, col. 2.

involved in the "official" musical life of their time.) His individualism and radical transcendence of long-established esthetic conventions made Partch, along with Ives, an especially important model for a number of younger American composers of the post–World War II period.

VARÈSE

In 1915, at the age of thirty-two, the French composer Edgard Varèse (1883–1965) boarded a ship to the United States for what he expected to be a short visit. As it turned out, the New World became Varèse's primary residence; he married an American, eventually acquired citizenship, and wrote all of his principal compositions in his adopted country. In many respects an "American" composer, he eventually seemed to view his move to the United States as a symbolic rejection of his European past, as part of a search for a new music, more fully reflective of the contemporary world and thus as independent as possible of Western music's traditional formal and expressive conventions.

Varèse's initial training was in mathematics and engineering, and this scientific background was to have a significant influence upon his future attitudes toward composition. Despite family objections, he began serious musical studies in 1903 in Paris, first at the Schola Cantorum and then at the Conservatory. Upon moving to Berlin in 1907, he encountered the most important influence of his early life, Busoni, whose appeal for extended musical resources, expressed in the just-published *Sketch of a New Musical Esthetic,* made a profound impression upon the young composer.

By the time he came to the United States Varèse had attracted considerable attention as one of the more interesting composers of his generation in Europe. Yet virtually all the compositions completed before his arrival in New York were either lost in a Berlin warehouse fire or destroyed by the composer himself, and are known only by hearsay. Varèse himself encouraged the idea of a clean break with his European past, and the first composition he conceived in the United States was called *Amériques*—a title intended not as "purely geographic but as symbolic of discoveries—new worlds on earth, in the sky, or in the minds of men." It was the first of a series of explorations of new musical terrain that occupied Varèse over the first two decades of his residence in the United States, a period that would prove by far the most productive of his life.

In a newspaper interview in March 1915, shortly after his arrival in New York, Varèse expressed a concern that would dominate his thinking from this point on: "Our musical alphabet must be enriched. We also need new instruments very badly. . . . Musicians should take up this question in deep earnest with the help of machinery specialists. I have always felt the need for new mediums of expression in my work. I refuse to submit myself only to sounds that have already been heard. What I am looking for are new technical mediums which can lend themselves to every expression of thought and can keep up with thought."[7] While recalling Busoni, these words also echo the Italian Futurists, whose interest in broadening the horizons of art to encompass all possible sounds and available materials Varèse shared. However, he thought the Futurists too concerned with noise for its own sake, and retained a more traditionalist belief in the artist as a shaper of materials. Fresh resources were certainly important to him; what the composer was able to do with them mattered even more.

Thus the new instruments Varèse was already searching for in the early years of the century were not just makers of novel noises. He envisaged sophisticated electronic machines that would make available such unprecedented sound possibilities as a continuous range of pitches, including all possible subdivisions of the tempered scale, which could also be precisely controlled by the composer. Throughout his life Varèse tried to persuade scientists and technicians to help him invent such instruments, and actively sought funding for such research. But few other musicians showed any interest in such innovations, and this aspect of his work met with general skepticism. Exceptions were several scientists involved in early work on electronic instruments, including Termen and Maurice Martenot (in *Ecuatorial* Varèse used a pair of the latter's instruments known as the ondes martenot). But applications for research grants to the Bell Telephone Company and the Guggenheim Foundation met with no success, and only after World War II, when electronic music began to come into its own, could Varèse begin to put into practice some of his long-cherished radical musical ideas.

In his earlier works, however, Varèse had to make do with existing instruments. *Amériques,* completed in 1921 after several years of work, is scored for a very large but essentially traditional orchestra, with one significant exception: an unprecedentedly large percussion section. Varèse saw the percussion as the only component of the standard orchestra that still offered opportunities for significant expansion and for the introduction of fresh timbral resources. *Amériques* uses a wide variety of percussion instruments not previously encountered in a symphonic context, many of non-Western origin. Moreover, whereas traditional Western music used percussion to support and emphasize accentual patterns associated with the pitched events produced by the other orchestral families, Varèse gave them essentially independent parts. They no longer "double" pitched elements but provide a separate orchestral strand, interacting with the pitched elements, coloring them and, in turn, being

7.   Quoted in Fernand Ouellette, *Edgard Varèse* (New York, 1968), pp. 46–47.

colored by them. *Amériques* even includes passages in which the percussion plays entirely alone, carrying the full musical burden on its own, but the principle of autonomy operates equally when the percussion is played off against other orchestral layers.

This emphasis on percussion writing, one of the most significant features of Varèse's style, stems not only from his desire for new timbral possibilities. At least as important is the fact that in his music pitch is no longer necessarily the musical element of primary significance. The focus of compositional activity has shifted to nonpitch elements—not only timbre but also rhythm, registration, dynamics, and texture—and the music's character and logic are determined at least as much by the structuring of these elements as by that of the pitches. In making this shift Varèse drew positive implications from one of the most characteristic "negative" features of post-tonal music: the static quality resulting from the absence of expected forward motion, of the sense that one pitch "needs" to move on to another. Most post-tonal composers of the first half of the century attempted to deemphasize this static quality by creating compositional contexts in which forward motion was at least strongly suggested despite the loss of traditional tonal functions. This is as true of the "atonalists" Schoenberg and Berg, for example, as it is of such "neo-tonalists" as Bartók and Hindemith. Yet, as we have seen, certain others—most notably Debussy and Stravinsky—accepted at least some of the implications of a static pitch framework in order to exploit the formal possibilities inherent therein. However, Varèse carried this tendency further than any of his contemporaries.

Although Varèse's new compositional conception was already evident to a large extent in *Amériques,* it achieved its fullest statement in a remarkable series of works for small ensembles written over the next several years: *Offrandes* (1921), *Hyperprism* (1923), *Octandre* (1923), *Intégrales* (1925), *Ionisation* (1931), and *Ecuatorial* (1934). *Ionisation* is scored entirely for percussion, and all the others except *Octandre* call for large percussion ensembles and a group of mixed instruments (plus voice in *Offrandes* and *Ecuatorial*). Strings are largely avoided; Varèse felt them to be too closely associated with the expressive features of nineteenth-century music, and also unsuited to producing the crisp, percussive attacks he wanted (another point of similarity with Stravinsky). In this group of works they appear only in *Offrandes,* where they are almost always used in an accompanimental—and often percussive—manner, and in *Octandre,* which calls for one double bass. The emphasis is thus on brass, woodwinds, and percussion, producing an unmistakable and unprecedented quality of sound. As the titles themselves suggest, these are compositions with a fundamentally new orientation—music reflecting the hard-edged intensity of modern urban landscapes and industrial technologies.

Most of these pieces are conceived in a single movement that can be parsed into several smaller sections. One of the most concentrated examples of Varèse's new way of structuring musical materials is the first section of *Intégrales,* whose opening measures (Example XIII-6; see p. 310) present the three principal units from which the entire section is constructed. The initial unit is presented by the E♭ clarinet (mm. 1–3) and immediately repeated and varied (mm. 4–6) in the same instrument. While this unit is essentially "melodic" in nature, the remaining two are chordal, presented by the upper woodwinds and trombones respectively (mm. 5–6). Not only is the entire section developed out of these three pitched elements; even more interesting, and most typical of Varèse's approach, is that all three remain essentially unchanged in pitch structure throughout the first twenty-four bars, comprising all but the last few measures of the opening section. Having completely relinquished any tendency toward forward—that is, linear—motion, they are essentially "stationary objects," quite unlike the "mobile" ones typical of tonal music. (The only exception to this is the first, melodic element, which adds new pitches in some of its restatements, but it too always begins with the identical grace-note figure, and B♭ always remains its highest and most emphasized pitch.) Thus the actual musical development depends not upon the transformation of these units themselves, at least as far as their pitch content is concerned, but upon their different combinations and juxtapositions.

Varèse handles these units as fixed components that, although largely immutable in themselves, are placed in different relationships to one another to produce different overall configurations. Even though all three are repeated continuously throughout the section, their relationship to one another changes constantly. For instance, in the second complete restatement of all three units (Example XIII-7; see p. 311) the melodic element, originally in the clarinet, is rhythmically and timbrally varied. Moreover, the woodwind and brass chords now enter together and have short durations (m. 11), and their entrance precedes the repetition of the melodic unit; when they are themselves repeated and sustained, the trombone chord now enters before the woodwind chord. In addition, the dynamic relationships have been significantly altered. (The importance of dynamics is, in general, greatly increased in such a static pitch context. For example, since the diminuendo in mm. 2–3 of Example XIII-6 is the only element of change at that point, it provides the essential musical content, presenting an idea that is picked up "motivically" by the two chordal elements, which similarly diminuendo at the end of their statements, and then by the clarinet itself, which has another diminuendo after the winds drop out at the end of m. 6.)

Throughout the section the percussion play an especially significant role in creating a sense of constant transformation despite the essentially

Example XIII-6: VARÈSE, *Intégrales,* mm. 1–6

Copyright assigned 1956 to G. Ricordi & Co., used by permission.

Example XIII-7: VARÈSE, *Intégrales,* mm. 10–11

unchanging pitch structure. Typically, they form a musical layer rhythmically independent of the pitched ones. Because they develop independently, they "color" the three pitch units differently at each repetition, associating them with continuously changing rhythmic and timbral patterns. This can be seen by comparing the percussion parts of Examples XIII-6 and XIII-7: although some elements recur, notably in the tenor drum (*caisse roulante*), the relationship of the percussion and pitch elements is completely changed. By offering such a continuous "reinterpretation" of the stationary pitch events, much as do the rhythmic, dynamic, and "combinational" aspects of the score, the percussion layer thus provides an essential part of the overall effect.

In this music, as in all of Varèse, the principal focus is on the general textural and timbral effect rather than on specific motivic or harmonic details. There is no clear distinction between melody and accompaniment. The individual notes are often not conceived as parts of "lines" or "harmonies," but as constituents of what the composer called "sound masses," whole configurations of notes that work together to produce a generalized sonic character. Thus the opening of *Intégrales* can be viewed as a "counterpoint of masses," in which multiple planes of musical activity interact with one another in varying combinations. The composer's own terms for the various techniques of combining and opposing such materials are revealing: "collision," "penetration," repulsion," "transmutation," etc.

Varèse once described his ultimate goal as the "liberation of sound," recalling Schoenberg's famous reference to the "emancipation of dissonance" in his atonal works. But whereas Schoenberg's revolution was directed toward a free use of conventional dissonances, Varèse's was concerned with an exploitation of the purely sonic attributes of musical sound, set free from traditional formal or expressive implications. Starting with the most basic features of his materials—instrumentation, registration, contour, rhythmic shape, etc.—he attempted to devise formal contexts in which they could function as "sound objects"—as plastic events to be shaped, combined, and fused by the composer, much as a sculptor works with physical materials. In this light, *Ionisation*—often considered Varèse's most revolutionary score, since it was the first concert work written for percussion alone—is entirely consistent with his other works. In a style wherein pitch is assigned a relatively "secondary" position, the compositional procedures used in a percussion piece can be basically the same as those of the other pieces.

During the period of these works for chamber ensembles, Varèse also composed *Arcana* (1927), a large-scale orchestral piece based on similar principles. After completing these works, he finished a brief piece for flute alone—*Density 21.5* (1936), now a standard in the modern flute repertory—but thereafter, for some twenty years, no new compositions. A number of explanations for Varèse's long silence are possible. One was his dissatisfaction with conventional instruments and their confinement by what he called the "tyranny of the tempered scale," combined with the failure of any acceptable new electronic instruments to emerge. A more general reason—one that affected a number of experimental composers of the day—was the general conservative trend of the 1930s and 1940s, which made Varèse (always looking to the future rather than the past) feel especially isolated.

In any event, although he undertook several projects during this period of silence, Varèse completed no new composition until *Déserts* appeared in 1954. Along with the reawakening of a more "progressive" musical atmosphere, Varèse's return to activity was stimulated by the recent availability of tape recorders and more reliable electronic instruments. *Déserts* combines exclusively electronic sections with purely instrumental ones featuring a wind and percussion ensemble similar to those Varèse had previously used—as if to demonstrate that there was no inherent inconsistency between what he had done in his earlier work with traditional instruments and what he could now do with the new technical possibilities. His next work, the *Poème électronique* (1958), was entirely electronic, but even this manifests a close affinity with the previous output. It too is a "counterpoint of masses," though encompassing a much broader range of sonic material, including both purely electronic sounds and recorded "natural" sounds—some musical (e.g., piano chords, human voices) and some not (e.g., machine noises)—transformed through electronic manipulation.

By the time *Poème électronique* was completed Varèse was seventy-five years old and near the end of his creative life. In his final years he worked on a couple of pieces for voice and chamber orchestra, one of which—*Nocturnal*—was completed by his student Chou Wen-chung and published after his death. To a large extent, the technical advances Varèse had called for throughout his life as a composer arrived too late for him to take full advantage of them. His two electronic pieces are among the most imaginative and innovative works produced during the infancy of this new musical medium, but the heart of Varèse's contribution lies in

Edgard Varèse at home in his New York apartment, April 14, 1959.

the ground-breaking instrumental pieces of the earlier years. There he fashioned a fresh approach to composition that not only inspired many of his contemporaries but has continued to exert an important influence on musical developments since World War II.

In addition to his work as a composer, Varèse contributed significantly to contemporary musical life in the United States between the wars. In 1919 he founded and led the New Symphony Orchestra, dedicated to performing challenging new works. Although this venture soon met with failure, two years later he joined with the French-American composer and harpist Carlos Salzédo to form the International Composers' Guild, which presented new scores by the most innovative American and European composers of the day, including Ives, Ruggles, Webern, and Berg. Largely responsible for choosing the guild's concert programs, Varèse frequently conducted its performances as well. After the dissolution of the guild in 1927, Varèse (with Henry Cowell and the Mexican composer Carlos Chávez) founded the Pan American Association of Composers, dedicated to performing new music by composers from throughout the Americas. (The international character of all of these organizations is especially characteristic.) Varèse's strong personality, unshakable conviction, and determined support of the most innovative tendencies in music made him one of the most charismatic figures in the arts of the time.

CHAPTER XIV

Latin America

As in the United States, art music in Latin America during the nineteenth century was almost entirely dominated by European models—in this case primarily by Italian opera. Among the Latin-American composers who wrote stage works firmly tied to Old World traditions, with nationalist elements confined primarily to the librettos, the most prominent was the Brazilian Carlos Gomes (1836–96), who like so many of his North American contemporaries went to Europe to study, but to Italy rather than France or Germany. Warmly praised by Verdi, he achieved international fame with the success of *Il Guarany* (1870) at La Scala in Milan, and his works have remained in the repertory in Brazil.

As in such European "fringe" areas as Scandinavia and Bohemia, the development of a more indigenous musical style in Latin America only took root with the rise of political nationalism in the later nineteenth century. At first this was limited to the introduction of native dances into their scores by Gomes and his contemporaries. The early years of the new century brought the first serious attempts to color a conception based mainly upon Italian *verismo* models with the consistent use of local musical elements: e.g., *Ollanta* (1901) by the Peruvian José Maria Valle Riestra and *Huemac* (1916) by the Italian-born Argentinian Pascual de Rogatis. Such works laid an essential foundation for the major twentieth-century Latin American composers, almost all of whom began their careers as ardent nationalists, committed to a reconciliation of the advanced techniques of European modernism with melodic and rhythmic elements derived from native folk sources.

VILLA-LOBOS

The first of these to achieve international recognition was the Brazilian Heitor Villa-Lobos (1887–1959), who developed a markedly individual compositional style strongly based on national elements. That Villa-Lobos was almost entirely self-taught as a musician is a point of some significance in explaining the unique and peculiarly Brazilian quality of his work. Determinedly individualistic in personality and distrustful of all academic training, he studied the cello formally (and played it in theater orchestras), but acquired most of his musical education within the context of popular Brazilian music, playing the guitar in small instrumental ensembles that worked the streets and cafés of Rio de Janeiro. This firsthand contact with urban music was complemented by a growing interest in the rural folk music of Brazil, stimulated by several journeys throughout the country.

Combining these diverse early musical experiences with an expanding awareness of contemporary European developments (especially those of France and Italy), Villa-Lobos fashioned the eclectic style of his maturity, blending popular elements with the techniques of modern concert music, especially the blocklike ostinato structures characteristic of Stravinsky. This orientation is especially evident in the series of fourteen *Chôros* written between 1920 and 1929 (the term refers to the genre of urban instrumental music he had played in the streets of Rio). Each *Chôro* is conceived in a single, multisectional movement, and each is scored for a different ensemble, ranging from solo guitar (No. 1) through small chamber groups of mixed instruments (Nos. 2, 4, 7) to full orchestra (Nos. 6, 8, 9) and orchestra and chorus (No. 10); they all reflect the essentially improvisatory and rhapsodic character and the syncopated rhythms of the popular music played by the bands for which they are named.

The entirely individual form of these pieces seems to derive more from a conception of free improvisational development than from conventional models. In *Chôro* No. 10, for example, a loosely structured orchestral opening, characterized by a number of different motivic ideas presented in abrupt juxtaposition, eventually leads to an extended final section announced by a chorus singing meaningless, constantly reiterated syllables. This last section is dominated by one of the earlier motives, acting as an almost constant ostinato-like element; although brief, simple, and entirely diatonic, this motive builds in intensity through its repetitions to produce, near the end, the work's biggest climactic point.

This rough, vigorous character is typical of much of Villa-Lobos's music of the 1920s. The extended, highly virtuosic piano piece *Rude-poema* (1926) features rich yet brutally percussive textures, brief and frequently reiterated melodic figures combined with ostinato accompaniments, and a conclusion of extraordinary primitive force in which the pianist, using the fist, bangs out a three-note cluster at the lower end of the keyboard. Also notable is the Nonet for winds, harp, piano, celesta, percussion, and textless chorus (1923), subtitled by the composer "a rapid impression of all Brazil." While resembling the *Chôros* in its sectionalized one-movement structure permeated with the flavor of Brazilian popular music, the Nonet is distinguished by its unusual combination of timbres and its percussion writing, exceptionally elaborate for that time, calling on an unprecedented range of instruments, including a number of indigenous Brazilian ones.

Between 1923 and 1930, assisted by the Brazilian government and wealthy patrons, Villa-Lobos spent much time in Europe, based in Paris but visiting other cities and also Africa. After 1929 he discontinued the series of *Chôros,* following it with a new series of nine compositions entitled *Bachianas brasileiras* (1930–45). In these he attempted to blend the character of Brazilian popular music with stylistic characteristics drawn from the music of J. S. Bach, a composer he especially admired and one who had, in his view, an affinity with Brazilian music. (Indeed, Villa-Lobos considered Bach to be an "intermediary between all cultures.")

Rather than attempting a neo-classical recreation of the spirit of Bach's music in modern-day terms, in the manner of Stravinsky or Hindemith, the *Bachianas* reexamine certain of Bach's general stylistic features—sequential melodic construction, chains of suspensions, contrapuntal textures, etc.—in the light of Villa-Lobos's own national musical heritage. Unlike the *Chôros,* they contain more than one movement, and most of the movements carry double titles, one of Baroque origin and the other indicating a Brazilian dance (e.g., Preludio / Modhina, Toccata / Picapao). Yet the diversity and originality of the scoring recall the earlier series; for example, *Bachianas brasileiras* No. 5, probably the best known of all Villa-Lobos's compositions, is for soprano soloist with an orchestra made up entirely of cellos. The first of its two movements, an extended cantilena with a broad, rhythmically flexible opening vocalise over an accompaniment loosely based on a Bachian slow-movement model, testifies to the composer's gift for sustained melodic lyricism.

Villa-Lobos was a composer of easy facility, who wrote music almost as if he were improvising; and his work list encompasses a remarkable range of music, including twelve symphonies, a large number of concertos (among them five for piano, one each for harp and harmonica), and seventeen string quartets, plus an extensive body of other chamber, vocal, and piano music. Since the approach tends to vary from composition to composition, a consistent style is difficult to find; however, all the music is tonal, and most of it features rich, triadically based harmonies derived from late Romantic and Impressionistic influences. Even in the more "abstract" works, such as the string quartets, the national element remains very pronounced. Quartet No. 1 (1915), for example, consists of six brief movements with the quality—and the titles—of Brazilian character pieces, and both the Fifth and Sixth Quartets are also openly nationalist in character.

The total number of Villa-Lobos's compositions has been estimated to exceed two thousand (many of them still in manuscript), although a number of these are adaptations and arrangements of other compositions. Given the size of his output, it is perhaps to be expected that the quality is uneven. In his later years, moreover, the composer lost some of his youthful individuality, and a quality of routine began to enter his work. Yet Villa-Lobos is a critical figure in the history of Latin-American music, its first unmistakably native musical voice.

CHÁVEZ

The Mexican Carlos Chávez (1899–1978) is in many respects a more typical composer of the twentieth century than his Brazilian colleague Villa-Lobos. Born some twelve years later, Chávez was more closely attuned to the main currents of international musical modernism, and eschewed Villa-Lobos's extremely personal, essentially Romantic approach in favor of a more objective and impersonal orientation, strongly akin to European neo-classicism. Yet he too relied upon native elements, though less consciously and consistently. As a gifted young musician maturing in postrevolutionary Mexico of the 1920s, when great emphasis was placed on the development of an independent national culture, Chávez assumed a major role in the so-called "Aztec Renaissance" of these years. Unlike Villa-Lobos, who based his work on current popular and folk music, Chávez and other Mexican artists of the time (most prominently the painters Diego Rivera and José Orozco) sought inspiration in the Indian culture of the pre-Columbian period, which they felt represented the only authentic embodiment of the Mexican spirit. In their view the yoke of European domination could be thrown off only by reaching back to this more distant past.

In several compositions, notably the *Sinfonia india* (1936), Chávez actually based his music on ancient Indian melodies (a few of which had been preserved) and employed native percussion instruments. With its repetitious primitivism tempered by sophisticated use of modern developmental techniques and instrumentation, the *Sinfonia india* impressed audiences as a work of undeniable contemporaneity yet also of distinctly Latin-American flavor.

More often Chávez avoided actual native materials, believing that national characteristics would inevitably appear in his music without conscious effort, the natural consequence of his Mexican heritage. Though named for the Aztec god of music and subtitled by the composer "An

In *The Departure of Quetzalcoatl,* José Clemente Orozco depicts the Aztec god's angry departure from his pyramid temple to the dismay of the natives. (Fresco mural, 1932–34; Baker Library, Dartmouth College, Hanover, New Hampshire)

Imagined Aztec Music," the chamber work *Xochipilli* (1940) contains no quoted material and is rather, as Chávez states in a preface to the score, "an attempt to reconstruct—as far as it is possible—the music of ancient Mexicans." Scored for four winds and six percussionists (the latter playing primitive instruments, which may, however, be replaced by their modern equivalents), the work represents an imaginative evocation of primitive musical ritualism through repetitions of brief and simple phrases. The austere melodic content, confined to a few pitches within a restricted range, and the propulsive rhythmic character project a stark dynamic force.

In still other compositions Chávez makes no conscious effort whatever to evoke a national flavor. Several of the symphonies, including the *Sinfonia de Antigona* (1933) and Symphonies No. 4 (*Sinfonia romantica,* 1953) and No. 5 (for string orchestra, 1954), are "abstract" in character and closely related to contemporary European symphonic models in general approach. Also significant is the Toccata for Percussion (1942), a three-movement work (played without pause) that was one of the first percussion pieces to be widely performed. Six players work with a large and varied group of instruments, whose broad range of timbral possibilities enables Chávez to explore his interest in unusual coloristic effects. The first movement is scored exclusively for drums, the second combines xylophone, glockenspiel, and chimes with cymbal and gongs (all metal except for the xylophone), while the last mixes different types of instruments in varying combinations.

Throughout his career Chávez played an active role in Mexican musical life beyond his activities as a composer. He helped establish the first permanent symphony orchestra in Mexico and served as its conductor from 1928 until 1948. In 1928 he became director of the National Conservatory, and during a brief seven-year reign initiated crucial reforms in the curriculum, developing the school into an important training center for Mexican musicians. He was also active as a writer, music critic for a Mexico City newspaper, and author of several books and articles (including one on Mexican music for Henry Cowell's *American Composers on American Music*). His book *Toward a New Music,* published in 1937 in the United States (where Chávez was active as both composer and conductor), focuses mainly upon the impact of modern technology—especially film, radio, and "electric" instruments—on twentieth-century music; it remains an interesting document of music in the Americas during the between-war years. Especially characteristic is the author's insistence on living entirely "in the present," making full use of all available technical possibilities. At the end of the book Chávez remarks: "I do not believe in futurism. I believe only in the present."

GINASTERA

The most prominent Latin-American composer of the next generation was the Argentinian Alberto Ginastera (1916–83). Like Villa-Lobos and Chávez, Ginastera made his early reputation as a composer of strongly nationalist sentiments, but he was also young enough to be significantly influenced by the more international flavor of musical developments after World War II.

In 1943 the premiere of an orchestral suite from Ginastera's first major work, the ballet *Estancia* (1941), consolidated his position in his native land. Depicting various scenes from country life in Argentina, the ballet is based on popular musical sources from rural areas. The *Danza del triga (Wheat Dance)* features a slow, lyrical melody accompanied by piano and pizzicato strings in a manner evocative of a guitar, and the *Danza finale* is a fast, heavily syncopated *gaucho* dance, a 6 / 8 *perpetuum mobile* whose driving rhythm produces a percussive, toccata-like quality that was to remain especially typical of the composer.

Other works of this first period include the *Danza argentinas* for piano (1937), the *5 Canciones populares argentinas* and *Las Horas de una estancia,* both for voice and piano (1943), and the *Pampeana* No. 1 for violin and piano (1947). Ginastera characterized this early period as one of "objective nationalism," in which definite features of folk music (including specific popular dances) are openly evoked. By contrast, in the "subjective nationalism" of his second period the ethnic attributes, though still present in "sublimated" form, are less consciously applied. The latter period is bounded by the composer's only two String Quartets, the first written in 1948, the second in 1958, and also includes the Piano Sonata

Ginastera's opera, *Don Rodrigo,* in the 1966 production of the New York City Opera. (Photo: Fred Fehl)

(1952) and the *Variaciones concertantes* for chamber orchestra (1953). As their titles suggest, these pieces are concerned more with matters of large-scale musical structure than with aspects of local color.

During this second period, beginning with the Piano Sonata, Ginastera adopted the twelve-tone technique, subsequently used in all his major works. Ginastera's conception of the technique always remained free and decidedly personal, however, and his music continued to display unmistakable nationalistic characteristics. The Second String Quartet features the same driving, propulsive rhythmic quality found in the earlier work, though now in conjunction with much more concentrated and extensive developmental processes. (Here can be felt the influence of Bartók, another "nationalist" who tried to reconcile the demands of large-scale musical structure with folk-inspired melodic materials.) Moreover, despite the use of dodecaphonic techniques, the Second Quartet remains essentially tonal: the outer movements are centered on G, and the two middle ones suggest D and C as points of emphasis.

The last phase of Ginastera's career, comprising the final quarter century of his life, brought a continued exploration of advanced technical procedures and a diminishing emphasis on explicitly national features. Along with an increasingly flexible approach to twelve–tone writing, he responded to some of the new currents of the post–World War II period, employing aspects of aleatory and microtonal composition that could be consistently integrated within his own general stylistic orientation. The most important works of this period were three operas, *Don Rodrigo* (1964), *Bomarzo* (1967), and *Beatrix Cenci* (1971), all of which enjoyed widespread success and established Ginastera as the leading Latin-American composer of the time. The librettos of these operas also reflect the more international and abstract character of the composer's later music: all three focus upon European rather than South American protagonists. The dramatic emphasis is upon modern psychological themes, coupled with an unusually explicit treatment of sexuality and violence. Other works from Ginastera's last period include two Piano Concertos (1961, 1972), a Violin Concerto (1963), and a Cello Concerto (1968), as well as the *Cantata para América mágica* (1960).

Although all Ginastera's later compositions fit comfortably within the worldwide musical mainstream of their time, they also affirm close ties with the older European modernist tradition. In *Don Rodrigo,* for example, which has three acts containing three scenes each, the scenes are shaped according to traditional formal types and connected by instrumental interludes—a concept clearly derived from Berg's *Wozzeck*—and the detailed system of symbolic associations between specific dramatic elements and specific aspects of the opera's twelve-tone structure recalls the same composer's *Lulu.* And the opera's archlike structure, in which corresponding scenes—the first and last, the second and the next to last, etc.—complement one another, recalls Bartók.

OTHER LATIN AMERICANS

Despite the strong predisposition toward musical nationalism throughout Latin America during the first half of the twentieth century, a small number of composers adopted a more experimental posture. Most remarkable among them was the Mexican Julián Carrillo (1875–1965), who developed an elaborate system of microtonal tuning called *Sonido 13* (The Thirteenth Sound). Carrillo's earliest work in the microtonal area apparently dates back to the last years of the nineteenth century (making him a remarkable pioneer), although the first compositions written within the new system did not appear until the 1920s; best known among them is the *Preludio a Colón* (1922), a chamber work for soprano, flute, guitar, violin, harp, and octavia (a string instrument of the composer's invention).

Although a number of younger composers have established solid reputations since World War II, Ginastera's recent death has left Latin-American music without a dominant figure. Following his example, the trend among the postwar generation has been to shun nationalism in favor of new formal and technical approaches. Two Argentinians have achieved international fame through careers centered in other parts of the world: Mauricio Kagel (b. 1931) in Germany and Mario Davidovsky (b. 1934) in the United States.

PART III

Innovation and Fragmentation: From World War II to the Present

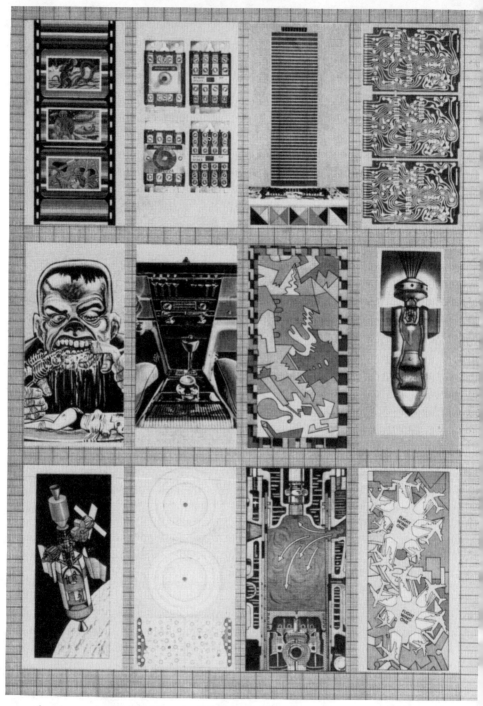

A screen-print by British artist Eduardo Paolozzi entitled *Will the Future Rule of the Earth come from the Ranks of the Insects?*, showing the imagery of modern life as increasingly drawn from technology, science fiction, and Pop art. Included are a printed circuit, the control panel of a car, an atomic bomb, a satellite space station, an internal combustion engine, and an airport stacking chart. Lithograph and screenprint from *Zero Energy Experimental Pile*, 1970.

CHAPTER XV

The Historical Context: The World after World War II

The twentieth century's second global military confrontation had even more far-reaching consequences than the first. The toll in human life was far greater. Not only was the number of military deaths much higher; the civilian fatalities approximately equaled them, producing a total estimated in the neighborhood of thirty million. The introduction of full-scale aerial bombing brought the conflict home to the common citizen in an unprecedented way. In addition, the racial and political policies of Nazi Germany resulted in the death of millions of Europeans.

The level of physical destruction was equally extensive. Many British and continental cities suffered massive damage, and countless dwelling places, historical monuments, and business, manufacturing, and transportation facilities were destroyed. By the war's end Europe was flooded with refugees uprooted from their residences and, often, from their native lands. Comparable devastation took place in the Far East, and the dropping of the first atomic bombs on Hiroshima and Nagasaki during the final days of the war virtually obliterated those two Japanese cities with a single blow. By the conclusion of hostilities, the world and its inhabitants seemed literally to have been torn to pieces by this second, more advanced version of modern technological warfare.

One by-product of the worsening European political situation of the 1930s had a significant impact on music after World War II: the emigration of large numbers of European musicians to the United States, where they found a haven from totalitarianism and, eventually, from the war itself. The largest group was German, mainly though by no means

325

exclusively Jewish, but many others came from Italy, France, and elsewhere. Especially notable was the large number of composers from Europe, many of them major figures, who resettled in the New World: to name only the most prominent, by 1940 Stravinsky, Schoenberg, Bartók, Hindemith, Weill, and Milhaud were all living and working in the United States, significantly realigning the cultural map and giving America a vastly more prominent position within the international musical configuration.

This immigration was but one of many factors that carried the United States from a peripheral position to the center of Western artistic and musical activities. Equally important were the political readjustments resulting from World War II, which changed the world's geopolitical shape even more drastically than had the previous war. With Europe in ruins, its cities devastated, its economy shattered, its culture in decline, and its military power eroded, and with no single European country in a position to assume political leadership, the United States and the Soviet Union emerged as the dominant powers of the postwar period.

Without significant political and military might of their own, the nations of Europe necessarily became aligned with one of these two great powers. The division of Germany into separate zones of Allied occupation by the terms of the Potsdam Agreement eventually hardened into two separate states, one allied with the West, the other with the Soviet Union. Eastern European countries such as Hungary, Czechoslovakia, and Poland, previously tied culturally to the West, were now politically and economically bound to the Soviet Union and effectively isolated from Western Europe—an isolation symbolized by the imaginary yet ideologically very real "Iron Curtain" that separated the two blocs. Correspondingly, the influence of the United States upon the Western European allies, its interaction in their affairs through joint economic, political, and military concerns, increased dramatically at the same time that the European countries were forced to relinquish some of their former sovereignty. As their individual colonial empires collapsed in the postwar years, they joined together in a new economic union, the so-called common market, which lent them something of the character of a single nation. The national traits of individual members, although by no means disappearing, were gradually less emphasized.

The eventual emergence of Communist China as a third great power served to draw the entire globe into a yet tighter and more complex network of tensions and shifting alliances. Other nations began to make their concerns felt on an international scale. The countries of the "Third World" (so called to distinguish them from the United States and its European allies on the one hand, and Russia and its Eastern allies on the other) emerged as a force in world affairs. Many of these poorer, less developed lands, located primarily in the Middle East, Africa, and South America, had only achieved their independence in the postwar years, with the collapse of the old colonial empires, and they often banded together in larger confederations wielding considerable political influence, no longer to be dismissed by the leading powers.

The world thus transformed politically also grew drastically smaller during the second half of the century. Important events in one part of the globe quickly generated significant repercussions elsewhere. The notably international, "one world" character of the postwar period is an outgrowth of rapidly expanding technological developments, particularly in transportation and communication. People and goods can now be moved with unprecedented speed and efficiency. The widespread use of telephones, phonographs, radio, television, and—most recently—computers, together with the proliferation of printed publications of all kinds and of libraries to house them, have produced a communications explosion that continues to have profound consequences for the way we live and the way we perceive ourselves, our neighbors, and, above all, those living at great distances from us. The cultural critic Marshall McLuhan foresaw the formation of a "global village, a unitary world of neo-tribesmen, sunk in their social roles and fraternally involved with one another." "Nowadays everything happens at once," remarked the composer John Cage, "and our souls are conveniently electronic, omniattentive."

The fact that we now know what is taking place across the globe almost as soon as it happens has made us much more conscious of other cultures than ever before, and has fostered the evolution of a single "world culture" shared by peoples living in greatly separated regions scattered throughout the world. A new musical development no sooner takes place in one country than it is reported—and even, in recorded or broadcast form, heard—everywhere. Internationally oriented composers who travel widely, participating in performances of their music in remote lands, are now commonplace, as are international musical festivals that bring together composers, listeners, and performers from great distances to hear new works and exchange new ideas. All this tends to blur cultural boundaries and support a new cultural supranationality. Scarcely a major European composer of the postwar years, for example, has not lived and worked for extended periods in the United States, some—including Boulez, Berio, and Penderecki—for significant portions of their professional lives.

This rapid, ever-expanding exchange of cultural goods and information fosters perhaps the most characteristic feature of contemporary culture: its pervasive pluralism. As distinct local cultures have been eroded by contact with the outside world and subjected to the impact of foreign influences, a new "world culture" has begun to piece itself together, drawing elements from a seemingly inexhaustible network of diverse sources. What differentiates this culture from previous ones, however, is the absence of any fixed technical and esthetic conventions—that is, just those features formerly assumed to constitute the necessary basis for any well-defined culture or style. As artistic products from distant lands and past eras have become instantaneously available by electronic means, brought to us daily by radio, television, and recordings, style has been redefined as an eclectic mix, a colorful mélange of materials and characteristics drawn from a vast storehouse of available resources. Among this new culture's most remarkable features is its ability to accommodate elements from many distinct subcultures that frequently cut across traditional geographic and esthetic boundaries. Such previously fundamental distinctions as those between popular and art music, or Western and Oriental music, are often blurred. Everything tends to fuse together in a new eclecticism.

The radical pluralism of contemporary culture first became broadly evident during the 1960s, when new artistic movements appeared to replace one another on an almost annual basis—or, rather, to join one another, for the old ones tended to persist. Encouraged by the absence of a common core of stable esthetic attitudes, a constant search for "something new" assumed an increasingly central role in the work of many artists. In painting, abstract expressionism, the prevailing artistic style of the 1950s, gave way in the 1960s to an unremitting series of new fashions: pop art, op art, minimalism, conceptual art, earth art, found art, photographic realism, neo-expressionism, and so on *ad infinitum*. Music followed a parallel course: serialism and indeterminacy, the two dominant compositional directions of the 1950s, were succeeded by textural music, quotation music, minimalism, ethnic music, environmental music, neo-tonality, and so on.

Such a mixture of styles, along with the concomitant instability and uncertainty of orientation manifested by individual artists, raised questions about the very nature of art—as if, throughout all the arts, something resembling a collective identity crisis had occurred. "I don't know what this is, 'Art,' " confessed the German conceptualist Hans Haacke, without the slightest hint of embarrassment.

The "tradition of the new," as the art critic Harold Rosenberg dubbed the phenomenon, gave expression to the deep feelings of alienation and discontent experienced by many during the postwar years. A principal—perhaps the principal—factor contributing to these feelings was the threat of nuclear warfare: the realization that at any moment entire cities and their populations could be instantaneously destroyed brought a new level of tension and unreality to contemporary life. Partly as a protest against the institutionalized political and cultural status quo, many artists and intellectuals conceived their work in direct opposition to the conventional forms of Western art, isolating them from a public largely attuned to traditional art.

Although some degree of separation between artist and public has characterized Western culture since the nineteenth century, the rift between the two now reached unprecedented dimensions. The atmosphere of artistic malaise achieved particularly pointed expression in the idea of a "theater of the absurd," propounding the conviction that since all discourse had become meaningless, artists should exalt the nonsensical, arbitrary, and capricious. As Eugène Ionesco, a leading playwright of the movement, explained: "Absurd is that which is devoid of purpose. . . . Cut off from his religious, metaphysical, and transcendental roots, man is lost; all his actions become senseless, absurd, useless." The spirit of Dada had returned, but on a scale unknown in the past.

Other signs of widespread alienation and dissatisfaction with traditional values became evident throughout the Western world in the 1960s. Significant numbers of the younger generation, disillusioned by constant international tension, by environmental pollution and the increasing encroachment of technology, rebelled against what they perceived as the monolithic centralism and elitism of the established cultural and political framework. (The accent on a "culture of youth" was so strong at one point that the phrase "You can't trust anyone over thirty" became a rallying cry.) Rejecting traditional modes of thought and behavior in favor of more direct and personalized ones, they explored a wide range of alternative "life-styles." Sexual emancipation, experimentation with drugs, interest in Oriental mysticism and non-Western philosophies— these were but some of the symptoms of a radical realignment of individual attitudes. The "establishment," despised as an impersonal force that victimized the average citizen, depriving him of any significant choice, was attacked by all available means—subversive political activity, guerrilla theater, cultural propaganda, or simply "dropping out." The general emphasis on individualism was reflected in a surge of concern for minority rights, primarily focused in its earliest stages (at least in the United States) on civil rights for blacks, but eventually encompassing such groups as American Indians, women, homosexuals, the aged, the disabled, and animals.

Mirroring the aura of alienation that has typified the arts in recent years is the sense of historical discontinuity characterizing the work of many composers, writers, and artists of the past quarter century. Here a feature typical of Western art for the past two centuries has been intensified to attain an entirely new level. Convinced that the modern situation is fundamentally different from anything previously known, many contemporary artists have sought to make a fundamental break with the past. Older traditions, the established and institutionalized ways

Andy Warhol drew attention to his pop art with endless rows of supermarket products, such as Coca Cola or Campbell soup. *100 Cans,* 1962. (Albright-Knox Art Gallery, Buffalo, New York, Gift of Seymour H. Knox, 1963)

of doing and perceiving things, are distrusted as inadequate and irrelevant for current circumstances. A need to try out radical new artistic approaches, evident to some degree throughout the twentieth century, has now become a basic esthetic stance.

Distrusted by the young as an extension and reflection of the status quo, "high" culture was felt to have reached a point of exhaustion. In its stead a "counterculture" was erected—in reality an indeterminate number of alternative cultures representing and responding to a variety of social and ethnic interests. The centralized culture would be replaced by a "democracy" of separate but equal cultures. One hoped-for result would be significant cultural renewal, giving rise to new forms of artistic expression able to speak more directly to a large and diverse public.

As high culture lost its former authority, popular culture gained in significance. "Has anyone been able completely to ignore *Sergeant Pepper's Lonely Hearts Club Band?*" asked the eminent literary critic Richard Poirier in a 1968 essay entitled "Learning from the Beatles." Distinctions between the two cultures were widely rejected, and there emerged a range of new cultural options that tended to cut across previously established demarcations. Andy Warhol, the artist who perhaps more than any other summed up the spirit of the 1960s and 1970s, drew openly upon the languages of popular culture and commercial art. His favored images included glamorous mass-media stars (Marilyn Monroe, Jacqueline Onassis), comic-book characters (Superman, Popeye), and artifacts of everyday life (Brillo boxes, Campbell's soup cans, automobile wrecks). Emphasizing the lack of uniqueness, the very ordinariness of his subjects, Warhol often filled his canvases with multiplications of a single image over undifferentiated columns and rows.

The erosion of old barriers between artistic "levels" encouraged the use of mixed genres and eclectic stylistic combinations. In architecture the severe consistency of the international style of modernism, which had completely dominated serious building since the 1920s, gave way to a new eclecticism termed "postmodernism." Based on a hybrid mixture of stylistic references drawn equally from historical (especially classical), vernacular, and commercial sources (the latter stressed by the architect Robert Venturi in his influential 1972 book *Learning from Las Vegas*), the new architecture revels in complexity, extravagance, pluralism, and humor.

People and environment oriented, postmodernism eschews a central esthetic tenet in favor of inconsistencies and differences. In place of the old modernist dogma "Form follows function," it promotes the freewheeling use of forms for their own sakes. And to Mies van der Rohe's famous modernist dictum, "Less is more," it seems to respond, "The more the better." Led by such figures as Michael Graves, James Stirling, Hans Hollein, and Minoru Takeyama, the movement has redefined architecture and transformed the appearance of cities throughout the world.

These developments in painting and architecture typify recent tendencies in all the arts, rendering them more diverse and inclusive than ever before. Indeed, with the decline of accepted conventions and standards of value, the present-day art world seems to be one in which almost anything is allowed. Positively considered, this lends recent artistic developments an extraordinary aura of excitement, daring, and experimentation. The variety of activity is remarkably high and the possibilities for personal expression virtually unrestricted.

Yet the lack of integration that makes this freedom and diversity possible has inevitably taken its toll. Today's cultural life manifests little sense of community. The absence of transpersonal conventions, of a common style and language equally accessible and congenial to all, has produced what many perceive as a wasteland of isolated, individual, and disconnected artistic activities. Not surprisingly, this pluralistic quality in contemporary culture has encouraged a countermovement: a desire to rediscover the past, to resurrect and revitalize its artistic traditions. Many composers of the last quarter century have therefore reincorporated traditional tonality in their work—however, not usually as an encompassing system (there is thus little sense of an actual *return*

In Michael Graves's Portland Building (View from Fifth Avenue), the postmodern aesthetic produces a far more ornate, colorful, and eclectic architecture than had characterized the International Style for so many decades. (Photo: Paschall/Taylor)

to the past), but as one among many possibilities that can be called upon to create formal coherence and expressive impact. In hopes of reducing the high degree of alienation that, on the part of many, has come to be taken as an inherent attribute of the modern situation, this turn to the past has gone hand in hand with attempts to write music with greater audience appeal.

Music since World War II, then, forms an unusually colorful and varied patchwork of apparently irreconcilable features, characterized perhaps more by diversity than by any other aspect. As a result, the developments dealt with in the last portion of this survey often seem to have little connection with one another. Unlike earlier phases of the twentieth century, the current one appears to reveal no larger stylistic or esthetic unity, no common thread tying together into a comprehensive whole at least a significant number of the different lines of development. Unless, of course, the unity of our present period can be said to reside in its very stylistic profusion—or, as is always possible, we are simply too close to it to be able to perceive the larger pattern.

We shall return to these more general cultural and esthetic considerations in the final chapter, but first we must examine the musical developments themselves. Because of the diversity and especially because of our lack of historical perspective, it will be more necessary than ever to be selective, focusing only on the developments most characteristic of the current age.

CHAPTER XVI

Integral Serialism

THE POSTWAR COMPOSITIONAL MOOD

Emerging from the material hardships and cultural isolation of the war years, the younger generation of European composers experienced a profound reaction against their cultural heritage. To them, the tradition of Western music seemed inextricably tied to the political and social failures of the past. If a new and better world was to be created out of the ashes of World War II, it would require a new kind of music, fundamentally different from anything known before. Neo-classicism, which in its various guises had dominated European music for over a quarter century, was regarded with suspicion and distaste by most younger composers, who saw it as a misguided attempt to reconcile the technical revolutions of the post-tonal era with the esthetic assumptions inherited from an earlier musical language. The overwhelming sense of disruption caused by the war made all hope of such reconciliation with the past seem futile. A complete break was needed with all previous notions of music, of how it should be composed and of how it should sound.

As Pierre Boulez, one of the leading figures of postwar European music, put it: "In 1945–46 nothing was ready and everything remained to be done: it was our privilege to make the discoveries and also to find ourselves faced with nothing—which may have its difficulties but also has many advantages."[1] Expressing a view shared by many of his con-

---

1. *Orientations,* ed. Jean-Jacques Nattiez, trans. Martin Cooper (Cambridge, Mass., 1986), p. 445.

temporaries, Boulez believed that earlier twentieth-century composers had failed to bring about a musical revolution sufficiently encompassing for a radically new age. More specifically, failing to recognize the full implications of the loss of tonality, they had clung to past assumptions of musical structure and expression instead of seizing the opportunity to completely rethink music according to new principles. In a famous and purposefully provocative essay entitled "Schoenberg Is Dead," written in 1952, not long after the Viennese composer's death, Boulez first praised the older master for inventing the twelve-tone system and then castigated him for not realizing its full potential. Schoenberg had treated the series as a "theme" rather than as an abstract configuration of intervals, and relied upon pre-Classical and Classical formal schemata instead of deriving explicitly serial structures from the characteristics of the row.

What was required, in Boulez's view, was a consistent treatment of all musical elements—not only pitch, but rhythm, dynamics, texture, and ultimately form itself—according to strictly serial procedures, resulting in a complete departure from previous musical assumptions. Debussy and Webern had shown the way; by breaking up traditional musical gestures through radical fragmentation, they had succeeded in treating musical sounds "objectively"—that is, on their own terms rather than as elements determined by a pre-established set of relationships. Boulez especially praised Webern for having reached the threshold of a new musical realm: "[He was] the only one . . . who was conscious of a new sound dimension, of the obliteration of the horizontal-vertical opposition [i.e., the traditional distinction between melody and harmony] so that he saw in the series only a way of giving structure to the sound-space."[2]

This single sentence, placing Webern—a composer almost completely ignored during his own lifetime—at the very center of current musical concerns, strikingly illustrates the vastly altered compositional point of view of the early postwar years. Nor was Boulez alone in hailing Webern as the harbinger of a new music. The German composer Karlheinz Stockhausen, whose numerous articles published during the 1950s made him the leading theorist of European serialism, wrote of Webern: "The Schoenbergian principle of the thematic row is broken. . . . What is essential is not a uniquely chosen Gestalt (a theme, or motive), but a chosen sequence of proportions for pitches, durations, and loudnesses."[3]

2.   *Relevés d'apprenti,* ed. Paul Thévenin (Paris, 1966), p. 150.
3.   "Weberns Konzert für 9 Instrumente, Op. 24," *Texte* (Cologne, 1963): 1:26.

THE SERIAL REVOLUTION IN FRANCE: MESSIAEN AND BOULEZ

Although integral serialism—composition according to exclusively serial principles—was developed mainly by composers who reached maturity after the conclusion of World War II, its history within a European context begins with a member of the previous generation: the Frenchman Olivier Messiaen (b. 1908). An established figure by the end of the war, Messiaen had a critical influence on the younger European serialists, many of whom—including both Boulez and Stockhausen—studied under him.

From his early years Messiaen favored a rigorous and objective approach to composition, which he eventually systematized in the book *Technique de mon langage musical* (1944). Here his inclination to treat the individual attributes of musical sound—pitch, rhythm, dynamics, timbre—as separable components, each with its own specific structural characteristics, is present in fully developed form. Pitch relationships, though still based upon various kinds of artificial scales (whole-tone, octatonic, etc.)—a practice common since Debussy—are treated in an unusually systematic manner. The most innovative aspect of the book— as of Messiaen's early music—concerns the treatment of rhythm. Electing to "replace the notions of 'measure' and 'beat' by the feeling of a short value (the sixteenth-note, for example) and its free multiplication," he moves toward an essentially "ametrical" conception.

Olivier Messiaen with his pupils. The composer's wife, pianist Yvonne Loriod, one of his foremost interpreters, is seated to his left.

Central is the idea of "added values," through which otherwise regular patterns acquire greater rhythmic flexibility: e.g., instead of ♩ ♫ ♩ , one uses ♩ ♫♩ (adding a sixteenth after the third note), or instead of ♫♫♫ , one substitutes ♫♩ ♫ (subtracting a sixteenth from the second and last note and adding one to the fourth). Messiaen also proposes a new type of augmentation and diminution, adding or subtracting a fixed rhythmic value to each member of a given unit (in contrast to the traditional procedure of multiplying or dividing values by a fixed unit): e.g., ♩ ♪♩ becomes ♩♪♪ ♩♪ (through augmentation of each member by a sixteenth) or ♪ ♪♪ (through diminution by a sixteenth).

These procedures, first apparent in the 1935 organ piece *La Nativité du Seigneur* (where they are explained in a preface), create complex yet pliable rhythmic successions, quite different from those of metrical music. A characteristic Messiaen innovation is the so-called "nonretrogradable rhythm"—i.e., a succession of durations that remains the same whether played forward or backward: e.g., ♫♩ ♩ ♫♩ . With reference to such symmetrical rhythmic structures, as well as to symmetrical pitch modes that allow only a limited number of transpositions (e.g., the whole-tone and octatonic scales), Messiaen speaks of "the charm of impossibilities." The inherent limitations of the materials themselves are for him a source of technical interest and esthetic value.

A brief excerpt from the sixth movement of the *Quatuor pour la fin du temps* (*Quartet for the End of Time,* 1940), for clarinet, violin, cello, and piano, illustrates aspects of Messiaen's rhythmic procedures. (In Example XVI-1 only the piano part is given; the remaining instruments simply double this part at the unison or octave.) Added rhythmic values appear

Example XVI-1: MESSIAEN, *Quartet for the End of Time,* sixth movement, mm. 1–4

frequently, and each measure consists of a nonretrogradable rhythm. Furthermore, in each successive measure the rhythmic values tend to become smaller.

Another important aspect of Messiaen's compositional method is the "borrowing" of pre-existent material and its transformation through what the composer calls the "prism" of his own musical consciousness. Avoiding more traditional models, Messiaen seeks inspiration from sources distantly removed from modern Western music. Not only are his rhythmic theories influenced by the study of Hindu music; actual Hindu rhythmic formulas are frequently employed. Another favored source is Gregorian chant, used as a starting point for melodic constructions that freely transform the original melodies to suit new expressive requirements.

The most consequential body of material appropriated by Messiaen is bird song. Most of his works refer at least briefly to bird calls, and some derive virtually all their melodic content from this source. For most of his life Messiaen has taken down in notation the songs of birds encountered on his extensive travels. As with other borrowings, his intention is not to "imitate" the source but to transform the bird calls so that they become musically meaningful. In compositions such as the *Réveil des oiseaux* (1953) the entire structure mirrors the changing sounds of birds located in a single habitat during a particular period of time (in this case, from midnight to midday).

A final ingredient shaping Messiaen's musical character is his deeply mystical and religious nature, which contributes significantly to the expressive detachment and structural rigor of his work. For Messiaen, music constitutes not a means of personal expression, but an "objective" embodiment of the beauty and perfection of God's universe. He therefore approaches his work as if from a distance, placing the structural demands of his compositional system—his "prism"—between himself and the material. The composer's description of plainchant applies equally well to his own work: music that is "truly religious because it is detached from all exterior effect and from all intention."

The *Quartet for the End of Time* marked the maturity of Messiaen's first style period, which continued through the *Turangalîla-symphonie* (1948). Already in the earlier work, the treatment of pitch and rhythm as independent elements interacting within a complex structural whole is firmly established. The first movement is made up largely of recurring cycles of predetermined material. The entire piano part comprises uninterrupted repetitions of a sequence of seventeen chords, set to a rhythmic ostinato comprising twenty-nine durations. (Pitch and rhythmic sequences thus never coincide, recalling the nonsynchronous *talea* and *color* of medieval and Renaissance music.) At the same time, the cello states a five-note pitch series in combination with a fifteen-note rhythmic series. These two parts form a sort of neutral background for the principal melodic line, played by the clarinet in a freely strophic pattern and accompanied by occasional bird calls in the violin. The effect of these similar or identical materials continuously recirculating in ever-changing configurations is one of static timelessness in the large, constant mutation in details.

Despite Messiaen's strong disposition toward such "serial" procedures (for the rhythmic and pitch ostinatos in the *Quartet for the End of Time* are essentially serial in conception), his pitch language in this earlier period remained freely tonal, based on scalar characteristics that lent the music a decided "Impressionist" tinge. However, during a brief yet critical "experimental" phase beginning in 1949, Messiaen employed still more rigorous structural methods and adopted total chromaticism. *Cantéyodjayâ* and the *Quatre Études de rythme,* two piano compositions of 1949, and the *Livre d'orgue* (1951) contain striking examples of systematic pre-compositional planning. In several sections of *Cantéyodjayâ* the musical material is limited entirely to a few rhythmic figures of Indian origin, each always associated with a single invariable pitch configuration. These several fixed pitch-rhythmic patterns are combined in collagelike sequences. Thus all the material within these sections is determined in advance, and the actual compositional process becomes a matter of distributing the predetermined units—and only these—in whatever patterns desired.

For the younger European composers, the critical Messiaen piece was the third of the *Quatre Études,* entitled "Mode de valeurs et d'intensités" (Mode of Values and Intensities). A preface to the score sets forth the three twelve-element series on which this composition is exclusively based (Example XVI-2a). Each member of each series is assigned a pitch in a given octave, a duration, a dynamic, and an attack type. The pitches comprise three different twelve-tone rows disposed in descending registral direction (the end of each row overlaps in register with the beginning of the next). In the first row, which begins with a thirty-second note, the durations are determined by adding a thirty-second to each successive note; the second row begins with a sixteenth note and adds successive sixteenths; the final row begins with an eighth and adds eighths. The attack types (of which there are also twelve, one being the absence of any indication) and the dynamic levels (only seven) are distributed freely rather than in "stepped" sequence.

These three series, prepared "pre-compositionally"—that is, prior to the actual writing of the piece—determine its entire content. All four musical elements remain absolutely fixed in relation to one another; any given pitch in a given octave always retains the duration, dynamic, and attack type assigned to it in the series. However, the composition itself is not serially structured: the rows are not transposed or inverted, nor

Example XVI-2: MESSIAEN, *Quatre Études de rythme,* "Mode de valeurs et d'intensités"

a. Series (from preface to score)

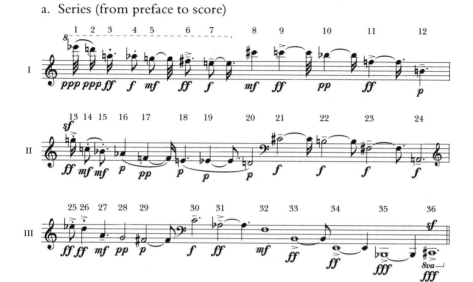

b. mm. 1–7

are their contents presented in the given pre-compositional order. Only the musical elements themselves are determined, not their succession. (As suggested by the title, the material is used like a "mode" rather than a "series.") Nevertheless, what attracted younger composers was the work's rigidly "constructivist" aspect—the fact that all four elements of pitch, rhythm, dynamics, and attacks were first uniquely predefined for the piece, and then compositionally manipulated through identical operations—a procedure they felt linked the elements through structural analogy.

The Étude's opening measures (Example XVI-2b) reveal the radical consequences of Messiaen's procedure. The score is laid out on three staves, one each for the three twelve-element "modes": i.e., each note on the top staff is drawn from the first, each on the second staff from the second, and each on the third from the third. (Although the order of notes is "free," Messiaen does choose to begin with the opening notes of the upper two rows.) The momentary effect is one of perpetual change, yet the overall character remains essentially constant throughout. There is no sense of directed motion. The notes seem to spin themselves out freely, as if in a state of suspended animation. When the piece is over, there is no "ending"; the music simply stops.

Although the younger generation took this Étude as a precedent for integral serialism, Messiaen himself followed a different course. While retaining a preference for chromaticism and for complex, abstract precompositional schemata (such as the elaborate table of numbers used to determine rhythmic values in Chronochromie, an orchestral work of 1960), he has never embraced serialism. Indeed, in many respects Messiaen's general compositional approach has remained consistent with his earlier work. His music has always relied on the type of mosaiclike formal structures he favored in the 1930s, in which discrete musical segments are abruptly juxtaposed, with certain elements recurring in static, refrainlike patterns. While this procedure suggests some kinship with Stravinsky or Varèse, the sound of Messiaen's music—its richly sonorous harmony and almost ecstatic expressive quality—is entirely his own.

Within an output largely dominated by instrumental music, Messiaen has been especially drawn to virtuosic music for piano and organ. (He was long active as the organist of Trinité in Paris, and his piano music was written for his wife Yvonne Loriod.) His Vingt Regards sur l'enfant Jésus (1945) and Catalogue d'oiseaux (1959) rank among the longest and most difficult piano pieces in the literature. Other large instrumental works include Oiseaux exotiques (1956), Couleurs de la cité céleste (1964), and Et exspecto resurrectionem mortuorum (1965), all scored for large chamber ensemble, the first two with prominent solo piano parts. More recently Messiaen completed his first opera, based on the life of St. Francis of Assisi, which was premiered in Paris in 1983.

When World War II came to an end Pierre Boulez (b. 1925) was in his twentieth year and just finishing his formal musical studies. With a strong background in mathematics as well as in music, Boulez—like Messiaen—was inclined to view composition from a perspective that was essentially logical rather than expressive. Convinced of the historical necessity of atonality, he adopted a rigorous conception of music as a consciously ordered structure of internal relationships.

Boulez's first major works, the Sonatine for Flute and Piano and the Piano Sonata No. 1, both completed in 1946 and heavily influenced by the Second Viennese School, caused a considerable stir when they first appeared. Suddenly, a French composer was making a fundamental break with neo-classicism, which had completely dominated the country's music since the early 1920s. These compositions, and other works Boulez composed over the following decade, played a decisive role in postwar musical developments. In addition to its uncommon technical achievement, the First Piano Sonata is a remarkably serious and ambitious work for so young a composer. Unquestionably, the influences of Webern and Schoenberg are evident, the former in the uncompromisingly "structural" approach, the latter in the density of texture and dramatic formal juxtapositions. Traces of traditional thematicism can also be detected, although the thematic content is radically fragmented into splintered motivic particles that appear in highly varied configurations. The passage in Example XVI-3, where a distinct motivic correspondence (the three-note stepwise figures circled in the example) emerges out of ongoing eighth-note motion in sudden, isolated crystallizations, is typical.

Boulez further developed the ideal of a more purely "structural" music in the Piano Sonata No. 2 (1948). Unlike the brief, two-movement First Sonata, the Second is an extended four-movement work. Here melodic content is almost completely dissolved. In Boulez's words: "It was probably the attempt of the Viennese school to revive older forms that made me want to destroy them completely: I mean I tried to destroy the first-movement sonata form, to disintegrate the slow movement

Example XVI-3: BOULEZ, Piano Sonata No. 1, second movement, mm. 11–12

form by the use of a trope, and repetitive scherzo form by the use of variation form, and finally, in the fourth movement, to demolish fugal and canonic form."[4] The work's textural opacity, its range of musical gestures, and its explosive violence and aggressiveness confirm his words. The Sonata can be viewed as a farewell to the tradition of earlier twelve-tone music, accomplished by subjecting its melodic gestures and rhythmic and formal conventions to radical pulverization.

Following the Second Sonata, and stimulated by the example of Messiaen's Third Étude, Boulez began working toward a completely integrated serialism, in which rhythmic, dynamic, and attack characteristics were strictly predetermined. (Previously he had applied serial procedures only to pitch, and even these in a decidedly unorthodox manner, preferring to break his pitch–rows into several smaller units treated as more or less independent entities.) Boulez's earlier work had already reflected Messiaen's influence, but mainly in his use of additive rhythmic structures. What interested Boulez in the Étude, however, was the rejection of such traditional musical categories as melody, accompaniment, and directional form, and the treatment of all the musical elements on an equal basis.

The first two works in which Boulez groped toward this more rigorous approach, the *Livre pour quatuor* (1949) and *Polyphony X* (1951), he found problematic and eventually withdrew. His next piece, *Structures I* for two pianos (1952), was a milestone in the evolution of integral serialism. Acknowledging his debt to Messiaen, Boulez used as the basic material of the first large section of his piece the first twelve pitches and durations of the pre-compositional material of the "Mode de valeurs et d'intensités" (see Example XVI-2a), as well as its twelve attack and seven dynamic types, increasing the latter by five new levels to make twelve for each of the four musical elements. This material he ordered into four "scales" of twelve units each, one for each musical element, assigning order numbers to each (see Table XVI-A).

Table XVI-A

Order No.	1	2	3	4	5	6	7	8	9	10	11	12
Pitch	E♭	D	A	A♭	G	F♯	E	C♯	C	B♭	F	B
Duration	♪	♪	♪.	♪	♪♪	♪.	♪..	♩	♩♪	♩♪	♩♪.	♩.
Attack	>	⌄	·	∧ *sfz*		⌢	,	*sfz* ∧	⌃	–	⌄	⌒
Dynamic	*pppp*	*ppp*	*pp*	*p*	quasi *p*	*mp*	*mf*	quasi *f*	*f*	*ff*	*fff*	*ffff*

(The absence of an attack at the fifth order number indicates "normal.")

4.   *Pierre Boulez: Conversations with Célestin Deliège* (London, 1975), pp. 41–42.

Table XVI-B

Order No.	7	1	10	3	4	5	11	2	8	12	6	9
Pitch	E	E♭	B♭	A	A♭	G	F	D	C♯	B	F♯	C
Duration	♪··	♪	♩♪	♪	♪·	♪	♪♪	♩♪·	♪	♩	♩·	♪·	♩♪
Attack	,	>	–	.	∧ sfz		⌐	≥	sfz ∧	⌒	⌢	≥
Dynamic	*mf*	*pppp*	*ff*	*pp*	*p*	quasi *p*	*fff*	*ppp*	quasi *f*	*ffff*	*mp*	*f*

Boulez then constructed two tables of numbers, one giving the order numbers of the twelve transpositions of the original form, the other the order numbers of the twelve transpositions of the inverted form, using the inverted pitch series to determine the latter. These order numbers remain attached to the same four elements with which they are associated in the original series (see Table XVI-A). The transposition of the pitch series up a semitone, for example, produces the new series shown in Table XVI-B.

The first section of *Structures I* was then composed by reading from the two numerical tables and writing down the pitches, rhythms, etc., indicated by the order numbers. The same series is not applied to two different elements at the same time, however; if the pitches are determined by reading off the original table, the durations will be determined by reading from the inverted one. (This means that the note E♭, for example, the first pitch of the original pitch series, will not normally be associated with the duration of a thirty-second note, but with some other value.) Dynamic and attack characteristics do not change with every note but only when an entire series of pitches and durations has been completed.

Once this method was established, the music could to some extent write itself "automatically," the result of a mechanical reading of the numerical tables, assigning the designated musical values accordingly. A "higher order" series even determines the sequence in which the numerical series is read. Certain critical aspects of the piece are, however, left to the composer's compositional (rather than "pre-compositional") choice, including tempo and the number of rows used at any given moment, both of which vary from section to section and significantly influence the music's overall character. Another important "freedom" concerns the choice of register. Boulez generally distributes the pitches over as wide a registral expanse as possible, creating a markedly fragmented quality—but if the same pitch recurs in close proximity (as often happens when two or more rows are used simultaneously), all its appearances are placed in the same register.

Example XVI-4: BOULEZ, *Structures I,* second segment, mm. 1–4

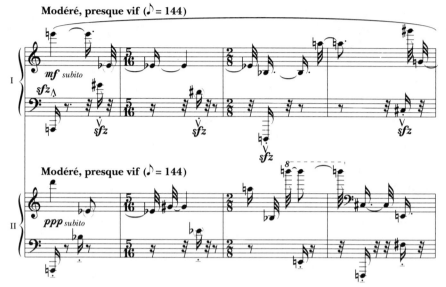

The opening measures of the second brief formal segment of *Structures I* (Example XVI-4) illustrate this feature, as well as something of the general character of the piece. In this segment four rows are employed simultaneously, two in each piano. The overall impression is of a "scattering" of pitches and durations, separated from one another in a radically pointillistic manner. Yet out of this seemingly amorphous and chaotic texture emerge a number of distinct pitch repetitions, most notably E♭ (or D♯), which appears no less than four times (once in each row, circled in the example) during the first two measures, always assigned to the octave above middle C. (The last two appearances occur simultaneously.)

This rigorous compositional approach was applied only in the first of the three main sections of *Structures I*. Here, carrying serialism to its furthest extremes, Boulez encountered the unexpected consequences following from such a rigidly predetermined structure. Not only was there the practical matter of whether performers or listeners could effectively distinguish so many gradations of dynamics and attacks; several more complex problems arose. First, although the chromatic scale used in modern Western music divides the natural pitch continuum into twelve discrete increments, and can thus be ordered in "scalar" form, the remaining elements—durations, dynamics, and attacks—exist in continua that do not readily lend themselves to precise scalar gradation. Moreover, whereas the pitch series given in Table XVI-B is a strict transposition of the original form in Table XVI-A, the other elements have been changed "arbitrarily," shuffled about solely according to the order numbers dictated by the transposed pitch series; the results are not in any sense analogous to "transpositions." Finally, and perhaps most tellingly, the overall effect of *Structures I* is paradoxically not that of logically planned and rationally structured music, but of music that, at least in its details, seems largely random. Even those relationships most clearly heard (such as the recurring E♭s of Example XVI-4) sound fortuitous.

Indeed, to a significant extent they *are* the result of chance, for once the rigid pre-compositional schema is set in motion, the composer has very little control over what will actually happen at any given moment. This is not to say that *Structures I* was a failure—it turned out to be a remarkably suggestive and influential composition, both for Boulez himself and for many of his contemporaries. In demonstrating that integral serialism, at least in this radical form, essentially dissolved all traditional aspects of musical structure, including melody, harmony, and formal direction, it opened up the possibility of a music in which individual details appear insignificant in relation to the overall, "global" effect. Musical texture, understood in a newer and wider sense, became the main focus of interest, providing a new area for compositional exploration.

Although European serialism quickly proved something of a dead end in a purely technical sense, it initiated a radical musical revolution whose consequences are still felt. And though Boulez himself already departed from the rigid conception of the first section of *Structures I* when composing the two remaining ones (the differences are especially noticeable in the middle section) and never again returned to such strict methods, his future music (as we shall see in the next chapter) was fundamentally colored by his early serial experience.

SERIALISM IN GERMANY: STOCKHAUSEN

Along with Boulez, the European composer most influential in the development of integral serialism was the German Karlheinz Stockhausen (b. 1928). A turning point in Stockhausen's early career was his attendance at the 1951 Darmstadt Summer Course in New Music, where he heard Messiaen's *Quatre Études de rythme*. There he also met the young Dutch composer Karel Goeyvaerts, who had already begun experimenting with total serialization and whose recently completed Sonata for Two Pianos (1951) made a strong impression. Immediately after leaving Darmstadt Stockhausen composed his first serial composition, *Kreuzspiel* for oboe, bass clarinet, piano, and three percussionists (1951), an abrupt departure from such earlier, more traditionally oriented student works as the Sonatine for violin and piano, completed earlier the same year.

Stockhausen spent 1952 in Paris, where he studied with Messiaen, befriended Boulez (then composing *Structures I*), and worked on two compositions: *Kontra-Punkte* for chamber orchestra and the set of Piano Pieces I-IV, both completed in 1953. To some extent his approach was similar to Boulez's in *Structures I:* the various musical elements are broken down into separate scales of relationships and individually permuted through serial operations. As in the Boulez work, the starting point is the single unit (pitch, duration, etc.), which is combined with other units to form textures consisting of widely separated individual events. Yet even in *Kreuzspiel,* his earliest serial composition, Stockhausen had created a larger structural framework to provide the pointillistic details with a more definite sense of growth and direction. In the first section, for example, a gradual registral transformation produces a "reversal" of the opening material: what is heard in the lowest register at the outset is gradually transferred to the highest register, and vice versa.

Kontra-Punkte reveals a similar concern for large-scale processes. The entire structure is shaped by a gradual tendency toward greater unification of its materials; the diversified, texturally and timbrally differentiated music of the opening (played by all ten instruments in an essentially pointillistic manner, with abrupt contrasts of register, dynamics, etc.) is progressively transformed into the continuous and monochromatic music of the close (played by the piano alone at a uniform dynamic level). The static quality of Boulez's *Structures I* is largely absent.

Comparison of the previously quoted Boulez passage (Example XVI-4) with the opening of Stockhausen's Piano Piece I (Example XVI-5) illustrates the essential differences. Though also based on serial principles, Stockhausen's method is considerably more flexible and differentiated. The pitches are organized into two chromatic hexachords, the first containing the six notes from C upward through F, the second the remaining six from F♯ through B. Since the internal order within these hexachords is constantly permuted, however, and the two hexachords are permuted by independent operations, the total chromatic series undergoes continuous transformation.

The differences of rhythmic character are equally marked. Boulez's rhythm is "additive" in nature: the basis is a very small value (a thirty-second note), from which all larger values are derived by adding this same value. The temporal dimension is thus conceived as an accumulation of individual units. Not only are the individual durations arrived at this way, but also the lengths of sections, which are determined by the statement of a single series of twelve of these durations. Stockhau-

Example XVI-5: STOCKHAUSEN, Piano Piece I, mm. 1–2

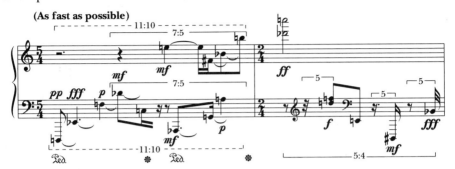

sen, on the other hand, takes a relatively large time segment as his basic unit and *divides* it to arrive at individual durations. In Piano Piece I these units are for the most part equal to the measure, and are themselves varied in length according to serial operations. This accounts for the extraordinary (and at times seemingly meaningless) complexity of the notated rhythmic relationships: the individual durations are conceived not so much as absolute values, calculated for their own worth, but as merely approximate subdivisions of larger values. Only these larger values are really "fixed," since—as the composer was certainly aware— no pianist could possibly play the indicated durations accurately.

The audible result—presumably intended by the composer to destroy any suggestion of traditional metrical regulation—is constantly changing rates of approximate speed, determined by the length of the measure and the degree of its subdivision, in a tempo simply labeled "as fast as possible." (In his subsequent work Stockhausen attempted to resolve the obvious "contradiction" between notation and actual result by employing a much freer and simpler rhythmic notation.) The first measure of the example—extreme but by no means atypical—calls for subdivision of the total duration into eleven equal units, of which the last five, taken collectively, are further subdivided into seven slightly shorter units. Within this abstract double frame of subdivisions, the notated durations tend to accelerate during the measure, though not consistently throughout.

These differences between the Stockhausen and Boulez pieces are not merely technical; they fundamentally affect the musical character. In *Structures I* the listener is mainly conscious of a consistent and generally homogeneous texture, the individual details dissolved within a larger "statistical" pattern. In Piano Piece I, however, one hears strongly pro-filed and differentiated gestures, grouped together to form well-defined larger shapes. For instance, the very dramatic, essentially rising and accelerating profile of the first measure of Example XVI-5 reaches an

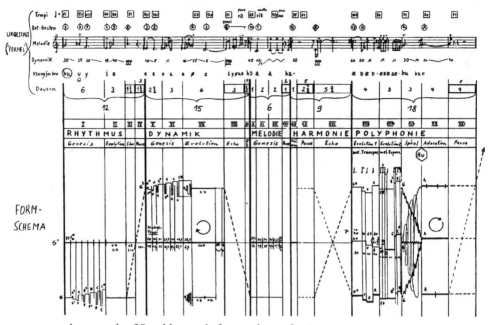

Autograph of Stockhausen's form-scheme for *Inori,* a 1973–74 composition for soloists, orchestra, and mime. (Courtesy of the composer)

upper goal in the sustained fortissimo major seventh at the beginning of the second measure, beneath which a more discontinuous shape rebounds downward as a kind of balancing counterweight. The impression is not entirely unlike the opening-closing pattern of a traditional antecedent-consequent phrase.

The inclination to think of music in terms of larger formal units rather than individual elements led Stockhausen away from strict serialism in the middle 1950s. Since then he has contributed significantly to many major musical developments of the postwar years, and we shall have occasion to return to his work later. Other prominent European composers involved in the serialist movement during the earlier 1950s were the Belgian Henri Pousseur (b. 1929) and the Italians Luigi Nono (b. 1924), Luciano Berio (b. 1925), and Bruno Maderna (1920–73). Indeed, with few exceptions, the most active younger Europeans of the time were all to some degree involved with serial techniques.

AMERICAN SERIALISM: BABBITT

Unlike Boulez and Stockhausen, who turned to serialism out of dissatisfaction with the principal musical developments of the earlier twentieth century and the esthetic attitudes they embodied, the American Milton Babbitt (b. 1916) conceived serial composition as a direct outgrowth and extension of the principles of "classical" twelve-tone music.

Musical life suffered much less disruption from the war in the United States than in Europe, and younger Americans at the time found it entirely natural to develop from within the European musical tradition, many of whose leading contemporary figures were then living in the country. Babbitt, who began exploring the idea of extending serial controls to elements other than pitch even before his European contemporaries, looked more to Schoenberg than to Webern for his musical precedents.

Antedating not only Boulez's and Stockhausen's earliest serial efforts but also Messiaen's *Mode de valeurs et d'intensités,* Babbitt's Three Compositions for Piano (1947) was the earliest work in which both pitch and nonpitch elements were strictly structured through serial operations. The opening measures of the first piece illustrate Babbitt's early approach (Example XVI-6). In mm. 1–2 the left hand unfolds the original form of a twelve-tone pitch series, while the right hand presents the same form transposed at the tritone. Since these two forms are combinatorial, the respective first two hexachords (m. 1) combine to form a twelve-tone aggregate, as do the last two (m. 2). (Here one recognizes the influence of Schoenberg, whose use of combinatoriality was discussed in Chapter IX.) In mm. 3–4 the left hand states the retrograde inversion, transposed up a semitone, while the right hand presents the untransposed retrograde, these two rows again forming combinatorial pairs of hexachords.

The durations in the piece are derived from a series of four numbers (5–1–4–2), which, like the pitch series, is retrograded (2–4–1–5), inverted (1–5–4–2), and retrograde-inverted (4–2–5–1). (By analogy with pitch

Example XVI-6: BABBITT, Three Compositions for Piano, No. 1, mm. 1–4

inversion, which can be represented mathematically as complementation modulo 12, Babbitt here uses complementation modulo 6 to determine rhythmic inversion: 5 inverts to 1 [5 + 1 = 6], 4 inverts to 2 [4 + 2 = 6], etc.) Since pitch and rhythmic series are always joined by type (original with original, etc.), the original form of the rhythmic series also appears in both hands in the opening two measures. The members of the series are rhythmically articulated by a longer duration at the end of a group of sixteenths (the single sixteenth, for the number 1, is followed by a rest). Thus 5–1–4–2 produces a group of five sixteenths of which the fifth is sustained (5), a single sixteenth followed by a rest (1), four sixteenths with the last sustained (4), and two sixteenths with the second sustained (2). (Other modes of articulating the rhythmic series are used later, including multiples of sixteenth notes— ♩ ♪ ♪ ♩ ♪—and a combination of slurs and accents: ♫♫♫ ♫♫♫ ♫♫ .) Dynamics are determined by associating each row form with a given level: all originals are played *mp* (thus only *mp* appears in mm. 1–2), retrogrades are *mf,* inversions are *f,* and retrograde inversions are *p.* In mm. 3–4 retrograde rhythmic and dynamic forms occur in the right hand and retrograde-inversion forms in the left, again corresponding to the pitch forms in each hand.

Differences between Babbitt's early serial music and that of Boulez and Stockhausen are immediately evident. Example XVI-6 is far more traditional in textural layout than the corresponding works of the two Europeans; the rows are presented in relatively straightforward two-part counterpoint, with the right hand in freely imitative relationship to the left. Successive notes within the series are grouped together to form clear linear patterns, rather than registrally isolated from one another. Finally, the rhythm is considerably more regular. (The fact that the four numbers of the rhythmic series add up to twelve is important, not only because this corresponds to the number of pitches in the pitch series, but also because later, when continuous sixteenth notes appear, it corresponds to the number of such notes in a bar of 3/4 meter.)

Babbitt has said that he wants "a piece of music to be literally as much as possible." He creates the maximum number of musical relationships within each composition, deriving as much "substance" as possible from his material. One characteristic technique (for which he found less systematic precedents in Schoenberg and Berg) is the formation of "derived" rows through serial permutations of segments of the original series. The principal (or "source") row for the Second String Quartet (1954), for example, is shown in Example XVI-7a. However, the Quartet opens with a derived row (Example XVI-7b), created entirely out of the first interval of the "source" row. Further such derived rows follow, based on successive intervals—or pairs of intervals—from the source row; each new row initiates a new formal section, until all the intervals in the source row's first hexachord have been introduced. At

Example XVI-7: BABBITT, String Quartet No. 2

a. Principal ("source") row

b. Derived row used at beginning of quartet

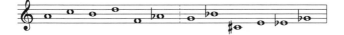

that point this hexachord is finally stated in complete form, rounding off the first part of the one-movement composition. The same procedure is then applied to the second hexachord, after which follows a final section where the complete source row appears for the first time. Thus the work's entire shape is derived from a systematic exploration of the source set's successive intervals.

Babbitt also employs a related technique to "partition" a single set into several distinct "voices" through various articulative means (e.g., timbre, accents, or dynamics). Recalling similar, though again less systematic, practices in Webern, the solo clarinet melody (Example XVI-8) that opens the Composition for Four Instruments (1948) uses register to define a recurring three-note cell that appears twice in each of four registral "voices" (indicated below the example), a basic pitch unit from which the entire sequence of pitches can be serially derived. Twelve-

Example XVI-8: BABBITT, Composition for Four Instruments, mm. 1–9

© 1949 Merion Music Inc. Used by permission of the publisher.

tone aggregates are formed, not only by the original note-by-note succession (two such aggregates appear in the excerpt), but also by adjacent pairs of the four registrally separated "voices": the four cells in the upper two voices form one aggregate, those in the lower ones another.

More recently, the idea of partitioning music into a succession of twelve-tone aggregates functioning as a constant unit of harmonic succession has led Babbitt to employ entire polyphonic complexes, or "arrays," of individually partitioned "layers" or "voices." The String Quartet No. 3 (1970) is based on an array of eight layers, each derived from a source set and each forming a succession of twelve-tone aggregates. In addition, the pitches are distributed vertically to form a series of "harmonic" twelve-tone aggregates. The total dimensions of the array are 8 x 8; that is, eight layers, each containing a sequence of eight twelve-tone rows. The number of vertical ("harmonic") aggregates formed by this particular array is seventy, of which the first three are shown in Example XVI-9. Within this brief segment no single layer completes a

Example XVI-9: BABBITT, Quartet No. 3, array segment including first three aggregates

	Aggregate 1					Aggregate 2					Aggregate 3			
Layer 1	G	D♯				D	G♯	C♯	A					
Layer 2						F	F♯	B	A♯	C	E			
Layer 3	F	E	B	C	A♯									
Layer 4						D♯						G	G♯	D	A
Layer 5												B	D♯	E	A♯
Layer 6	F♯	D	C♯			G								
Layer 7												C	C♯	F♯	F
Layer 8	A	G♯												

full twelve-tone structure (layer 1, for example, traverses only its first hexachord). The complete 8 x 8 array provides an abstract, background structure upon which the first large section of the quartet is based. (The three remaining sections are based on transformations of the same array by the three traditional twelve-tone operations: respectively, retrograde, inversion, and retrograde inversion.)

The Quartet's opening measures (Example XVI-10) are derived from the array segment in Example XVI-9. Each of the eight horizontal layers is articulated by a different "instrument" (Babbitt uses the distinction between arco and pizzicato to make a string quartet into "eight"

Example XVI-10: BABBITT, Quartet No. 3, mm. 1–6

instruments): layer 1 is played by Violin 1 arco, layer 2 by Violin 1 pizzicato, layer 3 by Violin 2 arco, etc. Derived from the pitch array is also a rhythmic array that determines the durational structure, its eight layers distinguished by eight dynamic levels, ranging from *fff* (layer 1) and *ff* (layer 2) down to *ppp* (layer 8).

A few of the many complex surface relationships within the opening measures can be noted: the initial rising major seventh in Violin 2 arco is transposed and inverted in the same instrument in m. 2; the initial rising minor sixth in Violin 1 arco is mirrored in the Viola's pizzicato falling major third (mm. 1–2), and its pitches are sounded simultaneously, pizzicato, by second Violin and Viola in m. 3; the four notes in the two pizzicato glissando figures in mm. 1–2 (the Cello's A-A♭ and the Viola's D-D♭) recur as the last four notes of the first-Violin line in m. 3. Such structural "density," with every note participating in many different structural connections on different levels, is especially characteristic of Babbitt.

Several factors may explain why Babbitt, unlike his European contemporaries, has remained committed to serialism. First, he came to serialism not as a way of avoiding traditional conceptions of musical structure but as a means of extending and expanding such conceptions—and it has satisfied that purpose. Second, in his serialism, pitch, traditionally the primary structural agency in Western music, retains priority; it is not simply one component within an equalized textural network. Finally, Babbitt's approach has remained conducive to further development and refinement. He has continued to extend his conception of composition with arrays, introducing new types (such as "weighted" arrays, in which partitions do not always yield twelve-tone aggregates) and new means for their articulation. The variety of musical results Babbitt achieves through these techniques is evident in such recent compositions as *Arie da capo* (1974), *Paraphrases* (1979), the Fifth String Quartet (1982), and *Canonical Form* (1983). Although all are works of formidable logic and complexity, the elegance and subtlety of the music seem to belie the rigor of its construction.

As composer, teacher, and writer, Babbitt has played an important role in recent American music. His seminal theoretical articles have revolutionized the study of twelve-tone music, and he has had a significant influence on several important younger American composers, among them Donald Martino (b. 1931) and Charles Wuorinen (b. 1938). Another American who has worked extensively with dodecaphonic technique, both as theorist and composer, developing it in quite novel ways for his own purposes, is George Perle (b. 1915).

The complexity of Babbitt's compositional thought has made him a "composer's composer" whose appeal has been largely limited to a specialized audience of professionals, and he has willingly accepted this position as a necessary consequence of the type of music he believes in. In a much-cited 1958 article published under the title "Who Cares if You Listen" (not the author's own), he argued that contemporary composers must be willing to accept the increasing specialization and corresponding isolation forced upon them by recent musical developments. They should see their work as comparable to that of highly specialized research scientists; now primarily of interest to a small group of peers, its true value will become evident to society at large only after many intervening years.

STRAVINSKY AND SERIALISM

No more convincing indication of serialism's centrality during the 1950s can be cited than the adoption of twelve-tone technique by Igor Stravinsky, the only member of the generation of composers who shaped musical developments in the first half of the century who lived long enough to take a prominent part in those of the second. In 1939, shortly before the outbreak of World War II, Stravinsky had emigrated to the United States, settling in Los Angeles, which remained his principal residence for the rest of his life. He lived until 1971, his eighty-ninth year, active as a composer almost to the end.

For the first decade or so after his move to America, Stravinsky continued to develop within the neo-classical framework, but a surprising turn was observed in the Cantata (1952), which shows a new interest in strict contrapuntal procedures and contains the composer's first use of strict serial technique. To be sure, the series appears in only part of the work, and has a strong tonal orientation (not all twelve notes are used, and some notes are repeated), but its use is clearly influenced by knowledge of Schoenberg's music (for example, all standard forms of the series appear).

While much in the Cantata—its tonality and textural clarity, for example—represents an extension of his previous music, the work initiates the third of Stravinsky's main stylistic periods, his serial phase. He progressively developed his personal approach to serialism in subsequent compositions: the Septet (1953), the Three Songs from William Shakespeare (1953), and *In Memoriam Dylan Thomas* (1954). The last, a setting of a Thomas poem for tenor, string quartet, and four trombones, was the composer's first wholly serial composition, derived entirely from a five-note row and its strict serial permutations. The opening phrase of the instrumental music that begins the piece (the first five measures are scored for strings, the last three for trombones) indicates Stravinsky's approach at this stage (Example XVI-11).

The passage exposes the series canonically, with all row forms rep-

Example XVI-11: STRAVINSKY, *In Memoriam Dylan Thomas*, Dirge-Canons (Prelude), mm. 1–10

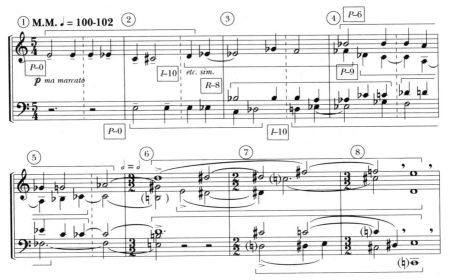

resented (the first few are indicated in the example). Yet the music remains unmistakably tonal, for both the row and the specific forms chosen are strongly oriented toward C. Especially telling are the four forms heard simultaneously at the end of the phrase (mm. 7–9), three of which end on either C or E (the tonic C is placed in the bass), while the fourth voice sounds a mildly dissonant D. (This C-D-E sonority reappears several times during the work's Prelude and Postlude, and also at its conclusion, thus serving as a sort of "tonic chord.")

The three middle movements of the next composition, the *Canticum sacrum* (1955), contain Stravinsky's first twelve-tone music; and the ballet *Agon* (1957), written for the choreographer George Balanchine (with whom Stravinsky enjoyed an especially fruitful association during his American years), is also in part twelve-tone. Since substantial portions of *Agon* were completed in 1953 (after which composition was interrupted until the *Canticum sacrum* was completed), the boundaries of this critical period of Stravinsky's evolution can be traced within this single work. Despite the juxtaposition of tonal and twelve-tone sections, *Agon* projects a remarkably unified compositional outlook: the tonal sections reveal distinct serial characteristics, while the serial ones, even those that are twelve-tone, reflect a definite tonal bias.

Finally, in 1958, Stravinsky completed an entirely twelve-tone composition: *Threni*, an extended setting of the Lamentations of Jeremiah for soloists, chorus, and orchestra. It was followed by a succession of pieces within which Stravinsky increasingly refined his very personal approach to twelve-tone serialism. A growing interest in the music of the younger postwar generation, especially that of Karlheinz Stockhausen and Pierre Boulez, brought him into close contact with the then-pervasive idea of total compositional control (it should be remembered that Stravinsky himself had always expressed a preference for conscious construction). Commenting on his *Movements* for piano and orchestra (1960), the composer noted: "They are the most advanced music from the point of view of construction of anything I have composed. . . . Every aspect of the composition was guided by serial forms." Yet the musical conception is entirely Stravinsky's own, the serial approach in fact completely undoctrinaire. As the composer himself liked to point out, no one could "determine the note order of many passages in the work simply from knowledge of the original row." An important technique employed in *Movements* and later compositions is "rotation," whereby the original form of the series is modified by such maneuvers as beginning with the second pitch and moving the first to the end of the row.

In the works of his final years, including the biblical allegory *The Flood* (1962), the Variations for orchestra (1964), and three sacred works for voices and orchestra, *A Sermon, a Narrative, and a Prayer* (1961),

A sketch for "Ad Tres Virtues Hortationes, Caritas," Part III of Stravinsky's *Canticum sacrum*, 1955. (Courtesy Sacher Stiftung)

Abraham and Isaac (1963), and *Requiem Canticles* (1965), Stravinsky continued to explore this newly discovered world of chromatic serialism with astonishing vigor and youthful enthusiasm. As if haunted by a fear of "not keeping up," he wrote music reflecting some of the most advanced compositional tendencies of the 1950s and 1960s. These final works, which carried the composer to the distant reaches of atonality and of "learned" contrapuntal devices, were extraordinary achievements for an octogenarian, comparable perhaps only to the operas of Verdi's last years.

Stravinsky's move toward serialism and dodecaphony sent a profound shock through the music world, for with it the rigidly doctrinaire divisions that had separated so many composers of the between-the-war years into Schoenbergians and Stravinskians seemed to dissolve. A number of Stravinsky's adherents followed him on his serial path, while others saw his move to dodecaphony as a betrayal of his former beliefs and viewed the compositions of this final phase as the misguided efforts of an old man turned against himself under the unhealthy influence of younger musicians. The young conductor and writer Robert Craft, who began working for Stravinsky in the late 1940s and remained his close associate and performing assistant until the composer's death, no doubt encouraged Stravinsky to keep up with the latest developments, and perhaps even helped to shape his changing musical attitudes. Yet it seems doubtful that such a forceful musical personality as Stravinsky could be so easily seduced by ideas foreign to his own temperament. More probably, his turn to serialism was simply the final stage of his ongoing creative interaction with the principal stylistic categories of Western music history. Significantly, Stravinsky's exploration of serial technique began within a year of Schoenberg's death—an event that suddenly rendered twelve-tone music a "historical" phenomenon, one Stravinsky could then approach as he did other historical materials. The music of the last period, including the most complex works of the final decade, retains a clearly audible Stravinskian flavor. Abrupt formal juxtapositions and polarized textures are still in evidence, as is the characteristic rhythmic vigor of the earlier music. The late style thus speaks eloquently, not only for the centrality of serial thought during Stravinsky's final years, but for the composer's undiminished ability, evident to the end, to absorb previously untapped "foreign elements" into his own distinctive musical language.

CHAPTER XVII

Indeterminacy

CAGE AND OTHER AMERICANS

Among the most significant postwar developments in music has been indeterminacy—the intentional utilization of some degree of chance in composition and / or performance. As we have noted, earlier twentieth-century composers such as Charles Ives and Henry Cowell made occasional and limited use of indeterminate elements in their work, and still earlier precedents go back at least to the Middle Ages. Yet musical indeterminacy emerged as a widespread, broadly influential phenomenon only in the 1950s, and is thus uniquely characteristic of the most recent period of music history.

Its acceptance, to some extent or other, by a broad spectrum of musicians during the 1950s stemmed largely from the influence of a single composer, the American John Cage (b. 1912). Born in California, Cage studied briefly in his early twenties with Cowell and Schoenberg. His remarkable individuality and originality were evident even then, and Schoenberg, despite fundamental reservations, acknowledged that he was an "inventor of genius." The schematic structure of Cage's early music, such as the Sonata for Two Voices (1933) and Composition for Three Voices (1934), reflects his debt to both these mentors.

Later Cage was significantly influenced by Varèse. In a 1937 talk entitled "The Future of Music: Credo," he set forth two basic principles of Varèsian origin that would shape his development over the following decade and ultimately lead him to indeterminacy: first, that music is an "organization of sound," with "sound" defined in the broadest possible sense, encompassing all types of noise as well as "normal" musical events; second, and as a consequence, that the "present methods of writing music, principally those which employ harmony and its reference to particular steps in the field of sound, will be inadequate for the composer, who will be faced with the entire field of sound."[1]

In a series of exploratory works written between the late 1930s and the early 1950s, Cage fashioned a new kind of music based upon these principles. The search for new sonic materials was a central consideration. Not content with available instruments, Cage wrote a series of three compositions entitled *Construction* (1939, 1940, 1941) that used various kinds of unconventional objects for percussive purposes. The *First Construction (in Metal),* for example, calls for brake drums, thunder sheets, and "string piano" (a normal piano played by plucking the strings rather than striking the keys). A second series, the five *Imaginary Landscapes* (1939, 1942, 1942, 1951, 1952), used different "electric devices," ranging from frequency recordings (whose fixed audio signals could be varied by changing the turntable speed, creating glissando-like effects) in *Imaginary Landscape No. 1* to a whole array of devices, including electrical buzzer, oscillator, generator whine, and contact microphone, in *Imaginary Landscape No. 3.* Cage's quest for unconventional sounds led him to anticipate indeterminacy in *Living Room Music* for percussion and speech quartet (1940), where the percussion parts may be played upon "any household or architectural elements" (tables, walls, etc.).

Among these early experiments in sonic extension were several compositions for "prepared piano"—a piano whose sound is altered by the application of screws, pieces of wood, rubber wedges, etc., to the strings. These works began with the *Bacchanale* (1940) and eventually included, in addition to individual pieces, three collections: *A Book of Music* (1944) and *Three Dances* (1945), both for two pianos, and the Sonatas and Interludes for solo piano (1948).

At the same time, Cage developed what he called a new "method of writing music" to accommodate these unusual materials. Treating musical form as a sort of "empty container," he set up for each composition a series of proportional time units measured by precise numerical calculations. Once this abstract durational structure—the "container"—had been determined, he could insert whatever sounds he wished, relying upon the prescribed proportional relationships to provide a larger temporal or rhythmic framework.

All Cage's compositions from this period are based upon such strictly measured temporal structures, segmenting the music into schematic, proportionally related units. The Fourth Sonata (from the *Sonatas and Interludes*) contains one hundred measures (of 2/2 meter) divided into ten segments of ten measures each, each further subdivided according to the pattern 3 + 3 + 2 + 2. The segments are then "filled in" with

1.   *Silence: Lectures and Writings* (Middletown, Conn., 1961), p. 4.

Example XVII-1: CAGE, *Sonatas and Interludes,* Sonata No. 4, mm. 1–10

the chosen musical materials, disposed according to the designated proportional lengths.

The first ten bars of the piece (Example XVII-1), comprising the first principal formal unit, reveal the underlying 3 + 3 + 2 + 2 pattern: the second three bars represent a slightly varied repetition of the first three, and the two final two-bar units are also closely related, each comprising a short event followed by silence.

Typical of Cage is the severely restricted nature of the musical "content" placed in this temporal structure. There are only five different "sounds"—though it should be remembered that the "prepared" piano produces timbres more varied than the notation suggests: of the five pitches used in this passage, only the outer ones, A and G, are unaltered and thus sound "normal." Also characteristic is the percentage of the example that consists of silence, mirroring Cage's belief that not only are all sounds equally "usable," but that silence is structurally equivalent to sound. The use of such abstract temporal containers, as receptive to one kind of musical content as to any other, enabled Cage to create "neutral" forms within which any possible sounds—as well as their absence (silence)—could be joined. The idea, as he later explained, was to "clarify" the structure through the content placed within it, to define it "either with sounds or with silences." From a musical point of view, the result is a succession of static alternations of material, presented objectively and dispassionately, with no attempt to create conventional musical "connections" among the different events.

The implications of Cage's new compositional methods were far-reaching. Although the specific materials for each composition were painstakingly chosen (and uniquely constructed), and the structure was precisely calculated, the relationship between the two—materials and structure—was essentially arbitrary. *Any* material could be placed into *any* structure. Commenting on how he composed the *Sonatas and Interludes* after he had determined the temporal structure, Cage noted: "The method was that of considered improvisation. . . . The materials, the piano preparations, were chosen as one chooses shells while walking along a beach."[2]

2.   "Composition as Process," ibid., p. 19.

For Cage, then, each musical unit existed more or less for itself, essentially independent of any relationship it might have with other units. A musical sound was not derived from the sounds that preceded it, nor did it imply those that followed. It simply "was." According to this conception, music is "purposeless." Its components have no meaning—that is, no discernible connections with one another. Moreover, Cage "purposefully" sought such purposelessness, and it was this search that eventually led him to adopt indeterminacy. By 1951 he had come to believe that the only way a truly purposeless music could be created was by doing away entirely with human intervention in the compositional process, removing the composer "from the activities of the sounds" so that they could simply "be themselves." The composer must "give up the desire to control sound, clear his mind of music, and set about discovering means to let sounds be themselves rather than vehicles for man-made theories or expressions of human sentiments."[3]

This belief led Cage to introduce chance operations into the compositional process. In *Music of Changes* (1951), an extended piece for piano, all elements of the musical structure—pitch, silence, duration, amplitude, tempo, and density—were chosen by using charts derived from *I Ching,* the Chinese book of oracles, and the tossing of coins. (Eastern mysticism, especially Zen Buddhism, crucially influenced Cage's development at this time.) In *Music for Piano* (1952–56), where the pitches were determined by tracing the imperfections in a piece of paper, the role of chance was further extended to include decisions made by the performers: durations (notated arbitrarily as quarter notes without stems) and dynamic levels were left entirely to the player's momentary impulse.

The most widely discussed work from this period was *4'33"*, in which Cage pursued indeterminacy and intentionlessness to their ultimate consequences. The score of this piece consists only of three Roman numerals, each followed by a numerically specified duration (all three add up to the four minutes and thirty-three seconds of the title) plus the word "tacet," indicating that the performer or performers (*4'33"* can be "played" by any number, and on any instrument or instruments) are to remain silent. The piece, in other words, consists solely of silence.

4'33" can be regarded in at least two ways. First, given Cage's belief that musical structure—in this case a temporal frame with three sectional subdivisions—is "as well expressed by the absence of . . . materials as by their presence," the piece simply constitutes the extreme case of the *complete* absence of musical material. But *4'33"* also embodies Cage's belief that "in this new music nothing takes place but sounds: those that are notated and those that are not." Accordingly, even in the total absence of notated sounds, there is the "music" provided by what-

3.   "Experimental Music," ibid., p. 10.

The activation of the sound system ot Cage's *Variations V* (1965) depends on the movement of the dancers as well as the manipulations of the musicians. Shown here in the foreground (left to right): John Cage, David Tudor, Gordon Mumma; background (left to right): Carolyn Brown, choreographer Merce Cunningham, Barbara Dilley. (Courtesy Cunningham Dance Foundation. Photo: Hervé Gloaguen)

ever ambient sounds occur during a "performance"—the humming of air-conditioning, the rustling of programs, the shuffling of feet, laughter from the audience, or whatever.

While *4'33"* may well exemplify Cage's musical philosophy more purely than any other composition (he still considers it his most significant work), it brought him to a difficult impasse. Either he could give up composing entirely, on the grounds that if all sounds can be viewed as music, musical "composition" is hardly necessary—or he could devise methods for preserving the activity of composition (and performance) as redefincd by this conception of radical intentionlessness.

Cage, of course, chose the latter course, and since the early 1950s he has devised various strategies permitting disciplined activity while discouraging "purpose." Among the seven compositions entitled Variations, the first four (1958–63) provide performers with transparent plastic sheets on which points, lines, and circles are drawn, along with instructions for overlapping the sheets and interpreting the resulting graphic configurations as performance indications. The score for the *Concert for Piano and Orchestra* (1958), for solo pianist and thirteen instrumentalists (any number of whom may participate in a given performance), mixes purely graphic indications and distorted musical ones, to be interpreted more or less at will by the performers. A page from the pianist's part

(Example XVII-2) illustrates both the notational freedom and the subtlety and skill of Cage's graphic style. (His scores are of sufficient visual interest to have been exhibited in a "one-man show" at a major New York museum.) Although minimal durations are provided concerning performance (the letters on the score refer to a set of general instructions), the pianist interprets largely at will.

Cage has influenced the development of music since 1950 more than any other American composer, possibly more than any composer of any nationality. Though perhaps more properly considered a musical philosopher than a composer, at least in any ordinary sense of that term (a view he himself appears to accept with complete equanimity), Cage's conception of what music can and should be has had a profound impact upon his contemporaries, including many who write music entirely different from his own.

In addition to being extremely prolific as a composer, Cage has also been active as a writer, and several of his books, which present his musical views with both wit and intelligence, have enjoyed as much currency as his compositions. He has also been an important force in other artistic areas, especially dance. The earliest prepared piano compositions were written for dance performances, and during the early 1940s Cage began a close, continuing association with the modern dancer Merce Cunningham, with whom he frequently toured and for whose company he served as musical director. Cage has also been active in developing innovative forms of musical theater, and we will have occasion to return to his work later.

Example XVII-2: CAGE, *Concert for Piano and Orchestra,* excerpt from piano part

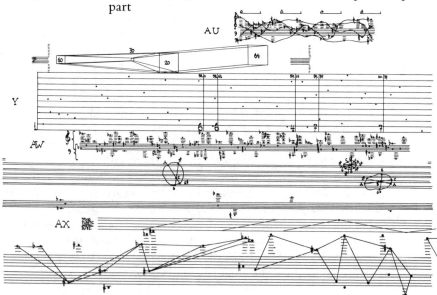

During the early 1950s Cage worked in close contact with a group of like-minded younger composers, including Morton Feldman (1926–87), Earle Brown (b. 1926), and, somewhat later, Christian Wolff (b. 1934). Despite Cage's greater prominence, the flow of influence within this group was to some extent mutual. All shared the view that more was to be learned about musical composition from visual artists, especially the abstract expressionist painters flourishing in New York at that time, than from other composers, past or present. This new painting, as Feldman remarked, led them to seek "a sound world more direct, more immediate, more physical" than anything known in the past.

Seeking a way of combining tones "as free and spontaneous as the way the abstract expressionists combined colors," Feldman was drawn to indeterminacy. In a series of five compositions entitled *Projection* (1950–51), he designed different types of graphic notation that would enable performers to make certain compositional choices within definitely prescribed limits. In *Projection 4* for violin and piano, the opening of which is given in Example XVII-3, the violin part is notated in the upper of two "systems" and the piano part in the lower. The signs P, A and ◇ indicate "timbre": whether the note is to be played pizzicato, arco, or as a harmonic (produced on the violin as usual, on the piano by pressing the string lightly while striking the key). The numbers in the piano part specify how many notes should be played simultaneously, while the position of the event within the larger squares indicates the attack point. Each square contains four "beats" (represented by the small boxes, each equal to approximately MM = 72). Since durations are shown by horizontal extensions within these smaller boxes, the rhythmic structure of the score is precisely, if unconventionally, fixed. Yet pitches are merely assigned to high, middle, or low registral areas, according to the vertical placement of the boxes within the larger squares (the latter placed on different levels depending on the timbre of the notes they contain);

Example XVII-3: FELDMAN, *Projection 4,* opening

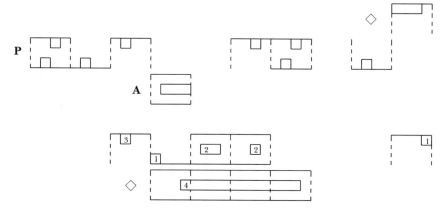

the performer selects the actual pitches. Everything is to be played extremely softly, emphasizing the fragmentary, pointillistic character of the texture.

As in many works by Cage, music is here reduced almost to silence, with individual notes sufficiently distanced from one another in time, register, and timbre to be heard as isolated events. Since no "normal" linear or harmonic connections are intended between these events, absolute pitch is of secondary importance. What matters is the extremely delicate textural atmosphere arising from the deliberate yet seemingly random placement of individual events against a neutral background of silence, producing a spontaneous play of colors and intersecting textural planes analogous to those on the canvases of such contemporary artists as Mark Rothko and Clifford Still.

Somewhat later Feldman experimented with textures in which pitches are specified but durations are indeterminate. In the Piece for Four Pianos (1957) four pianists are given identical music: a series of subtly changing, mildly dissonant chords that are notated conventionally, except that there are no bar lines and pitches appear as stemless quarter notes. All four pianists begin simultaneously and remain within a prescribed general tempo, which assures that all are clearly heard as playing the same thing. But since each is free to choose the exact durations of the individual chords, the four simultaneous renditions move gradually in and out of phase with one another. As in all of Feldman's music, the musical content of this "series of reverberations from an identical sound source" (the composer's description of the piece) is extremely limited, the pacing is slow, and the dynamic level is soft, "with a minimum of attack."

In later compositions, such as The Viola in My Life I–III (1970–71) and The Rothko Chapel (1972), Feldman avoided indeterminacy entirely, yet the general character of his music—the sparse, atmospheric, motionless textures produced by fragmentary events—remained largely unchanged. Even in the indeterminate scores, unspecified elements always appear within an unambiguous framework that controls the overall sonic character. Unlike Cage, Feldman's concern was more with musical effect than with social, political, or philosophical concerns. Moreover, he never used chance operations for compositional purposes, but only with reference to performance.

In this last respect, the music of Earle Brown resembles Feldman's, although Brown's application of indeterminacy for performance purposes (especially in his earlier compositions) has at times been considerably more drastic. In the influential collection of seven pieces entitled Folio (1952–53), Brown experimented with several different types and degrees of indeterminacy and with a number of different notational approaches. Some of the pieces use otherwise conventional notation but with no indications for duration (anticipating Feldman's *Durations* series), while others combine conventional elements with more purely graphic ones, leaving a broader range of interpretive choices to the performer. *November 1952 ("Synergy")*, for example, has a single clefless musical staff, of fifty lines instead of the usual five, on which are placed normally notated pitches, complete with durations and dynamics. The performer interprets this freely, choosing pitch register, tempo, instrumentation, articulations, and even order of events.

The most extreme application of indeterminacy in *Folio* appears in *December 1952,* possibly the earliest instance of a completely graphic musical score (Example XVII-4). This single page of purely abstract design, without conventional musical indications of any kind, is not unlike a nonrepresentational painting that the performer is to interpret musically. The brief instructions specify little more than that the piece is for "one or more instruments and / or sound-producing media," and that the score may be "performed in any direction from any point in

Example XVII-4: BROWN, *December 1952* (from *Folio*)

the defined space for any length of time and may be performed from any of the four rotational positions in any sequence." The score, then, is a point of departure for an essentially free improvisation, and it is quite possible—even likely—that any two performances will have little in common. (The exclusive use of short, straight lines of varying thickness may suggest common musical gestures to different musicians, but any resulting similarities would be so general as to preclude a precise sense of compositional identity.)

Brown has continued to use indeterminacy, although he has subsequently avoided the purely graphic approach of *December 1952*. Of special importance in his work are "variable forms"—that is, forms incorporating material written out in many details, but the order and combination of which are left to the performers and may vary from one performance to the next. (The term "open form" has also been used, to contrast with the "closed forms" of traditional Western music.) One such composition, the piano piece *Twenty-five Pages* (1953), contains twenty-five unbound sheets, which can be played by any number of players from one to twenty-five, in any order and / or combination—a sort of musical "mobile," analogous to the sculptural mobiles of such artists as Alexander Calder. (Like Feldman, Brown has been significantly open to the ideas and practices of visual artists.)

Alexander Calder's standing mobile *Red Petals* (1942) exemplifies open form through the variety of leaf shapes that can be assumed by the free-moving wire tendrils balanced in the air. (Collection of The Arts Club of Chicago)

Similarly, in *Available Forms I* for eighteen players (1961) and *Available Forms II* for large orchestra divided into two groups (1962), each with conductor, every musician is given a copy of the score, which consists of a number of unbound pages containing several musical events. The order of the pages and of the events they contain is determined by the conductor(s), whose hand signals indicate the choice and speed of events (including accelerandos, ritards, and the like). A typical page of *Available Forms II* (Example XVII-5) contains five events, each numbered in the score. Although some pitches are specifically prescribed,

Example XVII-5: BROWN, *Available Forms II*

elsewhere squiggly lines merely suggest general contour; durations are indicated only approximately, by spatial placement on the page.

Through such means, Brown was able to achieve complex yet spontaneous and flexible textural and formal relationships, of a sort that could be realized only with great difficulty using conventional notation. To achieve the freely flowing, nonmetrical rhythm of *Available Forms I* and *II* using precise rhythmic notation would require unreasonably complex metrical subdivisions, difficult if not impossible to realize exactly in performance. But in this type of music, accuracy, at least with respect to details, is no longer the point, nor even necessarily desirable. What matters is the overall effect, which can be achieved as satisfactorily— and with considerably greater ease—through the use of indeterminacy. What distinguishes Brown from Cage and his less specifically musical interest in indeterminacy is this focus on musical practicality, which also relates his work to that of numerous Europeans who adopted indeterminacy during the later 1950s and 1960s.

INDETERMINACY IN EUROPEAN MUSIC

Although integral serialism and indeterminacy apparently represent totally opposed positions—one a rational, largely calculated approach to composition, the other an essentially intuitive, nonsystematic one—they were in fact closely linked with each other from their beginnings. On a 1949 visit to Paris, Cage met Pierre Boulez and established a close association that lasted several years. Cage was intrigued by the constructivist character of Boulez's music, which he saw as assuring—much as did his own compositional methods—a certain "impersonality" and lack of expressive intent. Similarly, Boulez was drawn to the rigorous proportional structures found in Cage's compositions at that time. Both viewed the musical composition as a completely autonomous "object," quite independent of the composer's desires and feelings, and believed that the best way to produce such an object was through rigorous pre-compositional planning. Nor was Boulez the only younger European interested in Cage at this time: Stockhausen, in one of his earliest articles, praised the American for his tendency to invent uniquely constructed timbral materials for each composition, a tendency he regarded as consistent with integral serialism.

Cage returned to Europe in 1954 for a series of concerts with the pianist David Tudor, with whom he worked closely at that time. By this point Cage had passed through the first and most critical stage of the development of indeterminacy, and most Europeans reacted to his recent work with hostility. Yet some of the younger serialists recognized its affinity to what they were now doing. Stockhausen, Boulez, and their serialist colleagues had come to realize that the more precisely musical events were predetermined, the more random and haphazard they tended to sound. Since the nature of European serialism was to treat all musical elements as equal, the result often appeared to be a collection of disparate events with no perceptible effect upon, or connection with, one another. Any single event tended to sound "arbitrary" and could thus just as well be replaced by another.

Cage's European tour stimulated Stockhausen and Boulez to approach serialism in a somewhat freer and more intuitive way—a tendency present in two works already begun: Boulez's *Le Marteau sans maître* (1954; discussed further in Chapter XVIII) and Stockhausen's Piano Pieces V–XI (1956). No longer conceived primarily in terms of individual musical elements or "points," these pieces relied more on differentiations among larger formal units by degrees of relative "order" and "disorder" (terms introduced in this context by one of Stockhausen's influential articles) along a range extending from greater textural transparency, recurring elements, and tauter structures to textual opacity, constant transformation, and looser structures. From that point it was only a short additional step to the incorporation of explicitly "aleatory" methods (a designation, referring to the throw of a die, that most European composers preferred to "chance" or "indeterminate").

Stockhausen and Boulez and most of their continental colleagues had little interest in using indeterminacy as part of the process of composing, nor did they adopt it in a Cagean spirit of allowing sounds to "be themselves." Their concern was to create complex, multidimensional forms in which the overall structure remained in part variable. Moreover, the idea that the formal units of a composition could be rearranged without destroying their sense was not entirely inconsistent with serialism—itself a method in which all musical materials were equally subject to permutation.

In Piano Piece XI, his first aleatoric work, Stockhausen placed nineteen spatially separated musical segments on a single page and instructed the performer to move from one segment to the next according to momentary impulse; at the conclusion of each segment indications for playing the next segment are furnished, insuring that repeated segments would rarely sound identical. When any individual segment is played three times, a performance—one of countless possible versions of a mobile form—is concluded.

Zyklus (1959), for solo percussionist, takes a different approach. The spiral-bound score is so constructed that it can be read either forward or backward (turned upside down), and the performer may begin at any point on any page. However, once starting point and direction are decided, the overall sequence of events is fixed and the performance proceeds normally until the starting point is reattained, at which time

Example XVII-6: STOCKHAUSEN, *Zyklus,* excerpt

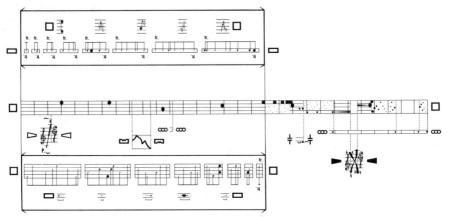

the piece is over. At the same time, the notation allows considerable leeway in playing individual events. In a sense, the procedure in *Zyklus* is thus the opposite of Piano Piece XI: the larger form is determined, the details are partially variable.

A page from the score (Example XVII-6) illustrates the complex interaction of specified and indeterminate elements. The thirty squares of equal size in the middle line mark off fixed units of time that remain constant throughout the composition. On this particular page this line contains the part for four tom-toms (designated, as are all the instruments, by a special graphic sign). The placement of the round note heads within the squares indicate the points of attack; their relative sizes indicate amplitude. Dotted lines coordinate events played on other instruments with the middle line's constant time frame. The outermost events on the page, in large bracketed boxes, can be "folded into" the more strictly measured music at any point and in any order within the time encompassed by the length of the box; the performer chooses which box to play, as the events in only one are used in a single performance. These procedures apply whether the score is read forward or (when turned upside down) backward. Where clef signs are used, they are provided for either possibility.

This highly calculated and carefully structured approach to indeterminacy sharply distinguishes *Zyklus* from the work of Cage and his American followers. Boulez's first venture into indeterminacy, the Piano Sonata No. 3 (1957), is similar in this respect. The middle movement, entitled *Constellation,* uses normal musical notation but is set up so that alternate continuations may be chosen at the end of each of a number of musical segments. Thus, not unlike Stockhausen's Piano Piece XI, the score is a "constellation" of separate units that can be arranged by the performer into different configurations. But here these segments are connected by a number of prescribed alternative paths; and the score requires that each event appear once, and only once, within a performance. Thus the possible routes, though multiple, are much more limited in number. And regardless of the path taken, the overall direction and outcome are fully determined. (Boulez has described his musical labyrinth as "a map to an unknown city.")

To date, only two of the projected five movements of Sonata No. 3 have been completed. Boulez has characteristically left many works unfinished, allowing them to be performed—if at all—only as "works in progress." Consequently, much of his creative activity in recent decades has been devoted to revising and amplifying already existing fragments. While this is partly explained by his heavy commitments as an internationally famous conductor (including the music directorship of the New York Philharmonic, 1971–78), it may also reflect uncertainty as to the possibility—or desirability—of producing "finished" works within the current cultural context. Like Ives, Boulez seems to prefer to think of his music as being in a state of constant flux and continuing evolution (lending it yet another aspect of "indeterminacy"). As he once remarked: "As long as my ideas have not exhausted every possibility of proliferation, they stay in my mind."

In two other compositions begun during the same period as the Third Piano Sonata, Boulez made extensive use of aleatory methods: *Structures II* for two pianos (1956–61) and *Pli selon pli (Fold upon Fold)* for soprano and orchestra (1957–62). Here again, a limited range of choice is allowed within a carefully prescribed larger plan. In *Structures II* an entire separate "movement" may be inserted into the work's ongoing structure at the performers' choice, yet this movement, if used, constitutes only a temporary interruption—rather like a cadenza—within a fixed and precisely controlled larger musical argument.

Although Boulez's interest in indeterminacy declined significantly after the middle 1960s, Stockhausen used it to an increasing degree throughout that decade. In a number of works written for a small performing group he established, including *Plus / Minus* (1963), *Prozession* (1967), and *Kurzwellen (Short Waves,* 1968), Stockhausen called for improvisation, following carefully worked out general instructions, on various types of pre-existing material: his own previous music, Beethoven's music, shortwave broadcasts. This reached an extreme stage in *Aus den sieben Tagen (From the Seven Days,* 1968), which does away entirely with "preformed" material and asks the performers to improvise freely on purely verbal texts supplied by the composer. Here is *Intensity,* one of these fifteen texts, in its entirety (in English translation):

Play the individual tones
with such dedication until
you sense the warmth
which radiates from you.
Play on and sustain them
as long as you can.

Stockhausen called such free improvisations "intuitive" music: "music
that as much as possible comes purely from intuition, which in the case
of a group of intuitively playing musicians, due to their mutual 'feedback,' is qualitatively more than the sum of their individual 'ideas.' "[4]

Stockhausen's intuitive music can be understood as an outgrowth of
the heady experimental atmosphere dominating much of the 1960s, when
free individual expression was accorded the highest priority. Systematic
constraints, including specific instructions from composer to performer
(as in conventional musical notation), came to be viewed as "repressive." Such attitudes inspired a revitalization of the extemporaneous
spirit unparalleled in modern Western concert music, and improvising
groups suddenly sprang up everywhere. Some worked within relatively fixed guidelines, among them the Improvisation Chamber
Ensemble, probably the earliest such group, formed in 1957 in Los
Angeles by the American composer Lukas Foss. Later many of these
ensembles were committed to "free-form" performances in which the
musicians were encouraged to do whatever they wished, constrained
only by a hoped-for spirit of mutual cooperation.

Among the most prominent such groups were the English ensemble
AMM and the Rome-based American ensemble MEV (Musica Elet-
tronica Viva), formed in 1965 and 1966 respectively. They combined
musicians with jazz experience and others from more traditional classical backgrounds, and the ambition was to create a completely "open"
situation in which any type of material, whatever its origins, could be
introduced. In addition to standard instruments, unconventional sound-
producing objects were often employed, and extensive use was made
of electronics. MEV especially favored informal concert presentations,
where friends and guests, as well as the audience at large, were encouraged to participate in the performance.

Despite Stockhausen's radical evolution during the 1960s, most other
European composers maintained a relatively cautious attitude toward
indeterminacy, using it mainly to achieve certain kinds of calculated
musical effects. Stockhausen himself returned to more traditional compositional methods with *Mantra* (1970), an extended work for two pianos
that was entirely specified and conventionally notated. Yet virtually

4.   *Texte III* (Cologne, 1973), p. 123.

every major European of the post–World War II generation made at least some use of indeterminacy, including such figures as Luciano Berio, Hans Werner Henze, Henri Pousseur, and Witold Lutosławski.

Born in Poland in 1913, Lutosławski is an interesting example of a composer somewhat older than most of those involved with indeterminacy, who accommodated aleatory techniques within a basically traditional compositional conception. By the time the significant postwar musical revolutions began, Lutosławski had an established style, based on folk sources and heavily indebted to Bartók. After his Concerto for Orchestra (1954), which already revealed a growing interest in texture and sonority, Lutosławski's work underwent significant transformations. During the later 1950s he adopted the twelve-tone method, and though soon abandoning it, he continued to treat pitch in terms of chromatic aggregates. In the early 1960s, in search of textural effects involving multiple yet uncoordinated layers of rhythmic activity, Lutosławski turned to aleatory procedures.

About his use of indeterminacy, Lutoslawski has written: "The point

Example XVII-7: LUTOSŁAWSKI, String Quartet, excerpt

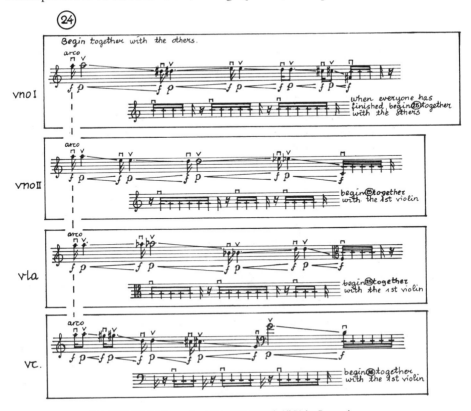

at issue is not a matter of differences between one performance and another. . . . I did not intend, either, to free myself of part of my responsibility for the work by transferring it to the players. The purpose of my endeavors was solely a particular result in sound."[5] Mirroring this view, the larger design of his 1964 String Quartet is a series of relatively brief, distinctly defined sections. Here there is no question of variable form; the aleatory features are essentially confined to matters of rhythmic detail and, especially, ensemble coordination within the sections.

Example XVII-7 is the complete score (also used as performing parts) for one of the Quartet's brief sections. While the music for the four instruments is distributed independently on the page, the starting points are aligned and the players begin simultaneously; thereafter, they move independently, creating shifting and flexible rhythmic relationships in the overall ensemble—an effect difficult to achieve otherwise, as any attempt to notate such rhythmic relationships by traditional means would produce unreasonable complexities. (The verbal instructions at the end of each part deal with coordinating the beginning of the next section.)

NOTATIONAL INNOVATIONS

One of the most characteristic features of later twentieth–century music has been the proliferation of new approaches to notation, most of them engendered by musical indeterminacy. The limitations of traditional notation with respect to new compositional procedures was already a source of concern earlier in the century; symptomatic are Schoenberg's use of accidentals before every note in his post–tonal music and Stravinsky's use of constantly changing meters (notably in the last section of *The Rite of Spring,* where even the basic pulse alternates between eighth and sixteenth notes). Even these practices could be handled by adjustments within the conventional system, and only a few isolated examples were so extreme as to require more basic departures; the radical notational experiments of Cowell or Russolo remained interesting curiosities, with no effect on other composers.

However, the introduction of indeterminacy on a broad scale required a fundamental rethinking of traditional notational practices and encouraged many composers to explore nonconventional methods. The degree to which standard notation is modified varies considerably from work to work, obviously depending on how much the music departs from traditional practices, especially those affecting pitch and rhythm. The examples already presented in this chapter suggest the range and variety

5.   Quoted in liner notes for recording, Deutsche Grammophon 137001.

of possibilities. Starting with the most traditional, Example XVII-7 is almost entirely "normal" except for the spatial layout. Example XVII-6 also uses many traditional elements, combined with nonconventional ones and placed within a purely graphic frame. In the somewhat similar graphic frame of Example XVII-3, no conventional musical signs are used at all, while Example XVII-2 distorts traditional elements so that

Example XVII-8: BUSSOTTI, *Siciliano*

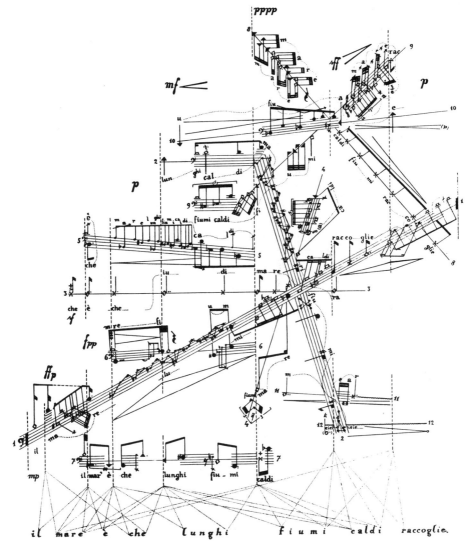

they lose virtually all their original meaning. Finally, Example XVII-4 is an entirely abstract design.

The emphasis on graphic values in recent scores has encouraged in some composers an unprecedented concern with the purely visual characteristics of their work. Cage, as mentioned, is widely admired as a graphic artist, and other composers with unusual graphic gifts include the Englishman Cornelius Cardew (see Chapter XXI) and the Italian Sylvano Bussotti (b. 1931). The American George Crumb (b. 1929), though a relatively traditional composer who relies almost exclusively upon conventional notation, commonly arranges his music into patterns of striking visual effect, often with an explicitly symbolic meaning, such as a cross or circle. As a final example, the score of Bussotti's *Siciliano* for twelve male voices (1962) combines musical, verbal, and graphic elements to produce an unusually complex and provocative visual design (Example XVII-8). Although no instructions are given for performing the score, close study reveals possible hints (e.g., numbered "parts" are included for each of the twelve singers).

Graphic notation offers composers virtually limitless opportunities to exercise their visual imagination. Yet the number and variety of new notational practices have made it difficult for any single method to win wide acceptance, and attempts at standardization and codification have met with little success. Most composers who use nonconventional notation continue to rely upon their own personal preferences in writing their scores, and often the explanation of the symbols and procedures proves longer than the score itself. When no such instructions are provided, the composition may have as much the quality of a puzzle as of a piece of music.

CHAPTER XVIII

Innovations in Form and Texture

THE IMPLICATIONS OF SERIALISM AND INDETERMINACY

We have already observed the surprising common ground between serialism and indeterminacy. In both approaches, "external" systems are to some degree arbitrarily imposed upon the musical materials they govern. Moreover, both produce results that are often analogous. Serialism and indeterminacy have also played a common role in certain far-reaching transformations of the way composers think about musical structure and time.

Music of the common-practice period is normally constructed to give listeners a strong feeling of temporal direction, a sense of where the music is located at any given moment within the overall continuum. This stems mainly from two interrelated factors: a relatively fixed set of hierarchical tonal relationships and a rhythmic framework, also hierarchically ordered, based upon the recurrence of regular durational units. In such music, time has a highly structured quality: a definite sense of beginning and end, and intermediate points of arrival and departure that are clearly marked off within the whole. Indeed, the listener not only knows where the music "is," but also knows how it got there and has some idea of where it is headed. The music has, in other words, a strongly directional, goal-oriented quality.

The breakdown of common-practice conventions in the early twentieth century inevitably compromised this directional quality, encouraging some composers, as we have seen, to develop a more "static" conception of musical form. Nevertheless, most composers, even those who adopted atonality, continued to use pitches in ways that preserved at least some goal-directed character, and most retained meter as the prevailing means of durational organization.

Only after World War II did a real change occur in this regard, when serialism and indeterminacy effected a complete dissolution of goal-oriented pitch structure and metrically organized rhythm. The mechanical permutation of both pitches and durations in serial music radically dissolved linear connections and rhythmic regularity, while aleatory procedures fostered "irrational" temporal relationships, giving rise to complex rhythmic situations that destroyed all sense of metrical order.

The absence of a central axis in both the tonal and durational dimensions of much recent music has fundamentally affected the character of musical form and time, seriously undercutting the basic assumptions of post-Renaissance Western music: linearity and logical forward progression. Some composers (for example, Cage and, in certain pieces, Stockhausen) have entirely abandoned such notions. More commonly, however, some degree of directionality has been retained, but of a more casual and ambiguous nature than before, so that the music loses much of its traditional "narrative" flow. This is closely tied to the use of "variable form" in so many recent compositions; no single, inevitable line connects individual formal segments. Since one event no longer leads inexorably to the next, formal units become interchangeable.

In extreme cases of variable form, individual units are entirely self-contained, with no implications whatever—either as consequences of what preceded or as initiators of what follows. Stockhausen refers to such self-enclosed segments as "moments" and speaks of "moment form," music that "does not tell a story, is not composed along a 'red ribbon' that one must follow from beginning to end in order to understand the whole. . . . It is thus not a dramatic form with exposition, increasing energy, development, climax, and effect of finality, but rather . . . every moment is a center connected with all others, but which can stand by itself."[1]

These transformations in musical structure are nowhere more clearly evident than in the thematic dimension, so critical in traditional music for defining forward motion (and determining musical character). In the 1950s the homogenization of texture and the concomitant loss of melodic and harmonic definition (as well as of other hierarchic textural differentiations) called into question the very possibility of creating convincing linear motion. The treatment of compositional elements as separable and permutable entities, the leveling of interval relationships through constant chromatic saturation and registral dispersion, the dissolution of metrical order in favor of an unbroken rhythmic contin-

1.   *Texte I* (Cologne, 1963), p. 190.

uum—all produced a neutralization of musical content that dissolved such traditionally distinguishable components as melody, counterpoint, and harmony into a single, generalized sound mass. Composers began to think about music in terms of such global attributes as textural density and timbral balance, requiring significant adjustments in basic compositional approach.

FROM POINTILLISM TO GROUP COMPOSITION

When the European serialists realized that so much emphasis on individual elements blurred distinctions in the overall structure (ironically, the more one produced unique musical gestures at each moment, the more the whole tended toward an undifferentiated sameness), they began extending the serial principle to larger formal categories: temporal relationships among sections, variations in textural density, registral transformations, etc. But the more they applied serial criteria to these larger dimensions, the more they had to relinquish control of individual details. As the details became subordinated to the overall effect, the focus shifted from the separate component to the total shape. This entailed a basic compositional reorientation: whereas previously the serialists had worked "pointillistically," starting with single elements and building up the larger structure through an essentially additive process, they now began with a conception of the whole and only afterward worked out the individual details that would achieve the desired overall result.

This development can be clearly traced in Stockhausen's music of the 1950s. His earliest serial compositions were uncompromisingly pointillistic in conception: "All forms should evolve from the point, the individual tone," he wrote in 1952.[2] He soon turned to what he called "group composition," in which emphasis was placed on larger musical segments made up of complex collections and on the manner in which large numbers of tones could be joined together, rather than on individual intervals and individual relationships.

Even in the relatively early Piano Piece I (1952), discussed briefly in the preceding chapter, this tendency was evident, but the most important composition reflecting Stockhausen's new approach was *Gruppen (Groups)* for three orchestras (1955–57). *Gruppen* consists of a number of distinct formal segments, or "groups," each with its own particular musical characteristics—determined not by such individual features as motives, specific intervals, or harmonies, but by such generalized properties as total interval content, average length of durations, registral extent, instrumental sonority, and textural density. The group idea

2. Ibid., p. 36.

A rehearsal for the first performance of Stockhausen's *Gruppen* at the West-deutscher Rundfunk, Cologne, 1958. The three conductors are the composer (orchestra 1, left), Bruno Maderna (orchestra 2, center), and Pierre Boulez (orchestra 3, right). (Photo Heinz Karnine)

reaches its most extreme form when the density of the texture becomes so great that individual notes can no longer be accurately perceived—everything tends to melt together into a generalized, total effect. In such cases Stockhausen speaks of "statistical music"—that is, music that depends upon only approximate designations. In a 1956 article on statistical form, he commented: "It is now a matter of degrees of density in the groups of notes, of direction of the motion, of speed, of the speed of transformations, of the average dynamic level, of changes in dynamics, of timbre, and of timbral mutation."[3] (Just such thinking would shortly thereafter lead Stockhausen to incorporate elements of indeterminacy in his work.)

The three orchestras of *Gruppen* project three simultaneous formal continuities, each with its own independent succession of groups, producing multilayered textures made up of two or three individual musical strands, each essentially complete in its own right. Such combinations of independent "musics" are rare in tonal music, because the different layers must be sufficiently coordinated in order not to cancel out the harmonic, melodic, and rhythmic content of the individual strands, and the level of contrast is thus severely restricted. But since a work like *Gruppen* does not depend upon specific harmonic or intervallic correspondences or on regular rhythmic patterns, the possibilities for combination are virtually limitless. And the more differentiated the layers, the more easily they can be perceived as separate entities when combined.

Separation is greatly aided in *Gruppen* because the simultaneous groups

3.   Ibid., p. 77.

Example XVIII-1: STOCKHAUSEN, *Gruppen*, excerpt

are assigned to three timbrally and spatially distinct orchestras, each with its own conductor. The composition projects a multidimensional time field within which the separate layers proceed at their own independent speeds, coordinated by a serially derived scale of metronomic relationships. (The passage shown in Example XVIII-1 illustrates how the relationship of the three orchestras is indicated notationally.) The orchestral separation seems to allow the sound literally to "move" from one strand to another. Stockhausen initially explored such temporal and spatial differentiations, respectively, in two earlier compositions completed in 1956: *Zeitmasse (Tempos)* for woodwind quintet and the electronic composition *Gesang der Jünglinge (Song of the Youths)*.

Gruppen represents a compositional approach adopted by many during the course of the 1950s, placing texture (defined in its broadest sense) at the center of musical concerns, as the main carrier of musical content. The structure of Stockhausen's score is conceived largely in terms of transformations in texture and timbre. At times the separate orchestral strands appear individually, at others they mix into joint complexes; occasionally they even synchronize momentarily at a common tempo, briefly sharing material before again going their separate ways. The textural types range from the purely pointillistic, with density sufficiently low for each individual event to be separately and distinctly heard, to statistical complexes in which so much happens at once that the listener has only a blurred impression of the whole.

Unlike Stockhausen, Boulez did not formulate a conscious theory of group composition, but his development after the radically pointillistic *Structures I* followed a somewhat similar course. His next composition, *Le Marteau sans maître (The Hammer without a Master, 1954)* for alto voice and six instrumentalists, abjured the detailed, note-by-note serial ordering characteristic of the earlier piece in favor of a more flexible, seemingly free musical succession, stubbornly resistant to straightforward serial explanation. In character, *Le Marteau* approaches a fanciful yet highly controlled and meticulously regulated improvisation.

As suggested by Boulez's choice of instruments, *Le Marteau* is especially distinguished by emphasis on timbre and texture: alto flute, xylophone, vibraphone, guitar, viola, and a battery of nonpitched percussion all fall within the middle to upper register, as does the alto voice. The music thus seems to have no bass (or base), but floats freely as if in a nongravitational field. Both similarities (e.g., between viola and alto voice) and differences (e.g., between short percussive attacks in the mallet instruments and sustained flute lines) among these registrally associated timbres are exploited. Constantly shifting layers of color and rhythmic activity lend the work a fluid, glittering quality, unprecedented at the time but soon copied by many others.

Le Marteau also reveals a new direction in Boulez's formal conceptions. Of the nine movements, all but two are scored for unique combinations drawn from the total ensemble. (The two exceptions, the sixth and ninth movements, are scored for the full group, and even these differ in the choice of nonpitched percussion.) Moreover, each movement has a distinct textural characteristic, so that—borrowing Stockhausen's terminology—each forms a "group" within the total structure. As in *Gruppen,* certain "groups" have relatively close correspondences with others, forming larger associations within the whole.

The overall layout is both complex and multivalent. The four vocal movements, settings of the surrealist poet René Char, are distributed asymmetrically (III, V, VI, and IX), while the five purely instrumental movements form "commentaries" on two of these. The two "uncommented" vocal movements are paired, being different settings of the same text. Though elusive, the correspondences among related movements are critical. For example, the vocal setting of the sixth movement and its three instrumental counterparts (II, IV, and VIII—two of them thus preceding the material they "comment" upon) all feature nonpitched percussion parts characterized by relatively regular, well-defined rhythmic patterns, set off against more florid and rhythmically elaborate pitched components. A passage from the second movement (Example XVIII-2) is typical.

The idea of commentaries—of extensive rephrasings or alternate versions of similar materials—has been a constant feature of Boulez's composing and is undoubtedly related to his previously mentioned inclination to leave compositions unfinished for later revision.

Although *Gruppen* and *Le Marteau sans maître* represent the same stage of European serialism and were equally influential, their differences are significant and mirror the temperaments and national heritages of their composers. The dramatic, sharply punctuated, and climax-oriented shape of the Stockhausen work, for example, contrasts markedly with Boulez's more lyrical and subtly inflected gestures. Stockhausen has since proved to be the more restless composer, ever searching for new areas

Example XVIII-2: BOULEZ, *Le Marteau sans maître,* second movement, mm. 67–69

of musical exploration, while Boulez has remained essentially constant in his development. Even Boulez's later, limited use of indeterminacy (discussed in Chapter XVII) can be seen as an extension of the idea of "multiple versions" embodied in the linked commentaries of *Le Marteau*.

After the 1950s serialism was largely abandoned by most younger European composers. One exception is the Englishman Brian Ferneyhough (b. 1943), who has more recently evolved a serially oriented style of staggering complexity, yielding richly detailed polyphonic textures transcending even those of *Gruppen* and *Le Marteau*. Ferneyhough's *Transit* (1975), a vast conception for six voices and chamber orchestra, demonstrates an unusual gift for fashioning meaningful statements out of the most complicated materials imaginable. Despite the great profusion of simultaneously competing details, the overall form is clear, defined by timbrally differentiated sectional contrasts mediated through carefully graded transitions.

Ferneyhough makes an explicit expressive point through the extreme difficulty of his scores. In the prefatory remarks to the score of his *Cassandra's Dream Song* for solo flute (1971), he writes:

> A "beautiful," cultivated performance is not aimed at: some of the combinations of actions specified are in any case either not literally realizable (certain dynamic groupings) or else lead to complex, partly unpredictable results. Nevertheless, a valid realization will only result from a rigorous attempt to reproduce as many of the textual details as possible; such divergencies and "impurities" as then follow from the natural limitations of the instrument itself may be taken to be the intention of the composer.

Here the notion of indeterminacy (as well as Messiaen's idea of "the charm of impossibilities") takes on a new dimension.

Relying upon a combination of strict serial procedures and more intuitively conceived modifications, reminiscent of Stockhausen in the 1950s, Ferneyhough has fashioned a distinctive niche in present-day music. He is definitely swimming against the tide of recent musical developments, however, at least as represented by other composers of his own generation, most of whom have avoided the textural and formal complexities engendered by integral serialism in favor of a simpler and more direct music.

TEXTURAL MUSIC

The trend of the later 1950s, toward shaping music through its larger sonic attributes rather than as an accumulation of individual details, was evident in an especially emphatic form in the work of two Eastern

Europeans, the Pole Krzysztof Penderecki (b. 1933) and the Hungarian György Ligeti (b. 1923).

In the years after 1956 Polish music enjoyed a remarkable openness to Western influence, manifested in the international tone of the annual Warsaw Autumn Festivals. Penderecki's earlier compositions, such as *Psalms of David* (1958) and *Strophe* (1959), though loosely serial, already reveal a preference for building chromatic pitch segments by coupling almost every note with one or both of its chromatic neighbors. This tendency eventually led Penderecki to shift his focus from individual pitches to "clusters," homogeneous bands of adjacent (usually chromatic) steps. Earlier composers, notably Henry Cowell, had used clusters, but normally as fixed and internally undifferentiated blocks of notes, functioning as complex doublings of a single note or as purely percussive sonorities. Penderecki, by contrast, took the cluster as a starting point for compositional development, subjecting it to various types of developmental processes—for example, variation through changes in registration, width, or density. But, just as in Cowell's clusters, the individual pitch is subordinated to the mass of sound within which it is embedded, and is more often than not completely imperceptible.

The *Threnody for the Victims of Hiroshima* for fifty-two string instruments, completed in 1960, was among Penderecki's earliest cluster compositions. Example XVIII-3 (see p. 388) shows a typical page from the score. Here ten cellos begin a new section (overlapping briefly with patterns held over from the previous one), playing a chromatic cluster that expands from a unison F before returning to its original position (indicated in the score by notating the entire cluster with a single black band of appropriate width, connecting the individual parts of the two outermost instruments). This wedgelike pattern is then imitated by other groups of instruments in contrasting registers: the first twelve violins, the contrabasses, the violas, and a second group of twelve violins. The imitation is quite free; the first twelve violins, for example, echo only the expanding part of the original idea, the violas only the contracting part.

Since it is impossible to hear individual pitches in such chromatic bands, the listener perceives only an undifferentiated mass, of a certain width and dynamic level. The effect, then, is of "noise," not of a group of distinguishable pitches. (Here, serialism's tendency to undermine pitch and interval differentiations has arrived at radical consequences.) Indeed, throughout this work and others written during this period, Penderecki essentially ignored all distinctions between pitch and noise, drawing freely from a wide spectrum of available sounds. Although *Threnody* is scored for normal string instruments, a number of special playing techniques are introduced to extend the range of sonic possibilities, such as playing between the bridge and tailpiece of the instrument, playing behind

Example XVIII-3: PENDERECKI, *Threnody for the Victims of Hiroshima,*
No. 10

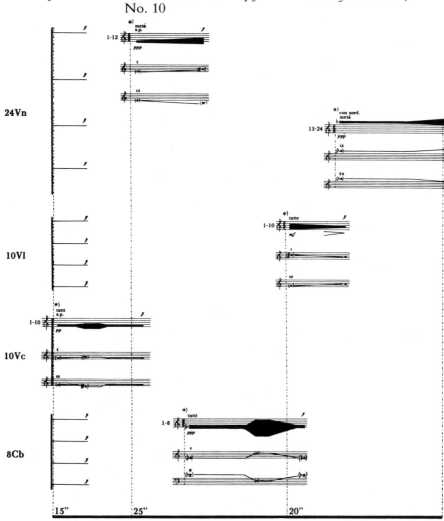

*) Dokładna realizacja w głosach. / Genaue Ausführung ist in den Stimmen angegeben.
Exact notation is given in the parts. / L'exécution précise est indiquée dans les parties.

the bridge or on the tailpiece itself, striking the sounding board with fingertips.

Threnody groups these unusual sounds into various textural patterns, transforming, developing, and mediating among them to create the overall form. Traditional notions of melody, harmony, and measured beat are completely absent. Rhythmic indications in Example XVIII-3 are given by reference to the number of seconds occupied by a given formal segment, the precise position of each event within the segment being only approximately designated. Nevertheless, much in *Threnody* remains traditional. The "imitative" aspect of Example XVIII-3 is one of many quasi-canonic techniques used throughout the score, and the larger form projects a clear A B A pattern: a more pointillistically conceived middle section sharply set off between more cluster-dominated outer sections.

Some ten years Penderecki's senior, Ligeti studied at the Budapest Academy of Music, where the postwar musical scene—and contact with the West—was more restricted than in Poland. While his early compositions, under the influence of Bartók, were largely based on folk music, Ligeti harbored a private interest in more experimental approaches. After fleeing Hungary during the 1956 uprising, he settled first in Germany (where he was associated with Stockhausen) and then in Vienna, quickly becoming one of the leading figures of the European avant-garde. Like Penderecki, Ligeti began working with clusters in the later 1950s; the most prominent in a series of works exploring their possibilities was the orchestral piece *Atmosphères* (1961).

Whereas Penderecki tended to treat clusters as "solid" blocks of sound made up of undifferentiated individual parts, Ligeti formed his clusters from separate components that, though for the most part not individually perceptible, changed constantly to produce subtly transforming internal patterns. Setting up a large number of moving parts, he would make them continuously exchange positions, producing a sense of internal motion within a textural complex that itself remained stationary. In one section of *Atmosphères* Ligeti employs strictly canonic procedures to reduce a widely spaced cluster, gradually and with careful control; initially spanning some four octaves, it ultimately collapses inward from both extremes to a four-note chromatic segment around middle C. This accomplishes, in a different way, the process carried out by the violas in the Penderecki excerpt (Example XVIII-3), but over a much longer period of time. It is also more precisely defined through carefully specified (and traditionally notated) rhythmic relationships, and involves a cluster that is in motion internally as well externally.

Both Penderecki's *Threnody* and Ligeti's *Atmosphères* proved remarkably successful with the public. Relatively easy to grasp in overall shape and intent, they were widely programmed (and imitated) during the 1960s and were welcomed by audiences as indications of a turn away from the rigors and austerities of integral serialism. Yet the limitations of such an uncompromisingly textural conception, with its tendency to emphasize purely surface effects, were severe, and both Penderecki and Ligeti turned in new directions during the 1960s.

The fact that they followed different courses reflected in part the dif-

ferences evident in the two works just considered. The more traditionally oriented and expressively direct of the two, Penderecki turned to
conventional genres and began juxtaposing more melodically and tonally
conceived segments against purely textural ones. His two large-scale
choral-orchestral works, the *St. Luke Passion* (1965) and *Utrenja* (1971),
faithfully follow the dramatic and formal structure of their sacred texts.
While the overall conception leans heavily upon Bach's passions, much
of the vocal writing is modeled upon liturgical chant. Triads, reintro-
duced to create stability at cadential points in the *Passion,* become still
more prominent throughout *Utrenja.* Similarly, the *Capriccio* for violin
and orchestra (1967) combines conventional motivic figurations with
clusterlike material, shaped into clearly articulated phrases with goal-
directed attributes echoing those of tonal music. In more recent works,
such as the opera *Paradise Lost* (1979), Penderecki has turned even more
overtly to triadic tonality, adopting a chromatic harmonic style with
strong ties to late nineteenth-century Romanticism.

Ligeti's later evolution has been more circuitous. During the 1960s
he began working in a more concentrated manner with the canonic
procedures employed in passing in *Atmosphères,* placing more emphasis
on linear structure. This progress can be traced in two orchestral pieces:
Lontano (1967) is almost entirely canonic in construction, although the
listener is still primarily conscious of overall texture rather than of clearly
etched individual voices, while in *Melodien* (1971) the textures are sufficiently thinned out for the linear structure to be heard as such. Both
works are less exclusively chromatic than *Atmosphères,* and a kind of
"tonality" is even evident in *Lontano,* where the clusters frequently expand
from and return to a single pitch, allowing individual tones to emerge
as momentary points of emphasis.

A composer who enjoys developing different compositional approaches
and working with different kinds of materials, Ligeti is difficult to cate-
gorize stylistically. Two of his most striking works, *Aventures* (1962)
and *Nouvelles aventures* (1965), are chamber pieces for voices employing
a specially created "language" consisting of a wide variety of unconventional sounds. More recently he has produced—with considerable
skill and humor—his own distinctive version of musical minimalism:
*Selbstporträt mit Reich und Riley (und Chopin ist auch dabei) (Self-Portrait
with Reich and Riley [and Chopin Is Also There]),* one of his Three Pieces
for Two Pianos (1976). His Horn Trio (1983), on the other hand, is
remarkably traditional in conception and, like his earliest works, owes
a heavy debt to Bartók.

NEW INSTRUMENTAL RESOURCES

One by-product of the emphasis on texture and on music's purely sonic
and coloristic aspects was the extension of traditional instrumental tech-

niques into previously unexplored areas. As the distinction between pitch and noise became increasingly blurred, the boundaries of what constituted "musical material" expanded dramatically. In a sense, *any* sound could now be taken as "musical" and incorporated within this new compositional framework. (This can be clearly connected to both developments in electronic music and the ideas of John Cage, and earlier to the Futurists and Varèse.)

In the area of instrumental performance a main line of development involved unconventional ways of playing conventional instruments. Often this necessitated a purposeful "misplaying" of the instrument to elicit sounds it was not originally intended to make. Some new kinds of string playing were mentioned in the discussion of Penderecki's *Threnody*. Other innovations include woodwind "multiphonics" (several pitches sounding simultaneously, produced with "false" fingerings and overblowing); breathing through brass instruments without producing a pitch; key clicks on woodwinds; humming and playing simultaneously on winds; blowing through a mouthpiece not attached to an instrument; playing a piano with a metal rod placed on the strings; playing on the strings of a double bass with percussion mallets (requiring two players, one to finger, one to strike); dipping a sounding tamtam into a bucket of water (thus "bending" its pitch); and playing timpani with crotales placed on the drum head.

During the 1960s certain performers began specializing in such unconventional performance techniques, and encouraged composers to write compositions exploiting them. Sometimes the performers were themselves composers: among many others, the oboist Heinz Holliger (b. 1939), the trombonists Vinko Globokar (b. 1934) and Stuart Dempster (b. 1936), and the clarinetist William O. Smith (b. 1926). Composers particularly active in this area include the Americans George Crumb and Robert Erickson (b. 1917), the Argentinian Mauricio Kagel and the Italian Luciano Berio. Berio has written a continuing series of pieces entitled *Sequenza* for various unaccompanied soloists, designed to display novel instrumental or vocal techniques within a virtuoso framework.

Despite its apparently innovative aspect, this development can be viewed as the most recent stage of a process that has been under way throughout the century, reflecting the emphasis on timbre characteristic of virtually all post-tonal music. Schoenberg's use of *Sprechstimme* and flutter-tongue and Bartók's employment of such relatively uncommon string techniques as *sul ponticello* and "snap pizzicato" are clear forerunners. During the first half of the century, however, such practices were primarily used as "departures" within a traditional context, whereas in recent music the new techniques often assume a role equal to, or more prominent than, "normal" modes of performance. And the number of composers using such techniques represents a far greater proportion of the whole.

STOCHASTIC MUSIC

A preference for massed blocks of sound also characterizes the music of the Greek composer Iannis Xenakis (b. 1922), although Xenakis's compositional ideas arose from assumptions quite foreign to serialism. Trained as an engineer and mathematician, he first pursued a career as assistant to the famed Swiss-French architect Le Corbusier and became interested in translating certain types of mathematical calculations into visual designs for architectural projects. Working in this manner, Xenakis had a major role in helping to design two noted Corbusier buildings: the convent of La Tourette and the Philips Pavilion for the 1958 Brussels World's Fair.

Xenakis had some musical training as a youth, and in 1950, shortly after meeting Le Corbusier, he again took up musical studies under Messiaen. Struck by the close analogies between music and architecture, both of which he felt could be viewed as concrete realizations of abstract mathematical calculations, Xenakis became increasingly preoccupied with questions of musical structure. His design for the Philips Pavilion was in fact an alternative realization, in a different medium, of ideas first developed for an orchestral composition, *Metastasis* (1954). One immediately evident point of contact between the two works, architectural and musical, can be seen in the continuously displaced, "flowing" straight lines of the building and the converging and diverging glissandos of the music.

Unlike most advanced European composers of the early 1950s, Xenakis was not influenced by serialism. In a 1954 article on "The Crisis in Serial Music" he commented that in such music the "linear polyphony destroys itself by its very complexity," producing "nothing but a mass of notes in different registers," and also noted the contradiction between the "deterministic causality" of serial methods and the actual effect of "an irrational and fortuitous dispersion of sounds over the whole extent of the sonic spectrum."[4] Nor did Xenakis accept the type of chance music then being developed by Cage. "For myself," he remarked in a later interview, "this . . . is an abuse of language and is an abrogation of a composer's function." Xenakis's own conception of complex textural configurations rejected both unrestricted irrationality and indeterminacy on the one hand and strict determinism on the other, attempting instead to incorporate both determinacy and indeterminacy within a more generalized theoretical framework.

Seeking a type of causality appropriate to massed sonic effects, he began applying theories of mathematical probability to music, especially the "law of large numbers" formulated by the eighteenth-century Swiss mathematician Jacques Bernoulli. In simple terms, this law states

4.   "La Crise de la musique sérielle," *Gravesaner Blätter,* 1 (1955): 2.

Iannis Xenakis played a major role in helping Le Corbusier design the Philips Pavilion for the Brussels World's Fair, 1958. Edgard Varèse's *Poème électronique* was composed for performance in this building during the fair. (Photograph courtesy The Museum of Modern Art, New York)

that as the number of occurrences of a chance event such as the flipping of a coin increases, the more the result will tend toward a determinate end—in this case an equal distribution of "heads" and "tails." Borrowing a term from Bernoulli, Xenakis spoke of music conceived in these terms as "stochastic music"—that is, music indeterminate in its details yet tending toward a definite goal.

The relationship of probability theory (and of related concepts such as the kinetic theory of gasses) to Xenakis's music can be illustrated by considering the types of musical complexes he favors, which he refers to by such figurative designations as "clouds" or "galaxies." Here the individual note is only one of a collection of complexly interacting notes, each with little weight or importance of its own (in which sense each can be said to be "indeterminate"). Yet the overall structure is carefully calculated to produce a definite, predictable result. And although Xenakis uses mathematical calculations to help shape these "probabilistic" or "statistical" musical events and to determine their distribution throughout a composition, he maintains that "music has to dominate." Mathematics is only a tool, and when translating the calculations into precisely notated musical indications, Xenakis adjusts them for purely musical purposes.

The process of constructing graphs based on mathematical calculations and then translating these into musical notation can be seen in an example cited in Xenakis's book *Formalized Music* (1963), which sets out his approach in considerable technical detail. The graph in Example XVIII-4a presents the original coordinates for a segment of glissandos in *Metastasis,* while Example XVIII-4b shows its musical realization.

The passage begins with two massed attacks on chromatic clusters, the first in the lower strings (m. 309) and the second in the upper ones (m. 310), after which both instrumental groups are quickly dispersed through glissandos, with some instruments dropping out, others continuing to m. 314, where they converge on a two-note, middle-register cluster (C♯ and D). Overlapping with the second half of this previous process, there is something approximating a reversal: instruments comprising two new string groups (consisting of those that had previously dropped out) enter separately in mm. 312–13 and glissando toward two chromatic clusters on the downbeat of m. 314 (followed, on the second sixteenth, by unison attacks on the highest note of each of these clusters).

The passage has been conceived according to a generalized process of textural transformation: a change of registral extent and density through continuous pitch motions (glissandos), first in a contracting direction and then in an expanding one. Typical of Xenakis, however, the process is not entirely "determined," in that not every part contributes to this pattern, which is the result of the total motion but not of any individual element. Indeed, certain parts directly contradict the pattern (e.g., the lower instruments in the cluster entering at m. 310). The passage thus only "tends" toward its definite, determinate goal.

Example XVIII-4: XENAKIS, *Metastasis*

a. Graph for mm. 309–17

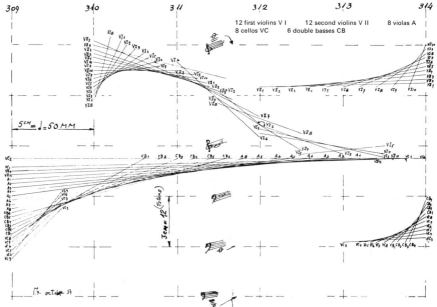

b. mm. 309–17

A second graph (Example XVIII-5) from Xenakis's book presents the formal "matrix" for an entire composition, *Achoripsis* for twenty-one instruments (1958). Here calculations have determined the frequency of various types of events (differentiated by timbre) and the distribution of these events throughout the composition. The eight boxes along the vertical axis correspond to the eight different timbral groups into which the ensemble has been divided. (These are indicated at the extreme right of the chart, "flute" here being shorthand for a trio of flute, clarinet, and bass clarinet, "oboe" for both oboe and bassoon.) The horizontal axis charts the temporal dimension, with each column equal to six and a half measures at MM = 26. As indicated below the matrix, the design of the individual box designates the extent of activity within that timbral group. (The word "event" here actually designates a mean level of activity, with a "single event" equaling approximately thirty-two "sounds" per box.)

Achoripsis thus contains twenty-eight sonic "fields" (corresponding roughly to Stockhausen's "groups"), one for each vertical column, with each field containing one or more textural layers defined by contrasting timbres and degrees of activity. The graph also reveals that the piece contains three formal sections clearly separated by two segments of complete silence (the eighth and twenty-fourth). After opening with a field containing only a single timbre, the music gradually builds in textural density during the first part. The densest field—and the only one

Example XVIII-5: XENAKIS, matrix of *Achoripsis*

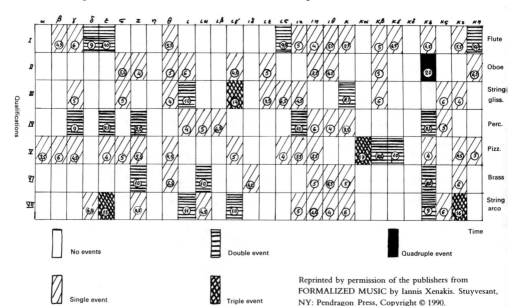

Reprinted by permission of the publishers from FORMALIZED MUSIC by Iannis Xenakis. Stuyvesant, NY: Pendragon Press, Copyright © 1990.

containing a "quadruple event"—follows the second silent segment, occupying (as the fourth unit from the end) a "traditional" position for the climax of the composition. There is, then, a musical as well as mathematical basis for the matrix.

The theory of games is closely related to probability theory, and Xenakis has composed two pieces based on ideas derived from this field— *Duel* (1959) and *Stratégie* (1962), in which two groups of players musically "compete" against each other according to carefully prescribed rules, with a "winner" designated at the end. Another group of compositions, including *Herma* for piano (1964) and *Nomos alpha* for cello (1966), contain what Xenakis calls "symbolic music," based on concepts drawn from symbolic logic. More recently, he has opened up his music to overt musico-historical allusions. *Medea,* a suite drawn from the score for a 1967 production of Seneca's tragedy, is not only texturally more transparent than earlier works but contains repetitive chant-like passages for male chorus, clearly intended to evoke the aura of ancient Greece.

Even if the complexity of Xenakis's work renders the specific technical details of his compositional methods accessible only to those with extensive mathematical background, the impact of his music is, for many, instantaneous. Indeed, Xenakis has claimed that the mathematical theorems he uses are in fact "universal laws" and are thus, when translated into musical terms, readily comprehensible to anyone who listens sympathetically.

CORRESPONDING DEVELOPMENTS IN AMERICAN MUSIC

Although developed independently of their European counterparts, the compositional styles of two important American composers, Elliott Carter and Ralph Shapey, incorporate similar ways of thinking about form and texture. Carter (b. 1908) studied for several years with Nadia Boulanger during the 1930s, and his earlier compositions, consistent with Boulanger's teaching and the prevailing temper of French and American music at the time, were neo-classical, even "populist" in nature. Yet certain works, such as the Symphony No. 1 (1942), revealed a degree of rhythmic and formal complexity, plus a concern for developmental processes, that became increasingly important to Carter, and ultimately led him away from what he came to consider the "static repetitiveness" and "squared-off articulation" of neo-classicism.

During the middle 1940s Carter became interested in fashioning a more continuous, unbroken rhythmic flow, focusing especially on processes of gradual change and evolution. This led him to devise a new rhythmic technique called "metrical modulation," first employed in the

Elliott Carter (right) conversing with Igor Stravinsky at an art gallery in late 1961.

Cello Sonata of 1948. The term (not coined by Carter) is actually a misnomer, since what is changed is not meter but tempo; the basic pulse is altered by taking some fractional subdivision (or multiple) of its total value and treating that as a new pulse of different value (faster or slower, respectively). The result is a proportional shift in rate of pulse—in other words, a change of tempo.

A passage from the opening section of the String Quartet No. 1 (1951) offers an illustration (Example XVIII-6). At the beginning of the excerpt the tempo is 𝅗𝅥 = 60 (or ♩ = 120). In m. 31, however, the triplet division of the original half note, previously established by the viola, becomes the "pivot" to the new tempo. Two of the viola's previous quarter-note triplets are now reinterpreted as a new half-note beat, producing an acceleration of the half-note pulse by one-third of the original value, so that it now equals 90 instead of 60. (This change is only fully carried out notationally in m. 32, when the tempo shift becomes explicit in the accelerated chords of the second violin.) In this instance the result is essentially the same as a hemiola, but Carter normally uses the technique to produce considerably more complex proportional relationships.

Carter's development took him increasingly in the direction of formal complexity and ambiguity, to a concern for "motion, change, progression in which literal or mechanical repetition finds little place." The technique of metrical modulation formed one aspect of a new compositional conception wherein all elements—tempo, rhythm, pitch structure, and even form itself—exist in a state of perpetual flux. Musical time is viewed as multilayered, as projecting simultaneous contrasts of character, with each textural component as individualized as possible. Thus, in Example XVIII-6 each instrument has not only its own char-

Example XVIII-6: CARTER, String Quartet No. 1, mm. 27–32

acteristic music but moves at its own rate of speed within the prevailing common meter. (All four have relatively consistent rhythmic patterns of their own, although the first violin breaks its pattern in m. 30.)

The First Quartet was the earliest work in which Carter explored these ideas extensively. The essentially tonal-diatonic style of the neo-classical works gave way to a flexible chromaticism, based on recurring sets of intervals (or "chords," as Carter prefers to call them). Most innovative, however, were the formal characteristics ensuing from

Carter's ideas of rhythmic continuity and change, which called into question the very concept of a "movement" as a unified and self-contained musical statement with a prevailing tempo and character. Since tempos shift constantly in the Quartet, and the four instruments have such independent roles, each tends to define itself as a separate entity— i.e., as a "movement" of its own.

These ideas, only partially realized in the First Quartet, eventually led Carter to completely abandon the concept of movements as separate, self-contained units, treating them rather as parts of an ongoing temporal structure in which different "movements" appear simultaneously, in which one "movement" may be suddenly interrupted—in midstream, as it were—and replaced by another, only to be resumed again later. The multidimensional formal structures Carter developed for this purpose bear certain resemblances to Stravinsky's crosscutting forms, but are considerably more dynamic in character.

This intensely individualized conception of music, with each instrument or instrumental group projecting its own unique "behavior pattern" (to use the composer's term), has led Carter to conceive form in largely dramatic terms: as a "large, unified musical action," an "auditory scenario for performers to act out on their instruments, dramatizing the players as individual participants in the ensemble." Typically, the larger shape is controlled by some overall process of transformation, frequently circular in nature, ultimately leading back to a musical condition similar to the one with which it began. But the logic depends more upon general rhythmic, textural, and dynamic matters—interval structure, instrumentation, register, mode of articulation, etc.—than upon specific thematic or motivic content. The return of a "behavior pattern" or "character continuity" (another Carter term) is not a matter of thematic recall, but a more generalized recurrence.

In Carter's String Quartet No. 3 (1971) these ideas appear in fully realized form. The ensemble is divided into two duos, spatially separated from each other as much as is practically possible. One duo has four different movements, the other six; but all movements are discontinuous. Each of the first duo's four movements is broken up into three separated segments, while the second duo's first five are broken up into two, its sixth into three segments, yielding for each duo a sequence of, respectively, twelve and thirteen interlocking sections. These are so arranged that each of the first duo's four movements is at some point heard in combination with each of the second duo's six. Since transitions between segments are usually gradual, the contrasting sections appear to grow out of one another in an unbroken evolution.

In one combination (Example XVIII-7) the upper duo (violin and viola) is playing its Grazioso movement, which contains sustained and lyrical music with fairly regular rhythmic patterns, performed *cantando* ("singing"). The lower duo's Leggerissimo features faster and more

Example XVIII-7: CARTER, String Quartet No. 3, m. 44

varied rhythmic values, frequent repetitions, and light, *spiccato* bowing (bounced off the strings). The two movements are also differentiated by interval content (the upper one emphasizes minor sevenths, the lower perfect fourths), dynamic levels, and tempo and meter (coordinated, however, so that measures correspond in length). In addition, the upper duo is instructed to play in strict tempo throughout, while the lower one plays more freely (quasi rubato).

Carter's mature scores, including the Third Quartet, Double Concerto for Harpsichord, Piano, and Two Chamber Orchestras (1961), Concerto for Orchestra (1969), and A Symphony of Three Orchestras (1977), share with the texturally oriented music of European composers of the 1950s and 1960s a common preference for massive sonorities and combinations of multiple textural layers, as well as a de-emphasis of specific thematic or motivic content in favor of overall sonic effect. Yet in Carter the individual event, never entirely subjugated to the whole, is stamped with its own special character. Nor is Carter interested in creating unusual sounds for their own sake (he rarely calls for special performance techniques of any kind). His concern, he once remarked, is for "the way each moment is being led up to and led away from." There is no question, then, of "open form"; the specific placement of each event is critical. Finally, Carter has never abandoned strictly measured rhythmic structures producing perceptible pulses, but has rather expanded the concept of pulse to encompass an entire system of proportional tempo relationships.

After concentrating for many years on instrumental music, Carter returned to vocal composition in three settings of poems by contemporary American poets, accompanied by chamber ensembles: *A Mirror on Which to Dwell* (1975), on poems by Elizabeth Bishop; *Syringa* (1978), which combines (simultaneously) a poem by John Ashbery with fragments from Greek literature; and *In Sleep, in Thunder* (1982), on poems by Robert Lowell. Here, simplifying his procedures somewhat, Carter reduced the density of the textural combinations so that voice and words assumed the dominant role. This tendency to greater transparency has also prevailed in more recent instrumental works, such as the String Quartet No. 4 (1986) and Oboe Concerto (1988), leading some to see a return to the more neo-classical orientation of the composer's youth.

Yet Carter's recent compositions retain his general stylistic focus. Indeed, the line of development he has traced since the late 1940s has been unusually direct, with each new work seeming to draw upon implications present but not yet fully realized in the preceding one. During a period characterized by stylistic uncertainty and change, Carter has followed a remarkably consistent course, rooted in the precedent of such earlier figures as Stravinsky, Ives, and Berg. In this sense he ranks among the principal "traditionalists" of later twentieth-century music.

Ralph Shapey (b. 1921) is a fiercely independent composer who has pursued his own compositional interests unconcerned with schools and fashions. In this respect he recalls Ives, although Shapey, unlike his predecessor, has lived his entire life as a professional musician, active as a composer, teacher, and conductor specializing in contemporary music. That his music was so long ignored, bringing him little public or professional recognition except from a small group of dedicated admirers, produced a certain degree of isolation in Shapey. (Between 1969 and 1976 he even refused to allow public performances of his work, though he continued to compose actively.) Only since completing his fifth decade has Shapey received more general recognition, and he is now widely viewed as one of the most distinctive voices in contemporary American music.

Shapey studied composition with Stefan Wolpe (1902–72), a German-born composer who settled in New York during the late 1930s and had considerable influence on a number of younger Americans. Wolpe, himself a student of Webern, developed an individual approach to twelve-tone composition unlike that of any of the members of the Second Viennese School. From him Shapey acquired a lasting commitment to total chromaticism, including an unsystematic use of twelve-tone procedures. Another influence was Varèse, whom Shapey knew in the 1950s in New York, although here too the common ground was more esthetic—especially a love of the concrete, "physical" qualities of sound—than specifically technical.

A recent photograph of composer Ralph Shapey in his role as a conductor specializing in new music.

Shapey has described his music—in notably Varèsian terms—as consisting of "aggregate sounds structured into concrete sculptured forms." As this suggests, he is not so much concerned with the development and transformation of musical materials as with the different possibilities of combining them. He tends to treat his musical ideas as fixed sonic objects, as concrete entities that can be set off against others in changing configurations. What changes is not so much the materials themselves as the "environments" in which they appear: "I think about setting masses against other masses. I'm interested in the relationships between things. Even if an object doesn't change, if you place that object against some other object, there is, I believe, a kind of subtle change."[5]

Shapey thus stresses the static nature of his work, its evocation of what he calls a "space of timelessness." Yet his music is also fundamentally dramatic. By setting opposed forces in confrontation, he creates extreme formal tensions and evokes strong emotional responses. The opening (Example XVIII-8) of the String Quartet No. 6 (1963), a one-movement composition in which the "spatial" aspect of Shapey's approach is strongly present, illustrates this clearly. These "measures" (bar lines are only intended to supply convenient divisions for the eye, not metrical articulations) contain most of the quartet's basic material, developed according to Shapey's "combinational" method. Notable are the extreme independence of the four separate voices and the extraordinary complexity of the rhythmic relationships employed to achieve this independence. Also typical is the recurrence, in the three upper parts, of relatively fixed musical units, which (despite some internal variation) consistently reappear in shifting textural combinations.

5.   Quoted in John Rockwell, *All American Music* (New York, 1983), p. 62.

Example XVIII-8: SHAPEY, String Quartet No. 6, opening

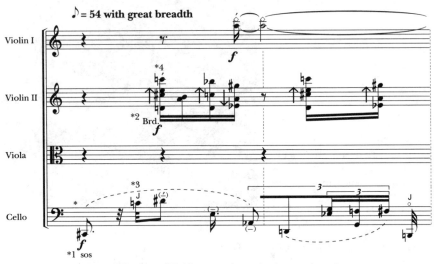

* Lower "C" string to "B". All notes on lowered string sound as written.

*1 sos = sostenuto
*2 Brd = broad
*3 ♩ = upbeat
*4 ′ = downbeat
*5 NE = non emotional—in a straight matter of fact manner (like steps) using enough vibration for a good sound.
*6 Brll. = brilliant
Barlines are only for the convenience of eye division (as small units) not to be interpreted under any of the existing bar line conepts.

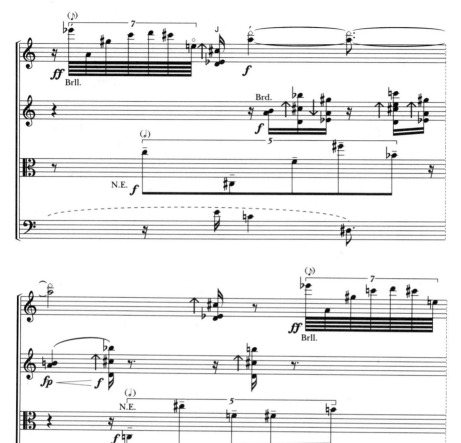

The entire quartet is constructed from staggered, cyclic returns of these materials, punctuated by occasional insertions of new gestures. The seemingly fixed elements are, however, quite flexible, constantly varied through pitch exchanges, permutations, interpolations, etc., while their contour, rhythm, and overall gestural characteristics remain sufficiently constant to assure recognition. The cello plays a special role. It too repeats material constantly, but in much larger cycles (Example XVIII-8 includes only the first part of the basic cello unit), and its larger repetitions (also featuring occasional interruptions) are largely responsible for determining the larger formal divisions. As a consequence, the music has something of the formal quality of a free passacaglia.

With reference to his general compositional outlook, Shapey once commented that he is concerned with "the concept of 'it is' rather than the traditional 'it becomes.' " This defines a basic difference with Carter: while the two composers share significant characteristics (extreme rhythmic complexity, maximum differentiation of individual parts), Carter's desire to transform his materials constantly, to turn them into something different, is antithetical to Shapey's wish to preserve the basic integrity of his musical units. Shapey allows his ideas to acquire a "history" mainly through their placement in altering contexts.

Shapey's large catalogue includes seven string quartets and a sizable body of chamber and orchestral music. In recent years he has been most closely associated with vocal music, and several of his most important works are extended settings for solo voice with accompanying ensembles of various sizes, from single instrument to full orchestra. The earlier *Incantations* (1961) was followed by a succession of such pieces, among them *Praise* (1971, with chorus), *Songs of Eos* (1975), *The Covenant* (1977), and *Song of Songs* (1980), the last an evening-long work in three parts for soprano, bass, large chamber ensemble, and tape. Here the underlying lyricism and extremely personal character of Shapey's music, its ritualistic and almost ecstatic expressivity, is perhaps most fully encountered.

The stylistic developments traced in the present chapter, encountered in composers of such diverse geographical backgrounds and compositional orientations, marked an important turn in post–World War II music. Though partly initiated by figures who had been central in the establishment of integral serialism, these developments reflected a withdrawal from the systematic rigors and detached rationalism of that approach. Renewed interest in the sensual aspects of sound, in richly detailed textures, coloristic nuances, and dramatic effects, gave evidence of a wish to move beyond the severely restricted range of musical possibilities available within the serial framework. The tendencies discussed here, widely evident by the late 1950s, were an early indication of serialism's loosening hold on the younger generation, from which would soon emerge a much more open musical atmosphere, encouraging experimentation with a broad spectrum of new compositional approaches. To this "second" phase of postwar music we now turn.

CHAPTER XIX

The New Pluralism

THE POST-SERIAL AGE

Music written since the 1960s is often referred to as "post-serial"—a usage that may seem to ascribe to serialism a disproportionate importance, considering the limited span of time during which it dominated contemporary Western composition. But the designation is apt because of the special historical position serialism occupied, as—for now and probably for some time to come—the last compositional development shared by enough composers of different stylistic persuasions and nationalities to have represented a sort of common, if not "universal," musical language. Like neo-classicism, it was international in scope and assumed, at least briefly, an almost official, even institutional character.

By contrast, indeterminacy, in the radical form practiced by John Cage during the years of serialism's reign, never enjoyed such status; in the early 1950s it was widely viewed as, at best, a marginal movement. Ironically, however, Cage himself can be seen as the first—and most influential—post-serialist (if we use the term purely conceptually rather than chronologically), for he too had a serial phase, first in the twelve-tone pieces of his student years and then in the mathematically determined "time-proportion" compositions of the 1940s. In passing beyond such consciously calculated procedures, Cage was the first to enter a new and largely uncharted area of musical experience, where literally anything seemed permissible and where, as a consequence, the composer faced an apparently unrestricted range of choices. Cage opted for indeterminacy, but of course there was no "necessity" in his decision. In fact, perhaps Cage's most far-reaching perception in the 1950s was his assumption that there were no longer any shared guidelines, that each composer had to make entirely personal—and thus essentially "arbitrary"—choices.

By 1960 most of the younger figures formerly committed to either serialism or indeterminacy had begun to view both approaches as simply the two extremes of a virtually unlimited range of compositional options, all equally available for exploration. The 1960s became a time of extraordinary experimentation in music, as also in the other arts, and were characterized by an explosion of new activity. The new developments were not clearly focused, nor did they point in any clear direction. On the contrary, the seemingly countless new compositional approaches appeared, at least on the surface, to have very little to do with one another.

This pluralism faithfully mirrored the changing social and political conditions of the time. As was briefly discussed in Chapter XV, the 1960s witnessed a strong reaction throughout most of the Western world against "the establishment"—against centralized governments and other forms of externally imposed authority. "Alternative life-styles" were cultivated. "High art"—regarded as the cultural equivalent of a centralized and repressive political force—was rejected in favor of a greatly expanded and more loosely related range of cultural choices. Wishing to break away from external restrictions (such as those imposed by serialism), many composers sought more personal and idiosyncratic forms of expression. If serialism was a final (and, some would say, desperate) attempt to impose centralized conventions on the musical community, post-serialism disdained all aspiration to universality, and often to coherence as well.

Technically considered, post-serial music represented an outgrowth of the destructive effect of serialism and indeterminacy on traditional compositional categories, an effect that gave rise to a musical revolution perhaps even more profound than the earlier one associated with the collapse of tonality. Fundamental questions were raised concerning the future of music: was the dissolution of conventional form to be welcomed as clearing the way for entirely new musical directions, or should it be taken as an indication that "progressive" musical developments this time had gone too far, leaving the composer with no alternative but to return to more traditional approaches?

The history of music since the late 1950s can be fruitfully viewed in terms of this question, although to date no clear consensus has emerged about its answer. The pendulum that now seems to be swinging toward more traditional values was during the 1960s moving just as clearly toward experimentation, even anarchy. Moreover, individual composers have responded variously to the question during different stages of their development, even within different parts of a single composition.

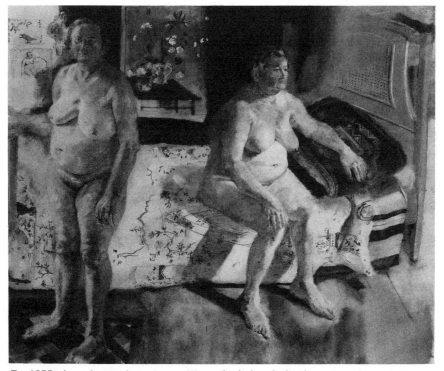

By 1955, American painter Larry Rivers had already broken away from the
nonrepresentational restrictions of abstract expressionism in his *Double Portrait
of Berdie,* a literal, explicit, and non-idealized nude study. (Collection of The
Whitney Museum of American Art. Anonymous gift.)

Yet whatever may be the future's answer, it is evident that the combined agencies of serialism and indeterminacy brought Western music
to a fundamental turning point, making anything and everything possible,
rendering all compositional choices problematic.

As important as the technical repercussions of serialism and indeterminacy was a new esthetic orientation to which both contributed. Indeterminacy, in particular, called into serious question the traditional
conception of a musical work as a fixed and objective entity, in some
sense separate from and independent of any given performance, instead
viewing a work as a continuous, ongoing process. Lacking a fixed set
of pitch and durational relationships realizable in performance only "after
the fact," an indeterminate composition often differed radically from
one performance to the next.

Composers began thinking of their work as a process of encouraging
certain kinds of activity rather than of creating immutable objects
(compositions). They took their music "out into the streets," linking it
to specific occasions and physical environments. The traditional con-

cept of the autonomous artwork, intended for a passive audience seated in a hushed auditorium, was seriously compromised, as was the notion of the "masterpiece," the work possessing a value that transcended the particular conditions of its creation and performance. Art conceived in terms of unique and momentary experiences no longer aspired to immortality.

The wide-open atmosphere of post-serialism's earlier stages encouraged the investigation of new modes of musical experience and innovative approaches to composition. This provided many composers with a surge of fresh creative energy, carrying them into previously unexplored regions of creative experimentation. In this and the next three chapters we will consider some of these developments and the composers most actively involved with them.

QUOTATION AND COLLAGE

Among the earliest symptoms of a significant shift in compositional outlook was the widespread quotation of traditional tonal music in new scores. Quotation in itself was not unknown to Western music; in addition to such earlier forms as Renaissance parody technique, direct quotation had formed a persistent, if relatively rare, practice throughout the nineteenth and earlier twentieth centuries, reflecting the dramatic growth of historical consciousness during this period. Because nineteenth-century quotations almost always shared a general tonal idiom with their new contexts, they tended to be carefully integrated. In the first half of the twentieth century, with the advent of nontriadic harmony and atonality, direct quotations of tonal music appeared less frequently, although when they did—as, for example, in Berg—great pains were still normally taken to attune them through compositional correspondences with their surroundings.

The reference to the opening of the *Tristan* Prelude in Berg's *Lyric Suite* passes almost unnoticed, so seamlessly is it embedded in its environment. Even the Bach chorale harmonization near the end of the same composer's Violin Concerto is carefully prepared by the equivalence of its opening four notes with the last four notes of the work's basic series, as also by the persistent allusions to triadic harmony. Stravinsky's "recompositions" of earlier music (*Pulcinella* and *The Fairy's Kiss*) achieve a similar congruence from the opposite direction: the "recycled" tonal materials are transformed to fit consistently within their new stylistic frameworks. Perhaps the only real exception is Charles Ives, whose blatant, undisguised employment of traditional tonal music (like many other features of his work) strikingly anticipates the music of the post-serial age.

The most distinctive new feature of musical quotations in the 1960s is that they are normally treated as "foreign objects"—as things drawn from other times and places, with stylistic conventions anachronous to their immediate contexts. Tonal music is typically set off against nontonal music, or against other, conflicting tonal music. More often than not, the quoted music is itself transformed through various processes of distortion. A second difference is that quoted material is no longer confined to an isolated moment and a dramatic purpose, but often appears consistently throughout a composition—some works even consist entirely of quotations and distortions thereof. Finally, the range of borrowings is unprecedented. Not only is material chosen from radically divergent sources—Gregorian chant, Renaissance polyphony, Baroque instrumental figuration, late nineteenth-century chromaticism, and so on—but these sources are freely joined in an eclectic mix; the most unlikely partners are intimately juxtaposed.

A common feature of these new approaches to quotation is a conscious effort to "distance" the borrowed material through distortions and juxtapositions. Though the musical past is evoked, it is also placed in unfamiliar surroundings, where it can be transformed into something new and strange, reinterpreted and revitalized through confrontation with the present. Indeed, the expressive effect of the music depends largely upon tensions produced by the contradictions between the quoted material and the manner of its employment.

The first composer since Ives to deal extensively with quotation was Bernd Alois Zimmermann (1918–70), a German who was already experimenting with borrowed materials in the early 1950s. By the time he completed his opera *Die Soldaten* (*The Soldiers,* 1960; revised version, 1964), Zimmermann had brought to fruition a complex method of combining materials from different stylistic periods and his "own" music (itself serial in origin) into a multileveled, collagelike structure. Zimmermann employed such "collages"—simultaneous strands of diverse music—to express temporal relativity. Discarding the traditional Western notion of time (and thus the work of art as well) as a closed system with definite beginning, middle, and end, he presented past, present, and future as simultaneously superimposed and inseparably interconnected. Corresponding to the fragmentary and disconnected nature of contemporary experience, time became pluralistic.

Overall, the four acts and fifteen scenes of *Die Soldaten* are organized through serial relationships. As in Berg's *Lulu,* a principal row forms the basis for a number of derived rows with specific dramatic functions. Quoted material (a Bach fugue, Gregorian chant, conventional jazz figures) occurs in only three of the scenes, always combined with other musical layers of Zimmermann's own invention. The quotations are

A scene the Stuttgart Opera production of Alois Zimmermann's *Die Soldaten*. The multi-dimensional staging mirrors the composer's multi-dimensional conception of musical time.

used to achieve what the composer termed "rotated time," a sudden opening up of the musical and dramatic action to the past and to distant musical cultures. The opera's stylistic plurality is mirrored in numerous other features: multiple sound sources (a pit orchestra, a percussion-dominated stage ensemble that shifts position with the action, a jazz group, and an electronic tape containing "concrete" sounds); an extensive range of vocal sounds, from spoken language through *Sprechstimme* and recitative to normal singing; and simultaneous presentation of several independent actions on multiple stage levels. The dissolution of the classical unity of time, place, and action permeates all aspects of the work.

The fact that despite its quotations, the opera is fundamentally serial in conception is revealing. Quotation technique and serialism may seem far removed from each other, yet they share at least one essential attribute: in both, the composer begins the compositional process with "pre-formed" material already at hand and manipulates it through various combinational and permutational methods. (Most of the earliest composers to turn to quotation in the 1960s had serial origins.) The connection is especially clear in Zimmermann's orchestral work *Musique pour les soupers du roi Ubu* (Music for the Repasts of King Ubu, 1966), which consists *entirely* of a carefully controlled assemblage of quotations, producing a complex mosaic "pieced together" through the composer's combinational skills.

Another example is the third movement of Luciano Berio's Sinfonia for eight solo voices and orchestra (1968), through virtually the whole of which runs the Scherzo of Mahler's Symphony No. 2. While largely responsible for determining form and temporal continuity, the Mahler supplies only one layer (albeit the main one) of a stratified structure, functioning as a sort of "carrier" for additional musical materials, most of them also quotations. Ranging from Monteverdi to Stockhausen, these additional quotations are fragmentary in nature and are joined together like the separate pieces of a puzzle. Berio has described the Mahler music as a "river, going through a constantly changing landscape, sometimes going underground and emerging in another, altogether different place, sometimes very evident in its journey, sometimes disappearing completely, present either as a fully recognizable form or as small details lost in the surrounding host of musical presences."[1] The movement also incorporates a largely spoken text, itself made up mainly of quotations (especially from Samuel Beckett's novel *The Unnameable*), yet another layer in a multidimensional whole whose various components impinge upon one another in a varied exchange of references and mutual commentaries.

A somewhat different approach was taken by the German-born American Lukas Foss (b. 1922) in his *Baroque Variations* for orchestra (1967). Each of the three movements is based exclusively on a single tonal composition. The second movement, for example, is drawn wholly from a movement of a Handel concerto grosso, heard in its entirety but in radically distorted form. Foss has said that he wished to "compose holes" in the original, with portions of it "submerging into inaudibility" so that a kind of "perforated" Handel would be heard, the fragmented remains of the original. Although the fragments are often played simultaneously, in different orchestral groups, or in different keys at different speeds, the original remains consistently recognizable. The result is curiously expressive, as if the tonal system itself were presented in a state of dissolution, coming apart before the listener's very ears.

Other works using quoted material extensively include Stockhausen's electronic *Hymnen* (Hymns, 1967), much of which is based on recorded versions of national anthems from all over the world; Henri Pousseur's opera *Votre Faust* (Your Faust, 1967), which mixes numerous musical references in an eclectic stylistic jumble; and Mauricio Kagel's *Ludwig van* (1970), derived entirely from music by Beethoven. More commonly, however, composers use quotations more sparingly. George Crumb has used borrowed material extensively since the 1960s, mainly to mark occasional points of dramatic emphasis, as in the fragmentary appearance of the Bach-attributed *Bist du bei mir,* played on a toy piano, in his *Ancient Voices of Children* (1970). Similarly, George Rochberg (b. 1918), in *Music for the Magic Theater* (1965), integrates pre-existing material from several sources, mainly a Mahler symphony and a Mozart divertimento, into a larger fabric shaped by his own music. In *Nach Bach*

1.   Quoted in the liner note for the recording on Columbia MS 7268.

(1964) Rochberg quotes fragments of Bach's E-minor Partita, filtering them in and out so that they appear as if through occasional "windows" in his score.

An excerpt from *Nach Bach* (Example XIX-1) shows how Rochberg mediates between the Bach fragments and his own music to create the impression that the latter grows directly out of the textural, intervallic, and expressive features of the former. First, a passage from the Air of the Partita is interrupted in mid-phrase by a brief pause. When it resumes, the right-hand figuration maintains the pattern established by the Bach passage, but expanding the upward leap from a sixth to a minor seventh. At the same time, the left hand slows down drastically, also expanding a rising sixth (imitating the right-hand sixths) to a seventh (in this case a major seventh). Finally, after another brief pause, the music moves away from the Bach work entirely in a rhythmically free and dissonant cadenza-like segment. Yet this too grows logically out of the preceding. Not only does the higher dissonance level of the second segment prepare for the third, but explicit linear and intervallic connections are made: e.g., the right hand's F#-Ab (beginning the third segment) sequentially carries the falling minor seventh that ended the preceding one (G-A) down an additional half step, and the left hand's simultaneous Eb-(C)-D similarly carries down its previous E-D#.

Since traditional tonal music stands out so clearly within a twentieth-

Example XIX-1: ROCHBERG, *Nach Bach,* excerpt

century compositional framework, it is also possible to allude to it without resorting to actual quotation, through the use of triads, traditional harmonic progressions, and the like. In Rochberg's String Quartet No. 3 (1972) extensive tonal sections evoking the styles of Beethoven and Mahler are set off against sections of more contemporary, nontriadic music—but all the music is Rochberg's own.

A somewhat special case is the English composer Peter Maxwell Davies (b. 1934), almost all of whose works have been based in some way on borrowed material, especially pre-Baroque music. *Alma redemptoris mater* for wind sextet (1957), one of Davies' earliest acknowledged compositions, is grounded on a plainchant and makes almost "programmatic" use of common late-medieval devices such as canon and isorhythm. Yet rather than attempting to evoke directly the character of pre-Baroque music, Davies relies on it to supply a sort of structural framework for his own music. The works of the immediately following years adhere to this practice: the two orchestral Fantasias (1962, 1964) based on music by John Taverner, the String Quartet (1961) based on Monteverdi, and the *Shakespeare Music* for chamber ensemble (1964), based on Elizabethan virginal pieces.

During the middle 1960s, reflecting the wider tendencies discussed above, Davies began to parody earlier styles in a more explicit way, and to incorporate a much wider range of references, including such popular genres as Viennese operetta (*Revelation and Fall,* 1966) and Victorian hymns (*Vesalii icones,* 1969), as well as earlier art music (e.g., a thirteenth-century motet in *Antechrist,* 1967). Although Davies's more recent work again avoids overt historical references, he continues to use borrowed material as a structural basis—e.g., the ballet *Salome* (1978), largely founded on plainchant. For Davies, then, the overt parodies, allusions, and quotations of the later 1960s and early 1970s represent but one particular phase of a reliance on pre-existing material that has formed a consistent feature of his entire creative development.

Although quotational procedures have in general declined in importance since the 1970s, their historical significance was great, touching many of the period's composers and encompassing figures of such opposed esthetic outlooks as the relatively traditional Hans Werner Henze (b. 1926), into whose opera *Die Bassariden* (The Bassarids, 1965) is woven a variety of historical references; the eclectic Russian Alfred Schnittke (b. 1934), who has used styles and quotations from many different historical periods, both to "tweak" the listener and to "create a tragic quality" (the latter, according to the composer, because early music represents "a beautiful way of writing that has disappeared and will never come back");[2] and the experimentally oriented Cage, who used recorded

2.   Quoted in the *New York Times,* May 22, 1988, section 2, p. 23.

excerpts of pre-existing music in several pieces dating back to his *Credo in Us* (1942), often in order to counter the "false" aura of musical masterpieces from the past. Moreover, quotation had a significant impact on the general musical climate of the time, loosening up the essentially "abstract" and "exclusive" musical language of serialism, enriching it with historical references that were structurally and expressively ambivalent. The "return to tonality" characteristic of so much recent music (see Chapter XX) can also be viewed as in part an outgrowth of this reintroduction of earlier music.

The prevalence of quotation also reflected a significant change in historical perspective, suggesting a critical impasse in the dynamic, evolutionary history of Western music. Perhaps the long-established tendency toward increasing chromaticism and rhythmic complexity had reached a point of maximum saturation, beyond which further development along the same lines had become pointless. Again, the role of serialism had been central, for after so fundamental a technical and esthetic reorientation, what was the logical "next step" to be? With no clear future in sight, composers returned to the past.

JAZZ, ROCK, AND POPULAR INFLUENCES

Transformed from an essentially autonomous, self-contained entity to one susceptible to "foreign" insertions, the musical work became susceptible to a broad range of new stylistic infusions. Quotation, whether of specific works or general stylistic features, was not confined to Western art music but soon encompassed other types of music as well. As composers turned away from both serialism and indeterminacy, they searched elsewhere for new lines of development. One of the most fertile sources was found in the richly varied popular music of the day, especially in the various forms of jazz and rock that flourished in the 1960s.

Interaction between popular and concert music has formed an important thread in Western music history, and we have had occasion to note its continued presence in this century: the importance of popular music to Stravinsky, Satie, and Weill, and of jazz both to native-born American composers (virtually all of whom were touched by it to some extent, although not always consciously) and to such Europeans as Debussy, Stravinsky, Hindemith, and Ravel. More recently, the so-called "Third Stream" movement of the 1950s, which produced such works as the Concertino for Jazz Quartet and Orchestra (1959) by the American Gunther Schuller (b. 1925), represented a fully conscious attempt to fuse elements of jazz and concert music into a new unity.

Not only did these influences persist in a particularly strong form during the 1960s; more unusually, branches of concert music and jazz and popular music began moving in parallel directions, at times becoming virtually indistinguishable from one another. One of the earliest and closest parallels is that between the music of the "free jazz" movement, initiated by the saxophonist Ornette Coleman (b. 1930) in the late 1950s, and such 1960s free-improvisation groups as MEV and Stockhausen's "intuitive music" ensemble. In his recordings *Free Jazz* and *Cross Breeding* (1960–61) Coleman rejected the well-defined conventions of form, meter, and harmonic progression that had previously regulated jazz practice, producing unprecedentedly extended, freely evolving, and polyphonically conceived group excursions that had much in common with their "art music" analogues. Although Coleman, along with similarly oriented jazz musicians such as John Coltrane (1926–67), Cecil Taylor (b. 1933), and Albert Ayler (1936–70), arrived at this common ground independently of their nonjazz colleagues, all shared a desire to renounce what they considered the arbitrary restrictions of an outmoded tradition in favor of a less restricted form of improvisation, characterized by flights of musical fancy limited only by the imagination. In subsequent years numerous prominent jazz artists, including Anthony Braxton (b. 1945), Anthony Davis (b. 1951), and George Lewis (b. 1952), as well as collaborative organizations such as the Art Ensemble of Chicago and the Globe-Unity Orchestra, have continued in this direction, developing complex and extended forms of jazz that draw extensively upon the language of contemporary concert music.

The points of contact with rock were equally pronounced. In an influential 1967 article Luciano Berio expressed admiration for the progressive tendencies of such then-popular rock groups as the Beatles, especially for the "performance-oriented" quality of their work. From the other direction, the leading rock publication *Rolling Stone* published a lengthy and adulatory interview with Stockhausen in 1971, stressing those features of his work that progressive rock musicians found stimulating.

Developments in contemporary concert music directly influenced a number of rock figures of the time, perhaps most prominently Frank Zappa (b. 1940) of the group The Mothers of Invention (Zappa has also composed concert works, some of which have been conducted and recorded by Pierre Boulez). Groups such as the Beatles and the Who made records that, instead of stringing together separate songs, were conceived as cycles, linked by an encompassing framework. The structure of the music became much freer and more complex than had traditionally been the case in popular forms of music. Instruments not normally associated with rock music, especially strings, were introduced, and electronic synthesizers made possible a dramatic expansion of timbral possibilities, producing a sound much closer to that of contemporary concert music.

The reverse flow of influence, from popular music to concert music, was even stronger. American composers were especially taken with the possibilities of drawing upon vernacular, jazz, and popular idioms. Much of the music of Terry Riley (b. 1935), exemplified in his recording *Poppy Nogood's Phantom Band* (1970), closely approaches the character of pop music with its repetitive diatonic melodic patterns, and some of the shorter compositions of Philip Glass (b. 1935), long associated with amplified keyboard and wind ensembles (similar in constitution to some rock bands), have been released on pop record labels. In a recent symptomatic collaboration Glass and the rock composer David Byrne (b. 1952), of the group Talking Heads, both contributed music to Robert Wilson's theatrical production *The Civil Wars: A Tree Is Best Measured When It Is Down* (1983–84).

In some cases the boundaries between popular and concert music have become blurred beyond recognition. The composer Glenn Branca (b. 1948), who began as a rock musician but has since moved into the concert area, writes extended "symphonies" for large ensembles consisting mainly of electric guitars and percussion, amplified to ear-splitting dynamic levels in a manner highly reminiscent of rock. Another American fitting uneasily into either the jazz-pop or classical category is John Zorn (b. 1953), whose recent recording *Spillane* (1987) contains pieces that use the scratching turntables of rap and also a work scored for string quartet, entitled *Forbidden Fruit*.

The composer-violinist-vocalist Laurie Anderson (b. 1947), after achieving pop stardom (her single *O Superman,* released in 1981, was an international hit), now works on larger and less commercial projects such as the collaborative theater piece *Set and Reset,* in which she supplied the music for choreography by Trisha Brown and designs by the painter Robert Rauschenberg. Her mammoth mixed-media "song cycle" *United States* (1983) combines film, slides, props, lighting, electronically altered voice, stylized body gestures, violin playing, story telling, poetry, and bits of singing in a two-evening-long solo entertainment that is at once a pop-art collage and a serious commentary on modern technology and the pursuit of the American Dream.

A paramount aspect of the pop influence on Anderson is the predominantly performance-oriented quality of her work, which is conceived entirely in terms of her own idiosyncratic manner of singing, playing violin and keyboard instruments, acting, and moving. (It is difficult to imagine her concert work being performed by anyone else, as it would undergo fundamental alteration.) This characteristic, pervasive in much recent music, has given rise to the term "performance art," a designation that applies equally to such other "borderline" pop-concert figures as the singer Meredith Monk, to certain forms of recent music theater, and even to minimalist composers like Steve Reich and Philip Glass,

Mixed-media artist Laurie Anderson, whose face is magnified in this scene from her film, *Home of the Brave* (1986), is acompanied by two back-up singers and a saxophonist. (Photo © 1986 Talk Normal Productions, Inc.)

much of whose music grows directly out of their own special playing skills and those of the small performing groups with which they are closely associated.

Other composers have chosen to make more oblique references to popular music. In his theater piece *Underworld* (1965) Salvatore Martirano (b. 1927) openly employed clichés from commercial music and jazz, but altered their expressive impact through fragmentation and through juxtaposition with other types of material (including electronically generated sounds). Martirano's *Cocktail Music* for piano (1962) and *Ballad* for "amplified nite-club singer" (1966) follow a similar course. Peter Maxwell Davies has on occasion drawn upon a range of "light" music, from jazz to operetta, but within works whose extreme formal complexity and expressive character have little in common with the world of popular music.

One of the most ambitious attempts to fuse popular and concert elements is *Songs of Innocence and Experience* (1981), a three-hour song cycle to poems of William Blake, for nine soloists, chorus, and large orchestra (including jazz, rock, and pop musicians) by the American composer William Bolcom (b. 1938). Bolcom, whose roots encompass both popular and concert traditions, took some twenty-five years to complete the work, producing an extraordinary potpourri spanning not only his own entire stylistic and technical development but every imaginable type of borrowed music as well, from folk song to reggae to Bergian counterpoint. The work's essentially dramatic conception is underscored by the composer's wish that, when possible, special lighting effects and slide projections of etchings by Blake accompany the performance.

A particularly rich area for interactions between popular and art music has been the American musical. Composers such as Leonard Bernstein (b. 1918) and Stephen Sondheim (b. 1930) have extended the genre's technical and expressive spectrum. Sondheim's recent *Sweeney Todd* (1979), *Sunday in the Park with George* (1984), and *Into the Woods* (1987) are fully operatic in conception: a continuous musical argument replaces the traditional Broadway alternation of set musical numbers (the so-called show tunes) and spoken dialogue. Bernstein, in addition to more or less conventional musicals, has written two full-scale operas (the second a belated sequel to the first), *Trouble in Tahiti* (1952) and *A Quiet Place* (1983), which maintain close ties to the Broadway idiom despite their more ambitious format. Bernstein's *West Side Story* (1957), a musical based on Shakespeare's *Romeo and Juliet,* has enjoyed great commercial success, and its use of techniques associated with symphonic music (e.g., fugal counterpoint) in combination with Latin-American and jazz elements has been widely imitated. Another significant example of use of vernacular idioms within an operatic framework is the opera *X* (1986) by the jazz composer Anthony Davis, based on the life of the black militant leader Malcolm X.

ETHNIC SOURCES

Many different types of folk and ethnic music have played a significant role in recent composition, with quotations or allusions ranging from simple American Indian songs to the complex musical styles of highly developed Oriental cultures. Representative are the String Quartet No. 4 (1973) of Ben Johnston (b. 1926), a microtonal work based on the American spiritual *Amazing Grace,* and Luciano Berio's *Cries of London* for small a cappella vocal group (1974, revised 1976), using the words and mimicking the character of London street vendors' cries. In *Coro* (1977), an extended work for voices and instruments, Berio takes a different course, employing the "techniques and modes of diverse folk music" without direct allusion or quotation.

Like Berio, George Crumb has drawn for his quotations upon a broad range of ethnic sources, including those of India and the Far East, and has employed a variety of instruments from other musical traditions (banjo and sitar, among many others), in addition to special instrumental and vocal effects (e.g., singing into an open piano while the sustaining pedal is depressed) that produce exotic and atmospheric effects. Crumb's music is notable for its combination of formal simplicity and timbral complexity. A passage (Example XIX-2) from *Lux aeterna* (1971) is clearly intended to evoke the character of Indian music, not only by

Example XIX-2: CRUMB, *Lux aeterna,* excerpt

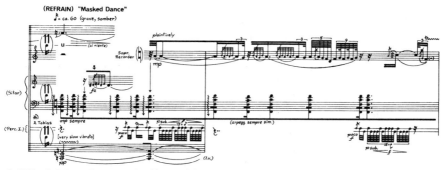

the use of Indian instruments (sitar and tablas), but also by the drone
effect of the reiterated open fifths (F–C). The combination of this static
harmony, the highly ornamented, modally colored melody in the soprano
recorder, and the brief, explosive percussion figure in the tablas that
seems to "summon" the recorder phrases produces a quasi-ritualistic
effect especially characteristic of the composer.

The use of foreign musical devices for exotic purposes is by no means
unprecedented in Western music. "Turkish" effects date back to the
eighteenth century, and "Eastern" scales and subjects attracted much
attention in the earlier twentieth century (e.g., in Debussy and Mahler).
But the current phase is distinguished (in both popular and concert music)
by a tendency to draw upon a very broad range of world idioms, often
in eclectic combinations. This interest in multiple cross-fertilization is
but one manifestation of the increasingly "global" nature of recent musical
developments. And whereas previous exotic influences on Western music
had for the most part only superficial effects (more on "color" than on
structure), now they have left their mark on the most basic compositional assumptions.

At one level, Cage's interest in Eastern philosophy played a critical
role in his decision to adopt indeterminacy. More generally, Oriental
conceptions of nondirectional time have inspired attempts to achieve a
more static and "motionless" type of music on the part of many contemporary Western composers, ranging from Cage through Glass to
Stockhausen. And Oriental features of a more particularly musical nature
have appeared in countless recent Western scores. The metallic sonorities and elaborately heterophonic textures in parts of Messiaen's orchestral piece *Chronochromie,* for example, and in Steve Reich's Music for
Mallet Instruments, Voices, and Organ clearly attest to a knowledge of
Balinese gamelan music. (In fact, Reich spent time in Bali studying the
native music.)

The most systematically rigorous attempt to exploit the music of other cultures has been Stockhausen's, in his vision of a "universal" art drawing on the entire gamut of the world's popular and art music. His electronic *Telemusik* (1966) is based on an astonishing range of prerecorded ethnic music (Japanese gagaku, Balinese, Chinese, Hungarian, even that of Peruvian Shipibos, to name only a few). These "found objects" are combined with originally composed electronic sounds, and are "intermodulated" with one another by electronically imposing a structural component from one source upon the music of another, thereby integrating the two into a combined "higher unity" (where the original sources are often distorted beyond recognition). Stockhausen refers to this technique as "metacollage," arguing that the electronic intermodulation allows the composer to go "beyond collage"—the mere juxtaposition of two or more unrelated entities—to achieve "total interpenetration."

The flow of influence has not been only from East to West. The Korean Isang Yun (b. 1917) and the Japanese Toshiro Mayuzumi (b. 1929) and Toru Takemitsu (b. 1930) have joined elements of their native musical cultures with those of Western music. The compositions of Takemitsu, who has written extensively for Western ensembles as well as for native instruments (sometimes combining the two), are delicate studies in textural shadings, almost always at a low dynamic level. While employing the full resources of Western chromaticism, Takemitsu uses subtle nuances of timbre and articulation to shape extremely ephemeral musical materials, whose quality of understatement and restraint recalls Japanese painting. As in Webern, the music's real life seems to be as much in the silences between the notes as in the notes themselves.

Takemitsu's words about the interaction of Eastern and Western elements in his own work could apply equally to many of his contemporaries:

> I would like to develop in two directions at once: as a Japanese with respect to tradition, and as a Westerner with respect to innovation. Deep down I would like to preserve both musical genres, each in its own legitimate form. But to take these fundamentally irreconcilable elements simply as a starting point for varied compositional uses is in my opinion no more than a first step. I do not want to remove the fruitful contradictions; on the contrary, I would like the two forces to struggle with one another. In that way I can avoid isolation from the tradition and yet also push toward the future in each new work.[3]

---

3.   Quoted in Ulrich Dibelius, *Moderne Musik II, 1965–1985* (Munich, 1988), p. 373.

CHAPTER XX

A Return to Simplicity: Minimalism and the New Tonality

The Oriental influences discussed briefly in the previous chapter have figured in another significant musical development since the 1960s: the tendency toward a simpler and more direct music, shorn of the technical complexities and emotional conflicts prominent in most forms of Western music. Like much Oriental art, this simpler music relies upon understatement rather than exaggeration, on veiled suggestion rather than overt expressivity, and it encourages a response of passive contemplation rather than active involvement. Technically, this entails static tonal structures, additive rhythms, textural consistency and transparency, and constant thematic repetition. Most typically, it finds expression in compositions that unfold slowly over extreme lengths of time, without dramatic incident or developmental goal.

A frequent attribute of pieces conceived in this spirit is their severely reduced "content," another indication of close ties with Eastern thought. John Cage's encounter with Zen Buddhism in the late 1940s not only influenced his turn toward indeterminacy, but reinforced his inclination to limit compositional materials to a minimum—a limitation that reached its most extreme form in *4'33"* (a work containing no musical "content" at all) but was also evident in many other works of Cage and his followers, notably Morton Feldman. And it eventually became a widespread stylistic trend.

MINIMALISM

During the 1960s a group of younger American composers began to explore the possibilities of working with drastically reduced means,

423

A minimalist work from the sculptor, Richard Serra, limited to a single strip of charcoal and synthetic polymer paint on paper. *Heir,* 1973. (9'6⅝" × 42¼". Collection, The Museum of Modern Art, New York. Gift of Mr. and Mrs. Samuel I. Newhouse, Jr. and the National Endowment for the Arts)

limiting themselves to the most basic musical elements. Although all were to some degree influenced by Cage, these composers, including La Monte Young, Terry Riley, Steve Reich, and Philip Glass, developed largely independently of him. Unconcerned with indeterminacy, they were, rather, interested in bringing music back to a more elemental foundation, freeing it from the accumulated weight of Western conventions, starting again from ground zero, as it were. The development they initiated, known as minimalism, has become one of the most influential forces in recent music.

In minimalism's earliest stages the leading figure was La Monte Young (b. 1935), who had matured in the heyday of serialism and, like most other young serialists of the day, was strongly drawn to the music of Webern. However, what seems to have appealed to him most in Webern was the sparseness of texture and the music's essentially static quality; as Young put it, "It uses the same information repeated over and over." For similar reasons, Young admired pre-Renaissance Western music, which "used stasis as a point of structure a little more the way Eastern musical systems have."[1]

Young's String Trio (1958), written while he was still a student in California, carried the principle of Webernian economy to unprecedented extremes. The work's opening five minutes contain only three notes, one for each of the three instruments, which enter slowly, one by one, and then sustain together for a very long period before slowly dropping out, again one by one. After a long silence a new event is finally introduced to begin the next section. Two years later Young had moved even further in this direction. *Composition 1960 No. 7* contained

1.   Quoted in Michael Nyman, *Experimental Music: Cage and Beyond* (London, 1974), p. 119.

only a single event, a perfect fifth (B–F♯) "to be held for a very long time," while *X for Henry Flynt,* from the same year, consisted simply of the uniform striking of an object (unspecified) every second or so over a very long period of time (its duration also unspecified). Through such unrelieved extensions or repetitions of a single sound, Young sought to make audible certain kinds of subtle acoustical events (including the minute variations resulting from human performance) that necessarily remain imperceptible when sounds appear as only passing instants within larger successions. (Such emphasis on the individual event can perhaps be said to represent the current stage—and perhaps the final one—of a development extending from Debussy through Varèse to Ligeti.)

In the light of later minimalist developments, Young's subsequent *Death Chant* (1961), for male chorus with optional carillon or bells, proved especially prophetic. The content is limited to a repeated diatonic melody sung in unison. At first only a two-note figure, the melody gradually expands through an additive process, acquiring one new note with each repetition. After the expansion encompasses five notes, the entire process is repeated (Example XX-1).

During the early 1960s Young began writing purely "conceptual" works consisting entirely of cryptic verbal instructions: e.g., "Build a fire in front of the audience," "Turn a butterfly (or any number of butterflies) loose in the performance area," "Draw a straight line and follow it." And he has since gone on to explore areas that have led him well beyond the boundaries of minimalism—e.g., improvisations within non-equal-tempered harmonic systems (*The Well-Tuned Piano*) and intensive study under the Indian singer Pran Nath, with whom he has performed on tambura. Yet Young's role in the initial stages of minimalism was critical, and the compositional approach of *Death Chant* supplied a foundation for the movement.

Example XX-1: LA MONTE YOUNG, *Death Chant,* excerpt

Slow (♩ = 54-68)

to be repeated many times or ad infinitum

DA DA   DA DA DI   DA DA DI DI   DA DA DI DI DI

+ = percussive slap on thigh

Closely associated with Young during the early 1960s when the two were fellow students in composition at the University of California in Berkeley, Terry Riley (b. 1935) may have been the first composer to focus almost exclusively on composing with constantly repeating melodic patterns. He began by experimenting with tape loops, which produced constant repetition of brief segments of recorded material at regular intervals. This was the basis of the tape compositions *I Can't Stop, No* and *Mescalin Mix* (both 1963) and, after adaptation of the idea to live performance, the instrumental works *Keyboard Studies* (1963) and *In C* (1964).

In C was a seminal work of the 1960s. Based entirely on fifty-three brief melodic figures derived from standard patterns of eighteenth-century tonal music, it was thus linked to the quotation music of the period. But Riley was more concerned with the structural possibilities of repeating and superimposing melodic units than with stylistic allusions. The fifty-three fragments, notated on a single page of score, are given to all the performers (the score is for "any number of melodic instruments"), who are instructed to play through the entire sequence in order. The surface rhythm is strictly dictated by regular eighth-note Cs, played without pause throughout in the upper register of the piano, but the other performers play their melodic fragments at their own rates of speed, repeating each one as many times as desired before passing on to the next. Since the players are also instructed to listen to one another so as not to stray too far apart, the execution depends upon a balance of precise notation, individual choice, and group cooperation.

Riley has likened his work to a "musical hall of mirrors," an apt description of *In C*. While one hears the same patterns over and over, they undergo constant transformation. Distortions are introduced both by conflicts between two or more simultaneous out-of-phase versions of the same pattern and by simultaneous juxtapositions of two or more different versions. "Modulations" also are heard, with different parts beginning and completing them at different times. Since the melodic figures vary significantly in length and contour, considerable overlapping in phrase structure also occurs. Despite all this, the work's final effect is of simplicity and directness. The melodic figures are diatonic; the only harmony is the result of chance combinations of simultaneously sounding melodic units; all rhythmic conflicts are ultimately resolved and coordinated by the piano's steadily pulsating Cs. *In C* offered a striking alternative to both the rigors of serialism and the randomness of indeterminacy, as well as to the sonic density of textural music. To many, it arrived on the new-music scene like a breath of fresh air.

Riley's earlier musical background had been primarily in jazz, and much of his compositional activity has centered on various forms of controlled improvisation, often involving elaborate tape-delay systems, which produce complex, echolike repetitions. Tape delay is used to virtuosic effect in the electronic keyboard composition *A Rainbow in the Curved Air* (1968), which—like much of the composer's work—is conceived much in the spirit of popular music. Following Young's example, Riley has also undertaken an extensive study of Indian music and has been actively involved in its performance.

Since the middle 1960s the two leading figures in the minimalist movement have been Steve Reich and Philip Glass. Reich (b. 1936) participated in the first performance and recording of Riley's *In C,* and, like Riley, developed a compositional approach heavily dependent upon repetition, first experimenting with multiple tape loops and then applying analogous procedures to instrumental composition. Yet Reich's evolution followed a rather different course. While working with tape loops he became fascinated with the possibilities of "phase shifting": i.e., playing two or more identical loops at slightly different speeds, so that the repetitions gradually move apart ("out of phase") from one another and eventually arrive again at synchronization. The two earliest compositions exploiting this technique, the tape pieces *It's Gonna Rain* (1965) and *Come Out* (1966), are based on prerecorded fragments of speech, while a third, *Melodica* (1966, also for tape), applies the idea to a simple melodic sequence.

Reich's earliest instrumental piece to incorporate phase shifting was *Piano Phase* for two pianos (1967). Its first section is based entirely upon a single melodic pattern of five different pitches. These are distributed in a rhythmic figure consisting of twelve successive sixteenth notes, alternating melodic sequences of three (left hand) and two (right hand) notes that, despite internal repetitions, produce changing pitch successions throughout. The opening line of the score (Example XX-2) presents this idea and indicates the first stage of its transformation.

One pianist begins alone, stating the pattern from four to eight times, after which (at No. 2 in the score) the second pianist "fades in," quickly reaching the same dynamic level as the first during his initial statement of the basic pattern. The two pianos then play together in unison from twelve to eighteen times, at which point the second pianist gradually begins to accelerate (indicated by dots in the score) while the first maintains the original tempo. Eventually the second piano again "locks in" with the first, but by then it has shifted one position out of phase: it

Example XX-2: REICH, *Piano Phase,* opening

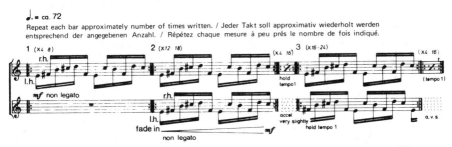

plays the second note of the basic unit as the first piano plays the first, etc. (at 3 in the score). The two pianos again maintain the same tempo, this time with sixteen to twenty-five repetitions, after which the second piano begins a second acceleration, eventually "locking in" again, but now *two* notes out of phase with the first (not shown in the example). This process continues throughout the first section, which ends when the second piano finally comes "all the way around" through twelve phase shifts and is once again in unison with the first. (The two subsequent sections of the piece are based on the same process, applied to increasingly shorter rhythmic patterns—respectively, eight and four sixteenth notes. The structure of the middle section is further complicated by the fact that the two pianos' melodic figures have different pitch contents.)

Piano Phase exemplifies several consistent stylistic features of Reich's music: brief diatonic melodic figures, steady rhythmic pulsation (almost always at a brisk pace), and percussive attacks played with machinelike precision. Structurally, the piece alternates segments of relative stability with passages in which gradual accelerations take place, producing minute variations in detail superimposed over ongoing patterns of constant repetition. Since the exterior surface remains largely unaffected by the variations, the listener must focus on the subtle "interior" modifications—otherwise the music simply seems to grind out mechanical replications of itself, spun out over extreme lengths of time.

During the late 1960s and early 1970s Reich explored different approaches to phase shifting in a series of works composed for his own performing ensemble, including *Violin Phase* (1967), *Phase Patterns* (1970), and *Clapping Music* (1972), the last a purely rhythmic piece for clapped hands. One work of this period, *Four Organs* (1970), exploited a somewhat different technique: the gradual lengthening, one by one, of the individual tones of an unchanging repeated chord.

During the 1970s Reich extended the phase approach of his earlier work with a new technique, in which melodic patterns are gradually built up by substituting attacks for rests—or, conversely, are broken down by substituting rests for attacks. *Drumming* (1971), an extended composition for unpitched percussion, was the first to use this new procedure. Its first section is based on the eight-note, twelve-beat pattern shown in Example XX-3. However, instead of beginning with a statement of the complete unit, Reich starts with only a single note from the pattern, replacing the others with additional rests. The remaining notes are then gradually substituted, one by one, for the rests, though not in linear order. Each time a new rhythmic pattern is generated by the addition of a new note, it is repeated a number of times before the next new note is added. The end of the third section is based on the reverse of this process: beginning with the full pattern, notes are gradually subtracted, one by one, until only one remains.

Example XX-3: REICH, *Drumming,* basic pattern of opening section

Reich continued to work with similar additive structures in *Six Pianos* and Music for Mallet Instruments, Voices, and Organ (both 1973). *Music for Eighteen Musicians* (1976) marked a turning point: it introduced a new technique involving pulsed durations determined by the breathing of the performers, and it employed a much larger ensemble than Reich had previously called for, including normal orchestral instruments (strings and woodwinds) in addition to the keyboard and percussion instruments of the earlier scores. Although *Music for Eighteen Musicians* preserved the constant surface rhythm and repetitive aspects of Reich's earlier music, it also reflected his increasing interest in richer textures and more full-bodied chordal sequences. The latter, though simple and repetitive in the extreme, give rise to slow-moving progressions with definite modal-tonal connotations. Indeed, an eleven-chord harmonic cycle is stated in complete form at the opening and close of the piece, providing a strong sense of tonal return, and individual chords from the cycle serve as structural pillars for each of the intervening sections. As Reich commented: "There is more harmonic movement in the first five minutes of *Music for Eighteen Musicians* than in any other complete work of mine to date."[2]

An enrichment of language through more differentiated polyphonic and harmonic textures has been characteristic of all Reich's more recent music. The concern for melodic construction and contrapuntal combination evident in the Octet (1979) and *Vermont Counterpoint* (1982) gives the music a much more traditional flavor than was present in his earlier work. And more recent large-scale conceptions such as *Tehillim* (1981), a setting of extracts from four Hebrew psalms scored for voices and small orchestra (later adapted for full orchestra), and *The Desert Music* (1982), for eight-part chorus with very large orchestra, project a "concert hall" image far removed from the small-scale orientation of the earlier works.

During the later 1960s Reich and Philip Glass (b. 1937) played in each other's performing ensembles. Glass's music resembles Reich's in many respects, similarly confining itself to a limited range of pitch material and emphasizing steady rhythmic pulsation and constant repetition, yet his compositional methods are on the whole different. Whereas Reich set out to achieve gradual transformations within an essentially repetitive melodic-rhythmic framework, Glass expanded basic melodic units through additive rhythmic processes, a technique he had developed while

2.   Quoted in liner notes for the recording, ECM 821–417–2.

studying Indian music in the mid-1960s. In Glass's early *Music in Fifths* (1969) an initial figure of eight notes is gradually expanded to encompass two hundred notes. In the initial stages (Example XX-4) the original eight-note unit is lengthened by additions to each of its two four-note subgroups, the first ascending in stepwise motion, the second descending. After the original unit is heard at No. 13, the first two notes of the first group are repeated at No. 14, and those of the second group at No. 15. Three-note repetitions are subsequently added at Nos. 16 and 17, followed by complete four-note repeats at Nos. 18 and 19.

Focusing in his earliest works almost exclusively on the melodic and rhythmic dimensions, and limiting texture to octave and unison doublings of a single line, Glass has undergone an evolution paralleling Reich's in which he gradually enriched his music's harmonic and textural components. *Music in Fifths* (1969) consisted of a single line doubled only in fifths, while *Music in Similar Motion* (1969) expanded slowly from a unison beginning to a rich web of chordal voices moving in similar motion. *Music in Changing Parts* (1970) introduced sustained notes for the first time and allowed for occasional exchanges of voices, thus breaking up the rigidly parallel voice-leading of the earlier scores. Finally, *Music in Twelve Parts* (1971–74) contained voices moving in contrary motion and exhibiting some degree of rhythmic independence. In addition, some sense of harmony began to emerge from a more extensive use of sustained voices. Although throughout most of the composition a single chord serves as the basis for each section, in the final two sections Glass fulfills the harmonic implications of the work's rich chordal

Example XX-4: GLASS, *Music in Fifths,* excerpt

The Phil Glass Ensemble performing at New York University, February 1971. Glass was a pioneer in the use of electronically amplified instruments in concert music. (Photo by Cynthia Guiraud)

sonorities by allowing different chords to link together so as to form simple harmonic progressions.

The title of Glass's next work, *Another Look at Harmony* (1975), explicitly acknowledged this turn, and all his more recent music has used simple harmonic progressions of an essentially traditional nature. Yet the manner in which he uses them remains consistent with his earlier approach: stripped of their normal contexts, they are obsessively repeated and are subjected to developmental techniques similar to those Glass used previously.

Since the middle 1970s Glass has concentrated largely on music for the stage. Three widely performed operas, *Einstein on the Beach* (1975), *Satyagraha* (1980), and *Akhnaten* (1983), have attracted considerable attention throughout the world. The first, an immensely long theater work conceived in collaboration with the dramatist-director Robert Wilson, is operatic in only a limited sense. A series of static, nonnarrative tableaux loosely focused around images related to the physicist Albert Einstein (a train, a trial, a spaceship), its music runs concurrently with, yet largely independently of, the dramatic action. And it is scored for Glass's own performing ensemble, consisting of amplified winds, keyboards, and voices, producing a sonic image unlike any heretofore associated with the traditional operatic stage. In addition, a solo violinist, dressed as Einstein, functions both as a musician and a character in the

A scene from the original production of *Einstein on the Beach*. Both the staging, by Robert Wilson (who also wrote the libretto), and the music, by Philip Glass, broke new ground for opera. (Photo Ken Howard)

opera, mediating between the other musicians and the stage performers, who are all actors and dancers rather than singers.

Glass's next opera, *Satyagraha,* was considerably more traditional in conception. Based on the life of the Indian political leader and pacifist Mahatma Gandhi, it is scored for a moderate-sized symphony orchestra (without brass)—a new stage in the composer's expansion of textural and timbral resources—and employs singers and music very much in the manner of traditional operatic conventions. Though the sound is noticeably different from his earlier music, especially the highly lyrical vocal writing (which almost brings Glass within the orbit of the "neo-romantic" movement), *Satyagraha* is in construction not fundamentally different from earlier Glass.

All Glass's operas have been accorded productions in opera houses of international importance, recordings, and enthusiastic public receptions. At a time of much speculation about opera's viability as a contemporary genre, Glass has played a significant role in revitalizing it, extending and reshaping its conventions to fit his own image of a more ceremonial, nonnarrative, and ritualistic music theater.

Although the music of Reich and Glass has little in common stylistically with non-Western music (beyond such general matters as length and a tendency to introduce change slowly and gradually), the rhythmic basis is in both cases derived primarily from non-Western sources. (Reich studied African and Balinese music in the United States and *in situ,* while Glass studied Indian music in Paris and traveled in India, North Africa, and central Asia.) Another shared influence is Cage, who in his early (pre-indeterminate) pieces, such as the *Book for Prepared Piano* and the String Quartet, similarly subjected a small number of sounds to establish a consistent and autonomous musical language, largely independent of traditional tonality. References to common-practice to strictly imposed rhythmic manipulations. And the idea of precisely specified processes of transformation also has a relationship with serialism. Yet Reich has stated that the musical processes used by both Cage and the serialists, since rarely audible, are of little use to him. "What I am interested in," he has written, "is a compositional process and a sounding music that are one and the same."[3]

Indeterminacy has interested neither Reich or Glass, nor has improvisation, except where its overall outcome is precisely determined. Yet the performance-oriented character of their music, most of which—at least in the early stages—was written to be played by the composers' own ensembles, is one of its essential features, a respect in which it resembles popular music, especially jazz and rock. (The relationship has been mutual: rock groups such as Tangerine Dream and Pink Floyd have often incorporated ideas borrowed from the minimalists.) This trait reflected a wish to break away from the specialized nature of modern Western concert music, in which composers turn out works exclusively for performance by others, usually without their own direct participation. Reich has stated: "In 1963 I first decided that despite my limitations as a performer I had to play in all my compositions. It seemed clear that a healthy musical situation would only result when the functions of composer and performer were united."[4]

Glass has described the kind of response required of listeners to fully appreciate his music as "one in which neither memory nor anticipation . . . has a place in sustaining . . . the musical experience. It is hoped that one would then be able to perceive the music as a 'presence,' freed of dramatic structure, a pure medium of sound."[5] This mode of listening, in which, ideally, one looses all sense of self (a mode more characteristically associated with non-Western than with Western music), has given rise to the designation "trance music." Other suggested terms have included "pulse music," "systemic music," and "process music," but "minimalism" remains the favored word, even though the resources called upon by Reich and Glass have in recent years become anything but minimal. Even pitch content, held to an absolute minimum in the earlier music, has expanded to the point where it makes little sense to speak of "reduced means." Yet the profound and continuing impact of the minimalist movement over the past two decades is undeniable.

---

3. *Writings about Music* (Halifax, Nova Scotia, 1974), p. 10.
4. Ibid., p. 45.
5. Quoted in Wem Martens, *American Minimal Music*, trans. J. Hautekiet (New York, 1983), p. 79.

THE REDISCOVERY OF TONALITY

A striking and highly characteristic attribute of twentieth-century music before the 1960s was the attempt, by virtually all its leading composers, conventions—especially functional harmonic progressions—were normally avoided. In its most extreme forms this gave rise to such proposals as the absolute proscription, in Schoenberg's early formulations of twelve-tone theory, of triads and octave doublings, on the grounds that such tonal allusions would be misleading, setting up expectations inconsistent with the inherent properties of the new compositional method, which should have its own "laws," quite distinct from and independent of those of tonality.

To be sure, Schoenberg later had second thoughts on this matter; deciding that such prohibitions had become unnecessary, he began employing triads and octave doublings in his own twelve-tone music, and even returned to tonal writing in several works of the late 1930s and 1940s. Many other leading figures eschewed hard-and-fast avoidance of tonal associations: e.g., Stravinsky, with his references to traditional formulas in his neo-classical works (treated, however, as conscious historical allusions), and Bartók, in his use of triads, especially in his later work. And of course a few conservative figures such as Rachmaninov and (in his later years) Strauss never discarded the basic principles of traditional composition at all. Yet the overall trend was to establish a self-contained, exclusively twentieth-century compositional language. Tonal allusions, when they occurred, were carefully integrated into a contemporary framework, avoiding any suggestion of a return to earlier stylistic conventions.

In the 1960s this attitude changed. The stripped-down diatonicism of the minimalists, the widespread use of tonal quotations, the allusions to common-practice style, to jazz, rock, and other forms of popular music—all combined to significantly erode the principle of a "pure" contemporary idiom. Thus "opened up" and made accessible to a much broader range of technical and expressive influences than it had previously known, new music became more "inclusive."

One telling outcome of this new eclecticism was that it encouraged reconsideration of the possibilities of traditional tonality. Unlike the tonal style of, say, Rachmaninov, this new tonality constituted a "return," a conscious repossession of a compositional manner that had temporarily been abandoned, rather than the extension of a tradition that, though outmoded in the eyes of many, persisted in the work of others. As the American composer David Del Tredici, who had worked in a dissonant, chromatic style throughout his earlier years, remarked: "For me tonality was virtually a daring discovery. I grew up in a climate in which, for a composer, only dissonance and atonality were acceptable. Right now, tonality is exciting for me. I think I invented it. In a sense,

In *Louis XIV* (1986), the American artist Jeff Koons returns to the techniques of representational art, but casts them in a material associated with the twentieth century, stainless steel. (The Gerald S. Elliott Collection of Contemporary Art, The Art Institute of Chicago)

I have. When you're a composer, you've got to feel that, on some level, you're doing something for the first time."[6]

After his uncompromisingly chromatic and atonal start, Del Tredici (b. 1937) began working in the late 1960s on what would become an extended series of Lewis Carroll settings, for which he adopted a more tonal and diatonic musical manner, often with direct references to popular music (emphasized by the use of pop-oriented instruments like electric guitar and saxophone). This manner reached an initial culmination in *Final Alice* (1976), an hour-long setting of the trial scene from Carroll's *Alice in Wonderland* for soprano and large orchestra, plus a "folk group" (two soprano saxophones, mandolin, banjo, and accordion) that functioned as a sort of concertino.

Final Alice's eclecticism is typical of much recent music. Although largely triadic and functional, the tonality sounds slightly askew, as if heard through filters supplied by a composer conversant with the entire gamut of twentieth-century musical style. The strongest influence is that of Richard Strauss, especially evident in the virtuoso handling of the large instrumental forces, but there are also references to popular song and even to atonality (used, however, as the composer remarked, "to suggest the eerie and frightening"). The work's essentially variational character, working over the same basic melodic elements in an obsessively repetitive fashion, recalls minimalism, although the opulence of Del Tredici's scoring and his preference for strong functional harmonic progressions produce a much more traditional flavor. Not simply a resurrection of late nineteenth-century style, however, *Final Alice* is a rethinking of the conventions of that style from the perspective of contemporary experience.

6.   Quoted in John Rockwell, *All American Music* (New York, 1983), p. 77.

Several distinct stages in the reincorporation of functional tonality can be traced in the music of the American George Rochberg, whom we considered briefly in the previous chapter. During the 1950s and early 1960s Rochberg wrote in a serial idiom of increasing rhythmic and textural complexity. Eventually bothered by what he came to consider the "extremely narrow confines" of total chromaticism, he began introducing quotations of tonal music into his scores (*Music for the Magic Theater* for fifteen instruments, 1965; *Nach Bach* for harpsichord or piano, 1966). These materials had a dramatic effect upon the subsequent evolution of Rochberg's musical language.

The String Quartet No. 3 (1972) eschewed actual quotation in favor of an eclectic style based upon several distinct historical sources, although all the music was in fact the composer's own creation. The most "radical" of the quartet's five movements was the third, a set of variations written throughout in a manner reminiscent of Beethoven. In the last movement extended tonal episodes evoke Mahler, but here the "foreign" allusions are set off against sections conceived in a more contemporary idiom. Stylistic discrepancies are thus purposely exploited to achieve a special sort of expressive tension. In later works, however, such as the String Quartets Nos. 4–6 (1977–78) and the opera *The Confidence Man* (1982), Rochberg has attempted to integrate traditional tonal elements as unexceptional components of a more "universal" musical language, capable of accommodating both free chromaticism and strict diatonicism, unadorned triads and dissonant harmonic complexes.

In recent years traditional tonality has drawn many composers. Such older figures as Penderecki and Henze have in a sense "returned to"— or at least "toward"—tonality after working exclusively in nontonal styles. Younger ones, including the German Wolfgang Rihm (b. 1952), the Englishman Robin Holloway (b. 1943), and the American John Adams (b. 1947), who came to maturity since the widespread reintroduction of tonality, have relied upon a partially tonal language throughout their careers. Indeed, the trend back to tonality is so prevalent, and so often combined with other traditional elements, as to lead commentators to speak of a "neo-romantic revival," characterized by such nineteenth-century stylistic features as strongly profiled melody, opulent orchestration, and rich texture, as well as a renewed concern for direct personal expression.

Nevertheless, most composers now using elements of traditional tonality in their work appear to have little interest in actually reviving common-practice style. Indeed, such a revival, even if desired, would be essentially impossible, since current conceptions of tonality are necessarily deformed by the post-tonal historical position. Contemporary composers necessarily view—or hear—tonality as if from a distance, as "outsiders" who must adopt its conventions by deliberate decision and must consequently use them by "calculation," in the self-conscious manner of someone employing a citation. Thus traditional gestures found in the new tonality, though in themselves quite conventional, are typically manipulated so that their larger coherence is distorted. Standard harmonic or melodic events appear as isolated units, cut off from their normal functional contexts. Thus neutralized, these disconnected modules must be pieced together again into new and (by traditional standards) "artificial" patterns. As with quotation, the goal is not to revive the past but to reconstruct it in a new image.

The music of Del Tredici, a composer who has adopted the language of common-practice tonality with unusual consequence, furnishes a good illustration, from *Vintage Alice* (1972), a Lewis Carroll setting for soprano and chamber orchestra. This passage (Example XX-5; see p. 438) closes one section ("Quodlibet-Return") during which several of the composition's principal melodic ideas have been combined contrapuntally, and provides a transition into the following (and, except for a coda, final) section. The latter, entitled "Hymn to the Queen," opens with the first full vocal statement of the British national anthem, *God Save the Queen,* which has been quoted prominently throughout, but previously only instrumentally, and either incompletely or in combination with other prominent material.

The transitional material thus serves to prepare an important dramatic moment in the piece, and does so in a most traditional manner, by means of a B♭-seventh chord, the dominant of the key of the following section. Yet the familiar effect has been drastically distorted. First, the passage is played on an accordion (part of a "folk group"), which, after landing briefly on the "correct" B♭ dominant (second half of the first measure), gropes uncertainly through a series of chromatic alterations before finally managing to find the chord again. After the accordion has apparently safely recovered the dominant, it is joined first by the folk group (on the same notes) and then by the strings and woodwinds, each playing its *own* dominant seventh, on D and F♯ respectively.

The effect is more than just intentionally humorous. The roots of the three major-third-related dominant sevenths form an augmented triad, part of a complex of whole-tone-derived relationships running through the piece. Moreover, the three dominants connect directly with the music of the new section, for the presentation of the tune in E♭ by voice and brass is accompanied by dislocated fragments of the same melody, in winds and strings, in G major and B major—that is, the tonics of the two additional dominants. Also typical of Del Tredici's compositional manner is the cumulative rhythmic diminution of the soprano phrase in the fragments, creating a kind of temporal telescoping.

Although the long-term historical significance of tonality's "rediscovery"—and of "neo-romanticism"—remains difficult to assess, little in recent music suggests that composers are now able simply to pick up

Example XX-5: DEL TREDICI, *Vintage Alice,* excerpt

HYMN TO THE QUEEN

again at an earlier and simpler stage of musical evolution, ignoring previous twentieth-century developments. That more traditional compositional approaches have, in the latter part of the twentieth century, again become an acceptable part of the composer's arsenal is certainly significant. Yet even for those most committed to it, tonality today does not, and cannot, provide a "universal" language as it did during the eighteenth and nineteenth centuries. Having lost its exclusivity, it is only one among many available resources, and thus susceptible to combination with alternative approaches. Though it can be used when wanted, it need be used only when wanted. In that respect, tonality today differs fundamentally from what it used to be.

MICROTONALITY

Ever since the apparent exhaustion of traditional tonality led to the musical upheavals of the early twentieth century, a few composers have sought fresh compositional possibilities in microtonal expansions of the standard Western twelve-note chromatic scale. Before 1950 this often took the form of additional chromatic extensions within a system still basically equal tempered: Alois Hába's microtonal music assumes the tempered scale as a point of departure, introducing new pitches through further subdivision (most frequently producing quarter tones). But another approach undertook to revitalize diatonic tonality through "purer" forms of tuning, based upon natural harmonic proportions. This type of tuning, known as "just intonation," produces intervals outside the equal-tempered system and is thus also microtonal, yet it preserves strictly graded distinctions between consonance and dissonance and remains fundamentally diatonic in conception.

Until recently, this second path to microtonality was less vigorously explored in twentieth-century music (Harry Partch being its chief proponent), but it now forms a significant element in the more general resurrection of tonality and diatonicism evident in today's music. Among many who have employed pure tunings, La Monte Young and Stockhausen have done so within an essentially minimalist context. Young's music uses sustained harmonies in pure tuning, changing them very slowly so that the listener can hear the resulting subtle pitch transformations as precisely as possible. And Stockhausen's *Stimmung* (1968), a composition for six solo voices lasting over an hour, limits its pitch material to a single six-note chord derived from the natural overtone series.

The American Ben Johnston (b. 1926), on the other hand, has not only explored just intonation with unusual rigor, but has subjected its tonal resources to a broad spectrum of compositional techniques. Johnston has used microtonal divisions derived from just-intonation scales containing, among other possibilities, thirty-one and fifty-three notes to the octave, in combination with techniques such as serialism (String Quartets Nos. 1 and 2, 1959 and 1964, and the Quintet for Groups, 1966), indeterminacy (*Four Do-It-Yourself Pieces,* 1969, and *In Memory Harry Partch,* 1975), and extended tonality (String Quartet No. 4, 1973). He has also developed a system for determining rhythmic proportions analogous to those used in his pitch systems.

Equal-tempered microtonality also continues to attract composers today, especially Americans. John Eaton (b. 1935) has used quarter-tone tuning for a number of years in a chromatic, nontriadic style, in which the microtonal relationships provide a more precisely inflected and richly colored repertory of pitches. A composer especially dedicated to opera, Eaton has found microtonalism an effective means for mirroring situations of dramatic conflict and emotional intensity in works such as *Danton and Robespierre* (1978) and *The Tempest* (1985).

Easley Blackwood (b. 1933), also a leading figure in tuning theory, has adopted an unusually systematic approach to equal-tempered tuning in some of his recent music. Each of his *Twelve Microtonal Études* for electronically synthesized sounds (1982) explores one of the twelve possible equal-tempered divisions of the octave from thirteen to twenty-four tones. In each case the tuning is exploited for its own particular structural characteristics, with preference given to harmonic procedures that correspond to traditional diatonic and chromatic relationships; for instance, since eighteen-tone tuning produces three—rather than the conventional two—whole-tone scales, Blackwood relies heavily upon whole-tone configurations in the étude composed in this tuning. The music consequently has a surprisingly traditional pitch quality (supported, moreover, by traditional rhythmic, textural, and formal features), yet sounds significantly different as a result of the nonconventional tunings.

In general, alternate tunings seem to be playing an increasingly important part in current music, not only when employed systematically by the composers mentioned above but when used more occasionally by many others. As an element in the assimilation of ethnic influences from other regions of the world, microtonal tunings supply intervallic configurations that sound fresh to Western ears and lend themselves to a wide variety of new expressive possibilities. (The appeal has been especially strong among musicians involved with improvisation, including not only such "art music" figures as Young or Terry Riley, but many jazz and popular artists as well, such as the saxophonist Ornette Coleman and the rock group Sonic Youth.) New tunings have opened up innovative approaches to harmony and melody, while the exploitation of unusual acoustical processes associated with just intonation, especially those involving interference patterns (or "beatings"), has introduced a spectrum of timbral effects largely untapped in previous Western music. Alternate tuning possibilities have been welcomed as a means to revitalize tonality without resort to high levels of chromaticism that have been the dominant manner of tonal extension in the West over the past two centuries or more. Like the return of triadic harmony and functionality, they attest to the widespread current interest in rethinking traditional tonal materials in contemporary terms.

CHAPTER XXI

Music and the External World

NEW APPROACHES TO LANGUAGE

There has been a dramatic shift in attitude among recent composers regarding text setting. When composers set texts to music during the common-practice period, the normal procedure was to preserve the text's linguistic integrity within its musical setting, to support—and even emphasize—both its syntactic and semantic components through the musical structure. This was, moreover, ultimately as true of composers like Mozart and Verdi, who professed the priority of music over text, as it was for those like Wagner, who claimed priority for the text. This attitude, which with minor exceptions remained in force throughout the earlier part of the twentieth century, has been seriously challenged by a sizable group of composers since World War II.

The first indication of a significant change appeared in serial music of the 1950s, where the fragmentation of line and texture produced by serial procedures tended to bring about corresponding dislocations in the verbal component in vocal compositions. The text, rather than being preserved as an integral whole, was broken up into its phonetic constituents, atomized by the pointillistic textures associated with this music. An interesting transitional example is provided by a passage from the end of Luigi Nono's *Cori di Didone* (*Choruses of Dido,* 1958), scored for chorus and nonpitched percussion (Example XXI-1). Here the isolation of individual pitches within each vocal part gives rise to syllabic fragmentation of the text; yet the syllables are sequentially distributed so that despite overlappings of syllables and occasional intensifications of purely phonetic elements (such as the phoneme "u" in "flu," the first

Example XXI-1: NONO, *Cori di Didone,* mm. 221–23

syllable of the Italian word "fumi," which is echoed in both tenors after being sung by the lower basses), one hears a continuous and meaningful text (which Nono prints out below the vocal parts) when all eight voices are performed together. The integrity of the original text is loosened, but not completely dissolved.

Other composers, however, wishing to integrate the text completely into the overall serial structure, chose to treat language purely phonetically, as a repository of "meaningless" vocal sounds that could be musically treated like any other sounds, arranged in combinations that, though musically (serially) organized, were without normal linguistic—syntactic or semantic—content. Stockhausen's electronic composition *Gesang der Jünglinge* (1956) thus attempts to integrate its biblical German text with all the other materials in the composition. To this end the composer set up a scale of sonic types, determined by spectral analysis, extending from pure noise at one extreme to pure pitch at the other. Vocal fragments of the text (sung by a boy soprano and subjected to electronic manipulation) were positioned in this continuum according to their own particular sonic characteristics (which vary, for example, depending upon whether the vocal sound is sung or spoken, dominated by vowels or consonants, etc.). Once established, this ordered

material, including its textual component, could be organized according to serial principles. A still more extreme example, as it avoids specific textural associations entirely, is offered by Milton Babbitt's vocal
compositions *Sounds and Words* (1960) and *Phonemena* (1970). Here the
vocal part is limited entirely to semantically meaningless phonemes,
which are subjected to serial operations analogous to those controlling
the pitches that accompany them.

A fragmentary and polyglot "reconstruction" of language out of
phonemes appears in Mauricio Kagel's *Anagramma* for four solo vocal-
ists, speaking chorus, and chamber ensemble (1960). Kagel, an Argentinian who has lived for many years in Germany, takes as his point of
departure a Latin palindrome (a text that forms its own "retrograde"):
In girum imus nocte et consumimur igni (We circle in the night and are
consumed by flames). The text is not itself heard, however, but merely
serves as a repository for phonetic material to be used in the piece, out
of which "anagrams"—i.e., new words derived from these phonemes—are constructed. Since the new words are completely different
from the original Latin ones, the text of the composition is freshly
"composed" out of the provided phonetic material. (Kagel refers to this
process as "acoustic translation.") The resulting text contains mixtures
of meaningful (though fragmentary) sequences of words, nonsensical
combinations, and "pure" phonemes. (Although the meaningful words
are limited to four languages [German, French, Italian, and Spanish],
there are also occasional "improvisatory" sections in which the performers are allowed to invent their own texts from the same phonetic
material in any language or dialect they wish.) As in the other pieces
mentioned, emphasis is placed on the sonic component of the text rather
than on its syntactic and semantic aspects. The creation of the text itself
becomes part of the compositional process. "The language combinations," in the words of the composer, "are—with regard to the permutation and variation of phonemes—essentially the same as the musical
combinations."[1]

Another innovative feature of recent vocal writing is found in the
unprecedented variety of the vocal resources employed. Luciano Berio
has been a leading figure in this regard. In such ground-breaking works
as *Circles* for voice, harp, and two percussionists (1960, on texts by E.
E. Cummings, a poet himself especially interested in the purely sonic
features of language), and *Sequenza III* for solo voice (1966), Berio
extended the boundaries of vocal production considerably beyond those
of "normal" singing.

The latter work employs a range of novel timbral effects comparable
to those introduced at this same time in instrumental music (a devel-

---

1.   Quoted in Dieter Schnebel, *Mauricio Kagel: Musik Theater Film* (Cologne, 1970), p.
     25.

opment discussed in Chapter XVIII). Thus *Sequenza III* calls upon the singer to produce sounds by breathing in, gasping, employing mouth clicks, holding hand over mouth while singing, singing with the mouth closed, whispering, laughing, and speaking, as well as normal singing. The work is shaped so that the music becomes more songlike as it progresses; and while in the earlier stages different types of vocal articulation are rapidly set off against one another, these gradually "resolve" into a single type of "pure," textless singing at the end. *Circles,* on the other hand, exploits the prominent "noise" component in many of these new vocal sounds by drawing correspondences between vocal and percussion timbres (for example, a sound heard in the voice may be mimicked and prolonged by sand block).

A few additional examples attest to the variety of recent vocal writing. An early instance of new resources exploited within a choral framework is Pauline Oliveros's (b. 1932) *Sound Patterns* for four-part unaccompanied chorus (1960). A number of different percussive sound types—tongue clicks, popped lips, snapped fingers in front of mouth, glissandos, etc.—are combined with occasional notes of definite pitch (specified only by general register) in a highly differentiated and rhythmically active texture, producing a musical surface of considerable variety.

Cage's *Aria* for solo voice (1958) employs a broad spectrum of vocal types within an essentially indeterminate context (see facing page for typical score page.) The score consists of isolated words and phrases in four languages, strung together in a meaningless sequence and presented in conjunction with a series of lines intended to suggest general melodic contours. These are drawn in different colors (ten in all), the singer being instructed to associate each color with a particular manner of singing, to be chosen by the performer. (In the recorded version sung by Cathy Berberian, an American singer closely associated with both Berio and Cage, the types include "jazz," "lyric coloratura," "Sprechstimme," "Oriental," "Marlene Dietrich," "nasal," and "baby.") The resulting mélange of different vocal styles, heard in close proximity, each with its own distinct expressive characteristics and personal associations, produces a disorienting, chaotic effect.

A final example, György Ligeti's *Aventures* for three singers and seven instrumentalists (1962), also has a purely phonetic text. Ligeti calls for many different types of vocal production, as well as gradual transitions from one type to another (e.g., a continuous change from singing through *Sprechstimme* to speaking). In addition, detailed instructions are provided for essentially dramatic aspects of the performance, including not only general indications of mood, but also explicit stage instructions such as "Turn to the soprano and gesture," "Pick up a book," "Blow into a paper bag," and "Sing through a megaphone." *Aventures* can be

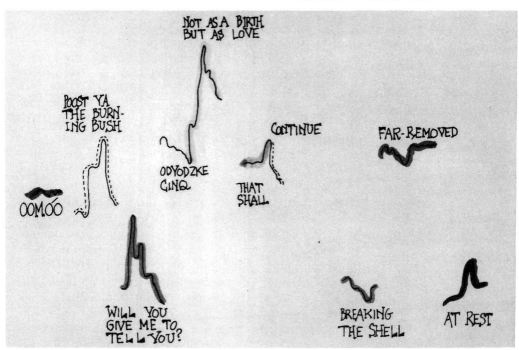

A page from the score of John Cage's *Aria*. (© 1960 by Henmar Press Inc. Used by permission of C. F. Peters Corporation)

heard as a sort of "imaginary drama" in a purely phonetic language, with both text and gestures treated as "music"—as essentially abstract elements, ordered without reference to linguistic or narrative meaning.

EXTENSIONS IN MUSIC THEATER

Ligeti's *Aventures,* with its prominent dramatic dimension, forms a convenient link leading from vocal music to music of an explicitly the-atrical nature. The twentieth century has in general been receptive to new forms of music theater introduced as alternatives to traditional opera. Stravinsky's theater works provide impressive examples, while others are found in the work of such varied composers as Satie, Weill, Hin-demith, and Partch. Only in the latter part of the century, however, have composers concentrated so heavily upon combining elements of music and drama into new types of composite art forms. The border-line nature of *Aventures,* situated somewhere between pure concert music and fully realized drama (an ambiguity underlined by Ligeti's revision of the work, four years after its inception, for stage presentation), is typical of a pervasive contemporary trend.

Many composers now incorporate some aspect of dramatic action or symbolism into what could otherwise be considered a pure concert piece. The compositions of George Crumb frequently contain a significant dramatic element: the soprano in his *Lux aeterna* for soprano, bass flute, sitar, and two percussionists (1971) is instructed to light a candle before the beginning of the performance and to blow it out at the end; the three performers in *Vox balaenae* for amplified flute, cello, and piano (1971) wear black masks; and members of the ensemble in the orchestral piece *Echoes of Time and the River* (1967) are called upon to form a "processional" that moves through the auditorium. Similarly, the soprano soloist in Berio's *Circles* changes positions during the performance, as do the wind players in Harrison Birtwistle's *Verses for Ensemble* (1969).

Frequently the dramatic component in recent concert works assumes a more integral role and becomes essentially inseparable from the overall compositional conception. During the late 1960s and early 1970s the English composer Peter Maxwell Davies wrote a series of compositions in which theatrical and concert elements are joined in roughly equal balance. His *Eight Songs for a Mad King* for male voice and six instruments (1969) is at once a song cycle on texts dealing with the madness of King George III of England (especially his efforts to teach his pet songbirds to sing) and a highly stylized dramatic presentation of the events depicted in the texts. The singer appears in costume as the king, and performs an extraordinarily complex and virtuosic part with a range extending from low-register "undertones" to high falsetto screams, intended to reflect (in the words of the composer) "certain extreme regions of experience." Four of the instrumentalists, also in costume, assume the roles of the king's birds and are positioned in large cages on the stage; and a fifth—the percussionist—plays the king's "keeper." Explicit dramatic events are acted out during the performance. (At one critical point the king seizes the violinist's instrument, eventually breaking it.) The music draws on a range of quotations and stylistic parodies, providing an additional dramatic dimension. Other Davies works of this period incorporating explicitly dramatic elements include *Revelation and Fall* (1965), *Missa super L'Homme armé* (1968), *Vesalii icones* (1969), and *Miss Donnithorne's Maggot* (1974).

The merging of music with drama, and of drama with music, achieves perhaps its most consequential form in works in which the performance, or concert, situation is itself treated as a dramatic or ritualistic occurrence. (Here again Cage can be considered a forerunner: his *4'33"*, in confronting an audience with silence, is literally "nothing" if not theatrical.) A typical instance is Berio's *Recital I* (1972, originally conceived in 1966), a thirty-minute "monodrama" for soprano and chamber orchestra whose only character is the singer herself and for which the dramatic context is itself a vocal recital. On one plane, then, the

Cathy Berberian performing the theater piece *Recital,* written for her by Luciano Berio. (Photo Courtesy of BMG Classics)

piece is about itself; on another it is about the presentation of a concert; and on a third it is about the disintegration of the character played by the singer (who, in a text of Joycean discontinuity, comments on various aspects of her life—including the recital itself—and sings fragmentary selections from the vocal literature, ranging from Monteverdi to Berio's own music).

Mauricio Kagel has been especially concerned with handling musical performance as a dramatic event. His *Match* for two cellists and a percussionist (1964) is structured like a contest, the cellists taking the role of competitors and the percussionist functioning as a referee. This lends itself readily to musical realization, with each cellist trying to outdo the other, interrupted by the "accompanying" percussionist, who offers various "rulings" (which the cellists occasionally ignore). Kagel's *Sur Scene* (1960) is an even more extreme example. Subtitled "Theatrical Chamber Music Work," it gives a speaker, a singer, a mime, and three instrumentalists elaborate stage directions (how to react to one another, what to do, where to look, etc.), yet provides them with no actual music to play. (There are only very general instructions, such as "play a staccato chord.") The only performed text is a purely verbal one for the speaker, consisting of a fragmentary assemblage of linguistic clichés.

All of the players, in fact, are really actors, who assume roles within a stylized, abstract chamber music performance for which there is no actual chamber music.

The dramatic possibilities of concert performance have also been explored in a less radical form in a number of compositions by the American composer Jacob Druckman (b. 1928). Druckman's *Animus I* for trombone and electronic sounds (1966), for example, is, like Kagel's *Match,* a dramatic contest, in this case between a live performer and tape. Despite an extremely elaborate, virtuosic part (with many special effects such as tongue clicks, singing while playing, etc.), the trombonist is twice "overwhelmed" by the louder taped music, reacting the first time by sitting silently on the stage and listening and the second time by retreating from the stage entirely. (The trombonist ultimately returns, however, to finish the piece; at least in this instance, man prevails over machine.)

Stockhausen's recent instrumental works also tend to have theatrical pretensions. His *Sternklang* (*Starsound,* 1971) is a three-hour, ritualistic "open-air" event, scored for five separate ensembles of five performers each positioned around a central percussionist—"as far as possible"— so as to form the five points of a star. These groups interact with one another musically, facilitated by "sound runners" who carry from group to group simple rhythmic and melodic models that are picked up and developed in repeated chant-like patterns by the players. The overall performance is coordinated by the percussionist, who acts as a signalman, hammering out common tempos at appropriate moments. As in all the pieces discussed in this section, one must see *Sternklang* as well as hear it in order to receive the full effect.

MULTIMEDIA

A common feature of much contemporary music theater is the use of various forms of multimedia, mixing vocal and instrumental performance with other modes of artistic expression such as acting, dancing, mime, film, and slides. Of course all music theater, including opera, involves juxtaposing different art forms, so in one sense there is nothing new in this development. Moreover, during the earlier twentieth century there was already some interest in experimenting with extramusical extensions in both symphonic and dramatic music (e.g., the color organ for Skryabin's tone poem *Prometheus,* the film in Milhaud's opera *Christophe Colomb,* a speaking narrator in Stravinsky's *Oedipus rex*). But the terms "multimedia" and "mixed media" have appeared only recently, introduced in response to a widespread interest in joining different artistic dimensions into new—and often startling—combinations, usually having little in common with traditional dramatic genres.

Frequently these new forms involve some degree of indeterminacy or audience participation. Here an important milestone was the first "happening" staged by John Cage in 1952 with, among others, the painter Robert Rauschenberg and the dancer Merce Cunningham. A group of audience participants were offered an especially constructed artistic "environment"—encompassing music, dance, painting, recited poetry, film, etc.—with which and within which they were invited to interact. A happening has no plot of predetermined action or plan; it is only an "event."

During the late 1950s and 1960s a number of loosely constituted composer collaboratives were formed in the United States that put on informal musical improvisations that were in essence happenings: freely evolving, essentially unstructured musical "occurrences" where virtually anything, musical or otherwise, could take place. Among the most prominent of these were the ONCE group in Ann Arbor (including Robert Ashley [b. 1930] and Gordon Mumma [b. 1935]) and the Flexus group in New York (including La Monte Young, Philip Corner, and the video artist Nam June Paik).

Multimedia conceptions, however, need not be loosely constructed. Examples of more structured presentations are found in works combining music with light shows or films, or compositions that simply use electronic sounds in conjunction with live performance. A typical, if unusually imaginative, illustration is Salvatore Martirano's *L's G.A.* (1968), in which a narrator, wearing a gas mask, gives a tortured reading of Lincoln's Gettysburg Address accompanied by a tape, slide, and film display projecting images of war and destruction. As the piece reaches its climactic ending, helium is released into the gas mask, causing the narrator's voice to rise hysterically as he delivers his final lines. A more recent case, *The Photographer* (1983), a theatrical collaboration based on the work of the nineteenth-century photographer Eadweard Muybridge, features music by Philip Glass. The work has a three-part structure, the first essentially spoken, the second a concert with slides, and the third a dance. Here, then, the different media are juxtaposed sequentially as well as simultaneously.

Perhaps the most elaborate, and largest, multimedia event yet staged was the premiere performance of John Cage and Lejaren Hiller's *HPSCHD*, which took place in 1969 in a large arena at the University of Illinois. The performance included seven harpsichordists (the work's title is a six-letter computerized version of the word "harpsichord"), several additional live performers, fifty-one tapes, multiple film, slide, and light shows, and several thousand listener-spectators, who moved about freely during a five-hour presentation.

TRADITIONAL OPERA

Despite these innovations in music theater, many works continue to be written for the traditional operatic stage. Some of these exploit new media and technologies and unconventional modes of dramatic presentation. Ground-breaking was Bernd Alois Zimmermann's *Die Soldaten* (discussed in Chapter XIX), which employs tape, slides, films, and multilevel staging. Other composers, however, such as the traditionally oriented Americans Gian Carlo Menotti (b. 1911), Dominick Argento (b. 1927), and Thomas Pasatieri (b. 1945), maintain an essentially conventional conception of the genre. Hans Werner Henze in Europe, Michael Tippett in England, and John Eaton in the United States have all devoted a substantial portion of their output to opera, while many leading figures of the postwar years, including Luigi Nono, Peter Maxwell Davies, Harrison Birtwistle, and George Rochberg, have made substantial contributions to the operatic repertory.

Stockhausen has also embraced the genre, devoting most of his recent activity to the composition of a seven-night cycle of Wagnerian scope entitled *Licht* (Light), containing one opera for each day of the week (for which that opera is named). The three operas completed to date typify much recent work in this area. They mix segments that are operatic in an essentially traditional sense with others of a more ritualistic nature, incorporating dances and purely instrumental works (e.g., the composer's Piano Piece XII, used in conjunction with a scene involving a music conservatory examination in *Donnerstag* [Thursday], the first of the operas, completed in 1980).

The recent work of Philip Glass for major opera houses, discussed in Chapter XX, testifies to the ongoing vitality of the genre and its challenge to contemporary composers. Among younger Americans working in the genre, the "postminimalist" John Adams (b. 1947) is notable. His recent *Nixon in China* (1987), conceived in collaboration with the director and designer Peter Sellars and the poet Alice Goodman, has attracted wide interest for its unprecedented—for the operatic stage— political currency (there are roles for Henry Kissinger and Mao Tsetung, for example, as well as for Richard and Pat Nixon, and of these, all but Mao are still living), as well as for the quality of its dramatic effect and vocal writing. The work has been remarkably successful, with three productions within its first year, each playing to consistently sold-out houses. (The unusual popularity of the operas of Glass and Adams even holds open the possibility that a significant creative revival of the genre may currently be under way in the United States.) Adams is now working on a second opera, again in collaboration with Sellars.

That opera nevertheless poses special problems for contemporary composers is indicated by the fact that many have found it impossible to deal with the genre except in an essentially detached and parodistic

A scene from Henri Pousseur's opera *Votre Faust* in the production at the Piccola Scala, Milan, 1968–69. (Photo Alfred A. Kalmus, Universal Edition, Ltd.)

manner. As its title already suggests, Luciano Berio's *Opera* (1970) concerns itself largely with the history of its own medium, taking Monteverdi's *Orfeo* as a point of departure for tracing the decline of the genre. Mauricio Kagel's *Staatstheater* (State Theater, 1971) intentionally misuses the elaborate resources of a modern opera house (singers, orchestra, ballet, etc.) in order to present a critical commentary on the institution of opera. The work is, in the composer's words, "not just the negation of opera but of the whole tradition of music theater." Finally, in Henri Pousseur's autobiographical *Votre Faust* (Your Faust, 1967) the main character, a composer named Henri, accepts a commission to write an opera on the Faust legend, the commission being treated as a symbolic equivalent to Faust's selling of his soul to Mephistopheles. The inclination of so much recent music to be "about music," especially evident in the use of quotation, is thus equally apparent in the area of opera and music theater.

THE ENCROACHMENT OF REALITY

Recent music history has even given rise to efforts by some composers to do away with all distinctions between what is and what is not music. Cage, for example, in focusing so heavily upon the *process* of musical composition (by using aleatory procedures) and of musical performance (by encouraging performers to make their own decisions), shows surprisingly little concern for what the sounding result may be. Indeed, in many of his works what one actually hears is so variable from one performance to the next that it raises questions as to whether there is an objective "work" there at all. Cage is not interested in compositions as "objects," as fixed entities that have a permanent existence as "work." Instead, he conceives of music primarily as an activity, and an activity that is—at least ideally—indistinguishable from any other.

Cage has himself expressed this eloquently: "When we separate music from life what we get is art (a compendium of masterpieces). With contemporary music, when it is actually contemporary, we have no time to make that separation (which protects us from living), and so contemporary music is not so much art as it is life."[2] Cage's work thus has a distinctly didactic character: it is intended to teach us to experience the world (and especially, though by no means exclusively, the way this world sounds) as directly as possible, unmediated by a predetermined network of relationships or associations. It is, quoting Cage again, "not an attempt to bring order out of chaos nor to suggest improvements in creation, but simply a way of waking up to the very life we're living."[3] For Cage, then, all of life—indeed the very act of living—becomes a form of art, with nature serving as a sort of ideal concert hall offering unlimited resources for "musical" experience.

It is just for this reason that Cage's work often seems to have little to do with what one ordinarily thinks of as music. The composer Robert Ashley has even suggested that the ultimate goal of Cage's thinking "would be a music that wouldn't necessarily involve anything but the presence of people. . . . It seems to me that the most radical redefinition of music that I could think of would be one that defines 'music' without reference to sound."[4]

The consequences of such views, though not always taken to this extreme, are evident in many facets of recent music and affect both the musical work (which tends to lose its status as a permanent artifact) and the work's relationship to performers and listeners (who are asked to give up their traditional roles as passive receptors and faithful interpreters in order to become active participants in a cooperative enterprise). Thus some contemporary composers feel that there should be no clear distinction at all between composer and performer. Ashley has written: "The only people I've ever been interested in . . . are people who make their own music."

Similarly, there are signs of dissatisfaction with the traditional notion of music as a compartmentalized area of experience that is purposely cut off from "normal" everyday activities, presented in specially designed

2.   "Communication," *Silence,* p. 44.
3.   "Experimental Music," ibid., p. 12.
4.   Quoted in Michael Nyman, *Experimental Music. Cage and Beyond* (London, 1974), p. 10.

concert halls where it is insulated from the rest of life. The tendency of much contemporary music to turn into a form of theater, discussed earlier in this chapter, is one symptom. Another is the conviction that music should be taken into the streets, presented outside of the normal concert framework, free from the formalities of traditional performance and made accessible to as broad a spectrum of people as possible.

ENVIRONMENTAL MUSIC

An especially vivid reflection of change in attitude is found in what might be termed "environmental" music. Since the early 1970s the American Max Neuhaus (b. 1939) has placed "sonic installations" in various locations not ordinarily associated with music: e.g., in a swimming pool in Germany, in the rotunda of an arboretum in St. Paul, in the stairway of a museum in Chicago, under a grate in the middle of Times Square in New York. When possible, these installations are intended to remain indefinitely, offering an unexpected auditory sensation for anyone who happens to pass within earshot. What one hears is not music, at least according to normal conceptions, but simple, recurring sonic events, usually played at such low dynamic levels that one must strain to hear them. As Neuhaus comments: "These pieces are not musical products; they're meant to be activities."

Alvin Lucier (b. 1931) is another American who has been concerned with the performance of loosely prescribed activities within a particular physical environment. His *Hartford Memory Space* (1969), for example, instructs the participants "to go out into an environment (urban, rural, hostile, benign), record the sound situation as precisely as possible by means of memory, sketches, tape recorders and so forth, returning to the concert place to duplicate as precisely as possible (without improvisations, additions, personal taste, one's own ideas) that outer sound situation by means of one's own voice or instrument."[5] Other works by Lucier include *Vespers* (1968), in which the participants are placed in a dark space so that they can explore it with the aid of echo-location (i.e., radar) devices; and *Music for Solo Performer* (1965), in which electrodes are attached to a performer's scalp so that alpha brain waves can be amplified in order to activate percussion instruments.

In such works Lucier's concern is less with sound than with the reciprocal interactions between the performers and some prescribed and usually unfamiliar terrain (in the case of the last piece, the performer's own brain); and a successful performance involves learning to cope with this landscape, to understand it by discovering one's own capacities for

---

5.   *Source: Music of the Avant-Garde,* 10 (1972): 98.

experiencing it. A "composition" of this type thus provides, in effect, a means for developing sensitivity to external events.

A similar focus is found in the recent work of the American Pauline Oliveros (b. 1932), although here less emphasis is placed on the external environment and more on group interactions, especially as interpreted within the context of the women's liberation movement. Her *Sonic Meditations* (1971), "intended for group use over a long period of time," consists entirely of verbal instructions dedicated to "the elevation and equalization of the feminine principle along with the masculine principle."[6] The score of "Teach Yourself to Fly," the first of several pieces in the set, reads: "Any number of persons sit in a circle facing the center. Illuminate the space with dim blue light. Begin by simply observing your own breathing. Always be an observer. Gradually observe your breathing become audible. Then gradually introduce your voice. Color your breathing very softly at first with sound. Let the intensity increase very slowly as you observe it. Continue as long as possible and until all others are quiet."

Probably the most elaborate collaborative performance to date is Neuhaus's *Radio Net,* presented in 1971 on a two-hour radio broadcast heard over some two hundred National Public Radio stations, all joined by telephone hookup to a central console manned by the composer. Listeners were invited to phone in and whistle anything they wished, their input being electronically altered by Neuhaus, mixed with the inputs of other listeners, and then broadcast over the participating stations. One could thus simultaneously be composer, performer, and listener—and presumably feel some sort of "communal" connection with countless other participants located throughout the United States.

Finally, the Canadian composer R. Murray Schafer (b. 1933) has undertaken a serious study, a "World Soundscape Project," devoted to examining the acoustic environment of the contemporary world. As Schafer describes the project, it consists of

> documenting important features, of notating differences, parallels and trends, of collecting sounds threatened with extinction, of studying the effects of new sounds before they are indiscriminately released into the environment, of studying the rich symbolism sounds have for man and of studying human behavior patterns in different sonic environments in order to use these insights in planning future environments for man. . . . The final question will be: is the soundscape of the world an indeterminate composition over which we have no control, or are *we* its composer and performers, responsible for giving it form and beauty?[7]

6.   Ibid., p. 104.
7.   *The Tuning of the World* (New York, 1977), pp. 4–5.

In addition to studying the acoustical environment, Schafer has also drawn inspiration from it for his own compositions. The rhythmic and formal structure of his String Quartet No. 2 (1976) is derived from the temporal patterns formed by waves breaking on a shore ("The duration from crest to crest usually falls between six and eleven seconds"). And he has written compositions specially designed for performance in particular physical environments (e.g., the shores of a lake near his home in Canada).

MUSIC AND POLITICS

The developments considered in this chapter represent a clear challenge to the dominant tendency of modern Western music to separate itself from the larger social context—to be, in a phrase introduced as a basic esthetic credo during the nineteenth century, "pure" or "absolute" music. According to the adherents of such music, art becomes most significant and meaningful precisely when it is furthest removed from everyday concerns, set apart in a privileged realm where it can acquire a "disembodied," almost religious aura, untouched by the practical concerns of ordinary life. As a direct reaction to this view, many contemporary composers have attempted to bring music back down to earth, so to speak, to integrate it with other types of experience in the hope of countering what has been termed the "inane isolation" of Western concert music.

Concern for questions of group interaction, social institutions, and the environment lends the work of many of these composers an unmistakable political dimension. For some this has become the central focus of their work. Of course, political consciousness is not unprecedented among composers. The work of Beethoven, Wagner, Weill, or Partch, among others, or of those working under totalitarian regimes (see Chapter X) can be fully comprehended and appreciated only in light of its political implications. Perhaps the most politically conscious composer of the earlier twentieth century was the German Hanns Eisler (1898–1962), a student of both Schoenberg and Webern, who during the 1920s came under the influence of Marxist thought, joined the Communist party, and participated in the German workers' movement. As a composer committed to political action, Eisler espoused a simpler, more practically applicable and "involved" music, intended for a proletarian public. He wrote, in addition to more ambitious projects, workers' songs and children's songs, as well as "festival" pieces composed in a sufficiently straightforward idiom to enable all to participate in their performance.

Although Eisler could be taken as the prototype for a number of

contemporary composers, he remained very much an exceptional figure during his own lifetime. The sudden blossoming of political consciousness in recent music, on the other hand, has been a remarkably
widespread phenomenon and constitutes an especially characteristic
feature of the present-day musical situation. Its growth was closely linked
to the cultural revolutions of the 1960s, when strong feelings of dissatisfaction and alienation encouraged attempts to use music as a tool for
social interaction and change. These developments were remarkably
pervasive, and were present not only in art music but in various forms
of popular music as well (rock groups like Jefferson Airplane were particularly prominent in the movement). Indeed, the politicization of music
was sufficiently widespread to suggest, at least for a time, that the revolutionary nature of twentieth-century music, which until recently has
been viewed primarily as a matter of musical language, might eventually come to embrace its social role as well.

There are a number of different ways, and degrees, in which a composer's work can claim political significance. Cage's music, for example,
might be said to be political in a passive sense, as the composer does
not overtly emphasize its political content. Yet Cage's attempt to
undermine assumptions about musical language, indeed to assert the
undesirability of a fixed language as a mediating—and thus falsifying—
agency between composer and composition, or listener and sound, can
readily be taken (and indeed has been by others) as a symbolic statement
about the tension between individual freedom and imposed institutionalized frameworks. Similarly, Cage's view of the composer-performer
relationship as one of shared responsibilities, and of the performer as a
free agent not subject to the "dictatorial" authority of composer or conductor, carries a distinct, if indirect, political message. Similar points
could be made about any number of other composers, including several
mentioned earlier in this chapter, such as Kagel, Ashley, Lucier, and
Oliveros.

Stockhausen has also remained aloof from overt political engage-
ment, yet he too aspires to enlighten and educate through his music.
Stockhausen even believes that he can aid the listener to achieve a new
stage of mankind as a "higher being." He writes, "Now we are in a
period in which the superconsciousness has become so strong in a few
people that they are close to becoming higher forms of life. . . . We
musicians are given a great power to ignite in other humans the first
fires of desire to exceed themselves."[8]

The German Hans Werner Henze offers an instance of a composer
whose style underwent significant transformations after political con-
version. Remarkably gifted and technically accomplished, Henze matured

8.   *Texte III* (Cologne, 1971), pp. 292, 294.

as a relatively traditional composer who concentrated heavily on opera. When he embraced Marxism in the late 1960s, however, Henze's work began to change: he adopted new forms of musical theater in preference to conventional opera (*Der langwierige Weg in die Wohnung der Natascha Ungeheuer*); began setting revolutionary texts (*Das Floss der Medusa, Versuch über Schweine*); largely abandoned the Italianate lyricism of his earlier vocal writing in favor of explorations of extreme tessituras and unorthodox techniques (*El Cimarrón*, Second Violin Concerto); and began employing musical quotations and direct stylistic allusions (*Voices, Tristan*). While Henze apparently viewed these new techniques as more appropriate expressions of his political views, like Cage and Stockhausen he has nevertheless remained detached from any active involvement in political affairs.

Others have sought a more consistent union of their musical activities with their political beliefs and actions. The Englishman Cornelius Cardew (1936–81), who in his early years was associated with Stockhausen (serving as his assistant from 1958 to 1960) and widely recognized as a leading figure of the English avant-garde, became increasingly interested during the 1960s in using music as a means of public motivation. He came to distrust the "elitism" of contemporary music and even to question the validity of musical education (since the most creative and responsive performers, he felt, were those without previous musical conceptions). In an effort to allow all who were interested, including nonmusicians, to share in his music, Cardew devised scores using graphic notation (*Treatise,* 1967), verbal instructions (*The Tiger's Mind,* 1967), or combinations of these with very simple musical notation (see p. 458: *The Great Learning,* 1970). Despite their "populist" aims, however, these works nevertheless remained within an avant-garde (though now essentially Cage-derived) framework.

In 1969 Cardew helped form the Scratch Orchestra, a cooperative organization of some fifty members representing various walks of life (musicians, artists, clerks, scholars, etc.) "willing and eager to engage in experimental musical activities." The idea was to put on concerts in which all participants, skilled and unskilled alike, would contribute equally in all phases of the undertaking. The repertory encompassed various types of pieces, including "improvisation rites," new compositions supplied by members, and paraphrases based on "popular classics." The history of the Scratch Orchestra was brief and turbulent, with considerable internal tensions leading to significant changes in policy; and Cardew himself eventually viewed the organization as too "individualistic" in orientation, placing too much emphasis on allowing each participant to do whatever he or she wanted.

Yet Cardew's work with the Scratch Orchestra had a critical impact on both his political and musical views. He became a committed com-

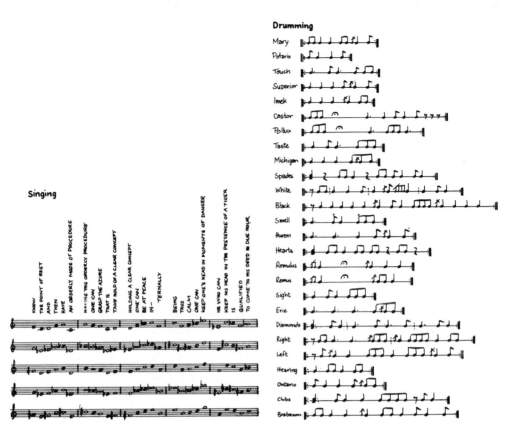

Paragraph 2 of *The Great Learning* by Cornelius Cardew. Cardew set the seven paragraphs of the classic Confucian text between 1968 and 1970.

munist who rejected the advanced idiom of his previous work as inappropriate for expressing (as he wrote in the preface to his *Piano Album* in 1973) "the vital struggles of the oppressed classes and peoples in their upsurge to seize political power." Cardew thus turned to a populist style firmly grounded in traditional tonality, writing workers' songs and political tunes intended for group performances at party meetings (here following Eisler) as well as concert pieces based on popular or folk melodies with strong political overtones. He also participated in political events, frequently performing as a pianist at rallies and in community halls.

Some of Cardew's later music is nevertheless quite virtuosic in quality and requires extremely skilled performers. An example is his *Boolavogue,* a four-movement composition for two pianos left unfinished at the composer's death in 1981. Its blend of simple and unassuming melodic and harmonic materials with extraordinarily brilliant piano figurations of conventional types (scales, arpeggios, etc.) evokes, curiously, perhaps nothing so much as nineteenth-century salon music.

Frederic Rzewski (b. 1938) is an American who has also adopted a populist style out of political conviction. In his recent work Rzewski has espoused what he calls musical "realism," directing his music toward a large and diverse audience not normally associated with concert music. *The People United Will Never Be Defeated!* (1975), a set of thirty-six virtuosic variations for piano, is based on a popular tune by the Chilean Sergio Ortega that has become a sort of anti-imperialist icon. The music's traditional tonal language and flashy virtuosic writing recall Cardew's late work; but the score is considerably more complex in structure, and its elaborate motivic developments reveal Rzewski's wide experience with the techniques of serialism. Christian Wolff (b. 1934), another American composer of Marxist persuasion (who has aptly described Rzewski's piece as "an image of popularity"), was closely associated with Cage during the 1950s. Wolff has himself avoided populist associations, however, focusing instead through aleatory means on the social dynamics of the performance situation, treating it as a sort of laboratory for the cultivation of political awareness.

An overtly political position thus need not be tied to a populist tonal style. Luigi Nono, one of the leading serialists of the 1950s, has since the early 1960s seen himself as "an instrument and living voice for the cultural and political advanced guard of the class struggle," and offered his work as an instance "of consciousness, of struggle, of provocation, of discussion, of participation." Nono has frequently performed his work in factories, conducting discussions on it with the workers; and he favors revolutionary texts and melodic materials (folk songs, for example) with overt political associations. He has also attempted to free himself from his self-proclaimed "European egocentricity," mainly through extended contacts with South America. Yet Nono has not been willing to relinquish any of the technical or technological resources available to the contemporary composer. He has consistently maintained an advanced and expressively "difficult" musical language (though the more rigorous serialism of his earlier scores has been abandoned in favor of a more flexible and varied style). Thus Nono subjects the folk materials he commonly uses to drastic distortions, precisely so that they will lose their popular flavor and become integrated components within a complex and fully contemporary musical statement. He has especially used electronic means for this purpose; and most of his pieces since 1960 feature combinations of live and electronic sound: e.g, *Como una cola de fuerza y luz* (*Like a Wave of Power and Light,* 1972), scored for solo piano, orchestra, and electronic sounds.

The stark contrast between the stylistic orientations of two composers like Cardew and Nono suggests that the present-day composer of radical persuasion who wishes to be politically engaged is confronted with a dilemma concerning what properly constitutes a "revolutionary" musical stance at the current moment in music history. Should the

music adopt the most up-to-date techniques and technologies, divorc-
ing itself from a suspect past in order to embrace the future (on the
assumption that a new world should give expression to a new music)?
Or should music maintain a popular and folklike flavor in order to be
accessible to all, especially those on the lower economic rungs for whose
benefit the struggle is, presumably, intended? There are risks either way:
on the one hand a failure to communicate, on the other a decline into
sentimentality and cliché. The new government in postrevolutionary
Russia, as we have seen in Chapter X, struggled with this problem
during the 1920s, first favoring an essentially experimental approach to
the arts but then, with Stalin's rise to power, quickly coming full circle
in assuming a rigorous antimodernist position. The history of more
recent music has failed to provide a definitive answer to the question,
nor is a resolution likely in the near future. The dilemma is itself a
reflection of the social and musical uncertainties that pervade our age.

CHAPTER XXII

Developments in Technology: Electronic Music

ANTECEDENTS

Innovations in musical technology, especially the creation of new instruments and modification of old ones, have been a normal feature of Western music history, moving hand in hand with the expansion of compositional resources. Such parallel development is understandable, since extensions in musical language often require new instruments for adequate realization, while new instruments open up previously untapped compositional possibilities and thus encourage stylistic transformation.

During the nineteenth century, however, expansion of compositional materials—increased chromaticism, broader instrumental palettes, wider registral ambits and dynamic ranges, and richer textures—accelerated at an almost geometric rate of change, culminating in the early years of the twentieth century, when musical "content" seems to have broken through a sort of barrier, stimulating a veritable explosion of new technical developments. The critical factor was the advent of atonality, which, by equalizing pitch relationships and abolishing distinctions between consonance and dissonance, posed the question of whether pitch still necessarily had to form the dominant element of musical construction.

Virtually contemporary with Schoenberg's earliest nontonal works came suggestions that post-tonal music could deal with materials altogether different from those previously used. As early as 1907 Busoni remarked in his *Sketch for a New Esthetic of Music* that the "exhaustion" of the old tradition would soon lead composers to "abstract sound, to unhampered technique, to unlimited tonal material." In the following decade the Futurists redefined music as an "art of noises," and Varèse made his first appeals for "new technical mediums that can lend themselves to every expression." No longer content with a highly limited, "specialized" body of specifically *musical* material, composers began to conceive of composition as the organization of all possible sounds, especially those made newly available by twentieth-century technology.

New instruments soon appeared to produce these new sounds. The expansion of the traditional orchestra, which throughout the nineteenth century had significantly increased its registral and timbral resources, represented a preliminary stage. (Especially important had been the addition of valves to brass instruments, making the full chromatic scale available on all pitched instruments in the orchestra.) The early twentieth century dramatically enlarged the size and variety of the percussion section, the orchestra's principal "noise" component, which up to this point had been largely excluded from orchestral developments.

In retrospect, however, the strongest portents of the post-tonal situation were early attempts to create electronic instruments, able to produce a variety of sounds far beyond any previously imagined. These included Thaddeus Cahill's telharmonium (1906), a two-hundred-ton instrument that produced "artificial" sounds with electronic generators; Lev Termen's theremin (1920), capable of performing a continuous range of pitches by altering the frequency of an electronic oscillator; Maurice Martenot's ondes martenot (1928), also capable of a continuous frequency range, but with improved pitch control and more timbral variety; and the first electronic organ invented by Louis Hammond in 1929. In addition, innovative mechanical (i.e., nonelectronic) instruments were introduced, notably the *intonarumori* (see p. 116) of the Futurist Luigi Russolo, and variable-speed phonographs were used to transform previously recorded sound, at first experimentally by Milhaud, Hindemith, and Varèse, and then in actual compositions by John Cage (beginning with his *Imaginary Landscape No. 1,* 1939).

Despite these developments, activity in electronic music and in the use of noise as a primary musical resource remained on the fringes of the main musical currents during this period. One reason was technical: early electronic instruments were quite primitive in both construction and sound-producing capacity. Moreover, there was as yet no efficient means for storing, transforming, and combining recorded musical sounds; recording on magnetic tape, though invented in 1935, did not become widely available until after World War II. Equally important, the general musical climate was not yet fully conducive to a radically new conception of music in which such experiments could prosper. Despite ground-breaking tonal and rhythmic innovations, dominant figures such

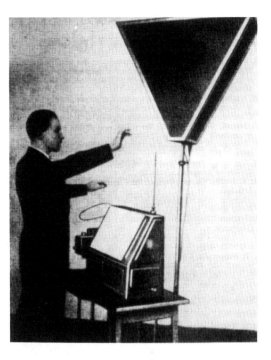

Lev Termen playing the
theremin, ca. 1927.

as Schoenberg and Stravinsky remained committed to the traditional
tempered pitch system—and thus also to traditional musical instruments. And although some of the inventions mentioned above were
put to practical use by composers, such cases as the original 1934 version of Varèse's *Ecuatorial* (with parts for two theremins) and Messiaen's 1937 *Fête des belles eaux* (scored for six ondes martenots) remained
exceptional.

MUSIQUE CONCRÈTE

The real inception of electronic music as a key compositional movement came after World War II, when new technologies and new attitudes joined to foster its advance. The earliest significant developments
took place in 1948 at the French National Radio, where the sound tech-
nician Pierre Schaeffer (b. 1910) began producing short tape studies based
on transformations of "natural" sounds, such as those of a train or a
piano. The transformational processes included editing out portions of
the sound, varying the playback speed, playing the sounds backward
("tape reversal"), and combining different sounds ("overdubbing"). Since
any natural sound could be treated as a "sound object" (Schaeffer's term
for a sonic event subjected to such manipulations), all sounds were equally

suitable as a basis for musical material. Schaeffer called this type of electronic music *musique concrète,* a name that has become standard (in its original French form) for all tape music based on natural, or "concrete," sounds, in distinction to "electronic music" in which the original sounds are produced artificially—that is, by purely electronic means.

Schaeffer was soon joined by the French composer Pierre Henry (b. 1927), with whom he produced the first extended work of *musique concrète, Symphonie pour un homme seul* (*Symphony for a Man Alone,* 1950), based mainly on various types of modified vocal sounds (breathing, laughing, whistling, speech), combined with other types of transformed sound (orchestral music, footsteps, etc.). In 1951 Schaeffer's studio was formally constituted as the Groupe de Musique Concrète. Many composers active during the 1950s became interested in the studio, and several prominent figures, including Messiaen, Varèse, Boulez, Stockhausen, and Xenakis, created *musique concrète* compositions there.

Similar studios were soon established elsewhere. In 1951 Vladimir Ussachevsky (b. 1911) and Otto Luening (b. 1900) founded a tape studio at Columbia University in New York, producing a number of collaborative tape works, including *Transposition* and *Reverberation* (both 1952, based on piano sounds), as well as independent works such as Ussachevsky's *Sonic Contours* (1952, also based on piano sounds) and Luening's *Fantasy in Space* (1952, based on prerecorded flute sounds). Unlike the French composers, the Americans almost exclusively used specifically "musical" sounds as a starting point.

ELECTRONIC STUDIOS

The first studio designed to produce music entirely by electronic means was founded in 1952 by the German composer Herbert Eimert (b. 1897) at the West German Radio in Cologne. In addition to variable-speed tape recorders and the filters, echo chambers, amplifiers, and the like found in *musique concrète* studios, Eimert's studio also contained electronic sound-producing devices: oscillators and noise generators. With these, composers could construct their own material "from the ground up," rather than relying upon natural sounds with predetermined timbral characteristics that, even when modified, could not be completely removed. To serial composers this was a critical distinction, for they saw in electronic music a means for controlling, not only pitches and durations, but also the sonic materials themselves. Besides generating the music's structure from a single integrated compositional plan, its timbre could be so derived as well. Stockhausen, who joined Eimert in Cologne after working briefly in Schaeffer's Paris studio, expressed this attitude in a 1952 article: "For a work X there will be only 'sounds' with X character, because the sounds are the result of the compositional process, not of 'pre-formed' timbres."[1]

Stockhausen's earliest compositions at the Cologne studio, *Study I* (1953) and *Study II* (1954), were the first examples of pure electronic music. They systematically explored one of the basic techniques of early electronic sound construction, "additive" synthesis, through which sounds are created by combining sine waves ("pure" pitches with no overtones) in order to create artificial overtone structures and thus new timbres. *Study II* eventually became the first published electronic score, in a graphic notation specially invented by the composer for the purpose (Example XXII-1 reproduces one of its pages). In the upper half of the page the horizontal axis represents time, the vertical axis frequency (pitch), and each rectangular box a single sonic event; the relative horizontal position of a rectangle indicates a note's pitch, the width its duration, and the height its overtone structure. (Since in this piece every sound is constructed of five equidistant sine tones, differences in height do not indicate differences in the number of overtones, but only differences in their placement relative to the fundamental.) The geometrical figures in the lower portion of the group indicate changes in dynamics.

The widespread dissatisfaction that arose in the middle 1950s with the limitations of a rigorously applied serialism was soon mirrored by a similar discontent with the possibilities of pure electronic synthesis.

Example XXII-1: STOCKHAUSEN, *Study II,* first page

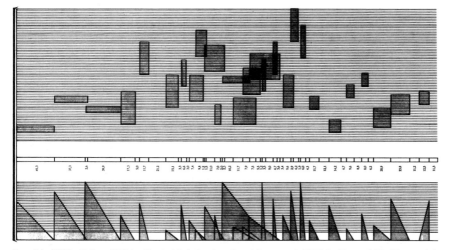

1.   *Texte I* (Cologne, 1963), p. 31.

Advantages of precision and complete control were offset by the timbral poverty of the sounds that could be achieved with techniques and equipment then available. The "dead" studio quality characteristic of pure electronic music troubled composers and listeners alike. Though of considerable historical importance and indicative of his remarkable ability to think within new compositional frameworks, Stockhausen's two early studies were in many respects quite primitive. Furthermore, Stockhausen himself was growing increasingly distrustful of an overly rigid approach, in which every sound was determined in advance, the result of the serial order of the elements.

His next electronic composition, *Gesang der Jünglinge* (1956), combined *concrète* sounds, based on a recording of a boy singing, with purely electronic sounds. The latter now included not only sine tones, both individually and in complexes, but filtered noise, achieved through a second basic technique of early electronic music: "subtractive" synthesis, in which components of a complex sound (usually electronically produced "white noise," containing the entire spectrum of audible frequencies) are filtered out in order to produce new timbres. (Subtractive synthesis applied to natural sounds had always been a standard technique of *musique concrète*.) Thus *Gesang der Jünglinge* deals with a much greater variety of sonic material than did the earlier studies. It is further enhanced by elaborate use of reverberation and of "spatial motion" produced by routing the sound through five independent loudspeakers placed in a circle around the listening space. The resulting work, of remarkable richness, was a milestone in electronic music, both as, arguably, the genre's first masterpiece and as the first composition to combine electronic and *concrète* elements.

Although Stockhausen's next tape piece, *Kontakte* (1960), was again purely electronic, his subsequent electronic compositions have all involved at least some *concrète* sources. Indeed, by the middle 1950s the sharp division between *musique concrète* and pure electronic music, previously viewed as two distinct methods based on essentially opposed compositional philosophies, had become academic.

New studios began to appear in which no rigid distinction was made between electronic and *concrète* sources. One of the earliest and most active was the Studio di Fonologia in Milan, founded in 1955, which maintained an entirely open attitude toward compositional approach. Henri Pousseur's *Scambi*, produced there in 1957, was purely electronic (its only sound source was "white noise"), while Luciano Berio's *Thema: Omaggio a Joyce* (*Theme: Homage to Joyce*, 1958) was entirely *concrète*, derived from a recorded recitation of a passage from James Joyce's *Ulysses*, first presented normally as a kind of prelude to the piece and then treated as a "sound system," broken up into its constituent elements and reassembled into a new, entirely "musical" structure. Berio's later *Visage* (1961), on the other hand, combined electronically generated sounds with *concrète* ones (again produced by voice, but consisting mainly of semantically meaningless vocal gestures rather than spoken language), producing what the composer described as a "bilevel" structure. Among many others who worked at the Milan studio during these early years was John Cage, whose several works produced there include *Fontana Mix* (1958).

During the later 1950s studios were founded in Tokyo (1956), Warsaw (1957), London (1958), Brussels (1958), and Stockholm (1958), all sponsored—like the earlier ones in Paris, Cologne, and Milan—by state-owned radio systems. At the same time, a number of private or university-affiliated studios appeared in the United States and Canada, among them Gordon Mumma and Robert Ashley's Cooperative Studio for Electronic Music in Ann Arbor, Michigan (1958), Morton Subotnick's San Francisco Tape Music Center (1959), and studios at the University of Illinois and the University of Toronto (both 1958). The first private studio had been founded some years previously by Louis and Bebe Baron in New York. (The Barons, primarily involved in commercial music, produced the first electronic score for a film, the science-fiction classic *Forbidden Planet*.) Here John Cage, who was among the first to be interested in the electronic medium, created his earliest tape works, *Imaginary Landscape No. 5* and *Williams Mix* (both 1952), the former based on material previously recorded on disc, the latter on a jumble of countless tape-recorded sounds, mostly *concrète* in nature. In both, the sound materials were spliced together in a collagelike manner, the length of tape used for each splice determined by chance operations.

SYNTHESIZERS

By 1960 electronic music was indisputably established as a vital element in contemporary music. Virtually every younger composer of importance, and many older ones, had made at least some use of the new medium. Moreover, electronic music had begun to assume commercial significance in radio, television, and film, mainly as a source of unusual background effects. With the growth of both professional and public interest in the medium, more research was directed toward new equipment for electronic studios. The most important advance was the discovery of a way to integrate the various available components— oscillators, amplifiers, envelope generators, filters, etc.—within one console, so that the individual units could be combined and controlled by a single voltage control device (usually a keyboard). This integrated unit, which with the simple addition of a tape recorder became a basic electronic studio, was called a "synthesizer"—that is, a machine capable of artificially combining, or synthesizing, purely electronic sounds.

The impact of synthesizers on the musical world was twofold: elec-

Milton Babbitt working at the Columbia-Princeton Electronic Music Center, New York City, ca. 1960.

tronic music was brought within the financial reach of a much larger group of musicians, and the amount of time required to complete basic electronic operations was greatly reduced. In a "classical studio" (the name given the standard presynthesizer studio, containing tape recorders and independent electronic components) the creation of a series of different pitches of different durations—a "melody"—required that each pitch be separately recorded on tape, each piece of recorded tape cut to the correct length for the desired duration, and the different pieces spliced together in the desired sequence. With a voltage-controlled synthesizer, on the other hand, variable voltages could be applied to a single oscillator to produce different pitches; thus a sequence of pitches and durations could be produced by pressing keys on a keyboard (for example) for the required lengths of time, as one does when playing a piano. What might have taken hours in a classical studio could be produced in "real time"—in seconds—on a synthesizer. To be sure, synthesizers had their disadvantages. The composer was limited to the particular modules placed in a given console, and the sound also tended to have a certain overall sameness—a "prepackaged" quality. The most flexible studios thus combined the capacities of a typical classical studio (encompassing *musique concrète*) with those of one or more synthesizers.

The first successful synthesizer was the RCA Mark II, developed at the Sarnoff Research Center in New Jersey, completed in 1955, and later given to the Columbia-Princeton Electronic Music Center, an outgrowth of the studio founded at Columbia by Ussachevsky and Luening. In addition to its new timbral resources, this instrument gave composers an unprecedented degree of control over their materials, enabling them to achieve absolutely precise "performances" of extremely complex conceptions. It appealed especially to those inclined toward strict compositional control, such as Milton Babbitt, who has realized all of his electronic music on the Mark II, beginning with his Composition for Synthesizer (1961) and including such ground-breaking works as *Philomel* (1964).

Though the most sophisticated electronic instrument of its time, the Mark II was heavy and bulky and in certain respects still tedious to use. It was superseded by a number of smaller and more practical synthesizers that lent themselves readily to mass production. Among the most important designers were Robert Moog and Donald Buchla, both of whom had produced commercially available synthesizers bearing their names by the middle 1960s.

The audio inventor Robert Moog testing his electronic instruments (photographed in the mid 70s).

The first composer to be closely identified with these smaller synthesizers was the American Morton Subotnick (b. 1933), who realized a series of large-scale electronic works on a Buchla. The earliest, *Silver Apples of the Moon* (1966), was the first electronic composition commissioned by a record company (Nonesuch), and it was followed by, among others, *The Wild Bull* (1967), *Touch* (1969), *Sidewinder* (1970), and *Until Spring* (1975). Subotnick employed a rich and varied spectrum of timbres, ranging from the clear, bell-like sonorities of *Touch* to the expressive "wailing" of *The Wild Bull,* and incorporated them in a relatively accessible style characterized by a judicious use of repetitive patterns (produced with the aid of a "sequencer," a standard component of most synthesizers). He was perhaps the first composer to make electronic music palatable to a relatively large group of listeners, and his works did much to bring electronic music and the synthesizer to public consciousness. An even more dramatic impetus to public acceptance was the phenomenal success of *Switched-On Bach* (1968), a commercial recording featuring virtuosic arrangements for Moog synthesizer, by Walter (later Wendy) Carlos, of compositions by J. S. Bach. With this disc, "synthesizer" became, almost overnight, a household word.

LIVE AND ELECTRONIC MIXTURES

From the earliest days of electronic music, both composers and audiences have been troubled by the seemingly "unnatural" phenomenon of concerts where there is nothing to look at but an amplifier, a tape recorder, and some loudspeakers. (As a result, a sizable portion of music for tape alone has been intended to accompany some sort of visual presentation, such as a film or dance.) The excitement and tension provided by a live performer—the uncertainty and the immediate expressive contact, as well as visual stimulus—is missing. Another peculiarity is that, once composed, an electronic piece is forever fixed in exactly the same form, deprived of the continuous enrichment that results from interaction with changing performers and performing traditions. Consequently, the combination of tape music with live performance played a significant part in electronic music virtually from its origin, and gained considerably in importance during the 1960s. The earliest work to combine tape and live instrumental music was the *Musica su due dimensioni (Music on Two Dimensions)* for flute, percussion, and tape, created by Bruno Maderna in the Cologne studio in 1952. Shortly thereafter Ussachevsky and Luening collaborated on two works for orchestra and tape: *Rhapsodic Variations* and *Poem in Cycles and Bells,* both completed in 1954. In this same year Varèse's *Déserts* appeared, alternating sections for chamber ensemble with segments of purely electronic music.

In these early works the tendency was to emphasize timbral contrasts between the taped and performed music. Later in the 1950s, however, composers also began to explore the possibilities of mediating between the two types of music, exploiting similarities as well as differences. Pousseur's *Rimes pour différentes sources sonores* (Rhymes for Different Sound Sources, 1959), for example, focuses on parallels (the "rhymes" of the title) between electronically generated sounds and the timbres of three orchestral groups, while Berio's *Différences* for chamber group and tape (1959) exploits the differences between the sounds of "live" instruments and those of the same instruments electronically modified on a prerecorded tape.

Most composers who have worked intensively with electronic music have written works combining live and electronic sounds, among them Stockhausen (whose *Kontakte* exists both as a separate tape piece and as a work for tape with two pianos and percussion) and Babbitt (whose compositions for voice and tape—*Vision and Prayer* and *Philomel*—rank among his most significant compositions). Mario Davidovsky (b. 1934), an Argentinian now living in the United States, has specialized in live-electronic mixtures. In eight compositions entitled *Synchronisms,* composed between 1962 and 1974, he has explored the possibilities of "dialogues" between taped music and various performing forces, ranging from a single instrument to full orchestra and chorus. Davidovsky's delicate sense of timbral balance and his ability to produce electronic sounds that subtly evoke the instruments with which they are paired (but without attempting to imitate them) have enabled him to create tape parts that assume an almost "unexceptional" role in the ensemble, that function as equal partners in a unified and integrated whole.

Purely electronic compositions rarely exist in score form, since none is needed for "performance," only to supply purely technical information about how the composition was made (Stockhausen's *Study II*—see Example XXII-1—is thus a rarity). However, pieces combining live and electronic music do require some kind of score to assure precise coordination of the two components. Three examples suggest the range of solutions that have been adopted (Example XXII-2). Davidovsky's *Synchronism No. 1* for flute and tape (2a) employs a radically simplified notation of the tape part, intended only as a cue for the flutist and mainly confined to indicating entrances and cutoffs. Stockhausen's *Kontakte* (2b), on the other hand, offers in its upper system a relatively detailed graphic depiction of how the electronic part sounds. Finally, the tape part of Babbitt's *Philomel* (2c) is represented entirely through ordinary notation, which in his case is possible because his electronic music is conceived in very much the same terms as his instrumental music (except for the extraordinary metrical complications, which would be impractical in live performance).

Example XXII-2: Examples of electronic music notation

a. DAVIDOVSKY, *Synchronism No. 1,* opening

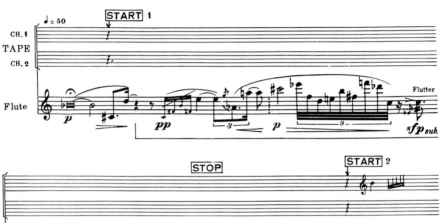

b. STOCKHAUSEN, *Kontakte,* excerpt

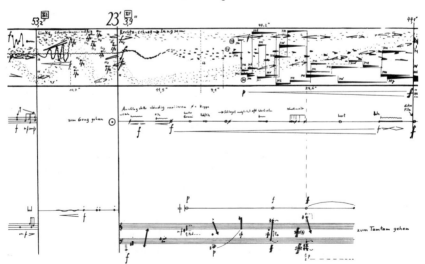

C. BABBITT, *Philomel,* excerpt

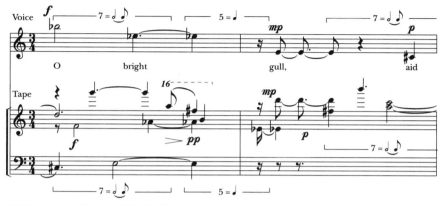

Used by permission of Associated Music Publishers, Inc.

LIVE ELECTRONIC MUSIC

Another way of overcoming the "fixed" character of taped music is to use the electronic medium itself as a vehicle for live performance. Cage was among the first to try to eliminate the "closed" nature of electronic music, a problem that affected his own tape compositions, despite their indeterminate nature, as much as those of others. One solution he offered was to combine performances of his electronic compositions with those of acoustic pieces: playing his *Fontana Mix* simultaneously with his *Aria* for solo voice, for example. Another solution was to manipulate the tape recorder during performances (by slowing it down, changing control settings, etc.). However, Cage's first truly "live" electronic piece—and probably the earliest work of its type—was *Cartridge Music* (1960), which calls for performers to activate small objects, such as toothpicks or feathers, that have been substituted for the stylus in a phonograph cartridge; or, in another version, to move large objects, such as tables or chairs, to which contact microphones have been attached. In both cases the result is amplified and transmitted through loudspeakers to the audience.

During the early 1960s Stockhausen sought close integration of electronic and instrumental music through the electronic manipulation of live performances. In his earliest work of this type, *Mikrophonie I* (1964), two performers produce various sounds on a large tam-tam (beating or scraping it with different objects), while two "microphonists" pick up the results and transmit them to a bank of electronic modules manned by two additional performers, who in turn subject the sounds to electronic modifications before sending them to loudspeakers. "The division of the musical process into three independent areas (sound production, sound recording, and sound transformation)," Stockhausen noted, "makes it possible to combine the possibilities of instrumental practice with those of electronic techniques. Any desired sound source (traditional instruments, sound events of whatever nature) can thus be integrated into a coherent sound composition."[2]

Stockhausen applied this idea to different sound sources in a series of works, including *Mixtur* (chamber orchestra, 1964) and *Mikrophonie II* (chorus, 1965). In 1964, having formed his own small performing group, the Stockhausen Ensemble, which specialized in partially improvisatory performances of live electronic music, he wrote a number of compositions utilizing real-time electronic transformations, including *Prozession* (1967), *Kurzwellen* (1968), and *Aus den sieben Tagen* (1968). By the later 1960s several exclusively improvisatory groups using live electronics had come into existence, including MEV in Rome and the English groups AMM, Gentle Fire, and Intermodulation.

An important factor in the growth of live electronics was the advent of relatively portable synthesizers, some designed expressly for concert purposes. A leading figure in the early use of these instruments was John Eaton, who began writing concert pieces for the Syn-Ket, a performance synthesizer—the first of its kind—designed for him by the sound engineer Paolo Ketoff in 1964. Between 1965 and 1970 Eaton composed several highly dramatic compositions for soprano accompanied by Syn-Ket, either alone or in combination with small instrumental ensembles, as well as solo Syn-Ket pieces and a concert piece for Syn-Ket and orchestra. Eaton's preference for microtonal tunings made electronic instruments, which have no particular disposition toward the equal-tempered twelve-note scale, especially useful. His *Mass* (1970), perhaps the most virtuosic of his electronic-vocal-instrumental mixtures, is scored for soprano, clarinet, three Syn-Kets, Moog synthesizer, and a tape-delay system. Extreme vocal gestures, clarinet multiphonics, and other timbral distortions are exploited to create close analogies between the live and electronic sounds, producing an unusually tightly knit ensemble effect and an intensely expressive statement.

A parallel development in live electronics involved the construction of electronic systems designed primarily for use in indeterminate performance situations. A simple example is the multiple-tape-loop system used in Cage's *Mozart Mix* (1965). The performer is instructed to make a large number of tape loops (brief segments of tape whose beginning and end are spliced together to form a loop, so that the recorded material repeats itself constantly), to choose some of these at random, and to play them simultaneously on several tape recorders. Other examples are Robert Ashley's *Wolfman,* for amplified singer and tape (1964), which employs a feedback system to achieve high volume levels

2.   *Texte III* (Cologne, 1971), p. 57.

that would be unattainable through normal amplification, and Gordon Mumma's *Hornpipe* (1967), for modified horn (the normal mouthpiece replaced by a double reed) and "cybersonic console" (a small sound-producing unit worn on the belt and designed to "react" to the sounds of the horn).

Composers have also worked with tape-delay systems, using two tape recorders, one recording material while the other plays it back after a brief delay. In the nature of such systems, a constant "feedback loop" is formed: what is played back by the second recorder is recorded again by the first one, then played back again (after another delay) by the second, and so forth. Among numerous works using tape delay are Stockhausen's *Solo* for any melody instrument (1966) and Alvin Lucier's *I Am Sitting in a Room* for speaking voice (1970).

By 1970 live electronics had also assumed a significant role in popular music and jazz. A number of rock groups active during the late 1960s, including The Velvet Underground, The Grateful Dead, and The Mothers of Invention, used electronic synthesizers extensively, and an early example of tape delay is found on Miles Davis's record *Bitches Brew,* a pioneering example of "fusion" (i.e., fusing elements of jazz and rock). Electronics, often used with remarkable technical sophistication, have since become a standard resource of virtually all popular music groups. The wide dissemination during the 1980s of digital synthesizers, capable of generating extraordinarily complex sounds with a remarkably modest physical apparatus, has further encouraged the development of electronic music, creating a wealth of new sonic possibilities currently being exploited by both composers and performers.

COMPUTER MUSIC

Unlike electronic synthesizers, computers are not themselves sound-producing instruments, but they have proved remarkably useful in connection with sound synthesis. Computer synthesis works on the principle that specifications for the various elements (or "parameters") of a desired sound (frequency, amplitude, duration, waveform) can be expressed in digital form; once thus encoded, this information can be fed into a computer, processed, and ultimately transformed by means of a digital-to-analogue converter (DAC) into electronically produced sound. A distinct advantage of generating sound through a computer is that it allows composers to design their own digital "instruments," rather than having to rely upon pre-existing electronic hardware, such as oscillators with already built-in timbral characteristics. (At least in principle, any conceivable sound can be achieved simply by inputting the proper digital information; the difficulty is in predicting the precise sound that will result from a given input.) Another advantage is that the most complex imaginable musical relationships—rhythmic, timbral, or whatever—can be exactly encoded and thus realized with absolute accuracy in recorded form. (Here the difficulty is to avoid a mechanical quality that may result from such exact specifications—for example, from rigidly proportioned subdivisions of a metrical unit.)

The application of computers to sound synthesis was pioneered by the American electrical engineer Max V. Matthews, who in 1957 at Bell Laboratories in New Jersey developed the first program capable of generating musical sound, the progressively more sophisticated successors of which culminated in the program known as Music V. Adaptations of Matthews's programs were installed in computers at Princeton University in 1964 and shortly thereafter at Stanford University. The earliest computer music studio in Europe was founded in Utrecht, Holland, also in 1964. Although interest in computers among musicians remained relatively limited during these early years, it eventually expanded until by the 1980s computer music facilities, some with considerable resources, were in operation throughout the world.

Among the pioneers in composition for computer synthesized sound were the Americans J. K. Randall (b. 1929), Hubert Howe (b. 1942), and James Tenney (b. 1934); New Zealand–born Barry Vercoe (b. 1937, now head of the computer music center at the Massachusetts Institute of Technology); and the German Gottfried Michael Koenig (b. 1926), who founded the Utrecht studio. Most of these composers have used computers primarily for producing purely electronic sounds, although computer music can also be combined with prerecorded vocal or instrumental parts (as in Randall's *Mudgett: Monologues by a Mass Murderer,* 1965) or with live performers. A composer who devotes a sizable portion of his output to combinations of the latter type is the American John Melby (b. 1941)—for example, his *Accelerazioni* for flute and computer-synthesized tape (1979).

Computers can also be used to transform prerecorded "natural" sounds, thus producing a computerized form of *musique concrète*. For his *Story of Our Lives* (1974), the American Charles Dodge (b. 1942) recorded normal spoken language, then converted the sounds into digital information (through an analogue-to-digital converter), analyzed and modified the results for compositional purposes, and resynthesized the modified material into sound. The composition thus consists of distortions of the original spoken sounds, with timbre, pitch, velocity, etc., altered, often so much so that distinctions between speech and song are obscured. An analogous technique was used by Hans Werner Henze in his *Tristan* (1974), a work for piano, orchestra, and a tape incorporating computer-assisted transformations of passages from Wagner's *Tristan und Isolde.* Another example, *Chronometer* (1971), by the English composer Harrison Birtwistle (b. 1934), is based on digital manipulation of sounds produced by various kinds of clocks.

Computers can also be used as control devices in electronic studios— that is, not to actually generate sound, which comes from the normal electronic equipment in the studio, but to send instructions to this equipment. This allows advance programming of elaborate changes in the settings and interconnections of the electronic modules and the making of these changes instantaneously and automatically, without manual assistance, according to a predetermined plan. In effect, this turns the electronic studio into a real-time instrument, programmed with its own "memory." Such so-called "hybrid" studios, in which synthesizers and other electronic equipment are interfaced with a computer, were increasingly common for a time, but now the digital synthesizers mentioned in the previous section seem to be replacing the older analogue electronic equipment.

Finally, computers have been used, though less widely, to actually "compose" music. Here the computer is programmed to make compositional decisions according to criteria derived from some arbitrarily chosen stylistic canon. Early examples include the attempt by a group working at Harvard in the 1950s under the direction of F. B. Brooks to produce computer-generated hymn tunes, and Lejaren Hiller and Leonard Isaacson's *Illiac Suite* for string quartet (1956), each movement of which was "composed" by a different computer program intended to mimic a particular compositional style (Bach, Bartók, etc.). Xenakis also used computer-assisted calculations in the composition of several of his works during the early 1960s (e.g., his *ST/4* for string quartet, completed in 1962). In general, however, there has been relatively little interest in this area since the 1960s.

A vivid indication of the growing importance of computer technology in the field of contemporary music is provided by the Institut de Recherche et de Coordination Acoustique / Musique (IRCAM) in Paris. Founded in 1976 under the general direction of Pierre Boulez (who greatly reduced his conducting career in order to assume this position) and funded by the French government, IRCAM is a large and active research organization devoted to the scientific study of musical phenomena and to bringing together scientists and musicians to work on common interests.

The IRCAM installation incorporates the most advanced computer facilities currently available, which are used both for sound synthesis and in connection with research on acoustics and on the physical and psychological aspects of aural perception. Considerable emphasis is placed on the use of computers as real-time performing instruments, especially to assist in transforming instrumental sounds. Boulez's still-unfinished *Répons,* for large chamber ensemble, widely performed as a work-in-progress, effectively exploits subtle real-time computer modifications of live instrumental music. Many prominent composers, representing stylistic persuasions ranging from Luciano Berio to the jazz composer George Lewis, have worked at IRCAM, and its former director of musical research, the American Tod Machover (b. 1952), is one of a growing number of young composers who are completely conversant with the computer and its musical applications.

THE IMPACT OF TECHNOLOGY ON TWENTIETH-CENTURY MUSIC

Electronic music is but one of a number of technological developments that have profoundly affected music and musical life during the twentieth century. One of the earliest and most significant of these was the phonograph, invented in the latter part of the previous century. By the interwar years recordings had become a normal part of the musical experience for many in the Western world. The phonograph's ability to preserve performances indelibly had a pronounced, if gradual, effect on attitudes about both performance and composition. With regard to the former, the phonograph, placing unprecedented emphasis on technical finish, tended to favor an objective and "streamlined" mode of presentation, as opposed to more personal and idiosyncratic ones, which were apt to sound increasingly stilted when repeated in exactly the same manner.

Recordings have also influenced views of what is practical in terms of performance difficulty for new music. The effort and cost of preparing an adequate realization of an unusually complex work are more easily justified when the results include a recording that can be made accessible to many more listeners than those attending a single concert. Extremely difficult compositions, which might otherwise be performed once and never heard again, can achieve a sort of instantaneous permanence, and composers are thereby encouraged to be less mindful of difficulty.

The phonograph brought the average listener a previously unimagined variety of music, and another innovation, the radio, dramatically extended that range. Although the first commercial radio station came into existence only in 1920, by the 1930s most Western countries had relatively comprehensive radio systems offering an extensive choice of programming. For the music listener, radio provided a sort of ideal music library, with access to both extensive record archives and broadcasts of live performances. As the century progressed, the repertory eventually encompassed popular, folk, and art music from all over the world, as well as a significant body of music from the past. Today the

The sophisticated equipment in this state-of-the-art recording studio includes a Solid State Logic 4056 recording console (center), various signal processors (at left), and 48-track analog or digital master tape recorders. The view is from the control room through to the studio. (Platinum Island Studios/NYC)

listener in a large city can, by simply turning a dial, move instantaneously through a remarkable panorama of musical styles and genres. Necessarily, this has altered our whole notion of what constitutes our own musical culture, a point to which we will return in the final chapter.

As for electronic music itself, the sheer number and variety of sounds it has placed at the composer's disposal has decisively influenced compositional practice. Perhaps most consequential has been the blurring of the distinction between musical sound and noise, with the latter becoming a more and more significant compositional element. The specific characteristics of certain electronic sounds have also suggested extensions in instrumental writing. There are, for example, definite correspondences between "ring-modulated" electronic sound and multiphonic woodwind sonorities. And simulations of tape-delay effects—by progressively reducing the volume of each figure in a repeating pattern—have become a cliché in recent instrumental music.

However, the invention with perhaps the greatest impact on compositional technique has been the tape recorder. We tend to think of the tape recorder as an essentially "passive" instrument, a means for storing sounds, and many composers, including those working with electronic music, continue to use it primarily for this purpose. But it can also be used as an active participant in the compositional process, as an instrument in its own right with definite characteristics, capable of impressing its personality on the music with which it is associated. Armed with a recorder, for example, a composer can collect and store material specifically chosen for a particular composition, taking sounds either from the "real world" (as in *musique concrète*) or synthetically constructed in an electronic studio. Once recorded, this material takes on an "object-like" quality quite unlike anything previously known in music: it exists in tangible form on a piece of tape, and can be worked with almost as a sculptor works with physical material, shaped in different ways to produce different sonic characteristics (through electronic transformation, fragmentation, juxtaposition, etc.). This possibility fundamentally transforms the way sound is conceived and compositionally manipulated, and its effects are almost as readily observable in some recent instrumental pieces as they are in electronic ones.

The process of putting together pretaped sound—whether by splicing together bits of heterogeneous materials or by combining individual events into complex simultaneous assemblages through multitrack recording—has led many composers to reinterpret what it means to "compose." The tape recorder seems to have decisively promoted the idea that any sound material whatever is appropriate for musical purposes, that any sound can be combined with, or set off against, any other material at all. A tendency to join diverse elements in collagelike textures can be perceived as early as Debussy and, especially, Ives (perhaps reflecting, in their cases, awareness of the new medium of film and its techniques of splicing and rapid crosscutting), and this tendency was carried on by Stravinsky and Varèse, among others, in the between-war years. But only since World War II have extremely abrupt oppositions of contrasting materials or their combination in multileveled structures become a dominant characteristic of a sizable portion of the music in the Western world.

CHAPTER XXIII

Epilogue: Music Today

THE CURRENT MUSICAL SCENE

In surveying the proliferation of new ideas and directions that have typified music of the post–World War II period, we have, for important historical reasons, focused mainly on works composed during the 1950s and 1960s. The two leading schools of the 1950s, serialism and indeterminacy, radically challenged traditional conceptions of musical structure and, in the second case, even brought into question previous beliefs about the very nature of music. The first phase of the post–World War II period, so largely dominated by these two "orthodoxies," expanded the horizons of compositional possibility—of what composers deemed feasible or imaginable—beyond anything previously envisioned. This set off a burst of fresh activity in the 1960s, with far-reaching explorations of untried compositional terrain, of regions formerly considered wholly outside of—indeed, alien to—the realm of musical consideration. The conception of musical form as an "open" structure, susceptible to various external influences, including the external world itself, unlocked entirely new vistas of compositional possibility: "noise" music, brain wave music, environmental music, political music, quotation music, music as theater, etc. But this radically new, largely unfocused activity could not be indefinitely sustained, and by the early 1970s most of the truly ground-breaking works in this extraordinary stage of music history had already appeared.

A survey that concentrates mainly upon new developments necessarily emphasizes the revolutionary events of these earlier postwar years. But there is no question that in more recent years compositional tendencies have become considerably less radical. Looking back over the 1970s, one can recognize a widespread movement, among composers of varied temperaments and stylistic persuasions, toward a more traditional and conservative orientation, especially evident in the wish to engage a broader and less specialized musical public. (Some of these tendencies were discussed in Chapter XX.) If the 1960s can be seen as a decade largely characterized by musical alienation, with its more radical manifestations often directed explicitly against the status quo, against traditional concert music, and against the concert situation itself, the 1970s represented a period of widespread reconciliation. Instead of searching out new possibilities, composers became interested in finding ways to incorporate what was already available into a more consistent and directly communicative musical language.

Taken as a whole, then, the music of the 1970s and 1980s seems decidedly more conventional in both conception and intention than the music of the earlier postwar years. Technically, this is most clearly reflected in the return to tonality, as well as in a desire to project a more direct kind of musical expressivity. The more sensual aspects of music—sustained melodic development, richly colored textures, and the like—have received new and general emphasis. Jacob Druckman (b. 1928), a leading figure in the adoption of a more traditional position, has written of the reemergence, in this most recent musical "revolution," of such "Dionysian" qualities as "sensuality, mystery, nostalgia, ecstasy, transcendency." It would be difficult to imagine a more drastic reaction against the quasi-scientific rigors of serialism or the expressive neutrality of indeterminacy than is reflected in these terms.

David Del Tredici and George Rochberg, whose efforts to "rediscover" tonality were discussed previously, are among those who began to adopt a more traditional and openly expressive tone at a relatively early stage. But many others, including composers such as Maxwell Davies, Penderecki, and Henze, whose earlier work has been treated here in quite different contexts, have embarked on similar courses, though with varying degrees of emphasis. If one defines the trend broadly enough, such figures as Stockhausen and the no-longer-so-minimalist Reich and Glass also belong within it, as distinct traces of more traditional thought are to be found in their latest work. Among the many young composers who reached maturity only after the trend was already well under way, and for whom the new conservativism is thus not so much a reaction as a norm, are the American John Adams, the Englishman Jonathan Lloyd (b. 1948), and the Dane Hans Abrahamsen (b. 1952).

These widespread developments have greatly affected the musical climate of the past fifteen years or so, giving rise to such descriptive catchphrases as "new simplicity" and "new romanticism." While the obvious importance of these tendencies cannot be denied, they must be seen and evaluated within a broad historical context. Neither the simplicity nor the romanticism found in recent music is really new; both of these attributes are equally applicable to any number of composers from all historical phases of twentieth-century music. And although the movement of so many composers of such varied persuasions in a conservative direction is perhaps unprecedented, the numbers are not yet sufficiently large or the musical results sufficiently focused in style or technique to confirm the turning of a critical historical corner, comparable to those turned in the years around 1910 and 1950.

Indeed, recent compositional developments have not put an end to—or even seriously weakened—the continued growth of either of the dominant "progressive" currents in twentieth-century music: the mainstream tradition of "advanced" concert music or the more radical tributaries of "alternative music." For example, in the first category it is possible to list a succession of prominent living American composers, the oldest born shortly after the turn of the century and the youngest at its midpoint, who have remained relatively untouched by the new conservatism, continuing to write concert music conceived in an essentially post-tonal language: Carter, Babbitt, Andrew Imbrie (b. 1921), Richard Wernick (b. 1934), Wuorinen, and Shulamit Ran (b. 1949). Similarly, most of the leading figures belonging in the second category, including Cage, Lucier, Ashley, and Oliveros (again to stay with Americans), have remained faithful to the esthetic positions they helped define in the 1950s and 1960s.

It is therefore too soon to say whether the compass of these recent trends will be sufficient to require a wholesale rethinking of the history of twentieth-century music. Conceivably, of course, they might prove so dominant and durable that the musical revolutions on which this survey has focused will come to be seen as part of a bizarre and only temporary diversion within a more extended period of common practice, spanning eighteenth- and nineteenth-century tonality and the new "neo-tonality" as well. If that is so, then certain twentieth-century repertories that have been slighted here—the later works of Richard Strauss come immediately to mind—may prove to be of much greater historial significance than now appears to be the case, as links between the old music and the new.

Nevertheless, the current musical scene offers scant evidence that things will turn out this way. Speaking strongly against it is the simultaneous existence of so many diverse compositional approaches, perhaps the most telling feature of contemporary musical life. As we have seen throughout the latter part of this survey, the remarkably pluralistic nature of music in the so-called "postmodern" (or, musically speaking, "post-serial") age has been manifested in a range of compositional attitudes and esthetic ideologies unprecedented in the history of Western music. Even basic distinctions between what is and is not music are no longer easily maintained, and lines between different types of music have often faded to the point of invisibility. Not merely do many different forms of music—various styles of concert music, popular music, folk music, etc.—exist simultaneously; that has to some extent always been the case. Now they impinge upon one another, both directly and indirectly, and often overlap entirely. We may well be at the beginning of an enduring "posthistorical" period during which different and often changing styles and esthetics will coexist simultaneously—at times peacefully, at times in conflict, but always in colorful profusion and interaction.

THE CULTURE OF MUSICAL PLURALISM

In discussing the historical background of modern music in Chapter I, we referred to the gradual erosion during the nineteenth century of the idea of a "universal" musical language. Viewed within this larger historical framework, the ultimate breakdown of the traditional tonal system in the early years of the present century was something like the last nail in the coffin: the final collapse of a communal form of musical expression that had flourished for several centuries but was by then in the advanced stages of decline. Once certain composers had made the decision to discard traditional tonality completely, music was suddenly free—or condemned, according to one's point of view—to develop in previously unthinkable ways. With no prevailing standard of reference to serve as a check, no "center," tonal or otherwise, to provide a focus, music could flourish as a free and seemingly unlimited field of activity, where all possible compositional resources and esthetic positions, no matter how inconsistent or contradictory, how outrageous or idiosyncratic, could stand equally at the composer's disposal. What we see today is thus simply the current stage—if the most fully developed one, and perhaps even the final one—of an ongoing historical process.

The extreme pluralism of current music seems to suggest that the present period actually does not have a musical culture of its own at all—at least not in the conventional sense of a set of interconnected beliefs and attitudes that, while possibly diverse and even partially in conflict, are sufficiently rooted in common ground to insure a significant degree of overall cohesion and comprehensibility. Instead, we have a whole range of subcultures that interact and influence one another in various ways, yet remain autonomous enough to permit independent development. Each of these subcultures has its own special audience, to which it caters and upon which it depends for its existence and continued growth, and each has its own communications system, encompassing specialized printed publications, concert networks, radio programs, etc. Some, like those associated with the most recent pop rage, may be ephemeral, enjoying a brief period of intense exposure and then slipping into anonymity; others, such as various forms of jazz, rock, and modern concert music, may enjoy lengthy life spans and show no sign of faltering. Some may be relatively small, appealing to highly specialized groups, while others embrace large segments of the population. But the most striking fact is that all seem able to coexist, usually more or less peacefully, without any one group representing a true consensus, and without the ascendancy of any one at a given moment necessarily affecting the health of the others.

Signs of this new esthetic environment are everywhere apparent. An abundance of specialized performing groups devote their energies to a range of music that, taken collectively, encompasses early Western music, avant-garde music, "exotic" music (at the moment in the United States, a number of composers are writing new music for Balinese gamelan ensembles), folk music, popular music, etc. Another symptom is that symphony orchestras and opera companies, which for years represented the two dominant genres of Western art music, have increasingly assumed the status of museums devoted to preserving the musical past. No longer linked to a clearly defined culture of their own day, these institutions have largely discarded their role as an outlet for current creative activity in favor of exhibiting artifacts from earlier musical periods.

The musical past is, in fact, now with us as much as—perhaps even more than—the musical present, providing a substantial component of the eclectic mix that makes up our current musical life. Thus the pluralism of contemporary music is not only esthetic (in that it encompasses different styles of music) and geographical (encompassing music from different parts of the world), it is also historical (encompassing different chronological epochs). Gregorian chant, medieval motets, and Renaissance madrigals, to take just three examples, form almost as "audible" a component of contemporary musical life as the music of our own day —and for some listeners, at least, older music is essentially the only music they hear.

To fit this fundamentally altered set of circumstances, our concept of musical culture needs to be fundamentally redefined. What we have today is a sort of global culture, of seemingly unlimited spatial and temporal scope, that provides a vast storehouse of stylistic and technical possibilities from which composers may draw at will, combining ingredients in any desired mixture. This explains why so many composers now seem to change their technical (and even esthetic) orientation from decade to decade, in some cases from composition to composition. Thus a new way of thinking about the whole notion of style is also required. Instead of a "current musical style" in any traditional sense of this term—that is, a set of shared principles and conventions—we have only a range of shifting alternatives and provisional choices. No common thread binds together today's composers, unless it be their common unwillingness to make a single, permanent choice. The very profusion of possibilities makes all dogmatism seem arbitrary and, ultimately, pointless.

Many composers consequently believe the only appropriate esthetic position for this age is a purposefully eclectic one, treating style not as a shared and stable framework but as a provisional—and basically personal—way of choosing and combining heterogeneous elements. The "music of our time" is, then, not a specific kind of music at all, but a sort of "total music" that, at least in principle, embraces all musics that have ever existed. We are only beginning to understand the far-reaching implications of this new, all-encompassing stylistic accessibility.

An important development, closely tied to the pluralistic character of recent music, is the growing number of composers from more diverse backgrounds who are becoming involved with concert music. The various "crossover" developments discussed in earlier chapters have brought together in common endeavors musicians, often rooted in very different cultures, from jazz, popular, and art backgrounds. Although this complex topic extends beyond the scope of the present survey, the enfranchisement of various ethnic and other minority groups forms a major issue of our day, as much so in the world of music as elsewhere. And it is evident that today's more inclusive compositional atmosphere has helped create possibilities for many groups previously excluded (with very rare exceptions) from the world of concert music. A large and active group of black composers has emerged, including T. J. Anderson (b. 1928) and Olly Wilson (b. 1937), as well as others mentioned previously in this text, whose works are widely performed and who occupy positions in major academic institutions. Many gifted women are also contributing significantly to the contemporary musical scene. Along with others already named, the Americans Ellen Taaffe Zwilich (b. 1939) and Joan Tower (b. 1938), the Scot Thea Musgrave (b. 1928), the Frenchwoman Betsy Jolas (b. 1926), and the Russian Sofia Gubaidulina (b. 1931) might be mentioned as representative of a group that, at least in the younger generation, approaches parity in size and importance with its male counterpart.

MUSICAL TRADITION TODAY

The unprecedented array of music that now colors our experience has made the contemporary musician acutely conscious of the musical past. Long a factor in Western thought, historical awareness has during the twentieth century become increasingly important in shaping musical attitudes. The past is now with us as never before, and the availability of such a breadth of historical repertory has fundamentally affected the way we perceive the past, the way we think about musical tradition, and consequently the way we view the music of our own day.

To clarify this, let us consider the older view of tradition—what can perhaps be called the "traditional" Western view of tradition. During the eighteenth century, for example, composers worked within a well-defined musical and cultural context, which provided them with definite professional and social obligations, and a stylistic framework against which all technical innovations could be measured and to which they ultimately had to be accommodated. The only music normally heard was contemporary music, which was specifically conceived to fulfill various functions required by the social conventions of the day. Since the composer was almost exclusively preoccupied with concerns of the present, interest in the past was minimal.

The position of eighteenth-century composers with regard to tradition can thus be described in terms of someone walking down a narrow corridor, with the past behind and the future ahead. Although fundamentally shaped by their past (since it completely determined the route they took), such composers were conscious of it only to the extent that they were of necessity walking out of it. Moreover, only one past—the one from which they were directly emerging—was available to them, and it offered them only very limited stylistic possibilities and alternatives; the further back into the distance they looked, the dimmer the view became and the less they were able to see (and hear). The immediate past, on the other hand, represented a "natural" extension of the composers' own historical moment—something with which they felt, on the whole, quite comfortable, which they could take more or less for granted precisely because they had no real choice in determining it.

Tradition, then, constituted a largely "fixed" component of the composers' makeup, something that had been assimilated unconsciously as a result of moving along a predetermined path. Although the more progressive composers (to carry the metaphor a step further) moved more quickly along the corridor and the more conservative ones more slowly, all moved in essentially the same direction. And all shared an essentially common origin: they carried the same past with them, so to speak, as they moved forward, modifying it according to whatever they might discover lying ahead.

This straight-line, two-dimensional conception of tradition gradually eroded during the nineteenth and twentieth centuries. As more and more emphasis was placed on stylistic uniqueness and on personal differences in musical expression and intent, the common stylistic and historical framework began breaking up. Similarly, as the older, stratified social structure eroded, so did the functional purposes to which music had always been previously tied. Instead of fulfilling a social role, composition became a matter of self-expression. Finally, when the sense of a shared language and culture had sufficiently dissolved, the idea of a definitely structured, all-encompassing musical present according to which everything else was measured gave way. Without a central focus to limit their perspective, composers could consider the entire past. The past was gradually able to overtake the present, and once it became fully and readily available, many found it more congenial than the chaotic picture the present had to offer.

For the composer today, then, tradition can no longer be represented as a simple unidirectional corridor. It has become more like a very large house with innumerable separate rooms, each containing some available component of the past. Although composers do not seem to have any single assigned room of their own in this house, the building is so designed that they have more or less immediate access to all rooms. Certain of these may seem to lie close at hand (the one for nineteenth-century Romanticism, for example) and thus be more easily entered, but all can in principle be visited. Composers are thus able to *choose* their past (or, if they wish, several pasts) for the purposes of any given piece. They simply walk into the room of choice and sift through its contents for whatever they want. Once they have what they want, they can then leave the room, shutting the door behind them until they should decide to return again.

Tradition thus takes on a multidimensional structure; it is "elective" in character, providing composers with a spectrum of stylistic options cutting across all previous historical, national, ethnic, and geographical boundaries. From this it follows that compositional choices, whatever they may be, take on a certain "arbitrary" quality. Choices, no matter how basic, are just that; other choices could just as well be made—and have been made. To take one pointed example discussed previously: attempts to return to tonality within the present cultural context are necessarily willful (though no more so, it should be added, than any other choices). Tonal music acquires a new meaning: no longer a given, it has become an elected attribute.

A GLIMPSE AT THE FUTURE

From one point of view, the present age offers a moment of exceptional musical excitement and opportunity. With so many technical and stylistic alternatives at hand, plus a constant stream of technological advances opening up ever new areas of exploration, today's composers would seem free to follow their imaginations at will, to the outermost reaches of what is musically possible. Yet the price is high. The openness and eclecticism of current musical life has been bought at the expense of a system of shared beliefs and values and a community of artistic concerns. The isolation of contemporary music from the larger social fabric, as well as the extreme strategies introduced to combat this isolation, are symptomatic of this condition. Music's very freedom, which has made possible the unusually varied character of recent developments, is inextricably tied to its lack of a clearly defined social function and its consequent (often desperate) search for a role in the larger order of things.

However one feels about contemporary music, one thing nevertheless seems clear: it faithfully reflects the fragmentary character of the larger world in which it exists. The absence of a consensus in such areas as politics and religion, to say nothing of such more ephemeral matters as clothing and furniture design, finds its precise corollary in the arts. In a period in which great emphasis is placed on "doing your own thing," music, following the general tendency, mirrors the world. Whether or not one likes what one hears, current music represents an honest, if perhaps unflattering, image of a cluttered and unfocused age.

Speculation on the permanence of this condition is naturally tempting. Will the future bring a new musical consensus, reflected in the emergence of a new set of commonly shared esthetic attitudes and a new musical language widely adopted by composers and understood by a broad spectrum of the public (and thus in some way comparable to tonality)? The answer, of course, lies beyond the scope of historical consideration. But if the present is examined for clues to the future, little indicates that such a consensus is apt to form itself in the foreseeable future. Some twenty-five years ago the music theorist and cultural historian Leonard B. Meyer wrote prophetically that "the coming epoch (if, indeed, we are not already in it) will be a period of stylistic stasis, a period characterized not by a linear, cumulative development of a single fundamental style, but by the coexistence of a multiplicity of quite different styles in a fluctuating and dynamic steady-state."[1] Little has happened since to contradict Meyer's view. To the extent that music can be said to express the general spirit of an age, moreover, it cannot be expected to mirror a consensus that does not exist elsewhere. At least until there is a profound shift in contemporary consciousness, it seems likely that music will retain its present pluralistic and uncentered quality. For music to change, the world will have to change.

1.   *Music, the Arts, and Ideas* (Chicago, 1967), p. 98.

Bibliography

The following bibliography is mainly confined to more recent publications and is intended for the general English-speaking reader rather than the specialist. It is organized for the most part by composer, although a few entries have also been given for each chapter heading. An asterisk preceding an entry indicates its availability in paperback. For those wishing additional bibliographic information, *The New Grove Dictionary of Music and Musicians,* ed. Stanley Sadie, 20 vols. (London: Macmillan, 1980), is recommended.

The following abbreviations are used:

CD	*Cahiers Debussy*
CM	*Current Musicology*
COH	*Cambridge Opera Handbooks*
DR	*Die Reihe*
ISAM	Institute for Studies in American Music
IABSN	*International Alban Berg Society Newsletter*
JAMS	*Journal of the American Musicological Society*
JASI	*Journal of the Arnold Schoenberg Institute*
JM	*Journal of Musicology*
JMR	*Journal of Musicological Research*
JMT	*Journal of Music Theory*
MA	*Music Analysis*
MF	*Music Forum*
ML	*Music and Letters*
MQ	*Musical Quarterly*
MR	*The Music Review*
MT	*The Musical Times*
NCS	*Norton Critical Score*
NZM	*Neue Zeitschrift für Musik*
PNM	*Perspectives of New Music*
PRMA	*Papers of the Royal Musical Association*
SMASH	*Studia Musicologica Academiae Scientiarum Hungaricae*
YIAMR	*Yearbook, Inter-American Institute for Music Research*
19CM	*19th Century Music*

GENERAL

Adorno, Theodor W. *Philosophy of Modern Music.* Trans. Anne G. Mitchell and Wesley V. Blomster. New York: Seabury Press, 1973.

Austin, William W. *Music in the Twentieth Century.* New York: Norton, 1966.

Mitchell, Donald. *The Language of Modern Music.* London: Faber & Faber, 1963.

Mellers, Wilfrid. *Caliban Reborn: Renewal in Twentieth-Century Music.* New York: Harper & Row, 1967, Reprint 1979.

*Salzman, Eric. *Twentieth-Century Music: An Introduction.* 2nd ed. Englewood Cliffs, N. J.: Prentice-Hall, 1974.

Simms, Bryan R. *Music of the Twentieth Century.* New York: Schirmer, 1986.

Slonimsky, Nicholas. *Music Since 1900.* 4th ed. New York: Scribner's, 1971. Supplement, 1986.

Vinton, John, ed. *Dictionary of Contemporary Music.* New York: Dutton, 1971.

Watkins, Glenn. *Soundings: Music in the Twentieth Century.* New York: Schirmer, 1988.

INTRODUCTION. THE NINETEENTH-CENTURY BACKGROUND

Bailey, Robert. "The Structure of the Ring and its Evolution," *19CM* 1 (July 1977): 48.

Bujic, Bojan, ed. *Music in European Thought. 1851–1912.* Cambridge: Cambridge Univ. Press, 1988.

Cinnamon, Howard. "Tonic Arpeggiation and Successive Equal Third Relations as Elements of Tonal Evolution in the Music of Franz Liszt." *MTS* 6 (1986): 1.

Dahlhaus, Carl. *Nineteenth-Century Music.* Trans. J. Bradford Robinson. Berkeley and Los Angeles: Univ. of California Press, 1989.

―――. *Between Romanticism and Modernism.* Trans. Mary Whittall. Berkeley and Los Angeles: Univ. of California Press, 1980.

Forte, Allen. "Liszt's Experimental Idiom and Music of the Early Twentieth Century." *19CM* 10 (1987): 209.

Morgan, Robert P. "Dissonant Prolongations: Theoretical and Compositional Precedents." *JMT* 20; 1 (1976): 49.

Plantinga, Leon. *Romantic Music.* New York: W. W. Norton, 1984.

Stein, Deborah J. *Hugo Wolf's Lieder and Extensions of Tonality.* Ann Arbor, Mich.: UMI Research Press, 1985.

Taruskin, Richard. "Chernomor to Kaschei: Harmonic Sorcery; or Stravinsky's 'Angle.' " *JAMS* 38 (1985): 72.

CHAPTER I. THE HISTORICAL CONTEXT: EUROPE AT THE TURN OF THE CENTURY

Janik, Allan, and Stephen Toulmin. *Wittgenstein's Vienna*. New York: Simon & Schuster, 1973.

Gollwitzer, Heinz. *Europe in the Age of Imperialism, 1880–1914*. Trans. David Adam and Stanley Baron. London: Thames & Hudson, 1969.

Kern, Stephen. *The Culture of Time and Space 1880–1918*. Cambridge: Harvard Univ. Press, 1983.

May, Arthur J. *Vienna in the Age of Franz Josef*. Norman: Univ. of Oklahoma Press, 1966.

Romein, Jan. *The Watershed of Two Eras: Europe in 1900*. Trans. Arnold Pomerans. Middletown, Conn.: Wesleyan Univ. Press, 1978.

Rudorff, Raymond. *The Belle Epoque: Paris in the Nineties*. London: Hamilton, 1972.

Schorske, Carl E. *Fin-de-Siècle Vienna: Politics and Culture*. New York: Knopf, 1980.

Shattuck, Roger. *The Banquet Years*. New York: Random House, 1955.

Tuchman, Barbara. *The Proud Tower*. New York: Macmillan, 1966.

Weber, Eugen. *France: Fin de Siècle*. Cambridge: Harvard Univ. Press, 1986.

Zweig, Stephan. *The World of Yesterday: An Autobiography*. New York: Viking Press, 1943.

CHAPTER II. SOME TRANSITIONAL FIGURES

Abraham, Gerald. *A Hundred Years of Music*. 2nd ed. London: Duckworth, 1949.

Brody, Elaine. *Paris: The Musical Kaleidoscope 1870–1925*. New York: George Braziller, 1987.

Byrnside, Ronald L. "Musical Impressionism: The Early History of the Term." *MQ* 66, no.4 (1980): 522.

*Cooper, Martin. *French Music from the Death of Berlioz to the Death of Fauré*. London: Oxford Univ. Press, 1969.

McGrath, William. *Dionysian Art and Populist Politics in Austria*. New Haven: Yale Univ. Press, 1974.

Myers, Rollo. *Modern French Music*. New York: Praeger, 1971. Reprint, 1989.

Newlin, Dika. *Bruckner, Mahler, Schoenberg*. New York: Norton, 1978.

Palmer, Christopher. *Impressionism in Music*. London: Hutchinson Univ. Library, 1973.

Samson, Jim. *Music in Transition*. London: Dent, 1977.

CHAPTER III. THE ATONAL REVOLUTION

Comini, Alessandra. "Through a Viennese Looking-Glass Darkly: Images of Arnold Schoenberg and His Circle." *Art Magazine* 58 (May 1984): 107.

Forte, Allen. *The Structure of Atonal Music*. New Haven: Yale Univ. Press, 1973.

Kandinsky, Wassily. *Kandinsky: The Complete Writings on Art*. 2 vols. London: Faber & Faber, 1982.

Leibowitz, René. *Schoenberg and His School: The Contemporary Stage of the Language of Music*. New York: Philosophical Library, 1949. *Reprint, 1975.

Lessem, Alan Philip. "Schoenberg and the Crisis of Expressionism." *ML* 55 (1974): 429.

Perle, George. *Serial Composition and Atonality*. 5th ed. Berkeley and Los Angeles: Univ. of California Press, 1982.

*Rahn, John. *Basic Atonal Theory*. New York: Longman, 1980.

Rognoni, Luigi. *The Second Vienna School: Expressionism and Dodecaphony*. Trans. Robert W. Mann. London: Calder, 1977.

Smith, Joan Allen. *Schoenberg and His Circle: A Viennese Portrait*. New York: Schirmer, 1986.

CHAPTER IV. NEW TONALITIES

Antokoletz, Elliott. "Interval Cycles in Stravinsky's Early Ballets." *JAMS* 39, no.3 (1986): 578.

————. "The Musical Language of Bartók's Fourteen Bagatelles for Piano." *Tempo* 137 (1981): 8.

Berger, Arthur. "Problems of Pitch Organization in Stravinsky." *PNM* 2, no.1 (1963): 11.

Reti, Rudolf. *Tonality, Atonality, Pantonality: A Study of Some Trends in Twentieth-Century Music*. New York: Macmillan, 1958. Reprint, 1978.

Taruskin, Richard. "*Chez Pétrouchka:* Harmony and Tonality *chez* Stravinsky." *19CM* 10, no.3 (1987): 265.

CHAPTER V. OTHER EUROPEAN CURRENTS

Russia

Abraham, Gerald. *Masters of Russian Music*. New York: Knopf, 1936. Reprint, 1971.

Asafiev, Boris. *Russian Music from the Beginning of the Nineteenth Century*. Trans. Alfred J. Swan. Ann Arbor, Mich.: Edwards, 1953.

Italy

Payton, Rodney J. "The Music of Futurism: Concerts and Polemics." *MQ* 62 (1976): 25.

Radice, Mark. "Futurismo: Its Origins, Context, Repertory, and Influence." *MQ* 73 (1989): 1.

Russolo, Luigi. *The Art of Noises*. Trans. Barclay Brown. New York: Pendragon, 1986.

*Tisdall, Caroline, and Angelo Bozolla. *Futurism*. London: Thames & Hudson, 1977.

Czechoslovakia

Berkovec, Jiři. *Five Chapters on Czech Music and Musicians*. Prague: Orbis, 1975.

Stepanek, Vladimir, and Bohumil Krasek. *An Outline of Czech and Slovak Music*. Prague: Orbis, 1964.

Hungary

Szabolcsi, Bence. *A Concise History of Hungarian Music*. Trans. Sara Karig and Fred Magnicol. 2nd ed. Budapest: Corvina, 1974.

Scandinavia

Horton, John. *Scandinavian Music*. London: Faber & Faber, 1963.

Yoell, John H. *The Nordic Sound. Explorations in the Music of Denmark, Norway, Sweden*. Boston: Crescendo, 1974.

CHAPTER VI. BEYOND THE CONTINENT

United States

Chase, Gilbert. *America's Music: From the Pilgrims to the Present*. 3rd ed. Urbana: Univ. of Illinois Press, 1987.

*Davis, Ronald L. *A History of Music in American Life*. Vol. 2. *The Gilded Years, 1865–1920*. Huntington, N. Y.: Kreiger, 1980.

Hamm, Charles. *Music in the New World*. New York: Norton, 1983.

*Hitchcock, H. *Wiley. Music in the United States*. 2nd ed. Engelwood Cliffs, N. J.: Prentice-Hall, 1974.

*Mellers, Wilfrid. *Music in a New-Found Land*. Rev. ed. Oxford: Oxford Univ. Press, 1987.

Tischler, Barbara L. *An American Music: The search for an American Musical Identity*. Oxford: Oxford Univ. Press, 1986.

England

Howes, Frank. *The English Musical Renaissance*. London: Secker & Warburg, 1966.

Mackerness, E. D. *A Social History of English Music*. London: Routledge & Kegan Paul, 1964. Reprint, 1976.

Pirie, Peter J. *The English Musical Renaissance*. London: Gollancz, 1979.

Walker, Ernest. *A History of Music in England*. 3rd rev. ed. Oxford: Clarendon Press, 1952. Reprint, 1978.

Young, Percy M. *A History of English Music*. London: Benn, 1967.

CHAPTER VII. THE HISTORICAL CONTEXT: EUROPE AFTER WORLD WAR I

Carr, Edward H. *The Russian Revolution: From Lenin to Stalin*. New York: Free Press, 1979.

Fowlie, Wallace. *The Age of Surrealism*. Bloomington: Indiana Univ. Press, 1960.

Gay, Peter. *Weimar Culture: The Outsider as Insider*. New York: Harper & Row, 1968.

Greene, Nathanael. *From Versailles to Vichy: The Third Republic, 1919–1940*. New York: Crowell, 1970.

Kindleberger, Charles P. *The World in Depression, 1929–1939*. Berkeley and Los Angeles: Univ. of California Press, 1973.

Motherwell, Robert, ed. *The Dada Painters and Poets: An Anthology*. 2nd ed. Boston: Hall, 1981.

Nolte, Ernst. *The Three Faces of Fascism*. New York: Holt, Reinhart & Winston, 1966.

Sontag, Raymond J. *A Broken World, 1919–1939*. New York: Harper & Row, 1971.

Steinberg, Michael. *The Meaning of the Salzburg Festival: Austria as Theater and Ideology, 1890–1938*. Ithaca, N.Y.: Cornell Univ. Press, 1990.

*Whitford, Frank. *Bauhaus*. London: Thames & Hudson, 1984.

CHAPTER VIII. NEO-CLASSICISM

Apollinaire. *Selected Writings*. Trans. Roger Shattuck. New York, n.p., n.d.

Cocteau, Jean. *A Call to Order*. Trans. Rollo H. Myers. London: 1926.

Harding, James. *The Ox on the Roof: Scenes from Musical Life in Paris in the Twenties*. London: Macdonald, 1972.

Lessem, Alan. "Schoenberg, Stravinsky, and Neo–Classicism: The Issues Reexamined." *MQ* 68, no. 4 (1982): 541.

Messing, Scott. *Neoclassicism in Music: From the Genesis of the Concept through the Schoenberg / Stravinsky Polemic.* Ann Arbor, Mich.: UMI Research Press, 1988.

Myers, Rollo. *Modern French Music.* New York: Praeger, 1971. Reprint, 1989.

Shead, Richard. *Music in the 1920s.* London: Duckworth, 1976.

Wiser, William. *The Crazy Years: Paris in the Twenties.* New York: Atheneum, 1983.

CHAPTER IX. THE TWELVE-TONE SYSTEM

Babbitt, Milton. "Some Aspects of Twelve-tone Composition." *The Score* 12 (1955): 53.

———. "Twelve-Tone Invariants as Compositional Determinants." *MQ* 46 (1960): 246.

Basart, Anne P. *Serial Music: A Classified Bibliography of Writings on Twelve-tone and Electronic Music.* 4th ed. Berkeley and Los Angeles: Univ. of California Press, 1977.

Mead, Andrew. "The State of Research in Twelve-Tone and Atonal Theory." (Includes extensive bibliography.) *MTS* 11, no.1 (1989): 40.

Perle, George. *Twelve-Tone Tonality.* Berkeley and Los Angeles: Univ. of California Press, 1978.

Rufer, Josef. *Composition with Twelve Notes.* Trans. Humphrey Searle. London: Rockcliff, 1954.

Schoenberg, Arnold. "Composition with Twelve Tones." In *Style and Idea.* Trans. Leo Black. 2nd ed. New York: Faber & Faber, 1975, p.214.

Stein, Erwin. *Orpheus in New Guises.* Trans. Hans Keller. Repr. of 1953 ed. London: Hyperion Press, 1980.

CHAPTER X. THE INFLUENCE OF POLITICS

Germany

Cook, Susan. *Opera During the Weimar Republic: The "Zeitopern" of Ernst Krenek, Kurt Weill, and Paul Hindemith.* Ann Arbor, Mich.: UMI Research Press, 1989.

Drew, David. "Music Theater in the Weimar Rebublic." *PRMA* 88 (1961–62): 89.

Sachs, Joel. "Some Aspects of Musical Politics in Pre-Nazi Germany." *PNM* 9, no.1 (1970): 74.

Russia

Gray, Camilla. *The Russian Experiment in Art, 1863–1922*. New York: Abrams, 1962.

Olkhovsky, Andrey. *Music Under the Soviets*. London: Routledge & Kegan Paul, 1955. Reprint, 1975.

Schwarz, Boris. *Music and Musical Life in Soviet Russia*. 2nd ed. Bloomington: Indiana Univ. Press, 1983.

CHAPTER XI. OTHER EUROPEANS

★Chase, Gilbert. *The Music of Spain*. 2nd. rev. ed. New York: Dover, 1959.

Erhardt, Ludwik. *Music in Poland*. Trans. Jan Aleksandrowicz. Warsaw: Interpress, 1975.

Livermore, Ann. *A Short History of Spanish Music*. New York: Vienna House, 1972.

Sachs, Harvey. *Music in Fascist Italy*. New York: Norton, 1988.

CHAPTER XII. ENGLAND AFTER WORLD WAR I

Demuth, Norman. *Musical Trends in the Twentieth Century*. London: Rockcliff, 1952.

Lambert, Constant. *Music Ho!* London: Faber & Faber, 1934. Reprint, 1966.

Routh, Francis. *Contemporary British Music. The Twenty-five Years from 1945 to 1970*. London: Macdonald, 1972.

Schafer, R. Murray. *British Composers in Interview*. London: Faber & Faber, 1963.

(See also the bibliography for Chapter VI.)

CHAPTER XIII. THE UNITED STATES

Cowell, Henry, ed. *American Composers on American Music: A Symposium*. New York: Ungar, 1933. Reprint, 1962.

★Davis, Ronald L. *A History of Music in American Life*. Vol. 3. *The Modern Era: 1920 to the Present*. New York: Krieger, 1981.

Du Pree, Mary Herron. "The Failure of American Music: The Critical View from the 1920s." *JM* 2, no. 3 (1983): 305.

Howard, John Tasker. *Our American Music*. 4th ed. New York: Crowell, 1965.

Tawa, Nicholas E. *Serenading the Reluctant Eagle. American Musical Life, 1925–1945*. New York: Schirmer, 1984.

(See also the bibliography for Chapter VI.)

CHAPTER XIV. LATIN AMERICA

Appleby, David P. *The Music of Brazil*. Austin: Univ. of Texas Press, 1983.

★Béhague, Gerard. *Music in Latin America: An Introduction*. Englewood Cliffs, N.J.: Prentice-Hall, 1977.

Stevenson, Robert M. *Music in Mexico*. New York: Crowell, 1952.

CHAPTER XV. THE HISTORICAL CONTEXT: THE WORLD AFTER WORLD WAR II

Battcock, Gregory. *Minimal Art: A Critical Anthology*. New York: Dutton, 1968.

Black, Cyril E. *The Dynamics of Modernization: A Study of Comparative History*. New York: Harper & Row, 1966.

Crane, Diana. *The Transformation of the Avant-Garde. The New York Art World, 1940–1985*. Chicago: The Univ. of Chicago Press, 1987.

Crouzet, Maurice. *The European Renaissance Since 1945*. London: Thames & Hudson, 1971.

De Porte, A. W. *Europe Between the Superpowers: The Enduring Balance*. 2nd ed. New Haven: Yale Univ. Press, 1986.

Krauss, Rosalind. *The Originality of the Avant-Garde and Other Modernist Myths*. Cambridge: MIT Press, 1985.

Laqueur, Walter. *The Recovery of Europe: From Devastation to Unity*. Rev. ed. New York: Penguin, 1982.

Rosenberg, Harold. *The De-definition of Art: Action Art to Pop to Earthworks*. New York: Horizon Press, 1972.

Toffler, Alvin. *Future Shock*. New York: Bantam, 1971.

Willis, Brian. *Art after Modernism: Rethinking Representation*. Boston: Godine, 1984.

Worsley, Peter. *The Third World*. London: Weidenfeld & Nicholson, 1967.

CHAPTER XVI. INTEGRAL SERIALISM

Babbitt, Milton. "Twelve-Tone Rhythmic Structure and the Electronic Medium." *PNM* 1 (1962): 49.

Ligeti, György. "Pierre Boulez: Decision and Automation in *Structures 1a.*" *DR* 4 (1960): 36.

Ruwet, N. "On the Contradictions in Serial Language."*DR* 3 (1959): 65.

*Smith Brindle, Reginald. *The New Music.* Oxford: Oxford Univ. Press,1974.

Stockhausen, Karlheinz. ". . . How Time Passes . . ." *DR* 3 (1959): 10.

Toop, Richard. "Messiaen / Goeyvaerts, Fano / Stockhausen, Boulez." *PNM* 13 (1974): 141.

CHAPTER XVII. INDETERMINACY

Boulez, Pierre. "Sonate, que me veux-tu?" *PNM* 1, no. 2 (1963): 32.

Cage, John. "Indeterminacy." In *Silence.* Middletown, Conn.: Wesleyan Univ. Press, 1961, p.35.

Clark, R. C. "Total Control and Chance in Music: A Philosophical Analysis." *Journal of Aesthetics and Art Criticism* 28 (1970): 335; 29 (1970): 53.

De Lio, Thomas. *Circumscribing the Open Universe.* Lanham, N.Y. and London: Univ. Press of America, 1984.

Karkoschka, Erhard. *Notation in New Music.* New York: Praeger, 1972.

*Meyer, Leonard B. *Music, the Arts, and Ideas.* Chicago: Univ. of Chicago Press, 1967.

O'Grady, Terrence J. "Aesthetic Value in Indeterminate Music." *MQ* 67 (1981): 366.

CHAPTER XVIII. INNOVATIONS IN FORM AND TEXTURE

Bartolozzi, Bruno. *New Sounds for Woodwind.* London: Oxford Univ. Press, 1967.

Carter, Elliott. "Music and the Time Screen." In *The Writings of Elliott Carter.* Bloomington: Indiana Univ. Press, 1977, p. 343.

Cogan, Robert. *New Images of Musical Sound.* Cambridge: Harvard Univ. Press, 1984.

Erickson, Robert. *Sound Structure in Music.* Berkeley and Los Angeles: Univ. of California Press, 1975.

Kramer, Jonathan. *The Time of Music. New Meanings, New Temporalities, New Listening Strategies.* New York: Schirmer, 1988.

Ligeti, György. "Metamorphoses of Musical Form." *DR* 7 (1965): 5.

Reynolds, Roger. *Mind Models. New Forms of Musical Experience.* New York: Praeger, 1975.

Xenakis, Iannis. "Elements of Stochastic Music." *Gravesaner Blätter* 18 (1960): 84; 19–20 (1960): 140; 21 (1961): 113; 22 (1961): 144.

CHAPTER XIX. THE NEW PLURALISM

Quotation and Collage

Griffiths, Paul. "Quotation, Integration." In *Modern Music: The Avant-Garde Since 1945.* London: Dent, 1981, p. 188.

Rochberg, George. "No Center." *Composer* 1, no.2 (1969): 86.

Watkins, Glenn. "Uses of the Past: A Synthesis." In *Soundings. Music in the Twentieth Century.* New York: Schirmer, 1988, p.640.

Jazz, Popular, and Ethnic Influences

Bohlman, Philip V. *The Study of Folk Music in the Modern World.* Bloomington: Indiana Univ. Press, 1988.

Budds, Michael J. *Jazz in the Sixties.* Iowa City: Univ. of Iowa Press, 1978.

Hamm, Charles. *Yesterdays: Popular Song in America.* New York: Norton, 1979.

Heifetz, Robin J. "European Influences upon Japanese Instrumental and Vocal Media: 1946–1977." *MR* 47 (1986–1987): 29.

Marcus, Greil. *Mystery Train: Images of American Rock 'n' Roll Music.* New York: Dutton, 1975.

May, Elizabeth, ed. *Music of Many Cultures.* Berkeley and Los Angeles: Univ. of California Press, 1980.

Poirier, Richard. "Learning from the Beatles." In *The Beatles Book.* Edward E. Davis, ed. New York: Cowles, 1968.

Rockwell, John. *All American Music: Composition in the Late Twentieth Century.* New York: Knopf, 1983.

Tirro, Frank. *Jazz: A History.* New York: Norton, 1977.

CHAPTER XX. A RETURN TO SIMPLICITY: MINIMALISM AND THE NEW TONALITY

Minimalism

Mertens, Wem. *American Minimal Music.* New York: 1983.

Nyman, Michael. *Experimental Music: Cage and Beyond.* London: Cassell and Collier Macmillan, 1974.

Osterreich, Norbert. "Music with Roots in the Aether." *PNM* 16, no. 1 (1977): 214.

Young, La Monte, and Marian Zazeela. *Selected Writings*. Munich: Heiner Friedrich, 1969.

Neo-Tonality and Microtonality

Johnston, Ben. "Proportionality and Expanded Pitch Relations." *PNM* 5, no.1 (1966): 112.

Rochberg, George. "Reflections on the Renewal of Music." *CM* 13 (1972): 75.

CHAPTER XXI. MUSIC AND THE EXTERNAL WORLD

Extensions in Music Theater

Griffiths, Paul. "Opera, Music Theater." In *Modern Music: The Avant Garde Since 1945*. London: Dent, 1981, p.248.

Kaprow, Allan. *Assemblage, Environments, and Happenings*. New York: Abrams, 1966.

Kostelanetz, Richard. *The Theater of Mixed Means*. New York: Dial Press, 1968.

Environmental Music

*Lucier, Alvin. "The Tools of My Trade." In *Contiguous Lines: Issues and Ideas in the Music of the Sixties and Seventies*. Thomas De Lio, ed. Lanham, N.Y. and London: Univ. Press of America, 1985, p.143

Nyman, Michael. *Experimental Music: Cage and Beyond*. London: Cassell and Collier Macmillan, 1974.

Schafer, R. Murray. *The Tuning of the World*. New York: Knopf, 1977.

Music and Politics

Attali, Jacques. *Noise: The Political Economy of Music*. Trans. Brian Massumi. Minneapolis: Univ. of Minnesota Press, 1985.

Cardew, Cornelius, ed. *Scratch Music*. Cambridge: MIT Press, 1972.

Shepherd, John, Phil Virden, Graham Vulliamy, and Trevor Wishard. *Whose Music? A Sociology of Musical Languages*. London: Latimer New Dimensions, 1977.

Small, Christopher. *Music, Society, Education*. New York: Schirmer, 1977.

*Wolf, Christian. "On Political Texts and New Music." In *Contiguous Lines: Issues and Ideas in the Music of the Sixties and Seventies*. Thomas De Lio, ed. Lanham, N.Y. and London: Univ. Press of America, 1985, p.193.

CHAPTER XXII. DEVELOPMENTS IN TECHNOLOGY: ELECTRONIC MUSIC

Electronic Music

Appleton, Jon, and Ronald Perera, eds. *The Development and Practice of Electronic Music*. Englewood Cliffs, N. J.: Prentice-Hall, 1974.

Babbitt, Milton. "An Introduction to the RCA Synthesizer." *JMT* 8 (1964): 251.

Basart, Anne P. *Serial Music: A Classified Bibliography of Writings on Twelve-tone and Electronic Music*. 4th ed. Berkeley and Los Angeles: Univ. of California Press, 1977.

Eimert, Herbert, and Karlheinz Stockhausen, eds. *DR* 1 (1965). Devoted entirely to electronic music; originally published in German in 1955.

Howe, Hubert S., Jr. *Electronic Music Synthesis*. New York: Norton, 1975.

Schwartz, Elliott. *Electronic Music. A Listener's Guide*. New York: Praeger, 1972.

Computer Music

Dodge, Charles and Thomas A. Jerse. *Computer Music: Synthesis, Composition, and Performance*. New York: Schirmer, 1985.

Kostka, Stefan M. *A Bibliography of Computer Applications in Music*. Hackensack, N.J.: Boonin, 1974.

Manning, Peter. *Electronic and Computer Music*. Oxford: Clarendon Press, 1985.

Mathews, Max. *The Technology of Computer Music*. Cambridge: MIT Press, 1969.

Roads, Curtis, and John Strawn, eds. *Foundations of Computer Music*. Cambridge: MIT Press, 1985.

COMPOSERS

Babbitt, Milton

Babbitt, Milton. "Who Cares if You Listen?" In *Contemporary Composers on Contemporary Music*. Elliott Schwartz and Barney Childs, eds. New York: Holt, Rinehart and Winston, 1967.

———. "Twelve-tone Rhythmic Structure and the Electronic Medium." *PNM* 1, no.1 (1962): 49.

———. "Contemporary Music Composition and Music Theory as Contemporary Intellectural History." In *Perspectives in Musicology*. Ed. Barry S. Brook, E. O. Downes, and Sherman Van Solkema. New York: Norton, 1971. Reprint,1985.

———. *Words about Music*. Ed. Stephen Dembski and Joseph N. Strauss. Madison: Univ. of Wisconsin Press, 1987.

Barkin, Elaine. "A Simple Approach to Milton Babbitt's 'Semi-Simple Variations.' " *MR* 28 (1967): 316.

Mackey, Steven. ". . . What Surfaces." *PNM* 25, nos.1 and 2 (1987): 258.

Mead, Andrew. "Recent Development in the Music of Milton Babbitt." *MQ* 77 (1984): 310.

Peel, John, and Cheryl Cramer. "Correspondences and Associations in Milton Babbitt's *Reflections*." *PNM* 26, no. 1 (1988): 144.

PNM, vol. 14, no. 2, and vol. 15, no. 1 (1976) Special issue devoted entirely to articles on Babbitt, with a response by the composer.

Westergaard, Peter. "Some Problems Raised by the Rhythmic Procedures in Milton Babbitt's Composition for Twelve Instruments." *PNM* 4, no.1 (1965): 109.

Bartók, Béla

Antokoletz, Elliot. *The Music of Béla Bartók: A Study of Tonality and Progression in Twentieth-Century Music*. Berkeley and Los Angeles: Univ. of California Press, 1984.

———. "The Musical Language of Bartók's Fourteen Bagatelles for Piano." *Tempo* 137 (1981): 8.

Babbitt, Milton. "The String Quartets of Bartók." *MQ* 35 (1949): 377.

Bachmann, T. and P. J. "An Analysis of Béla Bartók's Music through Fibonaccian Numbers and the Golden Mean." *MQ* 65 (1979): 72.

Bartók, Béla. "Bartók on His Own Music." John Vinton, ed. *JAMS* 19 (1966): 232.

———. *Essays*. Benjamin Suchoff, ed. London: Faber & Faber, 1976.

Bernard, Jonathan. "Space and Symmetry in Bartók." *JMT* 30, no. 2 (1986): 185.

Forte, Allen. "Bartók's Serial Composition." *MQ* 46 (1960): 233.

French, Gilbert. "Continuity and Discontinuity in Bartók's 'Concerto for Orchestra'." *MR* 28 (1967): 122.

Gillies, Malcolm. "Bartók's Notation: Tonality and Modality." *Tempo* 145 (1983): 4.

―――. "Bartók's Last Works: A Theory of Tonality and Modality." *Musicology* 7 (1982): 120.

Howat, Roy. "Bartók, Lendvai and the Principles of Proportional Analysis." *MA* 2, no. 1 (1983): 69.

Karpati, Janos. "Béla Bartók and the East." *SMASH* 6 (1964): 179.

*Lampert, Vera, and Laszlo Somfai. "Béla Bartók." In *The New Grove Modern Masters*. New York: Norton, 1984.

Lendvai, Ernö. *Béla Bartók: an Analysis of his Music*. New Jersey: Humanities, 1971.

Mason, Colin. "Béla Bartók and Folksong." *MR* 11 (1950): 292.

―――. "An Essay in Analysis: Tonality, Symmetry and Latent Serialism in Bartók's Fourth Quartet." *MR* 18 (1957): 189.

McCabe, John. *Bartók: Orchestral Music*. London: British Broadcasting Corporation, 1974.

Somfai, Laszlo. "Nineteenth-century Ideas Developed in Bartók's Piano Notation in the Years 1907–1914." *19CM* 11 (Summer 1987): 73.

―――. " 'Per finire': Some Aspects of the Finale in Bartók's Cyclic Form." *SMASH* 11 (1969): 391.

Stevens, Halsey. *The Life and Music of Béla Bartók*. Oxford: Oxford Univ. Press, 1953. Rev. ed. 1964.

Travis, Roy. "Tonal Coherence in the First Movement of Bartók's Fourth String Quartet." *MF* 2 (1970): 298.

Berg, Alban

Berg, Alban. *Letters to His Wife*. Trans. Bernard Grun. New York: St. Martin's Press, 1978.

Brand, Juliane, Christopher Hailey, and Donald Harris, eds. *The Berg-Schoenberg Correspondence*. New York: Norton, 1986.

Carner, Mosco. *Alban Berg*. London: Holmes & Meier, 1975. 2nd ed., 1983.

De Voto, Mark. "Some Notes on the Unknown *Altenberg Lieder*." *PNM* 5, no.1 (1966): 37.

Green, Douglas. "Berg's De Profundis: The Finale of the *Lyric Suite*." *IABSN* 5 (1977): 13.

Jarman, Douglas. *The Music of Alban Berg*. Berkeley and Los Angeles: Univ. of California Press, 1979.

―――. "Alban Berg, Wilhelm Fliess, and the Secret Programme of the Violin Concerto." *IABSN* 12 (1982): 5.

Perle, George. *The Operas of Alban Berg.* Vol. 1: *Wozzeck.* Vol. 2: *Lulu.* Berkeley and Los Angeles: Univ. of California Press, 1980–85.

————. "The Secret Program of the Lyric Suite." *IABSN* 5 (1977): 4.

————. "Alban Berg." In *The New Grove Second Viennese School.* New York: Norton, 1983.

Redlich, Hans F. *Alban Berg: The Man and His Music.* London: John Calder, 1957.

Reich, Willi. *Alban Berg.* Trans. Cornelius Cardew. London: Thames & Hudson, 1965.

Schmalfeldt, Janet. *Berg's "Wozzeck."* New Haven: Yale Univ. Press, 1983.

Stroh, Wolfgang. "Alban Berg's Constructive Rhythm." *PNM* 7, no.1 (1968): 18.

Berio, Luciano

Donat, Misha. "Berio and his Circles." *MT* 105 (1964): 105.

Flynn, George W. "Listening to Berio's Music." *MQ* 61 (1975): 388.

Hicks, Michael. "Text, Music, and Meaning in Berio's Sinfonia, Third Movement." *PNM* 20, nos. 1 and 2 (1981–82): 199.

Osmond-Smith, David. *Playing with Words: A Guide to Luciano Berio's Sinfonia.* London: Royal Music Association, 1985.

Santi, Piero. "Luciano Berio." *DR* 4 (1960): 98.

Usher, Nancy. "Sequenza VI for Solo Viola: Performance Practices." *PNM* 21, nos.1 and 2 (1982–83): 286.

Blitzstein, Marc

Dietz, Robert. "Marc Blitzstein and the 'Agit-Prop' Theater of the 1930s. *YIAMR* 6 (1970): 51.

Oja, Carol J. "Marc Blitzstein's *The Cradle Will Rock* and Mass-Song Style of the 1930's." *MQ* 73 (1989): 445.

Boulez, Pierre

Black, Robert. "Boulez's Third Piano Sonata: Surface and Sensibility." *PNM* 20, nos. 1 and 2 (1981–82): 182.

Boulez, Pierre. *Boulez on Music Today.* Trans Susan Bradshaw and Richard Rodney Bennett. Cambridge: Harvard Univ. Press, 1971.

————. *Orientations: Collected Writings.* Ed. Jean-Jacques Nattiez. Trans Martin Cooper. Cambridge: Harvard Univ. Press, 1986.

Cross, Anthony. "Form and Expression in Boulez' *Don.*" *MR* 36 (1975): 215.

Gable, David. "Ramifying Connections: An Interview with Pierre Boulez." *JM* 4, no.1 (1985–86): 105.

Glock, William, ed. *Pierre Boulez. A Symposium.* London: Eulenburg, 1986.

Griffiths, Paul. *Boulez.* London: New York Press, 1978.

*Hopkins, G. W. "Pierre Boulez." In *The New Grove Twentieth-Century French Masters.* New York: Norton, 1986.

McCalla, James. "Sea Changes: Boulez's *Improvisations sur Mallarmé.*" *JM* 6, no.1 (1988): 83.

Stacy, Peter F. *Boulez and the Modern Concept.* Lincoln: Univ. of Nebraska Press, 1987.

Trenkamp, Anne. "The Concept of 'Alea' in Boulez's 'Constellation-Miroir.'" *ML* 57 (1976): 1.

Britten, Benjamin

Alexander, Peter F. "A Study of the Origins of *Curlew River.*" *ML* 69 (1988): 229.

*Brett, Philip, ed. *Peter Grimes. (COH)* Cambridge: Cambridge Univ. Press, 1983.

Cooke, Mervyn. "Britten and Bali." *JMR* 7 (1987): 307.

Corse, Sandra and Larry Corse. "Britten's *Death in Venice:* Literary and Musical Structures." *MQ* 73 (1989): 344.

Evans, Peter. *The Music of Benjamin Britten.* Minneapolis: Univ. of Minnesota Press, 1979.

*———. "Benjamin Britten." In *The New Grove Twentieth-Century English Masters.* New York: Norton, 1986.

Flynn, William T. "Britten the Progressive." *MR* 44 (1983): 44.

Hindley, Clifford. "Love and Salvation in Britten's *Billy Budd.*" *ML* 70 (1989): 363.

Kennedy, Michael. *Britten.* London: Dent, 1981.

Mark, Christopher. "Contextually Transformed Tonality in Britten." *MA* 4, no.3 (1985): 259.

Mitchell, Donald. *Britten and Auden in the Thirties: The Year 1936.* Seattle: Univ. of Washington Press, 1981.

*Mitchell, Donald, ed. *Death in Venice. (COH)* Cambridge: Cambridge Univ. Press, 1987.

*Palmer, Christopher, ed. *The Britten Companion.* London and Boston: Faber & Faber, 1984.

White, Eric Walter. *Benjamin Britten: His Life and Operas.* London: Faber & Faber, 1970. Rev. 3rd ed. 1983.

Whittall, Arnold. "The Study of Britten: Triadic Harmony and Tonal Structure". *PRMA* 106 (1979–80): 27.

———. *The Music of Britten and Tippett: Studies in Themes and Techniques.* Cambridge and New York: Cambridge Univ. Press, 1982.

Busoni, Ferruccio

Beaumont, Antony. *Busoni the Composer*. London: Faber & Faber, 1985.

————. "Busoni and the Theater." *Opera* 37 (1986): 384.

————. "Dr. Faustus." *MT* 127 (1986): 196.

————. *Ferruccio Busoni Selected Letters*. New York: Columbia Univ. Press, 1987.

Busoni, Ferruccio. *Sketch of a New Esthetic of Music*. Trans. Th. Baker. New York: Schirmer, 1911.

Dent, Edward J. *Ferruccio Busoni: A Biography*. Oxford: Clarendon Press, 1933.

Raessler, Daniel M. "The 113 Scales of Ferruccio Busoni." *MR* 43 (1982): 51.

————. "Schoenberg and Busoni: Aspects of Their Relationship." *JASI* 7 (1983): 7.

Cage, John

Cage, John. *Silence: Lectures and Writings*. Middletown, Conn.: Wesleyan Univ. Press, 1973.

————. *M: Writings, 1967–73*. Middletown, Conn.: Wesleyan Univ. Press, 1973.

————. *Empty Words: Writings, 1973–78*. Middletown, Conn. Wesleyan Univ. Press, 1979.

————. *X: Writings, 1979–82*. Middletown, Conn. Wesleyan Univ. Press, 1983.

————. *For the Birds: In Conversation with Daniel Charles*. Trans. Richard Gardner. London: Boyars, 1981.

Gena, Peter, ed. *A John Cage Reader*. New York: Peters, 1982.

Griffiths, Paul. *Cage*. London: Oxford Univ. Press, 1981.

*Hamm, Charles. "John Cage." In *The New Grove Twentieth-Century American Masters*. New York: Norton, 1987.

Kostelanetz, Richard, ed. *John Cage*. New York: Praeger, 1970.

————. *Conversing with Cage*. New York: Limelight Editions, 1987.

Nyman, Michael. "Cage and Satie." *MT* 114 (1973): 1227.

Pritchett, James. "From Choice to Chance: John Cage's Concerto for Prepared Piano." *PNM* 26, no.1 (1988): 50.

Cardew, Cornelius

Cardew, Cornelius, ed. *Scratch Music*. Cambridge: MIT Press, 1974.

Dennis, Brian. "Cardew's 'The Great Learning.' " *MT* 112 (1971): 1066.

Potter, Keith. "Some Aspects of a Political Attitude: Cornelius Cardew Interviewed." *Contact* 10 (1974–75): 22.

Tilbury, John. "Cornelius Cardew." *Contact* 26 (1983): 4.

Carter, Elliott

Bernard, Jonathan. "Spatial Sets in Recent Music of Elliott Carter." *MA* 2, no.1 (1983): 5.

———. "The Evolution of Elliott Carter's Rhythmic Practice." *PNM* 26, no.2 (1988): 164.

Boretz, Benjamin. "Conversation with Elliott Carter." *PNM* 8, no.2 (1970): 1.

Carter, Elliott. *The Writings of Elliott Carter.* Ed. Else Stone and Kurt Stone. Bloomington: Univ. of Indiana Press, 1977.

Derby, Richard. "Carter's Duo for Violin and Piano." *PNM* 20, nos.1 and 2 (1981–82): 135.

Edwards, Allen. *Flawed Words and Stubborn Sounds. A Conversation with Elliott Carter.* New York: Norton, 1971.

Goldman, Richard F. "The Music of Elliott Carter." *MQ* 63 (1957): 151.

Mead, Andrew. "Pitch Structure in Elliott Carter's String Quartet No. 3." *PNM* 22, nos.1 and 2 (1983–84): 31.

Northcott, Bryan. "Carter in Perspective." *MT* 119 (1978): 1039.

———. "Carter's *Syringa.*" *Tempo:* 128 (1979): 31.

★———. "Elliott Carter." In *The New Grove Twentieth-Century American Masters.* New York: Norton, 1987.

Schiff, David. *The Music of Elliott Carter.* London: Eulenburg, 1983.

Chávez, Carlos

Chávez, Carlos. *Toward a New Music.* New York: Norton, 1937. Reprint, 1975.

———. *Musical Thought.* Cambridge: Harvard Univ. Press, 1961.

Parker, Robert L. *Carlos Chávez. Mexico's Modern-Day Orpheus.* Boston: Twayne, 1983.

Copland, Aaron

★Austin, William, and Vivian Perlis. "Aaron Copland." In *The New Grove Twentieth-Century American Masters.* New York: Norton, 1987.

Berger, Arthur. *Aaron Copland. His Work and Contribution to American Music.* New York: Oxford Univ. Press, 1955.

Butterworth, Neil. *The Music of Aaron Copland.* New York: Universe, 1986.

Cone, Edward T. "Conversation with Aaron Copland." *PNM* 6, no.2 (1968): 57.

Copland, Aaron, and Vivian Perlis. *Copland: 1900 through 1942.* New York: St. Martin's Press, 1984.

————. *Copland: Since 1943.* New York: St. Martin's Press, 1989.

Evans, Peter. "Copland on the Serial Road: An Analysis of Connotations." *PNM* 2, no.2 (1964): 141.

Hitchcock, H. Wiley. "Aaron Copland and American Music." *PNM* 19 (1980–81): 31.

Salzman, Eric, and Paul Des Marais. "Aaron Copland's Nonet: Two Views." *PNM* 1, no.1 (1962): 172.

Skowronski, JoAnn. *Aaron Copland: A Bio-bibliography.* Westport: Greenwood Press, 1985.

Starr, Lawrence. "Copland's Style." *PNM* 19 (1980–81): 68.

Sternfeld, Frederick W. "Copland as Film Composer." *MQ* 37 (1951): 161.

Cowell, Henry

Cowell, Henry. *New Musical Resources.* New York: Knopf, 1930.

Hitchcock, H. Wiley. "Henry Cowell's Ostinato Pianissimo." *MQ* 70 (1984): 23.

Lichtenwanger, William. *The Music of Henry Cowell: A Descriptive Catalog.* Brooklyn: ISAM, 1986.

Mead, Rita H. *Henry Cowell's New Music, 1925–1936: The Society, the Music Edition, and the Recordings.* Ann Arbor, Mich.: UMI Research, 1981.

Saylor, Bruce, and William Lichtenwanger. *The Writings of Henry Cowell.* Brooklyn: ISAM, 1977.

*————. "Henry Cowell." In *The New Grove Twentieth-Century American Masters.* New York: Norton, 1987.

Weisgall, Hugo. "The Music of Henry Cowell." *MQ* 14 (1959): 484.

Crumb, George

Dobay, Thomas R. de. "The Evolution of Harmonic Style in the Lorca Works of Crumb." *JMT* 27, no.2 (1984): 89.

Gillespie, Don, ed. *George Crumb: Profile of a Composer.* New York: Peters, 1985.

Lewis, Robert Hall. "George Crumb: *Night Music I.*" *PNM* 3, no.2 (1965): 13.

Moevs, Robert. "George Crumb: *Music for a Summer Evening (Makrokosmos III).*" *MQ* 62 (1976): 293.

Steinitz, Richard. "The Music of George Crumb." Contact 12 (1975): 3.

Dallapiccola, Luigi

Dallapiccola, Luigi. *Dallapiccola on Opera*. Trans and ed. Rudy Schackelford. Vol. 1. Gloucester, Eng.: Toccata Press, 1987.

Eckert, Michael. "Text and Form in Dallapiccola's Goethe-Lieder." *PNM* 17 (1979): 98.

———. "Octatonic Elements in the Music of Luigi Dallapiccola." *MR* 46 (1985): 35.

Mancini, David L. "Twelve-Tone Polarity in Late Works of Luigi Dallapiccola." *JMT* 30, no.2 (1986): 185.

Nathan, Hans. "The Twelve-tone Compositions of Luigi Dallapiccola." *MQ* 44 (1958): 289.

———. "On Dallapiccola's Working Methods. *PNM* 15, no.2 (1977): 34.

Petrobelli, Pierluigi: "Dallapiccola's Last Orchestral Piece." *Tempo* 123 (1977): 2.

Davies, Peter Maxwell

Griffiths, Paul. *Peter Maxwell Davies*. London: Robson, 1982.

Harbison, John. "Peter Maxwell Davies's *Taverner*." *PNM* 11, no.1 (1972): 233.

Pruslin, Stephen, ed. *Peter Maxwell Davies: Studies from Two Decades*. London: Boosey & Hawkes, 1970.

———. "Maxwell Davies's Piano Sonata." *Tempo* 140 (1982): 5.

Debussy, Claude

Abbate, Carolyn. *"Tristan* in the Composition of *Pelléas*." *19CM* 5 (1981–82): 117.

Allen, Judith Shatin. "Tonal Allusion and Illusion: Debussy's Sonata for Flute, Viola, and Harp." *CD* 7 (1983): 38.

★Austin, William, ed. *Prelude to "The Afternoon of a Faun."* (NCS) New York: Norton, 1970.

Berman, Laurence. "*Prelude to the Afternoon of a Faun* and *Jeux*: Debussy's Summer Rites." *19CM* 3, no. 3 (1980): 225.

Briscoe, James. "Debussy *d'après* Debussy: The Further Resonance of Two Early Melodies." *19CM* 5 (1981–82): 110.

Cobb, Margaret G. *The Poetic Debussy: A Collection of His Songs Texts and Selected Letters*. Boston: Northeastern Univ. Press, 1982.

Cox, David Vassall. *Debussy's Orchestral Music*. Seattle: Univ. of Washington Press, 1975.

Debussy, Claude. *Debussy on Music. The Critical Writings of the Great French Composer Claude Debussy*. Ed. François Lesure. Trans. Richard Langham Smith. New York: Knopf, 1977.

———. *Letters*. Ed. François Lesure and Roger Nichols. Trans. Roger Nichols. Cambridge: Harvard Univ. Press, 1987.

Eimert, Herbert. "Debussy's *Jeux.*" *DR* 5 (1961): 3.

Hepkoski, James A. "Formulaic Openings in Debussy." *19CM* 8 (Summer 1984): 44.

Holloway, Robin. *Debussy and Wagner*. London: Eulenburg, 1979.

Howat, Roy. *Debussy in Proportion: A Musical Analysis*. Cambridge: Cambridge Univ. Press, 1983.

————. "Dramatic Shape and Form in 'Jeux de Vagues' and Its Relationship to *Pelléas, Jeux,* and Other Scores." *CD* 7 (1983): 7.

Jarocinski, Stefan. *Debussy: Impressionism and Symbolism*. Trans. Rollo Myers. London: Eulenburg, 1976.

Lesure, François. "Claude Debussy after His Centenary." *MQ* 49 (1963): 277.

Lewin, David. "Some Instances of Parallel Voice-Leading in Debussy." *19CM* 11 (Summer 1987): 59.

Lockspeiser, Edward. *Debussy: His Life and Mind*. 2 vols. New York: Macmillan, 1965. Reprint, 1978.

Mueller, Richard. "Javanese Influence on Debussy's *Fantaisie* and Beyond." *19CM* 10 (Fall 1986): 157.

Myers, Rollo H. *Claude Debussy. The Story of His Life and Work*. London: Boosey & Hawkes, 1972.

*Nichols, Roger. "Claude Debussy." In *The New Grove Twentieth-Century French Masters*. New York: Norton, 1986.

*———— and Richard Langham Smith, ed. *Pelléas et Mélisande. (COH)* Cambridge: Cambridge Univ. Press, 1989

Orledge, Robert. *Debussy and the Theatre*. Cambridge: Cambridge Univ. Press, 1982.

Parks, Richard S. *The Music of Claude Debussy*. New Haven: Yale Univ. Press, 1989.

Pasler, Jann. "Debussy, *Jeux:* Playing with Time and Form." *19CM* 6 (1982–83): 60.

————. "*Pelléas* and Power: Forces Behind the Reception of Debussy's Opera." *19CM* 10 (Spring 1987): 243.

Rolf, Marie. "Orchestral Manuscripts of Claude Debussy, 1892–1905." *MQ* 70 (Fall 1984): 538.

Smith, Richard Langham. "Debussy and the Art of the Cinema." *ML* 54 (1973): 61.

————. "Debussy and the Pre-Raphaelites." *19CM* 5 (1981–82): 95.

Wenk, Arthur B. *Claude Debussy and the Poets*. Berkeley and Los Angeles: Univ. of California Press, 1976.

————. *Claude Debussy and Twentieth-Century Music*. Boston: Twayne, 1983.

Whittall, Arnold. "Tonality and the Whole-Tone Scale in the Music of Debussy." *MR* 36 (1975): 261.

Youens, Susan. "Music, Verse, and Prose Poetry: Debussy's *Trois Chansons de Bilitis.*" *JMR* 7, no. 1 (1986): 69.

Delius, Frederick

Carley, Lionel. *Delius: A Life in Letters.* 2 vols. Aldershot, Eng.: Scholar Press, 1983, 1988.

Cooke, Deryck. "Delius and Form: A Vindication." *MT* 103 (1962): 392; 461.

Fenby, Eric. *Delius.* London: Faber & Faber, 1971.

Palmer, Christopher. "Delius and Poetic Realism." *ML* 51 (1970): 404.

———. *Delius: Portrait of a Cosmopolitan.* New York: Holmes & Meier, 1976.

*Payne, Anthony. "Frederick Delius." In *The New Grove Twentieth-Century English Masters.* New York: Norton, 1986.

Redwood, Christopher, ed. *A Delius Companion.* London: Calder, 1976.

Warlock, Peter (Philip Heseltine). *Frederick Delius.* Reprint (orig. 1923). London: Bodley Head, 1952.

Del Tredici, David

Cole, Hugo. "Del Tredici's 'The Lobster Quadrille.' " *Tempo* 91 (1970): 20.

Earls, Paul. "David Del Tredici's *Syzygy.*" *PNM* 9, no. 2 (1971): 304.

Knussen, Oliver. "David Del Tredici and *Syzygy.*" *Tempo* 118 (1976): 8.

Eisler, Hans

Betz, Albrecht. *Hans Eisler: Political Musician.* Trans. Bill Hopkins. Cambridge: Cambridge Univ. Press, 1982.

Elgar, Edward

De La Noy, Michael. *Elgar: The Man.* London: Lane, 1983.

Elgar, Edward. *A Future for English Music and Other Essays.* Ed. Percy Young. London: Dobson, 1968.

———. *Letters.* Ed. Percy Young. London: Bles, 1956.

———. *Letters to Nimrod.* London: Dobson, 1965.

Kennedy, Michael. *Elgar: Orchestral Music.* London: British Broadcasting Corporation, 1970.

*McVeagh, Diana. "Edward Elgar." In *The New Grove Twentieth-Century English Masters.* New York: Norton, 1986.

Moore, Jerold N. *Edward Elgar.* Oxford: Oxford Univ. Press, 1984.

Mundy, Simon. *Elgar. His Life and Times.* New Jersey: Paganiniana, 1981.

Parrott, Ian. *Elgar.* London: Dent, 1971.

Whittall, Arnold. "Elgar's Last Judgement." *MR* 26 (1965): 23.

Falla Manuel de

Burnett, Manes. *Manuel de Falla and the Spanish Musical Renaissance.* London: Gollancz, 1979.

Chase, Gilbert. *Falla.* London: British Broadcasting Corporation, 1982.

——— and Andrew Budwig. *Manuel de Falla: A Bibliography and Research Guide.* New York: Garland, 1985.

Pahissa, Jaime. *Manuel de Falla: His Life and Works.* Trans. Jean Wagstaff. London: Museum Press, 1954.

Ferneyhough, Brian

Harvey, Jonathan. "Brian Ferneyhough." *MT* 120 (1979): 723.

Potter, Keith, et al. "Brian Ferneyhough." *Contact* 20 (1979): 4.

Toop, Richard. "Brian Ferneyhough in Interview." *Contact* 29 (1985): 4.

———. "Four Facets of 'The New Complexity.' " *Contact* 32 (1988): 4.

Ginastera, Alberto

Chase, Gilbert. "Alberto Ginastera: Argentine Composer." *MQ* 43 (1957): 439.

Glass, Philip

De Jong, Constance, and Philip Glass. *Satyagraha: The Historical Material and Libretto Comprising the Opera's Book.* New York: Tanam Press, 1983.

Jones, Robert T., ed. *Music by Philip Glass.* New York: Harper & Row, 1987.

Potter, Keith, and Dave Smith. "Interview with Philip Glass." *Contact* 12 (1976): 27.

Smith, Dave. "The Music of Phil Glass." *Contact* 11 (1975): 27.

York, Wesley. "Form and Process in Two Pages of Philip Glass." *Sonus* 1, no. 2 (1981): 28.

Griffes, Charles T.

Anderson, Donna K. *The Works of Charles T. Griffes: A Descriptive Catalogue.* Ann Arbor, Mich.: UMI Research Press, 1983.

Maisel, Edward. *Charles T. Griffes.* New York: Knopf, 1984.

Hába, Alois

Whitman, George. "Alois Hába: Seminal Works of Quarter-tone Music." *Tempo* 80 (1967): 11.

Henze, Hans Werner

Henderson, Robert. "Hans Werner Henze." *MT* 117 (1976): 566.
Stephan, Rudolph. "Hans Werner Henze." *DR* 4 (1960): 29.

Hindemith, Paul

Briner, Andres. "A New Comment on Tonality by Paul Hinde-mith." *JMT* 5 (1961): 109.
★Hindemith, Paul. *The Craft of Musical Composition*. Vol. 1. *Theoretical Part*. Trans. Arthur Mendel. New York: Associated Music, 1942. Vol. 2. *Exercises in Two-Part Writing*. Trans. Otto Ortmann. New York: Associated Music, 1941.
————. A Composer's World: *Horizons and Limitations*. Cambridge: Harvard Univ. Press, 1952.
Kemp, Ian. *Paul Hindemith*. London: Oxford Univ. Press, 1970.
★————. "Paul Hindemith." In *The New Grove Modern Masters*. New York: Norton, 1984.
Landau, Victor. "Paul Hindemith: A Case Study in Theory and Practice." *MR* 21 (1960): 38.
Neumeyer, David. *The Music of Paul Hindemith*. New Haven: Yale Univ. Press, 1986.
————. "Tonal Form and Proportional Design in Hindemith's Music." *MTS* 9 (1987): 93
Skelton, Geoffrey. *Paul Hindemith: The Man behind the Music*. New York: Crescendo, 1975.
Thomson, William. "Hindemith's Contribution to Music Theory." *JMT* 9 (1965): 52.

Holst, Gustav

Holst, Imogen. *A Thematic Catalogue of Gustav Holst's Music*. London: Faber & Faber, 1974.
————. *Gustav Holst: A Biography*. London: Oxford Univ. Press, 1938; 2nd ed. 1969.
————. *The Music of Gustav Holst*. London: Oxford Univ. Press, 1931; 3rd. ed., 1985.
Mellers, Wilfred. "Holst and the English Language." *MR* 2 (41): 228.
Rubbra, Edmund. *Collected Essays on Gustav Holst*. London: Triad Press, 1974.
Warrack, John. "Holst and the Linear Principle." *MT* 104 (1963): 732.

Honegger, Arthur

Honegger, Arthur. *I Am a Composer*. Trans. Wilson O. Clough with Arthur Willman. London: Faber & Faber, 1966.

Spratt, Geoffrey K. *The Music of Arthur Honegger*. Cork, Ire.: Cork Univ. Press, 1987.

———. "Honegger's *Le Roi David:* A Reassessment." *MR* 39 (1978): 54.

Ives, Charles

Blum, Stephen. "Ives's Position in Social and Musical History." *MQ* 63 (1977): 249.

Burkholder, J. Peter. *Charles Ives. The Ideas Behind the Music*. New Haven: Yale Univ. Press, 1985.

———. "Quotation and Emulation: Charles Ives's Uses of His Models." *MQ* 71 (1985): 1.

Clark, Sondra Rae. "The Elements of Choice in Ives's *Concord Sonata.*" *MQ* 60 (1974): 167.

Cyr, Gordon. "Intervallic Structural Elements in Ives' Fourth Symphony." *PNM* 9, no. 2 and 10, no. 1 (1971): 291.

Hitchcock, H. Wiley. *Ives*. London: Oxford Univ. Press, 1977.

——— and Vivian Perlis, eds. *An Ives Celebration: Papers and Panels of the Charles Ives Centennial Festival-Conference."* Urbana: Univ. of Illinois Press, 1977.

*Ives, Charles. *Essays Before a Sonata, The Majority, and Other Writings*. New York: W. W. Norton, 1970.

———. *Memos*. Ed. John Kirkpatrick. New York: W. W. Norton, 1972.

*Kirkpatrick, John and Paul Echols. "Charles Ives." *The New Grove Twentieth-Century American Masters*. New York: W. W. Norton, 1987.

Morgan, Robert P. "Rewriting Music History: Second Thoughts on Ives and Varèse." *Musical Newsletter* 3/1 (1973): 3; 3, no. 2 (1973): 15.

———. "Ives and Mahler: Mutual Responses at the End of an Era." *19CM* 2 (1978): 72.

Perison, Harry. "The Quarter-tone System of Charles Ives." *CM* 18 (1974): 96.

*Perlis, Vivian. *Charles Ives Remembered: An Oral History*. New York: W. W. Norton, 1976.

Perry, Rosalie Sandra. *Charles Ives and the American Mind*. Kent, Ohio: Kent State Univ. Press, 1974.

Rossiter, Frank R. *Charles Ives and His America*. New York: Liveright, 1975.

Soloman, Maynard. "Charles Ives: Some Questions of Veracity." *JAMS* 40 (1987): 443.

Tick, Judith. "Ragtime and the Music of Charles Ives." *CM* 18 (1974): 105.

Wooldridge, David. *From the Steeples and the Mountains: A Study of Charles Ives*. New York: Knopf, 1974.

Janáček, Leoš

Abraham, Gerald. "Realism in Janáček's Operas," in *Slavonic and Romantic Music*. New York: St. Martin's, 1963, 1983.

Evans, Michael. *Janáček's Tragic Operas*. London: Faber & Faber: 1977.

Horsbrugh, Ian. *Leoš Janáček*. London: David & Charles, 1981.

Janáček, Leoš. *Leaves from His Life*. Ed. and trans. Vilem and Margaret Tausky. London: Kahn & Averill, 1982.

———. *Letters and Reminiscences*. Ed. Bohumir Stedron. Trans. Geraldine Thomsen. Prague: Artia Prague, 1955.

Susskind, Charles. *Janáček and Brod*. New Haven: Yale Univ. Press, 1985.

*Tyrell, John. "Leoš Janáček." In *The New Grove Turn of the Century Masters*. New York: Norton, 1985.

———. "Janáček and the Speech-melody Myth." *MT* 111 (1970): 793.

*———. ed. *Kat'a Kabanova*. *(COH)* Cambridge: Cambridge Univ. Press, 1982.

Johnston Ben

Johnston, Ben. "Scalar Order as a Compositional Resource." *PNM* 2, no. (1964): 56.

———. "Extended Just Intonation: A Position Paper." *PNM* 25, nos.1&2 (1987): 517.

Shinn, Randall. "Ben Johnston's Fourth String Quartet." *PNM* 15, no.2 (1977): 145.

Kagel, Mauricio

Decarsin, François. "Liszt's *Nuage gris* and Kagel's *Unguis Incarnatus Est:* A Model and Its Issue." *MA* 6, no. 3 (1987): 207.

Perrin, Glyn. "Mauricio Kagel: Filmed Music / Composed Film." *Contact* 23 (1981): 10.

Kodály, Zoltán

Choksy, Lois. *The Kodály Method*. Englewood Cliffs, N. J.: Prentice-Hall, 1974.

*Eösze, László. *Zoltán Kodály: His Life and Work*. Trans. Istvan Farkas and Gyula Gulyas. London: Collet's, 1962.

Kodály, Zoltán. *Folk Music of Hungary*. Trans. Ronald Tempest and Cynthia Jolly. New York: Repr. 1987.

Lendvai, Ernö. *The Workshop of Bartók and Kodály*. Budapest: Editio Musica, 1983.

Krenek, Ernst

Erickson, Robert. "Krenek's Later Music." *MR* 9 (1948): 29.

Krenek, Ernst. "New Developments of the Twelve-tone Technique." *MR* 4 (1943): 81.

————. "Extents and Limits of Serial Techniques." *MQ* 46 (1960): 210.

————. *Horizons Circled: Reflections on My Life in Music*. Berkeley and Los Angeles: Univ. of California Press, 1974.

"A Krenek Festschrift." (Various articles on the composer.) *PNM* 24, no.1 (1985): 270.

Ligeti, György

Bernard, Jonathan. "Inaudible Structures, Audible Music: Ligeti's Problem, and His Solution." *MA* 6 / 3 (1987): 207.

Ligeti, György. "Metamorphoses of Musical Form." *DR* 7 (1965): 5.

————. "On Music and Politics." *PNM* 16, no.2 (1979): 19.

Sonus 9, no. 1 (1988). (Entire issue devoted to articles by and about Ligeti.)

Lutosławski, Witold

Casken, John. "Transition and Transformation in the Music of Witold Lutosławski." *Contact* 12 (1975): 3.

Kaczynski, Tadeusz. *Conversations with Witold Lutosławski*. Trans. Yolanta May. London: J. &. W. Chester, 1984.

Selleck, John. "Pitch and Duration as Textural Elements in Lutosławski's String Quartet." *PNM* 13, no. (1975): 150.

Stucky, Steven. *Lutosławski and His Music*. Cambridge: Cambridge Univ. Press, 1981.

Thomas, Adrian. "*Jeux vénitiens:* Lutosławski at the Crossroads." *Contact* 24 (1982): 4.

Mahler, Gustav

*Banks, Paul, and Donald Mitchell. "Gustav Mahler." In *The New Grove Turn of the Century Masters*. New York: Norton, 1985.

Bauer-Lechner, Natalie. *Recollections of Gustav Mahler*. Ed. Peter Franklin. Trans. Dika Newlin. London: Faber & Faber, 1980.

*Blaukopf, Kurt. *Gustav Mahler*. Trans. Inge Goodwin. New York and Washington: Praeger, 1973.

————, ed. *Mahler: A Documentary Study*. New York: Oxford Univ. Press, 1976.

Cardus, Neville. *Gustav Mahler, His Mind and Music*. London, 1965.

*Cooke, Deryck. *Gustav Mahler: An Introduction to His Music*. Cambridge: Cambridge Univ. Press, 1980. Reprint, 1985.

De La Grange, Henry-Louis. *Mahler*. Vol. 1. New York: Doubleday, 1973. (Translation of *Gustav Mahler I: Les chemins de la gloire [1860–1900]*. Paris: Fayard, 1973. Rev.1979. English translations of Vols. II and III [1983; 1984] are presently in progress.)

Forte, Allen. "Middleground Motives in the Adagietto of Mahler's Fifth Symphony." *19CM* 8 (1984): 153.

Greene, David B. *Mahler: Consciousness and Temporality*. New York: Gordon & Breach, 1984.

Hefling, Stephen E. "Mahler's *Todtenfeier* and the Problem of Program Music." *19CM* 12 (Summer 1988): 27.

Kennedy, Michael. *Mahler*. London: Dent, 1974. Reprint, 1977.

Kravitt, Edward F. "Mahler's Dirges for His Death: February 24, 1901." *MQ* 64 (1978): 329.

Lebrecht, Norman, ed. *Mahler Remembered*. New York: Norton, 1987.

Lewis, Christopher. *Tonal Coherence in Mahler's Ninth Symphony*. Ann Arbor, Mich.: UMI Research Press, 1982.

Mahler, Alma. *Gustav Mahler: Memories and Letters*. 3rd rev. ed. Ed. Donald Mitchell and Knud Martner. Trans. Basil Creighton. Seattle: Univ. of Washington Press, 1975.

Mahler, Gustav. *Gustav Mahler, Richard Strauss: Correspondence 1888–1911*. Ed. Herta Blaukopf. Trans. Edmund Jephcott. Chicago: Univ. of Chicago Press, 1984.

————. *Selected Letters of Gustav Mahler*. Ed. Knud Martner. Trans. Eithne Wilkins, Ernst Kaiser, and Bill Hopkins. London and Boston: Faber & Faber, 1979.

Mitchell, Donald. *Gustav Mahler: The Early Years*. London: Rockcliff, 1958. Rev. and Ed. Paul Banks and David Matthews. Berkeley and Los Angeles: Univ. of California Press, 1980.

*————. *Gustav Mahler: The Wunderhorn Years*. Berkeley and Los Angeles: Univ. of California Press, 1975.

————. *Gustav Mahler: Songs and Symphonies of Life and Death*. Berkeley and Los Angeles: Univ. of California Press, 1985.

Murphy, Edward. "Unusual Forms in Mahler's Fifth Symphony." *MR* 47 (May 1986–87): 101.

Roman, Zoltan. "Structure as a Factor in the Genesis of Mahler's Songs". *MR* 35 (1974): 157.

Stein, Erwin. "Mahler and the Vienna Opera." *Opera* 4 (1953): 4; 145; 200; 281.

Tischler, Hans. "Mahler's 'Das Lied von der Erde.' " *MR* 10 (1949): 111.

————. "Mahler's Impact on the Crisis of Tonality." *MR* 12 (1951): 113.

*Walter, Bruno. *Gustav Mahler*. Trans. James Galston. New York: Greystone Press, 1941. Reprint, 1973.

Wellesz, Egon. "The Symphonies of Gustav Mahler." *MR* 1 (1940): 2.

Wenk, Arthur. "The Composer as Poet in *Das Lied von der Erde*." *19CM* I (1977–1978): 33.

Youens, Susan. "Schubert, Mahler and the Weight of the Past: *Lieder eines fahrenden Gesellen* and *Winterreise*." *ML* 67 (July 1986): 256.

Malipiero, Gian Francesco

Keller, Marcello Sorce. "A 'Bent for Aphorisms': Some Remarks About Music and About His Own Music by Gian Francesco Malipiero." *MR* 39 (1978): 231.

Messiaen, Olivier

Drew, David. "Messiaen: A Provisional Study." *Score* 10 (1954): 33; 13 (1955): 59; 14 (1955): 41.

Griffiths, Paul. *Olivier Messiaen and the Music of Time*. Ithaca, N.Y.: Cornell Univ. Press, 1985.

*————. "Olivier Messiaen." In *The New Grove Twentieth-Century French Masters*. New York: Norton, 1986.

Hold, Trevor. "Messiaen's Birds." *ML* 52 (1971): 113.

Johnson, Robert Sherlaw. *Messiaen*. London: Dent, 1975.

Messiaen, Olivier. *The Technique of My Musical Language*. Paris: Leduc, 1944; English trans. 1957.

Morris, David. "A Semiotic Investigation of Messiaen's 'Abîme des oiseaux.' " *MA* 8, nos. 1&2 (1989): 125.

Nichols, Roger. *Messiaen*. London: Oxford Univ. Press, 1975.

Rössler, Almut. *Contributions to the Spiritual World of Olivier Messiaen*. Trans. Barbara Dagg and Nancy Poland. Duisberg, West Germany: Gilles & Francke, 1986.

Smalley, Roger. "Debussy and Messiaen." *MT* 109 (1968): 128.

Toop, Richard. "Messiaen's *Saint François*." *Contact* 28 (1984): 89.

Walker, Rosemary. "Modes and Pitch-Class Sets in Messiaen: A Brief Discussion of 'Première communion de la Vierge.' " *MA* 8, nos. 1&2 (1989): 159.

Milhaud, Darius

Collaer, Paul. *Darius Milhaud*. San Fransisco: San Francisco Press, 1988.

Drake, Jeremy. *The Operas of Darius Milhaud*. New York: Garland, 1989.

Mason, Colin. "The Chamber Music of Darius Milhaud." *MQ* 48 (1957): 326.

Milhaud, Darius. *Notes without Music*. Trans. Donald Evans. London: Dobson, 1952. Ed. Rollo Myers, London: Calder & Boyars, 1967.

Nielsen, Carl

Nielsen, Carl. *My Childhood*. Trans. Reginald Spink. London: Chester, 1953.

Simpson, Robert. *Carl Nielsen Symphonist*. London: Dent, 1952. 2nd rev. ed. New York: Taplinger, 1979.

Waterhouse, J. C. G. "Nielsen Reconsidered." *MT* 56 (1965): 425, 515, 593.

Nono, Luigi

Unger, Udo. "Luigi Nono." *DR* 4 (1960): 5.

Oliveros, Pauline

Subotnick, Morton. "Pauline Oliveros: Trio." *PNM* 2, no.1 (1963): 77.

Von Gunden, Heidi. *The Music of Pauline Oliveros*. Metuchen, N.J.: Scarecrow Press, 1983.

Partch, Harry

Earls, Paul. "Harry Partch: *Verses* in Preparation for *Delusion of the Fury*." *YIAMR* 3 (1967): 1.

Johnston, Ben. "The Corporealism of Harry Partch." *PNM* 13, no.2 (1975): 85.

*Partch, Harry. *Genesis of a Music*. 2nd ed. Madison: Univ. of Wisconsin Press, 1974.

Woodbury, A. "Harry Partch: Corporeality and Monophony." *Source* 1. no.(1967): 91.

Penderecki, Krzysztof

*Robinson, Ray. *Krzysztof Penderecki. A Guide to His Works*. Princeton, N.J.: Prestige, 1983.

Petrassi, Goffredo

Stone, Olga. "Petrassi's Concerto for Pianoforte and Orchestra: A Study of Twentieth-Century Neo-Classic Style." *MR* 39 (1978): 240.

Pfitzner, Hans

Franklin, Peter. "Palestrina and the Dangerous Futurists." *MQ* 70 (1984): 499.

Newsom, Jon. "Hans Pfitzner, Thomas Mann and 'The Magic Mountain.' " *ML* 55 (1974): 136.

Williamson, John. "Pfitzner and Ibsen." *ML* 67 (April 1986): 127.

Poulenc, Francis

Bernac, Pierre. *Francis Poulenc. The Man and His Songs.* New York; Norton, 1978.

*Daniel, Keith W. *Francis Poulenc: His Artistic Development & Musical Style.* Ann Arbor, Mich: UMI Research Press, 1982, 1988.

*Nichols, Roger. "Francis Poulenc." In *The New Grove Twentieth-Century French Masters.* New York: Norton, 1986.

Poulenc, Francis. *My Friends and Myself.* Geneva and Paris: La Palatine, 1963. Trans. James Harding. London: Dobson, 1978.

————. *Diary of My Songs.* (*Journal de mes mélodies,* 1964) Trans. Winifred Radford, London: Gollancz, 1985.

Prokofiev, Sergey

Abraham, Gerald. "Prokofiev as a Soviet Composer." *MR* 3 (1942): 241.

Bass, Richard. "Prokofiev's Technique of Chromatic Displacement." *JMT* 7, no. 2 (1988): 197.

Brown, Malcolm. "Prokofiev's *War and Peace.* A chronicle." *MQ* 63 (1977): 297.

Henderson, Lynn. "Prokofiev's Fifth Piano Concerto." *MR* 47 (1986–87): 267.

*McAllister, Rita. "Sergey Prokofiev." In *The New Grove Russian Masters 2.* New York: Norton, 1986.

Prokofiev, Sergey. *Materials, Articles, Interviews.* Moscow: Progress, 1978.

————. *Prokofiev by Prokofiev. A Composer's Memoir.* Ed. David H. Appel. Trans. Guy Daniels. New York: Doubleday, 1979.

————. *Autobiography, Articles, Reminiscences.* Moscow: Foreign Languages, n.d.

Saukina, Natalia. *Prokofiev*. Trans. Catherine Young. Neptune City, N.J.: Paganiniana, 1984.

Seroff, Victor. *Sergey Prokofiev: A Soviet Tragedy*. London: Frewin, 1969.

Puccini, Giacomo

*Ashbrook, William. *The Operas of Puccini*. Ithaca, N.Y.: Cornell Univ. Press, 1985.

*Carner, Mosco. "Giacomo Puccini." In *The New Grove Masters of Italian Opera*. New York: Norton, 1983.

*————. ed. *Tosca*. *(COH)* Cambridge: Cambridge Univ. Press, 1985.

*Groos, Arthur and Roger Parker. *La bohème*. *(COH)* Cambridge: Cambridge Univ. Press, 1986.

Marek, George R. *Puccini: A Biography*. New York: Simon & Schuster, 1951.

Puccini, Giacomo. *Letters*. Ed. Giuseppe Adami. Trans. Ena Makin. London: Harrap, 1931; Rev. ed. 1974.

Valente, Richard. *The Verismo of Giacomo Puccini*. Ann Arbor, Mich.: Braun-Blumfeld, 1971.

Weaver, William. *Puccini: The Man and His Music*. New York: Dutton, 1979.

Rachmaninov, Sergey

Bertensson, Sergei and Jay Leyda. *Sergei Rachmaninoff*. New York: New York Univ. Press, 1956.

Coolidge, Richard. "Architectonic Techniques and Innovation in the Rakhmaninov Piano Concertos." *MR* 40 (1979): 186.

Culshaw, John. *Sergei Rachmaninov*. London: Dobson, 1949.

*Norris, Geoffrey. *Rakmaninov*. London, 1976.

*————. "Sergey Rakmaninov." In *The New Grove Russian Masters 2*. New York: Norton, 1986.

*Piggot, Patrick. *Rachmaninov Orchestral Music*. London: British Broadcasting Corporation, 1974.

Threlfall, Robert and Geoffrey Norris. *A Catalogue of the Compositions of Sergey Rachmaninoff*. London: Scholars Press, 1982.

Ravel, Maurice

Davies, Laurence. *Ravel Orchestral Music*. Seattle: Univ. of Washington Press, 1971.

Demuth, Norman. *Ravel*. London: Dent, 1947. Reprint, 1979.

*Hopkins, G. W. "Maurice Ravel." In *The New Grove Twentieth-Century French Masters*. New York: Norton,1986.

Long, Marguerite. *At the Piano with Ravel*. Ed. Pierre Laumonier. Trans. Olive Senior-Ellis. London: Dent, 1973.

*Myers, Rollo. *Ravel: Life and Work*. London: Duckworth, 1960, 1971.

Nichols, Roger, ed. *Ravel Remembered*. New York: Norton, 1988.

Orenstein, Arbie. *Ravel: Man and Musician*. New York: Columbia Univ. Press, 1975.

Roland-Manuel. *Maurice Ravel*. Trans. Cynthia Jolly. London: Dobson, 1947.

*Stuckenschmidt, Hans Heinz. *Maurice Ravel: Variations on His Life*. Trans. Samuel R. Rosenbaum. Philadelphia: Chilton, 1968.

Reger, Max

Grim, William E. *Max Reger: A Bio-bibliography*. Westport, Conn.: Greenwood Press, 1988.

Popp, Susanne and Susanne Shigihara. *Max Reger: At the Turning Point of Modernism*. Bonn: Bouvier Verlag Herbert Grundmann, 1988.

Prince, P. "Reger and the Organ." *Diapason* 64, no.4 (1973): 1.

Reich, Steve

Potter, Keith. "The Recent Phases of Steve Reich." *Contact* 29 (1985): 28.

Reich, Steve. *Writings about Music*. New York: New York Univ. Press, 1974.

———. "Texture—Space—Survival." *PNM* 26, no. 2 (1988): 272.

Schwarz, K. Robert. "Steve Reich: Music as a Gradual Process." *PNM* 19 (1980–81): 373; 20 (1981–82): 225.

Rochberg, George

Block, Stephen. "George Rochberg: Progressive or Master Forger." *PNM* 21, nos. 1 & 2 (1982–83): 407.

Reise, Jay. "Rochberg the Progressive." *PNM* 19 (1980–81): 395.

Ringer, Alexander. "The Music of George Rochberg." *MQ* 52 (1966): 409.

Rochberg, George. *The Aesthetics of Survival. A Composer's View of Twentieth-Century Music*. Ed. William Bolcom. Ann Arbor: Univ. of Michigan Press, 1984.

Russolo, Luigi

Brown, Barclay. "The Noise Instruments of Luigi Russolo." *PNM* 20, nos.1&2 (1981–82): 31.

Payton, Rodney J. "The Music of Futurism: Concepts and Polemics." *MQ* 62 (1976): 25.

Russolo, Luigi. *The Art of Noises*. Trans. Barclay Brown. New York; Pendragon Press, 1986.

Rzewski, Frederic

Wason, Robert. "Tonality and Atonality in Frederic Rzewski's Variations on 'The People United Will Never Be Defeated!' " *PNM* 26 (1988): 108.

Satie, Erik

Austin, William. "Satie Before and After Cocteau." *MQ* 48 (1962): 216.

Cage, John, Roger Shattuck, and Alan Gillmor. "Erik Satie: A Conversation." *Contact* 25 (1982): 21.

Dickinson, Peter. "Erik Satie (1866–1925)." *MR* 28 (1967): 139.

Gillmor, Alan M. *Erik Satie*. Boston: Twayne, 1988.

Gowers, Patrick. "Satie's Rose Croix Music (1891–1895)." *PRMA* 92 (1965–66): 1.

*————. and Nigel Wilkins. "Eric Satie." In *The New Grove Twentieth-Century French Masters*. New York: Norton, 1986.

Harding, James. *Erik Satie*. London: Secker & Warburg, 1975.

Myers, Rollo. *Erik Satie*. London: Dobson, 1948: Reprint, 1969, 1988.

Shattuck, Roger. "Erik Satie, 1866–1925." In *The Banquet Years: The Origins of the Avant-Garde in France, 1885 to World War I*. Rev. ed. New York: Vintage, 1968.

Templier, Pierre-Daniel. *Erik Satie* (1932) Trans. Elena L. French and David S. Frick. Cambridge: MIT Press, 1969; Reprint, 1980.

Volta, Ornella. *Satie: His World through His Letters*. Trans. Michael Bullock. London and New York: Marion Boyars, 1989.

Wilkins, Nigel. "Erik Satie's Letters to Milhaud and Others." *MQ* 66 (1980): 404.

————, ed. and trans. *The Writings of Erik Satie*. London: Eulenberg, 1980.

Schoenberg, Arnold

Bailey, Walter B. *Programmatic Elements in the Works of Schoenberg*. Ann Arbor, Mich.: UMI Research Press, 1984.

Berg, Alban. "Why is Schoenberg's Music So Difficult to Understand?" (1924). Reprinted in Willi Reich. *Alban Berg*. Trans. Cornelius Cardew. London: Thames & Hudson, 1965. Reprint, 1974.

*Boretz, Benjamin and Edward Cone, eds. *Perspectives on Schoenberg & Stravinsky*. New York: Norton, 1972.

Cone, Edward T. "Sound and Syntax: An Introduction to Schoenberg's Harmony." *PNM* 13, no. 1 (1974): 21.

Crawford, John C. "Die glückliche Hand: Schoenberg's Gesamtkunstwerk." *MQ* 60 (1974): 583.

Dahlhaus, Carl. *Schoenberg and the New Music*. Trans. Derrick Puffett and Alfred Clayton. Cambridge: Cambridge Univ. Press, 1987.

Forte, Allen. "Schoenberg's Creative Evolution: The Path to Atonality." *MQ* 64, no.2 (April 1978): 133.

Frisch, Walter. "Thematic Form and the Genesis of Schoenberg's D-minor Quartet, Opus 7." *JAMS* 41 (1988): 289.

Goehr, Alexander. "The Theoretical Writings of Arnold Schoenberg." *PNM* 13 (1975): 3.

———. "Schoenberg and Karl Kraus: The Idea behind the Music." *MA* 4 (1985): 59.

Hyde, Martha Maclean. "The Format and Function of Schoenberg's Twelve-Tone Sketches." *JAMS* 36 (1983): 453.

Lessem, Alan Philip. *Music and Text in the Works of Arnold Schoenberg. The Critical Years, 1908–1922*. Ann Arbor, Mich.: UMI Research Press, 1982.

Lewis, Christopher. "Mirrors and Metaphors: Reflections on Schoenberg and Nineteenth-Century Tonality." *19CM* 11 (1987): 26.

———. " 'Tonal' Forms in Arnold Schoenberg's Twelve-Tone Music." *MTS* 9 (1987): 67.

*Neighbour, Oliver W. "Arnold Schoenberg." in *The New Grove Second Viennese School*. New York: Norton, 1983.

Payne, Anthony. *Schoenberg*. London: Oxford Univ. Press, 1968.

Reich, Willi. *Arnold Schoenberg: A Critical Biography*. Trans. Leo Black. London: Longman, 1971.

*Rosen, Charles. *Arnold Schoenberg*. Princeton, N.J.: Princeton Univ. Press, 1981.

Schoenberg, Arnold. *Letters*. Ed. Erwin Stein. Trans. Eithne Wilkins and Ernst Kaiser. London: Faber & Faber, 1964. Reprint, Berkeley and Los Angeles: Univ. of California Press, 1987.

*———. *Theory of Harmony*. Trans. [from 1911 *Harmonielehre*] Roy E. Carter. Berkeley and Los Angeles: Univ. of California Press. 1978.

*———. *Structural Functions of Harmony*. Rev. ed. New York: Norton, 1968.

*———. *Fundamentals of Musical Composition*. Ed. Gerald Strang and Leonard Stein. London: Faber & Faber, 1967, 1982.

*———. *Style and Idea: Selected Writings of Arnold Schoenberg*. Ed. Leonard Stein. Trans. Leo Black, London: Faber & Faber, 1975. New expanded ed., Berkeley and Los Angeles: Univ. of California Press, 1984.

"Schoenberg as Artist." *JASI* 2, no. 3 (1978) (special issue).

Stuckenschmidt, Hans H. *Arnold Schoenberg: His Life, World, and Work*. (1974). Trans. Humphrey Searle. London: Calder, 1977.

Swift, Richard. "1 / X / 99: Tonal Relations in Schoenberg's *Verklärte Nacht.*" *19CM* 1 (1977–78): 3.

White, Pamela. *Schoenberg and the God-Idea: The Opera "Moses und Aron."* Ann Arbor, Mich.: UMI Research Press, 1985.

*Whittall, Arnold. *Schoenberg Chamber Music*. London: British Broadcasting Corporation, 1972.

Sessions, Roger

Cone, Edward T. "In Honor of Roger Sessions." *PNM* 10, no. 2 (1972): 130.

———. "In Defense of Song: The Contribution of Roger Sessions." *Critical Inquiry* 2 (1975–1976): 93.

*Harbison, John and Andrea Olmstead. "Roger Sessions." In *The New Grove Twentieth-Century American Masters*. New York: Norton, 1987.

Imbrie, Andrew. "Roger Sessions: In Honor of His 65th Birthday." *PNM* 1, no. 1 (1962): 117.

*Sessions, Roger. *The Musical Experience of Composer, Performer, Listener*. Princeton, N.J.: Princeton Univ. Press, 1962.

*———. *Questions About Music*. New York, Norton, 1971.

*———. *Roger Sessions on Music: Collected Essays*. Ed. Edward T. Cone. Princeton, N.J.: Princeton Univ. Press, 1979.

———. *Conversations with Roger Sessions*. Ed. Andrea Olmstead. Lincoln: Univ. of Nebraska Press, 1987.

Shostakovich, Dimitry

Blokker, Roy and Robert Dearling. *The Music of Dimitri Shostakovich: The Symphonies*. London: Tantivy Press, 1979.

Fanning, David. *The Breath of the Symphonist: Shostakovich's Tenth*. London: Royal Musical Association, 1988.

*Kay, Norman. *Shostakovich*. London: Oxford Univ. Press, 1971.

Keller, Hans. "Shostakovich's Twelfth String Quartet." *Tempo* 94 (1970): 6.

Marothy, Janos. "Harmonic Disharmony: Shostakovich's Quintet." *Studia Musicologica* 19 (1977): 325.

Norris, Christopher, ed. *Shostakovich: The Man and His Music*. London: Laurence & Wishart, 1982.

Ottaway, Hugh. "Shostakovich: Some Later Works." *Tempo* 50 (1959): 2.

*Schwarz, Boris. "Dimitry Shostakovich." In *The New Grove Russian Masters 2*. New York: Norton, 1986.

Shostakovich, Dimitry. *Dimitry Shostakovich About Himself and His Times*. Ed. Lev Grigoryev and Yakov Platek. Moscow: Progress, 1981.

Sollertiusky, Dimitri and Ludmilla. *Pages from the Life of Dimitri Shostakovich*. London: Hale, 1981.

*Volkov, Solomon. *Testimony. The Memoirs of Dmitri Shostakovich as Related to and Edited by Solomon Volkov*. New York: Harper & Row, 1979.

Sibelius, Jean

Abraham, Gerald. *Sibelius: A Symposium*. London: Drummond, 1947; Reprint, Oxford Univ. Press, 1952.

Grey, Cecil. *Sibelius*. London: 1931; Reprint, Oxford Univ. Press, 1975.

Hill, W. G. "Some Aspects of Form in the Symphonies of Sibelius." *MR* 10 (1949): 165.

Layton, Robert. *The World of Sibelius*. London: Dent, 1965. Rev. ed., 1978.

*————. "Jean Sibelius," In *The New Grove Turn of the Century Masters*. New York: Norton, 1985.

McMullin, Michael. "Sibelius: An Essay on His Significance." *MR* 46 (1985): 199.

Tawastsjerna, Erik. *Jean Sibelius*. 4 vols. Helsinki: 1965–78. Eng. trans. of Vols. I and II: Berkeley and Los Angeles: Univ. of California Press, 1976, 1986.

Skryabin, Alexander

Baker, James. *The Music of Alexander Scriabin*. New Haven: Yale Univ. Press, 1986.

————. "Scriabin's Implicit Tonality." *MTS* 2 (1980): 1.

Bowers, Faubion. *The New Scriabin: Enigma and Answers*. New York: St. Martin's Press, 1973.

Brown, Malcolm. "Skryabin and Russian 'Mystic' Symbolism." *19CM* 3 (1979): 42.

Dickenson, Peter. "Skryabin's Later Music." *MR* (1965): 19.

Herndon, Claude H. "Skryabin's New Harmonic Vocabulary in his Sixth Piano Sonata." *JMR* 4, nos. 3 & 4 (1983): 353.

MacDonald, Hugh. *Skryabin*. London: Oxford Univ. Press, 1978.

*————, with Paul Echols. "Alexander Skryabin." In *The New Grove Russian Masters 2*. New York: Norton, 1986.

Perle, George. "Scriabin's Self-Analysis." *MA* 3, no. 2 (1984): 101.

Pople, Anthony. "Skriabin's Prelude, Op. 67, No. 1: Sets and Structure." *MA* 2, no.2 (1983): 151.

Reise, Jay. "Late Skriabin: Some Principles Behind the Style." *19CM* 6 (1983): 220.

Schloezer, Boris de. *Skryabin: Artist and Mystic.* Trans. Nicholas Slonimsky. Berkeley and Los Angeles: Univ. of California Press, 1987.

Stockhausen, Karlheinz

Cott, Jonathan. *Stockhausen: Conversations with the Composer.* New York: Simon & Schuster, 1973.

Harvey, Jonathan. *The Music of Stockhausen.* Berkeley and Los Angeles: Univ. of California Press, 1975.

Heikinheimo, Seppo. *The Electronic Music of Karlheinz Stockhausen: Studies of the Esthetical and Formal Problems of Its First Phase.* Trans. Brad Absetz. Helsinki: Suomen Musikkitieteellinin Seura, 1972.

*Maconie, Robin. *The Works of Karlheinz Stockhausen.* London: Oxford Univ. Press, 1976. Reprint, 1981.

Morgan, Robert P. "Stockhausen's Writings on Music." *MQ* 61 (1975): 1.

Stockhausen, Karlheinz. *Stockhausen on Music: Lectures and Interviews.* Robin Maconie, ed. London: Marion Boyars, 1989.

Tannenbaum, Mya. *Conversations with Stockhausen.* Oxford: Oxford Univ. Press, 1987.

Toop, Richard. "Stockhausen and the Kontarskys: A Vision, an Interval, and a Mantra." *MR* 47 (1986–87): 194.

Strauss, Richard

Adorno, Theodor W. "Richard Strauss: Born June 11, 1864." *PNM* 4. no. 1 (Fall-Winter 1965); 14, 4, no. 2 (Spring-Summer 1966): 113.

*Birkin, Kenneth, ed. *Arabella. (COH)* Cambridge: Cambridge Univ. Press, 1990.

Del Mar, Norman. *Richard Strauss: A Critical Commentary on His Life and Works.* 3 vols. Ithaca, N.Y.: Cornell Univ. Press, 1962. Reprint 1986.

Gilliam, Bryan. "Strauss's Preliminary Opera Sketches: Thematic Fragments and Symphonic Continuity." *19CM* 9 (Spring 1986): 176.

Jefferson, Alan. *The Life of Richard Strauss.* Newton Abbot, Eng.: David & Charles, 1973.

———. *The Lieder of Richard Strauss.* London: Praeger, 1972.

Kennedy, Michael. *Richard Strauss.* London: Dent, 1976.

*———. and Robert Bailey. "Richard Strauss." In *The New Grove Turn of the Century Masters.* New York: Norton, 1985.

Lockspeiser, Edward. "The Berlioz-Strauss Treatise on Instrumentation." *ML* 50 (1969): 37.

Mann, William. *Richard Strauss: A Critical Study of the Operas.* London: Cassell, 1964.

Murphy, E. "Tonal Organization in Five Strauss Tone Poems." *MR* 44 (1983): 223.

Newman, Ernst. *Richard Strauss.* London: Greenwood Press, 1908. Reprint, 1970.

Phipps, Graham H. "The Logic of Tonality in Strauss's *Don Quixote:* A Schoenbergian Evaluation." *19CM* 9 (Spring 1986): 189.

Potter, Pamela M. "Strauss's *Friedenstag:* A Pacifist Attempt at Political Resistance." *MQ* 69 (1983): 408.

★Puffett, Derrick, ed. *Elektra. (COH).* Cambridge: Cambridge Univ. Press, 1989.

★————. *Salome. (COH)* Cambridge: Cambridge Univ. Press, 1989.

Strauss, Richard. *Richard Strauss and Romain Rolland: Correspondence.* Ed. Rollo Myers. Berkeley and Los Angeles: Univ. of California Press, 1968.

————. *Correspondence: Hans von Bulow and Richard Strauss.* Ed. Willi Schuh and Franz Trenner. Trans. Anthony Gishford. London: Boosey & Hawkes, 1955.

————. *The Correspondence between Richard Strauss and Hugo von Hoffmansthal.* Trans. Hanns Hammelmann and Ewald Oesers. London: Cambridge Univ. Press, 1961. Reprint 1981.

————. *Recollections and Reflections.* Ed. Willi Schuh. Trans. L. J. Lawrence. London: Boosey & Hawkes, 1953, Reprint 1974.

Stravinsky, Igor

Asafiev, Boris. *A Book About Stravinsky* (1929). Trans. Richard F. French. Ann Arbor, Mich.: UMI Research Press, 1982.

★Boretz, Benjamin and Edward T. Cone, eds. *Perspectives on Schoenberg and Stravinsky.* New York: Norton, 1972.

Cone, Edward T. "Stravinsky: The Progress of a Method." *PNM* 1, no.1 (1962): 18.

————. "The Uses of Convention: Stravinsky and his Models." *MQ* 48, no.3 (1962): 287.

Craft, Robert. *Stravinsky: the Chronicle of a Friendship 1948–1971.* New York: Knopf, 1972.

Deli Ge, Celestin and Michael Lamb. "Stravinsky: Ideology-Language." *PNM* 26 (1988): 82.

Druskin, Mikhail. *Igor Stravinsky: His Personality, Works and Views.* (1974). Trans. Martin Cooper. Reprint, Cambridge: Cambridge Univ. Press, 1983.

Forte, Allen. *The Harmonic Organization of "The Rite of Spring."* New Haven: Yale Univ. Press, 1978.

Gordon, Tom. "The Cubist Metaphor: Picasso in Stravinsky Criticism." *CM* 40 (1985): 22.

*Griffiths, Paul. *The Rake's Progress. (COH)* Cambridge: Cambridge Univ. Press, 1982.

Haimo, Ethan, and Paul Johnson, eds. *Stravinsky Retrospectives.* Lincoln: Univ. of Nebraska Press, 1987.

Heyman, Barbara. "Stravinsky and Ragtime." *MQ* 68 (1982): 543.

*Joseph, Charles M. *Stravinsky and the Piano.* Ann Arbor, Mich.: UMI Research Press, 1983.

———. "Structural Coherence in Stravinsky's Piano-Rag-Music." *MTS* 4 (1982): 76.

Keller, Hans, and Milein Cosman. *Stravinsky Seen and Heard.* [1962] Reprint, London: Toccata Press, 1982, Reprint, 1985.

*Lang, Paul Henry, ed. *Stravinsky: A New Appraisal of his Work.* New York: Norton, 1963.

*Lederman, Minna. ed. *Stravinsky in the Theatre.* New York: Pelegrini & Cudahy, 1949, Reprint, 1975.

Libman, Lillian. *And Music at the Close: Stravinsky's Last Years.* New York: Norton, 1972.

Pasler, Jann. "Stravinsky and the Apaches." *MT* (1982): 403.

———. ed. *Confronting Stravinsky: Man, Musician, and Modernist.* Berkeley and Los Angeles: Univ. of California Press, 1986.

Philips, Paul Schuyler. "The Enigma of Variations." *MA* 3, no.1 (1984): 69.

Schwarz, Boris. "Stravinsky in Soviet Criticism." *MQ* 48, no. 3 (1962): 340.

Smalley, Roger. "The Sketchbook of *The Rite of Spring.*" *Tempo* 91 (1969–70): 2.

Strauss, Joseph. "A Principle of Voice Leading in the Music of Stravinsky." *MTS* 4 (1982): 106.

———. "Stravinsky's Tonal Axis." *JMT* 26, no.2 (1982): 261.

Stravinsky, Igor. *An Autobiography.* New York: Norton, 1962. (Trans. of *Chroniques de ma vie,* written in collaboration with Walter Nouvel. 2 vols. Paris: Denoel & Steel, 1935, 1936.)

———. *Poetics of Music: in the Form of Six Lessons.* New York: Knopf, 1960. (Trans. of *Poetique musicale: sous forme de six lecons.*]

———. *Selected Correspondence.* 3 vols. Ed. Robert Craft. London: Faber & Faber, 1982, 1984, 1985.

*Stravinsky, Igor and Robert Craft. *Conversations with Igor Stravinsky* (1959). Reprint. Berkeley and Los Angeles: Univ. of California Press, 1980.

———. *Memories and Commentaries* (1959). Reprint, Berkeley and Los Angeles: Univ. of California Press, 1981.

———. *Expositions and Developments* (1962). Reprint, Berkeley and Los Angeles: Univ. of California Press, 1981.

★———. *Dialogues and a Diary* (1963). Reprint, Berkeley and Los Angeles: Univ. of California Press, 1980.

———. *Themes and Episodes*. New York: Knopf, 1966.

———. *Retrospectives and Conclusions,* New York: Knopf, 1969.

★———. *Themes and Conclusions* (1972). Reprint, Berkeley and Los Angeles: Univ. of California Press, 1980.

———. *"The Rite of Spring": Sketches 1911–1913*. 3rd ed. London: Oxford Univ. Press, 1978.

Stravinsky, Theodore. *Catherine and Igor Stravinsky: A Family Album*. London: Boosey & Hawkes, 1973.

Stravinsky, Vera, and Robert Craft. *Stravinsky in Pictures and Documents*. New York: Simon & Schuster, 1978.

———. *A Stravinsky Scrapbook, 1940–1971*. London: Thames & Hudson, 1983.

Stravinsky, Vera, and Igor Stravinsky. *Dearest Bubushkin: The Correspondence of Vera & Igor Stravinsky. 1921–1954, with excerpts from Vera Stravinsky's Diaries*. Ed. Robert Craft. Trans. Lucia Davidova. New York and London: Thames & Hudson, 1985.

Taruskin, Richard. "Russian Folk Melodies in *The Rite of Spring*." *JAMS* 33 (1980): 501.

———. *"The Rite* Revisited: The Idea and Sources of the Scenario." In *Music & Civilization: Essays in Honor of Paul Henry Lang*. Ed. Maria Rika Maniates and Edmond Strainchamps. New York: Norton, 1984.

———. "Chernomor to Kashchei: Harmonic Sorcery; or, Stravinsky's 'Angle.' " *JAMS* 38, no.1 (1985): 72.

———. "Chez Pétrouchka: Harmony and Tonality chez Stravinsky." *19CM* 10, no.3 (Spring 1987): 265.

Toorn, Pieter C. van den. *The Music of Igor Stravinsky*. New Haven: Yale Univ. Press, 1983.

———. *Stravinsky and "The Rite of Spring": The Beginnings of A Musical Language*. Berkeley and Los Angeles: Univ. of California Press, 1987.

Vershinina, Irina. *Stravinsky's Early Ballets* (1967). Trans. L. G. Heien. Ann Arbor, Mich.: UMI Research Press, 1989.

Vlad, Roman. *Stravinsky* (1958). Trans. Frederick and Anne Fuller. London: Oxford Univ. Press., 1978.

Walsh, Stephen. *The Music of Stravinsky*. London: Routledge & Kegan Paul, 1988.

White, Eric Walter. *Stravinsky: The Composer and His Works*. Berkeley and Los Angeles: Univ. of California Press, 1966. 2nd ed., 1979.

★——— and Jeremy Noble. "Igor Stravinsky." In *The New Grove Modern Masters*. New York: Norton, 1984.

Subotnick, Morton

Perkins, John M. "Morton Subotnick: Serenade No. 1." *PNM* 2, no.2 (1964): 100.

Whipple, Harold W. "Beasts and Butterflies: Morton Subotnick's 'Ghost Scores.' " *MQ* 69 (1983): 425.

Szymanowski, Karol

McNamee, Ann K. "Bimodality, Mode, and Interval in the Music of Karol Szymanowski." *JMT* 29, no. 1 (1985): 61.

Thomson, Virgil

★Jackson, Richard. "Virgil Thomson." In *The New Grove Twentieth-Century American Masters*. New York: Norton, 1987.

Meckna, Michael. *Virgil Thomson: A Bio-bibliography*. New York: Greenwood Press, 1986.

Sonus 7, no.1 (1986). Entire issue is devoted to articles by and about Thomson.

Thomson, Virgil. *Virgil Thomson by Virgil Thomson*. New York: Knopf, 1966.

————. *A Virgil Thomson Reader*. Boston: Houghton Mifflin, 1981.

————. *Music with Words. A Composer's View*. New Haven: Yale Univ. Press, 1989.

Tommasini, Anthony. *Virgil Thomson's Musical Portraits*. New York: Pendragon Press, 1986.

Tippett, Michael

Bowen, Meirion. *Michael Tippett*. London: Robson , 1980.

Kemp, Ian. *Tippett. The Composer and His Music*. London: Eulenberg, 1984.

★————. "Michael Tippett." In *The New Grove Twentieth-Century English Masters*. New York: Norton, 1986.

★Mathews, David. *Michael Tippett. An Introductory Study*. London: Faber & Faber, 1980.

Puffett, Derrick. "The Fugue from Tippett's Second String Quartet." *MA* 5 (1986): 233.

Rodda, Richard E. "Genesis of a Symphony: Tippett's Symphony No. 3." *MR* 39 (1978): 110.

Tippett, Michael. *Moving into Aquarius*. 2nd ed. London: Palladin, 1974.

★————. *Music of the Angels*. London: Eulenburg, 1980.

White, Eric Walter. *Tippett and His Operas*. London: Barrie & Jenkins, 1979.

Whittall, Arnold. *The Music of Britten and Tippett: Studies in Themes and Techniques*. Cambridge and New York: Cambridge Univ. Press, 1982.

Varèse, Edgard

Babbitt, Milton. "Edgard Varèse: A Few Observations of His Music." *PNM* 4, no.2 (1966): 14.

Bernard, Jonathan. "Pitch / Register in the Music of Edgard Varèse." *MTS* 3 (1981): 1.

————. *The Music of Edgard Varèse*. New Haven: Yale Univ. Press, 1987.

Chou, Wen-chung. "Open Rather Than Bounded." *PNM* 5, no. 1 (1966): 1.

————. "A Varèse Chronology." *PNM* 5, no. 1 (1966): 7.

————. "Varèse: A Sketch of the Man and His Music." *MQ* 52 (1966): 151.

Morgan, Robert P. "Rewriting Music History: Second Thoughts on Ives and Varèse." Musical Newsletter 3, no. 1 (1973): 3; 3, no. 2 (1973): 15.

Ouellette, Fernand. *A Biography of Edgard Varèse*. New York: Orion Press, 1966. Reprint, 1981.

Schuller, Gunther. "Conversation with Varèse." *PNM* 3, no. 2 (1965): 32.

Stempel, Larry. "Varèse's 'Awkwardness' and the Symmetry in the 'Frame of Twelve Tones': An Analytic Approach." *MQ* 65 (1979) 148.

Strawn, John. "The *Intégrales* of Edgard Varèse: Space, Mass, Element, and Form." *PNM* 17, no.1 (1978): 38.

Van Solkema, Sherman, ed. *The New Worlds of Edgard Varèse: A Symposium*. Brooklyn: ISAM, 1979.

Varèse, Edgard. "The Liberation of Sound." *PNM* 5, no.1 (1966): 11.

Varèse, Louise. *Varèse. A Looking-Glass Diary 1883–1928*. New York: Norton, 1972.

Vaughan Williams, Ralph

Adams, Byron. "The Stages of Revision of Vaughan William's Sixth Symphony." *MQ* 73 (1989): 382.

Day, Douglas. *Working with Vaughan Williams: The Correspondence of Ralph Vaughan Williams and Roy Douglas*. London: The British Library Board, 1988.

Dickenson, A. E. F. "The Legacy of Ralph Vaughan Williams: A Retrospect." *MR* 19 (1958): 290.

Forbes, Anne-Marie. "Motivic Unity in Ralph Vaughan Williams' *Riders to the Sea.*" *MR* 44 (1983): 234.

Hurd, Michael. *Vaughan Williams.* London: Faber & Faber, 1970.

Kennedy, Michael. *Vaughan Williams.* London: Oxford Univ. Press, 1964.

★Ottaway, Hugh. *Vaughan Williams Symphonies.* London. British Broadcasting Corporation, 1972.

★————. "Vaughan Williams." In *The New Grove Twentieth-Century English Masters.* New York, Norton, 1986.

Payne, Elsie M. "Vaughan Williams and Folk Song." *MR* 15 (1954): 103.

Schwartz, Elliott S. *The Symphonies of Ralph Vaughan Williams.* Amherst: Univ. of Massachusetts Press, 1964, Reprint, 1982.

Vaughan Williams, Ralph. *Beethoven's Choral Symphony and Other Writings.* London: Oxford Univ. Press, 1953.

Vaughan Williams, Ursula. *R.V.W.: A Biography of Ralph Vaughan Williams.* London: Oxford Univ. Press, 1964.

Warrack, John. "Vaughan Williams and Opera." *Opera* 9 (1958): 698.

Villa-Lobos, Heitor

Appleby, David. *Heitor Villa-Lobos: A Bio-bibliography.* New York: Greenwood Press, 1988.

Mariz, Vasco. *Heitor Villa-Lobos.* Washington, D.C.: Brazilian American Cultural Institute, 1970.

Peppercorn, Lisa M. "Some Aspects of Villa-Lobos's Principles of Composition." *MR* 4, no.1 (1943): 28.

————. "Villa-Lobos's Last Years." *MR* 40 (1979): 284.

Walton, William

Craggs, Stewart R. *William Walton: A Thematic Catalogue of his Musical Works.* London: Oxford Univ. Press, 1977.

Howes, Frank S. *The Music of William Walton.* London: Oxford Univ. Press, 1965. 2nd Ed. 1974.

★Ottaway, Hugh. "William Walton." In *The New Grove Twentieth-Century English Masters.* New York: Norton, 1986.

Smith, Carolyn J. *William Walton: A Bio-bibliography.* New York: Greenwood Press, 1988.

Tierney, Niel. *William Walton.* London: Hale, 1984.

Walton, Susana. *William Walton: Behind the Facade.* Oxford: Oxford Univ. Press, 1988.

Webern, Anton

Archibald, Bruce. "Some Thoughts on Symmetry in Early Webern: Op. 5, No. 2." *PNM* 10, no.2 (1972): 159.

Cone, Edward T. "Webern's Apprenticeship." *MQ* 53 (1967): 39.

*Griffiths, Paul. "Anton Webern." In *The New Grove Second Viennese School*. New York: Norton, 1983.

Kolneder, Walter. *Anton Webern: An Introduction to His Work*. Trans Humphrey Searle. Berkeley and Los Angeles: Univ. of California Press, 1968.

Moldenhauer, Hans. *The Death of Webern*. London: Vision Press, 1962.

——, and Demar Irvine, eds. *Anton von Webern: Perspectives*. Seattle: Univ. of Washington Press, 1966, Reprint, 1978.

——, and Rosaleen Moldenhauer. *Anton von Webern: A Chronicle of His Life and Work*. New York: Knopf, 1979.

Roman, Zoltan, ed. *Anton von Webern. An Annotated Bibliography*. Detroit: Information Coordinators, 1983.

Smalley, Roger. "Webern's Sketches." *Tempo* 112 (1975): 2.

*Webern, Anton. *The Path to New Music*. Trans. Leo Black. Bryn Mawr, Pa.: Presser, 1963.

Westergaard, Peter. "Webern and 'Total Organization': an Analysis of the Second Movement of the Piano Variations, Op. 27." *PNM* 1, no. 2 (1963): 107.

Weill, Kurt

Borwick, Susan. "Weill and Brecht's Theories on Music in Drama." *JMR* 4, nos. 1 & 2 (1982): 39.

Drew, David. *Kurt Weill: A Handbook*. London: Faber & Faber, 1987.

Jarman, Douglas. *Kurt Weill, an Illustrated Biography*. Bloomington: Indiana Univ. Press, 1982.

Kowalke, Kim H. *Kurt Weill in Europe*. Ann Arbor, Mich.: UMI Research Press, 1979.

——, ed. *A New Orpheus. Essays on Kurt Weill*. New Haven: Yale Univ. Press, 1986.

Wolff, Christian

Fox, Christopher. "Music as Social Process: Some Aspects of the Work of Christian Wolff." *Contact* 28 (1984): 49.

Xenakis, Iannis

Bois, Mario. *Iannis Xenakis, the Man and His Music. A Conversation with the Composer and a Description of His Works*. London: Boosey & Hawkes, 1967, Reprint, 1980.

Butchers, Christopher. "The Random Arts: Xenakis, Mathematics and Music." *Tempo* 85 (1968): 2.

De Lio, Thomas. "Iannis Xenakis: *Nomos Alpha.*" *JMT* 24 / 1 (1980): 63.

Griffiths, Paul. "Xenakis: Logic and Disorder." *MT* 116 (1975): 329.

Waugh, Jane, and W. A. O'N. "Xenakis and Chance." *Contact* 10 (1974–1975): 6.

Xenakis, Iannis. *Arts, Sciences: Alloys.* Trans. Sharon Kanach. New York: Pendragon Press, 1985.

———. *Formalized Music: Thought and Mathematics in Composition.* Rev. ed. New York; Pendragon Press, 1990.

———. "Xenakis on Xenakis." *PNM* 25, nos. 1&2 (1987): 16.

Young, La Monte

Smith, Dave. "Following a Straight Line." *Contact* 18 (1977–78): 4.

Young, La Monte, and Marian Zazeela. *Selected Writings.* Munich: Heiner Friedrich, 1970.

Index

Page numbers in **boldface** refer to examples. Those in *italics* refer to illustrations.